Sociology

BRIEF EDITION

Exploring the Architecture of Everyday Life

David M. Newman

DePauw University

Los Angeles | London | New Delhi
Singapore | Washington DC

For information:

Pine Forge Press
An Imprint of SAGE Publications, Inc.
2455 Teller Road
Thousand Oaks, California 91320
E-mail: order@sagepub.com

SAGE Publications Ltd.
1 Oliver's Yard
55 City Road
London EC1Y 1SP
United Kingdom

SAGE Publications India Pvt. Ltd.
B 1/I 1 Mohan Cooperative Industrial Area
Mathura Road, New Delhi 110 044
India

SAGE Publications Asia-Pacific Pte. Ltd.
33 Pekin Street #02-01
Far East Square
Singapore 048763

Printed in the United States of America

Library of Congress Cataloging-in-Publication Data

Newman, David M., 1958-
Sociology : exploring the architecture of everyday life, brief edition / David M. Newman. — 2nd ed.
p. cm.
Includes bibliographical references and index.
ISBN 978-1-4129-8008-1 (pbk.)
1. Sociology. I. Title.

HM585.N485 2011
301—dc22 2010012093

This book is printed on acid-free paper.

10 11 12 13 14 10 9 8 7 6 5 4 3 2

Acquisitions Editor: David Repetto
Assistant Editor: Eve Oettinger
Editorial Assistant: Maggie Stanley
Production Editor: Brittany Bauhaus
Copy Editor: Megan Speer
Typesetter: C&M Digitals (P) Ltd.
Proofreader: Eleni-Maria Georgiou
Indexer: Diggs Publication Services, Inc.
Cover Designer: Candice Harman
Marketing Manager: Helen Salmon

Brief Contents

Detailed Contents

Preface

It was the first day of the fall semester in 1994. I had just finished making the final adjustments to the first edition of the full version of this book, which was due to be published the following January. I felt good, as though I'd just accomplished something monumental. Even my two sons were impressed with me (although not as impressed as the time we went to a professional hockey game and I leaped out of my seat to catch an errant, speeding puck barehanded). I walked into the first meeting of my Contemporary Society class eager to start teaching wide-eyed, first-year students a thing or two about sociology.

In my introductory comments to the class that day, I mentioned that I had just written this book. The panicked look in their eyes—a curious combination of awe and fear—calmed when I told them I wouldn't be requiring them to read it that semester. I assured them that the process of writing an introductory text helped me immensely in preparing for the course and that I hoped to pass on to them the knowledge I had accumulated.

The next day after class, one of the students—a bright, freshly scrubbed 18-year-old—approached me. The ensuing conversation would leave a humbling impression even 16 years later:

Student: Hi. Umm. Professor Newman. . . . I called my parents last night to, like, tell them how my first day in college went. I think they were, like, more nervous than I was. You know how parents can be.

Me: Yes, I sure do. I'm a parent myself, you know.

Student: Yeah, whatever. Anyway, I was telling them about my classes and my professors and stuff. I told them about this class and how I thought it would be pretty cool. I told them you were writing a book. I thought that would impress them, you know, make it seem like they were getting their money's worth and everything.

Me: Well, thanks.

Student: So, they go, "What's the book about?" [He laughs sheepishly.] I told them I didn't know, but I'd find out. So that's what I'm doing . . . finding out.

Me: Well, I'm glad you asked. You see, it's an introductory sociology textbook that uses everyday experiences and phenomena as a way of understanding important sociological theories and ideas. In it I've attempted to . . .

Student: Wait, did you say it was a textbook?

Me: Why, yes. You see, the purpose of the book is to provide the reader with a thorough and useful introduction to the sociological perspective. I want to convey . . .

Student: [quite embarrassed now] Oh. . . . Professor Newman, I'm really sorry. I misunderstood you. I thought you had written a real book.

Real book. *Real* book. *Real* book. Those words rang in my head like some relentless church bell. At first, I tried to dismiss the comment as the remarks of a naïve kid who didn't know any better. But the more I thought about it, the more I realized what his comment reflected. The perception that textbooks aren't *real* books is pervasive.

I once heard a radio ad for a local Red Cross book drive that asked listeners to donate any unused or unwanted books *as long as they weren't textbooks.* Torn copies of *The Cat in the Hat?* Fine, they'll take 'em. Grease-stained owners' manuals for 1976 Ford Pintos? Sure, glad to have 'em. Textbooks? No way!

Sadly, these sorts of perceptions are not altogether unwarranted. Textbooks hover on the margins of the literary world, somewhere between respectable, intellectual monographs on trailblazing research and Harlequin romance novels. Historically, they've been less than titillating: thick, heavy, expensive, and easily discarded for a measly five bucks at the end-of-semester "book buy-back."

My goal has always been to write a textbook that reads like a *real* book. The full version of this book is now in its eighth edition. Over the years, reviewers, instructors, and students who've read and used the book have indicated that they like the relaxed tone and appreciate the consistent theme that ties all the chapters together. Many instructors have commented on how the book enables students to truly understand the unique and useful elements of a sociological perspective.

But textbooks by their nature tend to be long and comprehensive. Recently, some instructors have suggested to me that I consider creating a smaller, more streamlined version of the full text. This way, they said, they could assign other books while still exposing students to the key points my book makes. That seemed like a good idea to me. And so, this condensed version of the book was born.

It would be impossible to write an introduction to the discipline of sociology without accounting for the life-altering occurrences—wars, natural disasters, political upheavals, legal developments, economic meltdowns, Lindsey Lohan's latest late-night escapades—that we hear about every day. Two events in particular have occurred since I wrote the last edition that have had—and will continue to have—a dramatic impact on sociological thought and on people's everyday lives: the global economic recession and the election of Barack Obama as the 44th president of the United States. As you will see throughout the book, it is impossible to understand what happens to us in our personal lives without taking into consideration broader social and historical phenomena. When the economy suffers, everyone—from tycoons to welfare recipients—experiences some kind of alteration in their day-to-day routines. Likewise, major political events can change what we know and what we take for granted. So throughout this book, I've made a special effort to provide some sociological insight into contemporary events and trends, both large and small. In the end, I hope to show you the pervasiveness and applicability of sociology in our ordinary everyday experiences in a way that rings familiar with you.

Throughout the book, I've also tried to provide the most current statistical information possible. Most of the statistical information is drawn from the most recent data from sources such as the U.S. Census Bureau, the Population Reference Bureau, the Centers for Disease Control and Prevention, the U.S. Bureau of Labor Statistics, and the U.S. Bureau of Justice Statistics.

COMPANION READER

Jodi O'Brien, a sociologist at Seattle University, and I have carefully edited a companion volume to this book, consisting of short articles, chapters, and excerpts written by other authors. These readings are provocative and eye-opening examples of the joys and insights of sociological thinking. Many of them vividly show how sociologists gather evidence through carefully designed research. Others are personal narratives that provide first-hand accounts of how social forces influence people's lives. The readings examine common, everyday experiences; important social issues; global concerns; and distinct historical events that illustrate the relationship between the individual and society. We've taken great pains to include readings that show how race, social class, gender, and sexual orientation intersect to influence everyday experiences.

Of the 40 or so selections in this edition of the reader, 17 are new. The new selections touch on important and relevant sociological issues such as diversity among same-sex couples, inner-city violence among teenage girls, the effect of pregnancy and post pregnancy on women's body image, ethnicity and youth identity, language difficulties in immigrant families, the social construction of legal and illegal drugs, compassion and poverty, teen childbearing in poor communities, the plight of Muslim Americans after 9/11, gentrification in African American neighborhoods, and the immigrant rights movement. In addition, we've moved several readings to different chapters to improve their usefulness and applicability.

TEACHING RESOURCES AND WEBSITE TO ACCOMPANY THE BOOK AND COMPANION READER

The *Teaching Resources Guide* is available for instructors at www.pineforge.com/newmanbrief2e/. The manual provides comprehensive, thorough coverage of the material in both the text and the companion reader, including the following:

- Chapter summaries
- Class exercises and discussion topics (suggestions for writing exercises, discussion topics, and student assignments to use both inside and outside class)
- Literary and visual resources
- Selected Internet resources
- Testing materials (multiple-choice, short-answer, and essay questions): the test bank was developed to test students' understanding of the material so instructors can encourage students to move beyond basic memorization of material toward application and critique. The multiple-choice questions are organized as recall questions and application questions. Recall questions are based more directly on the information presented in the textbook, and application questions assess students' comprehension of the material and their ability to apply concepts, theories, and research findings
- Summaries of classic sociological studies
- Teaching resource materials: these include an annotated bibliography of resources useful in preparing for and designing classes, suggestions for how to manage teaching interactions and elicit and evaluate student performance, and techniques for handling any challenges that arise in class

Students can also access an Internet study site for this book at www.pineforge.com. This site includes additional material not included in the book, as well as test questions that can be used to gauge understanding of the book's contents.

A WORD ABOUT THE "ARCHITECTURE OF SOCIETY"

I have chosen the image of architecture in the subtitle to convey one of the driving themes of this book: Society is a human construction. Society is not "out there" somewhere, waiting to be visited and examined. It exists in the minute details of our day-to-day lives. Whenever we follow its rules or break them, enter its roles or shed them, work to change things or keep them as they are, we are adding another nail, plank, or frame to the structure of our society. In short, society—like the buildings around us—couldn't exist were it not for the actions of people.

At the same time, however, this structure that we have created appears to exist independently of us. We don't usually spend much time thinking about the buildings we live, work, and play in as human constructions. We see them as finished products, not as the processes that created them. Only when something goes wrong—the pipes leak or the walls crack—do we realize that people made these structures and people are the ones who must fix them. When buildings outlive their usefulness or become dangerous to their inhabitants, people must renovate them or, if necessary, decide to tear them down.

Likewise, society is so massive and has been around for so long that it *appears* to stand on its own, at a level above and beyond the toiling hands of individual people. But here, too, when things begin to go wrong—widespread discrimination, massive poverty, lack of affordable health care, escalating crime rates—people must do something about it.

So the fascinating paradox of human life is that we build society, collectively "forget" that we've built it, and live under its massive and influential structure. But we are not "stuck" with society as it is. Human beings are the architects of their own social reality. Throughout this book, I examine the active roles individuals play in planning, maintaining, or fixing society.

A FINAL THOUGHT

One of the greatest challenges I face as a teacher of sociology is trying to get my students to see the personal relevance of the course material, to fully appreciate the connection between the individual and society. The true value of sociology lies in its unique ability to show the two-way connection between the most private elements of our lives—our characteristics, experiences, behaviors, and thoughts—and the cultures, groups, organizations, and social institutions to which we belong. The "everyday-life" approach in this book uses real-world examples and personal observations as a vehicle for understanding the relationship between individuals and society.

My purpose is to make the familiar unfamiliar—to help you critically examine the commonplace and the ordinary in your own life. Only when you step back and examine the taken-for-granted aspects of your personal experiences can you see that there is an inherent, sometimes unrecognized organization and predictability to them. At the same time, you will see that the structure of society is greater than the sum of the experiences and psychologies of the individuals in it.

It is my conviction that this intellectual excursion should be a thought-provoking and enjoyable one. Reading a textbook doesn't have to be boring or, even worse, the academic equivalent of a trip to the dentist (although I personally have nothing against dentists). I believe that part of my task as an instructor is to provide my students with a challenging but comfortable classroom atmosphere in which to learn. I have tried to do the same in this book. Your instructor has chosen this book not because it makes his or her job teaching your course any easier but because he or she wants you, the student, to see how sociology helps us understand how the small, private experiences of our everyday lives are connected to this thing we call society. I hope you learn to appreciate this important message, and I hope you enjoy reading this book as much as I enjoyed writing it.

Have fun,

—David M. Newman

Department of Sociology and Anthropology

DePauw University

Greencastle, IN 46135

E-mail: dnewman@depauw.edu

Acknowledgments

A book project such as this one takes an enormous amount of time to develop. I've spent thousands of hours on this book—typing away at my computer, searching the Web, fretting over what I should and shouldn't include—all while holed up in my isolated and very cluttered third-floor office. Yet as solitary as this project was, I could not have done it alone. Over the years, many people have provided invaluable assistance to make this book a reality. Without their generous help and support, it wouldn't have been written, and you'd be reading some other sociologist's list of people to thank.

I would like to extend my sincere gratitude to Dave Repetto, Brittany Bauhaus, Claudia Hoffman, and Megan Speer at SAGE Publications/Pine Forge Press for their insight and guidance in putting together this newest edition. I would also like to express my thanks to Beverly Bennett and William Todd Evans (Berkeley City College) for their contributions to development of the ancillary resources for the book, and to Karen Ehrmann for securing copyright permissions.

I appreciate the many helpful comments offered by the reviewers of the brief version of this book:

Sharon Abbott, Fairfield University

Deborah Abowitz, Bucknell University

Stephen Adair, Central Connecticut State University

Rebecca Adams, University of North Carolina, Greensboro

Ron Aminzade, University of Minnesota

Afroza Anwary, Carleton College

George Arquitt, Oklahoma State University

Carol Auster, Franklin and Marshall College

Ellen C. Baird, Arizona State University

Ellen Berg, California State University, Sacramento

David Bogen, Emerson College

Frances A. Boudreau, Connecticut College

David L. Briscoe, University of Arkansas at Little Rock

Todd Campbell, Loyola University, Chicago

Wanda Clark, South Plains College

Thomas Conroy, St. Peter's College

Norman Conti, Duquesne University

Maia Greenwell Cunningham, Citrus College

Doug Currivan, University of Massachusetts, Boston

Jeff Davidson, University of Delaware

Kimberly Davies, Augusta State University

Tricia Davis, North Carolina State University

James J. Dowd, University of Georgia

Laura A. Dowd, University of Georgia, Athens

Charlotte A. Dunham, Texas Tech University

Donald Eckard, Temple University

Charles Edgley, Oklahoma State University

Rachel Einhower, Purdue University

June Ellestad, Washington State University

Shalom Endleman, Quinnipiac College

Rebecca Erickson, University of Akron

Kimberly Faust, Winthrop University

Patrick Fontane, St. Louis College of Pharmacy

Michael J. Fraleigh, Bryant University

Sarah N. Gaston, Texas A&M University

Farah Gilanshah, University of Minnesota-Morris

Barry Goetz, University of Dayton

Lorie Schabo Grabowski, University of Minnesota

Valerie Gunter, University of New Orleans

Roger Guy, Texas Lutheran University

John R. Hall, University of California, Davis

Charles Harper, Creighton University

Douglas Harper, Duquesne University

Tara Hardinge, California State University, Long Beach

Lori Heald, North Carolina State University

Peter Hennen, University of Minnesota

Max Herman, Rutgers University

Cynthia Hewitt, Morehouse College

Christine L. Himes, Syracuse University

Susan Hoerbelt, Hillsborough Community College

Amy Holzgang, Cerritos College

Kate Hovey, Central New Mexico Community College

W. Jay Hughes, Georgia Southern University

Gary Hytreck, Georgia Southern University

Valerie Jenness, University of California, Irvine

Kathryn Johnson, Barat College

Richard Jones, Marquette University

Tom Kando, California State University, Sacramento

Steve Keto, Kent State University

Peter Kivisto, Augustana College

Lisa Konczal, Barry University

Marc LaFountain, State University of West Georgia

Sharon Melissa Latimer, West Virginia University

Joseph Lengermann, University of Maryland, College Park

Linda A. Litteral, Grossmont Community College

Julie L. Locher, University of Alabama, Birmingham

David G. LoConto, Jacksonville State University

David A. Lopez, California State University, Northridge

Fred Maher, Temple University

Kristen Marcussen, University of Iowa

Benjamin Mariante, Stonehill College

Joseph Marolla, Virginia Commonwealth University

Michallene McDaniel, University of Georgia

James R. McIntosh, Lehigh University

Jerome McKibben, Fitchburg State University

Ted P. McNeilsmith, Adams State College

Dan Miller, University of Dayton

Melinda Milligan, Sonoma State University

John R. Mitrano, Central Connecticut State University

Susannne Monahan, Montana State University

Kelly Murphy, University of Pittsburgh

Elizabeth Ehrhardt Mustaine, University of Central Florida

Daniel Myers, University of Notre Dame

Anne Nurse, College of Wooster

Marjukka Ollilainen, Weber State University

Toska Olson, Evergreen State College

Liza A. Pellerin, Ball State University

Larry Perkins, Oklahoma State University, Stillwater

Bernice Pescosolido, Indiana University, Bloomington

Mike Plummer, Boston College

Edward Ponczek, William Rainey Harper College

Tanya Poteet, Capital University

Sharon E. Preves, Grand Valley State University

Kennon J. Rice, North Carolina State University

Judith Richlin-Klonsky, University of California, Los Angeles

Robert Robinson, Indiana University, Bloomington

Mary Rogers, University of West Florida

Sally S. Rogers, Montgomery College

Wanda Rushing, University of Memphis

Michael Ryan, University of Louisiana, Lafayette

Scott Schaffer, Millersville University

Aileen Schulte, State University of New York, New Paltz

Dave Schweingruber, Iowa State University

Mark Shibley, Southern Oregon University

Thomas Shriver, Oklahoma State University

Toni Sims, University of Louisiana, Lafayette

Kathleen Slevin, College of William and Mary

Melissa Sloan, Drew University

Lisa White Smith, Christopher Newport University

Eldon E. Snyder, Bowling Green State University

Nicholas Sofios, Providence College

George Spilker, Clarkson College

Melanie Stander, University of Washington

Beverly Stiles, Midwestern State University

Kandi Stinson, Xavier University

Richard Tardanico, Florida International University

Robert Tellander, Sonoma State University

Kathleen Tiemann, University of North Dakota

Steven Vallas, George Mason University

Tom Vander Ven, Indiana University, South Bend

John Walsh, University of Illinois, Chicago

Gregory Weiss, Roanoke College

Marty Wenglinski, Quinnipiac College

Stephan Werba, Catonsville Community College

Cheryl E. Whitley, Marist College

Norma Williams, University of North Texas

Janelle Wilson, University of Minnesota, Duluth

Mark Winton, University of Central Florida

Judith Wittner, Loyola University, Chicago

Cynthia A. Woolever, Hartford Seminary

Don C. Yost, Mountain State University

Ashraf Zahedi, Stanford University

Stephen Zehr, University of Southern Indiana

And finally, I would like to express gratitude to my friends, colleagues, family, and above all, students who, throughout the years, have kept me curious and prevented me from taking myself too seriously.

About the Author

David M. Newman is professor of sociology at DePauw University. In addition to the introductory course, he teaches courses in research methods, family, social psychology, deviance, and mental illness. He has won teaching awards at both the University of Washington and DePauw University. His other written work includes *Identities and Inequalities: Exploring the Intersections of Race, Class, Gender, and Sexuality* (2005) and *Families: A Sociological Perspective* (2008). He received his PhD from the University of Washington.

PART I

The Individual and Society

CHAPTER 1
Taking a New Look at a Familiar World

CHAPTER 2
Seeing and Thinking Sociologically

What is the relationship between your private life and the social world around you? Part I introduces you to the guiding theme of this book: Our personal, everyday experiences affect and are affected by the larger society in which we live. Chapters 1 and 2 discuss the sociological perspective on human life and the ways in which it differs from the more individualistic approaches of psychology and biology. You will read about what society consists of and get a glimpse into sociologists' attempts to understand the two-way relationship between the individual and society.

As you read on, keep in mind a metaphor that will be used throughout the book to help explain the nature of society: architecture. Like buildings, societies have a design discernible to the alert eye. Both are constructed by bringing together a wide variety of materials in a complex process. Both, through their structure, shape the activities within. At the same time, both change. Sometimes they change subtly and gradually as the inhabitants go about their lives; other times they are deliberately redecorated or remodeled. As you make your way through this book, see if you can discover more ways in which buildings and societies are alike.

©iStockPhoto.com/Dmitry Galanternik

1 Taking a New Look at a Familiar World

André graduated from college in 2009. He had been a model student. When not studying, he found time to help kids read at the local elementary school and actively participated in student government at his own school. He got along well with his professors, his grades were excellent, he made the dean's list all 4 years, and he graduated Phi Beta Kappa. As a computer science major with a minor in economics, André thought his future was clear: He would land a job at a top software company or perhaps a stock brokerage firm and work his way up the ladder so that he'd be earning a six-figure income by the time he was 30.

But when André entered the job market and began applying for jobs, things didn't go exactly according to plan. Despite his credentials, nobody seemed willing to hire him full-time. He was able to survive only by taking temporary freelance programming jobs here and there and working nights at The Gap. Many of his friends from college had similar difficulties. Nevertheless, André began to question his own abilities: "Do I lack the skills that employers are looking for? Am I not trying hard enough? What the heck is wrong with me?" His friends and family were as encouraging as they could be, but some secretly wondered if André wasn't as smart as they had thought he was.

Michael and Carole were both juniors at a large university. They had been dating each other exclusively for the past 2 years. By all accounts, the relationship seemed to be going quite well. In fact, Michael was beginning to imagine them getting married, having children, and living happily ever after. Then one day out of the blue, Carole dropped a bombshell. She told Michael she thought their relationship was going nowhere and perhaps they ought to start seeing other people.

Michael was stunned. "What did I do?" he asked her. "I thought things were going great. Is it something I said? Something I did? I can change."

She said no, he hadn't done anything wrong, they had simply grown apart. She told him she just didn't feel as strongly about him as she used to.

After the breakup, Michael was devastated. He turned to his friends for support. "She wasn't any good for you anyway," they said. "We always thought she was a little flighty. She probably couldn't be in a serious relationship with anybody. It wasn't your fault; it was hers."

In both these stories, notice that people immediately try to explain an unhappy situation by focusing on the individual characteristics and attributes of the people involved. André blames himself for not being able to land a job; others question his intelligence and drive. Michael wonders what he did to sour his relationship with Carole; his friends question Carole's psychological stability. Such reactions are not uncommon. We have a marked tendency to rely on ***individualistic explanations,*** attributing people's achievements and failures to their personal qualities.

Why can't André, our highly intelligent, well-trained, talented college graduate, land a permanent job? It's certainly possible that he has some personal defect that makes him unemployable: lack of motivation, laziness, bad attitude, and so on. Or maybe he doesn't come across as particularly capable during job interviews.

But by focusing exclusively on such individual "deficiencies," we overlook the broader societal factors that may have affected André's job prospects. For instance, the employment situation for college graduates like André was part of a broader economic trend that began with the global financial crisis that began in 2008. From early 2008 to early 2009, 4.4 million jobs in the United States were lost (or 3.2% of all jobs); in the month of February 2009 alone, 651,000 jobs disappeared (cited in Goodman & Healy, 2009). At the time I was writing this chapter, close to 10% of American adults (more than 15 million people) were officially unemployed (U.S. Bureau of Labor Statistics, 2010). That figure didn't include several million other out-of-work people who didn't meet the government's official definition of "unemployed" because they hadn't been actively seeking employment in the past month. Indeed, an additional 9% of workers were employed part-time, although they wanted to work full-time (cited in Goodman & Healy, 2009).

Furthermore, college degrees are no longer the guarantee of fruitful employment they once were. According to the Collegiate Employment Research Institute (2009), job opportunities for college graduates improved in the mid-2000s, only to take a steep dive in 2009. Each year between 2004 and 2008, employers increased their hiring of college graduates by an average of 13% over the previous year (cited in Hunsinger, 2009). In fact, the job market became so good in the mid-2000s that newspapers began providing advice to college graduates on how to be "picky" when choosing a place to work (Knight, 2006). As late as May 2008, economists were still predicting a favorable job market for new graduates (Murphy, 2008).

But all that quickly changed. Of all long-term unemployed people, 17% are college graduates, up from 9.2% in 1979 (Mishel, Bernstein, & Allegretto, 2007). In 2009, employers hired nearly 22% *fewer* college graduates than the year before (cited in Hunsinger, 2009). In addition, between 2008 and 2009, the number of job openings for people with advanced college degrees dropped in just about all fields (Cohen, 2009).

Starting salaries for college graduates who did land jobs stagnated (National Association of Colleges and Employers, 2009). The "wage premium"—the taken-for-granted assumption that a college degree will bring higher wages—has lost steam recently. College graduates still earn nearly 45% more, on average, than people with high school diplomas. But the education-based wage gap has been shrinking for several years (Uchitelle, 2005).

So you see, André's employability and his chances of earning a good living were as much a result of the economic forces operating at the time he began looking for a job as of any of his personal qualifications. Had he graduated only a few years earlier, when the economy was doing better, his prospects would have been much brighter.

And what about Michael and Carole? It seems perfectly reasonable to conclude that something about either of them or the combination of the two caused their breakup. We tend to view dating relationships—not to mention marriages—as situations that succeed or fail solely because of the traits or behaviors of the two people involved.

But how would your assessment of the situation change if you found out that Jason—to whom Carole had always been secretly attracted—had just broken up with his longtime girlfriend and was now available? Like it or not, relationships are not exclusively private entities; they're always being influenced by outside forces. They take place within a larger network of friends, acquaintances, ex-partners, coworkers, fellow students, and people as yet unknown who may make desirable or, at the very least, acceptable dating partners. Social-networking websites such as MySpace and Facebook, as well as blogs where people can post word of their breakups, are becoming as popular as the more traditional places where people announce their weddings. As one columnist put it, "What good does it do to know that Joe and Jane are getting married? The news we really need is who's breaking up—so we can go and . . . hit on them" (quoted in Soukup, 2004, p. 15).

When people believe they have no better alternative, they tend to stay with their present partners, even if they are not particularly satisfied. When people think that better relationships are available to them, they may become less committed to staying in their present ones. Indeed, people's perceptions of what characterizes a good relationship (such as fairness, compatibility, affection) are less likely to determine when and if it ends than the presence or absence of favorable alternatives (Felmlee, Sprecher, & Bassin, 1990). Research shows that the risk of a relationship ending increases as the supply of potential alternative relationships increases (South & Lloyd, 1995).

In addition, Carole's decision to leave could have been indirectly affected by the sheer number of potentially available partners—a result of shifts in the birthrate 20 years or so earlier. Today, there are roughly 120 U.S. men in their 20s who have never been married, divorced, or widowed for every 100 women in the same category (Roberts, 2006). For a single, heterosexual woman such as Carole, such a surplus of college-age men increases the likelihood that she would eventually come across a better alternative to Michael. The number of available alternatives can even vary from state to state. For instance, Michael's attractiveness would have improved if he were living in New York (where there are more single women than men) but worsened if he were living in Alaska (where there are more single men than women; Kershaw, 2004). In sum, Michael's interpersonal value, and therefore the stability of his relationship with Carole, may have suffered not because of anything he did but because of population forces over which he had little, if any, control.

Let's take this notion beyond Carole and Michael's immediate dating network. For instance, the very characteristics and features that people consider desirable (or undesirable) in the first place reflect the values of the larger culture in which they live. Fashions and tastes are constantly changing, making particular characteristics (e.g., hairstyle, physique, clothing), behaviors (smoking, drinking, exercising), or life choices (occupation, political affiliation) more or less attractive.

The moral of these two stories is simple: To understand experiences in our personal lives, we must move past individual traits and examine broader societal characteristics and trends. External features beyond our immediate awareness and control often exert more influence on the circumstances of our day-to-day lives than our "internal" qualities. We can't begin to explain an individual's employability without examining current and past economic trends that affect the number of jobs available and the number of people who are looking for work. We can't begin to explain why relationships work or don't work without addressing the broader interpersonal network and culture in which they are embedded. By the same token, we can't begin to explain people's ordinary, everyday thoughts and actions without examining the social forces that influence them.

SOCIOLOGY AND THE INDIVIDUAL

Herein lies the fundamental theme of ***sociology***—the systematic study of human societies—and the theme that will guide us throughout this book: Everyday social life—our thoughts, actions, feelings, decisions, interactions, and so on—is the product of a complex interplay between societal forces and personal characteristics. To explain why people are the way they are or do the things they do, we must understand the interpersonal, historical, cultural, organizational, and global environments they inhabit. To understand either individuals or society, we must understand both (Mills, 1959).

Of course, seeing the relationship between individuals and social forces is not always so easy. The United States is a society built on the image of the rugged, self-reliant individual. Not surprisingly, it is also a society dominated by individualistic understandings of human behavior that seek to explain problems and processes by focusing exclusively on the personality, the psychology, or even the biochemistry of each individual. Consequently, most of us simply take for granted that what we choose to do, say, feel, and think are private phenomena. Everyday life seems to be a series of free personal choices. After all, we choose what to major in. We choose what to wear when we go out. We choose what and when to eat. We choose our lifestyles, our mates, and so on.

But how free are these decisions? Think about all the times your actions have been dictated or at least influenced by social circumstances over which you had little control. Have you ever felt that because of your age or gender or race, certain opportunities were closed to you? Your ability to legally drive a car, drink alcohol, or vote, for instance, is determined by society's prevailing definition of age. When you're older, you may be forced into retirement despite your skills and desire to continue working. Some occupations, such as bank executive and engineer, are still overwhelmingly male, whereas others, such as nurse and preschool teacher, are almost exclusively female. Likewise, the doctrines of your religion may limit your behavioral choices. For a devout Catholic, premarital sex or even divorce is unlikely. A strict Muslim is required to pause five times a day to pray. An Orthodox Jew would never drink milk and eat meat at the same meal.

Then there's the matter of personal style—your choices in hairstyle, dress, music, and the like. Large-scale marketing strategies can actually create a demand for particular products or images. Would the Jonas Brothers or Mylie Cyrus or Justin Timberlake have become so popular without a tightly managed and slickly packaged publicity program designed to appeal to adolescents and preadolescents? Your tastes, and therefore your choices as a consumer, are often influenced by decisions made in corporate boardrooms.

Broad economic trends also affect your everyday life. You may lose your job or, like André, face a tight job market as a result of economic fluctuations brought about by increased global competition or a severe recession. Or, because of the rapid development of certain types of technology, the college degree that may be your ticket to a rewarding career today may not qualify you even for a low-paying, entry-level position 10 years from now. And if you don't get a good job right out of college, you may have to live at home for years after you graduate—not because you can't face the idea of living apart from your beloved parents but because you can't earn enough to support yourself.

Government and politics affect our personal lives, too. A political decision made at the local, regional, national, or even international level may result in the closing of a government agency you depend on, make the goods and services to which you have grown accustomed either more expensive or less available, or change the amount of taxes you pay. Workplace family-leave policies established by the government may affect your decision whether and when to have a baby. If you are homosexual, the government can determine whether or not you can be covered by your partner's insurance policy and file a joint income tax return, whether or not you can inherit jointly acquired assets, or whether or not you can be involuntarily discharged from the military because of your sexual orientation. In the United States, decisions made by the U.S. Supreme Court can increase or limit your options for controlling your fertility, suing an employer for discrimination, using your property however you please, buying certain products, or keeping the details of your life a private matter.

THE INSIGHTS OF SOCIOLOGY

Sociologists do not deny that individuals make choices or that they must take personal responsibility for those choices. But they are quick to point out that we cannot fully understand the things happening in our lives, private and personal though they may be, without examining the influence of the people, events, and societal features that surround us. By showing how social processes can shape us and how individual action can in turn affect those processes, sociology provides unique insight into the taken-for-granted personal events and the large-scale cultural and global processes that make up our everyday existence.

Other disciplines study human life, too. Biologists study how the body works. Neurologists examine what goes on inside the brain. Psychologists study what goes on inside the mind to create human behavior. These disciplines focus almost exclusively on structures and processes that reside *within* the individual. In contrast, sociologists study what goes on *among* people as individuals, groups, or societies. How do social forces affect the way people interact with one another? How do people make sense of their private lives and the social worlds they occupy? How does everyday social interaction create "society"?

Personal issues such as love, sexuality, poverty, aging, and prejudice are better understood within the appropriate societal context. For instance, U.S. adults tend to believe that they marry purely for love, when in fact society pressures people to marry from the same social class, religion, and race (Berger, 1963). Sociology, unlike other disciplines, forces us to look outside the tight confines of individual anatomy and personality to understand the phenomena that shape us. Consider, for example, the following situations:

- A young high school girl, fearing she is overweight, begins systematically starving herself in the hope of becoming more attractive.
- A 55-year-old stockbroker, unable to find work since his firm laid him off, sinks into a depression after losing his family and his home. He now lives on the streets.
- A 36-year-old professor kills herself after learning that her position at the university will be terminated the following year.
- The student body president and valedictorian of the local high school cannot begin or end her day without several shots of whiskey.

What do these people have in common? Your first response might be that they are all suffering or have suffered terrible personal problems. If you saw them only for what they'd become—an "anorexic," a "homeless person," a "suicide victim," or an "alcoholic"—you might think they have some kind of personality defect, genetic flaw, or mental problem that renders them incapable of coping with the demands of contemporary life. Maybe they simply lack the willpower to pick themselves up and move on. In short, your immediate tendency may be to focus on the unique, perhaps "abnormal," characteristics of these people to explain their problems.

But we cannot downplay the importance of their *social* worlds. There is no denying that we live in a society that praises a lean body, encourages drinking to excess, and values individual achievement and economic success. Some people suffer under these conditions when they don't measure up. This is not to say that all people exposed to the same social messages inevitably fall victim to the same problems. Some people overcome wretched childhoods, others withstand the tragedy of economic failure and begin anew, and some people are immune to narrowly defined cultural images of beauty. But to understand fully the nature of human life or of particular social problems, we must acknowledge the broader social context in which these things occur.

THE SOCIOLOGICAL IMAGINATION

Unfortunately, we often don't see the connections between the personal events in our everyday lives and the larger society in which we live. People in a country such as the United States, which places such a high premium on individual achievement, have difficulty looking beyond their immediate situation. Someone who loses a job, gets divorced, or flunks out of school in such a society has trouble imagining that these experiences are somehow related to massive cultural or historical processes.

The ability to see the impact of these forces on our private lives is what the famous sociologist C. Wright Mills (1959) called the ***sociological imagination***. The sociological imagination enables us to understand the larger historical picture and its meaning in our own lives. Mills argued that no matter how personal we think our experiences are, many of them can be seen as products of society-wide forces. The task of sociology is to help us view our lives as the intersection between personal biography and societal history, to provide a means for us to interpret our lives and social circumstances.

Getting fired, for example, is a terrible, even traumatic private experience. Feelings of personal failure are inevitable when one loses a job. But if the unemployment rate in a community hovers around 20%—as it does in places hardest hit by the recent economic recession, such as Flint, Michigan—then we must see unemployment not as a personal malfunction but as a social problem that has its roots in the economic and political structures of society. Being unemployed is not a character flaw or personal failure if a significant number of people in one's community are also unemployed. We can't explain a spike in the unemployment rate as a sudden increase in the number of incompetent or unprepared individual workers in the labor force. As long as the economy is arranged so that employees are easily replaced or slumps inevitably occur, the social problem of unemployment cannot be solved at the personal level.

The same can be said for divorce, which people usually experience as an intimate tragedy. But in the United States, 4 out of every 10 marriages that begin this year will eventually end in divorce, and divorce rates are increasing in many countries around the world. We must therefore view divorce in the context of broader historical changes occurring throughout societies: in family, law, religion, economics, and the culture as a whole. It is impossible to explain significant changes in divorce rates over time by focusing exclusively on the personal characteristics and behaviors of divorcing individuals. Divorce rates don't rise simply because individual spouses have more difficulty getting along with each other than they used to, and they don't fall because more husbands and wives are suddenly being nicer to each other.

Mills did not mean to imply that the sociological imagination should debilitate us—that is, force us to powerlessly perceive our lives as wholly beyond our control. In fact, the opposite is true. An awareness of the impact of social forces or world history on our personal lives is a prerequisite to any efforts we make to change our social circumstances.

Indeed, the sociological imagination allows us to recognize that the solutions to many of our most serious social problems lie not in changing the personal situations and characteristics of individual people but in changing the social institutions and roles available to them (Mills, 1959). Drug addiction, homelessness, sexual violence, hate crimes, eating disorders, suicide, and other unfortunate situations will not go away simply by treating or punishing a person who is suffering from or engaging in the behavior.

CONCLUSION

In the 21st century, understanding our place within cultural, historical, and global contexts is more important than ever. The world is shrinking. Communication technology binds us to people on the other side of the planet. Increasing ecological awareness opens our eyes to the far-reaching effects of environmental degradations. The changes associated with colossal events in one country (political revolutions, terrorist attacks, natural disasters, economic crises, cultural upheavals) often quickly reverberate around the world. The consequences of such events often continue to be felt for years.

When we look at how people's lives are altered by such phenomena—as they sink into poverty or ascend to prosperity; stand in bread lines or work at a job previously unavailable; or find their sense of ethnic identity, personal safety, or self-worth altered—we can begin to understand the everyday importance of large-scale social change.

However, we must remember that individuals are not just helpless pawns of societal forces. They simultaneously influence and are influenced by society. The next chapter provides a more detailed treatment of this theme. Then, Part II examines how society and our social lives are constructed and ordered. It focuses on the interplay between individuals and the people, groups, organizations, institutions, and culture that collectively make up our society. Part III focuses on the structure of society, with particular attention to the various forms of social inequality.

CHAPTER HIGHLIGHTS

◆ The primary theme of sociology is that our everyday thoughts and actions are the product of a complex interplay between massive social forces and personal characteristics. We can't understand the relationship between individuals and societies without understanding both.

◆ The sociological imagination is the ability to see the impact of social forces on our private lives–an awareness that our lives lie at the intersection of personal biography and societal history.

◆ Rather than study what goes on within people, sociologists study what goes on among people, whether as individuals, groups, organizations, or entire societies. Sociology forces us to look outside the tight confines of our individual personalities to understand the phenomena that shape us.

KEY TERMS

individualistic explanation Tendency to attribute people's achievements and failures to their personal qualities

sociological imagination Ability to see the impact of social forces on our private lives

sociology Systematic study of human societies

©Stuart Dee/Photographer's Choice/Getty Images

2 Seeing and Thinking Sociologically

In 1994, ethnic violence erupted in the small African nation of Rwanda. The Hutu majority had begun a systematic program to exterminate the Tutsi minority. Soon, gruesome pictures of the tortured and dismembered bodies of Tutsi men, women, and children began to appear on television screens around the world. When it was over, close to a million Tutsis had been slaughtered—half of whom died within a 3-month period. Surely, we thought, such horror must have been perpetrated by bands of vicious, crazed thugs who derived some sort of twisted pleasure from committing acts of unspeakable cruelty. Or maybe these were the extreme acts of angry soldiers, trained killers who were committed to destroying the enemy as completely as possible.

Actually, much of the responsibility for these atrocities lay elsewhere, in a most unlikely place: among the ordinary, previously law-abiding Rwandan citizens. Many of the participants in the genocide were the least likely brutes you could imagine. For instance, Pauline Nyiramasuhuko, a former social worker who lectured on women's issues, promised the Tutsis in one village that they would be safe in a local stadium. When they arrived there, armed militia were waiting to kill them. She instructed one group of soldiers to burn alive a group of 70 women and girls, adding, "Before you kill the women, you need to rape them" (quoted in Zimbardo, 2007, p. 13).

Some of the most gruesome attacks took place in churches and missions (Lacey, 2006). Two Benedictine nuns and a University of Rwanda physics professor stood trial for their roles in the killings. The nuns were accused of informing the military that Tutsi refugees had sought sanctuary in the church and of standing by as the soldiers massacred them. One nun allegedly provided the death squads with cans of gasoline, which were used to set fire to a building where 500 Tutsis were hiding. The professor was accused of drawing up a list for the killers of Tutsi employees and students at the university and then killing at least seven Tutsis himself (Simons, 2001). A Catholic priest was sentenced to 15 years in prison for ordering his church to be demolished by bulldozers while 2,000 ethnic Tutsis sought refuge there.

A report by the civil rights organization African Rights provides evidence that members of the medical profession were deeply involved, too (Harris, 1996). The report details how doctors joined with militiamen to hunt down Tutsis, turning hospitals into slaughterhouses. Some helped soldiers drag sick and wounded refugees out of their beds to be killed. Others took advantage of their position of authority to organize road blocks, distribute ammunition, and compile lists of Tutsi colleagues, patients, and neighbors to be sought out and slaughtered. Many doctors who didn't participate in the actual killing refused to treat wounded Tutsis and withheld food and water from refugees who sought sanctuary in hospitals. In fact, the president of Rwanda and the minister of health were both physicians who were eventually tried as war criminals.

Ordinary, well-balanced people—teachers, social workers, priests and nuns devoted to the ideals of charity and mercy, and physicians trained to heal and save lives—had changed, almost overnight, into cold-hearted killers. How could something like this have happened? The answer to this question lies in the sociological claim that individual behavior is largely shaped by social forces and situational contingencies. The circumstances of large-scale ethnic hatred and war have the power to transform well-educated people with no previous history of violence into cruel butchers. Tragically, such forces were at work in many of the 20th and 21st centuries' most infamous examples of human brutality, such as the Nazi Holocaust during World War II and, more recently, large-scale ethnic massacres in Cambodia, Iraq, Bosnia, Kosovo, the Democratic Republic of Congo, and the Darfur region of Sudan, as well as Rwanda.

But social circumstances don't just create opportunities for brutality; they can also motivate ordinary people to engage in astounding acts of heroism. The 2004 film *Hotel Rwanda* depicts the true story of Paul Rusesabagina, a hotel manager in the Rwandan capital, Kigali, who risked his own life to shelter more than a thousand Tutsi refugees from certain death. Rusesabagina was a middle-class Hutu married to a Tutsi and the father of four children. He was a businessman with an eye toward turning a profit and a taste for the finer things in life. But when the genocide began, he used his guile, international contacts, and even water from the swimming pool to keep the refugees alive.

In this chapter, I examine the process by which individuals construct society and the way people's lives are linked to the social environment in which they live. The relationship between the individual and society is a powerful one—each continually affects the other.

HOW INDIVIDUALS STRUCTURE SOCIETY

Up to this point, I have used the word *society* rather loosely. Formally, sociologists define ***society*** as a population living in the same geographic area that shares a culture and a common identity and whose members are subject to the same political authority. Societies may consist of people with the same ethnic heritage or of hundreds of different groups who speak a multitude of languages. Some societies are highly industrialized and complex; others are primarily agricultural and relatively simple in structure. Some are very religious; others are distinctly secular.

According to the 19th-century French philosopher Auguste Comte, all societies, whatever their form, contain both forces for stability, which he called "social statics," and forces for change, which he called "social dynamics." Sometimes, however, people use the term *society* only to mean a "static" entity—a natural, permanent, and historical structure. They frequently talk about society "planning" or "shaping" our lives and describe it as a relatively unchanging set of organizations, institutions, systems, and cultural patterns into which successive generations of people are born and socialized.

As a result, sociology students often start out believing not only that society is powerfully influential (which, of course, it is) but also that it is something that exists "out there," completely separate and distinct from us (which it isn't). It is tempting to view society simply as a "top down" initiator of human activity, a massive entity that methodically shapes the lives of all individuals within it, like some gigantic puppeteer manipulating a bunch of marionettes. This characterization is not completely inaccurate. Society does exert influence on its members through certain identifiable structural features and historical circumstances. The concept of the sociological imagination discussed in Chapter 1 implies that structural forces beyond our direct control do shape our personal lives.

But this view is only one side of the sociological coin. The sociological imagination also encourages us to see that each individual has a role in forming a society and influencing the course of its history. As we navigate our social environments, we respond in ways that may modify the effects and even the nature of that environment (House, 1981). To fully understand society, then, we must see it as a human construction made up of people interacting with one another. Communication plays an important role in the construction of society. If we couldn't communicate with one another to reach an understanding about society's expectations, we couldn't live together. Through day-to-day communication, we construct, reaffirm, experience, and alter the reality of our society.

Imagine two people sitting on a park bench discussing the continuing "war on terror" in Iraq and Afghanistan. Person A is convinced that the actual threat to individual citizens, in the decade since the attacks of September 11, 2001, does not warrant the erosion of civil rights and personal privacy through measures such as the USA PATRIOT Act, which allows the government to gain access to citizens' tax records, credit records, library records, bookstore records, and medical records without probable cause, consent, or knowledge. She thinks that the war in Iraq began under false pretenses and the mounting number of U.S. casualties is reason enough to withdraw all our troops. Person B counters that more recent terrorist attacks, such as those in Madrid, London, Bali, and Mumbai, show that we're always potential targets and that any means of preventing U.S. deaths at the hands of foreign terrorists is worthwhile, even if it means sacrificing some freedoms. He believes that leaving Iraq and Afghanistan would be akin to surrender and would just embolden the terrorists. The debate becomes heated: One thinks that our nation's founding principles are the best protection for individual liberty; the other feels that individual liberty must be sacrificed if people's lives are in danger. These two people obviously don't agree on the need for or the effectiveness of a war on terror. But merely by discussing it, they are acknowledging that such a thing exists. In talking about such matters, people give shape and substance to society's ideals and values (Hewitt, 1988).

We live in a world in which our everyday lives are largely a product of structural, or ***macrolevel,*** societal and historical processes. Society is an objective fact that coerces, even creates us (Berger, 1963). At the same time, we are constantly creating, maintaining, reaffirming, and transforming society. Hence, society is part and parcel of individual-level human interaction (Collins, 1981). But although we create society, we then collectively "forget" we've done so, believe it is independent of us, and live our lives under its influence.

SOCIAL INFLUENCE: THE IMPACT OF OTHER PEOPLE IN OUR EVERYDAY LIVES

We live in a world with other people. I know that's not the most profound statement you've ever read, but it is key to understanding the sociology of human behavior. Our everyday lives are a collection of brief encounters, extended conversations, intimate interactions, and chance meetings with other people. In our early years, we may have our parents, siblings, uncles, aunts, and grandparents to contend with. Soon, we begin to form friendships with others outside our families. Over time, our lives also become filled with connections to other people—classmates, teachers, coworkers, bosses, spiritual leaders, therapists—who are neither family nor friends but who have an enormous impact on us. And, of course, we have frequent experiences with total strangers: the person at the local coffee shop who serves us our daily lattes, the travelers who sit next to us on airplanes, the tech support specialist who helps us when our laptops freeze.

If you think about it, understanding what it means to be alone requires that we know what it's like to be with other people. As I discuss in Chapters 5 and 6, much of our private identity—what we think of ourselves, the type of people we become, and the images of ourselves we project in public—comes from our contact with others.

Imagine for a moment what your life would be like if you had never had contact with other people (assuming you could have survived this long!). You wouldn't know what love is, or hate or jealousy or compassion or appreciation. You wouldn't know if you were wealthy or poor, bright or dumb, witty or boring. You'd lack some basic information, too. You wouldn't know what day it is, how much a pound weighs, where Belgium is, or how to read. Furthermore, you'd have no language, and because we use language to think, imagine, predict, plan, wonder, and reminisce, you'd lack these abilities as well. In short, you'd lack the key experiences that make you a functioning human being.

Contact with people is essential to a person's social development. But there is more to social life than simply bumping into other people from time to time. We act and react to things and people in our environment as a result of the meaning we attach to them. At the sight of a dog barrelling toward it, a squirrel instinctively runs away. A human, however, does not have such an automatic reaction. We've learned from past experiences that some animals are approachable and others aren't. So we can think, "Is this dog friendly or mean? Does it want to lick my face or tear me limb from limb?" and respond accordingly. In short, we usually interpret events in our environment before we react.

The presence of other people may motivate you to improve your performance—for example, when the quality of your tennis opponent makes you play the best match of your life. But their presence may at other times inhibit you—as when you forget your lines in the school play because your little brother's in the audience making faces at you. Even our physical well-being is affected by those around us. According to researchers in Japan, the risk of heart attack is three times higher among women who live with their husbands and their husbands' parents than among women who live with just their husbands (cited in Rabin, 2008).

Consider also the way people eat. Most of us assume that we eat when we're hungry and stop when we're full. But our eating tendencies reflect the social cues that surround us. For instance, when we eat with other people, we adjust our pace to their pace. We also tend to eat longer—and therefore more—when in groups than when we're by ourselves. One researcher found that people, on average, eat 35% more food when they're with one other person than when alone. That figure goes up to 75% more when eating with three other people (DeCastro, 1994, 2000). This may explain why a person's chance of becoming obese increases significantly if he or she has a close friend who is obese (Christakis & Fowler, 2007). As one researcher put it, "Weight can be inherited, but it can also be contagious" (Wansink, 2006, p. 99).

SOCIETAL INFLUENCE: THE EFFECT OF SOCIAL STRUCTURE ON OUR EVERYDAY LIVES

Social life is more than individual people affecting one another's lives. Society is not just a sum of its human parts; it's also the way those parts are put together, related to one another, and organized (Coulson & Riddell, 1980). Statuses, roles, groups, organizations, and institutions are the building blocks of society. Culture is the mortar that holds these blocks together. Although society is dynamic and constantly evolving, it has an underlying macrolevel structure that persists.

Statuses and Roles

One key element of any society is its collection of ***statuses***—the positions that individuals within the society occupy. When most of us hear the word *status,* we tend to associate it with rank or prestige. But here we're talking about a status as any socially defined position that a person can occupy: cook, daughter, anthropologist, husband, computer nerd, electrician, shoplifter, and so on. Some statuses may, in fact, be quite prestigious, such as president. But others carry very little prestige, such as gas station attendant. Some statuses require a tremendous amount of training, such as physician; others, such as ice-cream lover, require little effort or none at all.

We all occupy many statuses at the same time. I am a college professor, but I am also a son, uncle, father, brother, friend, sushi lover, occasional poker player, aging athlete, homeowner, and author. My behavior at any given moment is dictated to a large degree by the status that's most important at that particular point in time. When I am jogging, my status as professor is not particularly relevant. But if I decide to run in a half-marathon race instead of giving the final exam in my sociology course, I may be in trouble!

Sociologists often distinguish between ascribed and achieved statuses. An ***ascribed status*** is a social position that we acquire at birth or enter involuntarily later in life. Our race, sex, ethnicity, and identity as someone's child or grandchild are all ascribed statuses. As we get older, we enter the ascribed status of teenager and, eventually, old person. These aren't positions we choose to occupy. An ***achieved status,*** in contrast, is a social position we take on voluntarily or acquire through our own efforts or accomplishments, such as being a student or a spouse or an engineer.

Of course, the distinction between ascribed and achieved status is not always so clear. Some people become college students not because of their own efforts but because of their family's influence. Chances are the religion with which you identify is the one your parents belong to. However, many people decide to change their religious membership later in life. Moreover, as we'll see later in this book, certain ascribed statuses (sex, race, ethnicity, and age) influence our access to lucrative achieved statuses.

Statuses are important sociologically because they all come with a set of rights, obligations, behaviors, and duties that people occupying a certain position are expected or encouraged to perform. These expectations are referred to as ***roles***. For instance, the role of a "professor" includes teaching students, answering their questions, grading them impartially, and dressing appropriately. Any out-of-role behavior may be met with shock or suspicion. If I consistently showed up for class in a thong and a tank top, that would certainly violate my "scholarly" image and call into question my ability to teach.

Each person, as a result of her or his own skills, interests, and interactional experiences, defines roles differently. Students enter a class with the general expectation that their professor is going to teach them something. Each professor, however, may have a different method of meeting that expectation. Some professors are very animated; others remain stationary behind a podium. Some do not allow questions until after the lecture; others encourage probing questions from students. Some are meticulous and organized, others spontaneous and absentminded.

People engage in typical patterns of interaction based on the relationship between their roles and the roles of others. Employers are expected to interact with employees in a certain way, as are dentists with patients and salespeople with customers. In each case, actions are constrained by the role responsibilities and obligations associated with those particular statuses. We know, for instance, that lovers and spouses are supposed to interact with each other differently from the way acquaintances or friends are supposed to interact. In a parent-child relationship, both members are linked by certain rights, privileges, and obligations. Parents are responsible for providing their children with the basic necessities of life—food, clothing, shelter, and so forth. These expectations are so powerful that not meeting them may constitute the crime of negligence or abuse. Children, in turn, are expected to abide by their parents' wishes. Thus, interactions within a relationship are functions not only of the individual personalities of the people involved but also of the role requirements associated with the statuses they occupy.

We feel the power of role expectations most clearly when we have difficulty meeting them or when we occupy two conflicting statuses simultaneously. Sociologists use the term ***role strain*** to refer to situations in which people lack the necessary resources to fulfill the demands of a particular role, such as when parents can't afford to provide their children with adequate food, clothing, or shelter. ***Role conflict*** describes situations in which people encounter tension in trying to cope with the demands of incompatible roles. People may feel frustrated in their efforts to do what they feel they're supposed to do when the role expectations of one status clash with the role expectations of another. For instance, a mother may have an important out-of-town conference to attend (status of sociologist) on the same day her 10-year-old son is appearing as a talking pig in the school play (status of parent). Or a teenager who works hard at his job at the local ice-cream shop (status of employee) is frustrated when his buddies arrive and expect him to sit and chat or to give them free ice cream (status of friend).

Groups

Societies are not simply composed of people occupying statuses and living in accordance with roles. Sometimes individuals form well-defined units called groups. A ***group*** is a set of people who interact more or less regularly with one another and who are conscious of their identity as a group. Your family, your colleagues at work, and any clubs or sports teams to which you belong are all social groups.

Groups are not just collections of people who randomly come together for some purpose. Their structure defines the relationships among members. When groups are large, enduring, and complex, each individual within the group is likely to occupy some named position or status—mother, president, supervisor, linebacker, and so forth.

Group membership can also be a powerful force behind one's future actions and thoughts. Sociologists distinguish between ***in-groups***—those groups we belong to and toward which we feel a sense of loyalty—and ***out-groups***—the groups we don't belong to and toward which we feel a certain amount of antagonism. For instance, a girl who is not a member of the popular clique at school, but wants to be, is likely to structure many of her daily activities around gaining entry into that group. In addition, like statuses and roles, groups come with a set of general expectations. A person's actions within a group are judged according to a conventional set of ideas about how things ought to be. For example, a coworker who always arrives late for meetings or never takes his or her turn working an undesirable shift is violating the group's expectations and will be pressured to conform.

The smallest group, of course, is one that consists of two people, or a ***dyad.*** According to the renowned German sociologist Georg Simmel (1902/1950), dyads (marriages, close friendships, etc.) are among the most meaningful and intense connections we have. The problem, though, is that dyads are inherently unstable. If one person decides to leave, the group completely collapses. Hence, it's not surprising that for society's most important dyads (i.e., marriages), a variety of legal, religious, and cultural restrictions are in place that make it difficult for people to dissolve them.

The addition of one person to a dyad—forming what Simmel called a ***triad***—fundamentally changes the nature of the group. Although triads might appear more stable than dyads because the withdrawal of one person needn't destroy the group, they develop other problems. If you're one of three children in your family, you already know that triads always contain the potential for ***coalitions***—when two individuals pair up and perhaps conspire against the third.

Groups can also be classified by their influence on our everyday lives. A ***primary group*** consists of a small number of members who have direct contact with one another over a relatively long period of time. Emotional attachment is high in such groups, and members have intimate knowledge of one another's lives. Families and networks of close friends are primary groups. A ***secondary group,*** in contrast, is much more formal and impersonal. The group is established for a specific task, such as the production or sale of consumer goods, and members are less emotionally committed to one another. Their roles tend to be highly structured. Primary groups may form within secondary groups, as when close friendships form among coworkers, but in general, secondary groups require less emotional investment than primary groups.

Like societies, groups have a reality that is more than just the sum of their members; a change in a group's membership doesn't necessarily alter its basic structure. Secondary groups can endure changing membership relatively easily if some, or even all, individuals leave and new ones enter—as for example, when the senior class in a high school graduates and is replaced in the school the following year by a new group of students. Change in primary groups—perhaps through divorce or death—however, produces some dramatic effects on the nature and identity of the group, although the group itself still exists.

Although people of the same race, gender, ethnicity, or religion are not social groups in the strictest sense of the term, they function like groups in that members share certain characteristics and interests. They become an important source of a person's identity. For instance, members of a particular racial or ethnic group may organize into a well-defined unit to fight for a political cause. The feelings of "we-ness" or "they-ness" generated by such group membership can be constructive or dangerous, encouraging pride and unity in some cases and anger, bitterness, and hatred toward outsiders in others.

Organizations

At an even higher level of complexity are social units called ***organizations,*** networks of statuses and groups created for a specific purpose. The International Brotherhood of Teamsters, Oxford University, Microsoft, the Federal Emergency Management Agency, the National Organization for Women, and the Methodist Church are all examples of organizations. Organizations contain groups as well as individuals occupying clearly defined statuses and taking on clearly defined roles.

Some of the groups within organizations are transitory, some are more permanent. For instance, a university consists of individual classes that disband at the end of the semester, as well as more permanent groups such as the faculty, administration, secretarial staff, maintenance staff, and alumni.

Large, formal organizations are often characterized by a *hierarchical division of labor.* Each person in an organization occupies a position that has a specific set of duties and responsibilities, and those positions can be "ranked" according to their relative power and importance. At Honda, for instance, assembly-line workers typically don't make hiring decisions or set budgetary policies, and the vice president in charge of marketing doesn't spray paint the underbodies of newly assembled Accords. In general, people occupy certain positions in an organization because they have the skills to do the job that is required of them. When a person can no longer meet the requirements of the job, he or she can be replaced without seriously affecting the functioning of the organization.

Organizations are a profoundly common and visible feature of everyday social life, as you'll see in Chapter 9. Most of us cannot acquire food, get an education, pray, undergo lifesaving surgery, or earn a salary without coming into contact with or becoming a member of some organization. To be a full-fledged member of modern society is to be deeply involved in some form of organizational life.

Social Institutions

When stable sets of statuses, roles, groups, and organizations form, they provide the foundation for addressing fundamental societal needs. These enduring patterns of social life are called ***social institutions***. Sociologists usually think of institutions as the building blocks that organize society. They are the patterned ways of solving the problems and meeting the requirements of a particular society. Although there may be conflict over what society "needs" and how best to fulfill those needs, all societies must have some systematic way of organizing the various aspects of everyday life.

Key social institutions in modern society include the family, education, economics, politics and law, and religion. Some sociologists add health care, the military, and the mass media to the list.

Family. All societies must have a way of replacing their members, and reproduction is essential to the survival of human society as a whole. Within the institution of family, sexual relations among adults are regulated; people are cared for; children are born, protected, and socialized; and newcomers are provided an identity—a "lineage"—that gives them a sense of belonging. Just how these activities are carried out varies from society to society. Indeed, different societies have different ideas about which groups qualify for designation as family. But the institution of family, whatever its form, remains the hub of social life in virtually all societies (Turner, 1972).

Education. Young people need to be taught what it means to be a member of the society in which they live and how to survive in it. In small, simple societies, the family is the primary institution responsible for socializing new members into the culture. However, as societies become more complex, it becomes exceedingly difficult for a family to teach its members all they need to know to function and survive. Hence, most modern, complex societies have an elaborate system of schools—preschool, primary, secondary, college, professional—which not only create and disseminate knowledge and information but also train individuals for future careers and teach them their "place" in society.

Economy. From the beginning, human societies have faced the problems of securing enough food and protecting people from the environment (Turner, 1972). Today, modern societies have systematic ways of gathering resources, converting them into goods and commodities, and distributing them to members. In addition, societies provide ways of coordinating and facilitating the operation of this massive process. For instance, banks, accounting firms, insurance companies, stock brokerages, transportation agencies, and computer networks don't produce goods themselves but provide services that make the gathering, producing, and distributing of goods possible. To facilitate the distribution of both goods and services, economic institutions adopt a system of common currency and an identifiable mode of exchange. In some societies, the economy is driven by the value of efficient production and the need to maximize profits; in others, the collective well-being of the population is the primary focus.

Politics and Law. All societies face the problem of how to preserve order, avoid chaos, and make important social decisions. The legal system provides explicit laws or rules of conduct and mechanisms for enforcing those laws, settling disputes, and changing outdated laws or creating new ones (Turner, 1972). These activities take place within a larger system of governance that allocates and acknowledges power, authority, and leadership. In a democracy, the governance process includes the citizens, who have a say in who leads them; in a monarchy, kings or queens can claim that their birthright entitles them to positions of leadership. In some societies, the transfer of power is efficient and mannerly; in others, it is violent.

Religion. In the process of meeting the familial, educational, economic, and political needs of society, some individuals thrive, whereas others suffer. Hence, all societies also face the problem of providing their less successful members with a sense of purpose and meaning in their lives. Religion gives individuals a belief system for understanding their existence as well as a network of personal support in times of need. Although many members of a given society may actively reject religion, it remains one of the most enduring and powerful social institutions. Although religion provides enormous comfort to some people, it can also be a source of hatred and irreparable divisions.

Health Care. One of the profoundly universal facts of human life is that people get sick and die. In some societies, healing the sick and managing the transition to death involves spiritual or supernatural intervention; other societies rely on science and modern technology. Most modern societies have established a complex system of health care to disseminate medical treatments. Doctors, nurses, hospitals, pharmacies, drug and medical equipment manufacturers, insurance companies, and patients all play an active role in the health care system.

Military. To deal with the possibility of attack from outside and the protection of national interests, many societies maintain an active military defense. However, militaries are used not only to defend societies but also, at times, to attack other countries in order to acquire land, resources, or power. In other cases, the military is used for political change, as when the U.S. military was mobilized to overthrow the government of Saddam Hussein in Iraq in 2003.

Mass Media. In very small, relatively close-knit societies, information can be shared through word of mouth. However, as societies become more complex, the dissemination of information requires a massive coordinated system. The modern mass media—radio, newspapers, television, and the Internet—provide coverage of important societal events so individuals can make informed decisions about their own lives. But the media do more than report events of local, national, and international significance. They also actively mold public opinion and project and reinforce a society's values.

To individual members of society, social institutions appear huge, natural, and inevitable. Most of us couldn't imagine life without a family. Nor could most of us fathom what society would be like without a stable system of government, a common currency, schools to educate our children, or an effective military. It is very easy, then, to think that institutions exist independently of people.

But one of the important themes that will be revisited throughout this book is that we each have a role to play in maintaining or changing social institutions, as when citizens change the political shape of a country by voting out of office an administration with which they've grown displeased. Although the effects of changes can be felt at the organizational and institutional levels, they are ultimately initiated, implemented, or rejected, and, most importantly, experienced by individual people.

Culture

The most pervasive element of society is ***culture,*** which consists of the language, values, beliefs, rules, behaviors, and physical artifacts of a society. Think of it as a society's "personality." Culture gives us codes of conduct—the proper, acceptable ways of doing things. We usually don't think twice about it, yet it colors everything we experience.

Culture is particularly apparent when someone questions or violates it. Those who do not believe what the majority believes, value what the majority values, or obey the same rules the majority obeys are likely to experience punishment, psychiatric attention, or social ostracism. I discuss the power of culture in more detail in Chapter 4, but here we should look at two key aspects of culture that are thoroughly implicated in the workings of social structure and social influence: values and norms.

Values

Perhaps no word in the English language carries more baggage than values. People throw around terms such as *moral values, traditional values, family values,* and *American values* with little thought as to what they actually mean. Sociologically speaking, a ***value*** is a standard of judgment by which people decide on desirable goals and outcomes (Hewitt & Hewitt, 1986). Values represent the general criteria on which our lives and the lives of others can be judged. They justify the social rules that determine how we ought to behave. For instance, laws against theft clearly reflect the value we place on personal property.

Different societies emphasize different values. Success, independence, and individual achievement are seen as important values in U.S. society. In other societies, such as Vietnam, people are more likely to value group obligation and loyalty to family.

Values within a society sometimes come into conflict. The value of privacy ("stay out of other people's business") and the value of generosity ("help others in need") may clash when we are trying to decide whether to help a stranger who seems to need assistance. Similarly, although the value of cooperation is held in high esteem in contemporary U.S. society, when someone is taking a final exam in a sociology class, cooperation is likely to be defined as cheating. When the key values that characterize a particular social institution come into conflict, the result may be widespread legal and moral uncertainty among individuals.

Norms

Norms are culturally defined rules of conduct. They specify what people should do and how they should pursue values. They tell us what is proper or necessary behavior within particular roles, groups, organizations, and institutions. Thousands of norms guide the minor and the grand details of our lives, from the bedroom to the classroom to the boardroom. You can see, then, that norms serve as the fundamental building blocks of social order.

Norms make our interactions with others reasonably predictable. Americans expect that when they extend a hand to another person, that person will grasp it and a brief handshake will follow. They would be shocked if they held out their hand and the other person grabbed it and spit on it or wouldn't let go. In contrast, people in some societies commonly embrace or kiss each other's cheeks as a form of greeting, even when involved in a formal business relationship. A hearty handshake in those societies may be interpreted as an insult. In Thailand, people greet each other by placing the palms of their hands together in front of their bodies and slightly bowing their heads. This greeting is governed by strict norms. Slight differences in the placement of one's hands reflect the social position of the other person—the higher the hands, the higher the position of the person being greeted. Norms such as these make it easier to "live with others" in a relatively harmonious way (see Chapter 4).

Social Structure in a Global Context

A discussion of social structure would not be complete without acknowledging the fact that statuses, roles, groups, organizations, social institutions, and culture are sometimes influenced by broad societal and historical forces at work in the world. One such force with deep implications for contemporary society is ***globalization***, the process through which people's lives all around the world become increasingly interconnected—economically, politically, environmentally, and culturally (see Chapter 9 for more detail).

Cultures have rarely been completely isolated from outside influence, because throughout human history people have been moving from one place to another, spreading goods and ideas. What is different today, though, is the speed and scope of these changes. Several decades ago, overnight mail service and direct long-distance telephone dialing increased the velocity of cross-national interaction. Advances in transportation technology have made international trade more cost-effective and international travel more accessible to ordinary citizens. And recently, the Internet has given people around the world instantaneous access to the cultural artifacts and ideals of other societies. Through search engines such as Google, Yahoo!, and Bing, children in Bangkok, Beirut, or Baltimore can easily and immediately mine unlimited amounts of the same information on every conceivable topic.

Clearly, societies are more interdependent than ever, and that interdependence matters for individuals around the world. Sometimes the effects are positive. Pharmaceutical breakthroughs in the United States or Europe, for instance, can save lives around the world. Globalization gives us a chance to learn about other societies and learn from them. Other times, however, global influence can have disastrous consequences. Many of today's most pressing societal problems—widespread environmental devastation, large- and small-scale wars, economic crises, viral epidemics, and so on—are a function of globalization to some degree. Closer to home, the establishment of a toy factory in Southeast Asia or a clothing factory in Mexico may mean the loss of hundreds of manufacturing jobs in Kentucky or California.

In short, it is becoming increasingly difficult, if not impossible, to consider ourselves members of a single society unaffected by other societies. All of us are simultaneously members of our own society and citizens of a world community.

THREE PERSPECTIVES ON SOCIAL ORDER

The question of what holds all these elements of society together and how they combine to create social order has concerned sociologists for decades. Sociologists identify three broad intellectual orientations they often use to address this question: the structural-functionalist perspective, the conflict perspective, and symbolic interactionism. Each of these perspectives has its advantages and shortcomings. Each is helpful in answering particular types of questions. For instance, structural functionalism is useful in showing us how and why large, macrolevel structures, such as organizations and institutions, develop and persist. The conflict perspective sheds light on the various sources of social inequality that exist in this and other societies. And symbolic interactionism is helpful in explaining how individuals construct meaning to make sense of their social surroundings. At times, the perspectives complement one another; at other times, they contradict one another.

Throughout the remaining chapters of this book, I periodically return to these three perspectives—as well as several other specific perspectives—to apply them to specific social phenomena, experiences, and events.

The Structural-Functionalist Perspective

According to sociologists Talcott Parsons and Neil Smelser (1956), two theorists typically associated with the ***structural-functionalist perspective,*** a society is a complex system composed of various parts, much like a living organism. Just as the heart, lungs, and liver work together to keep an animal alive, so too do all the elements of a society's structure work together to keep society alive.

Social institutions play a key role in keeping a society stable. All societies require certain things to survive. They must ensure that the goods and services people need are produced and distributed; they must provide ways of dealing with conflicts between individuals, groups, and organizations; they must provide ways to ensure that individuals are made a part of the existing culture.

As we saw earlier in this chapter, institutions allow societies to attain their goals, adapt to a changing environment, reduce tension, and recruit individuals into statuses and roles. Economic institutions, for instance, allow adaptation to dwindling supplies of natural resources or to competition from other societies. Educational institutions train people for the future statuses they will have to fill to keep society going. Religions help maintain the existence of society by reaffirming people's values and maintaining social ties among people (Durkheim, 1915/1954).

Sociologist Robert Merton (1957) distinguishes between manifest and latent functions of social institutions. ***Manifest functions*** are the intended, obvious consequences of activities designed to help some part of the social system. For instance, the manifest function of going to college is to get an education and acquire the credentials necessary to establish a career. ***Latent functions*** are the *unintended,* sometimes unrecognized, consequences of actions that coincidentally help the system. The latent function of going to college is to meet people and establish close, enduring friendships. In addition, college informally teaches students how to live on their own, away from their parents. It also provides important lessons in negotiating the intricacies of large bureaucracies—registering for classes, filling out forms, learning important school policies—so that students figure out how to "get things done" in an organization. These latent lessons will certainly help students who enter the equally large and bureaucratic world of work after they graduate (Galles, 1989).

From the structural-functionalist perspective, if an aspect of social life does not contribute to society's survival—that is, if it is *dys*functional—it will eventually disappear. Things that persist, even if they seem to be disruptive, must persist because they contribute somehow to the survival of society (Durkheim, 1915/1954). Take prostitution, for example. A practice so widely condemned and punished would appear to be dysfunctional for society. But prostitution has existed since human civilization began. Some structural functionalists suggest that prostitution satisfies sexual needs that may not be met through more socially acceptable means, such as marriage. Customers can have their physical desires satisfied without having to establish the sort of emotional attachment to another person that would destroy a preexisting marriage, harm the institution of family, and ultimately threaten the entire society (Davis, 1937).

Structural functionalism was the dominant theoretical tradition in sociology for most of the 20th century, and it still shapes sociological thinking to a certain degree today. But it has been criticized for accepting existing social arrangements without examining how they might exploit or otherwise disadvantage certain groups or individuals within the society.

The Conflict Perspective

The ***conflict perspective*** addresses the deficiencies of structural functionalism by viewing the structure of society as a source of inequality, which benefits some groups at the expense of other groups. Conflict sociologists are likely to see society not in terms of stability and acceptance but in terms of conflict and struggle. They focus not on how all the elements of society contribute to its smooth operation and continued existence but on how these elements promote divisions and inequalities. Social order arises not from the societal pursuit of harmony but from dominance and coercion. The family, government, religion, and other institutions foster and legitimate the power and privilege of some individuals or groups at the expense of others.

Karl Marx, perhaps the most famous scholar associated with the conflict perspective, focused exclusively on economic arrangements. He argued that all human societies are structured around the production of goods that people need to survive. The individuals or groups who control the means of production—land in an agricultural society, factories in an industrial society, computer networks and information in a postindustrial society—have the power to create and maintain social institutions that serve their interests. Hence, economic, political, and educational systems in a modern society support the interests of those who control the wealth (see Chapter 10).

Marx believed that when resources are limited or scarce, conflict between the "haves" and the "have-nots" is inevitable and creates a situation in which those in power must enforce social order. He said this conflict is not caused by greedy, exploitative individuals; rather, it is a byproduct of a system in which those who benefit from inequality are motivated to act in ways that maintain it.

Contemporary conflict sociologists are interested in various sources of conflict and inequality. One version of the conflict perspective that has become particularly popular among sociologists in the past few decades is the ***feminist perspective.*** Feminist sociologists focus on gender as the most important source of conflict and inequality in social life. Compared with men, women in nearly every contemporary society have less power, influence, and opportunity. In families, especially in industrialized societies, women have traditionally been encouraged to perform unpaid household labor and child care duties, whereas men have been free to devote their energy and attention to earning money and power in the economic marketplace. Women's lower wages when they do work outside the home are often justified by the assumption that their paid labor is secondary to that of their husbands. But as women in many societies seek equality in education, politics, career, marriage, and other areas of social life, their activities inevitably affect social institutions (see Chapter 12 for more details). The feminist perspective helps us understand the difficulties men and women face in their everyday lives as they experience the changes taking place in society.

Because this perspective focuses so much on conflict, it tends to downplay or overlook the elements of society that different groups and individuals share. In addition, its emphasis on inequality has led some critics to argue that it is a perspective motivated by a particular political agenda and not the objective pursuit of knowledge.

Symbolic Interactionism

The structural-functionalist and the conflict perspectives differ in their assumptions about the nature of society, yet both analyze society mostly at the macro- or structural level, focusing on societal patterns and the consequences they produce. In contrast, ***symbolic interactionism*** attempts to understand society and social structure through an examination of the ***microlevel*** interactions of people as individuals, pairs, or groups.

These forms of interaction take place within a world of symbolic communication. A ***symbol*** is something used to represent or stand for something else (Charon, 1998). It can be a physical object (such as an engagement ring, standing for betrothal), a characteristic or property of objects (such as the pink color of a triangle, standing for gay rights), a gesture (such as a thumb pointed up, standing for "everything's OK"), or a word (such as the letters d-o-g, standing for a particular type of household pet).

Symbols are created, modified, and used by people through their interactions with others. We concoct them and come to agree on what they should stand for. Our lives depend on such agreement. For instance, imagine how chaotic—not to mention dangerous—automobile travel would be if we didn't all agree that green stands for "go" and red stands for "stop."

Symbols don't bear any necessary connection to nature. Rather, they're arbitrary human creations. There's nothing in the natural properties of "greenness" that automatically determines that green should stand for "go." We could have decided long ago that purple meant "go." It wouldn't have mattered as long as we all learned and understood this symbol.

Most human behavior is determined not by the objective facts of a given situation but by the symbolic meanings people attach to the facts (Weber, 1947). When we interact with others, we constantly attempt to interpret what they mean and what they're up to. A gentle pat on the shoulder symbolizes one thing if it comes from someone with whom you are romantically involved but something quite different if it comes from your mother or your boss.

Society, therefore, is not a structure that exists independent of human action. It is "socially constructed," emerging from the countless symbolic interactions that occur each day between individuals. Each time I refer to "U.S. society," "the school system," "the global economy," "the threat of terrorism," or "the Newman family" in my casual conversations with others, I am doing my part to reinforce the notion that these are real things. By examining how and why we interact with others, symbolic interactionism reveals how the everyday experiences of people help to construct and maintain social institutions and, ultimately, society itself.

This perspective reminds us that for all its structural elements, society is, in the end, people interacting with one another. But by highlighting these microlevel experiences, symbolic interactionism runs the risk of ignoring the larger social patterns and structures that create the influential historical, institutional, and cultural settings for people's everyday interactions.

CONCLUSION

Living with others, within a social structure, influences many aspects of our everyday lives. But we must be cautious not to overstate the case. Although the fundamental elements of society are not merely the direct expressions of the personalities of individuals, we must also remember that people are more than "robots programmed by social structure" (Swanson, 1992, p. 94).

The lesson I hope you take from this chapter—and, in fact, from this book—is that the relationship between the individual and society is reciprocal. One cannot be understood without accounting for the other. Yes, this thing we call "society" touches our lives in intimate, important, and sometimes not altogether obvious ways. And yes, this influence is often beyond our immediate control. But society is not simply a "forbidding prison" that mechanically determines who we are and what we do (Berger, 1963). We as individuals can affect the very social structure that affects us. We can modify role expectations, change norms, create or destroy organizations, revolutionize institutions, and even alter the path of world history.

CHAPTER HIGHLIGHTS

- Although society exists as an objective fact, it is also created, reaffirmed, and altered through the day-to-day interactions of the very people it influences and controls.

- Humans are social beings. We look to others to help define and interpret particular situations. Other people can influence what we see, feel, think, and do.

- Society consists of socially recognizable combinations of individuals—relationships, groups, and organizations—as well as the products of human action—statuses, roles, culture, institutions, and broad societal forces such as globalization.

- There are three major sociological perspectives. The structural-functionalist perspective focuses on the way various parts of society are structured and interrelated to maintain stability and order. The conflict perspective emphasizes how the various elements of society promote inequality and conflict among groups of people. Symbolic interactionism seeks to understand society and social structure through the interactions of people and the ways in which they subjectively define their worlds.

KEY TERMS

achieved status Social position acquired through our own efforts or accomplishments or taken on voluntarily

ascribed status Social position acquired at birth or taken on involuntarily later in life

coalition Subgroup of a triad, formed when two members unite against the third member

conflict perspective Theoretical perspective that views the structure of society as a source of inequality, which always benefits some groups at the expense of other groups

culture Language, values, beliefs, rules, behaviors, and artifacts that characterize a society

dyad Group consisting of two people

feminist perspective Theoretical perspective that focuses on gender as the most important source of conflict and inequality in social life

globalization Process through which people's lives all around the world become economically, politically, environmentally, and culturally interconnected

group Set of people who interact more or less regularly and who are conscious of their identity as a unit

in-groups Those groups we belong to and toward which we feel a sense of loyalty

latent function Unintended, unrecognized consequences of activities that help some part of the social system

macrolevel Way of examining human life that focuses on the broad social forces and structural features of society that exist above the level of individual people

manifest function Intended, obvious consequences of activities designed to help some part of the social system

microlevel Way of examining human life that focuses on the immediate, everyday experiences of individuals

norm Culturally defined standard or rule of conduct

organization Large, complex network of positions created for a specific purpose and characterized by a hierarchical division of labor

out-groups The groups we don't belong to and toward which we feel a certain amount of antagonism

primary group Collection of individuals who are together over a relatively long period, whose members have direct contact with and feel emotional attachment to one another

role Set of expectations—rights, obligations, behaviors, duties—associated with a particular status

role conflict Frustration people feel when the demands of one role they are expected to fulfill clash with the demands of another role

role strain Situations in which people lack the necessary resources to fulfill the demands of a particular role

secondary group Relatively impersonal collection of individuals that is established to perform a specific task

social institution Stable set of roles, statuses, groups, and organizations—such as the institutions of education, family, politics, religion, health care, or the economy—that provides a foundation for behavior in some major area of social life

society Population of people living in the same geographic area who share a culture and a common identity and whose members fall under the same political authority

status Any named social position that people can occupy

structural-functionalist perspective Theoretical perspective that posits that social institutions are structured to maintain stability and order in society

symbol Something used to represent or stand for something else

symbolic interactionism Theoretical perspective that explains society and social structure through an examination of the *micro*level, personal, day-to-day exchanges of people as individuals, pairs, or groups

triad Group consisting of three people

value Standard of judgment by which people decide on desirable goals and outcomes

PART II

The Construction of Self and Society

Part II examines the basic architecture of individual identities and of society: how reality and truth are constructed; how social order is created and maintained; how culture and history influence our personal experiences; how societal values, ideals, and norms are instilled; and how we acquire our sense of self. The tactical and strategic ways in which we present images of ourselves to others are also addressed. You will see how we form relationships and interact within small, intimate groups. The section closes with a look at how we define "acceptable" behavior and how we respond to those who "break the rules."

©iStockPhoto.com

3 Building Reality

The Social Construction of Knowledge

The year was 1897. Eight-year-old Virginia O'Hanlon became upset when her friends told her that there was no Santa Claus. Her father encouraged her to write a letter to *The New York Sun* to find out the truth. The editor's reply—which included the now famous phrase, "Yes, Virginia, there is a Santa Claus!"—has become a classic piece of American folklore. "Nobody sees Santa Claus" the editor wrote, "but that is no sign that there is no Santa Claus. The most real things in the world are those that neither children nor men [*sic*] can see" ("Is There a Santa Claus?" 1897).

In his book *Encounters With the Archdruid,* John McPhee (1971) examines the life and ideas of David Brower, who was one of the most successful and energetic environmentalists in the United States. McPhee recalls a lecture in which Brower claimed that the United States has 6% of the world's population and uses 60% of the world's resources and that only 1% of Americans use 60% of those resources. Afterward, McPhee asked Brower where he got these interesting statistics:

> Brower said the figures had been worked out in the head of a friend of his from data assembled "to the best of his recollection." . . . [He] assured me that figures in themselves are merely indices. *What matters is that they feel right* [italics added]. Brower feels things. (p. 86)

What do these two very different examples have in common? Both reflect the fickle nature of "truth" and "reality." Young Virginia was encouraged to believe in the reality of something she could never and would never perceive with her senses. She no doubt learned a different sort of truth about Santa Claus when she got older, but the editor urged her to take on faith that Santa Claus, or at least the idea of Santa Claus, exists despite the lack of objective proof. That sort of advice persists. A survey of 200 child psychologists around the United States found that 91% of them advised parents not to tell the truth when their young children asked about the existence of Santa Claus (cited in Stryker, 1997).

Likewise, David Brower urges people to believe in something that doesn't need to be seen. What's important is that the information "feels right," that it helps one's cause even if it is not based on hard evidence.

Such precarious uses of truth may appear foolish or deceitful. Yet much of our everyday knowledge is based on accepting as real the existence of things that can't be seen, touched, or proved—"the world taken-for-granted" (Berger, 1963, p. 147). Like Virginia, we learn to accept the existence of things such as electrons, the ozone layer, black holes in the universe, love, and God, even though we cannot see them. And like David Brower, we learn to believe and use facts and figures provided by "experts" as long as they sound right or support our interests.

How do we come to know what we know? How do we learn what is real and what isn't? In this chapter, I examine how sociologists discover truths about human life. But to provide the appropriate context, I must first present a sociological perspective on the nature of reality. How do individuals construct their realities? How do societal forces influence the process?

UNDERSTANDING THE SOCIAL CONSTRUCTION OF REALITY

In Chapter 2, I noted that the elements of society are human creations that provide structure to our everyday lives. They also give us a distinctive lens through which we perceive the world. For example, because of their different statuses and their respective occupational training, an architect, a real estate agent, a police officer, and a firefighter can each look at the same building and see very different things: "a beautiful example of Victorian architecture," "a moderately priced fixer-upper," "a target of opportunity for a thief," or "a fire hazard." Mark Twain often wrote about how the Mississippi River—a waterway he saw every day as a child—looked different after he became a riverboat pilot. What he once saw as a place for recreation and relaxation, he later saw for its treacherous currents, eddies, and other potential dangers.

What we know to be true or real is always a product of the culture and historical period in which we exist. It takes an exercise of the sociological imagination, however, to see that what we ourselves "know" to be true today—the laws of nature, the causes and treatments of certain diseases, and so forth—may not be true for everyone everywhere or may be replaced by different truths tomorrow (Babbie, 1986). For example, in some cultures, the existence of spirits, witches, and demons is a taken-for-granted part of everyday reality that others might easily dismiss as fanciful. On the other side of the coin, the Western faith in the curative powers of little pills—without the intervention of spiritual forces—might seem far-fetched and naïve to people living in cultures where illness and health are assumed to have supernatural causes.

The process through which facts, knowledge, truth, and so on are discovered, made known, reaffirmed, and altered by the members of a society is called the ***social construction of reality*** (Berger & Luckmann, 1966). This concept is based on the simple assumption that knowledge is a human creation. Ironically, most of us live our lives assuming that an objective reality exists, independent of us and accessible through our senses. We are quite sure trees and tables and trucks don't exist simply in our imaginations. We assume this reality is shared by others and can be taken for granted as reality (Lindesmith, Strauss, & Denzin, 1991).

Hence, reality often turns out to be more a matter of agreement than something inherent in the natural world. Sociologists, particularly those working from the conflict perspective and symbolic interactionism, strive to explain the social construction of reality in terms of both its causes and its consequences. Their insights help explain many of the phenomena that influence our daily lives.

LAYING THE FOUNDATION: THE BASES OF REALITY

Think of society as a building constructed by the people who live and work in it. The building's foundation, its underlying reality, determines its basic shape and dimensions. And the foundation is what makes that building solid and helps it stand up through time and weather. For students of architecture as well as sociology, the first thing to understand is the way the foundation is prepared.

Symbolic interactionism encourages us to see that people's actions toward one another and interpretations of situations are based on their definitions of reality, which are in turn learned from interactions with those around them. What we know to be real, we share with other members of our culture. Imagine how difficult it would be to believe in something no one else around you thought existed. Psychiatrists use terms such as *hallucination* and *delusion* to describe things experienced by people who see, hear, or believe things that others don't.

The social construction of reality is a process by which human-created ideas become so firmly accepted that to deny them is to deny common sense. Of course, some features of reality are grounded in physical evidence—fire is hot, sharp things hurt. But other features of reality are often based not on sensory experiences but on forces such as culture and language, self-fulfilling prophecies, and faith.

Culture and Language

As I mentioned in Chapter 2, we live in a symbolic world and interact chiefly through symbolic communication—that is, through language. Language gives meaning to the people, objects, events, and ideas of our lives. In fact, language reflects and often determines our reality (Sapir, 1949; Whorf, 1956). Thus, language is a key tool in the construction of society.

Within a culture, words evolve to reflect the phenomena that have practical significance. The Solomon Islanders have nine distinct words for "coconut," each specifying an important stage of its growth, but they have only one word for all the meals of the day (Lewis, 1948). The Hanunóo people of the Philippines have different names for 92 varieties of rice, allowing them to make distinctions all but invisible to English-speaking people, who lump all such grains under a single word: *rice* (Thomson, 2000). Yet a traditional Hanunóo coming to this country would be hard-pressed to see the distinction between the vehicles we call *sedans, SUVs hatchbacks,* and *station wagons.*

Language can also pack an enormous emotional wallop. Words can make us happy, sad, disgusted, angry, or even incite us to violence. Racial, ethnic, sexual, or religious slurs can be particularly volatile. Among heterosexual adolescents, for example, homophobic name-calling (*queer, fag, dyke*) is one of the most common modes of bullying and coercion in school (Thurlow, 2001). In 2007, a play called *Nigger Wetback Chink* opened in Hollywood. Although it was a comedy, it was an attempt to confront the pain of racial slurs. So volatile was the topic that the play was condemned by both neo-Nazis and the National Association for the Advancement of Colored People (Waxman, 2007). That same year, the popular radio personality Don Imus incited nationwide rage and was forced to resign after he referred to members of the Rutgers University women's basketball team as "nappy-headed hos."

The broader demands of everyday life influence the way language is used. For instance, as societies become more developed, the pace of life quickens and we become impatient. This phenomenon is reflected in the compression (and subsequent speedup) of language. Contractions (such as *we're* and *isn't*) shorten words. Portmanteaus combine two existing words into one, such as *brunch* for "breakfast and lunch" and *smog* for "smoke and fog" (Safire, 2008). Technology contracts language even further. If you do a lot of instant messaging or texting, you have no doubt made use of "shortspeak"—the reduction of words and sentences through the use of abbreviations, acronyms, and emoticons.

Within a culture, certain professions or groups sometimes develop a distinctive language, known as *jargon,* which allows members of the group to communicate with one another clearly and quickly. But jargon can sometimes create boundaries and therefore mystify and conceal meaning from outsiders (Farb, 1983). For instance, by using esoteric medical terminology when discussing a case in front of a patient, two physicians define who is and who isn't a member of their group, reinforce their image as highly trained experts, and keep the patient from interfering too much in their decision making. These communication roadblocks have become a cause for concern in the field of medicine. Many books and websites now help patients overcome their position of powerlessness by instructing them on how and when to ask physicians the right questions so they can make informed decisions about a course of treatment. For their part, many medical schools now require their students to be trained in how to avoid jargon and how to listen to their patients (Franklin, 2006).

In sum, words help frame or structure social reality and give it meaning. Language also provides people with a cultural and group identity. If you've ever spent a significant amount of time in a foreign country or even moved to a new school, you know you cannot be a fully participating member of a group or a culture until you share its language.

Self-Fulfilling Prophecies

As you will recall from Chapter 2, we do not respond directly and automatically to objects and situations; instead, as the symbolic-interactionist perspective points out, we use language to define and interpret them, and then we act on the basis of those interpretations. By acting on the basis of our definitions of reality, we often create the very conditions we believe exist. A ***self-fulfilling prophecy*** is an assumption or prediction that, purely as a result of having been made, causes the expected event to occur and thus confirms the prophecy's own "accuracy" (Merton, 1948; Watzlawick, 1984).

Every holiday season, we witness the stunning effects of self-fulfilling prophecies on a national scale. Each September, the toy industry releases the results of its annual survey of retailers, indicating what toys are predicted to be the top sellers at Christmas. Usually, one toy in particular emerges as the most popular, hard-to-get gift of the year. In the 1980s, it was Cabbage Patch Dolls. In the early 1990s, it was Mighty Morphin Power Rangers and Ninja Turtles. More recently, items such as Beanie Babies, SpongeBob SquarePants toys, Razor scooters, Wii video games, Bratz dolls, toy digital cameras, and Harry Potter paraphernalia have taken their turn as the "must-have" toy of the year. By around November, we begin to hear the hype about unprecedented demand for the toy and the likelihood of a shortage. Powerful retail store chains, such as Toys "R" Us and Wal-Mart, may announce the possibility of rationing: one toy per family. Fueled by the fear of seeing a disappointed child's face at Christmas, thousands of panicked parents and grandparents rush to stores to make sure they're not left without. Some hoard extras for other parents they know. As a result, supplies of the toy—which weren't perilously low in the first place—become severely depleted, thereby bringing about the predicted shortage. The mere belief in some version of the reality creates expectations that can actually make it happen.

Self-fulfilling prophecies are particularly powerful when they become an element of social institutions. In schools, teachers can subtly and unconsciously encourage the performance they expect to see in their students. For instance, if they believe their students are especially intelligent, they may spend more time with them or unintentionally show more enthusiasm when working with them. As a result, these students may come to feel more capable and intelligent and actually perform better (Rosenthal & Jacobson, 1968).

Faith and Incorrigible Propositions

David Blaine is a famous street performer and illusionist who combines sophisticated magic tricks with a hint of comedy. In one of his more astounding stunts, he appears to rise up and float several inches off the ground for a few seconds. Suppose you saw him perform such a feat in person. He looks as if he is levitating, but you "know better." Even though your eyes tell you he is floating in midair, you have learned that it's just not possible. Rather than use this experience to entirely abandon your belief that people can't float in midair, you'll probably come up with a series of "reasonable" explanations: "Maybe it's an optical illusion, and it just appears as though he's floating." "Perhaps there are wires holding him up." To acknowledge the possibility that he is literally floating is to challenge the fundamental reality on which your everyday life is based. It is an article of faith that people aren't capable of levitating.

Such an unquestionable assumption, called an ***incorrigible proposition,*** is a belief that cannot be proved wrong and has become so much a part of common sense that one continues to believe it even in the face of contradictory evidence. By explaining away contradictions with "reasonable" explanations, we strengthen the correctness of the initial proposition (Watzlawick, 1976). In the process, we participate in constructing a particular version of reality. For instance, if an incorrigible proposition for you is that women are inherently less aggressive than men, seeing an especially violent woman might lead you toward explanations that focus on the peculiar characteristics of *this particular* woman. Maybe *she's* responding to terrible circumstances in her life; maybe *she* has some kind of chemical imbalance or neurological disorder. By concluding that she is an exception to the rule, the rule is maintained.

BUILDING THE WALLS: CONFLICT, POWER, AND SOCIAL INSTITUTIONS

We, as individuals, play an important role in coordinating, reproducing, and giving meaning to society in our daily interactions. But we are certainly not completely free to create whatever version of social reality we want to create. We are, after all, born into a preexisting society with its norms, values, roles, relationships, groups, organizations, and institutions. Just as the walls of a building constrain the ability of the inhabitants to move about, directing them through certain predetermined doorways and corridors, these features of society influence our thoughts and deeds and consequently constrain our ability to freely construct our social world (Giddens, 1984). As Karl Marx (1869/1963) wrote, "[People] make their own history, but they do not make it just as they please; they do not make it under circumstances, chosen by themselves, but under circumstances directly encountered, given and transmitted from the past" (p. 15).

As the conflict perspective points out, certain people or groups of people are more influential in defining reality than others. In any modern society, where socioeconomic classes, ethnic and religious groups, age groups, and political interests struggle for control over resources, there is also a struggle for the power to determine or influence that society's conception of reality (Gans, 1971). Those who emerge successful gain control over information, define values, create myths, manipulate events, and influence what the rest of us take for granted. Conflict theorists therefore argue that people with more power, prestige, status, wealth, and access to high-level policymakers can turn their perceptions of the world into the entire culture's perception. In other words, "He who has the bigger stick has the better chance of imposing his definitions of reality" (Berger & Luckmann, 1966, p. 109). That "bigger stick" can be wielded in several ways. Powerful social institutions and the people who control them play a significant role in shaping and sustaining perceptions of reality for everybody else. But if you wish to develop the sociological imagination, you need to understand the role of not only these larger forces in shaping private lives but also private individuals who struggle to shape public reality.

The Economics of Reality

Definitions of reality frequently reflect underlying economic interests. The key concerns from the conflict perspective are who benefits economically and who loses from dominant versions of reality. Take mental illness, for example. The number of problems officially defined by the American Psychiatric Association (APA) as mental disorders and defects has now reached nearly 400 (Horwitz, 2002). In defining what constitutes a mental disorder, the APA unwittingly reflects the economic organization of U.S. society. In the United States, individuals seldom pay the total costs of health care services out of their own pockets. Most of the money for medical treatment comes from the federal and state governments or from private insurance companies. Only if problems such as gambling, depression, anorexia, and cocaine addiction are formally defined as illnesses is their treatment eligible for medical insurance coverage.

Similar economic considerations affect the general health care system. Approximately 50 million Americans are estimated to have some type of disability (Freedman, Martin, & Schoeni, 2004), which the 1990 Americans with Disabilities Act (ADA) defines as "a physical or mental impairment that substantially limits one or more of the major life activities of such individual" (U.S. Department of Labor, 2004, p. 1). Under this law, employers are required to accommodate employees who have a documented disability and are forbidden to fire them simply because of their disability. For instance, a company that has wheelchair-bound employees must have ramps or elevators that give these workers access to all areas of the building. Ironically, the added cost of employing disabled workers may actually work to their disadvantage by making them less attractive to potential hirers in the first place. One study found an 11% drop in the employment rate of people with disabilities after the ADA was enacted (DeLeire, 2000). Moreover, highly publicized stories of employees with questionable disabilities seeking accommodations—for example, an office worker allergic to artificial fragrances demanding that his employer install an expensive new air filtration system—give the impression that the ADA is placing an excessive economic burden on companies. Although powerful businesses and industries were not able to prevent this act from being passed in the first place, they have been able to create a reality that still works in their interest.

The Politics of Reality

The institution of politics is also linked to societal definitions of reality. To a great extent, politics is about controlling public perceptions so people will do things or think about issues in ways that political leaders want them to. During important political campaigns, we can see such attempts to influence public perception. Mudslinging, euphemistically called "negative campaigning," has become as common an element of the U.S. electoral process as speeches, debates, baby kissing, and patriotic songs.

Most politicians know that if you say something untrue or unproven about an opponent often enough, people will believe it. In fact, while companies that sell consumer products must meet some standard of accuracy in their advertising, we have no federal truth-in-advertising laws for political campaign ads. Candidates have the legal right to lie (National Public Radio, 2007). Ironically, a victim's constant public denials of the charges by the victim often reinforce their reality and keep them in the news. The actual validity of the claims becomes irrelevant as the accusations are transformed into "fact" and become solidified in the minds of the voting public. The problem has become so acute that a website, factcheck.org, exists solely to monitor the factual accuracy of what major U.S. politicians say in TV ads, debates, speeches, interviews, and news releases.

However, the relationship between politics and reality goes beyond the dishonesty or dirty campaigns of individual candidates. The social construction of reality itself is a massive political process. All governments live or die by their ability to manipulate public opinion so they can reinforce their claims to legitimacy. Information is selectively released, altered, or withheld in an attempt to gain public approval and support for their policies. During the Bush administration, at least 20 different federal agencies, including the Department of Defense and the Census Bureau, produced and distributed hundreds of suspicious "news" reports to local television networks. The reports looked like actual journalistic reports but were in fact prepackaged productions designed not just to inform but to build public support for governmental policy objectives, such as Medicare or Social Security reform (Barstow & Stein, 2005). For instance, in 2004, the Department of Health and Human Services distributed fake news (in the form of video news releases in which actors played the parts of reporters) to hundreds of local television stations in support of administration prescription drug policies (Alter, 2005). And in 2005, it was discovered that this department, as well as the Department of Education, had paid several sympathetic journalists and television commentators between $10,000 and $240,000 to present government policies in a favorable light in their columns and broadcasts.

When the lives of thousands of citizens are at stake and public opinion is crucial, such information control becomes particularly tight. Between September 2001 and the invasion of Iraq in March 2003, the Bush administration worked diligently to foster a belief that Iraq and its then dictator, Saddam Hussein, played a direct role in the September 11 attacks and had stockpiles of weapons of mass destruction. They were quite successful. Immediately after the attacks, national opinion polls showed that only 3% of Americans mentioned Iraq or Saddam Hussein when asked who was responsible. But by January 2003, 44% of Americans reported that either "most" or "some" of the hijackers were Iraqi citizens. In fact, none were (Feldmann, Marlantes, & Bowers, 2003). Two years after the attacks, 69% of Americans said in a *Washington Post* poll that they thought it at least likely that Hussein was involved in the attacks, even though the link between Iraq and al-Qaeda was never established (Milbank & Deane, 2003). Nevertheless, these beliefs provided the kind of public support necessary to justify the military invasion and occupation of Iraq that continues to this day. The Center for Public Integrity (2008) concluded that the administration had made close to 1,000 false public statements on either the existence of weapons of mass destruction or the link between al-Qaeda and Iraq. Such a molding of public perception is accomplished most notably through the media.

The Medium Is the Message

Communication media are the primary means by which we are entertained and informed about the world around us (see Chapter 5). But the messages we receive from the media also reflect dominant cultural values (Gitlin, 1979). In television shows and other works of fiction, the way characters are portrayed, the topics dealt with, and the solutions imposed on problems all link entertainment to the economic system and prevailing societal tastes in consumption.

The media are also our primary source of information about local, national, and international events and people. News broadcasts and newspapers tell us about things we cannot experience directly, making the most remote events meaningful (Molotch & Lester, 1974). The way we look at the world and define our lives within it is therefore shaped and influenced by what we see on Internet news sites, watch on TV news shows, hear on the radio, or read in our daily papers.

Because the news is the means by which political realities are disseminated to the public, it is an essential tool in maintaining social order (Hallin, 1986; Parenti, 1986). In many societies, news sources don't even try to hide the fact that they are mouthpieces of one faction or another. In repressive societies, the only news sources allowed to operate are those representing the government. In North Korea, for instance, the flow of news information is clearly controlled by the government. People who live in societies with a cultural tradition of press independence, in contrast, assume that news stories are purely factual—an accurate, objective reflection of the "world out there" (Molotch & Lester, 1974). Like everything else, however, news is a constructed reality.

Hundreds, perhaps thousands, of potentially newsworthy events occur every day. Yet we'll see maybe 10 of them on our favorite evening broadcast or the home page of our favorite online news service. These events exist as news not because of their inherent importance but because of the practical, political, or economic purposes they serve. The old newsroom adage "If it bleeds, it leads" attests to the fact that events with shocking details—which appeal to the public's fondness for the sensational—are the ones most likely to be chosen. At its most independent, the news is still the product of decisions made by reporters, editors, network executives, and corporation owners, all of whom have their own interests, biases, and values (Molotch & Lester, 1974).

Although "freedom of expression" and "freedom of the press" are core American values, manipulation of information has been not only tolerated but encouraged in some situations. Take the media coverage of the current military actions in Iraq and Afghanistan. During the initial stages of the war, the press coverage seemed to be relatively open. The Pentagon allowed hundreds of reporters to accompany fighting forces and transmit their stories from the front lines throughout the war. According to one study, 61% of their reports during the first 3 days of the war were live and unedited (Project for Excellence in Journalism, 2005). By granting such unprecedented access, Pentagon officials hoped that these "embedded" reporters would convey the "heroism and hard work" of American soldiers to a worldwide audience and in the process discredit Iraqi propaganda (Getlin & Wilkinson, 2003).

But even then, some media critics were concerned that the reporters were tools of the military, especially given their often close attachment to the soldiers with whom they were traveling. The Pentagon required embedded journalists to sign a contract giving the military control over the content of their stories (Jamail, 2007). According to one study, 80% of early embedded reports included no commentary at all from soldiers (Project for Excellence in Journalism, 2005). In addition, there is evidence that military personnel and news organizations fabricated stories to present the war in a favorable light. For instance, the famous footage of the dramatic rescue of the captured U.S. soldier Jessica Lynch from an Iraqi hospital in 2003 was staged for effect. Lynch testified before Congress in 2007 that details of her rescue were exaggerated (Alter, 2007).

For everyday news stories, even in societies that restrict the press, official censorship is usually unnecessary. Because of the economic pressures to attract audiences and keep their attention, TV networks and newspapers usually censor themselves (Bagdikian, 1991). Reporters pursue stories that are relatively easy to research and that have immediate interest for audiences. Less exciting, more complicated stories don't get enough journalistic resources or are cut in the editing process. We usually have no way of knowing which events have *not* been selected for inclusion in the day's news or which plausible alternatives are kept out of the public eye.

The economic and political motivation for such selectivity becomes apparent when we consider who owns the media. For instance, one company, Clear Channel, owns about 1,200 radio stations in all 50 states, reaching more than 110 million listeners every week (Clear Channel Communications, 2003). By comparison, the next top company, Cumulus Broadcasting, owns only 303 stations (Project for Excellence in Journalism, 2006). Another, the Sinclair Broadcast Group (2005), owns and operates 61 television stations in 38 markets and reaches an estimated 24% of the viewing population. In 1983, 50 companies controlled more than half of all U.S. media outlets; by 2000, six companies—General Electric, Viacom, Disney, Time Warner, Bertelsmann, and Rupert Murdoch's News Corporation—controlled more than half of all media outlets (Bagdikian, 2000). The 1996 Telecommunications Act allows one company to own up to six radio stations and two television stations in a single city. Many media observers fear that the concentration of corporate-owned news outlets twists certain stories to promote particular economic or political interests.

As the viewing and listening public, our recourse is difficult. To criticize unfair government policies and consider solutions to difficult social problems, we need solid information, which is frequently unavailable or difficult to obtain. The recent growth in popularity of podcasting, Internet-protocol television, microradio stations, and subscription satellite networks may be a sign that some citizens are growing weary of the filtered and sometimes partisan information they receive from traditional news sources. Indeed, distrust of the news media has become so acute that some people turn to deliberately fake news/comedy shows such as *The Daily Show* and *The Colbert Report* to keep abreast of national and world events.

So the challenge we face in our own private lives is to recognize the processes at work in the social construction of reality and to take them into account as we "consume" the news. A critical dimension of the sociological imagination is the ability to "read silences"—to be attentive to what the mass media *don't* say. Fortunately, one of the purposes of sociology is to scientifically amass a body of knowledge that we can use to assess how our society really works.

APPRECIATING THE CONTRIBUTIONS OF SOCIOLOGICAL RESEARCH

Up to this point, I've been describing how individuals, groups, organizations, and various social institutions go about constructing reality. We've seen that these realities sometimes shift with time, place, and individual perception. Faced with this type of fluctuation, sociologists, as well as scholars in other disciplines, seek to identify a more "real" reality through systematic, controlled research. The rules sociologists abide by when conducting research give them confidence that they are identifying more than just a personal version of reality. They hope to determine a reality as it exists for a community of people at a particular point in time.

Moving beyond the level of individual conclusions about the nature of social reality is crucial if we are to escape the distortions of personal interests and biases. A danger of relying solely on individual perceptions is that we are likely to conclude that what we experience is what everyone experiences. For example, the famous psychiatrist Sigmund Freud used his own childhood as the ultimate "proof" of the controversial concept called the Oedipus conflict (the belief that sons are secretly in love with their mothers and jealous of their fathers). He wrote to a friend in 1897, "I have found, in my own case too, being in love with the mother and jealous of the father, and I now consider it a universal event of early childhood" (quoted in Astbury, 1996, p. 73).

To avoid the risk of such overgeneralizations, sociologists try to determine what most people believe or how most people behave. But in doing so, they sometimes run the risk of simply restating what people already know. Indeed, a criticism of sociology you hear from time to time is that it is just a fancy version of common sense. A lot of the things that we think are obvious based on our personal observations, however, turn out not to be so straightforward under the closer scrutiny of social research. Consider the following "commonsense facts":

- Rape, assault, and murder occur most often between total strangers.
- Because of the high divorce rate in the United States, people are reluctant to get married.
- American children today are more likely to live in a single-parent household than they were 100 years ago.

Most of us probably assume these statements are true. Given what you've read or seen on television, they probably make a lot of sense. But how accurate are they?

According to the U.S. Bureau of Justice Statistics (Catalano, 2006), only 15.5% of homicides involving male victims and 8.8% of homicides involving female victims are perpetrated by strangers. In addition, only 44% of assaults, 28% of rapes, and 46% of attempted rapes involve strangers. The rest occur between acquaintances, friends, colleagues, romantic partners, and family members. In 61% of rapes and sexual assaults, the victim knew the attacker (U.S. Department of Justice, 2008). Among female college students, that figure increases to 74% (Hart, 2003).

According to the U.S. Bureau of the Census (2009), less than 7% of people between the ages of

55 and 64 have never been married. In fact, about two thirds of divorced women and three fourths of divorced men eventually remarry (Cherlin, 1992). Although we have become increasingly willing to end a bad marriage, we still tend to place a high value on the institution of marriage itself.

The percentage of children who live with one parent is roughly the same as it was a century ago. At that time, life expectancy was much lower than it is today, so it was highly likely that before reaching adulthood a child would lose at least one parent to death (Kain, 1990).

As you can see, sometimes commonsense "facts" don't hold up under the weight of evidence provided by social research.

The Empirical Nature of Sociological Research

Research is all around us. Throughout our lives, we are flooded with statistics that are supposedly the result of scientific studies—which detergents make clothes brighter, which soft drinks most people prefer, which chewing gum dentists recommend for their gum-chewing patients. Many of the important decisions we make, from purchasing a car to opting for a particular surgical procedure, are supported by some sort of research.

In addition, a significant proportion of our own lives is spent *doing* research. Every time we seek out the opinions of others, gauge the attitude of a group, or draw conclusions about an event, we engage in a form of research. Say, for example, you thought your exam scores would improve if you studied with others, so you formed a study group. After the exam, you compared your grade with the grade you received on the previous exam (when you just studied on your own) to see if there was any significant improvement. If there was, you would likely attribute your better performance to the study group. This is the essence of research: You had an idea about some social process, and you went out and tested it to see if you were correct.

Although useful and common, such casual research is fraught with problems. We may make inaccurate or selective observations, overgeneralize on the basis of a limited number of observations, or draw conclusions that protect our own interests (Babbie, 1992). Maybe your exam score would have improved even without the study group because you had a better understanding of the material this time and had a better sense of what the instructor expected.

Sociological research, which is a much more sophisticated and structured form of the sort of individual inquiry we use every day, can avoid some of these pitfalls. Of course, sociological researchers are human beings, and they too make errors in observation, generalization, and analysis. But they have a greater chance of avoiding these errors because, first and foremost, sociological research is an empirical endeavor. ***Empirical research*** operates on the assumption that answers to questions about human behavior can be ascertained through controlled, systematic observations in the real world. Individuals can reach naïve conclusions based on their personal impressions of what happens in society. Great scholars can spend years thinking about human life and developing logical explanations about particular social phenomena. But for most sociologists, the strength of an explanation depends on how much empirical support it has.

Another characteristic of sociological research that makes it a better reflection of social reality than individual inquiry is that it is ***probabilistic.*** Instead of making absolute predictions, most sociologists prefer to state that under certain conditions particular phenomena are likely to occur. In other words, human behavior operates within the laws of probability. Whenever sociologists set out to find the reasons, say, for why people hold prejudiced beliefs or why some countries have a higher birthrate than others, they are searching for the factors that would explain these phenomena most but not all of the time. For instance, adults with less than a high school education are more likely than adults with college degrees to be prejudiced against other ethnoracial groups. But that doesn't mean that every single high school dropout is a bigot or that every college graduate embraces people who are ethnically or racially different. By focusing on the probability of some phenomenon occurring while at the same time allowing for exceptions and variations, sociologists provide a view of reality that simultaneously reflects the way things are and the way they can be.

Qualitative and Quantitative Research

In contrast to the casual way we carry out our personal research, sociologists seek to define reality through a careful process of collecting information and answering questions. Some sociologists collect nonnumeric information (text, written words, phrases, symbols, observations) that describes people, actions, or events in social life (called ***qualitative research***; Neuman, 1994). Others collect numeric data and rely on precise statistical analysis (called ***quantitative research***). And some use a combination of both.

Qualitative researchers often go out and observe people and events as they happen in society. For instance, qualitative researchers interested in how additional children affect parents' ability to balance the demands of work and home may spend an entire day with a family, listening, observing, and asking questions (Upton, in press). Once they've collected enough information, they go about interpreting their observations, looking for identifiable patterns in people's everyday lives.

Quantitative sociological researchers methodically record observations across a variety of situations; they design and choose questions in advance and ask them in a consistent way of a large number of people; they use sophisticated techniques to ensure that the characteristics of the people in a study are similar to those of the population at large; and they use computers to generate statistics from which confident conclusions can be drawn.

Both kinds of sociological research are subjected to the scrutiny of peers, who will point out any mistakes and shortcomings. Researchers are obligated to report not only their results but also the methods they used to record observations or collect data and the conditions surrounding the study. Such detailed explanations allow other researchers to replicate a study—that is, to perform it themselves to see if the same results are obtained. The more a particular research result is replicated, the greater its acceptance as fact in the sociological community.

Theories, Variables, and Hypotheses

Whether qualitative or quantitative, social research is purposeful. Unlike personal research, which may be motivated by a hunch, whim, or immediate need, most social research is guided by a particular theory. A ***theory*** is a set of statements or propositions that seek to explain or predict a particular aspect of social life (Chafetz, 1978). Theory does not, as is popularly thought, mean conjecture or speculation. Ideally, theories explain the way things are, not the way they ought to be.

Research and theory closely depend on each other. Research without any underlying theoretical reasoning is simply a string of meaningless bits of information (Mills, 1959); theory without research is abstract and speculative.

Some theories—such as structural functionalism, conflict theory, and symbolic interactionism—are quite broad, seeking to explain why social order exists or how societies work overall. Other theories are more modest, seeking to explain more narrowly certain behaviors among specific groups of people. For example, Travis Hirschi (1969) developed a theory of juvenile delinquency called "social control theory," in which he argued that delinquent acts occur when an individual's bond to society is weak or broken. These bonds are derived from a person's attachments to others who obey the law, the rewards a person gains by acting nondelinquently (commitments), the amount of time a person engages in nondelinquent activity (involvements), and the degree to which a person is tied to society's conventional belief system.

To test theories, sociologists must translate abstract propositions into testable hypotheses. A ***hypothesis*** is a researchable prediction that specifies the relationship between two or more ***variables.*** A variable is any characteristic, attitude, behavior, or event that can take on two or more values or attributes. For example, the variable "marital status" has several categories: never married, cohabiting, married, separated, divorced, widowed. The variable "attitudes toward capital punishment" has categories ranging from "strongly in favor" to "strongly oppose."

Hirschi was interested in why juveniles engage in delinquent behavior. Such a question is far too general to study empirically, so he developed a clear, specific, empirically testable prediction, or hypothesis, specifying a relationship between two variables: Strong "social bonds" will be associated with low levels of "delinquency."

In developing their hypotheses, sociologists distinguish between independent and dependent variables. The ***independent variable*** is the factor presumed to influence or create changes in another variable. The ***dependent variable*** is the one assumed to depend on, be influenced by, or change as a result of the independent variable. If we believe that gender affects people's attitudes toward capital punishment, then "gender" would be the independent variable influencing "attitudes toward capital punishment," the dependent variable. For Hirschi's theory of juvenile delinquency, the strength of the social bond was the independent variable, and level of delinquency was the dependent variable.

The assumption behind most research that tests a hypothesis is that the independent variable *causes* changes to occur in the dependent variable—for instance, that a weak social bond *causes* a young person to become delinquent. But just because two variables seem to be related doesn't necessarily mean a causal relationship exists.

In fact, the two variables may not be related at all but merely seem to be associated with each other due to the effect of some third variable. Sociologists call such false relationships spurious. A classic example of a ***spurious relationship*** is the apparent association between children's shoe size and reading ability. It seems that as shoe size increases, reading ability improves (Babbie, 2007). Does this mean that the size of one's feet (independent variable) *causes* an improvement in reading skills (dependent variable)? Certainly not. This illusory relationship is caused by a third factor, age, that is related to both shoe size (older kids have bigger feet) and reading ability (older kids can read better than younger kids). Hence, when researchers attempt to make causal claims about the relationship between an independent and a dependent variable, they must control for—or rule out—other variables that may be creating a spurious relationship. Can you think of a third variable that might strengthen or weaken a person's social bond *and* influence his or her tendency toward delinquent behavior?

Aside from concern with spuriousness, quantitative social researchers, such as Hirschi, face the problem that many of the concepts that form the basis of theories are abstract and not easy to observe or measure empirically. We can't directly see concepts such as "attachments" or "commitments." So they must be translated into ***indicators:*** events, characteristics, or behaviors that can be observed or quantified.

In his survey of 1,200 boys in Grades 6 through 12, Hirschi derived a set of indicators for his independent variable, the strength of the social bond. To determine young people's attachments to law-abiding others, Hirschi measured their attraction to parents, peers, and school officials. To determine the degree to which they derived rewards from acting nondelinquently (commitment), he asked them to assess the importance of things such as getting good grades. To determine the proportion of their lives spent in conventional activities (involvement), he asked them how much time they spent in school-oriented activities. Finally, to determine their ties to a conventional belief system, he asked them questions about their respect for the law and the police.

Hirschi measured the dependent variable, delinquent activity, by asking the boys if they'd ever stolen things, taken cars for rides without the owners' permission, banged up something on purpose that belonged to somebody else, or beaten up or hurt someone on purpose. In addition, he used school records and police records to measure delinquent acts that had come to the attention of authorities.

The empirical data he collected supported his hypothesis. The boys who indicated close attachments to their parents and peers, who got good grades, who were involved in lots of school-related activities, and who had high levels of respect for the law were the boys who didn't get into trouble. He was therefore able to use these results to strengthen the power of his original theory.

Modes of Research

Although the answers to important sociological questions are not always simple or clear, the techniques sociologists use to collect and examine data allow them to draw informed and reliable conclusions about human behavior and social life. The most common techniques are experiments, field research, surveys, and unobtrusive research.

Experiments

An ***experiment*** is typically a research technique designed to elicit some sort of behavior under closely controlled laboratory circumstances. In its ideal form, the experimenter randomly places participants into two groups, then deliberately manipulates or introduces changes into the environment of one group of participants (called the experimental group) and not the other (called the control group). Care is taken to ensure that the groups are relatively alike except for the variable that the experimenter manipulates. Any observed or measured differences between the groups can then be attributed to the effects of the experimental manipulation.

Experiments have a significant advantage over other types of research because the researcher can directly control all the relevant variables. Thus, conclusions about the independent variable causing changes in the dependent variable can be made more convincingly. The artificial nature of most laboratory experiments, however, may make subjects behave differently than the way they would in their natural settings, leading some people to argue that laboratory experimentation in sociology is practically impossible (Silverman, 1982).

To overcome this difficulty, some sociologists have created experimental situations outside the laboratory. Arthur Beaman and his colleagues (Beaman, Klentz, Diener, & Svanum, 1979) conducted an experiment to see whether self-awareness decreases the likelihood of engaging in socially undesirable behavior—in this case, stealing. The researchers set up situations in which children arriving at several homes on Halloween night were sent into the living room alone to take candy from a bowl. The children were first asked their names and ages and then told, "You may take only one of the candies." For the experimental group, a large mirror was placed right next to the candy bowl so that the children couldn't help but see themselves. For the control group, there was no mirror.

In the control group, 37% of the children took more than one candy, but only 4% of the children in the experimental group took more than one candy. The researchers concluded from this experiment that self-awareness can significantly reduce dishonesty.

Field Research

In ***field research,*** qualitative sociologists observe events as they actually occur, without selecting experimental and control groups or purposely introducing any changes into the subjects' environment. Field research can take several forms. In ***nonparticipant observation***, the researcher observes people without directly interacting with them and without their knowing that they are being observed. Sociologist Lyn Lofland (1973), for example, studied how strangers relate to one another in public places by going to bus depots, airports, stores, restaurants, and parks and secretly recording everything she saw.

Participant observation requires that the researcher interact with subjects. In some cases, the researcher openly identifies himself or herself. For instance, to gain insight into how people balance work and family, sociologist Arlie Russell Hochschild (1997) observed employees at a large public relations company she called Amerco over a period of 3 years. She was particularly interested in why employees tend not to take advantage of available family leave policies. At Amerco, only 53 of 21,000 employees—all of them women—chose to switch to part-time work in response to the arrival of a new baby. Less than 1% of the employees shared a job or worked at home, even though the company permits it. Most of the workers worked a lot of overtime, coming in early and staying late. So why were these workers so unwilling to change their work lives to spend more time with their families even when the company would have supported them in doing so? Through her long-term observations of Amerco, Hochschild came to the conclusion that work has become a form of "home" and home has become "work." For many people at Amerco, home had become a place of frenzied activity and busy schedules, whereas work had become a sort of nurturing refuge where they could relax and share stories with friends. So they actually preferred spending more time at work.

This type of qualitative field research can be quite time-consuming. Researchers can conduct only a limited number of interviews and can observe only a limited number of people and events. Hochschild collected rich information about people's work-family trade-offs, but she could study only one corporation. It's risky to generalize from the experiences of a small group of workers in one company in one society to all workers in all sorts of work environments.

In more delicate situations where the people being studied don't want their actions made public, the researcher may have to conceal her or his identity in order to gather accurate information. For instance, researchers have gone "undercover" to study everything from doomsday cults (Festinger, Riecken, & Schacter, 1956) to college sororities (Robbins, 2004). Sociologist Julia O'Connell Davidson (2002) wanted to examine the issue of power and control in the relationships between prostitutes and their clients. In order to study this topic, she posed as a "receptionist" for a prostitute she called "Desiree," fielding phone calls and supervising the "waiting room" for the clients who had arrived to see Desiree. While Desiree knew O'Connell Davidson was a sociologist, the clients did not. If these men knew they were being studied, they might have altered their conversations and behaviors to cover up potentially damaging information.

Surveys

When it is impossible or impractical to carry out field observations or to set up a controlled experimental situation, social researchers use the survey method. ***Surveys*** require that the researcher pose a series of questions to respondents either orally, electronically, or on paper. The questions should be sufficiently clear so they are understood by the respondent the way the researcher wants them to be understood and measure what the researcher wants them to measure. In addition, the respondent is expected to answer the questions honestly and thoughtfully. The answers are often recorded in numerical form so they can be statistically analyzed.

All of us have experienced surveys of one form or another. Every 10 years, people who live in the United States are required to fill out questionnaires for the U.S. Census Bureau. You've probably filled out an evaluation form at the end of a college course. Or perhaps you've been interviewed in a shopping mall or have received an e-mail asking you to respond to a "brief survey" about a particular product or service.

Surveys typically use standardized formats. All subjects are asked the same questions in the same way, and large samples of people are used as subjects. One survey that has provided the basis for much sociological research on families is the *National Survey on Families and Households*. First conducted in the late 1980s, it includes information derived from interviews with more than 13,000 respondents. A second wave of the survey, conducted between 1992 and 1994, and a third wave between 2001 and 2003 include interviews with surviving members of the original sample. The sample covers a diverse array of households, including single-parent families, families with stepchildren, cohabiting couples, and recently married persons. A great deal of family information was collected from each respondent, including family arrangements in childhood, dating experiences, experiences of leaving home, marital and cohabitation experiences, details of contact with kin, and data on economic well-being, as well as education, childbearing, and employment histories. Some of the research discussed in this book is based on analyses of data collected from this survey.

When sociologists Philip Blumstein and Pepper Schwartz (1983) undertook a massive study of intimate couples in the United States, they sent questionnaires to people from every income level, age group, religion, political ideology, and educational background. Some of their respondents were cohabiting, others were married. Some had children, others were childless. Some were heterosexual, others homosexual. All couples filled out a 38-page questionnaire that asked questions about their leisure activities, emotional support, housework, finances, sexual relations, satisfaction, relations with children, and so forth. More than 6,000 couples participated. From these surveys, Blumstein and Schwartz were able to draw conclusions about the importance of money, work, sexuality, power, and gender in couples' lives.

Unobtrusive Research

All the methods I've discussed so far—whether quantitative or qualitative—require the researcher to have some contact with the people being studied: giving them tasks to do in an experiment, watching them (with or without their knowing that they are participating in social research), or asking them questions. But the very act of intruding into people's lives may influence the phenomena being studied. This problem, known as ***reactivity***, calls into question the accuracy of the data that are collected, thereby threatening the credibility of the research.

In the late 1920s, an engineer and a time study analyst (Roethlisberger & Dickson, 1939) were hired to study working conditions and worker productivity at an electric company in Hawthorne, Illinois. They were interested in finding out whether changing certain physical conditions in the plant could improve workers' productivity and satisfaction. They quickly discovered that increasing the lighting in the workroom was linked with workers producing more. Increasing the brightness of the lights again the next day increased productivity even further. To bolster their conclusion, they decided to dim the lights to see if productivity dropped. Much to their dismay, productivity increased again when they darkened the room. They soon realized that the workers were responding more to the attention they were receiving from the researchers than to changes in their working conditions. This phenomenon is known as the "Hawthorne effect."

To avoid such influence, sociologists sometimes use another research technique, unobtrusive research, which requires no contact with people at all. ***Unobtrusive research*** is an examination of the evidence of social behavior that people create or leave behind. There are several types of unobtrusive research.

Analysis of existing data (also known as secondary data) relies on data gathered earlier by someone else for some other purpose. One of the most popular and convenient sources of data is the U.S. Census. Studies that examine broad, nationwide trends (e.g., marriage, divorce, or premarital childbearing rates) typically use existing census data.

Content analysis is the study of recorded communications—books, speeches, poems, song lyrics, television commercials, websites, and so forth. For example, sociologists Bernice Pescosolido, Elizabeth Grauerholz, and Melissa Milkie (1997) analyzed close to 2,000 children's picture books published from 1937 to 1993 to see if there were any changes in the way African Americans were portrayed. They believed that these depictions could tell a lot about the shifting nature of race relations in the larger society. The researchers looked not only at the number of black characters in these books but also at whether they were portrayed positively or negatively. They found, among other things, that in times of high uncertainty in race relations and substantial protest and conflict over existing societal norms, Blacks virtually disappeared from picture books. Furthermore, depictions of intimate, equal interracial interactions and portrayals of Blacks as primary characters remained rare.

Historical analysis relies on existing historical documents as a source of research information. Sociologist Kai Erikson (1966) was interested in how communities construct definitions of acceptable and unacceptable behavior. For his book *Wayward Puritans,* he studied several "crime waves" among the Puritans of the Massachusetts Bay Colony in the late 17th century. Erikson examined court cases, diaries, birth and death records, letters, and other written documents of the period. Piecing together fragments of information 300 years old was not easy, but Erikson was able to draw some conclusions. He found that each time the colony was threatened in some way—by opposing religious groups, betrayals by community leaders, or the king of England's revocation of its charter—the number of convicted criminals and the severity of punishments significantly increased. Erikson believed that these fluctuations occurred because the community needed to restate its moral boundaries and reaffirm its authority.

All these methods allow sociological researchers to collect information without intruding on and possibly changing the behavior of the people and groups they're studying.

The Trustworthiness of Social Research

Most sociologists see research as not only personally valuable but central to improving human knowledge and understanding. However, as consumers of this research, we must always ask "How accurate is this information?" Sometimes it's difficult to interpret the information we come across in scholarly research articles. Moreover, because we have a tendency to believe what we read in print or see reported on television or posted on websites, much of what we see may be either inaccurate or misleading. To evaluate the results of social research, we must examine the researcher's samples, the indicators used to measure important variables, and the researcher's personal qualities—namely, values, interests, and ethics.

Samples

Frequently, sociological researchers are interested in the attitudes, behaviors, or characteristics of large groups—college students, women, sports enthusiasts, single parents, and so on. It would be impossible to interview, survey, or observe all these people directly. Hence, researchers must select a smaller ***sample*** of respondents from the larger population. The characteristics of this subgroup are supposed to approximate the characteristics of the entire population of interest. A sample is said to be ***representative*** if the small group being studied is in fact typical of the population as a whole. For instance, a sample of 100 students from your university should include roughly the same proportion of first-year students, sophomores, juniors, and seniors that characterizes the entire school population. Sampling techniques have become highly sophisticated, as illustrated by the relative accuracy of polls conducted to predict election results.

In the physical sciences, sampling is not such an issue. Certain physical or chemical elements are assumed to be identical. One need only study a small number of vials of liquid nitrogen, because one vial of nitrogen should be the same as any other. Human beings, however, vary widely on every imaginable characteristic. You couldn't make a general statement about all Americans on the basis of an interview with one person. For that matter, you couldn't draw conclusions about all people from observing a sample consisting only of Americans, men, or teenagers. Samples that are not representative can lead to inaccurate and misleading conclusions.

Note the sampling problems revealed in the following letter to the editor of a small-town newspaper in the rural Midwest:

> I went to a restaurant yesterday for lunch. I began to feel guilty, when I reached into my pocket for a cigarette. . . . I was thinking of the government figures which estimated cigarette smokers at 26% of the population of the United States. But everywhere I looked inside that room, people were smoking. I decided to count them. There were 22 people in the room. . . . I was surprised to discover that the government's figures were an outright fabrication. . . . Seventeen people out of the 22 were cigarette smokers . . . that accounts for over 77% of the people in that restaurant. . . . The government's figures are understated by 51% and just plain wrong! (*Greencastle Banner Graphic,* 1992)

This letter writer assumed that the 22 people who frequented a small restaurant in a small, relatively poor rural town on a single day were an adequate representation of the entire U.S. population. Such a conclusion overlooks some important factors. Government studies show that the lower a person's income, the greater the likelihood that person will be a smoker. Furthermore, people in blue-collar or service jobs are more likely to smoke than people in white-collar jobs. Finally, the prevalence of smoking tends to be higher in rural areas of the Midwest and South than in other parts of the country (U.S. Department of Health and Human Services, 2006).

Indicators

As you recall, one problem sociologists face when doing research is that the variables they are interested in studying are usually difficult to see. What does powerlessness look like? How can you "see" marital satisfaction? How would you recognize alienation or social class? Sociologists thus resign themselves to measuring indicators of things that cannot be measured directly. Researchers measure events and behaviors commonly thought to accompany a particular variable, hoping that what they are measuring is a valid indicator of the concept in which they are interested.

Suppose you believe that people's attitudes toward abortion are influenced by the strength of their religious beliefs, or "religiosity." You might hypothesize that the stronger a person's religious beliefs, the less accepting she or he will be of abortion rights. To test this hypothesis, you must first figure out what you mean by "religious." What might be an indicator of the strength of someone's religious beliefs? You could determine if the subjects of your study identify themselves as members of some organized religion. But this indicator might not tell you how religious your subjects are because many people identify themselves as, say, Catholic or Jewish but are not religious at all. Likewise, some people who consider themselves quite religious don't identify with any organized religion. So this measure would focus on group differences but would fail to capture the intensity of a person's beliefs or the degree of religious interest.

Perhaps a better indicator would be some quantifiable behavior, such as the frequency of attendance at formal religious services (Babbie, 1986). Arguably, the more someone attends church, synagogue, or mosque, the more religious that person is. But here, too, we run into problems. Attendance at a religious service, for instance, may reflect family pressure, habit, or the desire to visit with others rather than religious commitment. Furthermore, many very religious people are unable to attend services because they are sick or disabled. As you can see, indicators seldom perfectly reflect the concepts they are intended to measure.

Surveys are particularly susceptible to inaccurate indicators. A loaded phrase or an unfamiliar word in a survey question can dramatically affect people's responses in ways unintended by the researcher. The National Opinion Research Center asked in an annual survey of public attitudes if the United States was spending too much, too little, or about the right amount of money on "assistance to the poor." Two thirds of the respondents said the country was spending too little. But in a different study, the word *welfare* was substituted for "assistance to the poor" in the question. This time, nearly half of the respondents said the country was spending too much money (Kagay & Elder, 1992).

Values, Interests, and Ethics in Sociological Research

Along with samples and indicators, the researcher's own qualities can influence social research. Ideally, research is objective and nonbiased and measures what is and not what should be. However, the questions researchers ask and the way they interpret observations always take place in a particular cultural, political, and ideological context (Ballard, 1987; Denzin, 1989).

Consider the impact of values and interests. If prevailing social values identify an intact nuclear family as the best environment for children, then most researchers will be prone to notice the disadvantages and perhaps ignore the advantages of other family arrangements. Furthermore, research is sometimes carried out to support a narrowly defined political interest—as when environmental groups fund research showing the damaging effects of global warming—or economic interest—as when tobacco companies fund research that downplays the relationship between cigarette smoking and cancer. The researcher who has received such a grant may be pressured to withhold publishing negative results that may preclude further funding. In 2009, an investigation by the Department of Health and Human Services found that the Food and Drug Administration does almost nothing to monitor financial conflicts of interest of doctors who conduct clinical trials of drugs and medical devices (cited in Harris, 2009).

But it's not just a problem of unscrupulous researchers or financial benefactors. Academic journals are notoriously reluctant to publish studies that show no relationship between one variable and another. A reexamination of clinical trial studies of antidepressants conducted between 1987 and 2004 found that medical journals had a significant bias toward publishing studies with positive results (Turner, Matthews, Linardatos, Tell, & Rosenthal, 2008). This problem has become so bad that an organization of 12 major medical journals proposed that pharmaceutical companies be required to register clinical trials at *the beginning* of drug studies so that negative and not just positive results would be publicly available (Meier, 2004).

We must remember that sociologists are people too, with their own biases, preconceptions, and expectations. Sociologists' values determine the kinds of information they gather about a particular social phenomenon. If you were conducting research on whether the criminal justice system is fair, would you study criminals, politicians, law enforcement personnel, judges, or victims? Each group would likely provide a different perception of the system. The most accurate picture of reality is likely to be based on the views of all subgroups involved.

Ethics is another personal quality that affects the trustworthiness of social research. Research, as I mentioned earlier, often represents an intrusion into people's lives; it may disrupt their ordinary activities, and it often requires them to reveal personal information about themselves. Ethical researchers agree, therefore, that they should protect the rights of subjects and minimize the amount of harm or disruption subjects might experience as a result of being part of a study. Ethical researchers agree that no one should be forced to participate in research, that those who do participate ought to be fully informed of the possible risks involved, and that every precaution ought to be taken to protect the confidentiality and anonymity of participants. Sociologists almost always conduct their research under the scrutiny of university review committees for the protection of human participants.

At the same time, however, researchers must attempt to secure the most accurate—and perhaps most useful—information possible. Sometimes, this requirement conflicts with ethical considerations. In 2007, the federal government began a 5-year, $50 million project designed to improve the way hospital patients are treated after car accidents, shootings, heart attacks, and other emergencies. Because such patients are often unconscious when they arrive at the hospital, researchers are allowed to conduct medical experiments on them without their consent, something that goes against usual ethical research protocol (Stein, 2007).

And what about research that requires information about people who may be involved in dangerous behavior or who do not want or cannot have their identities revealed? Sociologist Patricia Adler (1985) was interested in studying the worlds of drug dealers and smugglers. The illegal nature of their work makes them, by necessity, secretive, deceitful, and mistrustful, not the sort of individuals who make ideal surveyor interview respondents. So Adler had to establish a significant level of rapport and trust. Although she never became actively involved in drug trafficking, she did become a part of the dealers' and smugglers' social world and participated in their daily activities. Only by studying these criminals in their natural setting was she able to see the full complexity of the world of drug smuggling. Her research, however, raises important questions related to trustworthiness and ethics: Did her closeness to her subjects make it impossible to study them objectively? Did she have an obligation to report illegal activity to law enforcement officials?

CONCLUSION

In this chapter, I have described some of the processes by which reality is constructed, communicated, manipulated, and accepted. Reality, whether in the form of casual observations or formal research, is ultimately a human creation. Different people can create different conceptions of reality.

This issue can be raised from a personal level to a global one. People in every culture believe that their reality is the paramount one. Who is right? Can we truly believe that a reality in direct conflict with ours is equally valid? If we profess that everyone should have the right to believe what she or he wants, are we acknowledging the socially constructed nature of reality or merely being tolerant of those who are not "smart enough" to think as we do? Do we have the right to tell other people or other cultures that what they do or believe is wrong only because it conflicts with our definition of reality? Exasperating and complex, these questions lie at the core of international relations, global commerce, and everyday life.

CHAPTER HIGHLIGHTS

◆ The social construction of reality (truth, knowledge, etc.) is the process by which reality is discovered, made known, reinforced, and changed by members of society.

◆ Language is the medium through which reality construction takes place. It enables us to think, interpret, and define. Linguistic categories reflect aspects of a culture that are relevant and meaningful to people's lives.

◆ Not all of us possess the same ability to define reality. Individuals and groups in positions of power have the ability to control information, define values, create myths, manipulate events, and ultimately influence what others take for granted.

◆ The purpose of a discipline such as sociology is to amass a body of knowledge that provides the public with useful information about how society works. This is done, quantitatively and qualitatively, through systematic social research—field research, surveys, and unobtrusive research. It is important to keep in mind, however, that this form of reality is also a social construction, shaped by the people who fund, conduct, and report on social research.

KEY TERMS

analysis of existing data Type of unobtrusive research that relies on data gathered earlier by someone else for some other purpose

content analysis Form of unobtrusive research that studies the content of recorded messages, such as books, speeches, poems, songs, television shows, websites, and advertisements

dependent variable Variable that is assumed to be caused by, or to change as a result of, the independent variable

empirical research Research that operates from the ideological position that questions about human behavior can be answered only through controlled, systematic observations in the real world

experiment Research method designed to elicit some sort of behavior, typically conducted under closely controlled laboratory circumstances

field research Type of social research in which the researcher observes events as they actually occur

historical analysis Form of social research that relies on existing historical documents as a source of data

hypothesis Researchable prediction that specifies the relationship between two or more variables

incorrigible proposition Unquestioned cultural belief that cannot be proved wrong no matter what happens to dispute it

independent variable Variable presumed to cause or influence the dependent variable

indicator Measurable event, characteristic, or behavior commonly thought to reflect a particular concept

nonparticipant observation Form of field research in which the researcher observes people without directly interacting with them and without letting them know that they are being observed

participant observation Form of field research in which the researcher interacts with subjects, sometimes hiding his or her identity

probabilistic Capable of identifying only those forces that have a high likelihood, but not a certainty, of influencing human action

qualitative research Sociological research based on nonnumerical information (text, written words, phrases, symbols, observations) that describes people, actions, or events in social life

quantitative research Sociological research based on the collection of numerical data that uses precise statistical analysis

reactivity A problem associated with certain forms of research in which the very act of intruding into people's lives may influence the phenomenon being studied

representative Typical of the whole population being studied

sample Subgroup chosen for a study because its characteristics approximate those of the entire population

self-fulfilling prophecy Assumption or prediction that in itself causes the expected event to occur, thus seeming to confirm the prophecy's accuracy

social construction of reality Process through which the members of a society discover, make known, reaffirm, and alter a collective version of facts, knowledge, and "truth"

spurious relationship A false association between two variables that is actually due to the effect of some third variable

survey Form of social research in which the researcher asks subjects a series of questions, either verbally, online, or on paper

theory Set of statements or proposition that seeks to explain or predict a particular aspect of social life

unobtrusive research Research technique in which the researcher, without direct contact with the subjects, examines the evidence of social behavior that people create or leave behind

variable Any characteristic, attitude, behavior, or event that can take on two or more values or attributes

©DEA/P. GHIROTTI/Getty Images

4 Building Order

Culture and History

In Madagascar, the harvest months of August and September mark the *famadihana*—the "turning of the bones." Families receive messages from *razana*—their dead loved ones—who may say they are uncomfortable or need new clothes. In an elaborate ceremony that can last for days, families feast, sing, and dig up the graves of the deceased. The bodies are wrapped in shrouds and seated at the dinner table. Family news is whispered to them, and toasts are drunk. Widows and widowers can often be seen dancing with the bones of their dead spouses. The exhumed bones are then oiled and perfumed and laid back onto their "beds" inside the family tomb (Perlez, 1991).

In the late 19th and early 20th centuries, dating and courtship in North America were based on a ritualized system known as "calling." Although the process varied by region and social class, the following general guidelines were involved:

> When a girl reached the proper age or had her first "season" (depending on her family's social level), she became eligible to receive male callers. At first her mother or guardian invited young men to call; in subsequent seasons the young lady . . . could bestow an invitation to call upon any unmarried man to whom she had been properly introduced at a private dance, dinner, or other "entertainment" . . . young men . . . could be brought to call by friends or relatives of the girl's family, subject to her prior permission. . . . The call itself

> was a complicated event. A myriad of rules governed everything: the proper amount of time between invitation and visit (two weeks or less); whether or not refreshments should be served . . . ; chaperonage (the first call must be made on mother and daughter . . .); appropriate topics of conversation (the man's interests, but never too personal); how leave should be taken (on no account should the woman accompany [her caller] to the door nor stand talking while he struggles with his coat). (Bailey, 1988, pp. 15–16)

How could anybody dig up the body of a dead relative? Why would young men and young women follow such elaborate rules just so that they could go on a date? Such practices seem peculiar, silly, or backward to most of us, but to the people involved, they are or were simply the taken-for-granted, "right" ways of doing things.

Some of the things you do may seem equally incomprehensible to an outside observer. For instance, you may not think twice about eating a bloody T-bone steak, but someone from a culture that views cows as sacred would be disgusted at the thought. You may think a Spaniard's fondness for bullfighting is "absurd," yet millions of people in the United States shell out a lot of money each year to watch large men in brightly colored shirts and helmets knock one another down while they chase, throw, carry, and kick an inflated object made from the hide of a dead animal. You may pity the turn-of-the-century woman who squeezed her body into an ultratight corset in order to achieve the wasp-waisted figure men considered attractive. Yet many women today (and some men) routinely use harsh chemicals to change the color of their hair, pay to have someone cut into their faces to decrease the size of their noses or tighten the skin around their chins, or reduce their food intake to the point of starvation in order to become slender.

The legitimacy of certain practices and ideas can be understood only within the unique context of the group or society in which they occur. What is considered abnormal in one case may be perfectly normal, even necessary, in another. It takes a sociological imagination to see that time and place have a great influence on what people consider normal.

Ancestor worship in Madagascar is a custom that has been around for centuries, impervious to the arrival of Christian churches and Western ideals. To the people who practice it, the ritual of burial, disinterment, and reburial is more important than marriage. The physical body may die, but the *fanahy,* or soul, lives on. The Malagasy believe that spirits stay with the bones and have needs for earthly goods such as food and clothing. It's up to the living to provide these things. In exchange, the dead take care of living relatives by determining their health, wealth, and fertility and by helping them communicate with God. In short, the custom is quite rational and beneficial: The individual's own earthly well-being and spiritual salvation depend on it.

Likewise, the practice of calling was an integral part of late-19th-century U.S. culture. It maintained the social class structure by serving as a test of suitability, breeding, and background (Bailey, 1988). Calling enabled the middle and upper classes to protect themselves from what many at the time considered the "intrusions" of urban life and to screen out the disruptive effects of social and geographic mobility, which reached unprecedented levels at the turn of the century. It also allowed parents to control the relationships of their children, thereby increasing the likelihood that their pedigree would remain intact.

These phenomena illustrate the important role played by culture and history in creating social order. Whether we're talking about our own ordinary rituals or those practiced by some distant society, the normative patterns that mark the millions of seemingly trivial actions and social encounters of our everyday lives are what make society possible. They tell us what to expect from others and what others should expect from us. In this chapter, by looking at the various taken-for-granted aspects of culture that lend structure to our daily lives, I examine how order is created and maintained in society. In the process, I compare specific aspects of our culture with others, past and present.

DIMENSIONS OF CULTURE

In Chapter 2, you saw that culture is one of the key elements that shape the structure of a society. It consists of the shared, taken-for-granted values, beliefs, objects, and rules that guide people's lives. In everyday conversation, however, the term *culture* is often used only when discussing something "foreign." We rarely feel the need to question why we do certain things in the course of our daily lives—we just do them. It's other people in other lands whose rituals and beliefs need explaining. What we often fail to realize is that culture is "doing its job" most effectively when it is unnoticed. Only in times of dramatic social change and moral uncertainty or when circumstances force us to compare our society with another—like when you travel abroad—do we become aware that a distinct set of cultural rules and values influences us, too.

To a large degree, we are products of the culture and historical epoch in which we live. From a very young age we learn, with startling accuracy, that certain types of shelter, food, tools, clothing, modes of transportation, music, sports, and art characterize our culture and make it different from others. Without much conscious effort, we also learn what to believe, what to value, and which actions are proper or improper both in public and in private.

Material and Nonmaterial Culture

Culture consists of all the products of a society that are created over time and shared by members of that society. These products may be tangible or intangible. The term ***nonmaterial culture*** refers to all the nonphysical products of society that are created over time and shared: knowledge, beliefs, customs, values, morals, symbols, and so on. Nonmaterial culture also includes common patterns of behavior and the forms of interaction appropriate in a particular society. It is a "design for living" that distinguishes one society from another. Like an owner's manual for social life, nonmaterial culture tells us how our society works, what is possible, what to value, how to conduct our everyday lives, and what to do if something breaks down. Without an understanding of a society's nonmaterial culture, people's behaviors—not to mention the symbolic significance of their material world—would be thoroughly incomprehensible.

Material culture includes the physical artifacts that shape or reflect the lives of members of a particular society: distinctive clothing and architecture, inventions, food, artwork, music, and so on. Some of the most important elements of material culture are technological achievements, which are the ways in which members of a society apply knowledge to adapt to changing social, economic, or environmental conditions. For instance, plastic products have provided people with cheaper and more convenient packaging of needed goods—and in the process have forever altered shopping and consumption patterns.

Similarly, the advent of the automobile in the early 20th century gave people greater mobility to take advantage of economic or residential opportunities elsewhere and thereby dramatically changed the way they lived. It's impossible to imagine society without cars. Today, the average number of cars per household (1.9) exceeds the average number of people per household (1.8). Since the interstate highway system was developed in 1956, the distance Americans drive annually has increased from 628 million miles to close to 3 billion (cited in Sullivan, 2006). This system made suburban living and cross-country travel possible. Moreover, our national economy would crumble without the ubiquitous long-haul trucks transporting needed goods to every corner of the country. The influence of the automobile is especially noticeable today in places such as Nepal and rural China, where it is just beginning to have a similar dramatic impact on people's lives.

Changes in material culture often transform the physical environment, creating the need for additional alterations in material and nonmaterial culture. The enormous amount of nonbiodegradable plastic piling up in overflowing landfills, for example, has spawned a vast array of advances in recycling and other eco-friendly technologies. Likewise, a heavy reliance on automobiles has created several serious problems throughout the world: air pollution, depletion of fossil fuel reserves, suburban sprawl, and constant traffic. These problems, in turn, have created the need for changes in travel patterns and arrangements, as well as further material developments, such as an entire "green" industry that includes pollution-reducing devices, hybrid automobiles, and alternative-fuel sources (for more, see Chapter 14).

Global Culture

Although culture gives each society its distinctive character, cultural "purity" is all but obsolete (Griswold, 1994). Transnational media, global communication and transportation systems, and centuries of international migration have contributed to a worldwide swapping of cultural elements. For instance, despite the recent economic downturn, U.S. retailers remain a common fixture around the globe. More than 175 million people worldwide shop at one of Wal-Mart's nearly 5,000 stores in Asia, Latin America, and North America each year (Landler & Barbaro, 2006). Starbucks has nearly 17,000 coffeehouses in 49 countries (Starbucks, 2008). American pizza, too, which originally came to us from Naples, Italy, has migrated to every corner of the globe. Domino's Pizza now has more than 8,600 stores in 55 countries (Domino's, 2008). And Yum! Brands—which owns fast-food chains such as Taco Bell, Kentucky Fried Chicken, Pizza Hut, and Long John Silver's—has more than 36,000 restaurants worldwide (Yum! Brands, 2008). According to the Canadian

Broadcasting Corporation (2003), only 30% of television shows, 18% of English-language magazines, 28% of books, 13% of music recordings, and 2% of feature films that Canadians consume are actually produced in Canada. What were once unique features of U.S. material culture—such as blue jeans and fast food—can now be found on nearly every continent.

In some societies, people see the imported elements of culture as dangerous encroachments on long-held traditions and national unity. Of special concern is the increasing influence of U.S. culture on other countries. About a decade ago, culture ministers from 20 different countries on four continents met to discuss how best to maintain their own cultures in a global environment dominated by U.S. media (Croteau & Hoynes, 2000). They were responding to examples such as these:

- Approximately two thirds of French respondents to a survey felt that the United States exerted too much cultural influence on Europe (Daley, 2000). A French sheep farmer named José Bové became something of a national hero for vandalizing McDonald's restaurants, a symbol of what many French consider to be the unwanted intrusion of U.S. food culture.

- In Austria, an organization called the Pro-Christkind Association launched a campaign against Santa Claus, claiming that he is nothing more than an advertising symbol of American culture and consumption habits (Landler, 2002).

- Okinawa, Japan, has historically had the highest proportion of people over the age of 100 in the world and the greatest life expectancy of any region in Japan. But, increasingly, Okinawans are living and eating like Americans. They walk less, eat fewer vegetables, and eat more hamburgers than they used to. Okinawa now has the most American-style fast-food restaurants of any city in Japan. As a result, average weight and rates of heart disease, cerebral hemorrhage, and lung cancer have all increased. Okinawans now rank 26th in life expectancy among the Japanese administrative regions (Onishi, 2004a; Takayama, 2003).

Emotions can run especially high when the integrity of a culture's language is at stake. About 60% of all existing languages have fewer than 10,000 speakers (Gordon, 2005). These languages are highly vulnerable to disappearance in a global culture. Indeed, linguists predict that of the 7,000 or so languages spoken worldwide today, nearly half are likely to disappear this century (cited in Wilford, 2007). Taking their place will be a handful of dominant languages that, in a technologically connected world, are seen as "linguistic passports" to education and a successful economic future (Lewis, 1998).

Foremost among these major languages is English, which today shapes communication all over the world. Japanese will order bottles of *bi-ru* (pronounced bee-roo) in pubs and spread *bata* on their bread. In many Spanish-speaking countries, people type e-mails on their *computadoras.* The French commonly use words such as *le weekend* and *le shopping.* People are recognizing that in a world of collapsing borders, a common language is useful. And because of pervasive U.S. cultural influences and technologies, English is an understandable choice. For instance, even though the number of non-English Internet users grows each year, about 80% of the world's electronically stored information is in English (Crystal, 2003). It is estimated that 500 million to 1 billion people now speak English as either a first or a second language (Cohen, 2006). In fact, there are more people who speak English as their second language than there are people who speak it as their first (Mydans, 2007).

The growth of English—and especially U.S. English—as a sort of "world" language has had a profound effect on the way people in other countries go about their business. For example, the Swiss government decreed that all Swiss children above the age of 6 must learn English. In Chile, the government wants to make all its 15 million citizens fluent in English within a generation (Rohter, 2004).

But not everyone is happy about such developments. In 1994, France enacted the Toubon Law, which makes French the mandatory language in a variety of situations, ranging from advertising to the workplace documents employees need to do their jobs.

In 2004, workers at a French branch of General Electric that manufactures health equipment sued the company for violating this law because all its internal e-mails, instruction manuals, and software applications are printed only in English. In 2006, the president of Iran proposed to ban English words such as *helicopter, chat,* and *pizza* (Cohen, 2006).

In the United States, many people are concerned with the encroaching influence not of English but of Spanish. More than 34 million U.S. residents speak Spanish as their first language; in Los Angeles 44%

of residents over the age of 5 speak Spanish at home (U.S. Bureau of the Census, 2009). Immigrants are actually making the transition to speaking English more quickly than in the past, and more than 90% of residents with a foreign-born parent prefer to speak only English at home (Kent & Lalasz, 2006). Indeed, about three quarters of the children who speak Spanish as their first language speak English "very well" (U.S. Bureau of the Census, 2009). Nevertheless, many U.S. citizens fret about the primacy of English when they see street signs, billboards, election ballots, and automated teller machines in Spanish. In 2009, a city councilman in Nashville, Tennessee, introduced a bill that would have prevented government workers from communicating in *any* language other than English. Even though the bill failed, it illustrated a deep-seated fear among many Americans that the United States is moving toward becoming a bilingual or multilingual nation. Indeed, 30 states (including Tennessee) and at least 19 cities have declared English as their official language (Brown, 2009).

Subcultures

Sociologists and anthropologists usually speak of culture as a characteristic of an entire society. But culture can also exist in smaller, more narrowly defined units. A ***subculture*** consists of the values, behaviors, and physical artifacts of a group that distinguish it from the larger culture. Think of it as a culture within a culture. Certain racial and ethnic groups, religions, age groups, and even geographic areas can all constitute subcultures.

To see a more common subculture, you don't have to look any farther than your own school. You're probably well aware of the material and nonmaterial subculture that is unique to your campus. Perhaps some landmark—a bell tower or ornate archway—is the defining symbol of the university, or maybe a boulder or tree or fountain occupies a hallowed place in campus lore. I'm sure you know your school mascot and the school colors. In addition, when you first arrived at school, you probably had to learn a tremendous amount of new information about the nonmaterial subculture just to survive—how to register for courses, how to address a professor, where to eat and study, what administrators, faculty, and fellow students expect of you, and so on. At my university, the student newspaper publishes a glossary of common words, phrases, acronyms, and nicknames at the beginning of each academic year to aid first-year students in their adjustment to life on campus. Just as you have to learn how to be a member of your society, you have to learn how to be a member of your university subculture.

CULTURAL EXPECTATIONS AND SOCIAL ORDER

Despite periodic shifts in the acceptability of certain acts, culture and history provide people with a common bond, a sense of shared personal experiences. That we can live together at all depends on the fact that we share a tremendous amount of cultural knowledge. This knowledge allows us to predict, with a fair amount of certainty, what most people will do in a given situation. For instance, I can assume that when I say "Hi, how are you?" you will reply, "Fine." You probably won't launch into some long-winded explanation of your mental, physical, and emotional condition at that precise moment, because doing so would violate the cultural rules governing such casual greetings.

The actions of individuals are not simply functions of personality types or psychological predispositions; rather, they are also a reflection of shared cultural expectations. Culture provides us with information about which of these actions are preferred, accepted, or disapproved of at a given time (McCall & Simmons, 1978). Take, for example, sexuality. American culture is often characterized as a ***heteronormative culture***—that is, a culture where heterosexuality is accepted as the normal, taken-for granted mode of sexual expression. Social institutions and social policies reinforce the belief that sexual relationships ought to exist between males and females. Cultural representations of just about every aspect of intimate and family life—dating, sex, marriage, childbearing, retirement, and so on—presume a world in which men are sexually and affectionately attracted to women and women to men (Macgillivray, 2000). Think of the flurry of magazine and TV advertisements we're subjected to in the weeks prior to Valentine's Day that depict men and women embracing, gazing longingly into each other's eyes, and buying each other expensive jewelry. Adolescent women seeing a gynecologist for the first time can expect to be given information on birth control, highlighting the assumption that they will have sex with men—it's just a matter of when. In 2008, the online dating service eHarmony was sued for discrimination because the site offered only two options to its customers: "man seeking woman" or "woman seeking man" (Miller, 2008). Even some sports reflect a heteronormative culture. In competitive figure skating, the "pairs" competition always consists of women partnered with men (Wildman & Davis, 2002). The 2007 film *Blades of Glory* humorously satirized this basic assumption by depicting two men skating with each other in the pairs event.

Recall from Chapter 2 that norms are the rules that govern the routine social encounters in which we all participate. Although many everyday norms are sometimes difficult to identify and describe, they reflect commonly held assumptions about conventional behavior. Consider the unspoken norms in a situation we've all experienced, shopping at a supermarket:

> There is a customer role to be played in grocery stores. There generally is a standard of orderliness. Shoppers are not seen pushing each other out of the way, picking things out of each other's shopping carts, or sitting on the floor eating from a recently opened can. How does one "know" how the role of customer is to be played? Aside from the "No Shirt. No Bare Feet" sign on the door . . . there is no clear listing of shopping rules. (Kearl & Gordon, 1992, p. 274)

Norms can be generalized to similar situations within a culture. That is, we can be reasonably certain that grocery store behavior that is appropriate in Baton Rouge will be appropriate in Bakersfield or Butte as well. The grocery store experience itself would be chaotic if there wasn't a certain degree of agreement over how we should act. Without such unspoken rules and expectations, every situation would have to be interpreted, analyzed, and responded to as if it were an entirely new occasion. Social life would be utterly unmanageable.

Social Institutions and Cultural Norms

Large social institutions are closely tied to culture. For one thing, some institutions reflect deeply held cultural values. A free-market economy, for instance, reflects the cultural values of achievement, competition, material acquisition, and so on. A democratic government reflects the values of individual freedom and citizen participation. As we'll see in the following chapter, other institutions—such as education, religion, and family—provide the mechanisms through which culture and subculture are transmitted across generations.

Institutions are also strongly supported by cultural norms. When a pattern of behavior becomes widely accepted within a particular social institution and is taken for granted in society, sociologists say it has become an ***institutionalized norm*** (DiMaggio & Powell, 1991). For instance, the institutionalized (i.e., culturally acceptable) way of becoming financially successful in many developed societies is to earn a college degree, get a job in an entry-level position somewhere, and eventually work your way to the top. Even things that most of us would condemn have, at times, been institutionalized and encouraged by society. Slavery, for example, was for several hundred years a culturally, politically, and economically acceptable practice in the United States. The buying and selling of slaves was strongly approved by the nation's most powerful forces, as well as by many ordinary people (Birenbaum & Sagarin, 1976).

Institutionalized norms constrain people's behavior by making some lines of action unthinkable. But they don't just limit options, they also establish the setting in which people discover their preferences and begin to see the world in a particular way (DiMaggio & Powell, 1991). The military ritualizes the process of becoming a full-fledged member through training, oaths of allegiance, and public recognition of the passage from one rank to another. In doing so, it ensures conformity to military norms and an understanding of the "rules of engagement," the specific norms that govern fighting on the battlefield. Religious congregations reinforce "appropriate" lifestyles and downplay inappropriate ones through collective worship services.

Shifts in one institution are often linked to shifts in another. The abolition of slavery in the United States, for instance, meant that the entire economic system of the South had to be restructured from a plantation economy to one characterized by smaller landholdings and more industry. In Russia, the collapse of communism close to two decades ago strengthened the role of religious organizations in providing people with normative guidelines. In the United States today, the fact that women are no longer expected to be the sole caretakers of children has meant an increase in the number of mothers who enter the paid labor force, which in turn has created a higher demand for organized day care as well as increased pressure on legislatures to enact laws protecting the interests of working parents.

Institutionalized Emotions

To illustrate the power of institutionalized norms in our private experiences, I turn to a common element of everyday life: emotions. We all experience emotions as physical, sometimes instantaneous responses to life events. Thus, we're inclined to see them as natural and universal. Yet emotional display comes under the strict control of cultural norms. In rural areas of Greece, widows traditionally are expected to mourn over the loss of their husbands—most notably by wearing black—for the rest of their lives. That would be seen as excessive in the United States, where more than 2 months of grieving might be considered a sign of major depression (Horwitz, 2002).

Every society has unwritten rules about which emotions are appropriate to feel, which are appropriate to display, and how intense the emotional display should be under specific circumstances. For instance, in our culture, we're supposed to be sad at funerals, happy at weddings, and angry when we are insulted. We're supposed to feel joy when we receive good news but not show too much of it if our good fortune is at someone else's expense. In extreme cases, the violation of emotional display norms can lead to grave sanctions, such as a diagnosis of mental illness (Pugliesi, 1987; Thoits, 1985).

When people hide or alter their emotions to fit the situation, they are playing a significant role in maintaining social order within broader social institutions. Take the popular TV show *American Idol,* for example. In the season finale, when the field is finally reduced to the last two contestants, the camera zooms in on both of them. They stand on stage holding hands in shaky anticipation of the final verdict. The lights are dimmed. When the winner is announced, the runner-up is the picture of grace and charm, all smiles and congratulations. But we know better. This person has just lost the contest of his or her life on national television and has got to be sad, angry, or at the very least disappointed. To add insult to injury, he or she is then gently escorted off stage so the winner can have the spotlight. Why does the runner-up suppress the urge to show true emotions? Part of the reason is that he or she understands that there's more at stake than personal feelings. Imagine what would happen to the *American Idol* phenomenon if the runners-up started displaying their bitterness on stage—screaming at the host, threatening the judges, shunning the winners, or demanding a recount.

Norms about expressing emotions are often linked to institutional concerns and needs. In her book *The Managed Heart,* Arlie Russell Hochschild (1983) describes the feeling rules required by occupations in which employees have a great deal of contact with the public. Flight attendants, for example, must constantly be good-natured and calm under dangerous conditions. They must make their work appear effortless and handle other people's feelings as deftly as their own. This ability is not just a matter of living up to social expectations—it is part of their job description. A "smile" becomes an economic asset and a public relations tool.

Likewise, doctors and nurses are trained to show kindness and concern for their patients, not disgust or alarm. Furthermore, they cannot become too emotionally involved with patients, because they see pain, suffering, and death every day. It is difficult not to become attached to patients, but such emotional outlay would inevitably lead to burnout, making effective job performance impossible. Doctors and nurses are more successful in their jobs when they can keep their emotions under control.

Although it is not surprising that organizations would have an interest in emotional displays by members, it is perhaps less obvious that particular emotions are linked to larger societal concerns such as politics and economics, often as a method of social control (Kearl & Gordon, 1992). For instance, the conflict perspective points out that some regimes may use fear to quell dissent and enforce obedience. In the early 20th century, in response to the increasing political and economic strength of African Americans, many white Southerners used fear to control Blacks, through the threat of lynching and other forms of violence. Similarly, religious leaders often use the fear of eternal damnation to make sure their followers cooperate.

The effectiveness of invoking emotions such as guilt, anxiety, and shame waxes and wanes as social climates change. In the past, when communities were smaller and more interdependent, social behavior could be easily regulated by the threat of shame. If people broke a law or violated some norm of morality, they would bring humiliation on themselves, their families, and the community at large. But as societies became more complex, such close ties began to disappear. Today, the political control of behavior through emotion is more likely to be directed inward, in the form of guilt and anxiety. For instance, if working mothers are implicated by politicians as contributing to the "breakdown" of the traditional family by leaving the raising of their children to others, more and more mothers will experience guilt when they seek employment outside the home (Berg, 1992).

Norms governing the expression of emotions give us a way to communicate and maintain social order. They perpetuate institutions by creating powerful cultural expectations that are difficult to violate.

Norms and Sanctions

Most norms provide only a general framework of expectations; rarely do they tell us exactly how to act, and rarely are they obeyed by all people at all times. Furthermore, norms may be ambiguous or contradictory. It is no surprise, then, that behavior sometimes departs markedly from normative expectations. When it does, negative ***sanctions*** may be applied. A sanction is a direct social response to some behavior; a negative sanction is one that punishes or otherwise discourages violations of social norms and symbolically reinforces the culture's values and morals.

Different norms evoke different sanctions when violated. ***Mores*** (pronounced MORE-ayz) are norms, sometimes codified into laws, that are taken very seriously by society. Violation of some mores can elicit severe, state-sponsored sanctions, such as serving time in prison for armed robbery. Other mores may be equally serious but are much less formally stated. Sanctions for violating these norms may take the form of public ostracism or exclusion from the group, as when one is excommunicated for going against the moral doctrine of one's church.

The vast majority of everyday norms are relatively minor, however; violation of these norms, called ***folkways***, carries much less serious punishment. For instance, if I chew with my mouth open and food dribbles down my chin, others may show outward signs of disapproval and consider me a "disgusting pig." I may receive fewer dinner invitations as a result, but I won't be arrested or banished from my community.

According to the structural-functionalist perspective, each time a community moves to sanction an act, it strengthens the boundaries between normative and nonnormative behavior (Erikson, 1966). In the process, the rest of us are warned of what is in store if we, too, violate the norms. In the 17th century, for example, criminals and religious heretics were executed at high noon in the public square for all to see. The spectacle was meant to be a vivid and symbolic reaffirmation of the community's norms. Today, such harsh sanctions are likely to be hidden from the public eye. However, the publicity surrounding executions, as well as the visibility of less severe sanctions, serves the same purpose—to declare to the community where the line between acceptable and unacceptable behavior lies. By sanctioning the person who violates a norm, society informs its members what type of person cannot live "normally" within its boundaries (Pfohl, 1994).

Cultural Relativism and Ethnocentrism

When it comes to examining the cultures of different societies, sociologists are inclined to adopt a position of ***cultural relativism***, the principle that people's beliefs and activities should be interpreted in terms of their own culture. In other words, cultural practices that might conflict with our cultural values are still considered valid because they reflect the values of that culture. Maintaining a culturally relativist position becomes especially difficult when the practice in question is considered brutal or oppressive. Take, for instance, the practice of female genital mutilation (FGM), a procedure that entails the removal of a young girl's clitoris and/or the destruction of the labia and vulva. In the African and Middle Eastern countries where FGM is practiced, women are expected to be virgins when they marry. The ritual therefore serves to control young women's sexuality and ensure their "marriageability." But to people in societies that acknowledge or even celebrate female sexuality, such a practice is abhorrent and a violation of human rights. A decades-long worldwide campaign to end FGM has led many countries to ban the practice. However, it persists as a local custom in 28 African countries and a few others in Asia and the Middle East. More than 3 million girls a year are at risk of genital cutting on the African continent alone (Population Reference Bureau, 2008a).

Cultural relativism is not part of the way most of us are raised. People tend to evaluate other cultures in comparison to their own. This tendency is called ***ethnocentrism***. As children, most people are taught that they live in the greatest country on earth. Many also learn to take pride in their religious, racial, or ethnic group. But the belief that one group or country is the "best" means that others are "not the best." Sixty percent of Americans believe that their culture is superior to others. The figure rises to 90% in South Korea and Indonesia (cited in Rieff, 2006).

Ethnocentrism results from the nature of human interaction itself. Much of our everyday lives are spent in groups and organizations. By their very character, these collectivities consist of individuals with some, though not necessarily all, shared interests. The same is true for larger cultures. To the extent that we spend a majority of our time with others "like us," our interactions with others "not like us" will be limited, and they will remain "foreign" or "mysterious." Similarity breeds comfort; difference breeds discomfort. For example, despite laws against the practice, many Japanese shopkeepers are so uncomfortable dealing with foreigners that they refuse to serve them (French, 1999a). In fact, when Japanese citizens who have lived abroad for a long time return to Japan, they find that they are no longer regarded as fully Japanese and are treated with the sort of cold disdain foreigners there often experience (French, 2000).

Another reason for the existence of ethnocentrism is the loyalty we develop to our particular culture or subculture (Charon, 1992). Different values, beliefs, and behaviors come to be seen not merely as different ways of thinking and acting but as threats to our own beliefs and values. Such perceptions, for instance, underlie much of the resentment and hostility toward recently arrived immigrants. Even groups whose position in society is strong and secure can find the encroachment of other ways of life threatening. For example, a school superintendent in Mustang, Oklahoma, got into trouble a few years ago for including references to Kwanzaa and Chanukah as well as Christmas in an annual school play and for removing a live nativity scene from the conclusion of the play so as not to highlight one faith too much over others. Christian parents became outraged, suing the school for discrimination and voting down an $11 million school bond (Zernike, 2004). In 1996, the national convention of Southern Baptists—the largest Protestant denomination in the United States—adopted a resolution calling for a major campaign to convert Jews to Christianity. Many Southern Baptists believe that Christianity is the culmination of Jewish history (Garment, 1996). More recently, some Southern Baptist congregations have targeted Hindus, Muslims, Mormons, and Jehovah's Witnesses for conversion as well ("Baptists Seek to 'Convert' Mormons," 2000).

Cultural loyalty is encouraged by institutional ritual and symbolism. In this country, saying the "Pledge of Allegiance" at the beginning of the school day, playing the "Star Spangled Banner" and "God Bless America" at sports events, and observing holidays such as Memorial Day, the Fourth of July, Veterans Day, and Flag Day all reinforce loyalty to U.S. culture. The American flag is considered such an important national symbol that an entire code of etiquette with specific instructions on how to display it exists to ensure that it is treated with reverence. These are the "sacred objects" of U.S. culture (Durkheim, 1915/1954). The importance of these objects is especially pronounced when people in society feel threatened. You will recall the enormous number of American flags, patriotic songs, pins, T-shirts, and magnetic ribbons on cars that exploded onto the cultural landscape after the September 11, 2001, attacks and during the wars in Iraq and Afghanistan. Religious artifacts and symbols, uniforms and team colors, and distinctive ethnic clothing all foster a sense of pride and identity and hold a community of similar people together, often to the exclusion of others.

Sometimes, respect for these cultural objects must be enforced under threat of punishment. In 2008, a fan at a New York Yankees' baseball game was forcibly removed by police for not standing by his seat as "God Bless America" was being played during the seventh-inning stretch. For years, some members of the U.S. Congress have been trying to ensure loyalty to the American flag by proposing a constitutional amendment banning its desecration. In Japan, 243 teachers were punished in 2004 for not standing and singing the national anthem at the beginning of the school day (Onishi, 2004b).

CULTURAL VARIATION AND EVERYDAY EXPERIENCE

As populations grow more ethnically and racially diverse and as the people of the world become linked

more closely by commerce, transportation, and communication, the likelihood of individuals from different cultures and subcultures living together increases. An awareness of cultural differences helps ease everyday interactions in a multicultural society and can be crucial in international relations.

In Iran, people are expected to give false praise and make insincere promises. They are expected to tell others what they want to hear in order to avoid conflict or offer hope when, clearly, there is none. This practice, known as *taarof,* is considered polite, not offensive. Children learn from an early age to pick up on nuances in others' comments. The practice has its historical roots in centuries of occupation by foreign powers, which taught Iranians the value of hiding their true feelings. As one Iranian psychologist put it, "When you tell lies, it can save your life" (quoted in Slackman, 2006, p. 5). You can see how important it is for diplomats and negotiators to know of such tendencies, especially because Iran is such an important player in volatile Middle Eastern politics.

In Afghanistan, the thumbs-up gesture—a sign of approval in the United States—is the equivalent of giving someone "the finger." To reduce potentially dangerous cultural clashes, the U.S. Marine Corps distributes "Culture Smart Cards" to U.S. military personnel on their arrival in Afghanistan and Iraq. The cards contain instructions on matters such as how to shake hands, what gestures are appropriate, and how to act when in Iraqi homes (Edidin, 2005).

Cultural variation reflects more than just differences in people's habits and customs. It indicates that even the most taken-for-granted truths in our lives, the things we assume are universal and unambiguous, are subject to different interpretations and definitions worldwide. Two important examples of such variation are beliefs about health and illness and definitions of sex.

Health and Illness

Medical beliefs and practices always reflect the cultural values of a society (Coe, 1978). We can't claim to have a disease that doesn't exist in our culture. In Malaysia, a man may be diagnosed with *koro,* a sudden, intense anxiety that his sexual organs will recede into his body, causing death. In some Latin American countries, a person can suffer from *susto,* an illness tied to a frightening event that makes the soul leave the body, causing unhappiness and sickness (American Psychiatric Association, 2000). One psychiatrist estimates that as many as 1 million Japanese (or about 1% of the population) suffer from *hikikomori,* a phenomenon whereby alienated adolescents withdraw from social life and sequester themselves in their rooms for 6 months or longer (some have lived in isolation for longer than a decade; Jones, 2006). None of these conditions exists as a medical diagnosis in other parts of the world. But they are not simply anthropological curiosities. They show that culture shapes everyday notions of health and illness.

Even more compelling, though, are the dramatic cultural differences in medical treatment among societies that share many other values, beliefs, norms, and structural elements. In the United States, medical treatment tends to derive from an aggressive "can-do" cultural spirit. Doctors in the United States are much more likely than European doctors to prescribe drugs and resort to surgery (Payer, 1988). Women in the United States are more likely than their European counterparts to undergo radical mastectomies, deliver their babies by cesarean section, and undergo routine hysterectomies while still in their 40s. People in the United States tend to see their bodies as machines that require annual checkups for routine maintenance. Diseases are enemies that need to be conquered as when people here try to "beat" their cancer.

In contrast, British medicine is much more subdued. British physicians don't recommend routine examinations, seldom prescribe drugs, and order about half as many X-ray studies as U.S. doctors do. British patients are also much less likely to have surgery. These attitudes also influence the perceptions of patients. People who are quiet and withdrawn—something U.S. doctors might consider symptoms of clinical depression—tend to be seen by British psychiatrists as perfectly normal.

Ironically, despite their more aggressive approach, Americans are much sicker than their British counterparts. They suffer higher rates of conditions such as diabetes, heart disease, and obesity and have a lower life expectancy. These differences exist even when controlling for social class. According to one study, the richest one third of U.S. citizens is in worse health than the poorest one third of the British (Banks, Marmot, Oldfield, & Smith, 2006).

In addition to determining the nature of illness, cultural attitudes also determine what it means to be sick and how sickness is experienced by individuals. Each society has a ***sick role***, a widely understood set of rules about how people are supposed to behave when sick (Parsons, 1951). The sick role entails certain obligations (things sick people are expected to do) as well as certain privileges (things to which sick people are entitled). Here are some common elements of the sick role in U.S. society:

- Because we tend to think of most illnesses as things that happen to people, individuals may be exempted from responsibility for the condition itself. At the same time, though, they're expected to recognize the condition as undesirable and something that should be overcome as soon as possible.

- Individuals who are allowed to occupy the sick role are excused from ordinary daily duties and expectations. This privilege varies with the severity of the illness. Compare someone with cancer to someone with a cold, for instance. National legislation—in the form of the Family and Medical Leave Act—and private workplace sick leave policies are the institutional manifestations of these expectations.

- Depending on the magnitude of the malady, sick people may be given relief from the ordinary norms of etiquette and propriety. Think of the nasty moods, actions, or insults you're able to "get away with" when you're sick that people wouldn't tolerate from you if you were well.

- Sick people are entitled to ask for and receive care and sympathy from others. But sympathy requests operate under their own set of cultural regulations. For instance, one should not claim too much sympathy, for too long, or for too many problems. In other words, sick people are expected to downplay their problems to avoid the appearance of self-pity. At the same time, though, they are expected to graciously accept some expressions of sympathy so as not to appear ungrateful (Clark, 1997).

- People occupying the sick role are required to take the culturally prescribed actions that will aid in the process of recovery, including, if the condition is serious enough, seeking help from a culturally appropriate health care professional (Parsons, 1951). Sometimes, to obtain the privilege of exemption from normal social obligations, people must be documented as officially ill from a culturally acceptable source. In the United States, that means a "doctor's note" (Lorber, 2000). Without such validation, your boss might not give you the day off, or your instructor might not allow you to take a makeup exam.

- Sick people are obligated to think of others as well as themselves. Hence, they are required to take precautions to avoid infecting those around them. In some cultures, sick people are expected to wear surgical masks in public to prevent contamination.

Failure on the part of sick people either to exercise their rights or to fulfill the obligations of the sick role—as when a person shows up at work with a persistent cough and a 102-degree fever—may elicit sanctions from the group (Crary, 2007). Moreover, those who do not appear to want to recover or who seem to enjoy being sick quickly lose sympathy. A person may also give up legal rights by not seeking or following expert advice. Parents who, because of their religious beliefs, prevent culturally approved medical intervention for their sick children have been arrested and charged with child endangerment or worse. If you are hospitalized and your attending physician doesn't think you ought to be discharged, but you leave anyway, your records will indicate that you have left "AMA"—against medical advice. This designation protects the doctor and the hospital from any liability should your condition worsen.

Like illness itself, sick role expectations are culturally influenced. For instance, when recent Latin American immigrants to the United States fall ill, they are likely to make a visit to the local *botanica* rather than a doctor. *Botanicas* are stores that sell all manner of folk remedies, religious objects, amulets, oils, perfumes, and other products purported to have curative powers. These practices, which combine alternative medicine with Roman Catholicism and other spiritual practices, are used to treat everything from arthritis to financial problems (Trotter & Chavira, 1997).

While different cultures define the sick role differently, it can also vary considerably along social class lines within the same culture (Freund & McGuire, 1991). Someone might have a debilitating disease, but without health insurance she or he may not have the wherewithal to seek the care of health professionals (and receive an official diagnosis) or may not be able to take time off from work for fear of losing her or his job. In short, socioeconomic factors may preclude such people from claiming sick role status.

Sex

The culture we grow up in shapes our most fundamental beliefs, even about what most people would consider the basic, universal facts of life. For instance, we take for granted that humans can be divided into two clearly identifiable sexes that are genetically determined at the time of conception. If you asked someone how to distinguish between males and females, the response would probably focus on observable physical characteristics—body shape, hair, voice, facial features, and so on. When biologists distinguish between the sexes, they too refer to biological traits—for example, chromosomes (XX for female, XY for male), sex glands (ovaries or testes), hormones (estrogen or testosterone), genitalia (vagina or penis), reproductive capacities (pregnancy or impregnation), germ cells produced (ova or sperm), and secondary sex characteristics (hips and breasts or facial hair and deep voice).

These characteristics, and hence the two sex categories, male and female, are usually assumed to be biologically determined, permanent, universal (males are males and females are females no matter what country or what era you live in), exhaustive (everyone can be placed into one or the other category), and mutually exclusive (you can be only one or the other sex, you can't be both). This set of beliefs is called the ***sexual dichotomy.***

If you think about it, our entire culture is built around the sexual dichotomy. We have separate clothing sections for men and women, separate hygienic products, separate sections in shoe stores, separate public restrooms, and so on. The sexual dichotomy is so obvious that we simply assume it to be in the nature of things. Our casual references to the "opposite" sex reinforce how much we take the sexual dichotomy for granted; when two things are opposite, it implies there's nothing in between.

But on closer inspection, the natural reality of the sexual dichotomy begins to break down. ***Transsexuals***—people who identify with a different sex and sometimes undergo hormone treatment and surgery to change their sex—challenge the idea that male and female are permanent biological characteristics. It's estimated that 1 in 30,000 men and 1 in 100,000 women in the United States undergo sex reassignment surgery, though many advocates consider this figure an underestimate (cited in Jost, 2006a). In 2008, a female-to-male transsexual named Thomas Beatie made international headlines when he gave birth to a baby girl. Though Thomas had his breasts removed, was taking testosterone, and was legally a man, he had kept his female reproductive organs.

The impermanence of sex received official recognition of sorts when the International Olympic Committee's Executive Board approved a proposal to allow transsexuals to compete in the 2004 Athens Olympics. Athletes who had undergone sex reassignment surgery were eligible to compete as long as they had been legally recognized as a member of the "new" sex and it had been at least 2 years since their surgery. Shortly afterward, the Ladies European Golf Tour enacted a similar policy, allowing a 37-year-old Danish male-to-female transsexual to play in one of their professional golf tournaments. In 2006, the city of New York began allowing people to change the sex listed on their birth certificates.

Other features of the sexual dichotomy—namely mutual exclusivity, exhaustiveness, and universality—are challenged when we examine sex categories cross-culturally. Throughout human history and across all societies, certain people have transcended the categories of male and female. They may be born with anatomical and/or genital configurations that are ambiguous. Or they may simply choose to live their lives in ways that don't conform to existing gender expectations associated with their sex (see Chapter 5 for more information about the distinction between sex and gender).

In Navajo culture, for instance, one could be identified as male, female, or *nadle*—a third sex assigned to those whose sex-typed anatomical characteristics were ambiguous at birth (Lang, 1998). Physically normal individuals also had the opportunity to choose to become *nadle* if they so desired. The gender status of *nadle* is simultaneously masculine and feminine. They are allowed to perform the tasks and take up the occupations of both men and women. For the Chuckchi of eastern Siberia, a biological male child with feminine physical traits gradually transforms into a "soft man."

Although he keeps his masculine name, he is expected to live as a woman (Williams, 1992). The *hijras* of India are born as men, but by choice they have their genitals surgically removed (Reddy, 2005). This operation transforms them not into women but into *hijras,* who appear feminine—dressing, standing, walking, and sitting as women. Many figures in Hindu mythology are neither male nor female. Hence, Indian culture not only accommodates the *hijras* but views them as meaningful, even powerful beings.

Such cross-cultural examples illustrate that our taken-for-granted beliefs about sex and gender are not held worldwide. In other cultures, sex is not dichotomous, exhaustive, or permanent.

The sexual dichotomy is not challenge-free in the United States either. ***Intersexuals,*** for instance, are individuals in whom sexual differentiation is either incomplete or ambiguous. They may have the chromosomal pattern of a female but the external genitals of a male, or they may have both ovaries and testicles. Experts estimate that about 1% of all babies born have some form of intersexuality, meaning that they are born with sexual organs that don't completely fit into the standard sex categories (Fausto-Sterling, 2000; Jost, 2006a).

It is interesting to note that the medical response to intersexuals supports the cultural and historical belief that there are two and only two sexes. Intersexuality is usually defined by doctors and medical researchers as a defective combination of the two existing categories and not as a third, fourth, or fifth category unto itself. Furthermore, on the diagnosis of intersexuality, a decision is always made to define the individual as either male or female. In societies with advanced medical technology, surgical and chemical means may be used to establish consistency between visible anatomy and the social label. Every month, dozens of sexually ambiguous newborns are "assigned" a sex and undergo surgery to confirm the designation (Cowley, 1997). About 90% are designated female because creating a vagina is considered surgically easier than creating a penis (Angier, 1997b).

However, an increasingly vocal group of intersexuals protest that many of the surgical techniques used to "correct" the problem of visually ambiguous genitals are mutilating and potentially harmful. They cite cases of intersexuals being robbed of any sexual sensation in the attempt to surgically "normalize" them—that is, give them the physical appearance of either a male or a female. The founder of the Intersex Society of North America eloquently summed up her organization's frustration: "They can't conceive of leaving someone alone" (quoted in Angier, 1997a, p. A10).

The medical profession can't leave these individuals alone because to do so would undermine our cultural understanding of sex. Drastic surgical intervention is undertaken not because the infant's life is threatened but because our entire social structure is organized around having two and only two sexes (Lorber, 1989). The male-female dichotomy in our culture is so essential to our way of life that those who challenge it are often considered disloyal to the most fundamental of biological "facts." To suggest that the labels "male" and "female" are not sufficient to categorize everyone is to threaten a basic organizing principle of social life. So pervasive is the sexual dichotomy that one doctor estimated her chances of persuading the parents of an intersexual child *not* to choose surgery at zero (Weil, 2006).

CONCLUSION

Over the span of a year or two, most cultures seem to have a stable set of norms about the acceptability of certain behaviors. This stability is illusory, however. From the perspective of a generation or even a decade later, that sense of order would give way to a sense of change (McCall & Simmons, 1978). Behaviors, values, beliefs, and morals fluctuate with startling frequency. Thus, comparisons across eras, in addition to comparisons across cultures, can provide rich insight into shifting definitions of acceptability, the nature of everyday life, and ultimately large-scale social change and stability.

The cultural and historical underpinnings of our private lives help us see the relationship among the individual, society, and social order. Cultural practices add continuity and order to social life.

To an individual, culture appears massive and unrelenting; but at the same time, it cannot exist without people. Norms govern our lives, whether we live by them or rebel against them. But to fully understand the relationship between the individual and society, we must look beyond the fact that culture and history shape our lives; we must see them as human constructions as well.

CHAPTER HIGHLIGHTS

◆ Culture provides members of a society with a common bond, a sense that we see certain facets of society in similar ways. That we can live together at all depends on the fact that members of a society share a certain amount of cultural knowledge.

◆ Norms—the rules and standards that govern all social encounters—provide order in our lives. They reflect commonly held assumptions about conventional behavior. Norm violations mark the boundaries of acceptable behavior and symbolically reaffirm what society defines as right and wrong.

◆ The more ethnically and culturally diverse a society is, the greater the likelihood of normative clashes between groups.

◆ Over the span of a few years, most cultures present an image of stability and agreement regarding normative boundaries. This agreement is illusory, however. Over a generation or even a decade, that sense of order is replaced by a sense of change.

KEY TERMS

cultural relativism Principle that people's beliefs and activities should be interpreted in terms of their own culture

ethnocentrism Tendency to judge other cultures using one's own as a standard

folkway Informal norm that is mildly punished when violated

heteronormative culture Culture in which heterosexuality is accepted as the normal, taken-for-granted mode of sexual expression

institutionalized norm Pattern of behavior within existing social institutions that is widely accepted in a society

intersexuals Individuals in whom sexual differentiation is either incomplete or ambiguous

material culture Artifacts of a society that represent adaptations to the social and physical environment

more Highly codified, formal, systematized norm that brings severe punishment when violated

nonmaterial culture Knowledge, beliefs, customs, values, morals, and symbols that are shared by members of a society and that distinguish the society from others

sanction Social response that punishes or otherwise discourages violations of a social norm

sexual dichotomy Belief that two biological sex categories, male and female, are permanent, universal, exhaustive, and mutually exclusive

sick role Set of norms governing how one is supposed to behave and what one is entitled to when sick

subculture Values, behaviors, and artifacts of a group that distinguish its members from the larger culture

transsexuals People who identify with a different sex and sometimes undergo hormone treatment and surgery to change their sex

©Sam Robinson/Digital Vision/Thinkstock

5 Building Identity

Socialization

My family once lived in a suburb just outside New York City. One day, when I was 9 years old, my parents sat me down and told me that we were going to be moving. They had narrowed down our ultimate destination to two possibilities: Laredo, Texas, or a suburb of Los Angeles called Burbank. After some rather intense debate, they chose Burbank. And so we headed "out West," where from age 9 to age 18, I lived in the shadow of the entertainment industry and all its glamour, glitz, and movie stars.

It wasn't long before I became a typical beach-loving Southern California kid. I often wonder how differently I would have turned out if my parents had chosen Laredo and I had spent my formative years along the Texas-Mexico border instead of in the middle of Tinseltown. Would I have a fondness for 10-gallon hats and snakeskin boots instead of tennis shoes and shorts? Would I have grown up with country music instead of the Beach Boys? Would my goals, beliefs, or sense of morality be different? In short, would I be a different person?

Try to imagine what your life would be like if you had grown up under different circumstances. What if your father had been a harpsichord enthusiast instead of a diehard Cubs fan? What if your family had been Jewish instead of Episcopalian? What if you had an older brother instead of a younger sister? What if you had lived on a farm instead of in a big city? What if you had been born in the 1960s instead of the 1990s? Your tastes, preferences, and hobbies, as well as your values, ambitions, and aspirations, would no doubt be different. But more profoundly, your self-concept, self-esteem, personality—the essence of who you are—would be altered, too.

Consider the broader social and historical circumstances of your life. What kind of impact might they have had on the type of person you are? Talk to elderly people who were children back in the 1930s, and they will speak of the permanent impact that the Great Depression had on them (Elder & Liker, 1982). Imagine spending your childhood as a Jew in Nazi Germany. That couldn't help but shape your outlook on life. The same can be said for growing up poor and black in the American South in the segregated 1950s or wealthy and white in Salt Lake City during the George W. Bush presidency.

Becoming the person you are cannot be separated from the people, historical events, and social circumstances that surround you. In this chapter, I examine the process of socialization—how we learn what's expected of us in our families, our communities, and our culture and how we learn to behave according to those expectations. The primary focus will be on the development of identity. ***Identity*** is our most essential and personal characteristic. It consists of our membership in various social groups (race, ethnicity, religion, gender, etc.), the traits we show to others, and the traits they ascribe to us. Our identity locates us in the social world, thoroughly affecting everything we do, feel, say, and think in our lives. Most people tend to believe that our self-concept, our sense of "maleness" or "femaleness," and our racial and ethnic identities are biologically or psychologically determined and therefore permanent and unchangeable. But as you will discover, these characteristics are social constructions: as much a product of our social setting and the significant people in our lives as a product of our physical traits and innate predispositions.

SOCIAL STRUCTURE AND THE CONSTRUCTION OF HUMAN BEINGS

The question of how we become who we are has for centuries occupied the attention of biologists, psychologists, anthropologists, sociologists, philosophers, and novelists. The issue is typically framed as a debate between *nature* (we are who we are because we were born that way) and *nurture* (we are who we are because of the way we were treated while growing up). Are we simply the predetermined product of our genes and biochemistry, or are we "created" from scratch by the people and the social institutions that surround us?

The answer to this question swings back and forth depending on the dominant cultural mood. In the late 19th and early 20th centuries, genetics became a popular explanation for human behavior, including a host of social problems ranging from poverty and crime to alcoholism and mental deficiency. Scientists, borrowing from the selective breeding practices used with racehorses and livestock, advocated programs of ***eugenics***, or controlled mating, to ensure that the "defective" genes of troublesome individuals would not be passed on to future generations. Theories of genetic inferiority became the cornerstone of Adolph Hitler's horrors in Nazi Germany during World War II. After the war, most people wanted to get as far away from such "nature" arguments as possible. So in the 1950s and 1960s, people heavily emphasized environmental influences on behavior, especially the role of early family experiences in shaping children's future personalities (Gould, 1997).

Today, because of the growing cultural emphasis on scientific technology, genetic explanations of human behavior have again become fashionable. In recent years, researchers have claimed that such diverse social phenomena as shyness, impulsiveness, intelligence, aggression, obesity, alcoholism, and addiction to gambling are at least partly due to heredity. Some political scientists even claim that people's emotional reactions to controversial issues such as the death penalty, taxes, and abortion are strongly influenced by their genetic inheritance (Carey, 2005b). The success of the Human Genome Project—an undertaking that mapped all the 20,000 to 25,000 genes in human DNA—will no doubt add fuel to "nature" arguments in the years to come.

Yet we are apparently not ready to say that nurture plays no role. When it comes to certain traits, heredity is meaningful only in the context of social experiences. Take intelligence. Many geneticists argue that heredity determines the limits of intelligence (Kirp, 2006). They base this claim on studies that have found that differences in IQ scores between identical twins (who share all their genes) are smaller than differences between fraternal twins (who share only half of their genes). But other researchers have found that a child's socioeconomic environment can make an enormous difference. One study of 7-year-old children found that while genetics accounts for most of the variation in IQ scores among twins with wealthy parents, the opposite is the case for twins from impoverished families. In these families, the IQs of identical twins vary just as much as the IQs of fraternal twins (Turkheimer, Haley, Waldron, D'Onofrio, & Gottesman, 2003). The researchers conclude that home life is critical for children at the lower end of the economic spectrum. In a chaotic and unstable environment, children's genetic potential cannot be reached. Conversely, affluent families are better equipped to provide the cognitive stimulation needed for neurological development.

Indeed, most sociologists would argue that human beings are much more than a collection of genetic predispositions and biological characteristics; they reflect society's influence as well. Certainly, our outward appearance, our physical strength, and our inherited predisposition to sickness have some effect on our personal development. Furthermore, our every thought and action is the result of a complex series of neurological and electrochemical events in our brains and bodies. When we feel the need to eat we are reacting to a physiological sensation—stomach contractions—brought about by a lowering of blood sugar. Satisfying hunger is clearly a biological process. But the way we react to this sensation cannot be predicted by physiology alone. What, when, how, and how often we eat are all matters of cultural forces that we learn over time. When you say something like "I'm starving, but it's too early to eat dinner," you're signaling the power of cultural training in overriding physiological demands.

Likewise, society can magnify physical differences or cover them up. We've collectively decided that some differences are socially irrelevant (e.g., eye color) and that some are important enough to be embedded in our most important social institutions (e.g., sex and skin color), giving rise to different rights, duties, expectations, and access to educational, economic, and political opportunities.

So who we become is influenced by the behaviors and attitudes of significant people in our lives as well as by cultural and institutional forces. As these things change, so do we. This proposition is not altogether comforting. It implies that who we are may in some ways be "accidental," the result of a series of social coincidences, chance encounters, decisions made by others, and political, economic, and historical events that are in large measure beyond our control—such as growing up in California rather than Texas.

SOCIALIZATION: BECOMING WHO WE ARE

The structural-functionalist perspective points out that the fundamental task of any society is to reproduce itself—to create members whose behaviors, desires, and goals correspond to those that that particular society deems appropriate and desirable. Through the powerful and ubiquitous process of ***socialization,*** the needs of the society become the needs of the individual.

Socialization is a process of learning. To socialize someone is to train that person to think, appear, and behave appropriately. It is the means by which people acquire a vast array of social skills, such as driving a car, converting fractions into decimals, speaking the language correctly, or using a fork instead of a knife to eat peas. But socialization is also the way we learn how to perceive our world; how to interact with others; what it means to be male or female; how, when, why, and with whom to be sexual; what we should and shouldn't do to and for others under certain circumstances; what our society defines as moral and immoral; and so on. In short, it is the process by which we internalize all the cultural information I discussed in Chapter 4.

This learning process is undertaken by the various individuals, groups, organizations, and institutions a person comes into contact with during the course of his or her life. These entities—whom sociologists refer to as ***agents of socialization***—can be family, friends, peers, teammates, teachers, schools, religious institutions, and the media. They can influence our self-concepts, attitudes, tastes, values, emotions, and behavior.

Although socialization occurs throughout our lives, the basic, formative instruction of life occurs early on. Young children must be taught the fundamental values, knowledge, and beliefs of their culture. Some of the socialization that occurs during childhood—often called ***anticipatory socialization***—is the primary means by which young individuals acquire the values and orientations found in the statuses they will likely enter in the future (Merton, 1957). Household chores, a childhood job, sports, dance lessons, dating, and many other types of experiences give youngsters an opportunity to rehearse for the kinds of roles that await them in adulthood.

The Acquisition of Self

The most important outcome of the socialization process is the development of a sense of self. The term *self* refers to the unique set of traits, behaviors, and attitudes that distinguishes one person from the next. The self is both the active source of behavior and its passive object (Mead, 1934).

As an active source, the self can initiate action, which is frequently directed toward others. Imagine, for example, that Donna and Robert are having dinner in a restaurant. Donna has a self that can perceive Robert, talk to him, evaluate him, and maybe even try to manipulate or persuade him to act in a way that is consistent with her interests. Donna also has a self that is a potential object of others' behavior: She can be perceived, talked to, evaluated, manipulated, or persuaded by Robert.

Donna can also direct these activities toward herself. She can perceive, evaluate, motivate, and even talk to herself. This is called ***reflexive behavior.*** To have a self is to have the ability to plan, observe, guide, and respond to one's own behavior (Mead, 1934). Think of all the times you have tried to motivate yourself to act by saying something such as, "All right, if I read 20 more pages of this boring sociology book, I'll make myself a hot fudge sundae." To engage in such an activity, you must simultaneously be the motivator and the one being motivated—the seer and the seen.

At this very moment, you are initiating an action: reading this book. But you also have the ability (now that I've mentioned it!) to be aware of your reading behavior, to reflexively observe yourself reading, and even to evaluate how well you are doing. This may sound like some sort of mystical out-of-body experience, but it isn't. Nothing is more fundamental to human thought and action than this capacity for self-awareness. It allows us to control our own behavior and interact smoothly with other self-aware individuals.

At birth, human babies have no sense of self. This is not to say that infants don't act on their own. Anyone who has been around babies knows that they have a tremendous ability to initiate action, ranging all the way from YouTube cute to downright disgusting. They cry, eat, sleep, play with squeaky rubber toys, and eliminate waste, all with exquisite flair and regularity. From the very first days of life, they respond to the sounds, sights, smells, and touches of others.

But this behavior is not characterized by the sort of reflexive self-consciousness that characterizes later behavior. Babies don't say to themselves, "I wonder if Mom will feed me if I scream" or "I can't *believe* how funny I sound." As children grow older, though, they begin to exert greater control over their conduct. Part of this transformation is biological. As they mature, they become more adept at muscle control. But physical development is only part of the picture. Humans must acquire certain cognitive capacities through interactions with others, including the abilities to differentiate between self and others, to understand and use symbolic language, and to take the roles of others.

Language Acquisition and the Looking-Glass Self

One of the most important steps in the acquisition of self is the development of speech (Hewitt, 1988). Symbolic interactionism points out that mastery of language is crucial in children's efforts to differentiate themselves as distinct social as well as physical objects (Denzin, 1977). Certainly, language acquisition relies on neurological development. But the ability to grasp the nuances of one's own language requires input from others. Most parents talk to their children from the start. Gradually, children learn to make sounds, imitate sounds, and use sounds as symbols for particular physical sensations or objects. Children learn that the sounds "Mama" and "Dada" are associated with two important objects in their life. Soon children learn that other objects—toys, animals, foods, Aunt Anita, Uncle Marc—have unique sounds associated with them as well.

This learning process gives the child access to the preexisting linguistic world in which his or her parents and others live (Hewitt, 1988). The objects named are not only those recognized within the larger culture but also those recognized within the child's family and social groups. The child learns the names of concrete objects (balls, buildings, furniture) as well as abstract ideas that cannot be directly perceived (God, happiness, peace, idea).

By learning that people and other objects have names, the child also begins to learn that these objects can be related to one another in a variety of ways. Depending on who is talking to whom, the same person can be called several different names. The object "Daddy" is called, by various other people, "David," "Dave," "Dov," "Dr. Newman," "Professor Newman," "Mr. Newman," and "Newman." Furthermore, the child learns that different people can be referred to by the same name. All those other toddlers playing in the park have someone they also call "Mama."

Amid these monumental discoveries, young children learn that they, too, are objects that have names. A child who learns that others are referring to her when they make the sound "Shayna," and that she, too, can use "Shayna" to refer to herself, has taken a significant leap forward in the acquisition of self. The child now can visualize herself as a part of the named world and the named relationships to which she belongs.

Children learn the meaning of named objects in their environment by observing the way other people act toward those objects. By observing people sitting on a chair, they learn what *chair* means. Parental warnings allow them to learn that a "hot stove" is something to be avoided. Similarly, by observing how people act toward them, they learn the meaning of themselves. People treat children in a variety of ways: care for them, punish them, love them, neglect them, teach them. If parents, relatives, and other agents of socialization perceive a child as smart, they will act toward him or her that way. Thus, the child eventually comes to believe he or she is a smart person. One of the earliest symbolic interactionists, Charles Horton Cooley (1902), referred to this process as the acquisition of the ***looking-glass self.*** He argued that we use the reaction of others toward us as mirrors in which we see ourselves and determine our self-worth. Through this process, we imagine how we might look to other people, we interpret their responses to us, and we form a self-concept. If we think people perceive us favorably, we're likely to develop a positive self-concept. Conversely, if we detect unfavorable reactions, our self-concept will likely be negative. Hence, self-evaluative feelings such as pride or shame are always the product of the reflected appraisals of others.

How the child-as-named-object is defined by others is also linked to larger societal considerations. Every culture has its own way of defining and valuing individuals at various stages of the life cycle. Children are not always defined, and have not always been defined, as a special subpopulation whose innocence requires nurturing and protection (Ariès, 1962). In some societies, they are expected to behave like adults and are held accountable for their actions just as adults would be. Under such cultural circumstances, a 5-year-old's self-concept may be derived from how well she or he contributes economically to the family, not from how cute or playful she or he is. Moreover, every society has its own standards of beauty and success. If thinness is a culturally desirable characteristic, a thin child is more likely to garner positive responses and develop a positive self-image than a child who violates this norm (i.e., an obese child).

The Development of Role Taking

The socialization process would be pretty simple if everyone in our lives saw us in exactly the same way. But different people expect or desire different things from us. Children eventually learn to modify their behavior to suit different people. Four-year-old Ahmed learns, for instance, that his 3-year-old sister loves it when he sticks his finger up his nose, but he also knows that his father doesn't find this behavior at all amusing. So Ahmed will avoid such conduct when his father is around but will proceed to amuse his sister with this trick when Papa is gone. The ability to use other people's perspectives and expectations in formulating one's own behavior is called ***role taking*** (Mead, 1934).

Role-taking ability develops gradually, paralleling the increasing maturation of linguistic abilities. Operating from the symbolic-interactionist perspective, George Herbert Mead (1934) identified two major stages in the development of role-taking ability and, ultimately, in the socialization of the self: the play stage and the game stage. The ***play stage*** occurs when children are just beginning to hone their language skills. Role taking at the play stage is quite simple in form, limited to taking the perspective of one other person at a time. Very young children cannot see themselves from different perspectives simultaneously. They have no idea that certain behaviors may be unacceptable to a variety of people across a range of situations. They know only that this particular person who is in their immediate presence will approve or disapprove of this conduct. Children cannot see that their father's displeasure with public nose picking reflects the attitudes of a larger group and is generally unacceptable. This more sophisticated form of self-control develops at the next stage of the socialization process: the game stage.

The ***game stage*** occurs about the time when children first begin to participate in organized activities such as school events and team sports. The difference between role taking at the play and game stages parallels the difference between childhood play and game behavior. "Play" is not guided by a specific set of rules. It has no ultimate object, no clearly organized competition, and no winners and losers.

Children playing baseball at the play stage have no sense of strategy and may not even be aware of the rules and object of the game. They may be able to hit, catch, and throw the ball but have no idea how their behavior is linked to that of their teammates. If a little girl is playing third base and a ground ball is hit to her, she may turn around and throw the ball to the left fielder, not because it will help her team win the game but because that's where her best friend happens to be.

Game behavior, in contrast, requires that children understand the object of the game. They realize that each player on the team is part of an organized network of roles determined by the rules of the game. Children know they must continually adapt their behavior to the team's needs in order to achieve a goal. To do so, they must imagine the group's perspective and anticipate how both their teammates and their opponents will act under certain circumstances.

With regard to role taking at the game stage, not only does the child learn to respond to the demands of several people, but he or she can also respond to the demands of the community or even society as a whole. Sociologists call the perspective of society and its constituent values and attitudes the ***generalized other***. The generalized other becomes larger as a child matures, growing to include family, peer group, school, and finally the larger social community. "Mama doesn't like it when I take off my pants in a restaurant" (play stage) eventually becomes, "It's never acceptable to take off one's pants in public" (game stage). Notice how such an understanding requires an ability to generalize behavior across a variety of situations and audiences. The child realizes that "public" consists of restaurants, shopping malls, school classrooms, neighbors' living rooms, and so forth.

This ability is crucial because it enables the individual to resist the influence of specific people who happen to be in his or her immediate presence. The boy who defies his peers by not joining them in an act of petty shoplifting is showing the power of the generalized other ("Stealing, no matter where or with whom, is bad"). During the game stage, the attitudes and expectations of the generalized other are incorporated into one's values and self-concept.

Real life is not always that simple, though. People from markedly different backgrounds are likely to internalize different sets of group attitudes and values. A devout Catholic contemplating divorce, for instance, is taking the role of a different generalized other than an atheist contemplating divorce. Likewise, the social worlds and social standards of men and women are different, as are those of children and adults, parents and nonparents, middle-class and working-class people, and people who grew up in different societies.

Nor is role-taking ability static. It changes in response to interactions with others. When people feel that they can understand another person's perspective—say, that of an intimate partner—they are likely to become concerned about or at least aware of how their behavior will affect that other person (Cast, 2004). Furthermore, as we move from one institutional setting to another, we adopt the perspective of the appropriate group and can become, for all intents and purposes, a different person. At school we behave one way, at church another, and at Grandma's house still another. We are as many different people as there are groups and organizations to which we belong.

In sum, the ability to imagine another person's attitudes and intentions and thereby to anticipate that person's behavior is essential for everyday social interaction. Through role taking, we can envision how others perceive us and imagine what their response may be to some action we're contemplating. Hence, we can select behaviors that are likely to meet with the approval of the person or persons with whom we are interacting and can avoid behaviors that might meet with their disapproval. Role taking is thus a crucial component of self-control and social order. It transforms a biological being into a social being who is capable of conforming his or her behavior to societal expectations. It is the means by which culture is incorporated into the self and makes group life possible (Cast, 2004).

Resocialization

Socialization does not end when childhood ends; it continues throughout our lives. Adults must be ***resocialized*** into a new set of norms, values, and expectations each time they leave behind old social contexts or roles and enter new ones (Ebaugh, 1988; Pescosolido, 1986; Simpson, 1979). For instance, we have to learn how to think and act like a spouse when we marry (Berger & Kellner, 1964), like a parent when we have kids (Rossi, 1968), and like a divorced person when a marriage ends (Vaughan, 1986).

Every new group or organization we enter, every new friendship we form, every new life-changing experience we have, requires the formation of new identities and socialization into new sets of norms and beliefs.

Certain occupations require the formal resocialization of new entrants. Often, the purpose is simply to make sure people who work in the organization share the same professional values, methods, and vocabulary. Many large companies, for example, have orientation programs for new employees to teach them what will be expected of them as they begin their new jobs. Sometimes the purpose is to make new entrants abandon their original expectations and adopt a more realistic view of the occupation. Police recruits who believe their job is to protect people must learn that deadly force is appropriate and sometimes necessary in the line of duty (Hunt, 1985). Many medical students become less idealistic and more realistic as they learn about the exhausting demands of their profession (Becker & Geer, 1958; Hafferty, 1991).

Sometimes resocialization is forceful and intense. According to sociologist Erving Goffman, this type of resocialization often occurs in ***total institutions*** (Goffman, 1961). Total institutions are physical settings in which groups of individuals are separated from the broader society and forced to lead an enclosed, formally administered life. Prisons, mental hospitals, monasteries, and military training camps are examples of total institutions. In these locations, previous socialization experiences are systematically destroyed and new ones developed to serve the interests of the larger group. Take the military training camp, for example. The Army alone spends several billion dollars a year and employs thousands of people to turn civilians into battle-ready warriors who look, act, and think like soldiers and learn to see the world from the soldier's perspective (Tietz, 2006). The process is called "total control." To aid in this transformation, recruits are stripped of old civilian identity markers (clothes, personal possessions, hairstyle) and forced to take on new ones that nullify individuality and also identify the newcomers' subordinate status (uniforms, identification numbers, similar haircuts). The newcomer is also subjected to constant scrutiny. Conformity is mandatory. Any misstep is met with punishment or humiliation.

Eventually, the individual learns to identify with the ideology of the total institution. In the boot camp, the uniformity of values and appearance is intended to create a sense of solidarity among the soldiers and thereby make the military more effective in carrying out its tasks. Part of the reason for all the controversy over diversity in the military—first with the inclusion of African Americans, then with women, and now with gay men and lesbians—is that it introduces diverse beliefs, values, appearances, and lifestyles into a context where, from an institutional perspective, similarity is essential.

The Self in a Cultural Context

When we imagine how others will respond to our actions, we choose from a limited set of lines of conduct that are part of the wider culture. In the United States, the self is likely to incorporate key cultural virtues such as self-reliance and individualism. Hence, personal goals tend to be favored over group goals (Bellah, Madsen, Sullivan, Swidler, & Tipton, 1985). In the United States, people will readily change their group membership as it suits them—leaving one career for another, moving from neighborhood to neighborhood, switching churches or even religions.

The United States is said to be an ***individualist culture,*** where personal accomplishments are a key part of a person's self-concept. We've always admired independent people whose success—usually measured in financial terms—is based on their own achievements and self-reliance (Bellah et al., 1985). Hence, the amount of respect people deserve is determined in large part by their level of expertise. For example, before a public speech, a guest lecturer in the United States will likely be introduced to her audience as "a distinguished scholar, a leader in her field," along with a list of academic credentials and scholarly achievements.

In many non-Western cultures, however, people are more likely to subordinate their individual goals to the goals of the larger group and to value obligations to others over personal achievements. In such a setting, known as a ***collectivist culture,*** personal identity is less important than group identity (Gergen, 1991). In India, for instance, feelings of self-esteem and prestige derive more from the reputation and honor of one's family than from any individual attainments (Roland, 1988). In a collectivist setting, a high value is placed on preserving one's public image so as not to bring shame on one's family, tribe, or community (Triandis, McCusker, & Hui, 1990). Overcoming personal interests and temptations to show loyalty to one's group and other authorities is celebrated. Guest lecturers in a collectivist culture would be considered self-centered and egotistical if they mentioned their personal accomplishments and credentials. Asian lecturers, for instance, usually begin their talk by telling the audience how *little* they know about the topic at hand (Goleman, 1990).

But even in an individualist society such as the United States, our personal identities are inseparable from the various groups and organizations to which we belong. Thus, to fully understand how we become who we are, we must know the norms and values of our culture, family, peers, coworkers, and all the other agents of socialization that are a part of our lives.

SOCIALIZATION AND STRATIFICATION: GROWING UP WITH INEQUALITY

Socialization does not take place in a vacuum. Your social class, your race and ethnicity, and your sex and gender all become significant features of your social identity. Were you born into a poor or a well-to-do family? Are you a member of a racial minority or a member of the dominant group? Are you male or female? These elements of identity shape your experiences with other people and the larger society and will direct you along a certain life path. In most societies, social class, race and ethnicity, and gender are the key determinants of people's opportunities throughout their lives.

Social Class

Social classes consist of people who occupy similar positions of power, privilege, and prestige. People's positions in the class system affect virtually every aspect of their lives, including political preferences, sexual behavior, religious affiliation, diet, and life expectancy. The conflict perspective points out that even in a relatively open society such as the United States, parents' social class determines children's access to certain educational, occupational, and residential opportunities. Affluent children grow up in more abundant surroundings than less affluent children and therefore have access to more material comforts and enriching opportunities such as good schools, opportunities to travel to far-off places, private music lessons, and so on. Furthermore, the lower the income of a child's family, the greater that child's risk of living in a single-parent household, having unemployed parents, having more than one disability, and dropping out of school (Mather & Adams, 2006).

But the relationship between class and socialization is not simply about parents providing (or not providing) their children with the trappings of a comfortable childhood. Parents' class standing also influences the values and orientations children learn and the identities they develop.

In Chapter 10, you will learn much more about how social class affects attitudes, behaviors, and opportunities. The important point here is that social class and socialization are linked. Sociologist Melvin L. Kohn (1979) interviewed 200 working-class and 200 middle-class American couples who had at least one child of fifth-grade age. He found that the middle-class parents were more likely to promote values such as self-direction, independence, and curiosity than were the working-class parents. A more recent study found that middle-class parents are more likely than working-class parents to foster their children's talents through organized leisure activities and experiences that require logical reasoning (Lareau, 2003). Other researchers have found this tendency especially strong among middle-class mothers (Xiao, 2000).

Conversely, working-class parents are more likely than middle-class parents to emphasize conformity to external authority, a common characteristic of the blue-collar jobs they're likely to have later on (Kohn, 1979). Principally, they want their children to be neat and clean and to follow the rules.

Of course, not all middle-class parents, or working-class parents, raise their children in these ways, and many factors other than social class influence parental values (Wright & Wright, 1976). Nevertheless, Kohn found that these general tendencies were consistent regardless of the sex of the child or the size and composition of the family. In a study of African American women, those from middle-class backgrounds reported that their parents had higher expectations of them and were more involved in their education than African American women from working-class backgrounds reported (Hill, 1997). Moreover, others have found that despite cultural differences, social class standing influences child socialization in European (Poland, Germany) and Asian (Japan, Taiwan; Schooler, 1996; Williamson, 1984; Yi, Chang, & Chang, 2004) societies.

Sudden shifts in social class standing—due, for instance, to an unexpected job loss—can also affect the way parents socialize their children. Parents who lose their jobs can become irritable, tense, and moody and their disciplinary style more arbitrary. They may come to rely less on reasoning and more on hostile comments and physical punishment. As a result, children's sense of self, their aspirations, and their school performance suffer (cited in Rothstein, 2001).

Class differences in socialization are also directly related to future goals. Working-class parents tend to believe that eventual occupational success and survival depend on their children's ability to conform to and obey authority (Kohn, 1979). Middle-class parents are likely to believe that their children's future success will result from assertiveness and initiative. Hence, middle-class children's feelings of control over their own destinies are likely to be much stronger than those of working-class children.

Race and Ethnicity

Similarly, race and ethnicity can have a powerful impact on socialization. For white children, learning about their racial identity is less about defining their race than it is about learning how to handle the privileges and behaviors associated with being white in a predominantly white society (Van Ausdale & Feagin, 2001). Chances are good that schools and religious organizations will reinforce the socialization messages expressed to white children in their families—for example, that "you can be anything you want as long as you work hard."

For children who are members of ethnoracial minorities, however, learning about their race occurs within a different and much more complex social environment (Hughes & Chen, 1997). These children must live simultaneously in two different worlds: their ethnoracial community and the "mainstream" (i.e., white) society. Hence, they're likely to be exposed to several different types of socialization experiences while growing up: those that include information about the mainstream culture, those that focus on their minority status in society, and those that focus on the history and cultural heritage of their ethnoracial group (Scott, 2003; Thornton, 1997). Parents often emphasize one type of orientation over others. In ethnoracial groups that have been able to overcome discrimination and achieve at high levels—such as some Asian American groups—ethnic socialization can focus simply on the values of their culture of origin. But among groups that by and large remain disadvantaged, such as African Americans, Native Americans, and Latino/as, parents' discussion of race is more likely to focus on preparing their children for prejudice, ethnic hatred, and mistreatment in a society set up to ignore or actively exclude them (McLoyd, Cauce, Takeuchi, & Wilson, 2000; Staples, 1992). For instance, these children may be taught that "hard work" alone may not be enough to get ahead in this society. Even African American children from affluent homes in racially integrated neighborhoods need reassurances about the racial conflicts they will inevitably encounter (Comer & Poussaint, 1992). These are lessons that children in the dominant racial group seldom require, for reasons explored in greater depth in Chapter 11.

Gender

As you recall from Chapter 4, the sexual dichotomy—the belief that there are two and only two sexes—is not universal. Cultures are even more likely to differ in what is expected of people based on their sex and in how male and female children are to be socialized.

Before discussing this aspect of socialization, it's necessary to distinguish between two concepts: sex and gender. ***Sex*** is typically used to refer to a person's biological maleness or femaleness. ***Gender*** designates masculinity and femininity, the psychological, social, and cultural aspects of maleness and femaleness (Kessler & McKenna, 1978). This distinction is important because it reminds us that male-female differences in behaviors or experiences do not spring naturally from biological differences between the sexes (Lips, 1993).

The gender socialization process begins the moment a child is born. A physician, nurse, or midwife immediately starts that infant on a career as a male or female by authoritatively declaring whether it is a boy or a girl. In most U.S. hospitals, the infant boy is wrapped in a blue blanket, the infant girl in a pink one. From that point on, the developmental paths of U.S. males and females diverge.

The subsequent messages that individuals receive from families, books, television, and schools not only teach and reinforce gender-typed expectations but also influence the formation of their self-concepts.

New parents can be very sensitive about the correct identification of their child's sex. Even parents who claim to consider sex and gender irrelevant may spend a great deal of time ensuring that their child has the culturally appropriate gender appearance. Parents of a girl baby who has yet to grow hair (a visible sign of gender in many cultures) often tape pink ribbons to their bald daughter's head to avoid potential misidentification. In many Latin American countries, families have infant girls' ears pierced and earrings placed in them to provide an unmistakable indicator of the child's sex and gender.

In a culture where sex and gender are centrally important and any ambiguity is distasteful, the correct gender identification of babies maintains social order. When my elder son was an infant, I dressed him on several occasions in a pink, frilly snowsuit in order to observe the reactions of others. (Having a sociologist for a father can be rather difficult from time to time!) Inevitably, someone would approach us and start playing with the baby and some variation of the following interchange would ensue:

Oh, she's so cute! What's your little girl's name?

Zachary.

Isn't Zachary a boy's name?

He's a boy.

At this point, the responses would range from stunned confusion and awkward laughter to nasty looks and outright anger. Clearly, people felt that I had emotionally abused my son somehow. I had purposely breached a fundamental gender norm and thereby created, in their minds, unnecessary trauma (for him) and interactional confusion (for them).

Both boys and girls learn at a very young age to adopt gender as an organizing principle (Howard & Hollander, 1997). By the age of 3 or so, most children can accurately answer the question "Are you a boy or a girl?" (e.g., Kohlberg, 1966). To a young child, being a boy or a girl is simply another characteristic, like having brown hair or 10 fingers. The child at this age has no conception that gender is a category into which every human can be placed (Kessler & McKenna, 1978). But by the age of 5 or so, most children have developed a fair number of gender stereotypes (often incorrect) that they then use to guide their own perceptions and activities (Martin & Ruble, 2004). They also use these stereotypes to form impressions of others. A boy, for instance, may avoid approaching a new girl who's moved into the neighborhood because he assumes that she will be interested in "girl" things. Acting on this assumption reinforces the original belief that boys and girls are different. Indeed, to children at this age, gender is typically seen as a characteristic that is fixed and permanent. Statements such as "Doctors are men" and "Nurses are women" are uttered as inflexible, objective "truths." A few years later, though, their attitudes toward gender become considerably more flexible, although such flexibility may not be reflected in their actual behaviors (Martin & Ruble, 2004).

It's important to note that gender socialization is not a passive process in which children simply absorb the information that bombards them. As part of the process of finding meaning in their social worlds, children actively construct gender as a social category (Liben & Bigler, 2002). From an early age, they are like "gender detectives," searching for cues about gender, such as who should and shouldn't engage in certain activities, who can play with whom, and why girls and boys differ (Martin & Ruble, 2004, p. 67).

Parents and other family members sometimes provide children with explicit instructions on proper gender behavior, such as "Big boys don't cry" or "Act like a young lady." Decades' worth of research shows that parents speak differently to and play differently with their sons and daughters. For instance, one study of mothers' reactions to their children's misbehaviors found that they tend to be more concerned about injuries and safety issues with their daughters and tend to focus more on disciplinary issues with their sons (Morrongiello & Hogg, 2004). In another study, parents were instructed to tell their children stories about their own childhoods. In doing so, they were more likely to highlight themes of autonomy and independence when they had sons than when they had daughters (Fiese & Skillman, 2000). Fathers spend more time with their sons and engage in more physical play than with their daughters, whereas mothers are more emotionally responsive to girls and encourage more independence with boys (Lanvers, 2004; Raley & Bianchi, 2006).

As children grow older, parents tend to encourage increasingly gender-typed activities (Liben & Bigler, 2002). Research consistently shows that children's household tasks differ along gender lines (Antill, Goodnow, Russell, & Cotton, 1996). For instance, boys are more likely to mow the lawn, shovel snow, take out the garbage, and do the yard work, whereas girls tend to clean the house, wash dishes, cook, and babysit their younger siblings (White & Brinkerhoff, 1981). These discrepancies are clearly linked to the different social roles ascribed to men and women, which are discussed in more detail in Chapter 12.

Parents participate in gender socialization through the things they routinely provide for their children: clothes, adornments, toys, books, videos, and so forth. Clothes, for example, not only provide visible markers of gender, they also send messages about how that person ought to be treated and direct behavior along traditional gender lines (Shakin, Shakin, & Sternglanz, 1985). Frilly outfits do not lend themselves easily to rough-and-tumble play. Likewise, it is difficult to walk quickly or assertively in high heels and tight miniskirts. Clothes for boys and men rarely restrict physical movement in this way. Toys and games are an especially influential source of gender information parents provide their children.

INSTITUTIONS AND SOCIALIZATION

It should be clear by now that becoming who we are is a complex process embedded in the larger social structure. We are much more than the sum of our anatomical and neurological parts. Not only can cultural attitudes toward class, race, and gender dramatically affect our personal identities, but various social institutions—in particular, the educational system, religious organizations, and the mass media—exert considerable influence on our self-concept, our values, and our perspectives as well.

Education

In contemporary industrial societies, the most powerful institutional agent of socialization, after the family, is education. In fact, according to the structural-functionalist perspective, the primary reason why schools exist is to socialize young people. Children formally enter the school system around age 5, when they begin kindergarten, although many enter earlier in preschool or nursery school. At this point, the "personalized" instruction of the family is replaced by the "impersonalized" instruction of the school, where children in most developed countries will remain for the next 13 years or longer. No other nonfamily institution has such extended and consistent control over a person's social growth.

Although schools are officially charged with equipping students with the knowledge and skills they need to fulfill various roles in society (e.g., reading, writing, mathematics), they also teach students important social, political, and economic values. When students set up simulated grocery stores or banks, they are learning about the importance of free enterprise and finance in a capitalist society; when they hold mock elections, they are being introduced to a democratic political system; when they spend time tending a school garden or setting up recycling bins, they are learning to nurture the earth.

More subtly, schools teach students what they can expect for themselves in the world. Ironically, although individual accomplishment is stressed in U.S. schools, through grades and report cards, students learn that their future success in society may be determined as much by who they are as by what they achieve. Ample evidence shows that teachers react to students on the basis of race, religion, social class, and gender (Wilkinson & Marrett, 1985). It is in school that many children are first exposed to the fact that people and groups are ranked in society, and soon, they get a sense of their own standing in the social hierarchy.

Some sociologists argue that schooling in most cultures is designed not so much to provide children with factual information and encourage creativity as to produce passive, nonproblematic conformists who will fit into the existing social order (Gracey, 1991). It may seem that the educational system is overwhelmingly dedicated to fitting every student into preordained roles. However, some teachers and alternative schools do instill values at odds with existing social arrangements. One school system in Minnesota, for example, is experimenting with a novel approach to teaching and learning in its elementary schools. Instead of forcing students to sit still during class time, teachers allow them to stand up and move around as much as they want. Even the desks are adjustable so students can stand at them to work if they like. Teachers claim that students sustain their attention longer and learn better than those in more traditional classrooms (Saulny, 2009).

Because formal education is so important in the everyday lives of most children, the agenda of a particular school system, regardless of its philosophy or method, cannot help but influence the types of people they will eventually become.

Religion

As the structural-functionalist perspective tells us, religion is the social institution that tends to the spiritual needs of individuals and serves as a major source of cultural knowledge. It plays a key role in developing people's ideas about right and wrong. It also helps form people's identities by providing coherence and continuity to the episodes that make up each individual's life (Kearl, 1980). Religious rites of passage, such as baptisms, bar and bat mitzvahs, confirmations, and weddings, reaffirm an individual's religious identity while impressing on her or him the rights and obligations attached to each new status (Turner, 1972).

Religion has always been a fundamental socializing agent in most Americans' lives. Indeed, compared to most other Western democracies—such as Canada, Germany, France, Great Britain, and Australia—people in the United States stand out for the depth of their religious beliefs (Zoll, 2005). Consider these facts:

- Eighty-four percent of U.S. adults say that religion plays a big role in their lives (cited in Zoll, 2005). In contrast, 52% of Norwegians and 55% of Swedes say that God doesn't matter to them at all (cited in Ferguson, 2004).
- Sixty-nine percent of Americans definitely believe there is a personal God, and another 12% believe in a "higher power," though not in a personal God (Kosmin & Keysar, 2009).
- Two thirds of Americans believe that God is best described as the all-powerful, all-knowing perfect creator of the universe who rules the world today (The Barna Group, 2007).
- Eighty-three percent of Americans pray in a given week (The Barna Group, 2007).
- Two thirds of Americans feel that it is important that an American president have strong religious beliefs (Pew Forum on Religion and Public Life, 2004) and that they'd be less likely to vote for a political candidate who didn't believe in God (cited in Luo, 2007).
- Two thirds of married Americans had religious weddings, and two thirds of Americans, in general, expect to have a religious funeral (Kosmin & Keysar, 2009).

In short, religion remains a significant part of U.S. life, even though most U.S. residents are actually quite ignorant about basic religious history and texts (Prothero, 2007). We still consider ourselves "one nation under God," and our money still proclaims our trust in God. It's virtually impossible these days to watch a music awards show without a winner acknowledging God's role in his or her success or a sporting event without seeing a baseball player cross himself before batting, a football player point skyward after scoring a touchdown, or a basketball player in a postgame interview thank God for guiding the shot that led to his team's victory. Sports stadiums around the country—including some major league ballparks—now offer "Faith Nights," religiously themed promotions that feature things such as Bible giveaways and revival-style testimonials from players (St. John, 2006). Sales of Christian books, computer games, videos, and toys are going up each year. Enrollment in evangelical colleges has grown steadily over the past decade, as has the number of families choosing to home school their children for religious reasons (Talbot, 2000).

Mass Media

Another powerful institutional agent of socialization is the media. Newspapers, magazines, television, radio, film, and the Internet transmit persuasive messages on the nature of reality. They are the gatekeepers of political, economic, and social information, defining what is and isn't important (Marger, 2005). They also tell us the type of people we "should" be, from how we should perform our jobs to how different social classes live to what our sexual relationships and families are supposed to look like. The media teach us about prevailing values, beliefs, myths, stereotypes, and trends (Gitlin, 1979) and provide an avenue through which we learn new attitudes and behavior (Bandura & Walters, 1963).

Media exposure is pervasive in the United States. Young people between the ages of 8 and 18 spend an average of six and a half hours a day—or about 45 hours a week—with some type of media, such as television, radio, magazines, and computers (Rideout, Roberts, & Foehr, 2005). Researchers estimate that U.S. children spend more time watching television than interacting directly with parents or teachers (Hofferth & Sandberg, 2001). So it's not surprising that sociologists, psychologists, and, of course, politicians continue to debate the degree to which sex and violence in film, television, and video games influence behavior, particularly among young people.

The socializing role of the media is especially apparent when it comes to gender. Children's books, for instance, teach youngsters what other little boys or girls in their culture do and what is expected of them. In the early 1970s, Lenore Weitzman and her colleagues studied the portrayal of gender in popular U.S. preschool books (Weitzman, Eifler, Hodada, & Ross, 1972). They found that boys played a more significant role in the stories than girls by a ratio of 11 to 1. Boys were more likely to be portrayed in adventurous pursuits or activities that required independence and strength; girls were likely to be confined to indoor activities and portrayed as passive and dependent. These gender stereotypes in children's books decreased only slightly over the next several decades (Peterson & Lach, 1990). Recent attempts to publish more nonsexist children's books have had little impact on the overall market. For instance, elementary school reading textbooks still primarily portray males as aggressive, argumentative, and competitive (Evans & Davies, 2000). "Gender equality" in children's books usually involves female characters taking on characteristics and roles typically associated with males. These books rarely, if ever, portray male characters exhibiting feminine traits (Diekman & Murnen, 2004).

Similarly, television continues to portray males and females in stereotypical ways. Although it's changed somewhat in recent years, men are typically shown as rational, competitive, and violent, while women are sensitive, romantic, peaceful, and submissive. Programming often emphasizes male characters' strength and skill and female characters' attractiveness and desirability (cited in Witt, 2005). A study of 41 Saturday morning cartoons found that male characters are more likely than female characters to occupy leadership roles, act aggressively, give guidance to or come to the rescue of others, express opinions, ask questions, and achieve their goals. In addition, males are more likely to be portrayed in some kind of recognizable occupation, whereas females are more likely to be cast in the role of caregiver (Thompson & Zerbinos, 1995). Even the media coverage of female sports events tends to focus on the physical appearance and sexual attractiveness of the athletes and not just their competitive accomplishments (Billings, Angelini, & Eastman, 2005; Shugart, 2003).

All these gender images have a strong influence on children's perceptions and behaviors (Witt, 2005). Children who watch a lot of television are more likely to hold stereotypical attitudes toward gender, exhibit gender-related characteristics, and engage in gender-related activities than children who watch little television (Morgan, 1987; Signorielli, 1990). In one study, girls who did not have stereotypical conceptions of gender to begin with showed a significant increase in such attitudes after 2 years of heavy television watching (Morgan, 1982). The more high school students watch talk shows and prime-time programs that depict a lot of sexual activity, the more likely they are to hold traditional sexual stereotypes (Ward & Friedman, 2006).

CONCLUSION

Becoming the people we are is a complex social process. Those intimate characteristics we hold so dear—our self-concept, our gender, and our racial and ethnic identity—reflect larger cultural attitudes, values, and expectations. Yet we are not perfect reflections of society's values. Despite all the powerful socializing institutions that pull our developmental strings, we continue to be and will always be individuals.

Sometimes we ignore our generalized others and strike out on our own with complete disregard for community standards and attitudes. Sometimes we form self-concepts that contradict the information we receive from others about ourselves. Sometimes we willingly violate the expectations associated with our social class, gender, or race. Societal influence can go only so far in explaining how we become who we are. The rest—that which makes us truly unique—remains a fascinating mystery.

CHAPTER HIGHLIGHTS

◆ Socialization is the process by which individuals learn their culture and learn to live according to the norms of a particular society. It is how we learn to perceive our world, gain a sense of our own identity, and interact appropriately with others. It also tells us what we should and should not do across a range of situations.

◆ One of the most important outcomes of socialization for an individual is the development of a sense of self. To acquire a self, children must learn to recognize themselves as unique physical objects, master language, learn to take the roles of others, and, in effect, see themselves from another's perspective.

◆ Socialization is not just a process that occurs during childhood. Adults must be resocialized into a new galaxy of norms, values, and expectations each time they leave or abandon old roles and enter new ones.

◆ Through socialization, we learn the social expectations that go with our social class, racial or ethnic group, and gender.

◆ Socialization occurs within the context of several social institutions—family first, and then schools, religious institutions, and the mass media.

KEY TERMS

agents of socialization Various individuals, groups, and organizations who influence the socialization process

anticipatory socialization Process through which people acquire the values and orientations found in statuses they will likely enter in the future

collectivist culture Culture in which personal accomplishments are less important in the formation of identity than group membership

eugenics Control of mating to ensure that "defective" genes of troublesome individuals will not be passed on to future generations

game stage Stage in the development of self during which a child acquires the ability to take the role of a group or community (the generalized other) and conform his or her behavior to broad, societal expectations

gender Psychological, social, and cultural aspects of maleness and femaleness

generalized other Perspective of the larger society and its constituent values and attitudes

identity Essential aspect of who we are, consisting of our sense of self, gender, race, ethnicity, and religion

individualist culture Culture in which personal accomplishments are a more important component of one's self-concept than group membership

looking-glass self Sense of who we are that is defined by incorporating the reflected appraisals of others

play stage Stage in the development of self during which a child develops the ability to take a role but only from the perspective of one person at a time

reflexive behavior Behavior in which the person initiating an action is the same as the person toward whom the action is directed

resocialization Process of learning new values, norms, and expectations when an adult leaves an old role and enters a new one

role taking Ability to see oneself from the perspective of others and to use that perspective in formulating one's own behavior

self Unique set of traits, behaviors, and attitudes that distinguishes one person from the next; the active source and passive object of behavior

sex Biological maleness or femaleness

socialization Process through which one learns how to act according to the rules and expectations of a particular culture

total institution Place where individuals are cut off from the wider society for an appreciable period and where together they lead an enclosed, formally administered life

©Jakez/Shutterstock

6 Supporting Identity

The Presentation of Self

On Christmas Day, 1981, I met my soon-to-be wife's family for the first time. For this group of important strangers, I knew I had to be on my best behavior and say and do all the right things. I wanted to make sure the impression they formed of me was that of a likable fellow whom they'd be proud to call a member of the family someday.

As people busily opened their presents, I noticed the wide and gleeful eyes of my wife's 14-year-old sister as she unwrapped what was to her a special gift—her very own basketball. Being the youngest in a family of eight kids, she didn't have much she could call her own, so this was a significant moment for her. She had finally broken away from a life filled with hand-me-downs and communal equipment. She hugged that ball as if it were a puppy.

I saw my chance to make the perfect first impression. "I'm not a bad basketball player," I thought to myself. "I'll take her outside to the basketball hoop in the driveway, impress her with my shooting skills, become her idol, and win family approval."

"Hey, Mary," I said, "let's go out and shoot some hoops." After we stepped outside, I grabbed the new ball from her. "Watch this," I said as I flung it toward the basket from about 40 feet away. We both watched as the ball arced gracefully toward its destination, and for a brief moment, I actually thought it was going to go in. But that was not to be.

As if guided by the taunting hand of fate, the ball struck an exposed bolt that protruded from the supporting pole of the hoop. There was a sickeningly loud pop, followed by a hissing sound as the ball fluttered to the ground like a deflated balloon. It sat there lifeless, never having experienced the joy of "swishing" through a net. For that matter, it had never even been bounced on the ground in its short-lived inflated state.

For a few seconds, we both stood numb and motionless. Then I turned to apologize to the 14-year-old girl, whose once cheerful eyes now harbored the kind of hate and resentment usually reserved for ax murderers and IRS auditors. In a flash, she burst into tears and ran into the house shrieking, "*That guy* popped my ball!" It was hardly the heroic identity I was striving for. As the angry mob poured into the backyard to stare at the villainous and still somewhat unknown perpetrator, I became painfully aware of the fragile nature of the self-images we try to project to others.

We all have been in situations—a first date, a job interview, a first meeting with a girlfriend or boyfriend's family—in which we feel compelled to "make a good impression." We try to present a favorable image of ourselves so that others will form positive judgments of us. This phenomenon is not only an important and universal aspect of our personal lives but a key element of social structure as well.

In this chapter, I examine the social creation of images. How do we form impressions of others? What do we do to control the impressions others form of us? I also discuss the broader sociological applications of these actions. What are the institutional motivations behind individuals' attempts to control others' impressions of them? How do groups and organizations present and manage collective impressions? Finally, what happens when these attempts fail and images are spoiled, as mine was in the story I just told?

FORMING IMPRESSIONS OF OTHERS

When we first meet someone, we form an immediate impression based on observable cues such as age, ascribed status characteristics such as race and gender, individual attributes such as physical appearance, and verbal and nonverbal expressions. This process of ***impression formation*** helps us form a quick picture of the other person's identity.

Keep in mind that the importance of this information—the value attached to a certain age, race, or gender; the particular physical or personality traits a society defines as desirable; the meaning of certain words and gestures—varies across time and place. Hence, the impressions that people form of others must always be understood within the appropriate cultural and historical contexts. For instance, an emotionally expressive person in the United States may give the impression of being energetic and outgoing; in the United Kingdom, such a person may seem boorish and rude; and in Thailand or Japan, that person may be considered dangerous or crazy.

Social Group Membership

Age, sex, race, and to a certain degree ethnicity can often be determined merely by looking at someone; social class is less obvious but sometimes becomes known early in an encounter with another person, through his or her language, mannerisms, or dress. Our socialization experiences have taught us to expect that people displaying these signs of social group membership have certain characteristics. For instance, if all you know about a person you've not yet met is that she's 85 years old, you might predict that she has low energy, a poor memory, and a conservative approach to life. Think about your expectations when you learn that a new roommate is from a different region of this country—or, for that matter, from a different country. Of course, such expectations are rarely completely accurate. Nevertheless, we begin social interactions with these culturally defined conceptions of how people from certain social groups are likely to act, what their tastes and preferences might be, and what values and attitudes they are likely to hold.

This information is so pervasive and so quickly processed that we usually notice it only when it isn't there. If you spend a lot of time texting or IMing with people you've never met, you may have noticed how difficult it can be to form a friendship or carry on a discussion when you don't know whether you are interacting with someone of the same sex or with someone of a different sex or whether the person is much older or much younger than you are. Social group membership provides the necessary backdrop to all encounters among people who have little if any prior knowledge of one another.

Physical Appearance

We confirm or modify early impressions based on social group membership by assessing other characteristics that are easily perceivable, such as a person's physical appearance (Berndt & Heller, 1986). The way people dress and decorate their bodies communicates their feelings, beliefs, and group identity to others. People's clothes, jewelry, hairstyles, and so on can also indicate their ethnicity, social class, age, cultural tastes, morality, and political attitudes.

But again, these impressions can be influenced by our cultural background. Physical appearance is enormously important in U.S. culture. Everywhere we turn, it seems, we are encouraged to believe that if our skin isn't free of blemishes, if we are too short or too tall, if we are over- or underweight, if our hair isn't stylish, if our clothes don't reflect the latest fashion trend, we have fallen short. Although we readily acknowledge that using a person's physical appearance to form an impression is shallow and unfair, most of us do it anyway.

Research confirms that physical appearance affects our perceptions and judgments of others. Attractive men are perceived as more masculine and attractive women more feminine than their less attractive counterparts (Gillen, 1981). Research on jury deliberations in legal trials suggests that attractive defendants are treated better (e.g., receive shorter jail sentences) than less attractive defendants (Stewart, 1980). In addition, we often assume that physically attractive people possess other desirable traits, such as sensitivity, kindness, strength, and sexual responsiveness (Dion, Berscheid, & Walster, 1972).

On the flip side, ugliness has always occupied a lowly place on the social landscape. In literature and film, ugliness is usually associated with evil and fear, characterizing all manner of monsters, witches, and villains (Kershaw, 2008). Beyond fictional portrayals, unattractiveness can have serious everyday consequences. For instance, one study estimated that plain-looking employees earn 5% to 10% less than more attractive workers (Hamermesh & Biddle, 1994). Another study found that even in occupations where looks have no bearing on a person's ability to do his or her job—such as computer programming—unattractive workers suffer discrimination (Mobius & Rosenblat, 2006). Many parents these days are becoming less tolerant of any flaw in their children's appearance. Numerous websites now offer retouching services so that parents can airbrush their child's school photo to remove blemishes, crooked teeth, and other facial imperfections (Bennett, 2008).

Physical attractiveness is still a more salient interpersonal and economic issue for women than for men, even though women have more money, political clout, and legal recognition today than ever. For instance, an article on a talented, all-female chamber music trio called Eroica stated, "The Eroica Trio not only plays beautiful music, it has also created a marketing sensation for being 'easy on the eye'" (W. Smith, 2002, p. 4). A fellow Democratic member of the House of Representatives once said of Speaker Nancy Pelosi: "She smiles too much in public. [But] she is an attractive woman who dresses very well" (quoted in Steinhauer, 2006, p. 20). Sarah Palin's unsuccessful 2008 vice-presidential campaign was marked by almost constant media focus on her clothing, glasses, and hairstyle. It's hard to imagine physical attractiveness being the hub of this kind of attention for male salespeople, classical musicians, or politicians.

Women around the world cause themselves serious pain and injury as they alter their bodies to conform to cultural definitions of beauty. In China, for example, hundreds of women each year, convinced that being taller would improve their job and marriage prospects, subject themselves to a procedure in which their leg bones are broken, separated, and stretched. Metal pins and screws pull the bones apart a fraction of a millimeter a day, sometimes for close to 2 years. Many Chinese women have lost the ability to walk from this treatment; others have suffered permanent, disfiguring bone damage (C. S. Smith, 2002). In the United States, a growing number of affluent women undergo potentially dangerous cosmetic foot surgery each year to reduce the size of their toes so that they can fit into today's fashionable, narrow high-heeled shoes (Harris, 2003).

At the individual level, the emphasis on physical appearance devalues a person's other attributes and accomplishments; at the institutional level, it plays an important role in the nation's economy by sustaining several multibillion-dollar enterprises, including the advertising, fashion, cosmetics, and weight loss industries (Schur, 1984).

Verbal and Nonverbal Expression

Another important piece of information we use in forming impressions of others is what people express to us verbally or nonverbally. Obviously, we form impressions of others based on what they tell us about themselves. But beyond speech, people's movements, postures, and gestures provide cues about their values, attitudes, sentiments, personality, and history (Stone, 1981). Sometimes people use these forms of communication purposely to convey meaning, as when they smile so that others will find them approachable. However, some physical expressions, such as a shaky voice, a flushed face, and trembling hands, are difficult to control. They transmit an impression whether we want to or not.

Most of us are quite proficient at "reading" even the subtlest nonverbal messages. We learn early on that a raised eyebrow, a nod of the head, or a slight hand gesture can mean something important in a social encounter. So crucial is this ability in maintaining orderly interactions that some psychologists consider a deficiency in it to be a learning disability akin to severe reading problems (Goleman, 1989).

MANAGING IMPRESSIONS

People form impressions of others and present impressions of themselves at the same time. This ability to create impressions is the defining feature of human interaction. Naturally, we try to create impressions of ourselves that give us advantages—by making us seem attractive or powerful or otherwise worthy of people's attention and esteem. Of course, that's what I was trying to do when I attempted the ill-fated jump shot with my future sister-in-law's new basketball.

The process by which people attempt to present a favorable public image of themselves is called ***impression management.*** Erving Goffman (1959), the sociologist most responsible for the scholarly examination of impression management, portrays everyday life as a series of social interactions in which a person is motivated to "sell" a particular image to others. The primary goal of impression management is to project a particular identity that will increase the likelihood of obtaining favorable outcomes from others in particular social situations (Jones & Pittman, 1982; Stryker, 1980). To do so, we can strategically furnish or conceal information. At times, we may need to advertise, exaggerate, or even fabricate our positive qualities; at other times, we conceal or camouflage behaviors or attributes that we believe others will find unappealing.

Obtaining favorable outcomes through impression management is usually associated with social approval—that is, with being respected and liked by others. However, different circumstances may require projecting different identities (Jones & Pittman, 1982). Perhaps you've been in situations where you tried to appear helpless in order to get someone else to do a task you really didn't want to do, or maybe you tried to appear as powerful and fearsome as you could to intimidate someone into doing something for you. Perhaps you "played dumb" to avoid challenging a superior (Gove, Hughes, & Geerkin, 1980). As social beings, we have the ability to tailor our images to fit the requirements of a particular situation.

Various psychologists argue that managing artificial impressions can sometimes have therapeutic value. For instance, during the 2009 economic recession, some therapists encouraged their laid-off clients to project the illusion of employment by maintaining their job routine—waking up early, dressing in their usual work clothes, and commuting—even though they didn't have a job to go to anymore. They claim that "keeping up appearances" may seem deceitful but can be useful in sustaining good habits and personal pride (Carey, 2009).

Goffman argues that impression management is not just used to present false or inflated images of ourselves. Many authentic attributes we possess are not immediately apparent to others; sometimes our actions may be misinterpreted. Imagine yourself taking the final exam in your sociology course. You look up from your paper and make brief eye contact with the instructor. You are not cheating, but you think the instructor may interpret your wandering eyes as an indication of cheating. What do you do? Chances are you will consciously overemphasize your noncheating behavior by acting as though you're deep in thought or by glancing up at the clock to highlight your "law-abiding" image.

Often people try to present a favorable image of themselves by altering their physical appearance. Clothing and body adornment can be used to manipulate and manage the impressions others form of us. People can dress to convey the impression that they are worthy of respect or, at the very least, attention (Lauer & Handel, 1977). Businesspeople are acutely aware of and usually conform to a corporate dress code, even if the code is "business casual"; those who dress too casually are not taken seriously. Children often signal their entry into the world of adolescence by wearing the clothing of their peers and refusing to wear the clothing chosen by their parents (Stone, 1981). The purveyors of pop, hip-hop, crunk, heavy metal, lounge, rave, dance/house/techno, goth, and other musical subcultures use clothing and hairstyle as an expression of identity and social rebellion. And as you are well aware, fashion is a significant element of the student subculture on most college campuses (Moffatt, 1989). In short, by what they wear, people tell one another who they are, where they come from, and what they stand for.

Image Making

In our individualistic, competitive society, appearances can sometimes provide a critically important edge. A person's desire to maximize prestige, wealth, and power can be the driving force behind a thorough makeover. These efforts are not things a person undertakes on her or his own. Whole industries have evolved that are devoted to making and remaking images for the public eye.

The desire to manage impressions by changing physical appearance motivates some people to do far more than try a new hairstyle, get a tattoo, or buy a new outfit or two. Even in economic hard times, people in the United States are willing to spend huge sums of money to medically alter their looks. According to the American Society of Plastic Surgeons (2009), 1.7 million cosmetic surgery procedures and more than 10 million nonsurgical procedures (such as Botox injections, cellulite treatments, and chemical peels) were performed in the United States in 2008. Ninety-one percent of patients are women. These figures are down slightly from 2007 but still represent a 63% increase over 2000. The overall cost for these procedures was about $10.2 billion.

The desire to surgically alter one's appearance is not unique to the United States. In China, the growing cosmetic surgery industry takes in more than $2.4 billion a year as people with newfound affluence rush to go under the knife to become *renzao meinu*, or "man-made beauties." In fact, China now hosts an "Artificial Beauty" contest, where people from all over the globe compete to become the world's most beautiful product of plastic surgery (Ang, 2004).

The growing popularity of cosmetic surgery reflects an alarming level of discontent among people about the way they look. Researchers estimate that 30% to 40% of U.S. adults have concerns about some aspect of their physical appearance (Gorbis & Kholodenko, 2005). And about 2% of the population is so self-conscious about their looks that their lives are constricted in some significant way, from feeling inhibited during lovemaking to becoming homebound or even suicidal. This condition, called "body dysmorphic disorder," has become more common over the past decade or so (Wartik, 2003). About half of these individuals seek some sort of professional medical intervention, such as surgery or dermatological treatment (Gorbis & Kholodenko, 2005).

Dramaturgy: Actors on a Social Stage

"All the world's a stage, / And all the men and women merely players: / They have their exits and their entrances; / And one man in his time plays many parts," wrote William Shakespeare in *As You Like It*. Analyzing social interaction as a series of theatrical performances—what sociologists call ***dramaturgy***—has been a staple of symbolic interactionism for decades. Like Shakespeare, sociologist Erving Goffman (1959) argues that people in everyday life are similar to actors on a stage. The "audience" consists of people who observe the behavior of others, the "roles" are the images people are trying to project, and the "script" consists of their communication with others. The goal is to enact a performance that is believable to a particular audience and that allows us to achieve the goals we desire. Just about every aspect of social life can be examined dramaturgically, from the ritualized greetings of strangers to the everyday dynamics of our family, school, and work lives.

Front Stage and Back Stage

A key structural element of dramaturgy is the distinction between front stage and back stage. In the theater, front stage is where the performance takes place for the audience. In contrast, back stage is where makeup is removed, lines are rehearsed, performances are rehashed, and people can fall "out of character."

In social interaction, ***front stage*** is where people maintain the appropriate appearance as they interact with others. For workers in a restaurant, front stage is the dining room where the customers (the audience) are present. Here, the servers (the actors) are expected to present themselves as upbeat, happy, competent, and courteous. ***Back stage***, however, is the region where people can knowingly violate their impression management performances. In the restaurant, back stage is the kitchen area where the once courteous servers now shout, shove dishes, and even complain about or mock the customers.

The barrier between front and back stage is crucial to successful impression management because it blocks the audience from seeing behavior that would ruin the performance. During a therapy session (front stage), psychiatrists usually appear extremely interested in everything their patients say and show considerable sympathy for their problems. At a dinner party with colleagues or at home with family (back stage), however, they may express total boredom with and disdain for their patients' disclosures. If patients were to see such back stage behavior, not only would it disrupt the performance, but it would damage the psychiatrist's professional credibility and reputation as well. One study found that beneath their mask of neutrality, many psychiatrists harbor strong and professionally inappropriate feelings—including hatred, fear, anger, and sexual arousal—toward their patients (cited in Goleman, 1993).

Props

Successful impression management also depends on the control of objects, called props, that convey identity. In the theater, props must be handled deftly for an effective performance. A gun that doesn't go off when it's supposed to or a chair that unexpectedly collapses can destroy an entire play. The same is true in social interaction. For instance, college students may make sure their schoolbooks are in clear view and beer bottles disposed of as they prepare for an upcoming visit from their parents. Similarly, someone may spend a great deal of time setting a romantic mood for a dinner date at home—the right music, the right lighting, pictures of former lovers hidden from view, and so on.

Sometimes people use props to create an environment that reinforces some individuals' authority over others. Note the way props were used to intimidate this professor as he testified before Congress:

> And then I was called to the witness stand. Now, the chair is something nobody talks about. It is low and extremely puffy. When you sit in it your butt just keeps sinking, and suddenly the tabletop is up to your chest. The senators peer down at you from above, and the power dynamic is terrifying. (Jenkins, 1999, p. 21)

Viewing impression management from a dramaturgical perspective reminds us that our everyday actions rarely occur in a social vacuum. Indeed, our behaviors are often structured with an eye toward how they might be perceived by particular "audiences."

Social Influences on Impression Management

Up to this point, I've described impression management and dramaturgy from the viewpoint of individual people driven by a personal desire to present themselves in the most advantageous light possible. But social group membership may also influence the sorts of images a person tries to present in social interaction. The elements of a person's identity—age, gender, race and ethnicity, religion, social class, occupational status—influence others' immediate expectations, which can be self-fulfilling. In other words, members of certain social groups may manage impressions somewhat differently than nonmembers because of society's preconceived notions about them. Race, ethnicity, and social status are among the most notable influences on impression management.

Race and Ethnicity

In a society in which race is a primary source of inequality, people of color often learn that they will be rewarded if they assimilate to "white norms" and "cover" the elements of their ethnoracial culture. According to Kenji Yoshino (2006), a law professor, the pressure to "act white" means that people of color must suppress the nonwhite aspects of their hairstyle, clothing, and speech. They must also monitor their social activities, participation in ethnic or race-based organizations or political causes, and friendship networks. The comedian Dave Chappelle once said that African Americans must be "bilingual" if they want to make it in this society. In other words, they become adept at identifying situations, such as job interviews, where they must eliminate "black" patterns of speech and "speak white" (Chaudhry, 2006).

Such impression management strategies may increase the likelihood of economic benefit, but they are not without their hazards. People of color who "act white" in some situations but perform a different version of their identity when with others like them run the risk of being considered sellouts or tagged as "Oreo cookies," "bananas," or "coconuts"—that is, black or yellow or brown on the outside and white on the inside—by members of their ethnoracial community (Chaudhry, 2006).

Moreover, it's only the relatively affluent who have the opportunity to learn how to act white. Others—Pakistani cab drivers, Latina housekeepers, Korean grocery store clerks, to name a few—have no such option. Indeed, living up (or down) to certain ethnoracial stereotypes may be one of the few ways people can participate actively in public life while retaining their own cultural identity. In the past, for example, Native Americans often complained that in interactions with members of other ethnoracial groups, they were expected to "act Indian" by wearing traditional garb or speaking in the stilted manner of media stereotypes. Contemporary rap and hip-hop stars are often criticized for conforming to unflattering black stereotypes in order to appeal to white, middle-class audiences. But while individuals from disadvantaged groups may appear to fit common racial or ethnic stereotypes in public (front stage), an analysis of private (back stage) behavior often indicates that they are keenly aware of the identities they've been forced to present.

Social Status

A person's relative position in society can also influence impression management. Some working-class youths, frustrated by their lack of access to the middle-class world and their inability to meet the requirements of "respectability" as defined by the dominant culture, may present themselves as malicious or dangerous. A tough image helps them gain attention or achieve status and respect within their group (Campbell, 1987; Cohen, 1955).

Conversely, those who occupy the dominant classes of society can get the attention and respect we all want with very little effort (Derber, 1979). They get special consideration in restaurants, shops, and other public settings. They monopolize the starring roles in politics and economics and also claim more than their share of attention in ordinary interactions. By displaying the symbolic props of material success—large homes, tasteful furnishings, luxury cars, expensive clothes and jewelry—people know that they can impress others and thereby reinforce their own sense of worth and status.

Prior to the recent economic recession, the visual trappings of social class had become harder to spot. When credit was easily available, more U.S. adults had access to the traditional high-end props of the well-to-do. A middle-class family could own a flat-screen television or a fancy sports car. Just a few years ago, 81% of respondents in one study indicated that they had felt some pressure to buy high-priced goods (cited in Steinhauer, 2005). So the truly wealthy ratcheted up the visual display of social status, buying even more expensive products, such as $130,000 cars and $400 bottles of wine, and using posh services such as personal chefs and private jets. Tough times, however, have led even the super rich to become a bit more discreet in their public displays of wealth: "Out are private jets, glitzy high-profile parties and see-and-be-seen vacations to hot spots such as St. Barts. In are flying first-class, tasteful low-profile affairs and getaways to more remote resorts in the likes of Laos and Panama" (Gomstyn, 2009, p. 1).

Indeed, ostentatious displays of wealth have become the object of public anger and ridicule. You may recall the firestorm that erupted in the media in 2009, when the chief executives of the major U.S. automakers flew to Washington, D.C., in their private jets to appeal for federal bailout money.

Status differences in impression management permeate the world of work as well. Those at the very top of an organization need not advertise their high status, because it is already known to the people with whom they interact regularly. Their occupational status is a permanently recognized "badge of ability" (Derber, 1979, p. 83). Others, however, must consciously solicit the attention to which they feel they are entitled. For example, physicians in hospitals may wear stethoscopes and white lab coats to communicate their high-status identity to patients; female doctors are especially inclined to wear the white coats so they will not be mistaken for nurses. These status markers become especially powerful when compared to patients, who are often required to shed their own clothes and don revealing hospital-issue garments. It's hard to appear powerful and be taken seriously in a conversation with a doctor when you're barefoot and naked under a paper gown (Franklin, 2006).

Impression management plays a prominent role in the socialization process within many professions (Hochschild, 1983). Managers and CEOs in large companies, for instance, become acutely aware through their rise up the corporate ladder of the image they must exude through their dress and demeanor. Salespeople are trained to present themselves as knowledgeable, trustworthy, and, above all, honest. Medical school students learn how to manage their emotions in front of patients and to present the image of "competent physicians."

In any given interaction, one person is likely to have more power than others (Wrong, 1988). When we first hear the word *power,* we think of it in terms of orders, threats, and coercion. But noncoercive forms of power—the signs and symbols of dominance, the subtle messages of threat, the gestures of submission—are much more common to impression management in social encounters (Henley, 1977). The humiliation of being powerless is felt by people who are ignored or interrupted, are intimidated by another's presence, are afraid to approach or touch a superior, or have their privacy freely invaded by another.

The norms that govern the way people address one another also reflect underlying power differences. For instance, the conversations that take place between friends or siblings are commonly marked by the mutual use of informal terms such as first names or nicknames. When status is unequal, though, the lower-status person is often required to use terms of respect such as *Sir* or *Ma'am* or *Doctor.* In the South in years past, every white person had the privilege of addressing any black person by first name and receiving the respectful form of address in return. A president's fondness for making up funny nicknames for people on his staff or members of Congress may appear amiable and friendly, but it also reinforces power differences. These people still must address him as "Mr. President."

MISMANAGING IMPRESSIONS: SPOILED IDENTITIES

While impression management is universal, it's not always successful. We may mishandle props, blow our lines, mistakenly allow the audience back stage, or otherwise destroy the credibility of our performances. Some of us manage to recover from ineffective impression management quite quickly; others suffer an extended devaluation of their identities. What happens when impression management is unsuccessful? What do we do to regain identities and restore social order?

Embarrassment

A common emotional reaction to impression mismanagement is ***embarrassment,*** the spontaneous feeling we experience when the identity we are presenting is suddenly and unexpectedly discredited in front of others (Gross & Stone, 1964). An adolescent boy trying to look "cool" in front of his friends may have his tough image shattered by the unexpected arrival of his mother in the family minivan. We can see his embarrassment in the fixed smile, the nervous hollow laugh, the busy hands, and the downward glance that hides his eyes from the gaze of others (Goffman, 1967). Embarrassment can come from a multitude of sources: lack of poise (e.g., stumbling, saying something stupid, spilling a drink, inappropriately exposing body parts), intrusion into the private settings of others (a man walking into a women's restroom), improper dress for a particular social occasion, and so on.

Embarrassment is sociologically important because it has the potential to destroy the orderliness of a social situation. Imagine being at your high school graduation. As the class valedictorian is giving the commencement address, a gust of wind blows her note cards off the podium. As she reaches down to collect them, she hits her head on the microphone and tears her gown. In front of hundreds of people she stands there, flustered, not knowing what to say or do. The situation would be uncomfortable and embarrassing not only for her but for you and the rest of the audience as well.

Because embarrassment is disruptive for all concerned, it is in everyone's best interest to cooperate in reducing or eliminating it. To call attention to such an act may be as embarrassing as the original episode itself, so we may pretend not to notice the faux pas (Lindesmith, Strauss, & Denzin, 1991). By suppressing signs of recognition, we make it easier for the person to regain composure (Goffman, 1967). A mutual commitment to supporting others' social identities, even when those identities are in danger, is a fundamental norm of social interaction.

At times, however, embarrassment is used strategically to disrupt another person's impression management. Practical jokes, for instance, are intentional attempts to cause someone else to lose identity. More seriously, groups and organizations may use embarrassment or the threat of embarrassment (e.g., hazing) to encourage a preferred activity or discourage behavior that may be damaging to the group. In that sense, practical jokes function as a check on arrogance and obliviousness (Carey, 2008). As a result, such embarrassment reasserts the power structure of the group, because only certain people can legitimately embarrass others. A low-status employee, for instance, has much less freedom to embarrass a superior or make him or her the target of a joke than vice versa (Coser, 1960).

Groups and organizations, as entities, can also suffer embarrassment. In 2009, the Colorado Veterans Alliance, an advocacy group that led a drive to help homeless veterans, announced that its founder—former Marine Captain Rick Duncan—was, in fact, never in the military. It turned out he was a 32-year-old drifter with a criminal record. The organization immediately disbanded. A few years earlier, the entire health care industry in New Zealand suffered an embarrassing blow to its image when it was discovered that a con artist pretending to be a Harvard-trained psychiatrist had been practicing medicine there for more than a year.

When events challenge an organization's public image, leaders are often compelled to engage in activities that protect, repair, and enhance that image (Ginzel, Kramer, & Sutton, 2004). For example, every year, *U.S. News & World Report* publishes its rankings of the top American universities. Schools that receive high rankings boast of that fact in their recruitment materials and on their websites. When a university falls in its ranking from one year to the next, though, officials face the unenviable task of scrambling to mend the school's reputation so that alumni continue to donate money and prospective students still consider applying. Typically, schools that have dropped in the rankings opt to downplay the rankings' relevance and criticize the magazine's methodology and ranking criteria, which only a year earlier (when they were ranked higher) were considered sound and trustworthy.

Most government agencies and large corporations now have public relations departments or crisis management teams that carefully oversee the organization's image by controlling negative publicity. One insurance company offers a corporate liability policy that pays policyholders up to $50,000 for the emergency hiring of an image consultant to help manage embarrassing public relations disasters (Landler, 1996). Southwest Airlines has a full-time employee, called "Senior Manager of Proactive Customer Communications," whose only job is to write apology letters to customers who are annoyed about flight delays, cancellations, or shoddy plane conditions. He writes about 20,000 such letters a year (Bailey, 2007).

Remedies for Spoiled Identities

Organizations and governments can enlist the aid of experts to overcome the debilitating effects of negative images, but individuals are left to their own devices. Fixing a spoiled identity is not easy. The mere knowledge that we are being evaluated negatively can impede our thoughts, speech, and action. Nevertheless, the major responsibility for restoring order lies with the person whose actions disrupted things in the first place.

To restore social order and overcome a spoiled identity, the transgressor will use an ***aligning action*** (Stokes & Hewitt, 1976). Sometimes aligning can be done easily and quickly. If you step on a person's foot while standing in line at a cafeteria, a simple apology may be all that's needed to avoid the impression that you're a clumsy oaf.

By apologizing, you acknowledge that such an act is wrong and send the message that you are not ordinarily a breaker of such social norms. Other situations, however, call for more detailed repair:

- An ***account*** is a verbal statement designed to explain unanticipated, embarrassing, or unacceptable behavior (Mills, 1940; Scott & Lyman, 1968). For example, an individual may cite events beyond her or his control ("I was late for the wedding because there was a lot of traffic on the highway") or blame others ("I spilled my milk because somebody pushed me"). An alternative is to define the offending behavior as appropriate under the circumstances, perhaps by denying that anyone was hurt by the act ("Yeah, I stole the car, but no one got hurt"), by claiming that the victim deserved to be victimized ("I beat him up, but he had it coming"), or by claiming higher, unselfish motives ("I stole food, but I did it to feed my family").

- A ***disclaimer*** is a verbal assertion given before the fact to forestall any complaints or negative implications (Hewitt & Stokes, 1975). If we think something we're about to do or say will threaten our identity or be used by others to judge us negatively, we may use a disclaimer. Phrases such as "I probably don't know what I'm talking about, but . . ." or "I'm not a racist, but . . ." introduce acts or expressions that ordinarily might be considered undesirable. As long as a disclaimer is provided, a self-proclaimed nonexpert can pretend to be an expert and a person claiming to be nonracist feels he or she can go ahead and make a racist statement.

Accounts and disclaimers are important links between the individual and society. We use them to explicitly define the relationship between our questionable conduct and prevailing cultural norms. That is, by using aligning actions, we publicly reaffirm our commitment to the social order that our conduct has violated and thereby defend the sanctity of our social identities and the "goodness" of society.

Other people may also try to deal with a transgressor's spoiled identity through a process called ***cooling out*** (Goffman, 1952): gently persuading someone who has lost face to accept a less desirable but still reasonable alternative identity. People engaged in cooling out seek to persuade rather than force offenders to change. It's an attempt to minimize distress. The challenge is to keep the offender from realizing that he or she is being persuaded.

Cooling out is a common element of social life; it is one of the major functions of consumer complaint departments. In addition, professionals who sometimes provide bad news—coaches who have to cut players, doctors who have to tell patients their poor prognoses, and so on—must also be deft practitioners of cooling out. Cooling out also plays a major part in informal relationships. A partner who terminates a dating or courting relationship might persuade the other person to remain a "good friend," gently pushing the person into a lesser role without completely destroying his or her self-worth.

Stigma

The permanent spoiling of someone's identity is called ***stigma.*** A stigma is a deeply discrediting characteristic, widely viewed as an insurmountable obstacle preventing competent or morally trustworthy behavior (Goffman, 1963). Stigmas spoil the identities of individuals regardless of other attributes those individuals might have. According to Goffman, the three types of stigma are (1) defects of the body (e.g., severe scars, blindness, paralyzed or missing limbs), (2) defects of character (e.g., dishonesty, a weak will, a history of imprisonment or substance abuse), and (3) membership in devalued social groups, such as certain races, religions, or ethnicities. The impression management task when faced with stigma is not so much to recapture a tarnished identity as to minimize the social damage.

Some stigmas are worse than others. For instance, the use of eyeglasses to compensate for one sensory deficiency (poor vision) is usually considered far less stigmatizing than the use of hearing aids to compensate for a different sensory deficiency (poor hearing). Contemporary hearing aids are designed to be as small and unnoticeable as possible. Eyeglasses, on the other hand, have become a common fashion accessory, often sold in their own trendy boutiques.

Stigma varies across time and culture as well. Being a Christian in the 21st century is very different from being one in AD 100, and being a Christian in the United States is different from being one in the Arab Middle East (Ainlay, Becker, & Coleman, 1986). Ancient Mayans considered being cross-eyed desirable, so parents encouraged babies to focus on objects that forced their eyes to cross (Link & Phelan, 2001). Obesity is stigmatized in contemporary Western societies but was seen as desirable, attractive, and symbolic of status and wealth in the past (Clinard & Meier, 1979) and is still seen that way in some other cultures today.

Interactions between the stigmatized and the nonstigmatized—called "mixed contacts"—can sometimes be uneasy. We have all felt uncomfortable with people who are "different" in appearance or behavior. Stigma initiates a judgment process that colors impressions and sets up barriers to interaction (Jones et al., 1984).

Whether intentionally or not, nonstigmatized individuals often pressure stigmatized people to conform to "inferior" identities. A person in a wheelchair who is discouraged from going camping or a blind person who is discouraged from living on his or her own is not given the chance to develop important skills and is thus kept dependent.

Nonstigmatized people often avoid mixed contacts because they anticipate discomfort and are unsure how to act (Goffman, 1963). Research shows that when interacting with a person who is physically disabled, an able-bodied person is likely to be more inhibited and more rigid and to end the interaction sooner than if the other person were also able-bodied (Kleck, 1968; Kleck, Ono, & Hastorf, 1966). On the one hand, the able-bodied person may fear that showing direct sympathy or interest in a disabled person's condition could be regarded as rude or intrusive. On the other hand, ignoring it may make the interaction artificial and awkward or create impossible demands (Michener, DeLamater, & Schwartz, 1986).

As for people with stigmatizing conditions, they often sense that others are evaluating them negatively. One study of people diagnosed with a mental disorder found that they had all at one time or another been shunned, avoided, patronized, or discriminated against when others found out about their condition (Wahl, 1999). Consider also the case of Mark Breimhorst, a Stanford University graduate. Mr. Breimhorst has no hands. When he was applying to business schools in 1998, he received permission to take the Graduate Management Admissions Test on a computer and was given 25% more time to accommodate his disability. His results were mailed out to prospective graduate schools with the notation "Scores obtained under special circumstances." Mr. Breimhorst was not admitted to any of the business schools to which he applied. He filed a federal lawsuit against the testing service, challenging the way they flagged the scores of students who needed accommodations. Such notations, he argued, were stigmatizing because they created suspicion that the scores were less valid than others (Lewin, 2000). In 2003, the testing service stopped flagging the results of students who receive special accommodations.

Faced with the strong possibility of discrimination, people with stigmatizing conditions often use coping strategies to establish the most favorable identity possible. One strategy is to try to hide the stigma. People who are hard of hearing, for instance, may learn to read lips or otherwise interact with people as if they could hear perfectly; those with bodily stigmas may opt for surgery to permanently conceal their condition.

Some stigmatized individuals, particularly those whose conditions are not immediately observable, use a strategy of selective disclosure. Sociologist Charlene E. Miall (1989) interviewed and surveyed 70 infertile women, nearly all of whom characterized infertility as something negative, an indication of failure, or an inability to function "normally." Most of the women were concerned that others' knowledge of their infertility would be stigmatizing. So they engaged in some form of information control. Many simply concealed the information from everyone except medical personnel and infertility counselors. Others used medical accounts, saying, "It's beyond my control." Some disclosed the information only to people they felt would not think ill of them. Some even used the disclosure of their infertility to gain control of a situation by deliberately shocking their "normal" audience (Miall, 1989).

Of course, not all stigmas can be hidden. Some individuals can only minimize the degree to which their stigmas intrude on and disrupt the interaction. One tactic is to use self-deprecating humor—telling little jokes about their shortcomings—to relieve the tension felt by the nonstigmatized. Others may try to focus attention on attributes unrelated to the stigma. For instance, a person in a wheelchair may carry around esoteric books in a conspicuous manner to show others that she or he still has a brain that works well.

Still others with stigmas boldly call attention to their condition by mastering areas thought to be closed to them (such as mountain climbing for an amputee). And some organize a movement to counter social oppression. For instance, the National Association to Advance Fat Acceptance helps fat people (*fat* is their preferred adjective, by the way) cope with a society that hates their size and lobbies state legislatures to combat "size discrimination." They have organized civil rights protests in Washington, D.C., lobbied health care professionals for tolerance and acceptance, and organized campaigns against insurance discrimination and the dubious "science" of weight loss programs (LeBesco, 2004).

But overcoming the problems created by stigma cannot be accomplished solely through individual impression management or collective demonstrations. Long-lasting improvements can be accomplished only by changing cultural beliefs about the nature of stigma (Link, Mirotznik, & Cullen, 1991). As long as we hold stigmatized individuals solely responsible for dealing with the stigma, only some of them will be able to overcome the social limitations of their condition.

CONCLUSION

After reading this chapter, you may have an image of human beings as cunning, manipulative, and cynical play actors whose lives are merely a string of phony performances carefully designed to fit the selfish needs of the moment. The impression manager comes across as someone who consciously and fraudulently presents an inaccurate image in order to take advantage of a particular situation. Even the person who seems not to care about his or her appearance may be consciously cultivating the image of "not caring."

There's no denying that people consciously manufacture images of themselves that allow them to achieve some desired goal. Most of us go through life trying to create the impression that we're attractive, honest, competent, and sincere. To that end, we carefully manage our appearance, present qualities we think others will admire, and hide qualities we think they won't. When caught in an act that may threaten the impression we're trying to foster, we strategically use statements that disclaim, excuse, or justify it.

So who is the real you? If people freely change their images to suit the expectations of a given audience, is there something more stable that characterizes them across all situations?

If you are aware that the impression you are managing is not the real you, then you must have some knowledge of what *is* the real you. And what you are may, in fact, transcend the demands of particular situations. Some basic, pervasive part of your being may allow you to choose from a repertoire of identities the one that best suits the immediate needs of the situation. As you ponder this possibility, realize that your feelings about impression management reflect your beliefs about the nature of individuals and the role society and others play in our everyday lives.

CHAPTER HIGHLIGHTS

- A significant portion of social life is influenced by the images we form of others and the images others form of us.
- Impression formation is based initially on our assessment of ascribed social group membership (race, age, gender, etc.), individual physical appearance, and verbal and nonverbal messages.
- While we are gathering information about others to form impressions of them, we are fully aware that they are doing the same thing. Impression management is the process by which we attempt to control and manipulate information about ourselves to influence the impressions others form of us. Impression management can be both individual and collective.
- Impression mismanagement can lead to the creation of damaged identities, which must be repaired in order to sustain social interaction.

KEY TERMS

account Statement designed to explain unanticipated, embarrassing, or unacceptable behavior after the behavior has occurred

aligning action Action taken to restore an identity that has been damaged

back stage Area of social interaction away from the view of an audience, where people can rehearse and rehash their behavior

cooling out Gently persuading someone who has lost face to accept a less desirable but still reasonable alternative identity

disclaimer Assertion designed to forestall any complaints or negative reactions to a behavior or statement that is about to occur

dramaturgy Study of social interaction as theater, in which people ("actors") project images ("play roles") in front of others ("the audience")

embarrassment Spontaneous feeling that is experienced when the identity someone is presenting is suddenly and unexpectedly discredited in front of others

front stage Area of social interaction where people perform and work to maintain appropriate impressions

impression formation The process by which we define others based on observable cues such as age, ascribed status characteristics such as race and gender, individual attributes such as physical appearance, and verbal and nonverbal expressions

impression management Act of presenting a favorable public image of oneself so that others will form positive judgments

stigma Deeply discrediting characteristic that is viewed as an obstacle to competent or morally trustworthy behavior

ever at work (Galinsky et al., 2006), perhaps to the detriment of relationships with our families. But for many people, forming ties with coworkers can be just as emotionally fulfilling (Wuthnow, 1994). And many of us spend a great deal of time in local hangouts (such as bars and coffee shops), where we can find comfort and good company (Oldenburg & Brissett, 1982). Many people find the sense of belonging they crave in these small groups of friends and like-minded neighbors and coworkers.

SOCIAL DIVERSITY AND INTIMATE CHOICES

Our bonds with coworkers, neighbors, relatives, and friends are certainly an important part of our social lives, but the sense of belonging and closeness that comes from intimate, romantic relationships has become one of the prime obsessions of the 21st century. Magazines, self-help books, supermarket tabloids, websites, blogs, and talk shows overflow with advice, warnings, and pseudoscientific analyses of every conceivable aspect of these relationships.

Most people in the United States assume that love is all they need to establish a fulfilling, long-lasting relationship. But their intimate choices are far from free and private. The choices they make regarding whom to date, live with, or marry are governed by two important social rules that limit the field of eligible partners: exogamy and endogamy.

Exogamy

At any given point in time, each one of us is a member of many groups simultaneously. We belong to a particular family, a friendship group, a set of coworkers, a religion, a race, an ethnicity, an age group, a social class, and so on. Entering into intimate relationships with fellow members of some of these groups is considered inappropriate. So society follows a set of customs referred to as ***exogamy*** rules, which require that an individual form a long-term romantic or sexual relationship with someone *outside* certain social groups to which he or she belongs. For instance, in almost all societies, exogamy rules define marrying or having sex with people in one's own immediate family—siblings, parents, and children—as incest. Presumably, these rules exist in order to prohibit procreation between people who are genetically related, thereby reducing the chance that offspring will inherit two copies of a defective gene.

Exogamy prohibitions typically extend to certain relatives outside the nuclear family too, such as cousins, grandparents, aunts, uncles, and, in some societies, stepsiblings. In the United States, 25 states completely prohibit marriage between first cousins; 6 others allow it under certain circumstances, such as when both partners are over 65 or when one is unable to reproduce (National Conference of State Legislatures, 2009). Informally, opposition to romantic relationships between coworkers or, on college campuses, between people who live on the same dorm floor (called "dormcest") illustrates a common belief that relationships work best when they occur between people who aren't in constant close proximity.

Different cultures apply the rules of exogamy differently. For example, in South Korea, it was once illegal to marry someone with the same surname—not a trivial law, considering that 55% of the population is named Kim, Park, Lee, Choi, or Chong (WuDunn, 1996b). This rule originated centuries ago as a way of preventing marriages between members of the same clan and was written into Korean law in 1957. The ban was deemed unconstitutional in 1997. However, most single people still try to avoid lovers with the same name. As one college student put it, "When I'm introduced to someone, I very casually ask what her name is, and if I find out that it's the same as mine, it puts a mark against her right there" (WuDunn, 1996b, p. A4).

In other places, the violation of exogamy rules can lead to severe sanctions. In 2003, a young Indian couple was beaten to death by members of their own families for being lovers. In their community, it was considered incest for two people from the same village to fall in love. A resident of the village said, "In our society all the families living in a village are all sons and daughters of the whole village. We are like brothers and sisters. The marriage of brothers and sisters is not accepted" (quoted in Waldman, 2003, p. A4).

Endogamy

Simultaneously, less formal, but just as powerful, are the rules of ***endogamy,*** which limit people's intimate choices to those *within* certain groups to which they belong. The vast majority of marriages in the United States, for example, occur between people from the same religion, ethnoracial group, and social class. These rules of endogamy increase the likelihood that the couple will have similar backgrounds and therefore share common beliefs, values, and experiences. But more importantly, from a sociological point of view, rules of endogamy reflect our society's traditional distaste for relationships that cross social-group boundaries.

Religious Endogamy

Throughout history, many societies have had endogamy rules relating to religion: Only people with the same religious background were allowed to marry. Marrying outside one's religion is more common than it once was in industrialized countries, however, because greater mobility and freer communication bring people from diverse religious backgrounds into contact. In the United States, it's estimated that between one quarter and one half of all marriages occur between people of different religions ("Breaking the Rules," 2002; Robinson, 1999).

Nevertheless, most religious leaders still actively discourage interfaith marriages. They worry about maintaining their religion's influence and its related ethnic identity within a diverse and complex society (Gordon, 1964). In 2004, the Vatican issued an official church document discouraging marriage between Catholics and non-Christians, especially Muslims (Feuer, 2004). The concern is that such marriages may further weaken people's religious beliefs and values, lead to the raising of children in a different faith, or encourage family members to abandon religion entirely.

The situation facing U.S. Jews provides a good example of the consequences of marriages that break rules of religious endogamy. The percentage of Jews in the U.S. population has declined from 4% to a little more than 1.7% in the past 50 years (Safire, 1995; U.S. Bureau of the Census, 2009). Although only 1 Jew in 10 married a non-Jew in 1945, close to 1 in 2 does so today. A lower birthrate among Jews compared with other groups, coupled with the likelihood that interfaith families will not raise children as Jews, explains, in part, why the Jewish population has been dropping steadily (Goodstein, 2003). Many Jewish leaders fear that the outcome of this trend will be not only the shrinking of the Jewish population but also the erosion and perhaps extinction of an entire way of life.

Racial and Ethnic Endogamy

Racial and ethnic endogamy is a global phenomenon, forming the basis of social structure in most societies worldwide (Murdock, 1949). The issue is an especially volatile one in U.S. society, however, given how racially and ethnically diverse we are. The first law against interracial marriage was enacted in Maryland in 1661, prohibiting Whites from marrying Native Americans or African slaves. Over the next 300 years or so, 38 more states put such laws on the books, expanding their coverage to include Chinese, Japanese, and Filipino Americans. It was believed that a mixing of the races (then referred to as "mongrelization") would destroy the racial purity (and superiority) of Whites. The irony, of course, is that racial mixing had been taking place since the 17th century, much of it through white slave owners raping and impregnating their black slaves.

Legal sanctions against interracial marriage persisted well into the 20th century. In 1958, for example, when Richard Loving (who was white) and his new wife, Mildred Jeter Loving (who was black), moved to their new home in Virginia, a sheriff arrived to arrest them for violating a state law that prohibited interracial marriages. The Lovings were sentenced to 1 year in jail but then learned that the judge would suspend the sentence if they left the state and promised not to return for 25 years. They agreed, but after leaving town, they sued the state of Virginia. In 1967, the U.S. Supreme Court ruled in their favor, concluding that using racial classifications to restrict the freedom to marry was unconstitutional. Sixteen states had their interracial marriage prohibition laws struck down with this ruling.

A half-century later, attitudes are becoming more tolerant, and people are no longer banished for violating racial endogamy rules. Although the vast majority of U.S. marriages remain racially endogamous, relationships that cross racial or ethnic lines are becoming more common. In 1970, there were 300,000 interracial married couples (or about 0.7% of all marriages). Today, there are 2.3 million interracial couples, constituting about 4% of all U.S. marriages. In addition, marriages between Latino/as and non-Latino/as (regardless of race) increased from 1.3% of all marriages in 1970 to 3.7% today. About 26% of married Latino/as are married to someone of a different ethnic group (U.S. Bureau of the Census, 2009).

Attitudes toward interracial marriage have steadily improved over the past 50 years. Nevertheless, people involved in interracial relationships report that they still face problems (Rosenblatt, Karis, & Powell, 1995). About half of the black-white couples in one study felt that biracial marriage makes things harder for them, and about two thirds reported that their parents had a problem with the relationship, at least initially (Fears & Deane, 2001). Many interracial couples—especially black-white couples—still experience a lack of family support when choosing to marry someone of a different race (Lewis & Yancey, 1997). Everyday activities may require more time and effort for interracial couples than for couples of the same race. For instance, when planning vacations, interracial couples often have to do extensive research of potential leisure destinations to see how accepting they are of relationships such as theirs (Hibbler & Shinew, 2005).

Social Class Endogamy

If we based our ideas about the formation of romantic relationships on what we see in movies, we might be tempted to conclude that divisions based on social class don't matter in U.S. society or perhaps don't exist at all. Popular films such as *Titanic, The Wedding Planner, Maid in Manhattan, Good Will Hunting, Sweet Home Alabama,* and *Pretty Woman* send the message that the power of love is strong enough to blow away differences in education, pedigree, resources, and tastes. When it comes to love, Hollywood's United States is a classless society.

In reality, however, social class is a powerful determinant of whom we choose to marry. Around the world, people face strong pressures to choose marital partners of similar social standing (Carter & Glick, 1976; Kalmijn, 1994). Even if two individuals from different races, ethnic groups, or religions marry, chances are they will have similar socioeconomic backgrounds (Rosenfeld, 2005). Certainly, some people do marry a person from a different social class, but the class tends to be an adjacent one—for instance, an upper-middle-class woman may marry a middle-class man. Cinderella-like marriages, between extremely wealthy and extremely poor people, are quite rare.

One reason this occurs is because individuals of similar social classes are more likely to participate in activities together, where they come into contact with people who share their values, tastes, goals, expectations, and backgrounds (Kalmijn & Flap, 2001). Our education system plays a particularly important role in bringing people from similar class backgrounds together. The proportion of married couples who share the same level of schooling is the highest it's been in 40 years. The odds of someone with only a high school education marrying a college graduate have been decreasing since the 1970s (Schwartz & Mare, 2005).

Moreover, neighborhoods—and thus neighborhood schools—tend to be made up of people from similar social classes. College often continues this class segregation. People from upper-class backgrounds are considerably more likely to attend costly private schools, whereas those from the middle class are most likely to enroll in state universities and those from the working class are most likely to enroll in community colleges. These structural conditions increase the odds that the people with whom college students form intimate relationships will come from the same class background.

FAMILY LIFE

To most people's way of thinking, committed intimate romantic relationships form the cornerstone of families. Of all the groups we belong to, family is usually the most significant. Our ancestors provide us with a personal history, and they, along with the families we build later in life, provide much of our identity. Because of its importance in everyday life, sociologists consider family one of the main social institutions, a social structure that addresses not only our personal needs but also the fundamental needs of society (see Chapter 2).

Defining Family

Ironically, as important as family is, it is an elusive term to define. When most people hear the word *family,* they usually think of the ***nuclear family:*** a unit consisting of parents and siblings. Others may think of the ***extended family:*** other kin, such as grandparents, aunts, uncles, and cousins. In everyday usage, people may use the word *family* more loosely to describe those with whom they've achieved a significant degree of emotional closeness and sharing, even if they're not related. If I choose to think of my father's best friend, my barber, and even my dog as members of my family, I can.

But we don't live our lives completely by ourselves, and so we don't have complete freedom to define our own families. Not only do we come into fairly regular contact with people who want to know what our family looks like, we also must navigate a vast array of organizations and agencies that have their own definitions of family and may, at times, impose them on us. Local, state, and federal governments manage many programs that provide certain benefits only to groups officially defined as "families."

The federal government regularly compiles up-to-date statistics on the number of individuals, married couples, and families that live in this country. Obviously, it must have some idea of what a family (or what a marriage) is before it can start counting. In its official statistics, the U.S. Bureau of the Census distinguishes between households and families. A ***household*** is composed of one or more people who occupy the same housing unit. A ***family*** consists of "two or more persons, including the householder, who are related by birth, marriage, or adoption, and who live together as one household" (U.S. Bureau of the Census, 2005). Not all households contain families. If we accept this narrow definition of family, then other arrangements—people living alone, same-sex and opposite-sex cohabitors, and various forms of group living—cannot be considered families in the strict sense of the word. According to the government's definition, more than 40% of U.S. households are not families (U.S. Bureau of the Census, 2009).

Having one's living arrangements legally recognized as family has many practical implications. Benefits such as inheritance rights, insurance coverage, spousal immigration benefits, savings from joint tax returns, the ability to make medical decisions for another person, and visitation rights in prisons and hospital intensive care units are determined by marital or family status. Members of relationships not defined as family relationships, no matter how committed, economically interdependent, or emotionally fulfilling, are not eligible. For instance, homosexual partners of victims of the September 11 attack on the Pentagon were not eligible for the same survivor benefits in the state of Virginia to which surviving heterosexual spouses were entitled (Farmer, 2002).

Historical Trends in Family Life

Many functionalist sociologists have voiced concern over the current state of family as a social institution. Over time, they argue, the family has lost many, if not all, of its traditional purposes (Lasch, 1977). Historically, the family was where children received most of their education and religious training. It was where both children and adults could expect to receive emotional nurturing and support. It was the institution that regulated sexual activity and reproduction. And it was also the economic center of society, where family members worked together to earn a living and support one another financially.

But as the economy shifted from a system based on small, privately owned agricultural enterprises to one based on massive industrial manufacturing, the role of family changed. Economic production moved from the home to the factory, and families became more dependent on the money that members earned outside the home. Schools began to take over the teaching of skills and values that were once a part of everyday home life. Even the family's role as a source of emotional security and nurturing began to diminish as it became less able to shield its members from the harsh realities of modern life (Lasch, 1977).

For all these reasons, many people are concerned about the survival of contemporary families. Anxiety over the future of families has generated some strident calls for a return to the "good ol' days" of family life. The belief in a lost "golden age" of family has led some to depict the present as a period of rapid decline and inevitable family breakdown (Coontz, 2005; Hareven, 1992; Skolnick, 1991). Critics often pessimistically cite high divorce rates, large numbers of out-of-wedlock births, changing gender roles (most notably, the increase in working mothers), and a de-emphasis on heterosexual marriage as troublesome characteristics of contemporary families. However, families have always been diverse in structure and have always faced difficulties in protecting members from economic hardship, internal violence, political upheaval, and social change. Calls for a return to the "good ol' days" are calls for a return to something that has never truly existed. By glorifying a mythical and idealized past, we artificially limit ourselves to an inaccurate image of what we think a "normal" family ought to look like.

Trends in Family Structure

The reality of U.S. family life has never quite fit its nostalgic image. In the 19th century, U.S. adults had a shorter life expectancy than adults today, so due to the death of a parent, children were actually more likely then than they are now to live in a single-parent home (Kain, 1990). Even children fortunate enough to come from intact families usually left home to work as servants or apprentices in other people's homes. Furthermore, although 18% of U.S. children live in poverty today (DeNavas-Walt, Proctor, & Smith, 2008), a comparable proportion lived in orphanages at the beginning of the 20th century—and not just because their parents had died. Many were there because their parents simply couldn't afford to raise them. Rates of alcohol and drug abuse, domestic violence, and school dropouts were also higher a century ago than they are today (Coontz, 1992).

Also contrary to popular belief, father-breadwinner/mother-homemaker households were not the universal family form in the 19th and early 20th centuries. For instance, by 1900, one fifth of U.S. women worked outside the home (Staggenborg, 1998). But the experiences of employed women varied along class and race lines. For middle- and upper-class white women, few professions other than teaching and nursing were available. Because their income was probably not essential for the survival of the household, most could enter and exit the labor force in response to family demands. In contrast, poor women were likely to work long hours, mostly in unskilled jobs in clothing factories, canning plants, or other industries.

Family life for women of color was even more affected by economic necessity. Black domestic servants, for instance, were often forced to leave their own families and live in their employer's home, where they were expected to work around the clock. And most of them had little choice. Throughout U.S. history, black women have rarely had the luxury of being stay-at-home spouses and parents. In 1880, 73% of black single women and 35% of black married women reported holding paid jobs. Only 23% of white single women and 7% of white married women reported being in the paid labor force at that time (cited in Kessler-Harris, 1982).

Trends in Household Size

Perhaps the most pervasive myth regarding U.S. families of the past is that of the primacy of the extended family with several generations living under the same roof. Today's more isolated nuclear family is often compared unfavorably with the image of these large, close-knit support networks. But research shows that U.S. families have always been fairly small and primarily nuclear (Blumstein & Schwartz, 1983; Goode, 1971; Hareven, 1992). This country has no strong tradition of large, extended multigenerational families living together. In fact, the highest proportion of extended family households ever recorded existed between 1850 and 1885 and was only around 20% of all households (Hareven, 1978). Because people didn't live as long then as they do today, most died before ever seeing their grandchildren. Even in the 1700s, the typical family consisted of a husband, a wife, and approximately three children.

When households of the past were large, it was probably due to the presence of nonfamily members: servants, apprentices, boarders, and visitors. The reduction in average household size we've seen over the past several centuries was caused not by a decline in the number of extended relatives but by a decrease in the number of nonfamily members living in a household, a reduction in the number of children in a family, and an increase in the number of young adults living alone (Kobrin, 1976).

As people migrated to the United States from countries that did have a tradition of extended families, such as China, Greece, and Italy, often their first order of business was to surrender their extended families so they could create their own households. Reducing the size of their families was seen as a clear sign that they had become American. Large, multigenerational families simply didn't make economic sense. Being able to move to a different state to pursue a job would be next to impossible with a bunch of grandparents, aunts, uncles, and cousins in tow.

In addition, it's not at all clear that families today are as isolated as some people make them out to be. More U.S. residents than ever have grandparents alive, and most adults see or talk to a parent on the phone at least once a week (Coontz, 1992). Extended family members may not live under the same roof, but they do stay in contact and provide advice, emotional support, and financial help when needed (Newman, 2005).

Trends in Divorce

Another oft-cited indicator of the demise of the U.S. family based on faulty conceptions of the past is the current high divorce rate. Many observers fear that the intact middle-class family depicted in 1950s television shows such as *Ozzie and Harriet*, *Father Knows Best*, and *Leave It to Beaver* has crumbled away forever. The rise in the divorce rate in the late 20th century has been attributed to the cultural movement toward swinging singles, open marriages, alternative lifestyles, and movements for women's equality in the 1960s and 1970s (Skolnick, 1991). True, this was a revolutionary period in U.S. history, and norms governing all aspects of social life were certainly changing.

What these conclusions overlook, however, is the longer historical trend in divorce in this country. Until World War II, it had been increasing steadily for more than 100 years. It rose sharply right after the war, most likely because of short courtships before the young men shipped out and the subsequent stress of separation. In the 1950s, the rate dropped just as sharply. The high divorce rates of the 1960s and 1970s, then, represented a return to a national trend that had been developing since the beginning of the 20th century. Indeed, since the mid-1980s, the rate has actually been declining (Eldridge & Sutton, 2007; Tejada-Vera & Sutton, 2009; U.S. Bureau of the Census, 2009).

Furthermore, the rate of "hidden" marital separation 100 years ago was probably not that much less than the rate of "visible" separation today (Sennett, 1984). For financial or religious reasons, divorce was not an option for many people in the past. For instance, divorce rates actually fell during the Great Depression of the 1930s. With jobs and housing scarce, many couples simply couldn't afford to divorce. Rates of marital unhappiness and domestic violence increased. A significant number of people turned to the functional equivalents of divorce—desertion and abandonment—which have been going on for centuries. So you can see that the divorce rate may have been lower in the past, but families found other ways to break up. The image of a warm, secure, stable family life in past times is at odds with the actual history of U.S. families (Skolnick, 1991).

Cultural Variation in Intimacy and Family

Families can be found in every human society, and from a structural-functionalist perspective, they all address similar societal needs. However, the way families go about meeting these needs—their structure, customs, patterns of authority, and so on—differs widely across cultures. Thus, ideas about what a family is and how people should behave within it are culturally determined.

Most of us take for granted that ***monogamy***, the practice of being married to only one person at a time, is the fundamental building block of the family. Some families do exist without a married couple, and some people may have several spouses over their lifetimes. But monogamous marriage is the core component of our image of family (Sudarkasa, 2001).

In the United States, monogamous marriage between one man and one woman continues to be the only adult intimate relationship that is legally recognized, culturally approved, and endorsed by the Internal Revenue Service. It's still the only relationship in which sexual activity between the partners is not only acceptable but expected. No other relationship has achieved such a status. Despite the growing number of couples choosing cohabitation over marriage, and the overall public concern with the disintegration of marriage, monogamous heterosexual marriage remains the cultural standard against which all other types of intimate relationships are judged.

It may be hard to imagine a society that is not structured around the practice of monogamy, but many societies allow an individual to have several husbands or wives at the same time. This type of marriage is called ***polygamy***. Some anthropologists estimate that about 75% of the world's societies prefer some type of polygamy, although few members within those societies actually have the resources to afford more than one spouse (Murdock, 1957; Nanda, 1994). Even in the United States, certain groups practice polygamy. Thousands of members of a dissident Mormon sect in Utah live in households that contain one husband and two or more wives (McCarthy, 2001). Although these marriages are technically illegal, few polygamists are ever prosecuted. For most of the past century, practitioners were tolerated as long as they kept to themselves. However, every once in a while, a case garners widespread publicity. For instance, in 2006, Warren Jeffs, leader of the Fundamentalist Church of Jesus Christ of Latter Day Saints, drew national attention when he was placed on the FBI's Ten Most Wanted List for unlawful flight to avoid prosecution on charges that he arranged illegal marriages between his adult male followers and underage girls. In 2007, he was convicted of this crime as well as rape and incest and sentenced to 10 years to life in a Utah prison. In 2008, law enforcement officials removed 400 children from his polygamous compound in Eldorado, Texas, and placed them in state custody.

Societies differ in other taken-for-granted facets of family life as well. Take living arrangements, for example. In U.S. society, families tend to follow the rules of ***neolocal residence;*** that is, young married couples are expected to establish their own households and separate from their respective families when financially possible. However, only about 5% of the world's societies are neolocal (Murdock, 1957; Nanda, 1994). In most places, married couples are expected to live with or near either the husband's relatives (called "patrilocal" residence) or the wife's relatives (called "matrilocal" residence).

Child-rearing philosophies vary cross-culturally, too. Most people in the United States believe that young children are inherently helpless and dependent: They feel that if parents attend to the child's drives and desires with consistency, warmth, and affection, that child will learn to trust the parents, adopt their values, develop a sturdy self-concept, and turn out to be a well-rounded, normal individual. In contrast, in the highlands of Guatemala, parents believe that their child's personality is determined by the date of birth. The parents are almost entirely uninvolved in the child's life, standing aside so he or she can grow as nature intended. In many societies—Nigeria, Russia, Haiti, the Dominican Republic, and Mexico, to name a few—most parents think that the best way to teach children to be respectful and studious is to beat them when they misbehave. In contrast, most U.S. child development experts believe that physical punishment can deaden the child's spirit and lead to violence later in life (Dugger, 1996). Despite these dramatic differences in child-rearing practices, most children in all these cultures grow up equally well adapted to their societies.

FAMILY AND SOCIAL STRUCTURE

All of us have experience with families of one form or another, so it's very tempting to look at this topic in individualistic, personal terms. However, the sociological imagination encourages us to think about how social forces affect this aspect of our private lives. As you will see, a focus on the influence of social structure—social institutions as well as sources of social inequality, such as gender, race, and class—can help us understand some of the dilemmas facing contemporary families.

How Other Institutions Influence Family

As a social institution, family is connected to other institutions in important ways. Consider, for instance, the effect that the wars in Iraq and Afghanistan have had on families. For as long as there have been wars, military families have been disrupted when one parent—almost always the father—either shipped out to sea or was deployed in another part of the world. But the structure of U.S. families had changed in many ways by the time the current war began. According to the Pentagon, the number of single mothers and fathers in the military increased from less than 50,000 in the Persian Gulf War of 1991 to about 140,000 in 2007 (cited in Associated Press, 2007; Piore, 2003). However, the military as an institution has no special programs in place to assist single parents when they are deployed. Raising a child in the military has always been hard, but being a single parent raises special challenges and difficult choices, not the least of which is what to do with the children while the parent is gone. According to the Service Members Civil Relief Act, military personnel cannot be evicted or have their property seized during deployment. But this law does not protect them from losing custody of their children, if that's what a judge decides.

The legal, political, religious, and economic forces that shape society are perhaps the institutions that most influence the identities and actions of individuals within family relationships. Keep in mind that individuals within families can act to influence society as well.

The Influence of Law and Politics

The relationship between the family and the law is obvious. Marriage, for instance, is a legal contract that determines lawful rights and responsibilities. In the United States, each state legislature determines the age at which two people can marry, the health requirements, the length of the waiting period required before marriage, rules determining inheritance, and the division of property in case of divorce (Baca Zinn & Eitzen, 1996). Sometimes the legislature sets limits on specific types of marriage. For instance, to protect noncitizens from potential abuse, the U.S. Congress enacted the International Marriage Broker Regulation Act, which requires that men who seek foreign brides over the Internet disclose information about their criminal record and marital history before any contracts are signed (Porter, 2006).

In the case of same-sex unions, the law's power to either forbid or grant family rights and privileges is especially obvious. In some countries, gay men and lesbians can have their relationships legally ratified. Belgium, Spain, Canada, South Africa, the Netherlands, Norway, and Sweden allow gay couples to legally marry. France, Denmark, Portugal, Germany, and many other European countries allow same-sex couples to enter "civil unions" (sometimes called "domestic partnerships" or "registered partnerships"), which grant them many of the legal and economic benefits and responsibilities of heterosexual marriage.

The matter is far from resolved in the United States, however. In 2004, Massachusetts became the first state to allow same-sex couples who are state residents to legally marry. Since then, Connecticut, Iowa, New Hampshire, Vermont, and the District of Columbia have followed suit. Though New York does not, at present, issue marriage licenses to same-sex couples, it does recognize same-sex marriages legally entered into in other states. California, New Jersey, Oregon, Hawaii, and Washington provide at least some spousal rights to same-sex couples (Human Rights Campaign, 2009). In addition, according to the Human Rights Campaign, more than 8,000 employers provide domestic partner benefits for their gay and lesbian workers (cited in Joyce, 2005).

But most states have moved in the opposite direction. Twenty-nine states have constitutional amendments restricting marriage to one man and one woman. (This number includes California, where a 2008 vote to amend the state constitution to prohibit same-sex marriage has been challenged and at the time of this writing remains unsettled.) Another 13 states have laws restricting marriage to one man and one woman (Human Rights Campaign, 2009). In 2005, the Michigan state legislature ruled that its law defining marriage as a relationship between one man and one woman meant that gay and lesbian state workers were not entitled to health benefits for their partners (Lyman, 2005). In 2006, the New York State Supreme Court ruled that denying same-sex couples the right to marry does *not* violate the state constitution. At the federal level, the 1996 Defense of Marriage Act formally reaffirms the definition of marriage as the union of one man and one woman; authorizes all states to refuse to accept same-sex marriages from other states if they ever become legal; and denies federal pension, health, and other benefits to same-sex couples.

State and federal laws usually reflect public opinion, which on the matter of legalizing same-sex marriage is indeed mixed. While acceptance of gays and lesbians in the workplace, as elementary school teachers, and as politicians has grown over the past several decades, support of laws allowing gay couples to marry has been slower to materialize. A 2008 poll found that while an overwhelming majority of respondents approved of inheritance rights, health insurance coverage, Social Security benefits, and hospital visitation rights for same-sex partners, only 39% approved of legal marital rights (Campo-Flores, 2008).

Yet support does seem to be growing. An April 2009 CBS/*New York Times* poll found that 42% of respondents felt same-sex couples should be allowed to legally marry (up from 33% the month before); only 28% thought same-sex couples should have no legal recognition (down from 35% the month before; Montopoli, 2009). And younger people seem especially inclined to support same-sex marriage. Sixty percent of 18- to 34-year-olds in a recent survey believed that not allowing same-sex couples to marry amounts to discrimination, compared with 38% of people over 55 (cited in Bai, 2009).

Politics and family are interconnected in other ways, too. Many of today's most pressing political issues, such as affordable health insurance, quality education, guaranteed parental leave in the workplace, Social Security, and government assistance for the poor, are fundamentally family problems. For example, abortion didn't become a significant political issue until the late 1960s, when it became part of the larger movement for women's rights and reproductive freedom. Later, the right-to-life movement framed the abortion debate not only as a moral and political issue but also as a symbolic crusade to define (or redefine) the role of motherhood and family within the larger society (Luker, 1984).

The Influence of Religion

You saw in Chapter 5 that religion is an important feature of everyday life and a powerful agent of socialization. Religion can also play a role in virtually every stage of family life. One of the key aspects of religion is that it constrains people's behavior, or at the very least encourages them to act in certain ways. This normative aspect of religion has important consequences for people's family experiences. For instance, all the major religions in the United States are strong supporters of marriage and childbearing.

In recent years, more churches have begun requiring engaged couples to participate in premarital counseling and education programs before the wedding. In addition, religions almost universally prohibit sexual relations outside marriage. Some religions prohibit divorce or don't permit remarriage after divorce. In 2003, the Roman Catholic Pope publicly urged women worldwide to pay heed to what he called their "lofty vocation" as wives and mothers ("Pope Exalts Women," 2003). In highly religious families, a sacred text such as the Bible, the Koran, or the Talmud may serve not only as a source of faith but as a literal guidebook for every aspect of family life, from dating, marriage, and sexuality to child discipline, responses to illness and death, and household division of labor.

Religion's influence on family life needn't be so direct, however. For example, among Muslims and members of certain Christian denominations, families are expected to tithe, or donate, a certain amount of their income (10% in most cases) to support their religious establishment. Although it is a charitable thing to do, tithing obligations can create problems for families that are already financially strapped.

Most evidence suggests that religious involvement has positive effects—especially for families raising children—such as higher levels of marital commitment (Larson & Goltz, 1989) and more positive parent-child relationships (Pearce & Axinn, 1998; Wilcox, 2000). "Spiritual wellness" is often cited as one of the most important qualities of family well-being (Stinnett & DeFrain, 1985).

However, in some situations, the link between religious beliefs and actual family behavior may not be as strong as we might think. Even in highly religious families, the practical demands of modern life make it difficult to always subscribe to religious teachings. For instance, although fundamentalist Christians believe wives should stay at home and submit to the authority of their husbands, many fundamentalist women do work outside the home and exert powerful influence over family decisions (Ammerman, 1987). Moreover, although many religions stress the value of keeping families intact, increased religious involvement does not do much to strengthen troubled marriages (Booth, Johnson, Branaman, & Sica, 1995). It may slightly decrease thoughts about divorce, but it doesn't necessarily enhance marital happiness or stop spouses from fighting.

The Influence of Economics

The economy affects virtually every aspect of family life, from the amount of money coming into the household to the day-to-day management of finances and major purchasing decisions. Money matters are closely tied to feelings of satisfaction within family relationships. When couples are disappointed with how much money they have or how it is spent, they find all aspects of their relationships less satisfying (Blumstein & Schwartz, 1983). Sustaining a supportive, nurturing family environment is nearly impossible without adequate income or health care. When economic foundations are weak, the emotional bonds that tie a family together can be stretched to the breaking point.

Financial problems are not just private troubles. Rather, they are directly linked to larger economic patterns. At the global level, the competitive pressures of the international marketplace have forced many businesses and industries to make greater use of so-called disposable workers—those who work part-time or on a temporary contract. These jobs offer no benefits and no security and therefore make family life less stable. Other companies have reduced their costs by cutting salaries, laying off workers, or encouraging early retirement. Some businesses relocate either to other countries or to other parts of the United States where they can pay lower wages (see Chapter 10 for a more detailed discussion). Relaxed rules on foreign investment and export duties have made it easy for U.S. companies to open low-wage assembly plants abroad. For instance, more than 11,500 U.S.-owned and -operated factories are located in Mexico along the 2,100-mile border with the United States (Vogeler, 2003). The companies obviously benefit from higher profits, and the impoverished workers in Mexico benefit from the added income, as these factories employ more than 1.2 million local workers (INEGI, 2007). But displaced U.S. workers and their families may suffer.

Major alterations in the national and local economies can also have a profound impact on families. When inflation or unemployment is high and wages low, families must search for ways to survive financially.

The financial strains of living in the 21st century have made it difficult for most young couples to survive on only one income. For instance, it now costs two-parent, middle-income families more than $204,000 to raise a child to the age of 17, up from $25,230 in 1970 (Lino, 2008; U.S. Department of Agriculture, 2001). Since the mid-1970s, the amount of an average family budget earmarked for mortgage payments increased 69%. And the cost of sending a child to college, when adjusted for inflation, is double what it was a generation ago (cited in Tyagi, 2004).

But incomes have not risen proportionately. In fact, in constant dollars, median household incomes have remained stagnant since 1999 (U.S. Bureau of the Census, 2009). Consequently, about 66% of married-couple households with at least one child under the age of 18 consist of two working parents. That figure is up from 39% in 1970 (Coontz, 2005; U.S. Bureau of the Census, 2009).

How Gender Influences Family

We cannot talk about structural influences on family life without discussing the role of gender. Gender is especially influential, explaining a variety of phenomena in intimate relationships, such as the way people communicate, how they express themselves sexually, how they deal with conflict, and what they feel their responsibilities are. Culturally defined gender expectations in families are certainly changing. But men and women are still likely to enter relationships with vastly different prospects, desires, and goals.

As you learned in Chapter 5, traditional gender role socialization encourages women to be sensitive, express affection, and reveal weakness, whereas men are taught to be competitive, strong, and emotionally inexpressive. These stereotypes have some basis in fact. Research has consistently shown that women have more close friends than men and are more romantic in their intimate relationships (Perlman & Fehr, 1987). Furthermore, women have been shown to be more concerned about, attentive to, and aware of the dynamics of their relationships than men are (see, e.g., Fincham & Bradbury, 1987; Rusbult, Zembrodt, & Iwaniszek, 1986). Women even think more and talk more about their relationships than men do (Acitelli, 1988; Holtzworth-Munroe & Jacobson, 1985).

Ironically, such attentiveness and concern do not necessarily mean that women get more satisfaction out of family relationships than men do. In fact, the opposite may be true. According to one sociologist, every marriage actually contains two marriages: "his" and "hers"—and "his" seems to be the better deal (Bernard, 1972). Both married men and married women live longer and healthier lives than their single counterparts, but husbands typically are sick less often and have fewer emotional problems (Gove, Style, & Hughes, 1990; Ross, Mirowsky, & Goldstein, 1990; Waite & Gallagher, 2000). One study found that compared with married men, married women suffer from higher rates of back pain, headaches, serious psychological distress, and physical inactivity (Schoenborn, 2004).

The reason for these differences lies in the relationship between cultural gender expectations and family demands. Because of the continued pressures of gender-typed family responsibilities, married women are more likely than married men to experience the stresses associated with parenthood and homemaking. Men have historically been able to feel they are fulfilling their family obligations by simply being financial providers. Most people still interpret a father's long hours on the job as an understandable sacrifice for his family's sake. Fathers rarely spend as much time worrying about the effect their work will have on their children as mothers do.

In contrast, even in the relatively "liberated" United States, women's employment outside the home is often perceived as optional or, more seriously, as potentially damaging to the family. Even though women work for the same reasons men work—because they need the money—and bring home paychecks that cover a major chunk of the family's bills (Warren & Tyagi, 2007), women have traditionally had to justify why their working outside the home is not an abandonment of their family duties. You'd be hard-pressed to find many journalists and scholars fearfully describing the perilous effects of men's outside employment on the family. But a mountain of articles and editorials in popular magazines, newspapers, and academic journals over the years focuses on the difficulties women have in juggling the demands of work and family and on the negative effects of mothers' employment on their children's well-being. Newspaper accounts of studies showing that children who spend time in day care have more behavioral problems than children who don't—even if the effect is slight—perpetuate the idea that mothers' labor force choices can have dire consequences (Carey, 2007).

FAMILY CHALLENGES

Given all the pressures on families from the society around them, it should be no surprise that some families experience serious problems. Those problems include divorce and its aftereffects and family violence.

Divorce

Although divorce is more common and more acceptable in some places than in others, virtually all societies have provisions—legal, communal, or religious—for dissolving marriages (McKenry & Price, 1995). In Chile, for example, divorce was illegal until 2005. Up to that point, many unhappy couples had opted for civil annulments, which required that they persuade a court that the marriage had not met legal requirements. Often they'd leave themselves legal loopholes on their wedding day so that if the relationship soured some time in the future they could end it. For instance, witnesses to a wedding would sometimes deliberately misspell their names or give an incorrect address. Or a couple might "illegally" marry in a town in which neither lived (Rohter, 2005).

Worldwide, divorce rates tend to be associated with socioeconomic development. The developing countries of Latin America (e.g., Ecuador, Nicaragua, and Panama) and Asia (e.g., Malaysia, Mongolia, and Sri Lanka) have substantially lower divorce rates than the developed countries of Western Europe and North America (Nugman, 2002).

But even in societies that we would consider modern and developed, powerful religious forces can suppress divorce. For instance, in 1995, the Irish government began a campaign against the Catholic Church over the country's constitutional ban on divorce. The government estimated at that time that at least 80,000 people were trapped in broken marriages and that they deserved the right to end them and remarry. The Catholic bishops launched a massive advertising counterattack, arguing that even unhappily married people have an obligation to keep their marriages intact to provide a good example for society. The referendum passed by a minuscule margin, and in 1997, for the first time, people in Ireland had the right to legally divorce.

Although the dissolution of marriage is virtually universal, no society values divorce highly. In fact, in most societies, people who divorce are somehow penalized, either through formal controls such as fines, prohibitions against remarriage, excommunication, and forced alimony and child support or through informal means such as censure, gossip, and stigmatization.

The Normalization of Divorce

Fifty years ago, divorce was a topic people talked about in whispers if they talked about it at all. Today, of course, things are quite different. You'd be hard-pressed to find an 8-year-old who doesn't know what the word *divorce* means or who hasn't witnessed the end of a marriage, either that of her or his parents or of someone close. Divorce has become a part of everyday life. It's in our movies, television shows, and novels. The children's sections of bookstores stock picture books showing little dinosaurs or bears worrying about the possibility of their parents divorcing. Hallmark has an entire line of greeting cards for parents whose children live elsewhere.

Although the U.S. divorce rate has declined a bit since reaching a peak in 1981 (Stevenson & Wolfers, 2007), it still remains high, especially compared with other industrialized countries. Consider these statistics:

- In 2001, more than 2 million U.S. adults divorced (Kreider, 2005). That works out to a little less than 20 divorces per 1,000 existing marriages.
- About 40% of men and women in their 50s have been divorced at least once (U.S. Bureau of the Census, 2007).
- About 20% of all first marriages in the United States have been disrupted after 5 years, either because of separation or divorce. The figure jumps to 33% after 10 years and to 43% after 15 years (Bramlett & Mosher, 2002).

Such figures frighten people who are about to enter a "lifetime" relationship and distress those already married who want some sense of permanence.

Despite the traditional "family values" rhetoric we hear so much about these days, divorce in the United States tends to be unaffected by religious restrictions or political conservatism. For instance, several studies have found that born-again Christians are just as likely as anyone else to divorce (cited in Belluck, 2004). In addition, divorce rates are lowest in the so-called liberal states of the Northeast and upper Midwest and are highest in the conservative, heavily religious states of the South, such as Arkansas, Oklahoma, and Kentucky (U.S. Bureau of the Census, 2009). Some sociologists argue that other factors more commonly found in these states—namely younger age at marriage, less education, and lower socioeconomic status—render religiosity irrelevant. No matter how religious they are, young people who drop out of school and marry quickly not only lack emotional maturity but are highly susceptible to the economic strains that can create insurmountable problems in a marriage.

At a cultural level, the causes of the high divorce rates in Western societies include things such as the weakening of the family's traditional economic bonds and the stress of shifting gender roles (Popenoe, 1993). One particularly important factor has been a cultural change in the perception of marriage. Marriage has become a voluntary contract system that can be ended at the discretion of either spouse. In the past, when economic needs—not to mention constraints such as parental expectations or religious norms—held couples together, people "made do" with loveless, unsatisfying marriages because they had to. But when these constraints do not exist, people are less willing to make do (Coontz, 2005). Women's increasing earning power and decreasing economic dependence on men have made it easier to end an unsatisfying marriage.

In addition, people's overall attitudes toward divorce have become more accepting. In the 1960s, a divorced politician didn't stand a chance of being elected in the United States. Today, many of our most influential lawmakers are divorced. In the 1980s, Ronald Reagan's divorce and remarriage didn't prevent him from being elected—twice. In the 2008 presidential election, people barely mentioned candidate John McCain's divorce and remarriage. Most people now recognize that a divorce may be preferable to an unhappy marriage. In short, divorce is as much a part of U.S. family life as, well, marriage.

Changing perceptions of marriage and changing cultural attitudes toward divorce are typically accompanied by other institutional changes. In the United States, modifications of existing divorce laws in the past 3 decades have made it easier for people to end an unsatisfying marriage. Historically, evidence of wrongdoing—adultery, desertion, abuse, and so forth—was required for courts to grant a divorce. But since the early 1970s, every state has adopted a form of no-fault divorce. "No-fault" laws have eliminated the requirement that one partner be found guilty of some transgression. Instead, marriages are simply declared unworkable and are terminated.

Many critics argue that these laws and innovations have made divorce *too* easy and *too* quick. Indeed, there seems to be a desire in some areas of the country to return to more restrictive divorce laws. One survey found that 55% of U.S. citizens favor making it harder to leave a marriage when one partner wants to maintain it (cited in Leland, 1996). Some states—Indiana, New Hampshire, Colorado, and Georgia, to name a few—have laws that impose mandatory waiting periods for couples contemplating divorce. Other states have toyed with the idea of providing discounted marriage licenses to couples who participate in premarital counseling. In 1997, the Louisiana State Legislature passed a measure forcing engaged couples to choose between a standard marriage contract that permits no-fault divorce and a "covenant marriage," which could be dissolved only by a mutually agreed-on 2-year separation or proof of fault, chiefly adultery, abandonment, or abuse (Loe, 1997). Arizona followed suit in 1998, as did Arkansas in 2001. Critics of such measures note that instead of having a positive impact on family life, the result might be an increase in contentious, expensive, potentially child-harming divorces and unhappy, perhaps even dangerous marriages.

Children, Divorce, and Single Parenting

More than 1 million U.S. children see their parents divorce each year (U.S. Divorce Statistics, 2006). When we combine divorce, separation, widowhood, and out-of-wedlock births, a significant number of children grow up living with one parent. In 1960, 9% of children under 18 lived with a single parent; by 2008, the figure had increased to 26%. Another 4% of children live with neither parent (Fields, 2003; U.S. Bureau of the Census, 2008).

Although divorce can be traumatic for adults, most recover after a period of years. Children, however, have a more difficult time adjusting. For them, divorce may set a series of potentially disruptive changes in motion. They may have to move to a new home in a new neighborhood, make new friends, and go to a new school. Because the overwhelming majority of children of divorced parents live with their mothers (Newman, 2009), they often experience a decline in their standard of living. The earning capacity of women is generally lower than that of men to begin with. Furthermore, noncustodial fathers do not always pay child support. In 61.4% of divorces in which mothers have sole physical custody, fathers are required to pay child support (Grall, 2007). Of these, only 36.7% of noncustodial fathers pay the full amount, 40.8% pay a partial amount, and 22.5% pay nothing. Hence, more than half of divorced mothers with custody of children don't receive the total financial assistance they have been awarded. Award rates are especially low for African American and Latina women, who are likely to suffer from higher poverty rates to begin with (Grall, 2007).

The relationship that children have with their noncustodial parent also tends to deteriorate over time. Some research indicates that noncustodial fathers rarely see their children regularly or maintain close relationships with them (Furstenberg & Harris, 1992). What contact they do have with their children often diminishes over time (Manning & Smock, 1999). One study found that 75% of noncustodial fathers never attend their child's school events, 85% never help them with their homework, and 65% never take them on vacations (Teachman, 1991). Another found that fewer than one in five noncustodial fathers have a significant influence over their children's health care, education, religion, or other matters important to their welfare (Arendell, 1995).

What are the long-term effects of divorce on children? A substantial body of research shows that regardless of race or education of parents, children raised in single-parent homes have more problems at every stage of life than children from two-parent families. An extensive review of studies published during the 1990s found that children from divorced families fare worse in terms of academic success, psychological adjustment, self-concept, social competence, and long-term health than children from intact, two-parent families (Amato, 2000). When they reach adulthood, they are at greater risk of low socioeconomic attainment, increased marital difficulties, and divorce (Diekmann & Engelhardt, 1999).

These differences are typically attributed to factors such as the absence of a father, increased strain on the custodial parent to keep the household running, and emotional stress and anger associated with the separation. However, the causes of these problems are more likely to be factors that can also be found in two-parent families: low income, poor living conditions, lack of parental supervision, and marital discord (Amato & Sobolewski, 2001; Cherlin, 1992).

Some critics argue that the standard research design in studies on the impact of divorce on children—comparing children whose parents have divorced with children in happy, intact families—is flawed. Indeed, if we compare kids from divorced families with kids from intact families whose parents are unhappily married or whose families experience a great deal of conflict, we find that the type and frequency of emotional and interpersonal problems are similar for both sets of children (Cherlin et al., 1991). In fact, children who grow up in intact families marked by frequent conflict may actually suffer more. This research suggests that behavioral problems are caused not by the divorce itself but by exposure to conflict between the parents both before and after the divorce (Stewart, Copeland, Chester, Malley, & Barenbaum, 1997). In short, simply witnessing his or her parents' divorce may not be as important in the development of a child as the way parents relate to each other and to the child.

Family Violence

Ironically, relationships in families—with the people who are supposed to nourish us when the outside world has sucked away our life energy—can also be some of the most violent relationships in a society.

Intimate-Partner Violence

Wife beating occurs in about 85% of the world's societies. According to the World Health Organization, women everywhere face the greatest threat of violence in their own homes (Garcia-Moreno, Jansen, Ellsberg, Heise, & Watts, 2006). A study of intimate violence in developing countries found that about one third of women in Egypt and Nicaragua and close to one half of women in Peru, Colombia, and

Zambia have been beaten by their spouses or partners (Kishor & Johnson, 2004).

Husband beating occurs less frequently—in about 27% of societies—and occurs less often than wife beating in those societies where both are present (Levinson, 1989). In the United States, for instance, women are eight times more likely than men to be beaten by an intimate partner (Rand, 2008).

Exact statistics about the prevalence of violence among intimates are difficult to collect. In the United States, domestic violence typically occurs in private, beyond the watchful eyes of relatives, neighbors, and strangers. Even with the more stringent rules for police reporting that have been instituted in the past decade or two, most incidents of domestic violence are never reported; others are dismissed as accidents. It's been estimated that only about half of the cases of nonlethal violence against women are reported to the police (Rennison & Welchans, 2000).

The statistics on intimate-partner violence that do exist indicate that it remains a widespread problem, even though it has declined by about 50% in the past decade (Prah, 2006). According to the U.S. Bureau of Justice Statistics (Rand, 2008), about 623,000 nonlethal violent acts (including rape, sexual assault, aggravated assault, and simple assault) were committed by current spouses, former spouses, boyfriends, or girlfriends in 2007 (the last year for which such figures were available at the time of this writing).

Other studies place the prevalence rate for intimate partner violence significantly higher. For instance, the National Violence Against Women Survey of 16,000 women and men across the country found that nearly 25% of surveyed women and 7.6% of men said they'd been raped or physically assaulted by a spouse, partner, or date at some point in their lifetimes. Within the previous 12 months, 1.5% of women and 0.9% of men reported being raped or physically assaulted. According to these estimates, about 1.5 million women and more than 800,000 men are assaulted by an intimate partner annually in the United States, well above the official Bureau of Justice Statistics figures. And if we add relatively minor acts of violence—pushing, grabbing, shoving, and slapping—the figures would rise to more than 3 million incidents for men and more than 5 million for women (Tjaden & Thoennes, 2000).

In 2005, more than 1,500 murders were attributed to intimate partners, and 78% of the victims were women. Overall, about 30% of all female murder victims were killed by an intimate partner (Fox & Zawitz, 2007). One study found that almost half the women murdered by their intimate partners had visited the emergency room within the 2 years before they were killed (Crandall, Nathens, Kernic, Holt, & Rivara, 2004).

Women don't just suffer disproportionate physical consequences. Female victims of intimate violence are also more likely than male victims to suffer psychologically (e.g., from depression, anxiety, or low self-esteem) and socially (such as isolation from friends). The economic costs can be steep, too. It's estimated that intimate violence costs about $4.1 billion in direct costs (medical and mental health care) and $1.8 billion in indirect costs (lost productivity) each year. Women who experience severe forms of abuse are also more likely than women who experience less serious forms of abuse to lose their jobs or to go on public assistance (Centers for Disease Control and Prevention, 2006).

Although domestic violence between heterosexual partners gets most of the attention, same-sex couples are not immune to the problem. Indeed, same-sex intimate violence is widespread. It's estimated that between 42% and 79% of gay men and 25% to 50% of lesbians have experienced some type of intimate violence (cited in Burke & Owen, 2006). In fact, some researchers claim that more violence occurs in long-term homosexual relationships than in heterosexual relationships (Cameron, 2003).

Child Abuse

Children are even more likely to be victims of intimate violence than adult family members. In some poverty-stricken countries, children may be consigned to unpleasant and dangerous labor, sold to buy food for the rest of the family, or even murdered in infancy if their parents don't want them or can't afford them. In the United States, there were close to 900,000 substantiated cases of child abuse and/or neglect in 2006 (U.S. Bureau of the Census, 2009). Because the vast majority of child abuse incidents involve victims who can't protect themselves or report the abuse and remain hidden from the police and social service agencies, many researchers think the actual figure is much higher. And if we take violence against children to mean any act of physical aggression directed by an adult toward a child—including spanking and slapping—perhaps as many as 9 of every 10 U.S. children under the age of 3 have been the object of violence at the hands of their parents or caretakers (Straus & Gelles, 1990).

Because of the relative size of victims and abusers, child abuse can sometimes be fatal. It's estimated that 1,760 children nationally died from abuse or neglect in 2007, and 70% were killed by one or both parents. More than 75% of them were younger than 4 at the time of their death (Administration for Children and Families, 2009).

Intimate Violence in Cultural Context

Individual-level factors such as frustration over money, stress, and alcohol and drug use are frequently cited as major causes of domestic violence. To some analysts, batterers are either psychopaths or people who are just plain prone to violence. Although it would be comforting to believe that domestic violence is rare and occurs only in families that harbor a "sick" parent or spouse, it actually happens with alarming frequency and is likely to be committed by people we would otherwise consider "normal." Spouse or partner abuse and child abuse—not to mention elder abuse and violence between siblings—occur in every culture, class, race, and religion. It is not an aberration; it is a fundamental characteristic of the way we relate to one another in private, intimate settings. So to fully understand domestic violence, we must take a look at some important characteristics of the society in which it occurs.

The United States is fundamentally committed to the use of violence to achieve desirable ends (Straus, 1977). For many people, violence is considered the appropriate means by which to resolve certain problems. Furthermore, violence pervades the culture. It is in our schools, our movies, our toy stores, our video games, our spectator sports, and our government. It's even in our everyday language. How many times have you heard a parent "playfully" warn a misbehaving child that he or she is "cruising for a bruising"?

In addition to the pervasiveness of violence in the culture, families have several characteristics that increase the probability of conflict. For instance, we spend a lot of time with family members and interact with them across a wide range of situations. The intimacy of these interactions is intense. Emotions run deep. The anger we may feel toward a stranger or an acquaintance never approaches the intensity of the anger we feel toward a spouse—or for that matter, toward a sibling or a child.

Moreover, we also know more about family members than we know about other people in our lives. We know their likes and dislikes, their fears, and their desires. And they know these things about us, too. If someone in your family insults you, you know immediately what you can say to get even. Spouses usually know the "buttons" they can push to hurt or infuriate each other. Arguments can escalate into violence when one partner focuses on the other's vulnerabilities and insecurities.

Finally, family life contains endless sources of stress and tension. For one thing, we expect a lot from our families: emotional and financial support, warmth, comfort, and intimacy. When these expectations aren't fulfilled, stress levels escalate. Life circumstances also contribute to family tension (Gelles & Straus, 1988). The birth and raising of a child, financial problems, employment transitions, illness, old age, death, and so on are all events that potentially increase stress. Indeed, a pregnant or recently pregnant woman is more likely to be the victim of a homicide than to die of any other cause (Horon & Cheng, 2001).

We must also look at the broader conceptions of gender that exist within a society. Male dominance in human societies has a long and rather infamous history. Roman law, for instance, justified a husband's killing his wife for reasons such as adultery, wine drinking, and other so-called inappropriate behaviors (Steinmetz, Clavan, & Stein, 1990). Most societies in the world remain dominated by and built around the interests of men. Men typically occupy the high-status positions, make important decisions and exercise political power, tend to dominate interpersonal relationships, and occupy the roles society defines as most valuable.

Men who beat their partners are not necessarily psychotic, deranged, "sick" individuals. Rather, they are often men who believe that male dominance is their birthright. Such men are actually living up to cultural prescriptions that are cherished in many societies—aggressiveness, male dominance, and female subordination (Dobash & Dobash, 1979). We have a deeply entrenched tendency to perceive domestic violence as "normal," as something that, though not necessarily desirable, is not surprising or unexpected either. Consequently, much of the research in this area has focused on the victims rather than on the perpetrators.

Personal and Institutional Responses to Intimate Violence

One question that has captured the attention of many marriage and family researchers is why people, especially women, stay in abusive relationships in societies where divorce is readily available. During the 1960s, the masochism thesis—that is, that women like being humiliated and hurt—was the predominant reason offered by psychiatrists (see, e.g., Saul, 1972). Even today, many psychiatrists believe that masochism—or self-defeating personality disorder, as it is now called—is a "legitimate" medical explanation for women who stay in abusive relationships. Other contemporary explanations focus on the woman's character flaws, such as a weak will or a pathological emotional attachment.

All these explanations focus on the victim while paying little attention to her social situation. From a conflict perspective, we can see that in a society reluctant to punish male abusers, many women may perceive that they have no alternatives and may feel physically, economically, and emotionally trapped in their relationships. Many of them leave, sometimes on several occasions, but find that the opportunities outside the relationship are not sufficient and end up returning (Anderson, 2003). Indeed, the broader economic structure conspires to keep vulnerable women in abusive relationships. Women who are unemployed and cannot support themselves financially are significantly less likely to leave an abusive marriage than women who are employed and who therefore have their own source of income (Strube & Barbour, 1983).

But the very social organizations and institutions that are designed to help battered women may be more to blame for their inability to escape abuse than psychological shortcomings. As recently as 20 years ago, for instance, emergency room workers routinely interviewed battered women about their injuries with their husbands or boyfriends present. The courts, too, historically treated spousal violence less seriously than other crimes, making it even more difficult for women to seek help. Even today, about 80% of domestic violence victims don't have lawyers to guide them through the legal process (Prah, 2006). Most states require that volunteers who work on domestic violence hotlines complete 40 to 50 hours of training, but no such training is required for police personnel, lawyers, and judges (Prah, 2006).

Sometimes the resources in place to assist battered women are simply inadequate. Several states have waiting lists of intimate violence victims in need of counseling. If shelters are filled—as is often the case—victims may have to be bused hundreds of miles away to a place where shelter is available. This remedy may get them out of harm's way, but it may also wreck their work lives, endanger welfare checks, take them away from the support of extended family and friends, and disrupt their children's schooling.

In rural areas, there may be no services available at all. And if there's no public transportation, the shelters that do exist may be inaccessible to women who live miles away and don't own a car. In small towns, confidentiality is virtually impossible. The fact that people tend to know one another can dissuade a woman from calling a local sheriff's office for help, because the person answering might be a friend or relative of her abusive partner.

Broader societal circumstances may also play a role. In the months following the September 11, 2001, attacks, for instance, many battered women made the decision not to leave their relationship, clinging to familiar surroundings and coming to believe that a bad home was better than none in such unstable times. As a consequence, shelters reported dwindling demand for beds in their facilities in the immediate aftermath of the attacks (Lewin, 2001). In their need to acknowledge such realities, battered women are no different from any other individuals seeking to negotiate the complexities of social life.

CONCLUSION

Close relationships form the center of our personal universes. Life with intimates provides us with the sense of belonging that most of us need. However, although these relationships are the principal source of identity, community, happiness, and satisfaction for many, they can be the source of tremendous anguish and suffering for others.

Family, the most structured and culturally valued intimate relationship, is simultaneously a public and a private institution. True, most intimate and family behavior occurs away from the watchful eyes of others; we alone have access to our thoughts, desires, and feelings regarding those with whom we are intimately involved. But people around us, the government, and even society as a whole have a vested interest in what happens in our intimate lives.

The social institutions and culture that make up our society also shape the very nature and definition of "family." Today, the boundaries of that definition are being pushed by rapidly increasing numbers of "nontraditional" families—dual-earner couples, single-parent households, cohabitors, same-sex couples, and so on.

Every family relationship, whether it violates or conforms to current social norms, reflects the dominant ideals and beliefs regarding what a marriage or a family ought to look like. Although each relationship is unique, this uniqueness will always be bounded by the broader constraints of our cultural, group, and institutional values.

CHAPTER HIGHLIGHTS

◆ In this culture, close relationships are the standard against which we judge the quality and happiness of our everyday lives. Yet in complex, individualistic societies, they are becoming more difficult to establish and sustain.

◆ Many people in the United States long for a return to the "golden age" of the family. But the image of the U.S. family of the past is largely a myth.

◆ Although monogamous marriage is the only sexual relationship that has achieved widespread cultural legitimacy in the United States, other forms of intimacy (e.g., extra- and premarital sex, polygamy) are considered legitimate in other societies.

◆ Although we like to think that the things we do in our family relationships are completely private experiences, they are continually influenced by large-scale political interests and economic pressures. Furthermore, our choices of romantic partners are governed to some degree by cultural rules that encourage us to form relationships within certain social groups and outside others.

◆ Divorce is not a solely private experience either. It occurs within a cultural, historical, and community context. The high rate of remarriage after divorce indicates that people still view the institution of marriage as desirable.

◆ Instead of viewing domestic violence (spouse abuse and child abuse) as a product of "sick" individuals, sociologists are likely to view it as the product of a culture that tolerates violence in a variety of situations, traditionally grants men authority over women in family roles, and values family privacy and autonomy over the well-being of individual members.

KEY TERMS

endogamy Marriage within one's social group

exogamy Marriage outside one's social group

extended family Family unit consisting of the parent-child nuclear family and other relatives, such as grandparents, aunts, uncles, and cousins

family Two or more persons, including the householder, who are related by birth, marriage, or adoption and who live together as one household

household Living arrangement composed of one or more people who occupy a housing unit

monogamy The practice of being married to only one person at a time

neolocal residence Living arrangement in which a married couple sets up residence separate from either spouse's family

nuclear family Family unit consisting of at least one parent and one child

polygamy Marriage of one person to more than one spouse at the same time

©Zack Seckler/Corbis

8 Constructing Difference

Social Deviance

In 1984, 22-year-old Kelly Michaels moved to New York to pursue her dream of becoming an actress. She was a mild-mannered, devout Catholic who loved children. To support herself, she began working at the Wee Care Preschool in a New Jersey suburb. By all accounts, the kids there loved her (Hass, 1995).

Two weeks after Michaels left Wee Care for a better-paying job at another preschool, a 4-year-old boy who was enrolled at Wee Care was taken to a doctor. A nurse rubbed his back and explained that she was going to take his temperature rectally. He said something like "That's what teacher [Michaels] does to me at nap time." Although it was unclear exactly what he meant by this—Michaels sometimes rubbed children's backs to get them to sleep and did take their temperature with a plastic forehead strip—the boy's alarmed mother, who happened to be the daughter of a local judge, called the school and the police (Michaels, 1993). The police questioned the child, as well as other children at Wee Care, searching for evidence that Michaels had sexually abused them. As word spread of the investigation, worried parents phoned other parents to share stories about the latest allegations. The police encouraged parents to seek state-funded psychological help for themselves as well as their children. In turn, the therapists encouraged the parents to cooperate with authorities in investigating Michaels.

That casual comment made by one little boy in a doctor's office touched off a 16-month investigation by the Division of Youth and Family Services, which eventually ended in a 235-count indictment against Michaels. During the investigation, scores of parents became convinced that Michaels had raped their children with silverware, wooden spoons, LEGOs, and light bulbs; that she had played "Jingle Bells" on the piano while naked; and that she had licked peanut butter off children's genitals, made them drink her urine, and forced them to eat excrement off the floor (Hass, 1995).

By the time the trial began, Kelly was being called the most hated woman in New Jersey. The 10-month trial was filled with a host of inconsistencies and questionable legal tactics. Prosecutors never provided any substantiated evidence of abuse, yet they portrayed Michaels as "actressy" and "deviously charming." Everything she did was interpreted from the assumption that she was a "monster." For instance, if she was kind and patient with the children, that meant she was trying to seduce them.

None of the other teachers at the day care center had heard or seen anything, even though most of the alleged abuse took place during the children's nap time in a room set off only by a plastic curtain. The judge in the trial allowed the children to testify on closed-circuit TV while seated on his lap and denied the defense attorneys the opportunity to cross-examine them. One of the prosecution's witnesses—a child therapist—testified that the children who denied being molested by Ms. Michaels suffered from something called "child sexual abuse accommodation syndrome," a psychological condition that made them deny the abuse. In fact, the more the children denied it, the more certain the child therapist was that the abuse had actually happened.

Michaels was found guilty on 115 counts of assault, sexual abuse, and terrorist threats and sentenced to 47 years in prison. In 1993, after she had spent 5 years in prison—including an 18-month stint in solitary confinement—a state appellate court overturned the conviction. Later, the New Jersey State Supreme Court upheld the appellate court's decision, decrying the original conviction with outrage. The court wrote that all 20 children who testified against Michaels had been led, bribed, or threatened (Hass, 1995).

You might think that a formal declaration of innocence from such a powerful body as a state supreme court would change people's feelings about Kelly Michaels. Yet she remained a target of hate. Several civil suits were filed against Michaels by parents who still believed their children had been sexually abused. One mother said she would try to kill Michaels with her bare hands if she had the chance. Long after Michaels's conviction on sexual abuse charges had been overturned, the media continued to identify her as a criminal. For instance, an Associated Press news release about her thwarted attempt to sue the county and the state was titled "Sex Offender's Case Denied in Court" (2001).

Why was it so hard for people to admit that Michaels was innocent? For one thing, at a time when child molestation was becoming a national obsession, the case reflected our darkest collective fears. The terrifying message was that our children could be hurt not only by creepy, middle-aged men but also by seemingly safe, 22-year-old college women. In the frenzy over children's safety, no one seemed willing to protect the principle that a defendant is innocent until proven guilty.

Even more striking about this case is what it says about the way people think. Once members of the community concluded that Kelly Michaels had committed these horrible acts, no amount of conflicting evidence was going to sway them to believe otherwise. Deviant labels and what they imply in people's minds can overshadow everything else about that person. When Michaels was convicted and formally tagged a criminal, the public degradation acquired legal legitimacy. From that point on, she would never again be able to reclaim a normal life and in many people's minds would forever be a "child molester."

Few of us have spent 5 years in prison as a wrongly convicted child molester. But people are unjustifiably tagged as deviant all the time. Perhaps there have been times in your life when you acquired some sort of inaccurate reputation that you couldn't shed. In this chapter, I examine several questions related to this phenomenon: What is deviance? How does society attempt to control deviant behavior? Who gets to define what is and is not deviant? And what are the consequences of being identified by others as deviant?

DEFINING DEVIANCE

In its broadest sense, the term ***deviance*** refers to socially disapproved behavior—the violation of some agreed-on norm that prevails in a community or in society at large. Staring at a stranger in an elevator, talking to oneself in public, wearing outlandish clothes, robbing a bank, and methodically shooting dozens of students on a college campus can all be considered deviant acts. If we define deviance simply as any norm violation, then most deviance is rather trivial—even "normal"—like driving over the speed limit or walking across an intersection when the light is red. Most of us, at some point in our lives, occupy statuses or engage in behaviors that others could regard as deviant. But most sociologists focus on deviant acts that are assaults on mores, the most serious of a society's norms. It's this type of deviance to which I will devote most of my attention in this chapter.

The determination of which behaviors or characteristics are deviant and which are normal is complex. We usually assume that there's a fair amount of agreement in a society about what and who is deviant. For instance, no one would challenge the notion that child abuse is bad and that child abusers ought to be punished. But the level of agreement within a given society over what specific acts constitute child abuse can vary tremendously. Spanking may be a perfectly acceptable method of discipline to one person but can be considered a cruel form of abuse by another.

To further complicate the issue, some sociologists who are identified with structural functionalism (e.g., Durkheim, 1895/1958; Erikson, 1966) argue that deviance, as a class of behaviors, is not always bad for society and may actually serve a useful purpose. As you recall from Chapter 4, norm violations help define the cultural and moral boundaries that distinguish right from wrong and increase feelings of in-group togetherness among those who unite in opposition to deviance from group norms. At the surface level, individual acts of deviance are disruptive and generate varying degrees of social disapproval, but at a deeper level, they can contribute to the maintenance and continuity of every society. Deviance can also lead to needed change in a society (Durkheim, 1895/1958). During the 1950s and 1960s, civil rights protestors purposely broke laws they considered discriminatory, such as those that prevented Blacks from entering certain establishments or attending certain schools. These acts of deviance eventually helped convince many voters and politicians to support legislation ending legal segregation.

As you may have guessed, sociologists usually don't judge whether a given behavior should or shouldn't be considered deviant. Instead, they examine how deviance comes about and what it means to society. One of their primary concerns is whether people respond to deviance from the perspective that all human behavior can be classified as essentially good or bad (absolutists) or from the perspective that definitions of deviance are socially constructed (relativists).

Absolutist Definitions of Deviance

According to ***absolutism***, there are two fundamental types of human behavior: (1) that which is inherently proper and good and (2) that which is obviously improper, immoral, evil, and bad. The distinction is clear and identifiable. The rightness or wrongness of an act exists prior to socially created rules, norms, and customs and independently of people's subjective judgments (Goode, 1994).

Absolutist definitions of deviance imply something about society's relationship with the person who is considered deviant. Many people consider "deviants" to be psychologically, and perhaps even anatomically, different from ordinary, conforming people. The attribute or behavior that serves as the basic reason for defining a person as deviant in the first place is considered pervasive and essential to his or her entire character (Hills, 1980). Respectable, conventional qualities become insignificant. It doesn't matter, for instance, that the "sexual deviant" has an otherwise ordinary life, that the "alcoholic" has recovered, or that the violent act of the "wife batterer" was completely atypical of the rest of his life. In short, the deviant act or trait determines the overall worth of the individual (Katz, 1975). Being defined as deviant means being identified as someone who cannot and should not be treated as an ordinary member of society.

There's another element of unfairness involved in the absolutist approach to deviance. People routinely make judgments about deviants based on strongly held stereotypes. If you ask someone to imagine what a typical drug addict looks like, for instance, chances are that the person will describe a dirty, poor, strung-out young man living on the streets and resorting to theft to support his habit. The image probably wouldn't be one of a middle-class alcoholic, stay-at-home mother, or a clean-shaven, hardworking physician hooked on prescription drugs, even though these groups constitute a higher percentage of drug addicts than any other in U.S. society (Pfohl, 1994).

In U.S. society, the consequences of absolute deviant stereotypes fall heavily on members of ethnoracial minorities. Latinos and African Americans make up more than 60% of the male population in state and federal prisons, even though they constitute only about 28% of the general male population (U.S. Bureau of the Census, 2009; West & Sabol, 2009).

The U.S. Bureau of Justice Statistics (2009) estimates that 1 in 21 black males is incarcerated compared with 1 in 138 white males. According to the Justice Policy Institute (2002), the number of black men in jail or prison has grown so much in the past 2 decades that there are now more black men behind bars than are enrolled in colleges and universities.

Although some people may see such figures as clear evidence of higher rates of minority involvement in crime, other statistics seem to suggest something different. For instance, African Americans make up about 13% of the nation's population and constitute about the same percentage of all illegal drug users (National Institute on Drug Abuse, 2003); yet they account for 45% of people in state prisons for drug offenses (cited in Moore, 2009). In 75% of cases in which a federal prosecutor sought the death penalty between 1995 and 2000, the defendant was a member of an ethnoracial minority group; and in half the cases, the defendant was black (cited in Bonner & Lacey, 2000).

Absolutist images of deviants are often oversimplified and fall short of accounting for every individual. The vast majority of African Americans do not commit crimes, just as the vast majority of gay men are not sexual predators, the vast majority of Italians are not involved in the Mafia, and the vast majority of Muslims are not terrorists. Nevertheless, the degree to which an entire group is characterized by an absolutist stereotype is important, because it determines individual and societal responses. If affluent housewives and businesspeople who abuse drugs are not considered typical drug addicts, they will never be the focus of law enforcement attention, collective moral outrage, political rhetoric, or public policy.

Relativist Definitions of Deviance

Reliance on a strict absolutist definition of deviance can lead to narrow and often inaccurate perceptions of many important social problems. This shortcoming can be avoided by employing a second approach to defining deviance, ***relativism***, which draws from symbolic interactionism and the conflict perspective. This approach—which parallels the more general "cultural relativism" discussed in Chapter 4—states that deviance is not inherent in any particular act, belief, or condition; instead, it is socially constructed, a creation of collective human judgments and ideas. Like beauty, it is in the eye of the beholder. Consequently, no act is universally or "naturally" deviant. The relativist approach is useful when the focus of study is the process by which some group of people or some type of behavior is defined as deviant.

For the relativist, complex societies consist of different groups with different values and interests. Sometimes these groups agree and cooperate to achieve a common goal, as when different segments of society join together to fight a foreign enemy. But more often than not, there is conflict and struggle among groups to realize their own interests and goals.

Different people or groups can thus have dramatically different interpretations of the same event. In 1995, a 35-year-old white former Marine named William Masters was taking his usual armed, late-night walk through a barren neighborhood in Los Angeles. He came upon two young Latino men spray painting graffiti beneath a freeway overpass. Masters wrote down the license number of their car on a small piece of paper. When the men saw him and demanded the paper, Masters pulled out his 9-millimeter pistol and shot them, wounding one and killing the other. He told the police that the men had threatened him with a screwdriver and he had acted in self-defense, even though both were shot in the back. He was not charged with murder. Eventually, he was found guilty on one count of carrying a concealed gun in public and one count of carrying a loaded gun in public—charges that carried a maximum of 18 months in jail and a $2,000 fine.

Shortly after his arrest, Masters made a case for why his actions shouldn't be defined as deviant. He told one interviewer he was sure people were glad that as an intended victim he had gotten away and that no jury would ever convict him (Mydans, 1995). Many people agreed. Callers to radio talk shows and letters to newspapers applauded him for his vigilant anti-graffiti efforts and for his foresight in carrying a weapon for self-protection. A few suggested that society would be better off with more people like William around (Mydans, 1995). But others expressed dismay at the verdict and argued that Masters was simply a racist out looking for trouble. They felt he was a deviant who literally got away with murder.

All those who expressed opinions on this case would likely agree on one thing: "Murder" is a deviant act at the far end of the spectrum of social acceptability. However, their perceptions of whether William Masters was a "murderer" were quite different. Was he a "hero" or a "killer"? The answer lies not in the objective act of taking another's life but in the way others define and respond to such an act.

To fully understand the societal and personal implications of deviance designations, we must look at how these definitions are created and perpetuated. One key factor is who is doing the defining. One person's crime is another person's act of moral conscience; one group's evil is another group's virtue; one culture's terrorist is another culture's freedom fighter.

Definitions of deviance are also relative to particular cultural standards.

- In Singapore, a young vandal is a serious deviant (punishable by caning), as is a person who leaves chewed gum where it can be stepped on. The fine for simply bringing one stick of gum into Singapore is $10,000.
- In Malaysia, a Muslim woman can be whipped for drinking alcohol in public or arrested for snacking during the daylight fasting hours of Ramadan.
- In Russia, convicted drunk drivers automatically lose their licenses for life; in El Salvador, a drunk driver could face a firing squad for his or her first offense.

Deviance definitions undergo changes over time as well. For instance, several states at one time had laws that were designed specifically to protect women's virtue. Florida had a law that prohibited women from parachuting on Sundays. Michigan law made it a crime for men to use profanity in front of women. In Texas, it was a crime for women to adjust their stockings in public. The state of Washington still has a law on the books that makes it illegal to call a woman a "hussy" or "strumpet" in public (Kershaw, 2005).

Conflict over deviance definitions often reflects differing cultural expectations. In 2005, for instance, an appeals court in Florida upheld a judge's earlier ruling that a Muslim woman could not wear a burka—a traditional veil that covers all but a woman's eyes—in her driver's license photo. In 2005, the U.S. Supreme Court ruled that the federal government could prohibit the medicinal use of marijuana even in the 11 states that explicitly permit it (Greenhouse, 2005). Even though people in the United States who wear burkas or smoke marijuana for medical purposes don't consider themselves deviant, these court rulings meant they could be defined and treated as such by the dominant culture.

The absolutist approach assumes that certain individual characteristics are typical of all deviants, but the relativist approach acknowledges that there is no typical deviant. In fact, the same act committed by two different people may yield very different community responses. In 1980, a Bayonne, New Jersey, teacher named Diane Cherchio was caught kissing and groping a 13-year-old male student at an 8th-grade dance. A few years later, after being promoted to guidance counselor, she had sex with an 11th grader, became pregnant, and eventually married him upon his graduation in 1985. Yet instead of being fired or even reprimanded, she was allowed to continue working in the public school district for 2 decades. When the son she gave birth to grew up to be a teenager, Ms. Cherchio began having sex with one of his friends. She used her school authority to rearrange the boy's schedule so they had time for their sexual trysts. When that boy's parents found out and complained to the police, she was arrested. Again, she was not fired. School officials instead allowed her to take an early retirement package that increased her pension. They even gave her a gala farewell party. When she finally pled guilty to sexual assault charges in 2005, glowing references from coworkers convinced the judge to sentence her to probation and to spare her from registering as a sex offender (Kocieniewski, 2006).

Cherchio was eventually punished, as have other older women who've had sexual relationships with teenage boys. Nevertheless, it's hard to imagine a school accommodating or defending a male teacher who seduced teenage girls in such a way. Because she was a young, attractive, intelligent woman whose victims were willing teenage boys, people in this community looked the other way. When *she* did it, somehow it wasn't so bad. One author summed up the public response to such incidents: "A teenage boy who gets to live his fantasy? What can be the harm?" (Levy, 2006, p. 2).

From a relativist approach, immediate situational circumstances, such as the time and location of an act, can also influence definitions of deviance. For example, drinking alcohol on the weekend is more acceptable than drinking during the week, and drinking in the evening is more acceptable than drinking in the morning. In 2005, the state of Florida expanded its self-defense law so that people could use concealed guns or other deadly force to defend themselves in public places without first trying to escape the attacker (Goodnough, 2005). In fact, 15 states have adopted "stand-your-ground" laws that allow victims to use deadly force in situations that aren't life threatening (Liptak, 2006). Had William Masters lived in any of these places instead of Los Angeles, he wouldn't have even faced minor criminal charges; he would have simply been a citizen exercising his legal right.

If deviance is relative, then even acts of extreme violence may be defined as acceptable under certain circumstances. Killings committed under the auspices of the government—shooting looters during a riot, killing enemy soldiers during wartime, or executing convicted murderers—fall outside the category of behaviors deemed deviant and problematic in society. However, a relativist approach to defining deviance doesn't mean that we can't be upset by activities that some people consider acceptable:

> Relativity does not require moral indifference, and it does not mean that one can never be . . . horrified by what one experiences in another group or culture. . . . [It] just reminds us that our personal beliefs or our cultural understandings are not necessarily found everywhere. (Curra, 2000, p. 13)

Relativists, like absolutists, acknowledge that every society identifies certain individuals and certain behaviors as bothersome and disruptive and therefore as justifiable targets of social control, whether through treatment, punishment, spiritual healing, or correction. However, to a relativist, the main concerns in defining deviance are not so much what is committed but rather who commits the act, who labels it, and where and when it occurs. Some people have the wherewithal to avoid having their acts defined as deviant; others may fit a certain profile and be defined as deviant even if they've done nothing wrong. Definitions of deviant behavior change over time, and certain acts are acceptable to some groups and not others. The definitions most likely to persevere and become part of the dominant culture are those that have the support of influential segments of the population or have widespread agreement among the members of that society.

The Elements of Deviance

The two perspectives on defining deviance raise some complex and controversial issues. The definition of deviance that is most applicable to both perspectives is this: behavior (how people act), ideas (how people think), or attributes (how people appear) that some people in society—though not necessarily all people—find offensive, wrong, immoral, sinful, evil, strange, or disgusting.

This definition has three important elements (Aday, 1990):

- *Expectation:* Some sort of behavioral expectation must exist, a norm that defines appropriate, acceptable behavior, ideas, or characteristics. The expectations may be implicit or explicit, formal or informal, and more or less widely shared.

- *Violation:* Deviance implies some violation of normative expectations. The violation may be real or alleged; that is, an accusation of wrongdoing may be enough to give someone the reputation of being a deviant.

- *Reaction:* An individual, group, or society must react to the deviance. The reaction is likely to lead to some sort of response: avoidance, criticism, warnings, punishment, or treatment. The reaction may accurately reflect the facts, or it may bear little relation to what really happened, as when people are punished or ostracized for acts they did not commit.

Deviance, then, cannot exist if people don't have some idea of what's appropriate, if someone hasn't been perceived as or accused of violating some social norm, and if others haven't reacted to the alleged transgression.

EXPLAINING DEVIANT BEHAVIOR

The question of how certain acts and certain people come to be defined as deviant is different from the question of why people do or don't commit acts that are considered deviant. Psychological or biological theories addressing this question might focus on the personality or physical characteristics that give rise to deviant behavior, such as proneness to violence or addiction, genetic predispositions, chemical imbalances, or neurological defects. Most sociological theories, however, focus on the environmental forces that act on people and the effectiveness of various methods to control them.

The structural-functionalist perspective, for instance, tells us that it is in society's interest to socialize everyone to strive for success so that the most able and talented people will come to occupy the most important positions. Sociologist Robert Merton's

(1957) "strain theory" argues that the probability of committing deviant acts increases when people experience a strain or contradiction between these culturally defined success goals and access to legitimate means by which to achieve them. The despair and hopelessness that accompany sudden economic hardship can sometimes evoke anger and blame, leading to violence. For instance, some criminologists noted an unprecedented spike in mass murders during the economic recession of 2009. In the span of one month, there were eight mass murders that took the lives of 57 people (cited in Rucker, 2009).

More commonly, though, those who believe that being wealthy and achieving the "American dream" are important goals but have no money, employment opportunities, or access to higher education will be inclined to achieve the goal of success through illegitimate means (Merton, 1957). One of the most consistent findings in criminal research is the correlation between unemployment (a factor closely associated with economic disadvantage) and property crime (Hagan, 2000). In this sense, people who sell, say, illegal drugs or stolen cell phones to get rich are motivated by the same desire as people who sell real estate to get rich. But people who lack access to legitimate means to achieve success may also reject the culturally defined goal of success and retreat from society altogether. According to Merton, deviants such as vagrants, chronic drunks, drug addicts, and the mentally ill fall into this category.

Another sociologist, Edwin Sutherland, bases his theory of deviance (Sutherland & Cressey, 1955) on the symbolic-interactionist principle that we all interpret life through the symbols and meanings we learn in our interactions with others. Sutherland argues that individuals learn deviant patterns of behavior from the people with whom they associate on a regular basis: friends, family members, peers. Through our associations with these influential individuals, we learn not only the techniques for committing deviant acts (e.g., how to pick a lock or how to snort cocaine) but also a set of beliefs and attitudes that justify or rationalize such behavior (Sykes & Matza, 1957). To commit deviant acts on a regular basis, we must learn how to perceive those acts as normal.

Deterring Deviance

Some sociologists have turned away from the issue of why some people violate norms to the issue of why most people don't (see, e.g., Hirschi, 1969). Their concern is with the mechanisms society has in place to control or constrain people's behavior. ***Deterrence theory*** assumes that people are rational decision makers who calculate the potential costs and benefits of a behavior before they act. If the benefits of a deviant act (e.g., money or psychological satisfaction) outweigh the costs (e.g., getting caught and punished), we will be inclined to do it. Conversely, if the costs exceed the benefits, the theory predicts that we'll decide it's not worth the risk (van den Haag, 1975).

The controversy surrounding capital punishment is, essentially, a debate over its true capacity to deter potentially violent criminals. According to deterrence theory, a punishment, to be effective, must be swift as well as certain and severe. However, capital punishment is anything but swift. Currently, more than 3,200 inmates are on death row in the United States, but only 1,136 prisoners have been executed since 1977, when the death penalty was reinstated. On average, death row inmates spend almost 13 years awaiting execution, a figure that has been growing steadily for 3 decades (Snell, 2008).

In addition, opponents of the death penalty argue that violent offenders are often under the influence of drugs or alcohol or are consumed by passion when they commit an act of violence; their violence is more or less spontaneous. Hence, they may not be thinking rationally (weighing the potential benefits of the act against the costs of punishment) at the time of the crime. The threat of being condemned to death may not deter such people when they are committing the act. Researchers have, indeed, found little empirical support for the argument that the publicized threat of capital punishment reduces murders (Bailey, 1990; Galliher & Galliher, 2002). Nor have they found that well-publicized executions deter homicides (Peterson & Bailey, 1991). In fact, over the past several decades, the homicide rate in the 38 states with the death penalty has been 48% to 100% higher than in the 12 states without the death penalty (Bonner & Fessenden, 2000).

Most societies around the world have abandoned the use of capital punishment for both moral and practical reasons: It isn't humane, and it doesn't deter crime. Even in China, a country responsible for most of the world's court-ordered executions, legislators voted in 2006 to bar all but the nation's highest court from approving death sentences

("China Changes," 2006). Nevertheless, the majority of U.S. citizens—about 64% according to one recent study—continue to favor the death penalty (Pew Research Center, 2007b). Legislative efforts to increase the number of offenses punishable by death and to reduce the number of "death row" appeals an offender can file reflect this popular attitude. However, such a position can sometimes conflict with economic realities. During the recession of 2009, lawmakers in several states pushed bills to abolish the death penalty, not on moral grounds but to cut costs. Some have argued that capital punishment cases cost states nearly three times as much as homicide cases where the death penalty is not sought (Urbina, 2009).

Labeling Deviants

These theories help us explain why some people engage in deviant acts and others don't, but they bypass the question of why certain acts committed by certain people are considered deviant in the first place. ***Labeling theory*** attempts to answer this question by characterizing a deviant person as someone—such as the preschool teacher Kelly Michaels—to whom the label "deviant" has been successfully applied (Becker, 1963; Lemert, 1972). According to this theory, the process of being singled out, defined, and reacted to as deviant changes a person in the eyes of others and has important life consequences for the individual. Once the label sticks, others may react to the labeled deviant with rejection, suspicion, withdrawal, fear, mistrust, and hatred (Cohen, 1966). A deviant label suggests that the person holding it is habitually given to the types of undesirable motives and behavior thought to be typical of others so labeled. The "ex-convict" is seen as a cold-blooded and ruthless character incapable of reforming, the "mental patient" as dangerous and unpredictable, the "drug addict" as weak willed, the "prostitute" as dirty and immoral.

The problem, of course, is that such labels overgeneralize and can be misleading. For instance, a study by two marketing professors found that convicted felons showed just as much integrity as MBA students on a test of ethics related to difficult business situations. In fact, the convicts were less likely than the students to indicate that they'd steal employees from competitors or scrimp on customer service to increase profits ("MBA vs. Prison," 1999).

The type of deviant who receives the harshest expressions of public outrage changes with some regularity. At various points in time, child molesters, crack addicts, and drug dealers have claimed the title of society's most despised deviant. Currently, foreign terrorists and greedy Wall Street executives fit the bill. Often, collective hostility is directed toward people who don't seem to pose a grave societal threat, such as those who talk loudly on cell phones. Cigarette smoking used to be seen as a sign of sophistication; nowadays, many people consider smoking filthy and disgusting, and smokers are often banished from buildings and forced to keep their distance from entryways. Across the country, landlords of privately owned multiple housing units have begun to forbid smoking *inside* people's apartments.

Cities around the country sometimes use humiliating labels as an alternative to incarceration. For example, an Illinois man convicted of assault was once required to place a large sign at the end of his driveway that read "Warning: A Violent Felon Lives Here. Travel at Your Own Risk." In some states, convicted drunk drivers have to put special license plates on their cars, and convicted shoplifters must take out ads in local newspapers that use their photograph and announce their crimes. Such penalties are designed to shame the labeled individuals into behaving properly and to deter others from committing such crimes. In the process, they satisfy the public's need for dramatic moral condemnation of deviants (Hoffman, 1997).

Deviant labels can impair an individual's eligibility to enter a broad range of socially acceptable roles. Consider the impact of the 1994 Federal Crime Bill on convicted sex offenders. This law requires states to register and track convicted sex offenders for 10 years after their release from prison and to privately notify police departments when the sex offenders move into their community. A website, familysafetyguardian.com, provides information on released sexual offenders in all 50 states, including their names, addresses, and photographs. Many states have "sexually violent predator" statutes that give officials the power to commit violent sex offenders to mental hospitals involuntarily or to retain them in prison indefinitely *after* their prison terms are up (Goldberg, 2001). These convicts have "paid their debt" to society by serving their mandated prison sentence. But under these laws, convicted sex offenders can never fully shed their deviant identity. Finding a decent place to live or a decent job may be a problem for the rest of their lives.

All ex-offenders experience the "stickiness" of labels to some degree. Potential employers often refuse to hire ex-convicts, even when the crime has nothing to do with the job requirements. Like the public at large, many employers believe that prisons do not rehabilitate but actually make convicts more deviant by teaching them better ways to commit crime and by providing social networks for criminal activity outside the prison (Johnson, 1987). These suspicions can vary by race. A study of ex-offenders in New York found that white men with prison records receive far more job offers than black men with identical records (cited in von Zielbauer, 2005). In fact, other research has found that white ex-offenders are more likely to be hired than black men who have led law-abiding lives (Pager, 2003).

Deviant labels are so powerful that a mere accusation of dangerous activity can taint a person's character. In 2007, Andrew Speaker, in Rome for his honeymoon, learned he had an extreme form of tuberculosis (TB). Nevertheless, he flew to Montreal. When he attempted to return to the United States, he was quarantined by government officials, sparking a nationwide TB scare. A month later, he found out he wasn't infected after all. Yet even to this day, he occasionally gets e-mail death threats, and he and his wife have separated. His life has been so irreparably damaged that he has since sued the Centers for Disease Control and Prevention (CDC) for knowingly releasing false information about his medical history.

LINKING POWER, DEVIANCE, AND SOCIAL CONTROL

Because deviance is socially defined, the behaviors and conditions that come to be called "deviant" can at times appear somewhat arbitrary. Sociologists working from the conflict perspective would say that definitions of and responses to deviance are often a form of social control exerted by more powerful people and groups over less powerful people and groups. In U.S. society, the predominant means of controlling those whose behavior does not conform to the norms established by the powerful are criminalization and medicalization. Labeling people either as criminals or as sick people gives socially powerful individuals, groups, and organizations a way to marginalize and discount certain people who challenge the status quo. Criminalization and medicalization also have economic and other benefits for certain powerful groups.

The Criminalization of Deviance

Presumably, certain acts are defined as crimes because they offend the majority of people in a given society. Most of us trust our legal institutions—legislators, courts, the police, and prisons—to regulate social behavior in the interest of the common good. But according to the conflict perspective, most societies ensure that those offenders who are processed through the criminal justice system are members of the lowest socioeconomic class (Reiman, 2007). Poor people are more likely to get arrested, be formally charged with a crime, have their cases go to trial, get convicted, and receive harsher sentences than more affluent citizens (Parenti, 1995; Reiman, 2007). In 2002, 69 poor people in Atlanta who had been arrested on petty charges—shoplifting, trespassing, public drunkenness—and who couldn't afford bail remained in jail for weeks, and in some cases months, awaiting a lawyer and a court date, despite a law that requires anyone arrested for a misdemeanor to go before a judge or lawyer within 48 hours. All of them had spent more time behind bars than they would have had they been convicted (Rimer, 2002).

The quality of legal representation for defendants in criminal cases is also skewed along socioeconomic lines. When wealthy or powerful individuals are tried for capital crimes (an occurrence that, in and of itself, is rare), they are usually able to afford effective legal representation. In contrast, poor defendants in such cases are often represented by public defenders, who have fewer resources available for investigative work and who may have little, if any, experience in such matters. For instance, in one Alabama case, the public defender for a poor man facing the death penalty had never tried a capital case and had no money to hire an investigator before the case went to trial. The defendant was sentenced to death. In 2008, three North Carolina death row inmates were released in a span of 6 months because appeals courts found that evidence that would have favored the defendants was withheld during their trials. As one critic of capital punishment put it, "The problem with the death penalty [is] not the method of execution, but instead [is] poor people getting lousy lawyers" (quoted in Dewan, 2008, p. A1).

Cases like these have intensified the national debate over class—not to mention racial—disparities in the quality of legal representation. Ninety-eight percent of chief district attorneys in death penalty states are white; 1% are black. Since 1977, 15 white defendants have been executed for murdering black victims; during the same time period, 235 black defendants have been executed for killing white victims (Death Penalty Information Center, 2009).

Persistent imbalances in the justice system go beyond the way disadvantaged people are treated by the police, judges, attorneys, and juries. If these imbalances were simply a matter of discrimination, the situation would be relatively easy to address. Instead, they occur because the actions of poor individuals are more likely to be ***criminalized***—that is, officially defined as crimes in the first place. When poor people do commit certain crimes—car theft, burglary, assault, illegal drug use, and so on—they become "typical criminals" in the public eye (Reiman, 2007).

The Social Reality of Crime

Followers of the conflict perspective point out that powerful groups often try to foster a belief that society's rules are under attack by deviants and that official action against them is needed. The strategy has worked well. In polls taken in the United States in the 1980s and 1990s, an average of 83% of respondents felt that the justice system was not harsh enough in dealing with criminals (Gaubatz, 1995). Governments at the state and federal level responded to the popular sentiment by "getting tough on crime"—cracking down on drug users and dealers, reviving the death penalty, scaling back parole eligibility, lengthening prison sentences, and building more prisons. By 1999, 15 states had abolished parole boards and early-release programs, resulting in more prisoners serving their full sentences (Butterfield, 1999).

Not surprisingly, the inmate population in this country has swelled. According to the U.S. Justice Department, the number of prisoners has grown exponentially over the past several decades. In 1970, there were fewer than 200,000 people in state and federal prisons; by 2008, that figure had grown to more than 2.3 million (Sabol, Minton, & Harrison, 2007; West & Sabol, 2009). More than 7.2 million U.S. adults (or more than 3% of the adult population) are either on probation, in jail or prison, or on parole (U.S. Bureau of the Census, 2009), at a cost of close to $50 billion a year (Moore, 2009). No other country comes close to incarcerating as large a proportion of its population as the United States does (International Centre for Prison Studies, 2007).

But other problems have popped up. For instance, increasing rates of incarceration have been accompanied by heightened police surveillance and supervision in poor communities. The number of police per capita has increased dramatically in the past several decades (Goffman, 2009). Video cameras mounted on street lights and hovering police helicopters have become the ubiquitous markers of poor urban neighborhoods. As a consequence, a climate of fear and suspicion has gripped these communities. In such an environment, life for everyone is anxious and unsettled: "Family members and friends are pressured to inform on one another and young men live as suspects and fugitives, with the daily fear of confinement" (Goffman, 2009, p. 353).

Newly released inmates—who are likely to be poor and members of ethnoracial minorities—are also significantly less likely than their counterparts of 2 decades ago to find jobs and stay out of the kind of trouble that leads to further imprisonment (Butterfield, 2000). Many states have sharply curtailed education, job training, and other rehabilitation programs inside prison. In addition, parole officers are quicker to rescind a newly released inmate's parole for relatively minor infractions, such as failing a drug test. In California, for instance, four out of five former inmates who return to prison do so *not* for committing new crimes but for violating the conditions of their parole.

The question you might ask is, "Who benefits when it becomes so hard for ex-convicts to stay out of prison?" According to advocates of the conflict perspective, the law is not merely a mechanism that protects good people from bad people; it is a political instrument used by specific groups to further their own interests, often at the expense of others' (Chambliss, 1964; Quinney, 1970). Law is, of course, determined by legislative action. But legislatures are greatly influenced by powerful segments of society, such as lobbying groups, political action committees, individual campaign contributors, and so on.

Tellingly, the acts that threaten the economic or political interests of the groups that have the power to influence public policy are more likely to be criminalized (and more likely to be punished) than are the deviant acts these groups commit. For instance, it's against the law to fail to report income on one's annual tax return. But poor working people are far more likely to be audited by the Internal Revenue Service (IRS) than wealthy people (Johnston, 2002). That's not surprising, given that the IRS looks for tax cheating by wage earners much more closely than it does by corporations or by people whose money comes from their own businesses, investments, partnerships, and trusts.

Through the mass media, dominant groups influence the public to look at crime in ways that are favorable to them. The selective portrayal of crime plays an important role in shaping public perceptions of the "crime problem" and therefore its "official" definition. For instance, decades of research show that the crimes depicted on television are significantly more likely to be violent than actual crimes committed in the real world (cited in Reiman, 2007). When politicians talk about fighting the U.S. crime problem or when news shows report fluctuations in crime rates, they are almost always referring to street crimes (illegal drug use, robbery, burglary, murder, assault, etc.) rather than corporate crimes, governmental crimes, or crimes committed by people in influential positions.

Such coverage creates a way of perceiving crime that becomes social reality. We accept the "fact" that certain people or actions are a threat to the well-being of the entire society and therefore a threat to our own personal interests.

Corporate and White-Collar Crime

Consequently, people in the United States take for granted that street crime is our worst social problem and that corporate crime is not as dangerous or as costly (Reiman, 2007). U.S. citizens simply shake their heads over the exploitative practices of corporations or wealthy despots in places such as the rain forests of Brazil and Indonesia and the sweatshops of Southeast Asia. However, unsafe work conditions; dangerous chemicals in the air, water, and food; faulty products; and unnecessary surgery actually put people who live in the United States in more constant and imminent physical danger than do ordinary street crimes. A little more than 18,000 U.S. residents were murdered in 2005 (U.S. Bureau of the Census, 2009). At the same time, it's estimated that 56,000 U.S. workers die each year on the job or from occupational diseases such as black lung and asbestos. Hundreds of thousands more die from pollution, contaminated foods, hazardous consumer products, and hospital malpractice (Mokhiber, 1999). The CDC estimates that almost 100,000 people die each year from infections they contracted in hospitals or clinics (Klevens et al., 2007).

Corporate and white-collar crimes also pose greater economic threats to U.S. citizens than does street crime. The FBI estimates that burglary and robbery cost the United States $3.8 billion a year. The total cost of white-collar crimes such as corporate fraud, bribery, embezzlement, insurance fraud, and securities fraud amounts to perhaps as much as $500 billion a year (Reiman, 2007).

To be fair, some people actually do view certain types of corporate crime as more serious than street crimes (Mokhiber, 2000). Indeed, the financial crisis that first gripped the nation in 2008 created a firestorm of public anger that cast unprecedented scrutiny on white-collar misbehavior. Across the country, attorneys began to indict loan processors, mortgage brokers, and bank officials on various types of financial fraud. Congress and the Justice Department plotted strategies for an all-out federal attack. As one lawyer who represents white-collar clients put it, "It's going to be open season" on corporate officials (Segal, 2009, p. A19).

In a few high-profile cases, executives convicted of corporate malfeasance have actually received harsh prison sentences. In 2006, Jeffrey Skilling, former CEO of Enron, received a 24-year sentence for securities fraud and other crimes. Bernard Ebbers, mastermind of an $11 billion accounting fraud scheme at WorldCom, received a 25-year sentence. In 2009, a wealthy stockbroker and financial adviser named Bernard Madoff pled guilty to charges of securities fraud, investment fraud, mail fraud, wire fraud, money laundering, and theft from an employee benefit plan, to name a few. Prosecutors estimated that these schemes cost his clients about $65 billion. The judge called Madoff's actions "extraordinarily evil" and sentenced him to 150 years in prison, an act that was largely symbolic considering that Madoff was 71 years old at the time (Henriques, 2009).

But responses such as these have been directed largely at individual white-collar criminals. Corporations themselves rarely receive heavy criminal punishment when their dangerous actions violate the law (Reiman, 2007). For example, in 2004, the pharmaceutical company GlaxoSmithKline agreed to settle a $2.5 million lawsuit brought by the state of New York alleging that the company had hidden the results of drug trials showing that its antidepressant Paxil might have dangerous side effects, such as increasing suicidal thoughts in children.

At congressional hearings, lawmakers berated executives from GlaxoSmithKline and other drug companies for hiding study results that challenged the effectiveness of their drugs. The companies promised to do better. But according to studies financed by the National Institutes of Health, crucial facts about many clinical trials continue to be withheld from the Food and Drug Administration (cited in Berenson, 2005).

To ease the inconvenience of prosecution for corporate wrongdoers, the U.S. Justice Department has instituted a form of corporate probation. Several major companies that have been charged with billions of dollars worth of accounting fraud, bid rigging, and other illegal financial schemes—including American International Group, PNC Financial Services Group, Merrill Lynch, AOL-Time Warner, and American Express—have agreed to *deferred prosecutions,* in which they accept responsibility for wrongdoing, agree not to fight the charges, agree to cooperate, pay a fine, and implement changes in their corporate structure to prevent future criminal wrongdoing. If the company abides by the agreement for a specified period of time—usually 12 months—prosecutors will drop all charges (Mokhiber & Weissman, 2004). Between 2005 and 2008, the Justice Department made deferred prosecution agreements with more than 50 companies accused of wrongdoing (Lichtblau, 2008).

Such arrangements are meant to avoid more drastic punishment, which could destroy these companies and cost thousands of innocent employees their jobs. For instance, when the government aggressively prosecuted the Arthur Andersen accounting firm in 2002 for its criminal role in the famous Enron scandal, 28,000 employees lost their jobs (Lichtblau, 2008). But the penalties companies do receive are relatively minor and don't deter their future law violations. For instance, as punishment for its involvement in an illegal bid-rigging scheme for a NASA contract in 2006, Boeing was forced to pay a $615 million fine—a relatively small amount for a multibillion dollar company. The government agreed not to file any criminal charges because the company had cooperated with the investigation. It then went one step further and designated the fine as a "monetary penalty" rather than a "criminal penalty," thereby making the payment tax deductible (Mokhiber & Weissman, 2006). In 2009, UBS AG, Switzerland's largest bank, entered a deferred prosecution agreement on charges that it had helped U.S. taxpayers hide accounts from the IRS. In exchange for a dismissal of the charges, the bank agreed to pay $780 million in fines, penalties, interest, and restitution; acknowledge responsibility for its actions and omissions; and continue cooperating with Justice Department officials (U.S. Department of Justice, 2009). It's no wonder that many large corporations consider the punishments they receive for wrongdoing simply a cost of doing business.

The imbalance in the legal response to these crimes versus street crimes is glaring. If you were an individual thief who had robbed a bank at gunpoint, a shop owner who had defrauded your customers of millions of dollars, or a small businessperson who had knowingly manufactured a potentially lethal product, it's highly unlikely that you would be allowed to avoid any criminal prosecution simply by "cooperating with the investigation." Our massive law enforcement and criminal justice machinery would no doubt mobilize its vast resources to see that you were prosecuted to the fullest extent of the law. Yet large corporations engage in such activities every day, largely without much public outcry or moral panic. In fact, most aren't even prosecuted under criminal statutes. Between 1982 and 2002, about 170,000 American workers died on the job. During that same period, federal and state workplace safety agencies investigated 1,798 fatality cases in which companies had *willfully* violated workplace safety laws—for instance, by removing safety devices to speed up production, denying workers proper safety gear, or simply ignoring explicit safety warnings. But only 104 of these cases were ever prosecuted. And of those, only 16 resulted in criminal convictions (Barstow, 2003).

Why aren't these dangerous and costly corporate acts considered deviant the way face-to-face street crimes are? According to sociologist Jeffrey Reiman (2007), the answer resides in the perceived circumstances surrounding these acts. People typically see the injuries caused by corporate crime as unintentional, indirect, and a consequence of an endeavor defined in this culture as legitimate or socially productive: making a profit. In most people's minds, someone who tries to harm someone else is usually considered more evil than someone who harms without intending to. Moreover, harming someone directly seems more deviant than harming someone indirectly. Finally, harm that results from illegitimate activities is usually considered more serious than harm that is a byproduct of standard business activities.

The Menace of "Illegal" Drugs

Different cultures show varying levels of tolerance when it comes to drug use. For instance, throughout the South Pacific, people commonly chew betel nuts for their stimulant effects. In the Bolivian and Peruvian Andes, people chew coca leaves during their ordinary workday. The Huichol of Central Mexico ingest peyote—a small cactus that produces hallucinations—as part of their religious rituals. And in the United States, we wink at the use of many substances that alter people's state of mind, such as coffee, chocolate, and alcohol.

But when it comes to illegal drugs, U.S. attitudes change dramatically. Like the term *terrorist,* the term *drugs* is an easy and popular scapegoat on which to heap our collective hatred. The United States has been described as a *temperance culture* (Levine, 1992)—one in which self-control and industriousness are perceived as desirable characteristics of productive citizens. In such an environment, drug-induced states of altered consciousness are likely to be perceived as a loss of control and thus feared as a threat to the economic and physical well-being of the population.

The United States has been in an ill-defined, undeclared, but highly publicized "war" against illegal drugs for many years. The Drug Enforcement Administration, the FBI, and the U.S. Customs Service seized more than 3.6 million pounds of illegal drugs in 2007, five times as much as was seized in 1990 (U.S. Bureau of the Census, 2009). During that same period, the drug arrest rate increased from 435 people per 100,000 to about 600 per 100,000. More people are behind bars in the United States for drug offenses than are in prison for all crimes in England, France, Germany, and Japan combined (Egan, 1999). Federal spending on antidrug campaigns increased from $420 million in 1973 to $12.7 billion in 2006 (Katel, 2006).

With so much attention and resources now focused on homeland security and the threat of terrorism, it would seem that the fight against drug dealers and users could no longer be a national priority. Indeed, cuts in the federal budget have reduced the availability of resources devoted to drug enforcement, and some antidrug programs and agencies have been folded into antiterrorism efforts. Nevertheless, there remains a widespread belief that although terrorists pose an external danger, drug users and drug dealers are slowly destroying the country from within and therefore need to be stopped.

Many conflict sociologists, though, argue that antidrug campaigns and legislative activities are driven chiefly by political interests (see, e.g., Goode, 1989). The war on drugs in the United States has permitted greater social control over groups perceived to be threatening, such as young minority men, and has mobilized voter support for candidates who profess to be "tough" on drugs. Capitalizing on the "drug menace" as a personal and societal threat is a common and effective political tactic (Ben-Yehuda, 1990).

As with deviance in general, the very definition of which substances are "illegal" is influenced by powerful interests. Behind the phrase "war on drugs" is the assumption that illegal drugs (marijuana, ecstasy, cocaine, methamphetamines, heroin, etc.) are the most dangerous substances and the ones that must be eradicated. However, the difference between legal and illegal drugs is not necessarily a function of their relative danger.

For instance, each year, about 1,700 college students die from alcohol-related injuries, nearly 100,000 are victims of alcohol-related sexual assault and rape, 700,000 are assaulted by another student who has been drinking, and close to 3 million are cited for drunken driving (National Institute on Alcohol Abuse and Alcoholism, 2007). But alcohol is big business: Sales of alcoholic beverages topped $157 billion in 2006 (U.S. Bureau of the Census, 2009). Hence, efforts to completely criminalize it are few and far between. While most colleges now offer "alcohol-free" housing, encourage students to "drink responsibly," or sponsor alcohol-free social events, few have banned alcohol outright.

Tobacco is an even clearer health risk than alcohol—or marijuana and heroin for that matter

(Reiman, 2007). But aside from some age restrictions, it is legally available to anyone. According to the CDC (2008a), cigarette smoking is responsible for 1 in 5 deaths annually (or about 443,000 deaths a year). If those figures are accurate, more people die from smoking-related causes than from AIDS, illegal drug use, alcohol use, motor vehicle injuries, suicides, and murders combined. The costs of smoking are financial as well as physical. It's estimated that smoking costs the U.S. economy nearly $193 billion annually in both health care costs and lost productivity due to illness (American Lung Association, 2008).

In 2003, the U.S. Justice Department took the unprecedented step of demanding that the nation's biggest cigarette makers forfeit $289 billion in profits derived from more than 50 years of dangerous and "fraudulent" marketing practices, such as manipulating nicotine levels, lying to customers about the health effects of smoking, and directing advertising campaigns at children (Lichtblau, 2003). Yet knowing the hazards of selling and smoking cigarettes has not prompted our society to outlaw it entirely, as we have marijuana smoking and cocaine use. It's true that some states have enacted smoking bans in bars, restaurants, and other enclosed public places and some cities have banned outdoor smoking as well (Springen, 2006). And in 2009, President Obama signed into law the Family Smoking Prevention and Tobacco Control Act, which gives the FDA more power to impose stricter controls on the production and sale of cigarettes (Wilson, 2009b). But this bill stopped short of completely criminalizing tobacco, which would have had a disastrous impact on many large corporations and on several states whose economies depend on this crop. The tobacco industry has one of the most powerful lobbies in Washington. In fact, in 2005, the Justice Department decided to reduce the amount it sought in its case from $289 billion to a mere $10 billion, out of concern over the financial impact that the original amount would have on the tobacco companies (Leonnig, 2005).

The response to illegal drug users also shows how conceptions of deviance are socially constructed. Take, for instance, discrepancies in prison sentences for the possession and use of cocaine. Although the two types of cocaine—powdered and crack—cause similar physical reactions, the sentences for those convicted of selling them are vastly different. The average length of a sentence for selling less than 25 grams of crack cocaine is 65 months; for powdered cocaine, it is 14 months (Coyle, 2003). According to federal law, it would take 500 grams of powdered cocaine (or 5,000 doses) to draw the same mandatory minimum sentence of 5 years in prison that a person convicted of possessing 5 grams (or 10 doses) of crack cocaine would get (Greenhouse, 2007a).

Many law enforcement officials argue that the different levels of punishment are justified because crack cocaine is more closely associated with violence than powdered cocaine, it is more dangerous to the user, and it is more likely to cause birth defects in babies whose mothers use it while pregnant. However, a study of the physiological and psychoactive effects of different forms of cocaine found that they are so similar as to make the existing discrepancy in punishment "excessive." In addition, other research has found that the effects of crack use by pregnant women on fetuses are no different from those of tobacco or alcohol use (cited in Coyle, 2003).

Some sociologists argue that the problems associated with crack use have as much to do with poverty and race as with the drug itself. Harsh sentences for crack offenses have had a disproportionate effect on black and Latino men in poor urban areas, where crack is much more common than the powdered cocaine favored by white users. In 2000, 93% of those convicted of crack possession were black and Latino/a; only 6% were white. In contrast, 30.3% of those convicted of powdered cocaine possession were black, 18% were white, and 51% were Latino/a (though most of these individuals are white; Coyle, 2003). In 2009, the Judiciary Committee of the U.S. House of Representatives began hearings on the mandatory sentence disparity between crack and powdered cocaine.

Meanwhile, little has been accomplished in the way of stopping the illegal activities of the rich and powerful interests that participate in the drug industry. Established financial institutions often launder drug money, despite laws against it (Parenti, 1995). Massive international crime organizations that ensure the flow of illicit drugs into the country have grown bigger and richer, despite a decades-long attempt to stop them (Bullington, 1993). Unlike low-status users and small-time dealers of illegal drugs, these organizations wield tremendous economic power and political influence (Godson & Olson, 1995).

The Medicalization of Deviance

One of the most powerful forces in defining deviance in the United States today is the medical profession. Throughout the 20th century, the medical profession gained in prestige, influence, and authority. This professional dominance gave medicine jurisdiction over anything that could be designated "healthy" or "sick" (Conrad & Leiter, 2004). This trend, what sociologists call ***medicalization,*** is the process through which deviant behavior is defined as a medical problem or illness and the medical profession is mandated or licensed to provide some type of treatment for it (Conrad, 2005). Each time we automatically refer to troublesome behavior or people as "sick," we help perpetuate the perception that deviance is like an illness. Many physicians, psychologists, psychiatrists, therapists, and insurance agents, as well as the entire pharmaceutical industry in the United States, benefit from a medicalized view of certain deviant acts.

According to some, we're currently in the midst of an "epidemic of diagnoses" (Welch, Schwartz, & Woloshin, 2007), meaning that actions once categorized simply as misbehaviors or problems in living are being redefined as psychiatric diseases, disorders, or syndromes. Between 1952 and 2000, the number of mental disorders officially recognized by the American Psychiatric Association increased from 110 to close to 400 (Caplan, 1995; Horwitz, 2002). Many of these designations seem to have nothing to do with illness. Take for instance a malady called Conduct Disorder, a diagnosis restricted to children and adolescents. According to the American Psychiatric Association (2000), the "symptoms" of this disorder include bullying or threatening behavior toward others, physical cruelty, destruction of property, theft, and violations of other rules such as staying out late despite parental prohibition. In another era, this sort of misbehavior was called "juvenile delinquency."

To accommodate the growing number of "illnesses," the number of psychiatric professionals has almost tripled over the past 2 decades, as has the number of people seeking psychiatric help. The combined indirect and related costs of mental "illness" in this society, including lost productivity, lost earnings due to illness, and social costs, are estimated to be at least $193 billion annually (National Institute of Mental Health, 2008). According to the National Institute of Mental Health (2009), 26.2% of U.S. adults suffer from a diagnosable mental disorder. It also estimates that 55% of Americans will suffer from a diagnosable mental disorder sometime during their lifetime (cited in Carey, 2005a). Along with alcoholism, drug addiction, and serious mental illness, these disorders now include overeating, undereating, shyness, school stress, distress over a failed romance, poor performance in school, addiction to using the Internet, and excessive gambling, shopping, and sex.

For their part, drug companies sometimes create medicalized conceptions of deviance by marketing diseases and selling drugs to treat those diseases. In 1997, Congress passed the Food and Drug Administration Modernization Act, allowing drug companies to advertise directly to the public and create heightened demand for their products. Between 1996 and 2000, drug company spending on television advertising increased by 600%, to $2.5 billion, and it's been rising ever since. They now spend as much money on this direct-to-consumer advertising as they spend on advertising to physicians in medical journals (Conrad, 2005).

Why has the medical view of deviance become so dominant? One reason is that medical explanations of troublesome social problems and deviant behaviors are appealing to a society that wants simple explanations for complex social problems. If violent behavior is the result of a dysfunction in a person's brain, it then becomes a problem of defective, violent individuals, not of the larger societal context within which violent acts occur. Likewise, when our doctor or therapist tells us our anxiety, depression, crabbiness, and insecurity will vanish if we simply take a drug, we are spared the difficult task of looking at the social complexities of our lives or the structure of our society.

The medicalization of deviance also appeals to humanitarian values. The designation of a problem as an illness removes legal and moral scrutiny or punishment in favor of therapeutic treatment (Zola, 1986). The alcoholic is no longer a sinner or a criminal but a victim, someone whose behavior is an "illness," beyond his or her control. Children who have trouble learning in school aren't disobedient and disruptive, they are "sick." If people are violating norms because of a disease that has invaded their bodies, they should not be held morally responsible. Medicalization creates less social stigma and condemnation of people labeled deviant.

Despite its enormous public appeal, the tendency to medicalize deviance has serious social consequences (Conrad & Schneider, 1992). These include the individualization of complex social issues and the depoliticization of deviance.

Individualizing Complex Social Issues

Individualistic medical explanations of deviance are not necessarily wrong. Some violent people do have brain diseases, and some people diagnosed with clinical depression do have imbalances of chemicals in their brains. But when we focus exclusively on these explanations for everyone whose behavior diverges from social expectations, the solutions we seek focus on the perpetrator alone, to the exclusion of everything else.

Consider the problem of attention-deficit/hyperactivity disorder (ADHD), one of the most commonly diagnosed maladies among U.S. children today. A child diagnosed with ADHD is difficult to deal with at home and in the classroom. He or she fidgets and squirms, has difficulty remaining seated, can't sustain attention in tasks or play activities, can't follow rules, talks excessively, and is easily distracted (American Psychiatric Association, 2000).

Fifty years ago, such children were considered bad or troublesome and would have been subjected to punishment or even expulsion from school. Today, however, most hyperactive behavior is diagnosed as a symptom of a mental disorder, and drugs are prescribed to treat it. An estimated 4 million children in the United States are taking drugs to curb their overactivity or inattentiveness (President's Council on Bioethics, 2003). Between 2000 and 2003, spending for drugs used to treat ADHD increased 183% for all children and 369% for children under the age of 5 (AIS Health, 2004). The number of prescriptions for these drugs written for U.S. children is growing at a faster rate than for any other drug; more prescriptions are written for them than for antibiotics or asthma medication (Conrad, 2005).

This growth is part of an alarming trend toward the increased use of drugs for children in general (Safer, Zito, & dosReis, 2003). For instance, prescriptions for sleeping pills among children increased 85% between 2000 and 2004 (Harris, 2005b). Between one quarter and one half of all kids who attend summer camps take daily prescription medications (Gross, 2006). Critics worry not only about the safety of these drugs but also about the mixed messages children receive when they are handed a daily pill to medicate away their troublesome behavior while at the same time being told to say no to drugs (Koch, 1999).

Despite occasional adverse side effects, the drugs used to treat ADHD are generally successful in quieting unruly and annoying behavior (Whalen & Henker, 1977). But are we ignoring the possibility that hyperactive behavior may be a child's adaptation to his or her social environment? In some cases, it may be a response to an educational system that discourages individual expression (Conrad, 1975) or that expects more self-control from young children than they're capable of exercising (Duncan, 2007). Narrowly defined norms of acceptable behavior make it difficult if not impossible for children to pursue their own desires and needs. Some pediatricians argue that the symptoms of ADHD may just be children's natural reaction to living in a fast-paced, stressful world (Diller, 1998).

I'm not suggesting that all children who are diagnosed with ADHD are disruptive simply because they are bored in school or because their individual creativity and vitality have been squashed by unsympathetic teachers. Some children do have debilitating problems that require treatment. The point is that from an institutional perspective, the tendency to label disruptiveness as an individual disorder protects the school system's legitimacy and authority. The institution cannot function if disruptiveness is tolerated (Tobin, Wu, & Davidson, 1989). But imagine if our educational system promoted and encouraged free individual expression rather than obedience and discipline. In such an environment, overactivity wouldn't be considered disruptive and wouldn't be a problem in need of a medical solution.

When inconvenient behavior is translated into an individual sickness, medical remedies (usually drugs) become a convenient tool for enforcing conformity and upholding the values of society. When parents say they want "better children," they typically mean they want children who are in line with our culture's values: "well adjusted, well-behaved, sociable, attentive, high-performing, and academically adept" (President's Council on Bioethics, 2003, p. 73).

Parents who *don't* want their children to have these characteristics become objects of suspicion.

Depoliticizing Deviance

The process of individualizing and medicalizing social problems robs deviant behavior of its power to send a message about malfunctioning elements in society. Disruptive behaviors or statements automatically lose their power to prompt social change when they are seen simply as symptoms of individual defects or illnesses. We need not pay attention to the critical remarks of an opponent if that opponent is labeled as mentally ill. Totalitarian regimes often declare political dissidents insane and confine them to hospitals in an attempt to quiet dangerous political criticism. The Chinese government, for instance, has forcibly hospitalized and medicated hundreds of followers of the outlawed spiritual movement Falun Gong, which it has condemned as a dangerous cult (Eckholm, 2001). In 2007, a Russian activist was held in a psychiatric clinic for months after publishing an article detailing the harsh treatment of patients in the same hospital.

Such practices are not found only in foreign countries. In the early 1990s, a *Dallas Morning News* investigation discovered that high-ranking U.S. military commanders were trying to discredit and intimidate subordinates who reported security and safety violations or military overpricing by ordering them to undergo psychiatric evaluations or sending them to a mental ward (Timms & McGonigle, 1992). When a low-ranking naval officer reported that fellow sailors had raped three women while stationed in Bermuda, he was committed to a psychiatric hospital for a week (Zwerdling, 2004). A chief petty officer in the Air Force contended that his forced hospitalization was part of retaliation for reporting payroll abuses at Dallas Naval Air Station. He insightfully describes the power of medical labels to discredit his political criticism: "What happened was nobody would speak to me. Let's face it. After someone has gone to a mental ward, you kind of question what's going on. It was a nice ploy, and it worked. What they did was totally neutralize me" (quoted in Timms & McGonigle, 1992, p. F1).

Creating the image of deviants as sick people who must be dealt with through medical therapies is a powerful way for dominant groups in society to maintain conformity and protect themselves from those whom they fear or who challenge the way "normal" social life is organized (Pfohl, 1994). The seemingly merciful medical labels not only reduce individual responsibility but also reduce the likelihood that such potentially contagious political criticism will be taken seriously (Hills, 1980).

CONCLUSION

When we talk about deviance, we usually speak of extreme forms: crime, mental illness, substance abuse, and so on. These activities are indeed troublesome, but for most people, they remain comfortably distant phenomena. I think most of us would like to cling to the belief that deviants are "them" and normal people are "us."

The lesson I hope you take away from this chapter, however, is that the issue of deviance is, essentially, an issue of social definition. As a group, community, or society, we decide which differences are benign and which are dangerous. Standards and expectations change. Norms come and go. The consequence is that each of us could be considered deviant to some degree by some audience. We have all broken unspoken interactional norms; many of us have even broken the law. To a lesser degree, we are all potentially like Kelly Michaels, subject to being erroneously labeled deviant and unfairly treated as a result. Given the right—or wrong—circumstances, all of us risk being negatively labeled or acquiring a bad reputation.

This chapter has examined deviance as both a microlevel and a macrolevel sociological phenomenon, as something that plays a profound role in individual lives and in society as a whole. Although sociologists are interested in the broad social and political processes that create cultural definitions of deviance, they are also interested in the ways these definitions are applied in everyday life. Societal definitions have their most potent effect when expressed face-to-face. We can talk about powerful institutions such as medicine creating definitions of deviance that are consistent with broader political or economic interests, but if these definitions aren't accepted as appropriate to some degree by the majority, they will be ineffectual. Again, we see the value of developing the sociological imagination, which helps us understand the complex interplay between individuals and the culture and community within which they live.

CHAPTER HIGHLIGHTS

◆ According to an absolutist definition of deviance, there are two fundamental types of behavior: that which is inherently acceptable and that which is inherently unacceptable. In contrast, a relativist definition of deviance suggests that it is not a property inherent in any particular act, belief, or condition. Instead, deviance is a definition of behavior that is socially created by collective human judgments. Hence, like beauty, deviance is in the eye of the beholder.

◆ The labeling theory of deviance argues that deviance is a consequence of the application of rules and sanctions to an offender. Deviant labels can impede individuals' everyday social lives by forming expectations of them in the minds of others.

◆ According to conflict theory, the definition of deviance is a form of social control exerted by more powerful people and groups over less powerful ones.

◆ The criminal justice system and the medical profession have had a great deal of influence in defining, explaining, and controlling deviant behavior. Criminalization is the process by which certain behaviors come to be defined as crimes. Medicalization is the depiction of deviance as a medical problem or illness.

KEY TERMS

absolutism Approach to defining deviance that rests on the assumption that all human behavior can be considered either inherently good or inherently bad

criminalization Official definition of an act of deviance as a crime

deterrence theory Theory of deviance positing that people will be prevented from engaging in deviant acts if they judge the costs of such an act to outweigh its benefits

deviance Behavior, ideas, or attributes of an individual or group that some people in society find offensive

labeling theory Theory stating that deviance is the consequence of the application of rules and sanctions to an offender; a deviant is an individual to whom the identity "deviant" has been successfully applied

medicalization Definition of behavior as a medical problem, mandating the medical profession to provide some kind of treatment for it

relativism Approach to defining deviance that rests on the assumption that deviance is socially created by collective human judgments and ideas

PART III

Social Structure, Institutions, and Everyday Life

Up to this point, I have been discussing how our everyday lives are constructed and ordered. But this is only part of the picture. What does social life look like from the top down? Once the architecture is constructed and in place, what influence does it exert on our everyday lives? To answer these questions, the remaining chapters investigate the organizational and institutional pressures on everyday life and the various sources of structural inequality in society: social class and wealth, race and ethnicity, and gender. Global institutions and population trends are other structural influences on everyday life. These facets of society may seem ominous and impenetrable. However, you will see that our lives don't completely fall under the control of the social structure. As the concept of the sociological imagination suggests, the collective actions of individuals often bring about fundamental changes in society.

©PATRICK BAZ/AFP/Getty Images

9 The Structure of Society

Organizations, Social Institutions, and Globalization

History will no doubt mark the 2000 U.S. presidential election as one of the most bizarre political events of all time. The chaos began on election night. Early in the evening, Al Gore, the Democratic candidate, was projected as the winner of Florida's 25 electoral votes, giving him the inside track to the presidency; a few hours later, that projection was rescinded, and Florida was labeled "too close to call." In the early morning hours of the following day, George W. Bush, the Republican candidate, was projected as the winner of Florida, and therefore the election, only to have that projection withdrawn when Florida, again, was declared "too close to call." The ensuing month brought a daily dose of street protests, charges of voter fraud, recounts, debates over absentee votes, lawsuits, countersuits, and legal rulings. On November 26th, the Florida State canvassing board certified that George Bush was the winner. The Florida Supreme Court overruled and ordered another recount. But on December 13, the U.S. Supreme Court issued its definitive ruling, on a 5–4 vote, that the Florida recount was unconstitutional. George W. Bush was thus declared the next president of the United States, even though he had received more than 500,000 fewer votes nationwide than his challenger.

To listen to the domestic and foreign news media describe it at the time, the most powerful country in the world was in a state of utter political confusion. The situation was described in either mocking or apocalyptic terms. U.S. citizens were losing their moral authority to lecture other countries about the virtues of democracy. We were about to face a "constitutional crisis." We were going to be a country without a leader. We were on the brink of anarchy.

Of course, none of that happened. As one journalist put it, "The apparatus of government is still in place, skilled politicians and career civil servants still keep things running, and ultimately nothing apocalyptic is likely to happen. . . . The system will work and life will go on" (Belluck, 2001, p. A9). Indeed, for the average U.S. citizen, nothing really changed during the electoral confusion. Buses, trains, and planes still ran on time. Food was still delivered to grocery store shelves. Government services were still provided. Even the stock market remained solid. We all simply went about our business, pausing now and then to witness the political spectacle or to debate with friends, family, and coworkers.

Why didn't the country collapse during this electoral epic? To answer that question, we must turn to one of the key concepts of this book: social structure. Despite strong emotions, dire predictions, and confrontational behavior, the political system remained intact. Whether we agreed with the ultimate outcome of that election or not, our legal and political institutions worked as they were designed to. From local precincts and campaign organizations to state legislatures to the highest court in the land, the system continued to function. To be sure, the motives of some of the individual players were highly partisan. But the structure itself rose above the actions of these individuals and prevented the sort of large-scale catastrophe that media pundits predicted. One of the great sociological paradoxes of human existence is that we are capable of producing a social structure that we then experience as something other than a human product. It is ironic that we spend most of our lives either within or responding to the influence of larger structural entities—particularly in a society such as the United States, which so fiercely extols the virtues of rugged individualism and personal accomplishment.

This chapter focuses on our relationship with the social structure we construct and maintain, both locally and globally. This focus requires us to examine the structure not only from the individual's perspective but also from the macrosociological perspective of the organizations and institutions themselves. Many important social issues look quite different depending on the perspective we use to understand them.

SOCIAL STRUCTURE AND EVERYDAY LIFE

As you recall from Chapter 2, ***social structure*** is the framework of society that exists above the level of individuals and provides the social setting in which individuals interact with one another to form relationships. It includes the organizations, groups, statuses and roles, cultural beliefs, and institutions that add order and predictability to our lives. The concept of social structure is important because it implies a patterned regularity in the way we live and in the way societies work. We could not draw any meaningful conclusions about human behavior if we started with the notion that society is haphazard and that things occur by chance alone.

If you know what to look for, you can see social structure everywhere. Consider, for instance, the components of social structure that affect the experience of going to high school. Within this broad U.S. educational institution, there are examples of every component of social structure:

- *Organizations:* National Education Association, state teachers' associations, accrediting agencies, local school boards, and so on
- *Groups:* faculty, administrators, students, classes, clubs, cafeteria staff, and so on
- *Statuses:* teacher, student, principal, nurse, custodian, coach, librarian, and so on
- *Role expectations:* teaching, learning, disciplining, making and taking tests, coaching, and so on
- *Cultural beliefs:* for example, the belief that education is the principal means of achieving financial success, that it makes possible a complex division of labor, and that it makes a technologically advanced society possible
- *Institutionalized norms:* for example, the expectation that everyone attend school until at least the age of 16, school rules that determine acceptable behavior (not running in the halls, not screaming in class, staying on the school grounds until classes are over) (Saunders, 1991)

The massive structure of the educational system is a reality that determines life chances and choices. You can choose which science class to take in high school, whether to go on to college, and what to major in once you get there, but the admissions policies of potential colleges and the availability of jobs to people with and without a college degree are factors beyond your control. You're reading this book right now not because of your fondness for fine literature but because of the structural requirements of being a college student. You know you must graduate to increase your chances of getting a good job, and to graduate you must get good grades in your classes. To get good grades in your classes, you must keep up with the material so you're prepared for exams. You probably would rather be doing a number of other things right now—reading a better book, making love, watching TV, texting a friend, sleeping, staring into space—but personal preferences must take a back seat for the time being to the more immediate structural demands of college life.

The structural requirements of the educational system have a broader impact as well. Course grades, standardized test scores, and class rankings are emphasized so much and create such personal anxiety for students that they may actually overshadow learning and intellectual growth.

A competitive educational atmosphere can also create incompatibility between the needs of the individual student and the needs of the system. Suppose your sociology instructor told you that she was going to give everyone in the class an "A" as long as they showed up each day. Your immediate reaction might be joy, because such a grade would no doubt improve your grade point average (GPA). But what if all instructors in all courses at your school decided to do the same thing? Everybody who simply showed up for class would graduate with a perfect GPA. How would you feel then? Your joy might be tempered by the knowledge that the reputation of your school would suffer. As long as our educational system is structured on the principle of "survival of the fittest"—the assumption that only the smartest or hardest-working students earn the top grades—such changes would be perceived by others as a sign that your school is academically inferior. Hence, your long-term personal interests may actually be best served by a highly competitive system that ensures that some of your fellow students will get lower grades than you.

Structural factors can also sometimes overwhelm individuals' best efforts to exercise their will. Take, for example, the tsunami disaster of 2004, which killed more than 200,000 people in South Asia and eastern Africa and left millions homeless. Millions of ordinary people around the world pledged to help the victims, alongside promises of billions of dollars in aid and military assistance made by 19 nations. Close to 30% of U.S. citizens donated money to the cause, and another 37% indicated that they intended to do so (Lester, 2005). Two weeks after the disaster, the charitable organization "Save the Children" had received more than $10 million in donations over the Internet alone. In a typical month, the organization receives between $30,000 and $50,000 (Strom, 2005).

But such dramatic individual benevolence was hobbled and almost crushed at the organizational level. When two dozen government and aid organizations arrived in the hardest-hit regions of Indonesia a week or two after the tsunami hit, they found that looters and black market traders had already descended on the wreckage. Some devastated areas had yet to see any relief workers, while others were swarming with doctors and nurses. Moreover, the presence of foreign military and relief workers soon created resentment in the Indonesian government. In response, it imposed travel restrictions on foreign aid workers, citing security concerns, and demanded that all foreign military personnel leave the country within 3 months. In one of the hardest-hit areas, Banda Aceh, relief organizations found themselves in the middle of a civil war, operating alongside paramilitary rebels (officially regarded as terrorists by the U.S. government) and an Indonesian military known for its corruption and rights abuses (Wehrfritz & Cochrane, 2005). Despite the presence of thousands of caring and generous individuals who came to help, these structural factors conspired to slow down the relief process.

Even when it's operating as it's designed to, social structure can cause problems. Mistakes are sometimes the end result of a chain of events set in motion by a system that either induces errors or makes them difficult to detect and correct. For instance, an annual study of patient safety in U.S. hospitals estimates that between 2005 and 2007, there were more than 900,000 safety incidents and close to 100,000 preventable deaths attributable to medical errors such as anesthesia complications, infections due to medical care, accidental lacerations, and various other postoperative complications. These incidents resulted in nearly $7 billion in excess medical costs (Health Grades, 2009). Another study found that one in five Medicare patients ends up back in the hospital within a month of being discharged and more than half return within a year. The annual cost of these unplanned readmissions is more than $17 billion (Jencks, Williams, & Coleman, 2009).

The tendency to sue individual doctors or nurses for malpractice in such cases demonstrates an overwhelming cultural perception that these errors are caused by individual incompetence.

But what appear to be obvious errors in human judgment are often, on closer inspection, linked to broader structural failures. Up to a quarter of unanticipated injuries and deaths among hospital patients occur because of a systemwide shortage of nurses (Health Resources and Services Administration, 2005). In 2005, 10% of nursing positions were unfilled. That figure is expected to grow to 27% by 2015 and to 36% by 2020 (Health Resources and Services Administration, 2004). The problem is not solely one of too few staff. An analysis of 334 drug errors in hospitals found that structural failure was responsible for most of them—for example, poor dissemination of drug knowledge to doctors, inadequate availability of patient information, faulty systems for checking correct dosage, and inefficient hospital procedure (Leape & Bates, 1995).

More than a decade ago, a report by the Institute of Medicine (1999) recognized that the problem of unnecessary hospital injuries and deaths lies beyond the actions of individual health care workers. It recommended that the health care system build safety concerns into its operations at all levels. It suggested creating a national center for patient safety, establishing a mandatory nationwide reporting system, placing greater emphasis on safety and training in licensing and accreditation evaluations, and developing a "culture of safety" that would help make the reduction of medical errors a top professional priority.

To date, however, the United States, unlike some European countries, has no federal agency charged with hospital oversight. Instead, responsibility for protecting the health and safety of hospital patients lies with a patchwork of state health departments and a nonprofit group called the Joint Commission on Accreditation of Hospitals, which sets quality standards. As a result, bad hospitals are rarely closed and are seldom hit with significant financial penalties for patient suffering (Berenson, 2008).

SOCIAL DILEMMAS: INDIVIDUAL INTERESTS AND STRUCTURAL NEEDS

Although social structure can clearly affect the lives of individuals, individual actions can also have an enormous effect on social structure and stability. Sometimes those actions are coordinated to benefit a collection of individuals, and sometimes they're undertaken independently and for personal gain. Let's say a group of residents want to make sure that their neighborhood is free of crime. Each individual could go on a personal crusade to stop crime, but it seems more logical and efficient for everyone to volunteer at some point to "patrol" at night or to chip in money to improve street lighting.

In actuality, though, people seldom voluntarily act to achieve a common objective unless forced to do so. Instead, they usually act to ensure their own personal interests (Cross & Guyer, 1980; Dawes & Messick, 2000; Olsen, 1965). Say that your neighbors decide to fight crime by improving street lighting. They ask people in the community for voluntary donations. Some may decide that the rational thing to do is not to donate money for a new streetlight because they figure others will do so. That way, they could enjoy the benefits of safer streets without spending their own money. But if every person individually decides not to donate, they may save some cash in the short run, but the new streetlight will never be purchased, and everyone will suffer in the long run. The experience of each person in a group pursuing his or her self-interest regardless of the potential ruin for everyone is known as a ***social dilemma*** (Messick & Brewer, 1983).

Major social problems, such as environmental pollution, can be understood as stemming, at least in part, from social dilemmas. If I fling one bag of trash out my car window and onto the highway, it won't seem significant or destructive. Large numbers of people doing the same thing, though, would be very destructive. If we think of nations as individual actors and the planet as the community to which they belong, many problems that have global significance—including energy shortages, massive climate change, and species extinction—can be understood from this perspective. Two important types of social dilemmas, at both the local level and broader levels, are the tragedy of the commons and the free-rider problem.

The Tragedy of the Commons

The term *commons* was originally used to describe the public pasture ground, often located in the center of medieval towns, where all the local herders could bring their animals to graze. When villagers used the commons in moderation, the grass could regenerate, resulting in a perpetual supply of food for the herds (Hardin & Baden, 1977). However, each herder soon realized that he or she could benefit individually by letting the animals eat as much as they wanted, thereby increasing their size and the price they could fetch at market. Unfortunately, when many of the herders came to this same conclusion and allowed their herds to eat without limit, the grass in the commons could not regenerate fast enough to feed them all. The tragic result was that the commons collapsed and the herds that grazed on it died or were sold off. The short-term needs of the individual overshadowed the long-term collective needs of the group.

In this illustration, the common resource was grazing land, and the group was relatively small. However, the ***tragedy of the commons*** model can be applied to any situation in which indispensable but finite resources are available to everyone. For example, during periods of extremely hot temperatures, people increase their use of fans and air conditioners. Such heightened energy demand can sometimes overwhelm power companies, resulting in isolated or total electrical outages, which hurts everyone.

The impulse to seek individual gain over the collective good becomes particularly tempting when personal well-being is at stake. In the flood-prone summer of 1993, a river overflowed its banks in Des Moines, Iowa, wiping out a filtration system and making the municipal water supply unsafe. To restore full water service, the system had to be refilled with clean water. The situation was urgent. Without full water pressure in the city's water pipes, not only were the residents without regular water service, but fire engines also couldn't use the hydrants. Local officials asked everyone to voluntarily refrain from using tap water in their homes and businesses for a few days. If all the city's residents had complied, everyone in the community would have had water within a couple of days. For some individuals, however, the temptation to use water secretly in the privacy of their own homes was too hard to resist. So many residents violated the city's request that the resumption of full water service had to be delayed for many more days (Bradsher, 1993). The entire community suffered as a result of individuals seeking their own short-term benefits.

Why do such dilemmas occur? Part of the problem is lack of communication and lack of trust among individual members of a community. I may want to be a good citizen and conserve water by using it sparingly, but if I think my neighbors are hoarding it, I too will hoard it to make sure I don't go without. Hence, I may follow a line of action that results in a positive outcome for me but that may eventually have a negative outcome for the community.

The problem is made worse when individuals think that meeting their individual needs won't have a noticeable effect on the community. "Is my using an extra gallon of water during a drought *really* going to harm the community?" The tragedy of the commons arises when everyone, or at least a substantial number of people, concludes that it will not. As we collectively ignore or downplay the consequences of our actions, we collectively overuse the resource and pave the way for disasters that none of us has caused individually (Edney, 1979).

The Free-Rider Problem

Social dilemmas can also occur when people refrain from contributing something to a common resource because the resource is available regardless of their contribution. Why pay for something that's available for free? For example, it is irrational, from an individual's point of view, to donate money to public television. I can enjoy *Sesame Street, Nova,* and *Frontline* without paying a penny. My small personal donation wouldn't be more than a tiny drop in public television's budgetary bucket anyway. I have no incentive to incur any costs when I don't have to. If everyone acted this way, however, we would all eventually lose the resource. If public television depended solely on voluntary donations made during those annoying fund drives—corporate grants and sponsorships actually keep it going—it would have disappeared a long time ago.

Sociologists sometimes refer to this situation as the ***free-rider problem*** (Olsen, 1965). As the term implies, a free rider is an individual who acquires a good or service without risking any personal costs or contributing anything in return. Free-rider behavior can be seen in a variety of everyday activities, from reading a magazine at a newsstand without buying it to downloading music files for free from other people's online collections. We all enjoy the benefits our tax dollars provide—police, firefighters, smooth roads, and many other municipal services. But if taxes were voluntary, would anyone willingly pay for these services?

We can see evidence of the free-rider problem at the institutional level. People often talk about children as a vital resource on whom the future of the country and the planet depend. The care and education of all children can be seen as a public resource. The whole society benefits when our children are well educated and in good physical and psychological health. Yet taxpayers—especially those without children—often protest against tax increases to improve schools, raise teachers' salaries, or hire more youth social workers, because they fail to see how such increases will benefit them personally in the long run.

THE STRUCTURE OF FORMAL ORGANIZATIONS

Social life has far more complex functions than simply trying to balance individual and collective interests. Those of us who live in a complex society are all, to varying degrees, organizational creatures. We're born in formal organizations, educated in them, spend most of our adult lives working for them, and will most likely die in them (Gross & Etzioni, 1985). Organizations help meet our most basic needs.

Think about the food on your dinner plate. The farm where the food is produced is probably a huge organization, as are the unions that protect the workers who produce the food and the trucking companies that bring it to your local stores. And all this is controlled by a vast network of financial organizations that set prices and by governmental agencies that ensure the food's safety.

To prepare the food that is produced, delivered, and sold, you have to use products made by other organizations—a sink, a refrigerator, a microwave, a stove. To use those appliances, you have to make arrangements with organizations such as the water and power departments, the gas company, and the electric company. And to pay these bills, you must use still other organizations—the postal service, your Internet provider, your bank, credit companies, and so on.

Most likely, the money to pay the bills comes from a job someone in your household has. If you are employed, you probably work for yet another organization. And when you receive a paycheck, the Internal Revenue Service steps in to take its share.

What about the car you use to get to that job? No doubt a huge, multinational corporation manufactured it. Such corporations also produced and delivered the fuel on which the car runs. The roads you travel on to get to your destinations are built and maintained by massive organizations within the state and federal governments. You aren't even allowed to drive unless you are covered by insurance, which is available only through an authorized organization.

And what if things aren't going well? If you become sick, have an accident, or have a dispute with someone, you have to use organizations such as hospitals, police departments, and courts.

You get the picture? Life in a complex society is a life touched by public and private organizations at every turn. In such a society, things must be done in a formal, planned, and unified way. For instance, the people responsible for producing our food can't informally and spontaneously make decisions about what to grow and when to grow it, and the people responsible for selling it to us can't make its availability random and unpredictable. Imagine what a mess your life would be if you didn't know when your local supermarket would be open or what sorts of food would be available for purchase. What if one day it sold nothing but elbow macaroni, the next day only bell peppers, and the day after that just peach yogurt?

In a small-scale community where people grow their own food and the local mom-and-pop store provides everything else, the lack of structure might not be a problem. But this type of informal arrangement can't work in a massive society. There must be a relatively efficient and predictable system of providing goods and services to large numbers of people. The tasks that need to be carried out just to keep that system going are too complex for a single person to manage. This complexity makes bureaucracy necessary.

Bureaucracies: Playing by the Rules

The famous 19th-century sociologist Max Weber (VAY-ber) was vitally interested in understanding the complexities of modern society. He noted that human beings could not accomplish feats such as building cities, running huge enterprises, and governing large and diverse populations without bureaucracies. Bureaucracies were certainly an efficient and rational means of managing large groups of people, although Weber acknowledged that these qualities could easily dehumanize those who work in and are served by these organizations.

Today we tend to see bureaucracies primarily as impersonal, rigid machines that trespass into our personal lives. Bureaucracies conjure up images of rows of desks occupied by faceless workers, endless lines and forms to fill out, and frustration over "red tape" and senseless policies. Indeed, the word *bureaucrat* has taken on such a negative connotation that to be called one is an insult. Keep in mind, however, that in a sociological sense, ***bureaucracy*** is simply a large hierarchical organization that is governed by formal rules and regulations and that has a clear specification of work tasks.

This specific type of organization has three important characteristics:

Division of labor: The bureaucracy has a clear-cut ***division of labor,*** which is carefully specified by written job descriptions for each position. Theoretically, a clear division of labor is efficient because it employs only specialized experts, with every one of them responsible only for the effective performance of her or his narrowly defined duties (Blau & Meyer, 1987). Division of labor enables large organizations to accomplish more ambitious goals than would be possible if everyone acted independently. Tasks become highly specific, sometimes to the point that it is illegal to perform someone else's task. In hospitals, for instance, orderlies don't prescribe drugs, nurses don't perform surgery, and doctors don't help patients fill out their insurance forms.

Hierarchy of authority: Not only are tasks divided in a bureaucracy, but they are also ranked in a ***hierarchy of authority*** (Weber, 1946). Most U.S. bureaucracies are organized in a pyramid shape with a small number of people at the top who have a lot of power and many at the bottom who have virtually none. In such a chain of command, people at one level are responsible to those above them and can exert authority over those below. Authority tends to be attached to the position and not to the person occupying the position so that the bureaucracy will not stop functioning in the event of a retirement or a death. The hierarchy of authority in bureaucracies not only allows some people to control others, it also justifies paying some people higher salaries than others. When applied to political organizations, the hierarchy of authority can create an ***oligarchy,*** a system in which many people are ruled by a privileged few (Michels, 1911/1949). In such a setting, leaders can often distance themselves from the public, becoming less accountable for their actions in the process.

Impersonality: Bureaucracies are governed by an elaborate system of rules and regulations that ensure a particular task will be done the same way by each person occupying a position. Rules help ensure that bureaucrats perform their tasks impartially and impersonally. Ironically, the very factors that make the typical bureaucrat unpopular with the public—an aloof attitude, lack of genuine concern—actually allow the organization to run more efficiently. We may want the person administering our driver's license examination to care about us, but think of how you'd feel if the examiner had decided to stop for a bite to eat with the person who was taking the driver's test before you.

Your university is a clear example of a bureaucratic organization. It has a definite division of labor that involves janitors, secretaries, librarians, coaches, professors, administrators, trustees, and students. The tasks that people are responsible for are highly specialized. Professors in the Spanish department don't teach courses in biology. In large universities, the specialization of tasks is even more narrowly defined. Sociology professors who teach criminology probably don't teach courses on family.

Although the power afforded different positions varies from school to school, all universities have some sort of hierarchy of authority. Usually, this hierarchy consists of janitors, groundskeepers, and food service workers at the bottom, followed by students, staff employees, teaching assistants, part-time instructors, professors, and department chairs. At the administrative level are associate deans, deans, vice presidents, and ultimately the president of the university and the board of trustees.

In addition, universities are governed by strict and sometimes exasperating sets of bureaucratic rules. There are rules regarding when students can register for classes and when grades must be turned in by professors, graduation requirements, and behavioral policies. Strict adherence by university employees to these rules and policies is likely to give universities their final characteristic: impersonality.

As people are fitted into roles within bureaucracies that completely determine their duties, responsibilities, and rights, they often become rigid and inflexible and are less concerned with the quality of their work than with whether they and others are playing by the rules. Hence, people become oriented more toward conformity than toward problem solving and critical thinking. They are the source of frustrating procedures and practices that often seem designed not to permit but to prevent things from happening (Morgan, 1986).

Although he stressed the functional necessity of bureaucracies in complex Western societies, Weber (1947) warned that they could take on a life of their own, becoming impersonal "iron cages" for those within them. He feared that bureaucracies might one day dominate every part of society, locking people in a system that allows movement only from one dehumanizing bureaucracy to another. Weber's fears have been largely realized. The bureaucratic model pervades every corner of modern society. The most successful bureaucracies not only dominate the business landscape but have come to influence our entire way of life.

The Construction of Organizational Reality

According to the symbolic-interactionist perspective, organizations are created, maintained, and changed through the everyday actions of their members (Morgan, 1986). The language of an organization is one of the ways it creates its own reality. At one level, new members must learn the jargon of the organization to survive within it. To function within the military system, for example, a recruit must learn the meaning of a dizzying array of words, phrases, acronyms, slang, sounds, and symbols that are unintelligible to outsiders (Evered, 1983). More importantly, language helps generate and maintain the organization by marking boundaries between insiders and outsiders.

For an organization to work well, everyone must also internalize the same rules, values, and beliefs. But people still have their own ideas and may develop their own informal structure within the larger formal structure of the organization (Meyer & Rowan, 1977). For example, many college instructors tell their students that class discussion is important and that they may use it as a criterion for assigning a final grade. Yet rarely does every student in a class, or even a majority of students, participate. Most college students know that a few classmates can usually be counted on to respond to questions asked by the professor or to comment on any issue raised in class. These students relieve the remainder of the class from the burden of having to talk at all (Karp & Yoels, 1976). But although these talkative students are carrying the discussion for the entire class, they tend to be disliked by others. A strong norm among many students is that people shouldn't talk too much in class (Karp & Yoels, 1976). Students who speak up all the time upset the normative arrangement of the classroom and, in the students' eyes, may increase the instructor's expectations, hurting everyone in the long run. Other students indicate their annoyance by audibly sighing, rolling their eyes, or openly snickering when a classmate talks too much.

One of the ironies of large complex organizations is that if everyone followed every rule exactly and literally, the organization would eventually self-destruct. For example, the goal of the highly bureaucratized criminal court system is to ensure justice by punishing those who have violated society's laws. The U.S. Constitution guarantees each person accused of committing a serious crime a timely trial by a jury of peers. However, public defenders, district attorneys, private attorneys, and judges actually work closely together to bypass the courtroom and move offenders through the system in an orderly fashion (Sudnow, 1965). In 2008, only 3.7% of federal convictions resulted from court trials (U.S. Sentencing Commission, 2008).

If judges and attorneys followed the procedural rules to the letter and provided all their clients with the jury trial that is their constitutional right, the system would break down. The courts, already overtaxed, would be incapable of handling the volume of cases. Thus, the informal system of plea bargaining has taken root, allowing the courts to continue functioning. Those who play exclusively by the rules, such as a young, idealistic public defender who wants to take all her or his cases to trial, are subjected to informal sanctions by judges and superiors, such as inconvenient trial dates or heavier caseloads.

In sum, organizational life is a combination of formal structural rules and informal patterns of behavior. Codified rules are sometimes violated and new, unspoken ones created instead. Stated organizational goals often conflict with the real ones. Despite what may appear to be a clear chain of command, the informal structure often has more of an impact on how things are done.

ORGANIZATIONS AND INSTITUTIONS

Understanding the influence of organizations on our everyday lives tells only part of the story. Organizations themselves exist within a larger structural context, acting as a sort of liaison between people and major social institutions such as the economic system, government, religion, health care, and education. As we saw in Chapter 2, institutions are stable sets of statuses, roles, groups, and organizations that provide the foundation for behavior in certain major areas of social life. They are patterned ways of solving the problems and meeting the needs of a particular society.

Organizational Networks Within Institutions

Like individual people, organizations are born, grow, become overweight, slim down, migrate, form relationships with others, break up, and die. They interact with one another, too, cooperating on some occasions and competing on others, depending on the prevailing economic and political winds. They even lie, cheat, and steal from time to time. As with people, some organizations are extremely powerful and can dictate the manner in which other organizations go about their business.

The state of Texas accounts for about 15% of the entire national textbook market (Stille, 2002). A provision in the Texas Education Code states that textbooks should promote decency, democracy, patriotism, and the free-enterprise system. A coalition of various watchdog organizations in Texas scours textbooks each year in search of material they consider inappropriate or offensive. For instance, in 2004, the Texas Board of Education approved new high school health textbooks that emphasized abstinence and contained no mention of condoms. It approved these books only after the publishers agreed to replace the term "married partners" with "husband and wife," and the term "when two people marry" with "when a man and a woman marry" (Gott, 2004). Over the past few years, the Texas Board of Education has also asked publishers to delete favorable references to Islam, discussions of global warming, and illustrations of breast and testicular self-examinations (Simon, 2009). The economic importance of Texas forces many publishers to write their books with that state's rules in mind.

Similarly, when giant corporations, such as General Electric, Apple, and Coca-Cola, decide to downsize or expand their operations, the effects are felt throughout the entire financial community. But even powerful organizations such as these cannot stand alone. Massive networks of organizations are linked by common goals and needs. The networks are often so complex that organizations from very different fields find themselves dependent on one another for survival.

Institutional Pressures Toward Similarity

If you think about how many varieties of organizations exist in the world, you might be tempted to focus on their obvious differences. Some are large, others small. Some are formal and complex, others informal and simple. Some have a pyramid-shaped chain of command, others are more egalitarian (Gross & Etzioni, 1985). Sociologists have long been interested in the unique ways in which different organizations adapt to changing political, economic, cultural, or environmental circumstances. However, organizations seem to be more similar than different and even tend to imitate one another's actions as they become established in a particular institution (DiMaggio & Powell, 1983).

Organizational similarity is not really that surprising. Because of the nature of the problems that organizations in the same industry have to address, they come to adopt similar methods of dealing with them. For instance, the major U.S. commercial television networks—NBC, ABC, CBS, and Fox—see the success one network has with a particular type of program and try to attract viewers in much the same way. As you well know, the perceived popularity of a certain type of television show creates an irritating avalanche of similar shows on other networks—such as shows where people compete with one another to see who will perform the grossest or the most fearsome feats (*Survivor* and *Fear Factor*), home improvement shows (*While You Were Out, Flip This House,* and *Trading Spaces*), glorified talent contests (*American Idol, America's Got Talent, Dancing With the Stars,* and *Top Chef*), model/fashion shows (*Project Runway* and *America's Next Top Model*), and weight loss shows (*Biggest Loser,*

Weighing In, and *Celebrity Fit Club*). In short, instead of adjusting directly to changes in the social environment, such as the shifting tastes of the television-viewing public, organizations end up adjusting to what other organizations are doing (DiMaggio & Powell, 1983).

The surprising fact is that the imitated practices are not necessarily more effective or successful. After once-novel strategies have spread throughout an industry, they may no longer improve the organization's performance. Viewers eventually get sick of seeing the same types of shows. The net effect of the imitations is to reduce innovation within the industry.

In times of institutional uncertainty, the tendency for organizations to emulate one another is heightened (DiMaggio & Powell, 1983). When new technologies are poorly understood, when the physical environment is undergoing dramatic changes, or when local, state, and federal governments are creating new regulations or setting new agendas, organizations are likely to be somewhat confused about how things ought to be done. Just as individuals look to one another to help define ambiguous situations and determine an appropriate course of action, so do organizations.

Take changes in the field of higher education. Many colleges and universities across the country face the problem of how to attract more students. Such was the case several years ago at the university where I teach. An outside consultant was called in to design a new marketing program for the school. He had some clear strategies for "packaging" the school's image to make it more attractive to prospective students: redesigned brochures, a new recruitment video, a flashy website, and so on. But he was also consulting for several other schools competing for the same shrinking pool of students and admitted that many of the "novel" strategies he advised us to use were things other universities were already using. We were addressing a new and uncertain dilemma by replicating the practices of other organizations in the network.

Likewise, when economic times are difficult and organizations are struggling to survive, there is a tendency for companies—even competitors—to imitate one another. During the recession of 2009, some of the nation's largest retailers began implementing similar business strategies. Wal-Mart, Target, and K-Mart, for instance, reduced their on-site inventories and began carrying fewer name brands. J. C. Penney and Sears installed self-service computers in their stores so that customers could browse collections, compare prices with other retailers, and buy out-of-stock items (Rosenbloom, 2009).

In sum, certain organizational forms dominate not necessarily because they are the most effective means of achieving goals but because social forces such as institutional uncertainty and the power of professions to provide individuals with a single normative standard create pressures toward similarity. Such similarity makes it easier for organizations to interact with one another and to be acknowledged as legitimate and reputable within the field (DiMaggio & Powell, 1983). But this homogeneity is not without its costs. When organizations replicate one another, institutional change becomes difficult and the iron cage of bureaucracy becomes harder to escape.

GLOBALIZATION AND SOCIAL INSTITUTIONS

You've seen in this book so far the enormous effect that globalization is having on everyday life. Many of our important social institutions have become international in scope—notably economics, education, and religion. How do such global institutions meet the needs of human beings around the world?

Economics

Looking around my office at this moment, I notice that my telephone and computer were made in Japan; my desk and chair in the United States, my watch in Switzerland, my stapler in Great Britain, my calculator in Taiwan, my shoes in Korea, my pants in Hong Kong, my bottle of water in France, the frame holding my kids' picture in Thailand, and my paper clips, scissors, cell phone, and iPod in China. Because of the rapid increase in recent years in the economic links among producing nations, your life is probably similarly filled with products made in other countries. Japan is experiencing a troubling shortage of blue fin tuna—the most desirable fish used in sushi—because of growing demand in the United States, Europe, and other countries in Asia (Issenberg, 2007).

Economic globalization is more than just a matter of more goods being shipped from one place to another. For instance, there's a pretty good chance that if you contact someone online or by phone to prepare your taxes, provide legal advice, track your lost luggage, solve your software problem, or review your long-distance phone bill, you'll be dealing with someone working at a call center in India (Friedman, 2005). The large pool of English-speaking, technologically savvy Indian workers willing to work for low wages has attracted the phone service operations of companies such as American Express, Sprint, Citibank, General Electric, Ford, Hewlett-Packard, and IBM (Lakshmi, 2005).

If a product wasn't entirely manufactured in another country, it's a good bet that some of its component ingredients were. Even domestic products can have a complex international pedigree. Take, for instance, a loaf of good old American white bread. Its ingredients include honey (Vietnam, Brazil, Uruguay, Canada, Mexico, and Argentina), calcium propionate (Netherlands), guar gum (India), flour enrichments (China), beta-carotene (Switzerland), vitamin D3 (China), and wheat gluten (France, Poland, Russia, and Australia; Barrionuevo, 2007).

The economic processes involved in globalization have made national boundaries less relevant. ***Multinational corporations,*** businesses that have extended their markets and production facilities globally, have become increasingly powerful over the past several decades. U.S.-based multinational corporations alone employ more than 32 million workers worldwide (Mataloni, 2007). These companies control a significant portion of the world's wealth, heavily influence the tastes of people everywhere, and don't owe their allegiance to any one country's political authority or culture. At the same time, international financial organizations, such as the World Bank, the World Trade Organization, and the International Monetary Fund, loan money to countries all over the world to finance development and reconstruction projects. (For more on the global economic impact of international financial organizations and multinational corporations, see Chapter 10.) With the costs of communication and computing falling rapidly, barriers of time and space that traditionally separated national markets have also been falling. Even the most remote rural villagers are linked to the global economy as they carry out transactions over the Internet and send and receive goods around the world.

A global economy has its everyday advantages. Goods manufactured and services provided in a country where wages are lower are less expensive for consumers in other countries. Universally accepted credit cards make international travel more convenient. Snack bars in overseas airports accept American money, as do foreign establishments around the world that are near U.S. borders or military bases. Global economic influence has also enabled a significant portion of the world's population to be healthier, eat better, and live longer than the royalty of past civilizations (Kurtz, 1995).

We may barely be aware of how the taken-for-granted elements of our daily lives connect to the economic well-being of people in faraway places. For instance, most of today's popular electronic gadgets could not work without a little-known, gritty, super-heavy mud called coltan. Once it is refined in U.S., Japanese, and European factories, coltan becomes tantalum, a remarkably heat-resistant conductor of electricity. Capacitors made of tantalum can be found inside practically every laptop computer, pager, personal digital assistant, MP3 player, and cell phone in the world (Harden, 2001). But there isn't nearly enough coltan in the United States, Europe, or Japan to meet these needs. Its largest quantities lie in the rain forests of the Republic of the Congo, where it is mined in much the same way as gold was mined in California in the 1800s. Miners spend days in the muck, digging up mud and sloshing it around in plastic tubs until the coltan settles to the bottom. On a good day, a miner can produce about a kilogram of the stuff. Miners earn up to $50 a week, quite a high figure considering that most people in this region live on the equivalent of $10 a month ("What Is Coltan?" 2002).

But global trade has also created some interesting everyday dilemmas. For instance, for centuries, workers in Spain and other Latin American countries have enjoyed the workday *siesta,* a long afternoon nap or an extended lunch, sometimes lasting until 5:00 PM. But the owners of some Spanish factories and retail stores have realized that shutting down operations every afternoon so workers can take their siestas is incompatible with Spain's growing integration into the global economy. As the president of a Spanish research group that advocates doing away with the siesta put it, "In a globalized world, we have to have schedules that are more similar to those in the rest of the world so we can be better connected" (quoted in McLean, 2005, p. 4). Spain officially cut lunch breaks from 3 hours to 1 hour for government workers in 2006 (McLean, 2006).

Global financial institutions must also keep close track of holidays around the world to avoid trying to do business on nonbusiness days. In some countries, holidays are determined by the lunar calendar, which not only varies from year to year but may vary from area to area within a country based on local customs. In other countries, such as France, the dates of some bank holidays are a matter of negotiations between the banks and the unions that represent their employees. Even weekends are defined differently in different countries. In Taiwan, the weekend consists of every Sunday and the second and fourth Saturdays of each month. In Malaysia, it is every Sunday and only the first Saturday of every month. And in Lithuania, 1-day weekends are occasionally followed by 4-day weekends (Henriques, 1999).

Economic globalization has fostered more serious social problems as well, including higher levels of unemployment in countries that maintain labor and environmental protections and exploitation of people in poor, developing countries. The result is a worldwide system of inequality, whose problems are often invisible to consumers (see Chapter 10). For instance, many of the best and most beautiful roses Americans buy for their loved ones each year come from the rich volcanic soil of Ecuador. These flowers help generate about $240 million a year and tens of thousands of jobs for this once impoverished region. But the Ecuadorian workers who harvest roses are exposed each day to a toxic mix of pesticides and fungicides (Thompson, 2003). They work with severe headaches and rashes for the benefit of wealthier customers around the world, who are largely unaware of the conditions under which these fragrant symbols of romance are produced. We may wish to do our part to make life better for the rose harvesters of Ecuador, as well as other poor workers around the world, but it's hard to take any effective action. For instance, boycotts of exploitative manufacturers are a double-edged sword. The origin of products is seldom clear-cut, and local workers are typically glad to have jobs they wouldn't have had otherwise. Pressure to compete in the global marketplace also erodes the ability of governments to set their own economic policies, protect national interests, or adequately protect workers and the environment.

Education

The prospect of international competition in a global economy can foster changes in a country's educational system. For instance, U.S. students attend school an average of 180 days a year, compared with 190 days in Germany and 208 days in Eastern Asian nations. Moreover, during the 4 years of high school, the average American student devotes approximately 1,462 hours to math, science, language, and social studies. The average Japanese student will spend 3,190 hours studying these subjects. In Germany, the figure is 3,628 hours (cited in Bainbridge, 2005). Not surprisingly, students in these and other industrialized countries consistently outperform U.S. students in fields such as math and science, causing alarm among many educational experts and political leaders.

Concern over our ability to compete in the global marketplace has led to nationwide calls for educational reforms such as heavier emphasis on math and science; more time spent on foundational skills, such as reading and writing; increased computer literacy; and training in political geography and international relations. Many school districts around the country have adopted longer school days (Lehigh, 2005) and a year-round schedule to improve student performance. Competitive pressures have become so great in some schools that administrators have been forced to make students slow down. For instance, at a high school in Briarcliff Manor, New York, many students are so caught up in the achievement frenzy that they barely have time to eat or sleep. A third of the students take classes during lunch period. Some take five or six Advanced Placement classes at a time. To reduce stress levels, school officials decided to rearrange the schedule to cut the number of minutes each class meets over the year and to *require* every student to take a 20-minute lunch break (Hu, 2008).

Pressures to achieve academically are present from the beginning. Even though research shows that play is essential for healthy development, children as early as kindergarten spend significantly more time on lessons and testing than on play, exercise, and imagination. According to a study of New York and Los Angeles kindergartens (Miller & Almon, 2009), children spend four to six times as long being instructed and tested in math skills and literacy (2 to 3 hours a day) than in free play (20 to 30 minutes a day). Standardized testing and preparation for testing are now a daily activity in most kindergartens. Play materials such as blocks, sand, water tables, and props for dramatic play have largely disappeared from the classroom. Some school districts in Atlanta, New York, Chicago, New Jersey, and Connecticut have opted to eliminate recess, even to the point of building new schools in their districts without playgrounds (Sindelar, 2004).

Ironically, at a time when concern over global competitiveness is more acute than ever, economic hard times are forcing schools to cut back. School districts in major cities across the country have laid off thousands of teachers, school psychologists, and custodians. Some districts have trimmed bus service, discontinued field trips, and even shortened the school day (Dillon, 2008).

Moreover, some critics still feel that we already place far too much emphasis on performance and achievement in this society and that children end up suffering as a result (Mannon, 1997). They often point to Japan, not as a model but as a cautionary tale. Many Japanese children attend classes all day, then go to one of the many private "cram" schools, where they study for college entrance exams until 10 or 11 P.M. Even 3-year-olds may spend hours a day memorizing stories, learning vocabulary, and taking achievement tests (WuDunn, 1996a). But Japanese educational accomplishments often come at a steep price. Some Japanese sociologists blame the intense competitive pressures children face for the dramatic rise in youth crime over the past few years. Historically, passing grueling exams and getting into the top high schools and elite colleges was a virtual guarantee of a prestigious job. But Japan's economic stagnation and record unemployment in the 2000s shattered the implicit social contract that had once justified all the hard work and sacrifice. Many Japanese youth rebel when they discover that not only do they not have much of a social life, they have no job prospects either (French, 1999b). About one in three Japanese elementary school teachers have experienced at least one disruptive classroom incident, such as students mocking their authority, walking out of class, or even physically attacking them (cited in French, 2002).

Few people in the United States would argue that we should emulate the pressurized Japanese educational model. At the same time, though, the demands of the global economy and concerns over Americans' ability to compete internationally will continue to exert influence on legislators and education reformers.

Religion

Another institution influenced by globalization is religion. Despite the enormous variety of cultures and ethnicities that exist today, nearly two thirds of the world's population belong to just three major religions—Christianity, Hinduism, and Islam—which have successfully crossed national boundaries for centuries.

Some denominations are globalizing to deal with shrinking memberships in the countries where they originated. For example, outside the United States and Canada, the Mormon Church has grown by more than 500% since 1980 (cited in Kress, 2005). The Methodist Church lost 1 million U.S. members between 1980 and 1995 but gained about 500,000 elsewhere, mostly in Africa (Niebuhr, 1998). Indeed, during the 20th century, the population of Christians in Africa grew from 10 million to 360 million. The Anglican Church, in particular, is growing faster in Africa than in its traditional bases, Great Britain and North America; Nigeria alone has 25% of the world's Anglicans (Rice, 2009).

Ironically, this globalization of religion is creating crises for religious communities. Exposure to competing worldviews challenges traditional beliefs. In some cases, religions have reacted with a forceful revitalization of ancient, fundamentalist traditions (Kurtz, 1995). Witness the growing trend toward governments defining themselves in narrowly religious terms. The ascension of fundamentalist Islamic government in Iran, the growing influence of Orthodox Jews in Israeli politics, and the continuing conflict between Hindus and Muslims in Kashmir and between Sunni and Shiite Muslims in Iraq attest to the fact that many people today believe religion cannot be separated from a nation's social and political destiny.

The rise of religious nationalism around the world has created an obvious threat to global security. The attacks of September 11, 2001, are the most glaring illustration. Radical elements sometimes use religious texts—in this case the Koran—as a justification for violence against societies that they blame for moral decline and economic exploitation. Elsewhere, the possibility of violence by supporters of religious nationalist movements has brought down political regimes, changed the outcomes of elections, strained international relations, and made some parts of the world dangerous places for travelers (Juergensmeyer, 1996).

But religion has also played a positive role in world affairs and has created dramatic social changes. According to Max Weber (1904/1977), the spread of Protestant beliefs throughout Europe made the growth of modern capitalism possible. Protestantism maintained that worldly achievements, such as the accumulation of wealth through hard work, are a sign of God's favor. But the early Protestants also believed that God frowns on vulgar displays of wealth, such as big houses, fancy clothes, and so forth.

So people were motivated to save and reinvest their wealth rather than spend it frivolously. You can see how such beliefs made large-scale and long-term economic growth possible (Weber, 1904/1977). A study of 59 Christian, Buddhist, Muslim, and Hindu countries found that strong religious beliefs tend to stimulate economic growth because of their association with individual traits such as honesty, work ethic, thrift, and openness to strangers (Barro & McCleary, 2003).

The influence of religious movements on social life continues. In the 1960s, television pictures of Buddhist monks setting themselves on fire in Vietnam to protest the war fed the growing antiwar movement in the United States. In the 1970s and 1980s, images of Catholic priests and nuns challenging government policies in Central and South America provoked a heightened awareness worldwide of the plight of indigenous people there. In the early 2000s, followers of the Dalai Lama raised global awareness of the plight of Tibetans who seek independence from China, leading to the establishment of the worldwide International Campaign for Tibet. In 2007, tens of thousands of Buddhist monks in Myanmar marched in the streets to protest against that country's oppressive military regime. Their actions sparked organized protests in more than two dozen Asian, European, and North American cities.

CONCLUSION

More than 3 centuries ago, John Donne wrote, "No man is an island, entire of itself; every man is a piece of the continent, a part of the main." The same can be said of contemporary social life. We are not isolated individuals whose lives are simply functions of personal characteristics and predispositions. We are social beings. We are part of aggregations of other social beings. We have a powerful need to belong to something larger than ourselves. As a result, we constantly affect and are affected by our associations with others, whether face-to-face or in well-structured groups, massive bureaucratic organizations, or all-encompassing social institutions.

Throughout Part II of this book, I discussed how society and culture affect everyday experiences and how those experiences help construct and maintain social order. The development of self and self-controlled behavior, the influence of cultural norms, responses to deviance, and so on are all topics that provide insight into how we are able to live together in a relatively orderly and predictable way. In this chapter, however, you can see that the social structure, though created and maintained by the actions of individuals, is more than just the sum of those actions. Organizations interact at a level well above the individual; institutions are organized in a massive, global system.

Social structure is bigger than any of us, exerts enormous control over our lives, and is an objectified reality that appears to exist independently of us. But it cannot exist without us. I'm reminded of a skit from the old British comedy show *Monty Python's Flying Circus,* in which a high-rise apartment building stood erect only because its inhabitants believed in it. When they doubted its existence, it began to crumble. Like that building, social structure requires constant human support. Once we as a society are no longer able to sustain our organizations or believe in our institutions, they fall apart.

CHAPTER HIGHLIGHTS

◆ Social structure is both a source of predictability and a source of problems in our everyday lives. Sometimes individual interests coincide with structural needs; other times they conflict.

◆ By virtue of living in society, we are all organizational creatures. We are born in organizations, educated in them, spend most of our adult lives working in them, and will probably die in them.

◆ A common form of organization in a complex society is the bureaucracy. A bureaucracy is a large hierarchical organization that is governed by a system of rules and regulations, has a clear specification of work tasks, and has a well-defined division of labor.

◆ Organizations are more than structures, rules, policies, goals, job descriptions, and standard operating procedures. Each organization, and each division within an organization, develops its own norms, values, and language.

◆ Organizations exist within highly interconnected networks. In times of institutional or environmental uncertainty, organizations tend to imitate one another, adopting similar activities, policies, and goals.

◆ As national borders become increasingly permeable, cultures and social institutions become more global in nature.

KEY TERMS

bureaucracy Large hierarchical organization governed by formal rules and regulations and having clearly specified work tasks

division of labor Specialization of different people or groups in different tasks, characteristic of most bureaucracies

free-rider problem Tendency for people to refrain from contributing to the common good when a resource is available without requiring any personal cost or contribution

hierarchy of authority Ranking of people or tasks in a bureaucracy from those at the top, where there is a great deal of power and authority, to those at the bottom, where there is very little power and authority

multinational corporation Company that has manufacturing, production, and marketing divisions in multiple countries

oligarchy System of authority in which many people are ruled by a privileged few

social dilemma Potential for a society's long-term ruin because of individuals' tendency to pursue their own short-term interests

social structure Framework of society—social institutions, organizations, groups, statuses and roles, cultural beliefs, and institutionalized norms—which adds order and predictability to our private lives

tragedy of the commons Situation in which people acting individually and in their own interest use up commonly available (but limited) resources, creating disaster for the entire community

©iStockPhoto.com/Tomasz Pietryszek

10 The Architecture of Stratification

Social Class and Inequality

If you've seen the 1997 Hollywood film *Titanic,* you know that the famous ship had every amenity and comfort: Turkish baths, the finest orchestras, intricately tiled walls, the best cuisine. What it didn't have when it hit an iceberg and began to sink were enough lifeboats. There was room for only 1,178 of the 2,207 passengers and crew members on board. Over the span of 2 hours on that cold April night in 1912, as the "unsinkable" ocean liner was engulfed by the frigid waters of the North Atlantic, more than 1,500 people lost their lives.

This part of the story is well-known. What is less well-known is that some of the passengers actually had a much better chance of survival than others. More than 60% of the people from the wealthy first-class deck survived, compared with 36% of the people from the second-class deck and 24% of the people from the lowest, or "steerage," class. The figures were even more striking for women and children, who, by virtue of mannerly tradition, were entitled to be spared first. In first class, 97% of the women and children survived; in second class, 89% survived. However, only 42% of the women and children in steerage were saved (Hall, 1986).

One reason why so many wealthier passengers survived was that the lifeboats were accessed from the higher first- and second-class decks. The locked doors and other barriers erected to keep third-class passengers from venturing to the upper decks during the cruise remained in place when disaster struck. In addition, little effort was made to save the people in steerage. Some were forcibly kept down by crew members standing guard.

For passengers on the *Titanic,* social inequality meant more than just differences in the comfort of accommodations or the quality of the food they ate. It literally meant life or death. This situation serves as a metaphor for what many people face in today's society. Those at the top have easy access to various "lifeboats" in times of social or economic disaster; others face locked gates, segregated decks, and policies that make even survival exceedingly difficult (Sidel, 1986).

Let's turn the clock ahead to the summer of 2005, when Hurricane Katrina killed more than 1,000 people in the Gulf Coast region of the U.S. South. Most of these people died not because of the hurricane's torrential rains and high winds but because of the flooding that occurred when the levees that ordinarily protect the low-lying areas of New Orleans (which were in need of repair to begin with) were breached. In addition to the fatalities, hundreds of thousands of people lost everything they owned and were forced to relocate.

The storm and its aftermath did not affect all residents equally. The neighborhoods with significant flooding had a lower median income, a higher poverty rate, and a higher percentage of households without a vehicle than the areas that experienced little or no flooding (Schwartz, Revkin, & Wald, 2005). Those of us watching the tragedy unfold on television could not help but notice the obvious fact that the vast majority of the evacuees who suffered for days in the sweltering darkness of the Superdome and convention center in New Orleans were poor people of color who came from the most vulnerable parts of the city. These were individuals who either didn't have the necessary transportation to evacuate prior to the hurricane or who stayed behind to tend to sick and elderly relatives who couldn't be moved. Even today, poor, displaced children who were forced to live in ramshackle government trailer parks after the hurricane continue to suffer from various ailments including anemia, respiratory infections, and depression (Carmichael, 2008). Again we see how the lack of economic resources can have direct, physical consequences in people's lives.

In this chapter, I look at class inequality and stratification. In subsequent chapters, I explore two other facets of inequality: race and/or ethnicity and gender. It's important to note, however, that although class, race and ethnicity, and gender are covered in separate chapters, these components of our identities are not experienced separately. They are all interrelated, and they combine to determine individuals' positions in society. For instance, a person doesn't live his life just as a working-class person, just as a man, or just as an Asian American. He is all these things—and more—simultaneously (Newman, 2007).

STRATIFICATION SYSTEMS

Inequality is woven into the fabric of all societies through a structured system of ***stratification,*** the ranking of entire groups of people that perpetuates unequal rewards and life chances in a society. Just as geologists talk about strata of rock, which are layered one on top of another, the "social strata" of people are arranged from low to high. All societies, past and present, have had some form of stratification, although they vary in the degree of inequality between strata. The four main forms of stratification that sociologists have identified—all of which continue to exist in contemporary societies—are slavery, caste systems, estate systems, and social class systems.

Slavery

One of the most persistent forms of stratification in the world is slavery. ***Slavery*** is an economic form of inequality in which some people are the property of others. Their lives are owned, controlled, coerced, and restricted. One can become a slave in a variety of ways: through birth, military defeat, debt, or, as in the United States until the mid-19th century, capture and commercial trade (Kerbo, 1991). Because slaves are considered possessions, they are denied the rights and life chances other people take for granted. Slavery has occurred in various forms almost everywhere in the world at some time. Mexico, Great Britain, France, Russia, and Holland all abolished slavery before the United States; Spain and Brazil did so afterward (Davis, 2006). Today, tens of thousands of people in the West African nations of Niger, Burkina Faso, Mali, and Mauritania are born into slavery ("A Continuing Abomination," 2008). In South Asia, there are millions of "bonded laborers," whose employers force them to work for nothing so as to pay off a debt (Appiah, 2007).

Caste Systems

Some societies today retain a second form of stratification: a ***caste system***. Traditionally, one's caste, which determines lifestyle, prestige, and occupational choices, was fixed at birth and couldn't be changed. Ancient Hindu scriptures, for instance, identified the strict hierarchy of elite, warrior, merchant, servant, and untouchable castes. The rights and duties associated with membership in each caste were clear. In India, "untouchables"—members of the lowest caste—were once required by law to hide from or, if that wasn't possible, to bow in the presence of anyone from a higher caste. They were routinely denied the right to enter Hindu temples or to draw water from wells reserved for members of the higher castes, who feared they would be contaminated if they touched or otherwise came in contact with an untouchable.

According to Human Rights Watch (2001), more than 250 million people worldwide continue to suffer severe caste discrimination. They are victims of exploitation and violence and face massive obstacles to their full attainment of civil, political, economic, and cultural rights.

Things are beginning to change, however. In India, for instance, laws have been passed that prohibit caste-based discrimination. More untouchables (or *Dalits*, as they prefer to be called) now vote than members of the upper caste (Dugger, 1999a). In fact, the benefits Dalits now receive—such as reserved spaces in universities and governmental jobs—have prompted members of the next highest caste of farmers and shepherds to lobby the government to have its caste status downgraded so as to be eligible for these benefits (Gentleman, 2007).

But the caste system still serves as a powerful source of stratification and oppression in India, especially in rural areas. Cultural norms still encourage people to take the occupation of their parents and marry within their caste (Weber, 1970). Even Indians living in the United States find that caste sometimes colors their experiences with friends and business associates (Berger, 2004).

Estate Systems

A third form of stratification is the ***estate system***, or ***feudal system***, which develops when high-status groups own land and have power based on their noble birth (Kerbo, 1991). Estate systems were most commonly found in preindustrial societies. In medieval Europe, the highest "estate" in society was occupied by the aristocracy, who derived their wealth and power from large-scale landholdings. The clergy formed the next estate. Although they had lower status than the aristocracy, they still claimed considerable status because the Catholic Church itself owned a great deal of land and exerted influence over people's lives. The last, or "third," estate was reserved for commoners: serfs, peasants, artisans, and merchants. Movement between estates was possible, though infrequent. Occasionally, a commoner might be knighted, or a wealthy merchant might become an aristocrat.

Some reminders of the estate system can still be seen today. In Great Britain, for instance, Parliament's House of Lords is still occupied primarily by people of "noble birth," and a small group of aristocratic families still sits at the top of the social ladder, where the members enjoy tremendous inherited wealth and exercise significant political power. Attempts have been made to change the system, however. In 2007, the British House of Commons (the so-called lower house) voted overwhelmingly to introduce elections to the House of Lords. It also voted to remove the last remaining "hereditary peers," whose presence in the House of Lords is based solely on their noble lineage (Cowell, 2007). A week later, the House of Lords soundly rejected the measure.

Social Class Systems

Stratification systems in contemporary industrialized societies are most likely to be based on social class. A ***social class*** is a group of people who share a similar economic position in society based on their wealth and income. Class is essentially, therefore, an economic stratification system. It is a means of ranking people or groups that determines access to important resources and life chances. Less obviously perhaps, social-class standing provides people with a particular understanding of the world and where they fit into it compared with others.

Class systems differ from other systems of stratification in that they raise no legal barriers to ***social mobility***, the movement of people or groups from one level to another. Theoretically, all members of a class system, no matter how destitute they are, can rise to the top. In practice, however, mobility between classes may be difficult for some people. Recent economic studies have found that it takes five or six generations to erase the advantages or disadvantages of a person's economic origins (Krueger,

2002). Within the span of a single generation, there isn't much social mobility—wealthy parents tend to have wealthy children; poor parents tend to have poor children. Likewise, race and gender have historically determined a person's access to educational, social, and employment opportunities. Women of color are especially likely to face barriers to upward mobility, in terms of both economic disadvantage and lack of emotional support from their families (Higginbotham & Weber, 1992).

SOCIOLOGICAL PERSPECTIVES ON STRATIFICATION

Sociologists have long been interested in figuring out why societies are stratified. Two perspectives—the structural-functionalist perspective and the conflict perspective—offer insights into the sources and purposes of social inequality. They are often presumed to be competing views, but we can actually use them together to deepen our understanding of why social inequality exists, how it develops, and why it is so persistent.

The Structural-Functionalist View of Stratification

From a structural-functionalist perspective, the cause of stratification lies in a society's inevitable need for order. Because social inequality is found in some form in all societies and thus is apparently unavoidable, inequality must somehow be necessary for societies to run smoothly.

As with bureaucracies, the efficient functioning of society requires that various tasks be allocated through a strictly defined division of labor. If the tasks associated with all social positions in a society were equally pleasant and equally important and required the same talents, it wouldn't make a difference who occupied which position. But structural functionalists argue that it does make a difference. Some occupations, such as teaching and medicine, are more important for the well-being of society than others and require greater talent and training. Society's dilemma is to make sure that the most talented people perform the most important tasks. One way to ensure this distribution of tasks is to assign higher rewards—better pay, greater prestige, more social privileges—to some positions in society so that they will be attractive to people with the necessary abilities (Davis & Moore, 1945). Presumably, if these talented people were not offered sufficiently high rewards, they would have no reason to take on the difficult and demanding tasks associated with important positions. Why would someone go through the agony and costs of many years of medical school, for instance, without some promise of compensation and high prestige?

Just because an important position is easily filled, however, does not mean it is generously rewarded (Davis & Moore, 1945). Imagine what our society would be like without people who remove our trash. Not only would our streets be unsightly, but our collective health would suffer. Therefore, garbage collectors serve a vital social function. But they don't get paid very much, and trash removal is certainly not a highly respected occupation. Why aren't garbage collectors higher up in the hierarchy of occupations? According to the structural-functionalist perspective, it is because we have no shortage of people with the skills needed to collect garbage. Physicians also serve the collective health needs of a society. But because of the skills and training needed to be a doctor, society must offer rewards high enough to ensure that qualified people will want to enter the medical profession.

This explanation may make some sense. But when we examine the pay scales of actual occupations, it comes up short. One look at the salary structure in today's society reveals obvious instances of highly paid positions that are not as functionally important as positions that receive smaller rewards. For instance, Oprah Winfrey makes about $275 million a year. Hip-hop star 50 Cent makes $150 million. Filmmaker Steven Spielberg earns more than $100 million a year and comedian Jerry Seinfeld, $85 million. You might say that talk show hosts, rappers, filmmakers, and comedians serve important social functions by providing the rest of us with a recreational release from the demands of ordinary life; and the best entertainers and athletes do have rare skills, indeed. However, society probably can do without another TV show, concert, or megahit movie more easily than it can do without competent physicians, scientists, computer programmers, teachers, or even trash collectors, who earn substantially less in a year than what many celebrities earn in a day.

Furthermore, the structural-functionalist argument that only a limited number of talented people are around to occupy important social positions is probably overstated. Many people have the talent to become doctors. What they lack is access to training. And why are some people—women and members of racial and ethnic minorities—paid less for or excluded entirely from certain jobs? The debates over equal employment opportunity and equal pay for equal work are essentially debates over how the functional importance of certain positions is determined.

Finally, when functionalists claim that stratification serves the needs of society, we must ask, Whose needs? A system of slavery obviously meets the economic needs of one group at the expense of another, but that doesn't make it acceptable. In a class-stratified society, those individuals who receive the greatest rewards have the resources to make sure they continue receiving such rewards. Over time, the competition for the most desirable positions will become less open and less competitive. The offspring of "talented"—that is, high-status—parents will inevitably have an advantage over equally talented people who are born into less successful families. Hence, social background and not personal aptitude may become the primary criterion for filling important social positions (Tumin, 1953).

The structural-functionalist perspective gives us important insight into how societies ensure that all positions in the division of labor are filled. Every society, no matter how simple or complex, differentiates people in terms of prestige and esteem and possesses a certain amount of institutional inequality. But this perspective doesn't address the fact that stratification can be unjust and divisive, a source of social *disorder* (Tumin, 1953).

The Conflict View of Stratification

Conflict theorists are among those who argue that social inequality is neither a societal necessity nor a source of social order. They see it as a primary source of conflict, coercion, and unhappiness. Stratification ultimately rests on the unequal distribution of resources—some people have them, others don't. Important resources include money, land, information, education, health care, safety, and adequate housing. Those high in the stratification system can control these resources because they are the ones who set the rules. The conflict perspective takes it as a fundamental truth that stratification systems serve the interests of those at the top and not the survival needs of the entire society.

Resources are an especially important source of inequality when they are scarce. Sometimes, their scarcity is natural. For instance, there's only a finite amount of land on earth that can be used, inhabited, and owned. At other times, however, the scarcity of a resource is artificially created. For instance, in 1890, the founder of DeBeers, the South African company that currently controls two thirds of the international diamond market, realized that the sheer abundance of diamonds in southern Africa would make them virtually worthless on the international market. So the company decided to carefully limit the number of diamonds released for sale each year. This artificially created rarity, coupled with a carefully cultivated image of romance, is what made diamonds so expensive and what continues to make companies such as DeBeers so powerful today (Harden, 2000).

Rich and politically powerful individuals frequently work together to create or maintain privilege, often at the expense of the middle and lower classes (Phillips, 2002). The U.S. Congress is dominated by both Republicans and Democrats who are far wealthier than the citizens they represent. The average net worth of a U.S. senator is more than $10 million; House representatives average more than $5 million. When he was a senator, Barack Obama's net worth ranged from $2 to $7 million, placing him only 31st among all members of the Senate (Center for Responsive Politics, 2008). Thus, from the conflict perspective, it's not at all surprising that politicians would make decisions that benefit the wealthy. For instance, on the same day in 2005 that the U.S. House of Representatives voted for a full gradual repeal of the estate tax—a tax that affects only the wealthiest Americans—it also passed a bill that made it more difficult for debt-ridden lower-income individuals and families to file for bankruptcy protection (Labaton, 2005; Rosenbaum, 2005). To provide financial aid to the victims of Hurricane Katrina, many members of Congress favored cutting the budgets of existing social programs that helped other needy citizens rather than repealing tax cuts for upper-class Americans.

What the conflict perspective gives us that the structural-functionalist perspective doesn't is an acknowledgment of the interconnected roles that economic and political institutions play in creating and maintaining a stratified society.

The Marxian Class Model

Karl Marx and Friedrich Engels (1848/1982) were the original proponents of the view that societies are divided into conflicting classes. They felt that in modern societies, two major classes emerge: capitalists (or the bourgeoisie), who control the ***means of production***—land, commercial enterprises, factories, and wealth—and are able to purchase the labor of others, and workers (or the proletariat), who neither own the means of production nor have the ability to purchase the labor of others. Workers, instead, must sell their own labor to others in order to survive. Some workers, including store managers and factory supervisors, may control other workers, but their power is minimal compared with the power exerted over them by those in the capitalist class. Marx and Engels supplemented this two-tiered conception of class by adding a third tier, the petite bourgeoisie, which is a transitional class of people who own the means of production but don't purchase the labor power of others. This class consists of self-employed skilled laborers and businesspeople who are economically self-sufficient but don't have a staff of subordinate workers (Robinson & Kelley, 1979).

Capitalists have considerable sway over what and how much will be produced, who will get it, how much money people will be paid to produce it, and so forth. Such influence allows them to control other people's livelihoods, the communities in which people live, and the economic decisions that affect the entire society. In such a structure, the rich inevitably tend to get richer, to use their wealth to create more wealth for themselves, and to act in ways that will protect their interests and positions in society.

Ultimately, the wealthy segments of society gain the ability to influence important social institutions such as the government, the media, the schools, and the courts. They have access to the means necessary to create and promote a reality that justifies their exploitative actions. Their version of reality is so influential that even those who are harmed by it come to accept it. Marx and Engels called this phenomenon ***false consciousness***. False consciousness is crucial because it is the primary means by which the powerful classes in society prevent protest and revolution. As long as large numbers of poor people continue to believe that wealth and success are solely the products of individual hard work and effort rather than structured inequalities in society—that is, they believe what in the United States has been called the American Dream—resentment and animosity toward the rich will be minimized and people will perceive the inequalities as fair and deserved (Robinson & Bell, 1978).

Neo-Marxist Models of Stratification

In Marx's time—the heyday of industrial development in the mid-19th century—ownership of property and control of labor were synonymous. Most jobs were either on farms or in factories. Lumping all those who owned productive resources into one class and all those who didn't into another made sense. However, the nature of capitalism has changed a lot since then. Today, a person with a novel idea for a product or service, a computer with high-speed Internet access, and a smart phone can go into business and make a lot of money. Corporations have become much larger and more bureaucratic, with a long, multilevel chain of command. Ownership of corporations lies in the hands of stockholders (foreign as well as domestic), who often have no connection at all to the everyday workings of the business. Thus, ownership and management are separated. The powerful people who run large businesses and control workers on a day-to-day basis are frequently not the same people who own the businesses.

In light of changing realities, more contemporary conflict sociologists, such as Ralf Dahrendorf (1959), have offered models that focus primarily on differing levels of authority among the members of society. What's important is not just who owns the means of production but who can exercise influence over others. ***Authority*** is the possession of some status or quality that compels others to obey (Starr, 1982). A person with authority has the power to order or forbid behavior in others (Wrong, 1988). Such commands don't require the use of force or persuasion, nor do they need to be explained or justified. Rulers simply have authority over the ruled, as do teachers over students, employers over employees, and parents over children. These authority relationships are not fixed, of course: Children fight with their parents, students challenge their teachers, and workers protest against their bosses. But though the legitimacy of the authority may sometimes be called into question, the ongoing dependence of the subordinates maintains it. The worker may disagree with the boss, and the student may disagree with the teacher; but the boss still signs the paycheck, and the teacher still assigns final grades.

Like Marx and Engels, Dahrendorf believed that relations between classes inherently involve conflicts of interest. Rulers often maintain their position in society by ordering or forcing people with less authority to do things that benefit the rulers. But by emphasizing authority, Dahrendorf argued that stratification is not exclusively an economic phenomenon. Instead, it comes from the social relations between people who possess different degrees of power.

Dahrendorf's ideas about the motivating force behind social stratification have since been expanded. Sociologist Erik Olin Wright and his colleagues (Wright, 1976; Wright, Costello, Hachen, & Sprague, 1982; Wright & Perrone, 1977) developed a model that incorporates both the ownership of means of production and the exercise of authority over others. The capitalist and petite bourgeoisie classes in this scheme are identical to those of Marx and Engels. What is different is that the classes of people who do not own society's productive resources (Marx and Engels's worker class) are divided into two classes: managers and workers.

Wright's approach gives us a sense that social class is not simply a reflection of income or the extent to which one group exercises authority over another. Lawyers, plumbers, or cooks, for instance, could conceivably fall into any of the four class categories. They may own their own businesses and hire assistants (placing them in the capitalist class), work for a large company and have subordinates (placing them in the manager class), work for a large company without any subordinates (placing them in the worker class), or be self-employed (placing them in the petite bourgeoisie; Robinson & Kelley, 1979).

Wright's approach also emphasizes that class conflict is more than just a clash between the rich and the poor. Societies have, in fact, multiple lines of conflict—economic, political, administrative, and social. Some positions, or what Wright calls *contradictory class locations,* fall between two major classes. Individuals in these positions have trouble identifying with one side or the other. Middle managers and supervisors, for instance, can align with workers because both are subordinates of capitalist owners. Yet because middle managers and supervisors can exercise authority over some people, they may also share the interests and concerns of owners.

Weber's Model of Stratification

Other conflict sociologists have likewise questioned Marx's heavy emphasis on wealth and income as the sole factors that stratify society. Max Weber (1921/1978) agreed with Marx that social class is an important determinant of stratification. However, he observed that the way people are ranked is not just a matter of economic inequality. Weber added two other dimensions—prestige and power—to his model of stratification, preferring the term ***socioeconomic status*** rather than class to describe social inequality (Weber, 1970).

The existence of these other dimensions makes the conflict model of stratification more complex than simply a battle between the rich and the poor. ***Prestige*** is the respect and honor given to some people in society. It is obviously influenced by wealth and income, but it can also be derived from *achieved* characteristics, such as educational attainment and occupational status, and from *ascribed* characteristics, such as race, ethnicity, gender, and family pedigree. While wealth and prestige often go hand in hand, they don't necessarily have to. Drug dealers, for example, may be multimillionaires, but they aren't well respected and therefore aren't ranked high in the stratification system. On the flip side, professors may earn a modest salary, but they command a fair amount of respect. ***Power,*** for Weber, is a person's ability to affect decisions in ways that benefit him or her. Again, power is usually related to wealth and prestige, but it need not be. Sometimes low-income individuals can band together and influence decisions at the societal level, as when workers strike for better working conditions.

CLASS INEQUALITY IN THE UNITED STATES

One of the ideological cornerstones of U.S. society is the belief that all people are created equal and that only personal shortcomings can impede a person's progress up the social ladder. After all, the United States is billed as the "land of opportunity." Our folklore is filled with stories of disadvantaged individuals who use their courage and resolve to overcome all adversity. We don't like to acknowledge that class inequality exists. But sociologists tell us that our place in the stratification system determines the course of our lives, in obvious and subtle ways.

Class and Everyday Life

Class standing in the United States has always determined a whole host of life chances, including access to higher education; better-paying jobs; and healthier, safer, and more comfortable lives:

- In fire-prone regions of the West, insurance companies offer "premium" protection plans to wealthy policyholders. At the first sign of a wildfire in the vicinity, someone will come out and spray special fire retardant on the policy owner's house to prevent it from burning (Yardley, 2007).

- A study of street repair work in Indianapolis found that the average time it took between the filing of a complaint and the fixing of a pothole was 11 days in neighborhoods with an average annual income of more than $55,000; in neighborhoods with an average income of less than $25,000, it took an average of nearly 25 days (Evans & Nichols, 2009).

- For an annual fee, which could be as much as $20,000, wealthy individuals can buy "boutique" or "concierge" medical care, which includes special access to their physician via 24/7 cell phone and e-mail; same-day appointments with a guaranteed waiting time of no more than 15 minutes; nutrition and exercise physiology exams at the patients' homes; nurses to accompany them when they go to see specialists; and routine physicals that are so thorough they can last up to 3 days (Belluck, 2002; Garfinkel, 2003; Zuger, 2005). The recent economic recession has not dampened the desire for this type of personalized health care among the very wealthy (Sack, 2009).

Such exclusive personal attention reinforces feelings of power and privilege. Conversely, people in the lower classes routinely face frustrating barriers in their daily lives. They must often make use of public facilities (health clinics, laundromats, public transportation, and so on) to carry out the day-to-day tasks that wealthier people can carry out privately.

Class can also determine access to other resources and thereby contribute to long-term advantages. Consider, for instance, admission to college. We would like to think that admissions decisions are based solely on a student's merit: high academic achievement (reflected in high school grades) and strong intellectual potential (reflected in scores on standardized aptitude tests such as the SAT). What could be fairer than the use of these sorts of objective measures as the primary criteria for determining who gets an elite education that will open doors for a lifetime?

Would it disturb you to know that your SAT score may depend as much on your parents' financial status as on your own intellect? Obviously, simply coming from a well-to-do family doesn't guarantee a high score on the SAT, but it can help. If you were fortunate enough to attend high school in an affluent, upper-class neighborhood, chances are your school offered SAT preparation courses. In some of these schools, students take practice SAT exams every year until they take the real one in their senior year. Wealthy high schools are also significantly more likely than midlevel or poor high schools to offer advanced placement courses, another important tool that college admissions officers use to measure applicants (Berthelsen, 1999). Even if a school doesn't provide such opportunities, private lessons from test preparation coaches are available to those who can afford them.

Access to these opportunities pays off. In 2007, the average combined SAT score for students whose families earned less than $10,000 a year was 1301. The average score for students whose families earned more than $100,000 a year was 1637 (National Center for Fair and Open Testing, 2008).

Class Distinctions

Class distinctions go beyond differences in access to educational or economic opportunities, however. People create and maintain class boundaries through their perceptions of moral, cultural, and lifestyle distinctions (Lamont, 1992). For example, some communities forbid residents to dry their clothes outdoors on clotheslines because it gives the neighborhood a shabby appearance. A few years ago, the town of Wilson, North Carolina, voted to prohibit people from keeping old sofas on their front porches (Bragg, 1998). For generations, poor people in the area—unable to purchase expensive outdoor furniture—have kept their worn-out sofas and chairs on the porch, where they can still be used. But more affluent residents saw the practice as "low class" and approved the ban to make neighborhoods more presentable.

Although the boundaries between classes tend to be fuzzy and subjective, distinct class designations remain a part of everyday thinking, political initiatives, and social research. The ***upper class*** (which some sociologists define as the highest-earning 5% of the U.S. population) is usually believed to include owners of vast amounts of property and other forms of wealth, major shareholders and owners of large corporations, top financiers, rich celebrities and politicians, and members of prestigious families. The ***middle class*** (roughly 45% of the population) is likely to include college-educated managers, supervisors, executives, owners of small businesses, and professionals. The ***working class*** (about 35% of the population) typically includes industrial and factory workers, office workers, clerks, and farm and manual laborers. Most working-class people don't own their own homes and don't attend college. Finally, about 15% of the population consists of people who work for minimum wages or who are chronically unemployed. They are the ***poor*** (sometimes referred to as the underclass or the lower class; Walton, 1990; Wright et al., 1982).

The Upper Class

The upper class in the United States is a small, exclusive group that occupies the highest levels of status and prestige. For some, membership in the upper class is relatively recent, acquired through personal financial achievement. These families are usually headed by high-level executives in large corporations and highly compensated lawyers, doctors, scientists, entertainers, and professional athletes. Such individuals may have been born into poor, working-class, or middle-class families, but they have been able to climb the social ladder and create a comfortable life. They are sometimes called "the new rich."

Others, however, are born into wealth gained by earlier generations in their families (Langman, 1988). The formidable pedigree of "old wealth," not to mention the wealth itself, provides them with insulation from the rest of society. Their position in the stratification system is perpetuated through a set of exclusive clubs, resorts, charitable and cultural organizations, and social activities that provides members with a distinctive lifestyle and a perspective on the world that distinguishes them from the rest of society.

Sociologists G. William Domhoff (1983, 1998) and C. Wright Mills (1956) have made the case that members of the upper class can structure other social institutions to ensure that their personal interests are met and that the class itself endures. They control the government, large corporations, the majority of privately held corporate stock, the media, universities, councils for national and international affairs, and so on (Domhoff, 1998). Hence, members of this class enjoy political and economic power to a degree not available to members of other classes.

For example, the educational system plays not only a key socializing role (see Chapter 5) but also an important role in perpetuating or reproducing the U.S. class structure. Children of the upper class often attend private schools, boarding schools, and well-endowed private universities (Domhoff, 1998). In addition to the standard curriculum, these schools teach vocabulary, inflection, styles of dress, aesthetic tastes, values, and manners (Collins, 1971). Required attendance at school functions; participation in esoteric sports such as lacrosse, squash, and crew; the wearing of school blazers or ties; and other "character-building" activities are designed to teach young people the unique lifestyle of the ruling class. In many ways, boarding schools function like "total institutions" such as prisons and convents (Goffman, 1961), isolating members from the outside world and providing them with routines and traditions that are highly effective agents of socialization.

In a study of more than 60 elite boarding schools in the United States and Great Britain, Peter Cookson and Caroline Persell (1985) showed how the philosophies and programs of boarding schools help transmit power and privilege. This school experience forms an everlasting social, political, and economic bond among all graduates, and the schools act as gatekeepers into prestigious universities. After graduates leave these universities, they connect with one another at the highest levels in the world of business, finance, and government.

The privileged social status that is produced and maintained through the elite educational system practically guarantees that the people who occupy key political and economic positions will form a like-minded, cohesive group with little resemblance to the majority whose lives depend on their decisions.

The Middle Class

In discussing the U.S. class system, it is tempting to focus attention on the very top or the very bottom, overlooking the chunk of the population that falls somewhere in the ill-defined center: the middle class.

Ironically, the middle class has always been important in defining U.S. culture. Every other class is measured and judged against the values and norms of the middle class. It is a universal class, a class that supposedly represents everyone (Ehrenreich, 1990). Not surprisingly, the middle class is a coveted political constituency. Liberal and conservative politicians alike court it. Policies are proclaimed on its behalf.

But the lofty cultural status of the middle class in U.S. society belies the difficulties it experiences. While corporate profits rose sharply during the early 2000s, the take-home pay of middle-income U.S. workers failed to keep up (Greenhouse & Leonhardt, 2006). Median household incomes rose steadily throughout the 1980s and 1990s but have leveled off and even fallen a bit ever since. Between 1989 and 2000, middle-class earnings grew by 9%; between 2000 and 2006, however, earnings shrunk by 1.3% (Mishel, Bernstein, & Shierholz, 2009).

The recent economic recession has taken its toll on every sector of the population, including the middle class. Hourly earnings, weekly earnings, and employer-provided benefits such as pensions and retirement accounts have all fallen since 2007 (Mishel et al., 2009). The number of workers who earn at least $20 an hour (a wage that once symbolized "middle class") has dropped nearly 60% over the past 3 decades (cited in Uchitelle, 2008). Indeed, after adjusting for inflation, the median hourly wage today is only $15.57 (U.S. Bureau of Labor Statistics, 2008c). In addition to lower wages, many workers across the country are also seeing their hours cut—for instance, by being moved from full-time to part-time or by losing opportunities for overtime (Goodman, 2008). According to data from the U.S. Bureau of Labor Statistics, in 2009, 6.7 million workers had to cut their hours to fewer than 35 a week due to slack work conditions, nearly double the number a year earlier (cited in Luo, 2009).

Even before the recession, only about a third of U.S. adults said they earned enough money to lead the kind of life they want, and about two thirds worried that good jobs would move overseas and that workers here would be left with jobs that don't pay enough (Kohut, 1999). Today, even families with good incomes live close to the financial edge, one layoff or medical emergency away from financial crisis. The proportion of middle-class families that could weather an economic emergency equal to 3 months of lost income decreased from 39% in 2000 to 29% in 2007 (Weller & Logan, 2008). Many urban areas around the country are beginning to see a new form of homelessness: formerly middle-class families who've lost their homes and now must live week-to-week in cramped motel rooms (Eckholm, 2009).

To make matters worse, the rising cost of health care coupled with higher insurance premiums, higher out-of-pocket payments, and less extensive coverage is making it increasingly difficult even for middle-class families to afford medical coverage (Abelson & Freudenheim, 2008). According to the Kaiser Family Foundation (2009), because of cost-trimming actions over the past 2 years, an estimated 11.1 million Americans have lost the health insurance they received through their employers. In fact, 39% of the uninsured have incomes more than $50,000 a year (DeNavas-Walt, Proctor, & Smith, 2008).

Not only do middle-class jobs pay less than they used to, but there are fewer of them to go around. Many people who have followed the institutionalized path to success—getting college degrees, developing marketable skills, building impressive résumés—are finding themselves out of work as companies cut costs to stay afloat. Hundreds of thousands of once-solid jobs in high tech, communication, and finance have disappeared. And with a national unemployment rate that hovers between 9% and 10%, many people who were once middle class are either marginally attached to the labor force or completely discouraged over their job prospects (U.S. Bureau of Labor Statistics, 2009).

To make matters worse, economists predict that even when the economy turns around, the job market will be weak. Many companies that are currently laying people off don't plan to rehire at prerecession levels once things get better (Lowenstein, 2009). Moreover, the types of jobs that will be available in the future may not be the sort that will strengthen people's middle-class status. According to the U.S. Bureau of Labor Statistics, 7 out of 10 occupations that are forecasted to show the greatest growth between now and 2012 are in low-wage service fields that require little, if any, education or training: retail sales, customer service, food service, cashier, janitor, waitperson, nursing aide, and hospital orderly (cited in Greenhouse, 2004). Most of these jobs pay less than $18,000 a year. By most accounts, high-paying jobs will continue to be in short supply, meaning that many college-educated people will be thwarted in their attempts to earn a comfortable living. It's no wonder that many middle-class adults feel as though they're on a treadmill that constantly threatens to throw them into a less desirable social class.

The Working Class

Members of the working class—people who work in factory, clerical, or low-paying sales jobs—are even more susceptible than those in the middle class to economic fluctuations. Most working-class people have only a high school education and earn an hourly wage rather than a weekly or monthly salary. Although they may earn enough money to survive, they typically don't earn enough to accumulate significant savings or other assets. Under the best circumstances, they usually have difficulty buying a home or paying for a child's education. When times are bad, they live their lives under the constant threat of layoffs, factory closings, and unemployment.

The working class has suffered disproportionately from downturns in the U.S. economy. For instance, to save money, many large companies have reduced their low-wage workforce. The year 2008 was the worst year for layoffs and job losses since World War II. Companies as diverse as Starbucks, Alcoa, Linens 'n Things, Bennigan's Restaurants, and DHL laid off tens of thousands of low-wage workers (Kells, 2009). Chrysler and General Motors alone cut more than 50,000 factory jobs in 2009.

Many working-class people haven't had raises in years but have seen the cost of living (in particular, food, energy, and health care) rise steadily. One in five people living in households with an income between $25,000 and $49,000 had no health insurance during 2007 (DeNavas-Walt et al., 2008). And about 80% of low-wage earners get no paid sick days off from work (Herbert, 2007).

The Poor

In an affluent society such as the United States, the people at the very bottom of the social class structure face constant humiliation in their everyday lives. You've heard the old saying "Money can't buy happiness." The implication is that true satisfaction in life is more than just a matter of being wealthy. Indeed, research shows that compared with others, people with high incomes aren't happier, don't spend more time in enjoyable activities, and tend to be more tense (Kahneman, Krueger, Schkade, Schwarz, & Stone, 2006). Yet such information provides little comfort to people who can't pay their bills, don't know where their next meal is coming from or whether their job will exist tomorrow, suffer from ill health, or have no home. The legendary vaudeville singer Sophie Tucker once said, "I've been rich and I've been poor—and believe me, rich is better."

Poverty clearly influences people's physical well-being. With each step down the income ladder comes an increased risk of headaches, varicose veins, respiratory infection, hypertension, stress-related illness, low-birth-weight babies, stroke, diabetes, and heart disease (Krugman, 2008; Perez-Peña, 2003; Shweder, 1997). Among children, decades of research show that rates of chronic illness, injury, ear disease, asthma, and physical inactivity all increase as socioeconomic status decreases (Chen, Matthews, & Boyce, 2002). Not surprisingly, research consistently shows that those at lower levels of the stratification system are more likely to die prematurely from inadequate health care than people at higher levels. Even after controlling for age, sex, race, family size, and education, the risk of death steadily decreases as income goes up (Marmot, 2004). And the gap is growing. According to data from the U.S. Department of Health and Human Services, in 1980, the most affluent U.S. citizens could expect to live 2.8 years longer than the poorest citizens; by 1998, the difference had increased to 4.5 years, and it continues to widen today (cited in Pear, 2008a). The health status of poor people in the United States is so bad that volunteer medical groups that were created to provide free medical services in destitute third-world countries such as Ghana, Tanzania, and Haiti have begun setting up mobile medical facilities in poor rural areas of the United States (Towell, 2007).

One of the obvious reasons for these health gaps is lack of access to adequate health care. According to the U.S. Bureau of the Census (2009), 32% of poor people have no health insurance, even though they may be eligible for government health insurance (Medicaid). In fact, only 42.3% of poor people have Medicaid (U.S. Bureau of the Census, 2009). The dangers of having no health insurance are undeniable. Uninsured people are less likely than people who have health insurance to see a doctor when needed and are more likely to report being in poor health (Robert Wood Johnson Foundation, 2005).

They are also more likely than those with private health insurance to receive diagnoses of cancer in its late stages, diminishing their chances of survival (Virning, 2008). Recently passed health care reform legislation may eventually alleviate this problem, but at the time of this writing, the changes had not yet taken effect.

In addition, approximately 11% of U.S. households are "food insecure"—meaning that some members don't have enough to eat or the family uses strategies such as eating less varied diets, participating in food assistance programs, or getting emergency food from community food pantries. And 4% of U.S. households were food insecure to the extent that one or more members were hungry at least some time during the year because they could not afford enough food (Nord, Andrews, & Carlson, 2006). In 2008, demand at U.S. food banks increased by 30% over the previous year (Bosman, 2009).

To make matters worse, lower-income families actually pay higher-than-average prices for basic necessities, including food (Brookings Institution, 2006). Large supermarket chains, for example, hesitate to open stores in very poor neighborhoods because of security fears. Hence, residents who are without transportation must rely on small neighborhood grocery stores, which charge higher prices for food than larger supermarkets do.

The educational deck is likewise stacked against poor people. A report by The Education Trust (2002) showed that in most states, those school districts with the neediest students receive far less state and local tax money—on average, just under $1,000 less per student—than those districts with the fewest poor students. Teachers in poor districts tend to be less experienced and are paid less than teachers in more affluent districts (LaCoste-Caputo, 2007). Without adequate resources, teachers become frustrated and do not teach; children become cynical and do not learn. Consequently, the worst-performing school districts typically have the largest percentages of students from poor families (cited in "Student Performance," 2007).

Even if they graduate from high school, most poor children can't afford to attend college. Those who do are more likely to attend community colleges or state universities, which are less expensive but lack the prestige, and often the quality, of their more expensive counterparts. To add insult to injury, the proportion of income that poor families must spend for children to attend public universities—about 25% of their total annual income—has almost doubled since 1980. For wealthy families, who spend an average of only about 2% of their annual income on their children's education, there was no increase (Steinberg, 2002).

Thus, despite nationwide efforts to increase access to higher education, a greater proportion of college students today come from wealthy families than was the case 2 decades ago. Of course, students without family wealth do sometimes attend top universities with the help of need-based scholarships. But these schools, by and large, have no systematic plans for identifying, recruiting, or admitting low-income students. Only 3% of students in elite U.S. universities come from the poorest quarter of the population, and only 10% come from the poorest half (Carnevale & Rose, 2003). Furthermore, once they get into college, poor students don't fare as well as their more affluent counterparts. According to the Department of Education, a little more than 25% of college students from families with annual incomes of less than $25,000 earn a bachelor's degree within 6 years. For students from families with incomes more than $70,000, the figure is 56% (Hebel, 2007).

What Poverty Means in the United States

We hear the word *poverty* all the time. In common usage, poverty is usually conceived in economic terms as the lack of sufficient money to ensure an adequate lifestyle. Sociologists, though, often distinguish between absolute and relative poverty. The term ***absolute poverty*** refers to the minimal requirements a human being needs to survive. The term ***relative poverty*** refers to one's economic position compared with the living standards of the majority in a given society. Absolute poverty means not having enough money for minimal food, clothing, and shelter. But relative poverty is more difficult to gauge. It reflects culturally defined aspirations and expectations. Poor people "generally feel better if they know that their position in life does not compare too badly with others in society" (quoted in Altman, 2003, p. 21). An annual family income of $5,000, which constitutes abject poverty in the United States, is perhaps five times higher than the *average* income in many developing countries. Life in a U.S. slum might be considered luxurious compared with the plight of tens of millions of destitute people in other parts of the world.

The Poverty Line

The U.S. government uses an absolute definition of poverty to identify those people who can't afford what they need to survive. The official U.S. ***poverty line*** identifies the amount of yearly income a family requires to meet its basic needs. Those who fall below the line are considered officially poor. The poverty line is based on pretax money income only, which does not include food stamps, Medicaid, public housing, and other noncash benefits. The figure does vary according to family size, and it is adjusted each year to account for inflation. But it doesn't take into account regional differences in cost of living. In 2009, the official poverty line for a family of four—two parents and two children—was an annual income of $21,756.

That dollar amount is established by the U.S. Department of Agriculture and for decades has been computed from something called the Thrifty Food Plan. This plan, developed in the early 1960s, is used to calculate the cost of a subsistence diet, which is the bare minimum a family needs to survive. This cost is then multiplied by 3 because research at the time showed that the average family spent one third of its income on food each year. The resulting amount was adopted in 1969 as the government's official poverty line. Even though the plan is modified periodically to account for changes in dietary recommendations, the formula itself and the basic definition of poverty have remained the same for about 4 decades.

Many policymakers, economists, sociologists, and concerned citizens question whether the current poverty line provides an accurate picture of basic needs in the United States. Several things have changed since the early 1960s. For instance, today, food costs account for less than 13% of the average family's budget because the price of other things, such as housing and medical care, has inflated at much higher rates (U.S. Bureau of Labor Statistics, 2007). In addition, there were fewer dual-earner or single-parent families in the past, meaning that fewer families had to pay for childcare at that time. In short, today's family has many more expenses and therefore probably spends a greater proportion of its total income on nonfood items. The consequence is that the official poverty line is probably set too low and therefore underestimates the hardships that struggling Americans experience (Swarns, 2008a).

Deciding who is and isn't officially poor is not just a matter of words and labels. When the poverty line is too low, we fail to recognize the problems of the many families who have difficulty making ends meet but who are not officially defined as poor. A needy family making slightly more than the poverty line may not qualify for a variety of public assistance programs, such as housing benefits, Head Start, Medicaid, or Temporary Assistance for Needy Families. As a result, its standard of living may not be as good as that of a family that earns slightly less but qualifies for these programs.

Some economists suggest that the exclusive focus on income in setting the poverty line underestimates the harmful long-term effects of poverty. Obviously, when families don't have enough income, they can't buy adequate food, clothing, and shelter. But when families don't have any assets, such as savings and home equity, they lose economic security and their ability to plan, dream, and pass on opportunities to their children (Boshara, 2002).

The Near-Poor

Interestingly, the government seems to agree implicitly that the poverty line is too low. The U.S. Bureau of the Census defines individuals or families who earn up to 25% more than the official poverty line amount as the ***near-poor*** or ***working poor***. Their existence is fraught with irony. Because they fall above the poverty line, they escape academic attention and tend not to be the recipients of large-scale governmental assistance programs. At the same time, they are everywhere, doing the tasks with which others come into contact and on which they depend on a daily basis:

> They serve you Big Macs and help you find merchandise at Wal-Mart. They harvest your food, clean your offices, and sew your clothes. In a California factory, they package lights for your kids' bikes. In a New Hampshire plant, they assemble books of wallpaper samples to help you redecorate. (Shipler, 2004, p. 3)

When nothing out of the ordinary happens, the near-poor can manage. But an unexpected event—a sickness, an injury, the breakdown of a major appliance or automobile—can destroy a family financially and sink it into poverty.

It has been estimated that about one quarter of U.S. residents hovering just above the poverty line will fall below it at some point in their lives, and then they have some difficult decisions to make. One study of 34,000 people nationwide found that during the cold winter months, families spend less on food and reduce their caloric intake by an average of 10% in order to pay their fuel bills (Bhattacharya, DeLeire, Haider, & Currie, 2003). Imagine being a poor single mother with a sick child. One trip to the doctor might cost an entire week's food budget or a month of rent. Dental work or an eye examination is easily sacrificed when other pressing bills need to be paid. If she depends on a car to get to work and it breaks down, a few hundred dollars to fix it might mean not paying the electric bill that month. When gasoline prices approach $5 a gallon—as they did for a while in 2008—many near-poor families find that they have to cut down on food purchases so they can afford to drive to work. These are choices that wealthier families never face.

The Poverty Rate

The ***poverty rate,*** the percentage of residents whose income falls below the official poverty line, is the measure that the U.S. government uses to track the success of its efforts to reduce poverty. In 2008 (the most recent year for which data are available), 13.2% of the population—or more than 39 million Americans—fell below the poverty line, up from 11.3% in 2000 (DeNavas-Walt et al., 2009). If we add the near-poor, the number increases to more than 53 million (DeNavas-Walt et al., 2009). Economists project a spike of as many as 10.3 million additional poor people in the next few years, the result of high unemployment and the economic recession (Parrott, 2008).

When used to describe national trends in poverty, the overall poverty rate can obscure important differences among subgroups of the population. For example, although two out of every three poor people in the United States are white, the poverty rate for non-Hispanic Whites (8.6%) is lower than that for Asian Americans (11.8%) and considerably lower than that for nonwhite Latino/as (23.2%) and African Americans (24.7%). The poverty rates in the South (14.3%) and West (13.5%) are higher than the rates in the Midwest (12.4%) and Northeast (11.6%; DeNavas-Walt et al., 2009).

Although racial and ethnic minorities have consistently been rated among the poorest Americans, other groups have seen their status change over time. Before Social Security was instituted in 1935, many of the most destitute were those over age 65. As recently as 1970, 25% of U.S. residents over age 65 fell below the poverty line. Today, only 9.7% of the people in this age group are poor (DeNavas-Walt et al., 2009).

Taking their place among the poor, however, are children. Although the rate of child poverty has declined a bit since the mid-1990s, 19% of U.S. residents under the age of 18 are poor, and children under 6 are the poorest age group in the nation (21.3%; DeNavas-Walt et al., 2009). Children represent 25% of the U.S. population but constitute about 35% of all Americans living in poverty. The figures are especially bad for children of color: 26.9% of Latino/a children and 33.4% of African American children live in poor households (U.S. Bureau of the Census, 2009). The 18% poverty rate among U.S. children is the highest of any industrialized country. In Sweden, Norway, and Finland, for example, between 3% and 4% of all children live in poverty (Mishel et al., 2009).

Several factors explain why the poverty rate among U.S. children is high compared with that of older U.S. residents. For one thing, family structure is closely related to child poverty. The poverty rate for families headed by single mothers is 28.7%, compared with 13.8% for families headed by single fathers and 5.5% for married-couple families (DeNavas-Walt et al., 2009). Half of all poor families are headed by single women. More than half of all children under the age of 6 who live in a female-headed household are poor, about five times the rate of children in married-couple families (Federal Interagency Forum on Child and Family Statistics, 2007).

In addition, government spending on programs for the elderly (Medicaid, Medicare, Social Security) has increased over the past 4 decades, while spending on children (cash assistance, health care, food and nutritional aid, etc.) has dropped and will continue to drop into the foreseeable future (Steuerle, 2007). Worldwide, there is a strong correlation between the amount of money a country spends on social programs and rates of child poverty (Mishel, Bernstein, & Allegretto, 2007).

Why Poverty Persists

Even in the best of times, a prosperous country such as the United States has a sizable population of poor people. Why, in such an affluent society, is poverty a permanent fixture? To explain the persistence of poverty, we must look at enduring imbalances in income and wealth, the structural role poverty plays in larger social institutions, and the dominant cultural beliefs and attitudes that help support it.

Enduring Disparities in Income and Wealth

One obvious reason why poverty is so persistent in the United States is the way income and wealth are distributed. In 2006, the annual income of the top 5% of U.S. families averaged $174,012, and the annual income of the bottom 20% of families averaged $20,035 (U.S. Bureau of the Census, 2009).

This wide income gap between the richest and poorest segments of the population has been growing steadily over the past few decades, although the recent recession may have slowed this trend by taking a bite out of sources of income common among the very wealthy, such as stock dividends and real estate (Leonhardt & Fabrikant, 2009). The share of the nation's income earned by the richest Americans grew dramatically between the 1970s and the mid-2000s; at the same time, the share earned by the rest of the population remained flat. Between 1979 and 2006, the average income for the lowest-earning 90% of Americans grew by only 16%. During the same time span, the average income of the nation's top 1% of earners grew by 144%, and the income of the top 0.1% grew by an astonishing 324% (Mishel et al., 2009).

In 2007, after 10 years of debate, Congress finally approved a measure to increase the minimum wage from $5.15 an hour to $7.25 an hour. It's unclear, however, whether this increase will do much to close the income gap. In those states that already have a higher minimum wage than the federal level, millions of workers still fall into poverty (Uchitelle, 2006a).

Meanwhile, compensation for those at the very top continues to soar. The average American chief executive makes more than $10 million a year. In 2008, the average annual compensation for the 10 highest-paid executives was more than $53 million (AFL-CIO, 2009). In 1945, chief executives earned $51 for every $1 earned by the average worker; by 2007, that figure had increased to $275 (Billitteri, 2007; Mishel et al., 2009). We may want to believe that personal effort and hard work solely determine our success, but it's hard to imagine that a CEO of, say, an electronics company works 275 times harder than a person who actually assembles the TVs and cell phones.

Tax laws also work to the advantage of those at the top. The rich do pay a lot of taxes as a total percentage of all taxes collected; however, they don't pay a lot of taxes as a percentage of what they earn and can afford. In the 1940s, the tax rate for the wealthiest tax bracket was about 90%; today it's 35%. Incidentally, the threshold for that top bracket is $357,000. Any income above that is taxed at the same rate. In other words, someone earning $40 million a year pays the same tax percentage as someone earning $360,000 a year (Leonhardt, 2009).

Although most U.S. residents paid more taxes as a percentage of income during the late 1990s and early 2000s than in previous decades, many of the wealthiest citizens paid less. Families earning more than $1 million a year have seen their federal tax rates drop more sharply than any other group in the country (Andrews, 2007). In fact, in 2008, the Bush tax cuts had virtually no effect on low-income families. However, families in the top 1% of income earners saw tax reductions of more than $50,000 (Mishel et al., 2009).

The United States has the greatest income inequality between poor and wealthy citizens of any industrialized nation. The wealthiest fifth of U.S. families earns almost nine times more than the poorest fifth (U.S. Bureau of the Census, 2009). In France, the richest fifth earns seven times more than the poorest fifth, and it's four times more in Japan (Phillips, 2002). But to be fair, the income gap between rich and poor is worse in developing countries. For example, the richest 20% of Brazilians earn 64% of the country's income, whereas the poorest 20% earn 2.5% (Romero, 1999). Similar disparities exist in other Latin American countries and in most of sub-Saharan Africa.

Inequalities in income lead to even more striking inequalities in wealth. A lifetime of high earnings and inheritance from privileged parents creates a lasting advantage in ownership of property; of durable consumer goods such as cars, houses, and furniture; and of financial assets such as stocks, bonds, savings, and life insurance. The wealthiest 1% of U.S. households control a larger share of the national wealth than the entire bottom 90% (Mishel et al., 2009). There are four times as many households with a net worth of more than $10 million today than there were in 1989 (Uchitelle, 2006b). At the same time, one in six households has zero or negative net wealth.

We will never live in a society with a perfectly equal distribution of income and wealth. Some people will always earn more, have more, and maybe even deserve more than others. But the magnitude of the gap between rich and poor in the United States challenges the notion that we live in a society where everyone is valued equally. As disparities in income and wealth grow, so too does the gap in quality of life and access to opportunity between those at the top of society and those at the bottom.

The Social "Benefits" of Poverty

Recall the structural-functionalist assertion that stratification is necessary because it ensures that the most qualified and valuable people in society will occupy the most important positions. Social conditions exist and persist only if they are functional to society in some way. But functional for whom? If you were to survey people on the street and ask them if poverty is a good or bad thing, most, I'm sure, would say, "Bad." Yet according to sociologist Herbert Gans (1971, 1996), within a free-market economy and competitive society such as the United States, poverty plays a necessary institutional role. Although structural functionalism has often been criticized for its propensity to justify the status quo, Gans combines it with conflict thinking to identify several economic and social "functions" served by poverty that benefit all other classes in society:

- Poverty provides a ready pool of low-wage laborers who are available to do society's "dirty work." Poor people work at low wages primarily because they have little choice. When large numbers of poor people compete for scarce jobs, business owners can pay lower wages.

- Poverty ensures that there will be enough individuals, especially during times of high unemployment, to populate an all-volunteer military. To people with limited educational and occupational opportunities, military service holds out the promise of stable employment, comprehensive insurance coverage, a living wage, free schooling, the development of marketable skills, and an escape from poverty. In Iraq and Afghanistan, U.S. military personnel have been disproportionately ethnoracial minorities from poor and working-class families (Halbfinger & Holmes, 2003). As you might guess, American casualties have also overwhelmingly been from families of modest means who live in sparsely populated rural counties (Cushing & Bishop, 2005; Golway, 2004). By 2006, 34% of U.S. military personnel killed in Iraq came from the poorest quarter of families, while only 17% came from the richest quarter (cited in "Price Paid," 2006).

- Poverty supports occupations that either serve the poor or protect the rest of society from them: police officers, penologists, welfare workers, social workers, lawyers, pawnshop owners, and so on. Even drug dealers and loan sharks depend on the presence of a large population of poor people willing to pay for their illegal services.

- Poverty is the reason why some people purchase goods and services that would otherwise go unused: secondhand appliances; day-old bread, fruits, and vegetables; deteriorated housing; dilapidated cars; incompetent physicians; and so forth. In 2002, dozens of Coca-Cola employees in Texas revealed that, for years, they were required to sell expired Coke to stores in poor neighborhoods. They were instructed to strip cans from their boxes, stuff them into fresh boxes with new dates stamped on the side, and stock them on store shelves in poor neighborhoods as if they were new (Winter, 2002). Clearly, this merchandise had little or no monetary value outside the poverty market; it was believed that the beverages couldn't be sold to wealthier Coke drinkers because they'd have noticed the difference.

- Poverty is a visible reminder to the rest of society of the "legitimacy" of the conventional values of hard work, thrift, and honesty. By violating, or seeming to violate, these mainstream values, the poor reaffirm these virtues. If poor people are thought to be lazy, their presence reinforces the ethic of hard work; if the poor single mother is condemned, the two-parent family is legitimated as the ideal.

- Poverty provides scapegoats for society's institutional problems. The alleged laziness of the jobless poor and the anger aimed at street people and beggars distract us from the failure of the economic system to adequately deal with the needs of all citizens. Likewise, the alleged personal shortcomings of slum dwellers and the homeless deflect attention from shoddy practices within the housing industry.

This explanation of poverty can easily be dismissed as cold and heartless. We certainly don't want to admit that poor people allow the rest of us to avoid unpleasant or even dangerous tasks and enjoy comfortable and pleasant lifestyles. Yet this explanation is quite compelling. Just as society needs talented people to fill its important occupational positions, it also needs a stable population of poor people to fill its "less important" positions. If society fostered full equality, who would do the dirty work?

If we are truly serious about reducing poverty, we must find alternative ways of performing the societal functions it currently fulfills. But such a change will assuredly come at a cost to those who can now take advantage of poverty's presence. In short, poverty will be eliminated only when it becomes dysfunctional for people who *aren't* poor.

The Ideology of Competitive Individualism

Poverty also persists because of cultural beliefs and values that support the economic status quo. An important component of this value system in U.S. society is the belief in ***competitive individualism*** (Feagin, 1975; Lewis, 1978; Neubeck, 1986). As children, most of us are taught that nobody deserves a free ride. The way to be successful is to work hard, strive toward goals, and compete well against others. We are taught that we are fully responsible for our own economic fates. Rags-to-riches stories of people who rose above terrible conditions to make it to the top reinforce the notion that anybody can be successful if he or she simply has the desire and puts in the necessary effort.

The dark side of the U.S. belief in competitive individualism is that it all too easily justifies the unequal distribution of rewards and the existence of poverty. If people who are financially successful are thought to deserve their advantages allegedly because of individual hard work and desire, then the people who are struggling financially must likewise deserve their plight—because of their *lack* of hard work and desire. People in the United States have an intense need to believe that good things happen to good people and bad things happen to bad people (Huber & Form, 1973; Lerner, 1970). In short, most of us want to believe that if a poor person is suffering, she or he "must have" done something to deserve it. The people who succeed, in contrast, "must have" been born smarter, stayed in school longer, or worked harder. The belief in competitive individualism gives people the sense that they can control their own fate.

But the depth of such beliefs depends on where people are located in the stratification system. When asked why people succeed, lower-income people are more likely than wealthy people to downplay competitive individualism and cite reasons such as "coming from a wealthy family" or "knowing the right people." Upper-class individuals, on the other hand, are more likely than their lower-income counterparts to contend that opportunities for success and advancement are available to everyone, meaning that success is a result of individual merit. They are likely to cite "natural ability," "a good education," and "hard work" as factors that are essential to get ahead in life. Hence, they can justify inequality by emphasizing equal chances (cited in Scott & Leonhardt, 2005).

The belief system that such a comment reflects doesn't take into consideration the possibility that the competition itself may not be fair. Competitive individualism assumes that opportunities to learn a high-level trade or skill or enter a profession are available to everyone. Every person is supposed to have the chance to "be all that he or she can be." But the system may be rigged to favor those who already have power and privilege.

The contemporary U.S. welfare system does not seek to alter these conditions. Instead, it reflects the belief that the best way to reduce poverty is to change poor people's lifestyles. In 1994, more than 5 million U.S. families were on government assistance. By 2006, that figure had dropped to 1.8 million (U.S. Bureau of the Census, 2009). You might think that a booming economy is what helped reduce U.S. citizens' dependence on government aid, but much of the reduction was actually due to the eligibility limitations of a new welfare system that began in 1996. This system includes a mandatory work requirement (or enrollment in vocational training or community service) after 2 years of receiving assistance and a 5-year lifetime limit to benefits for any family. Despite soaring unemployment rates and the worst economic recession in decades, 18 states cut back their cash assistance welfare programs in 2009 (DeParle, 2009).

Some of the people who left welfare have, in fact, found sustained employment (Duncan & Chase-Lansdale, 2001). However, more than half of the decrease in welfare rolls in the first decade after welfare reform went into effect reflects a decline in government assistance to families that are poor enough to qualify for aid rather than an increase in the number of families who no longer need the assistance. Indeed, in the 1990s, the poverty rate decreased by only 14% (U.S. Bureau of the Census, 2009) and has increased significantly ever since. Moreover, the number of people living in "deep" poverty—that is, below *half* the poverty line—has increased significantly in recent years (Parrott & Sherman, 2006).

You'd think that with all the political rhetoric over "ending welfare as we know it," the welfare system represented the largest drain on the federal budget. However, the amount of money the government spends on aid to the poor is a fraction of what it spends on assistance programs that serve predominantly middle-class recipients. In 2006, the federal government paid individuals approximately $47 billion in poverty assistance under the Temporary Assistance to Needy Families and Food Stamp programs. That same year, it spent more than $470 billion on Social Security, unemployment insurance, and Medicare, the government-subsidized health care program for the elderly (U.S. Bureau of the Census, 2009).

Nonetheless, the assumptions behind welfare reform are clear: Making work mandatory will teach welfare recipients important work values and habits, make poor single mothers models of these values for their children, and cut the nation's welfare rolls. The underlying idea is that hard work will lead to the moral and financial rewards of family self-reliance. It will cure poverty and welfare dependence and ensure that new generations of children from single-parent families will be able to enter the American mainstream. Like competitive individualism, however, this ideology protects the nonpoor, the larger social structure, and the economic system while blaming poor people for their own plight.

GLOBAL DEVELOPMENT AND INEQUALITY

As you've seen elsewhere in this book, it is becoming increasingly difficult to understand life in any one society without understanding that society's place in the larger global context. The trend toward globalization (see Chapter 9) may have brought the world's inhabitants closer together, but they are not all benefiting equally. Nations have differing amounts of power to ensure that their interests are met. The more developed and less developed countries of the world experience serious inequalities in wealth that have immediate consequences for their citizens.

The Global Economic Gap

Just as an economic gap exists between rich and poor citizens within a single country, so too do economic gaps exist between rich and poor countries. Consider these facts:

- The average per capita yearly income in Western Europe, the United States, Canada, and Japan is $31,200; in the less developed countries of the world, it's less than $5,000 (Population Reference Bureau, 2008b).
- About 0.13% of the world's population controls 25% of the world's financial assets. On the other end of the economic spectrum, more than 2.6 billion people in less developed countries live on the equivalent of less than $2 a day (Shah, 2009), and close to half of all people living in sub-Saharan Africa survive on $1 a day (World Bank, 2006).
- The wealthiest 20% of the world accounts for about 77% of all private consumption (Shah, 2009). Twelve percent of the world's population (who happen to reside in developed countries) use 85% of its water. The United States alone consumes one quarter of the world's oil ("Burning Through Oil," 2008).

Explanations for Global Stratification

How has global stratification come about? The conflict perspective explains not only stratification within a society but also stratification between societies. One way a country can use its power to control another is through ***colonization***—invading and establishing control over a weaker country and its people in order to expand the colonizer's markets. Typically, the native people of the colony are forced to give up their culture. The colony serves as a source of labor and raw materials for the colonizer's industries and a market for their high-priced goods. Much of North and South America, Africa, and Asia were at one time or another under the colonial control of European countries such as Great Britain, France, Spain, Holland, and Portugal. The United States once controlled territories in Central and South America.

Although the direct conquest of weak countries is rare today, wealthy countries are still able to exploit them for commercial gain. Powerful countries can use weaker countries as a source of cheap raw materials and cheap labor. They can also exert financial pressure on poorer nations by setting world prices on certain goods (Chase-Dunn & Rubinson, 1977). Because their economic base is weak, poor countries often have to borrow money or buy manufactured goods on credit from wealthy countries. The huge debt they build up locks them into a downward spiral of exploitation and poverty. They cannot develop an independent economy of their own and thus remain dependent on wealthy countries for their very survival (Frank, 1969).

Global Financial Organizations

It's not just powerful nations that have the ability to hold poor nations in their grip. Several international financial organizations play a significant role in determining the economic and social policies of developing countries. For instance, the World Bank funds reconstruction and development in poor countries through investments and loans. It spends about $55 billion annually to better the lives of destitute people worldwide (Dugger, 2004b). Similarly, the International Monetary Fund (IMF) tries to foster economic growth and international monetary cooperation through financial and technical assistance. The World Trade Organization (WTO) oversees the rules of trade between nations.

Although these organizations spend a lot of money to improve the standard of living in many poor countries by funding projects such as new roads or water treatment plants, they may, from time to time, do more harm than good. The WTO, for example, can impose fines and sanctions on debtor countries that don't act as it dictates. It has, in the past, forced Japan to accept greater levels of pesticide residue on imported food, prevented Guatemala from outlawing deceptive advertising on baby food, and eliminated asbestos bans and car emission standards in various countries (Parenti, 2006).

In fact, the countries that receive the aid of these organizations sometimes end up even more impoverished than before. When the World Bank and the IMF provide development credit, they do so with certain conditions attached. The conditions, referred to as "structural adjustments," typically reflect a Western-style, free-market approach: reducing government spending, eliminating barriers to foreign ownership, privatizing public services, and paying high interest rates (Brutus, 1999). For instance, countries might be required to lift trade restrictions, cut social spending, or balance their budgets in exchange for aid.

You can see that global financial relationships between international lending institutions and poor countries are a double-edged sword. The countries certainly receive much-needed financial assistance. But in the process, they sometimes become even more dependent and less able to improve conditions for their citizens.

Multinational Corporations

Global stratification has been made even more complex by the growth of massive multinational corporations, which can go outside their country's borders to pursue their financial interests if domestic opportunities aren't promising. They can invest their money in more lucrative foreign corporations or establish their businesses or factories abroad. U.S.-based multinational corporations employ close to 22 million people worldwide and have total assets of $16.7 trillion (U.S. Bureau of the Census, 2009).

Often, such success comes at a price. The largest U.S.-based multinational corporations achieved record earnings at the end of the 20th century while hiring fewer Americans than ever. Between 1980 and 1999, the 500 largest corporations tripled their assets. At the same time, though, they eliminated almost 5 million U.S. jobs (Phillips, 2002). In 2005, IBM laid off 13,000 American and European workers at the same time that it was adding 14,000 workers in India to its payroll (Lohr, 2005).

With their ability to quickly shift operations to friendly countries, multinational corporations find it easy to evade the governance of any one country. Their decisions reflect corporate goals and not necessarily the well-being or interests of any particular country.

From a structural-functionalist perspective, a U.S. company locating a production facility in a poor country would seem to benefit everyone involved. The host country benefits from the creation of new jobs and a higher standard of living. The corporation, of course, benefits from increased profits. And consumers in the country where the corporation is based benefit from paying lower prices for products that would cost more if manufactured at home. Furthermore, the entire planet benefits because these firms form allegiances with many different countries and therefore might help pressure them into settling their political disputes peacefully.

Multinational corporations are indeed a valuable part of the international economy, as we saw in Chapter 9. However, the conflict perspective argues that in the long run, multinationals can actually perpetuate or even worsen global stratification. One common criticism of multinationals is that they exploit local workers and communities. Employees in foreign plants or factories often work under conditions that wouldn't be tolerated in wealthier countries. The most obvious inequity is the wage people earn. For example, according to the National Labor Committee for Worker and Human Rights (2001), senior seamstresses with 6 years' experience at a Bangladesh factory that makes Disney clothing earn 17 cents an hour. Most work more than 15 hours a day, 7 days a week.

In addition, environmental regulations and occupational safety requirements that tend to drive up the cost of finished products, such as protection against dangerous conditions or substances, sometimes don't exist in other countries. Hence, local workers may become sicker and the environment more polluted when foreign manufacturers set up facilities.

The host countries themselves are equally likely to be exploited. The money that multinational corporations earn is rarely reinvested in the host country. In fact, 85% of the profit from exported products ends up in the hands of the multinational corporations, bankers, traders, and distributors (Braun, 1997). For example, in Brazil, one of the world's largest agricultural exporters, shipments abroad of fruits, vegetables, and soybeans have grown considerably over the past several decades. During the same period, however, the number of Brazilians who were undernourished grew from one third to two thirds of the population (Braun, 1997).

Local economies can suffer as well. For instance, supermarket chains owned by large multinational corporations have revolutionized food distribution worldwide. They are popular with consumers all over the world because of their lower prices and greater variety and convenience (Dugger, 2004a). But these stores tend to get their produce from large companies that have more money and marketing know-how than small, local suppliers and can therefore provide cheaper fruits and vegetables. Hence, the livelihoods of millions of struggling small farmers have been destroyed, widening the gap between the haves and the have-nots in developing countries.

Not all multinationals are hard-hearted organizations that ignore the well-being of their workers abroad, the well-being of the workforce at home whose jobs are being exported to other countries, or the health and welfare of poor people in developing nations. For many multinationals, relocating manufacturing facilities to another country where labor is less expensive is a necessary response to global economic pressures as well as the demands of domestic consumers for inexpensive products. But those processes that drive corporate decisions do sometimes drive individuals out of work, contribute to environmental and health problems, and reinforce global inequality.

CONCLUSION

In Chapter 1, I pondered the question of how free we really are to act as we wish. I described some of the personal, interpersonal, and structural considerations that limit or constrain our choices. In this chapter, you have seen that this fundamental issue is affected by social stratification and inequality. Certain groups of people have a greater capacity to control their own lives than others. Your position in the stratification system can determine not only your ability to influence people and exert authority but a whole host of life chances as well, from financial stability to housing, education, and health care. The unequal distribution of economic resources, whether between wealthy and poor individuals in the same society or between wealthy and poor countries worldwide, has created a seemingly indestructible system of haves and have-nots.

The profound imbalances in wealth, power, and prestige that exist in the United States are especially ironic given how loudly and frequently U.S. citizens boast of their cultural commitment to the values of equality and justice. Nevertheless, the U.S. system is set up, like most others in the world, to promote, enhance, and protect the interests of those who reside at or near the top of the stratification system. Authority, wealth, and influence grant rights that are unknown to the vast majority of people.

It's rather shocking that in a country as wealthy as the United States, a comfortable, healthy, and stable life is well beyond the reach of tens of millions of people. Constant media images of wealth remind poor and working-class people that they are outsiders who can only watch and long to be part of that affluent world. And when disaster strikes, such as Hurricane Katrina or the 2010 earthquake in Haiti, poor people receive the message once again that their marginal status in society can have deadly consequences.

We speak of the poor as if they were an unchanging and faceless group to be pitied, despised, or feared. To talk of the "poverty problem" is to talk about some depersonalized, permanent fixture on the U.S. landscape. But poverty is people. It's people standing in soup kitchen lines and welfare lines. It's people living in rat-infested projects. It's people sleeping on sidewalks. It's people struggling to acquire things the rest of society takes for granted. It's people coming up short in their quest for the American Dream.

When we look at the institutional causes of poverty, we see that the personality or "cultural" traits often associated with poverty—low ambition, rejection of the work ethic, inability to plan for the future—might be better understood as the consequences of poverty rather than its causes. As long as the structural obstacles to stable employment, adequate wages, and a decent education continue to exist, so will the characteristic hopelessness associated with poverty.

CHAPTER HIGHLIGHTS

◆ Stratification is a ranking of entire groups of people, based on race, gender, or social class, that perpetuates unequal rewards and life chances in society.

◆ Social class is the primary means of stratification in many societies, including the United States. Contemporary sociologists are likely to define one's class standing as a combination of income, wealth, occupational prestige, and educational attainment. Social class is more than an economic position; it is a way of life that affects how we experience every facet of our lives.

◆ The structural-functionalist explanation of stratification is that higher rewards, such as prestige and large salaries, are afforded to the most important positions in society, thereby ensuring that the most qualified individuals will occupy the highest positions. Conflict theory argues that stratification reflects an unequal distribution of power in society and is a primary source of conflict and tension.

◆ The official U.S. poverty line, the dollar cutoff point that defines the amount of income necessary for subsistence living, may actually be set too low, thereby underestimating the proportion of the population that is suffering financially.

◆ Poverty persists because it serves economic and social functions. The ideology of competitive individualism–that to succeed in life all one has to do is work hard and win in competition with others–creates a belief that poor people are to blame for their own suffering. In addition, poverty receives institutional "support" from a distribution of wealth and income that is growing increasingly unequal.

◆ Stratification exists not only among different groups within the same society but also among different societies within a global community. Wealthy nations are better able to control the world's financial resources than poor nations are.

KEY TERMS

absolute poverty Inability to afford the minimal requirements for sustaining a reasonably healthy existence

authority Possession of some status or quality that compels others to obey one's directives or commands

caste system Stratification system based on heredity, with little movement allowed across strata

colonization Process of expanding economic markets by invading and establishing control over a weaker country and its people

competitive individualism Cultural belief that those who succeed in society are those who work the hardest and have the best abilities and that those who suffer don't work hard enough or lack the necessary traits or abilities

estate system (feudal system) Stratification system in which high-status groups own land and have power based on noble birth

false consciousness Situation in which people in the lower classes come to accept a belief system that harms them; the primary means by which powerful classes in society prevent protest and revolution

means of production Land, commercial enterprises, factories, and wealth, which form the economic basis of class societies

middle class In a society stratified by social class, a group of people who have an intermediate level of wealth, income, and prestige, such as managers, supervisors, executives, small business owners, and professionals

near-poor Individuals or families whose earnings are between 100% and 125% of the poverty line (see also **working poor**)

poor In a society stratified by social class, a group of people who work for minimum wage or are chronically unemployed

poverty line Amount of yearly income a family requires to meet its basic needs, according to the federal government

poverty rate Percentage of people whose income falls below the poverty line

power Ability to affect decisions in ways that benefit a person or protect his or her interests

prestige Respect and honor given to some people in society

relative poverty Individuals' economic position compared with the living standards of the majority in the society

slavery Economic form of inequality in which some people are the property of others

social class Group of people who share a similar economic position in a society, based on their wealth and income

social mobility Movement of people or groups from one class to another

socioeconomic status Prestige, honor, respect, and lifestyle associated with different positions or groups in society

stratification Ranking system for groups of people that perpetuates unequal rewards and life chances in society

upper class In a society stratified by social class, a group of people who have high income and prestige and who own vast amounts of property and other forms of wealth, such as owners of large corporations, top financiers, rich celebrities and politicians, and members of prestigious families

working class In a society stratified by social class, a group of people who have a low level of wealth, income, and prestige, such as industrial and factory workers, office workers, clerks, and farm and manual laborers

working poor Employed people who consistently earn wages but do not make enough to survive (see also **near-poor**).

©Tyrone Turner/National Geographic/Getty Images

11 The Architecture of Inequality

Race and Ethnicity

Just like millions of other Americans, I sat transfixed in front of my television on the night of November 4, 2008, watching the presidential election results trickle in. At about 11:00 PM Eastern time, the networks made the astounding projection: Barack Obama—a man with a black Kenyan father and a white American mother—would be the 44th president of the United States. I sat in semi-disbelief. Had this country, one with such a difficult, painful, and deadly racial history, really just elected a black man to the highest office in the land? A development that would have been unthinkable 50, 25, or even 10 years ago had just happened. People of all colors and classes here and abroad danced in the streets. Jesse Jackson, Oprah Winfrey, Colin Powell, and countless other less famous people wept with joy. Parents named their newborns "Barack." One African American columnist wrote a letter to her 4-month-old son that night:

> What does Barack Obama's election mean to you? When you are older we will talk about how African American children, like their parents and grandparents, have struggled to overcome the feeling that no matter how hard they study and work and try, there are barriers—some visible, others hidden but still there—that block their way. The feeling that we can rise, but only so far. I did not want you to grow up believing

> that bitter remnants of the past could hold power over your future. I wanted to be able to tell you that it wasn't true—that you could be anything you wanted to be. But I couldn't quite believe it myself. Now I do. (Kelley, 2008, p. 29)

Sociologists, columnists, and political pundits struggled to find the most memorable and most articulate way to capture the historical significance of the moment. Some speculated that it might mark the end of racial inequality and exclusion in this country; others wondered if we'd become a "postracial" society, where traditional racial categories no longer matter. In a national poll the day before Obama's inauguration, more than two thirds of African Americans said they believed that Martin Luther King's famous 1963 dream (of a country where race and ethnicity are losing their status as major criteria for judging the content of a person's character) had been fulfilled (CNN.com, 2009). As I tried to absorb the magnitude of what took place that night, I began to think about the other important but less dramatic educational, economic, political, and cultural gains that people of color have made over the past few years:

- The percentage of African American and Latino/a college graduates has risen steadily over the past 10 years, as has the proportion of ethnoracial minority families that could be considered middle or upper class.
- The number of black and Latino/a families headed by married couples is increasing.
- More Latino/as, Asian Americans, and Native Americans are in elected offices at the national, state, and local levels than ever before. In 2009, Sonia Sotomayor became the first Latina to be appointed to the U.S. Supreme Court.
- African American artists such as Jay-Z, Flo Rida, Kanye West, Beyoncé, and 50 Cent have achieved remarkable crossover success, and Oprah Winfrey is one of the highest-paid entertainers in the country. The most successful athletes in what were once exclusively white sports—tennis and golf—are people of color: Serena and Venus Williams and Tiger Woods. Twenty-seven percent of all major league baseball players are Latino, and 10.2% are African American (Lapchick, 2009).

Yet as I think of the significant strides ethnoracial minorities have made, I can't forget a more troubling reality. Despite the progress they've attained, African Americans, Latino/as, and Native Americans still remain, on average, the poorest and most disadvantaged of all groups in the United States. Their average annual income is still substantially lower than that of Whites and Asian Americans (U.S. Bureau of the Census, 2009). Half of black men in their 20s who didn't attend college are unemployed (compared with 21% of Whites; Eckholm, 2006b). The rate of home ownership among minority groups passed 50% for the first time in 2004, but rates of foreclosures have more than doubled since then (Bajaj & Nixon, 2006). In New York City, foreclosures occur three times as often in black and Latino/a neighborhoods as in mostly white ones (Powell & Roberts, 2009). Of all ethnoracial groups in this society, African Americans have the lowest life expectancy; highest rate of infant mortality; highest rate of most cancers, diabetes, heart disease, high blood pressure, and HIV/AIDS; and highest rate of death from treatable illnesses, gunshot wounds, and drug- or alcohol-induced causes (American Sociological Association, 2005; U.S. Bureau of the Census, 2009).

I also thought of some specific violent events in the recent past that further belie the image of racial progress and harmony. On the same day in 2009 that *The New York Times* reported that people's views on race relations might be more positive and optimistic than ever before (Stolberg & Connelly, 2009), it ran a story about two white teenagers facing trial for killing a 25-year-old Mexican man after calling him a "spic" and telling him, "This is Shenandoah [Pennsylvania]. You don't belong here" (quoted in Hamill, 2009, p. A3). In one New York suburb, attacks on Latinos are such an established pastime among some white youths that attackers have a common derogatory term for it: "Beaner hopping" (Barnard, 2009). According to the Federal Bureau of Investigation (2008), in 2007, about 7,500 hate-related offenses were motivated by race, religion, or ethnicity, a number that increases each year. Indeed, in response to reports of the growth in racial hate groups, the Department of Homeland Security stated that the election of the country's first African American president coupled with the current economic downturn "present unique drivers for right-wing radicalization and recruitment" (quoted in Conant, 2009, p. 32).

So how far have we really come? Which is the real United States? Is it the one that Martin Luther King Jr. dreamed about? Or is it the one perpetually plagued by racial inequality, prejudice, and hatred?

In the previous chapter, I examined the class stratification system. But social class doesn't create unequal life chances on its own. This chapter focuses on another important determinant of social inequality: race and ethnicity.

RACE AND ETHNICITY: MORE THAN JUST BIOLOGY

To most people, ***race*** is a category of individuals labeled and treated as similar because of common inborn biological traits, such as skin color, color and texture of hair, and shape of eyes, nose, or head. It is widely assumed that people who are placed in the same racial category share behavioral, psychological, and personality traits that are linked to their physical similarities. But sociologists typically use the term ***ethnicity*** to refer to the nonbiological traits—such as shared ancestry, culture, history, language, patterns of behavior, and beliefs—that provide members of a group with a sense of common identity. Whereas ethnicity is thought to be something that we learn from other people, race is commonly portrayed as an inherited and permanent biological characteristic that can easily be used to divide people into mutually exclusive groups.

But the concept of race isn't nearly so straightforward. For instance, people who consider themselves "white" may actually have darker skin and curlier hair than some people who consider themselves "black." In addition, some groups have features that do not neatly place them in one race or another. Australian Aboriginals have black skin and "Negroid" facial features but have blond, wavy hair. The black-skinned !Kung who live in various countries in southern Africa have epicanthic eye folds, a characteristic typical of East Asian peoples.

Not surprisingly, there are no universal racial categories. Brazilians have three primary races—*branco* (white), *prêto* (black), and *pardo* (mulatto)—but use dozens of more precise terms to categorize people based on minute differences in skin color, hair texture and length, and facial features. South Africa has four legally defined races—black, white, colored, and Indian—but in England and Ireland the term *black* is used to refer to all people who are not white. In one small Irish town that experienced an unprecedented influx of refugees in the late 1990s, anyone who wasn't Irish was considered black. As one resident put it, "Either Romanians or Nigerians, we don't know the difference. They're all the same. They're all black" (quoted in Lyall, 2000, p. A6). Conversely, some African Americans visiting Ghana are shocked when people there refer to them as *obruni,* or "white foreigner" (Polgreen, 2005).

In some places, racial identification can change throughout the course of a person's life, reflecting economic standing more than skin color. For instance, as Brazilians climb the class ladder through educational and economic achievement, their racial classification changes, as illustrated by popular Brazilian expressions such as "Money whitens" or "A rich Negro is a white man, and a poor white man is a Negro" (Marger, 1994, p. 441). In Puerto Rico, a U.S. territory, conceptions of race are markedly more fluid than they are in the United States. Race is seen as a continuum of categories with different shades of color as the norm and classifications that can change as one's socioeconomic circumstances change (Rodriguez & Cordero-Guzman, 2004). In fact, a nationwide survey of African Americans found that 37% of respondents believe that because of a widening gap between middle-class and poor Blacks, "black" can no longer be thought of as a single race (cited in Gates, 2007).

The complex issue of defining race points to a complicated biological reality. Since the earliest humans appeared, they have consistently tended to migrate and interbreed. Some surveys estimate that at least 75% of U.S. Blacks have some white ancestry (cited in Mathews, 1996). Indeed, there is no gene that is 100% of one form in one race and 100% of a different form in another race (Brown, 1998).

That is not to say that race has absolutely *no* connection to biology. Geneticists have known for quite a while that some diseases are not evenly distributed across racial groups. The overwhelming majority of cases of sickle cell anemia, for instance, are among people of African descent; it is rare among non-Hispanic Whites (Black Health Care.com, 2003). In 2005, the Food and Drug Administration approved the cardiac drug BiDil, which is intended to be used exclusively by African Americans, who have shown to be genetically predisposed to heart disease. Hemochromatosis, a disorder that causes the body to absorb too much iron, is virtually absent among people from India and China but occurs in 7.5% of Scandinavians (Wade, 2002). However, no disease is found *exclusively* in one racial group. Furthermore, it's unclear whether these differences are solely due to some inherited biological trait or to the life experiences and historical, geographical, and/or environmental location of certain groups.

For most sociologists, then, race is more meaningful as a social category than as a biological one (Gans, 2005). That is, the characteristics a society selects to distinguish one ethnoracial group from another shape social rankings and determine access to important resources. But they have less to do with innate physical or genetic differences than with what the prevailing culture defines as socially significant (American Sociological Association, 2002). For instance, Jews, Irish, Italians, and even some Germans were once defined as members of inferior races. They came to be seen as "white" only when they entered the mainstream culture and gained economic and political power (Bronner, 1998a). Sociologists have noted that more and more U.S. adults feel comfortable simply changing out of the ethnic identities they were born into and taking on new ones (Hitt, 2005).

Historical changes in the categories used by the U.S. government in its decennial population censuses further illustrate shifting conceptions of race (Lee, 1993):

- In 1790, the first U.S. census used the following classifications: Free White Males, Free White Females, All Other Free Persons, and Slaves.
- In 1870, there were five races: White, Colored (Black), Mulatto (people with some black blood), Chinese, and Indian.
- Race categories in the 1890 census reflected white people's concern with race mixing and racial purity. Eight races were listed, half of them applying to black or partly black populations: White, Colored (Black), Mulatto (people with three eighths to five eighths black blood), Quadroon (people with one fourth black blood), Octoroon (people with one eighth black blood), Chinese, Japanese, and Indian.
- In 1900, Mulatto, Quadroon, and Octoroon were dropped, so any amount of "black blood" meant a person had to be classified as "Black."
- In 1910 and 1920, Mulatto returned to the census form, only to disappear for good in 1930.
- Between 1930 and 2000, some racial classifications (such as Hindu, Eskimo, part-Hawaiian, and Mexican) appeared and disappeared. Others (Filipino, Korean, Hawaiian) made an appearance and have remained ever since.
- Individuals filling out the 2010 census form will have a wide array of racial categories from which to choose: White, Black, American Indian or Alaska Native, Asian Indian, Chinese, Filipino, Japanese, Korean, Vietnamese, Guamanian or Chamorro, Native Hawaiian or Samoan.

You might have noticed that Latino/a is not included in the list of races on the latest census form. With the exception of the inclusion of "Mexican" in 1930, Spanish-speaking people have routinely been classified as "White." But because Latino/as can be members of any race, "Hispanic Origin" is included in the census form, not as a race but as an ethnicity. In fact, the 2010 form explicitly states that "Hispanic Origins are not races." Many Latino/as are upset that they are not officially recognized as a racial group. In fact, 42% of Latino/a respondents to the 2000 census refused to identify themselves by any of the categories available on the census form. As a result, "some other race" became the fastest-growing racial category in the United States (Swarns, 2004).

In short, racial categories are not natural, biological groupings. They are created, inhabited, transformed, applied, and destroyed by people (Omi & Winant, 1992). What ties individuals together in a particular racial group is not a set of shared physical characteristics—because there aren't any physical characteristics shared by all members of a particular racial group—but the shared experience of identifying, and being identified by others, as members of that group (Piper, 1992). The power of this experience is reflected by the fact that people who identify as one race but are perceived by others as a member of another race suffer higher levels of depression and psychological distress than people who are "correctly" classified (Campbell & Troyer, 2007).

HISTORIES OF OPPRESSION AND INEQUALITY

A quick glance at the history of the United States reveals a record of not just freedom, justice, and equality but also of conquest, discrimination, and exclusion. Racial and ethnic inequalities have manifested themselves in phenomena such as slavery and fraud; widespread economic, educational, and political deprivation; the violent and nonviolent protests of the civil rights movement; and racially motivated hate crimes. Along the way, such injustices have constricted people's access to basic necessities, including housing, health care, a stable family life, and a means of making a decent living.

Every ethnoracial minority has its own story of persecution. European immigrants—Irish, Italians, Poles, Jews, Greeks—were objects of hatred, suspicion, and discrimination when they first arrived in significant numbers in the United States. Nineteenth-century newspaper job ads routinely noted, "No Irish need apply." Jews were refused admission to many U.S. universities until the mid-20th century.

The National Origins Act of 1924 restricted immigration from southern Europe (mainly Greece and Italy) until the 1960s. Because these groups had the same skin color as the dominant white Protestants, however, they eventually overcame most of these obstacles and gained entry into mainstream society. Most recently, immigrants from Asia, Latin America, and the Middle East have become popular targets of hostility. For people of color in this country, racial equality has always been elusive.

Native Americans

The story of Native Americans includes racially inspired massacres, takeover of their ancestral lands, confinement on reservations, and unending governmental exploitation. Successive waves of white settlers seeking westward expansion in the 18th and 19th centuries pushed Native Americans off any land that the settlers considered desirable (U.S. Commission on Human Rights, 1992). A commonly held European belief that Native Americans were "savages" who should be displaced to make way for civilized Whites provided the ideological justification for conquering them.

According to the Fourteenth Amendment to the U.S. Constitution, "All persons born or naturalized in the United States, and subject to the jurisdiction thereof, are citizens of the United States and of the state wherein they reside." But despite the broad wording of this amendment, Native Americans were excluded from citizenship. In 1884, the U.S. Supreme Court ruled that Native Americans owed their primary allegiance to their tribe and so did not automatically acquire citizenship at birth. Not until 1940 were all Native Americans born in the United States considered U.S. citizens (Haney López, 1996).

Despite their history of severe oppression, Native Americans have shown a remarkable ability to endure and in some cases to shrewdly promote their own economic interests. In the Pacific Northwest, for instance, some Indian tribes have successfully protected their rights to lucrative fishing waters (Cohen, 1986). Casinos and resorts have made some tribes wealthy. The Connecticut Sun, a professional women's basketball franchise, plays its home games on the grounds of a casino owned by the Mohegan tribe. Elsewhere, organizations have been formed to advance the financial concerns of Native Americans in industries such as gas, oil, and coal, where substantial reserves exist on Indian land (Snipp, 1986). However, intense struggles between large multinational corporations and Native American tribes continue today over control of these reserves.

Latino/as

The history of Latino/as in this country has been diverse. Some groups have had a relatively positive experience. For instance, Cuban immigrants who streamed into this country in the late 1950s, fleeing Fidel Castro's communist political regime, received an enthusiastic welcome (Suarez, 1998). Many early Cuban immigrants were wealthy business owners who set up lucrative companies, particularly in South Florida. Today, Cuban American families are the most financially successful of any Latino/a group.

But other groups have experienced extreme resentment and oppression. For instance, when the United States expanded into the Southwest, white Americans moved into areas that were already inhabited by Mexicans. After a war that lasted from 1846 to 1848, Mexico lost half its national territory, including what are now the states of Arizona, California, Colorado, New Mexico, Texas, Nevada, and Utah, as well as parts of Kansas, Oklahoma, and Wyoming.

In theory, Mexicans living on the U.S. side of the new border were to be given all the rights of U.S. citizens. In practice, however, their property rights were frequently violated, and they lost control of their mining, ranching, and farming industries. The exploitation of Mexican workers coincided with a developing economic system built around mining and large-scale agriculture, activities that demanded a large pool of cheap labor (Farley, 1982). Workers often had to house their families in primitive shacks with no electricity or plumbing for months on end while they performed seasonal labor.

Today, the status of Latino/as is mixed. They represent a bigger proportion of the U.S. population than Blacks (U.S. Bureau of the Census, 2009). Larger numbers mean not only greater influence on the culture but more political clout. An estimated 11.8 million Latino/as voted in the 2008 presidential election (Gimpel, 2009), and they voted for Barack Obama over his Republican opponent John McCain by a margin of more than 2 to 1. In swing states with heavy Latino/a populations, such as Florida and California, their vote was key to Obama's victory (Lopez, 2008).

Economically and educationally, though, the situation is less rosy. The average annual income for Latino/a individuals and families is still substantially lower than that of other groups (U.S. Bureau of the Census, 2009). Latino/as are significantly more likely to drop out of school and less likely to go to college than are white, Asian American, or African American children.

African Americans

The experience of African Americans has been unique among ethnoracial groups in this country because of the direct and indirect influences of slavery. From 1619, when the first black slaves were sold in Jamestown, Virginia, to 1865, when the Thirteenth Amendment was passed outlawing slavery, several million Blacks in this country endured the brutal reality of forced servitude. Slave owners controlled every aspect of a slave's life. They determined which slaves could marry and which marriages could be dissolved. The economic value of children (i.e., future slaves) meant that slave owners had an interest in keeping slave marriages intact. But even the possibility of stable family life was an illusion. When economic troubles forced the sale of slaves to raise money, slave owners didn't hesitate to separate the very slave families they had once advocated. The threat of separation hung over every slave family.

Even after slavery was abolished, the conditions of life for U.S. Blacks showed little improvement. "Jim Crow" laws established rigid lines between the races. In 1896, the U.S. Supreme Court ruled that racial segregation in public facilities was constitutional. Unequal access to public transportation, schools, hotels, theaters, restaurants, campgrounds, drinking fountains, the military, and practically every other aspect of social life continued until the middle of the 20th century.

Despite advances, the quality of life for most African Americans remains below that of Whites. The median annual income for black households is $31,969, compared with $50,673 for white households (U.S. Bureau of the Census, 2009). Black unemployment is twice as high as that of Whites. Fewer than half of African American families own their own homes, compared with more than 70% of white families (National Urban League, 2004). Nevertheless, blatant discrimination has declined in the past 4 decades, and some economic, educational, and political advances have been made. For instance, between 1997 and 2002, the number of black-owned businesses grew by 45% and generated nearly $89 billion in revenues (U.S. Bureau of the Census, 2006a). The average annual household income of $31,969 represents a significant increase over the average income of black households in 1980 ($25,076). And the median income of black women is only slightly less than that of white women (U.S. Bureau of the Census, 2009).

Asian Americans

When large numbers of Chinese men came to this country in the second half of the 19th century to work in the mines and on the expanding railroad system, they were treated with hostility. The image of the "yellow peril" was fostered by rampant fears that hordes of Chinese workers would take away scarce jobs and eventually overrun native-born Whites. U.S. law prevented Chinese laborers from becoming permanent citizens, from bringing their wives with them, and from marrying Whites when they got here. Eventually, laws were passed that put limits on and even prohibited Chinese immigration.

Early Japanese Americans faced similar circumstances. Like the Chinese, Japanese families created tight-knit, insulated communities where they were able to pool money and resources and achieve relative success. But their perceived success motivated lawmakers to enact legislation that barred all further Japanese immigration. Hostility toward the Japanese reached a peak in 1941, following Japan's attack on Pearl Harbor. President Franklin Roosevelt signed an executive order authorizing the relocation and internment of Japanese immigrants and U.S. citizens of Japanese descent in camps surrounded by barbed wire, watch towers, and armed guards.

The irony of race for Chinese, Japanese, Koreans, Vietnamese, Cambodians, Laotians, Indians, and other Asian groups is that they are often perceived as "model minorities" or "America's greatest success story." For instance, the average total SAT scores for Asian high school seniors is 1605, compared with 1579 for Whites and 1511 for the general population (National Center for Fair and Open Testing, 2008). Almost twice as many Asian Americans as Whites complete college, and their average household income is actually higher than that of the population as a whole (U.S. Bureau of the Census, 2009). Of the 11 finalists in the 2009 National Spelling Bee, 7 were of Asian descent.

But the expectations and resentment associated with being the "model minority" can be as confining and oppressive as those created by more negative labels. By overemphasizing Asian American success, the label downplays the problems Asian Americans continue to face from racial discrimination in all areas of public and private life. Furthermore, it portrays Asian American success as proof that the United States provides equal opportunities for those who conform and work hard, even though many ethnoracial groups continue to suffer.

The "model minority" image can also turn ugly when equated with perceptions that Asians are overstudious loners who can't be trusted. These stereotypes bubbled to the surface in the immediate aftermath of the 2007 massacre at Virginia Tech University, in which a Korean American student went on a rampage and killed 32 people. Although it turned out that the gunman suffered from serious mental problems and the feared anti-Korean backlash never materialized, media portrayals continued to highlight both his ethnicity and his lack of social skills, perpetuating the idea that shy, bookish Asian American college students might be ticking time bombs.

Muslim Americans

Though their numbers are small compared with other ethnoracial minority groups and their arrival more recent, few groups have evoked stronger negative feelings or are as misunderstood as Muslim Americans. While the tendency is to see them as a monolithic homogeneous group, they are actually quite culturally and racially diverse. Sixty-five percent of Muslim Americans are first-generation immigrants. About a third come from the Arabic-speaking countries of the Middle East and North Africa and another 27% from South Asia. Despite the heavy presence of immigrants, more than three quarters of Muslims in this country are U.S. citizens (Pew Research Center, 2007a).

In terms of educational attainment and income level, Muslim Americans mirror the rest of U.S. society. The proportion of Muslims who have earned college degrees is the same as in the general population. In addition, 41% of Muslim American adults report annual household incomes of more than $50,000, compared with 44% of all U.S. adults. In fact, Muslims in the United States are in far better shape economically than those in France, Spain, Germany, or Great Britain (Pew Research Center, 2007a).

Overall, Muslim Americans are quite assimilated into mainstream U.S. society. The vast majority believe that their communities are good places in which to live and that hard work will pay off. Most are happy to be in the United States and condemn Islamic extremism.

Nevertheless, the equation of Muslims with violent terrorism has been a common prejudice for decades, dating back to the murder of 11 Israeli athletes during the 1972 Summer Olympics in Munich. The September 11, 2001, attacks bolstered anti-Muslim prejudice and have made their lives significantly more difficult. Most believe that the government singles them out for increased surveillance and monitoring (Pew Research Center, 2007a).

Despite knowing more about Islam than ever before, almost half of U.S. adults have an unfavorable view of Muslims. And since 2002, there has been a marked increase in the percentage of people who believe that Islam encourages violence more than other religions (Jost, 2006b). One study found that a high level of anti-Islamic imagery in the media supports the negative portrayal of Muslims and furthers the stereotype that all Muslims are terrorists (Khalema & Wannas-Jones, 2003). Indeed, the mere suggestion that someone *is* a Muslim can sometimes be enough to disparage that person. False rumors that he is a Muslim dogged Barack Obama throughout his entire presidential campaign. The fact that he and his representatives felt it was something that had to be vigorously denied reinforced its negative status in the culture.

The expression of anti-Muslim sentiment is more open than such sentiments applied to other ethnoracial groups. According to the Council on American-Islamic Relations, incidents of harassment of and violence against Muslims increased 70% between 2002 and 2003 ("Anti-Muslim Incidents Increase," 2004). In fact, negative perceptions are often fueled by well-known religious leaders. A famous evangelist once called Islam "a very wicked and evil religion." Others have called Muhammad, Islam's founder and prophet, "a demon-possessed pedophile" and "a terrorist" (Jost, 2006b, p. 919). And in 2006, Pope Benedict XVI quoted a 14th-century Christian ruler's view that Muhammad had brought only evil to the world. Such statements have helped make Muslim Americans one of the most openly despised ethnoracial groups in the country today.

RACIAL AND ETHNIC RELATIONS

U.S. society's long history of racial tension is unlikely to fade away any time soon. Increasing numbers of ethnoracial minorities and an influx of non-English-speaking immigrants are heightening competition and conflict over society's resources, including various forms of wealth, prestige, and power. The unequal distribution of resources is often motivated by ***racism,*** the belief that humans are subdivided into distinct groups so different in their social behavior and mental and physical capacities that they can be ranked as superior or inferior (Marger, 1994). Racism can be expressed at the personal level through individual attitudes and behavior, at the cultural level in language and collective ideologies, and at the macrostructural level in the everyday workings of social institutions.

Personal Racism

Personal racism is the expression of racist attitudes or behaviors by individual people. This type of racism takes many obvious forms, such as individuals who use derogatory names when they refer to other ethnoracial groups or those who show clear disdain for and hostility toward members of other groups during face-to-face contacts. However, subtle forms of personal racism, such as the high school guidance counselor who steers minority students away from "hard" subjects toward those that do not prepare them for higher-paying jobs, are much more common. Whether blatant or subtle, personal racism rests on two important psychological constructs—stereotypes and prejudice.

Stereotypes

The word ***stereotype*** was first used by the political commentator Walter Lippmann in 1922. He defined it as an oversimplified picture of the world, one that satisfies our need to see our social environment as a more understandable and manageable place than it really is (Lippmann, 1922). When applied to race, it is the overgeneralized belief that a certain trait, behavior, or attitude characterizes all members of some identifiable group.

Casual observations easily refute the accuracy of common racial or ethnic stereotypes. Most African Americans aren't on welfare, most Jews aren't greedy, few Italians belong to the Mafia, not all Asian Americans excel in math, and so on. Overgeneralizations are never true for every member of a group. Yet despite their obvious inaccuracy, stereotypes remain a common part of our everyday thinking. We all know what the stereotypes are, even if most of us choose not to express them or act on them.

The contemporary view is that stereotyping is a universal aspect of human thought (Hamilton, 1981). Our brains tend to divide the world into distinct categories: good and bad, strong and weak, them and us (Rothenberg, 1992). By allowing us to group information into easily identifiable categories, stereotypes make the processing of information and the formation of impressions more efficient. As you saw in Chapter 6, our lives would be utterly chaotic if we weren't able to quickly categorize and form expectations about people in terms of gender, race, age, ethnicity, and so on. What's important to remember, though, is that the actual content of stereotypes is by no means natural; it must be learned.

The media provide large audiences with both real and fantasized images of racial, religious, and ethnic groups: the savage American Indian; the sassy, confrontational, overweight black woman; the spoiled, pampered, shopping-obsessed Jewish daughter; the fanatical Arab terrorist; and so on. Asians are frequently depicted as camera-wielding tourists, scholastic overachievers, or sinister warlords. Latino/as have historically been cast as "Latin lovers," "banditos," "greasers," or "lazy good-for-nothings" (Reyes & Rubie, 1994).

An analysis of a random sample of television news shows aired in Los Angeles and Orange counties in California revealed that Whites are more likely than African Americans and Latino/as to be portrayed on television news as victims of crime. Conversely, African Americans and Latino/as are more likely to be portrayed on news shows as lawbreakers than as crime victims (Dixon & Linz, 2000). Another study found that although people of color appear regularly in prime-time TV commercials, they usually appear as secondary characters. Furthermore, Whites are more likely to appear in ads for upscale products, beauty products, and home products. People of color, in contrast, are more likely to appear in ads for low-cost, low-nutrition products (such as fast foods and soft drinks) and in athletic or sports equipment ads (Henderson & Baldasty, 2003).

Prejudice and Discrimination

When stereotypes form the basis of a set of rigidly held, unfavorable attitudes, beliefs, and feelings about members of a racial or ethnic group, they constitute ***prejudice*** (Allport, 1954). A good example of how prejudice affects social interaction is a study in which a group of Whites was shown a photograph of a white person holding a razor blade while arguing with a black person on a New York subway. Subjects were shown the picture for a split second and then asked to write down what they saw. More than half said they saw the black man holding the razor against the white man's throat (cited in Helmreich, 1992). The belief that all Blacks are violent was so powerful that it distorted people's perceptions. Similarly, a day after Hurricane Katrina hit in 2005, several Internet news outlets posted two similar photographs—one of a white victim wading in chest-high water, the other of a black victim doing the same thing. The caption that accompanied the photo of the white person said that she had "found" bread and water from a local grocery store. The caption for the photo of the black man said that he had just "looted" a local grocery store.

These sorts of perceptions can, at times, be life threatening. In New York City, for example, undercover black police officers have, on occasion, been shot and wounded or killed by white officers who mistook them for dangerous criminals. As one black officer put it, "If you speak with nine out of 10 [undercover] officers of color they would tell you that when they hear sirens, in their head they are thinking: 'I hope these cops know that I'm one of the good guys'" (quoted in Powell, 2009a, p. 18). Over the years, there have been calls for the department to appoint panels to examine the underlying racial assumptions of white officers and to provide cadets with extra training.

Prejudices can change as social conditions change. When people feel their cultural integrity or their economic livelihood is being threatened—by either the real or the perceived infiltration of other ethnoracial groups—prejudicial attitudes can become more open and hostile. For instance, widespread anti-Catholic sentiment became especially virulent in the late 19th and early 20th centuries as waves of Catholic immigrants entered the country looking for a better life (Gusfield, 1963).

Prejudiced beliefs would be of little significance if they didn't lead sometimes to discrimination. ***Discrimination*** is the unfair treatment of people based on some social characteristic. The 1964 Civil Rights Act prohibits discrimination or segregation on the grounds of race, color, religion, or national origin. This act has produced tremendous progress in U.S. race relations. Nevertheless, discrimination still exists.

When we think of discrimination, we usually think of its most blatant forms—racial epithets, racially inspired hate crimes, barriers to employment, and so on. Most of the time, though, discrimination is much more subtle, expressed as suspicion or avoidance. We are generally so unaware of our own nonverbal behavior that if we unwittingly give off signs of our dislike, we don't interpret others' subsequent behavior as a reaction to our nonverbal cues. Rather, we attribute it to some inherent trait in them. We may unknowingly prompt the very actions that we then use as evidence of some flaw or deficiency in that group.

From the point of view of those discriminated against, these subtle forms of discrimination are often harder to fight than overt bigotry. If you are excluded from a job because you're Asian or denied membership in a club because you're Jewish, you can fight to open those doors. Today, quite a few people have made it in (Blauner, 1992). But once inside, they still have many interpersonal barriers to overcome.

When such subtle behavior becomes common among large numbers of people, prejudice and discrimination become mutually reinforcing. Defining one group as inferior and thus denying its members access to a decent education and jobs becomes a self-fulfilling prophecy, producing the very inferiority that the group was believed to possess in the first place.

Prejudice and discrimination based on skin color may also occur *within* a particular ethnoracial group. Some see this phenomenon, known as ***colorism,*** as just as bad a problem as racial hatred expressed toward the group by outsiders. For instance, skin tone has been associated with social advantage among Blacks since the days of slavery, when light-skinned slaves were often allowed to work in the main house but dark-skinned slaves were relegated to the fields (Graham, 1999). During the early to mid-20th century, many African American churches, social clubs, fraternities, and other organizations still used skin color to determine the suitability of candidates for membership. The so-called brown bag test restricted membership to those whose skin was lighter than the color of a brown paper bag (Graham, 1999). Contemporary studies have found that lighter-skinned Blacks have higher educational attainment, more prestigious occupations, and higher annual incomes than darker-skinned Blacks, regardless of their sex, region of residence, age, marital status, or parents' socioeconomic status (Hill, 2000; Keith & Herring, 1991). As a result, darker-skinned Blacks sometimes resent light-skinned Blacks, accusing them of "selling out" in an attempt to conform to white standards of beauty as well as behavior (Davis, 1991).

Colorism is not limited to African Americans. Among Latino/as, the degree of "Indianness," or the darkness of one's skin, has long determined a person's status. After controlling for all other relevant factors, researchers have found that dark-skinned Mexican Americans who have a Native American physical appearance have fewer years of education than light-skinned Mexican Americans who appear more European (Murguia & Telles, 1996); they are more likely to live in segregated, low-income neighborhoods (Relethford, Stern, Caskill, & Hazuda, 1983); and they consistently earn lower wages (Telles & Murguia, 1990).

The Privilege of Having No Color

People who are members of a racial majority sometimes have trouble appreciating the humiliating effects of everyday encounters with prejudice and discrimination. They don't have to experience the petty indignities of racism, such as repeatedly being watched with suspicion in stores and on streets. Consequently, many Whites in the United States pay little attention to their own race, think people of color are obsessed with their race and ethnicity, and find it difficult to understand the emotional and intellectual energy people of color devote to the subject (Haney López, 1996).

In a society in which they dominate statistically and culturally, U.S. Whites rarely define their identity in terms of race. Whiteness is so obvious and normative that white people's racial identity is, for all intents and purposes, invisible. Whites enjoy the luxury of ***racial transparency,*** or "having no color" (Haney López, 1996). People in the United States are far more likely to hear "black" or "Asian" or "Latino" used as an adjective (e.g., the black lawyer, the Latino teacher) than "white" (the white lawyer, the white teacher). Whites have the luxury of choosing whether or not to include their specific ancestry in descriptions of their identity (Waters, 2008). In this sense, ethnicity is optional, voluntary, and perhaps even recreational—as when white people celebrate their Irishness on St. Patrick's Day. In short, Whites for the most part enjoy the privilege of not having to constantly think about race or identify their ethnicity.

Such a luxury provides advantages to Whites whether or not they approve of the way dominance has been conferred on them. One white author (McIntosh, 2001) catalogued all the everyday privileges she enjoyed (and often didn't notice) simply because she was white. They included advantages such as the ability to shop alone in a department store without being followed by suspicious salespeople, to buy greeting cards or children's picture books featuring people of her race, and to find bandages that match her skin color. In other words, Whites need not be bigots or feel racially superior or more deserving than others to enjoy the privileges that their skin color brings.

Class, Race, and Discrimination

Some sociologists have argued that discriminatory treatment, as well as the unequal social and political status of some racial groups, is more a function of social class than of race. If this belief were accurate, the lives of middle- and upper-class people of color should be relatively free of discrimination. The election of Barack Obama clearly shows that well-educated, highly qualified members of ethnoracial minorities are no longer barred from the highest positions in society. However, some civil rights advocates believe Obama's victory was an isolated one and fear that many people will conclude that racial discrimination is over (Swarns, 2008b). After all, African Americans still remain twice as likely as Whites to be unemployed, three times as likely to live in poverty, and six times as likely to be incarcerated (National Urban League, 2009). As the former chair of the U.S. Civil Rights Commission put it, "It's like saying that because some poor white person made it, there's no poverty" (quoted in Cose, 2009, p. 43).

Indeed, even for many highly successful minority professionals, lack of respect, faint praise, low expectations, and outright harassment and exclusion continue to be common features of their lives (Feagin & McKinney, 2003). In 2009, the famous African American historian and prominent Harvard professor Henry Louis Gates Jr. was arrested for disorderly conduct in his own home as police investigated a report of a break-in there. The charge was later dropped but not before angry accusations of racial profiling were being heard all around the country.

More generally, minority professionals often bemoan the tendency of others to assume they bring to every interaction the perspective of their entire group. A successful law professor, who happens to be Chinese American, once said, "I suspect . . . that at every appearance . . . my audience continues to see and hear me as a spokesperson on behalf of Asian Americans" (Wu, 2002, p. 37).

Everyday life can be trying as well. Wealthy black residents of affluent neighborhoods all over the country sometimes complain that they are watched closely when shopping in upscale stores or that the police view them with suspicion simply because their skin color doesn't match the neighborhood. Some upper-middle-class black couples complain about the difficulties they face finding live-in caretakers for their young children. Many prospective nannies—some of whom are women of color themselves—balk at the idea of working for black employers. The reasons they give often include accusations of low pay and fears that the employing family will look down on them. As one African American mother put it, "We've attained whatever level society says is successful, we're included at work, but when we need the support for our children and we can afford it, why do we get treated this way? It's a slap in the face" (quoted in Kantor, 2006, p. 1). For some, the problem is so bad that they've had to turn down job offers and stay at home because they couldn't find someone to care for their children.

Situations such as these are disturbing and frustrating not only because of the racist attitudes that lie behind them but also because the people who experience them had come to believe that their upward social mobility protected them from such treatment. The stigma of color is still very important in the lives of members of ethnoracial minorities, including those who are affluent. In fact, such discrimination is more apparent than that experienced by low-income people because the affluent individuals have entered previously inaccessible social spaces (Bonilla-Silva, 2008). One study even found that Blacks with college degrees experience more discrimination than those without degrees (Forman, Williams, & Jackson, 1997).

The days of "No Negroes" and "No Indians" signs on public facilities may be gone, but less blatant contemporary expressions of personal racism serve as a constant reminder that in the 21st century, members of ethnoracial minorities—no matter what their class standing—are still stereotyped, prejudged, and discriminated against every day.

Quiet Racism

The nature of public attitudes in the United States toward racial and ethnic groups has changed over the past few decades, prompting many sociologists to rethink their ideas of what constitutes personal racism. One nationwide poll found that the proportion of U.S. residents who feel that race relations are improving and that progress has been made in reducing racial discrimination is the highest it's been since the early 1990s (cited in Cohen & Agiesta, 2008). However, other surveys indicate that different groups have very different perceptions of the state of race relations (cited in Blow, 2008, 2009):

- Twice as many Blacks as Whites think racism is a big problem; twice as many Whites as Blacks think that Blacks have achieved racial equality.
- Seventy-two percent of Whites believe that Blacks overestimate the amount of discrimination against them; conversely, 82% of Blacks believe that Whites underestimate the amount of discrimination Blacks suffer.
- Almost half of white respondents oppose programs that make special efforts to help minorities get ahead; 27% feel that too much has been made of the problems facing black people.

These paradoxes have led some to argue that a subtle form of racism has emerged (Ansell, 2000; Bonilla-Silva, 2008; Sniderman & Tetlock, 1986). ***Quiet racism*** is linked to the traditional forms of personal racism by negative feelings toward certain groups.

However, the feelings common to quiet racism are not hate or hostility but discomfort, uneasiness, and sometimes fear, which tend to motivate avoidance rather than outright negative acts. Quiet racists are people who maintain that discrimination against a person because of his or her race or ethnicity is wrong but who nonetheless cannot entirely escape the cultural forces that give rise to racist beliefs in the first place. What complicates the situation is that this type of racism is often expressed by people who consider themselves unbiased and nonprejudiced.

The changing face of racism has serious institutional consequences as well. When racism remains quiet, people are tempted to assume that it has disappeared and thus to forget about helping groups that have traditionally been the objects of discrimination (Bonilla-Silva, 2003). Recent efforts to eliminate programs designed to help ethnoracial minorities exemplify this trend. Many Whites now believe that the only reason so many Blacks are unsuccessful is that they lack motivation and aren't committed to the "white" values of hard work, individualism, delayed gratification, and so on (Schuman & Krysan, 1999). Although these beliefs are more subtle than overt acts of bigotry, they have the same effect: On the basis of stereotypes, they promote prejudice toward individuals.

The Cultural Ideology of Racism

If I stopped here in my discussion of racism, you might be inclined to consider it an individual-level phenomenon that could best be stopped by changing the way people think or by personal acts of kindness and respect. But the sociologically important thing about racism is that it exists not just in the minds and actions of individuals but in a cultural ideology that both justifies the domination of some groups over others and provides a set of social norms that encourages differential treatment for these groups (O'Sullivan-See & Wilson, 1988). From a conflict perspective, the ideology of racism that exists in our language and in our prevailing cultural beliefs contributes to racial and ethnic inequality.

Racism in Language

Certainly, racial slurs and derogatory words reflect underlying racism. But racism in language is often less obvious. Consider the use of ***panethnic labels***—general terms applied to diverse subgroups that are assumed to have something in common (Newman, 2007). Today, we use the general terms "Native American" or "American Indian" to refer to all the 560 or so native nations living in the United States, despite their different languages and cultures. "Asian American" refers to a variety of peoples from dozens of countries whose ethnic heritages and lifestyles are quite different from one another. Similarly, "Hispanic" or "Latino" refers to people whose backgrounds include culturally diverse areas such as Mexico, the Caribbean, Central America, and South America. To some, even the term African American, which is widely considered to be a positive racial label, glosses over the thousands of ethnic groups, class interests, and indigenous religions that exist on the continent of Africa. Reliance on panethnic labels allows users to overlook and ignore variations within a particular labeled group, thereby reinforcing stereotypes.

Racial identifiers often become equated with negative meanings. Consider, for instance, connotations of the words *black* and *white*. Among the definitions of *black* in *Webster's New Universal Unabridged Dictionary* are soiled and dirty, thoroughly evil, wicked, gloomy, marked by disaster, hostile, and disgraceful. The definition of *white*, in contrast, includes fairness of complexion, innocent, favorable, fortunate, pure, and spotless. The pervasive "goodness" of white and "badness" of black affects children at a very young age and provides white children with a false sense of superiority (Moore, 1992). Young children know the difference between a black lie, which is harmful and inexcusable, and a white lie, which is small, insignificant, and harmless.

Language is just a small part of the overall problem of racist ideology in U.S. society. It seemingly pales in comparison with more visible issues such as racial violence and economic discrimination. We must remember, however, that language filters our perceptions. It affects the way people think from the time they first learn to speak. Fortunately, efforts are being made today to address the issue of language and its crucial role in maintaining racism and oppression. People are becoming more aware of the capacity of words to both glorify and degrade (Moore, 1992).

The Myth of Innate Racial Inferiority

Scientific-sounding theories of the innate inferiority of certain ethnoracial groups have long been used to explain why some groups lag behind others in areas such as educational achievement and financial success. These theories combine with the belief in competitive individualism (see Chapter 10) to justify all forms of prejudice and discrimination.

Appeals to biology and nature have been used throughout history to define the existing stratification system as proper and inevitable (Gould, 1981). What would you think of a person who harbored the following beliefs about Blacks?

> [Blacks] have less hair on the face and body. They secrete less by the kidnies [*sic*], and more by the glands of the skin, which gives them a very strong and disagreeable odour. . . . They are at least as brave, and more adventuresome. But this may perhaps proceed from a want of forethought, which prevents their seeing a danger till it be present. . . . In imagination, they are dull, tasteless, and anomalous. . . . The improvement of the blacks in body and mind, in the first instance of their mixture with the whites, has been observed by everyone, and proves that their inferiority is not the effect merely of their condition of life. . . . I advance it therefore . . . that the blacks . . . are inferior to the whites in the endowments both of body and mind.

A white supremacist? A raving bigot? An ignorant fanatic? How would your assessment of this person change if you found out that this passage was written by none other than Thomas Jefferson (1781/1955, pp. 138–143)? In the 18th and 19th centuries, no white person—not even one apparently committed to protecting people's right to "life, liberty and the pursuit of happiness"—doubted the correctness of natural racial rankings: Indians below Whites, and Blacks below everyone else. Other idols of Western culture—George Washington, Abraham Lincoln, Charles Darwin—held similar beliefs about the "natural inferiority" of some races, beliefs that were commonly accepted knowledge at the time but would at the very least be considered racially insensitive today.

The approval given by white scientists to conventional racial rankings arose not from objective data and careful research but from a cultural belief in the "goodness" and inevitability of racial stratification. Such beliefs were then twisted into independent, "scientific" support. Scientists, like everybody else, have attitudes and values that shape what they see. Such thinking is not the result of outright dishonesty or hypocrisy; rather, it is the combination of the way human minds work and the generally accepted knowledge of the day.

From a conflict perspective, beliefs about racial inferiority provide advantages for the dominant group. These beliefs discourage subordinate groups from questioning their disadvantaged status. In addition, they provide moral justification for maintaining a society in which some groups are routinely deprived of their rights and privileges. White Americans could justify the enslavement of Blacks, and Nazis could justify the extermination of Jews and other "undesirables," by promoting the belief that those groups were biologically subhuman.

Despite energetic searches over the centuries, a link between "inferior" race-based genes and certain traits and abilities has not been found (Hacker, 1992). For one thing, comparing racial groups on, say, intelligence overlooks the range of differences within and between groups. Many African Americans are more intelligent than the average white person; many Whites are less intelligent than the average Native American.

Variations such as these are difficult to explain in terms of the genetic superiority of one race. Moreover, treating the more than 200 million "white" people in the United States as a single (and intellectually superior) group is problematic at best and misleading at worst. It can't account for the wide variation in academic achievement among Whites of different national backgrounds. For instance, at the end of the 20th century, 21% of white Americans of Irish descent completed college, whereas 22% of Italian Americans, 33% of Scottish Americans, and 51% of Russian Americans did so (Hacker, 1994). Finally, such comparisons also ignore a problem I described earlier in this chapter: that race itself is a meaningless biological category. How can we attribute racial differences in intelligence to genes when race itself is not traceable to a single gene?

Nevertheless, the idea that racial inferiority is innate remains appealing. If observable, physical differences among races are inherited, the argument goes, then why not differences in social behavior, intelligence, and leadership ability? Like the belief in competitive individualism we examined in the previous chapter, the belief in innate racial inferiority places the blame for suffering and economic failure on the individual rather than on the society in which that individual exists.

Institutional Racism: Injustice Built Into the System

Anyone can be personally racist, whether overtly or quietly. And members of any ethnoracial group can develop a set of beliefs or a vocabulary that denigrates outsiders. But one form of racism, less obvious and perhaps more dangerous, can work only to the advantage of those who wield power in society: institutional racism. ***Institutional racism*** consists of established laws, customs, and practices that systematically reflect and produce racial inequalities in society, whether or not the individuals maintaining these practices have racist intentions (Jones, 1986). Thus, a society can be racist even if only a small proportion of its members harbor racist beliefs. Because African Americans, Latino/as, Asian Americans, Native Americans, and other groups have historically been excluded from key positions of authority in social institutions, they often find themselves victimized by the routine workings of such structures.

Sometimes institutional discrimination is obvious and codified into the law. Until the early 1990s, for example, South Africa operated under an official system of *apartheid:* Nonwhite groups were legally segregated and subjected to sanctioned forms of political and economic discrimination. In the United States, the forceful relocation of Native Americans in the 19th century, the repressive Jim Crow laws in the 20th-century South, and the internment of Japanese Americans during World War II are all examples of legislated policies that purposely worked to the detriment of already disadvantaged groups.

But understanding the less obvious forms of institutional racism is a test of the sociological imagination. Because it is a built-in feature of social arrangements, some forms of institutional racism are often much more difficult to detect than acts of personal racism. Consider one well-established practice for granting home mortgage or home improvement loans. Many banks use zip codes to mark off the neighborhoods they consider high risk—that is, where property values are low and liable to drop even further. These practices make it virtually impossible for individuals in such areas to borrow money to buy or improve a home. Unfortunately, these are precisely the areas where minorities, with lower than average incomes, are most likely to find an affordable home to purchase. Thus, although individual bank officers are not denying loans to people because of their race—they are merely following their employers' policy—the resulting discrimination is the same.

Sometimes institutional racism is camouflaged behind claims that seem quite reasonable on their face. For instance, taxi companies protect the safety of their drivers by refusing service to what they consider dangerous neighborhoods. Similarly, home delivery businesses, such as pizza parlors, sometimes refuse to deliver to certain neighborhoods. Several years ago, Domino's Pizza was criticized in the media when it was revealed that the company was distributing software to its outlets to let them mark addresses on computers as green (deliver), yellow (curbside only), or red (no delivery). Businesses defend such policies as a rational response to the threat of sending easy-to-spot delivery personnel with cash into unsafe areas ("Pizza Must Go," 1996). Although such practices may be considered "good" business policy and are not intentionally racist, their consequences are discriminatory because high-risk neighborhoods tend to be inhabited predominantly by people of color. Institutional racism is difficult to address in these cases because no individual "bad guy," no identifiable bigot, is the source of the discrimination.

The National Fair Housing Alliance (2009) conservatively estimates that there are approximately 4 million fair-housing violations each year. Apart from incidents of landlords discriminating against families with small children, most of these cases involve ethnoracial minorities. Indeed, there were more official reports of such housing discrimination made to private, state, and federal agencies in 2008 than in any previous year. For instance, of the 2,176 cases of racial discrimination in housing filed with the Ohio Civil Rights Commission between 1988 and 2003, 80% involved victims of color (Roscigno, Karafin, & Tester, 2009). On occasion, such housing discrimination is personal, the result of individuals' blatant "we don't want you people here" attitudes. More commonly, though, it is institutional, politely and subtly driven by company policies (Pearce, 1979). Discriminatory policies include making fewer houses or rental units available to minorities, limiting their access to financial assistance, and steering them toward particular neighborhoods.

One study found that African Americans were twice as likely as Whites, and Latino/as one and a half times as likely as Whites to be denied a conventional 30-year home loan (cited in Kilborn, 1999). When they do receive home loans, African Americans and Latino/as are twice as likely as Whites to have to pay substantially higher "subprime" interest rates (cited in Bajaj & Fessenden, 2007). Some argue that the discrepancy in rates is justified because borrowers who have poor credit histories are higher risks or because Blacks and Latino/as have fewer assets and therefore have less money for down payments than white borrowers (Blanton, 2007). But the discrepancy is even found between minority and white borrowers with similar credit scores (Bocian, Ernst, & Li, 2006). In 2009, the city of Baltimore sued Wells Fargo Bank for systematically steering Blacks into subprime mortgages, which sent hundreds of homeowners into foreclosure and cost the city tens of millions of dollars (Powell, 2009b).

Racial Inequality in the Economic System

Institutional racism is readily apparent throughout the U.S. economy. Consider participation in the labor force. In general, workers of color have always been concentrated in lower-paying jobs. African Americans make up 11% of the entire civilian U.S. workforce but only 4.9% of lawyers, 5.6% of physicians, and 5.3% of architects and engineers. Similarly, Latino/as make up 14% of the labor force, but they are underrepresented in the fields of law (4.3%), medicine (5.2%), and engineering (6.4%; U.S. Bureau of the Census, 2009). The underrepresentation becomes more acute in the higher echelons of certain professions. For instance, while 17% of attorneys in U.S. law firms are members of ethnoracial minorities, only 5% ever become partners in those firms (cited in Glater, 2006).

Because ethnoracial minorities are occupationally concentrated in low-paying jobs, they are particularly vulnerable to economic downturns. The recent recession, for instance, has not hit all races equally. In April 2009 (the most recent data available at the time of this writing), the overall unemployment rate was close to 10%. However, the rate varied dramatically by race. Whites (9.0%) and Asian Americans (6.8%) had significantly lower unemployment rates than Blacks (16.5%) and Latino/as (12.5%; U.S. Bureau of Labor Statistics, 2010). Rates of homeownership among Blacks and Latino/as—which had been growing steadily for a decade—have fallen more sharply than rates for Whites (Kochhar, Gonzalez-Barrera, & Dockterman, 2009).

People of color also remain marginal participants in the economy as owners of their own small businesses. Loan companies usually demand a credit history, some form of collateral, and evidence of potential success before they will lend money to prospective businesses. These are standard practices—and not in and of themselves racist—but they perpetuate racial inequalities because members of groups that have been exploited in the past tend to be poorer and thus have poor credit ratings and no collateral. Admittedly, poor people are greater credit risks than those with economic resources, and businesses in poorer communities must pay more for insurance because of the greater likelihood of theft or property damage. But the higher costs of doing business in a poor community usually make small business loans to minority members even more necessary.

As long as companies are motivated to maximize their own interests (and profits), they are likely to adapt to market tastes. To the extent that those tastes reflect underlying prejudice, discrimination will continue. This structural-functionalist explanation of institutional racism is important because it enables us to see why discrimination is so difficult to end. The problem is not individual bigotry; it is the mistreatment that has been built into the system so effectively that it is sometimes difficult to see, let alone remove.

Racial Inequality in the Health Care System

As I pointed out at the beginning of this chapter, the economic and educational advances of ethnoracial minority groups over the past decade or so have been tempered by continuing disadvantages in health and health care. For example, members of ethnoracial minorities are routinely underrepresented as subjects in research on medical and psychiatric drug treatments (Vedantam, 2005). Members of ethnoracial minorities are also less likely than Whites to have access to health insurance. More than 33% of Latino/as (especially those from Mexico and Central America) and 19.7% of African Americans lack any kind of health insurance, compared with 10.7% of non-Hispanic

Whites (DeNavas-Walt, Proctor, & Smith, 2009). As the president of the American Medical Association put it, "When people don't have health insurance, they live sicker and they die younger" (quoted in Wilson, 2009a, p. 16).

Ethnoracial health imbalances are most glaring when it comes to the most serious diseases. For instance, a study of heart failure among 5,000 black and white men and women over a 20-year period found that Blacks had a rate 20 times higher than Whites (Bibbins-Domingo, 2009). African Americans make up about 13% of the population in this country but account for 43% of all people living with HIV/AIDS (U.S. Bureau of the Census, 2009). Death rates from HIV/AIDS also vary widely between different ethnoracial groups (U.S. Bureau of the Census, 2009). It is now the leading cause of death among African Americans between the ages of 25 and 44—ahead of heart disease, cancer, accidents, and homicides (Andriote, 2005).

Sometimes personal stereotyping and bias are to blame for these outcomes. For instance, in one study, doctors described African American patients—no matter what their education and income levels—as less intelligent, less likely to follow medical advice, less likely to participate in rehabilitation, and more likely to abuse alcohol and drugs than white patients (Van Ryn & Burke, 2000). Another study found that doctors often stereotype Asian patients as compliant and "problem free" (cited in American Sociological Association, 2005). When time and medical resources are limited, such beliefs can drive the treatment decisions doctors make.

But we can't simply blame ruthless and bigoted individuals for all racial imbalances in the health care system. Instead, the financial considerations that drive the health care system create a context ripe for institutional racism. Consider racial differences in organ transplants. According to the Organ Procurement and Transplant Network (2009), the 2009 national kidney transplant waiting list consisted of 39% Whites and 34% African Americans. (This figure in and of itself is telling: African Americans make up only about 13% of the population yet account for more than one third of people in need of kidney transplants.) However, that same year, Whites received 52% of all kidney transplants, while African Americans received only 27%. Such a discrepancy is likely linked to hospitals determining a candidate's ability to pay before approving a procedure. These policies are sometimes referred to as "green screens" or "wallet biopsies." A liver transplant, for example, can cost anywhere from $100,000 to $400,000, so it's not surprising that most hospitals would screen potential recipients for some kind of evidence up front that their insurance will cover the procedure. Because ethnoracial minorities are less likely than Whites to have medical insurance, they are less likely to receive a referral for transplant surgery (Stolberg, 1998). Financial concerns, not outright racial prejudice, lie at the heart of these policies.

Sometimes the institutional racism underlying threats to people's health is less obvious than shoddy medical care or unethical research. For instance, people in neighborhoods where hazardous waste treatment plants or other sources of industrial pollution exist are disproportionately exposed to the unhealthful effects of air pollution, water pollution, and pesticides. The decisions on where to place such facilities are usually based not on the ethnoracial makeup of an area but on factors such as the cost of land, population density, and geological conditions. However, because the less desirable residential areas (and hence more desirable industrial areas) are disproportionately inhabited by poor people of color, these decisions have the effect of discriminating against them. For instance, Native American reservations, which have less stringent environmental regulations than other areas, have been targeted by the U.S. military for stockpiles of nuclear, chemical, and biological weapons and by private companies for solid waste landfills, hazardous waste incinerators, and nuclear waste storage facilities (Hooks & Smith, 2004). When it comes to the federal government cleaning up polluted areas, predominantly white communities see faster action, better results, and stiffer penalties for polluters than do communities where ethnoracial minorities predominate (Bullard, 2001).

Poor African American communities often have the worst conditions. Seven oil refineries and several hundred heavy industrial plants are situated along a stretch of the Mississippi River between Baton Rouge and New Orleans known as "cancer alley" (Koeppel, 1999). An early study of toxic emissions in this area by the Environmental Protection Agency showed that 9 of the 10 major sources of industrial pollution were in predominantly black neighborhoods (Cushman, 1993). Overall, the greater the proportion of black residents in a community, the more likely it is that there will be industrial sources of air pollution within a 2-mile radius of people's homes (Perlin, Sexton, & Wong, 1999). Indeed, Blacks are 79% more likely than Whites to live in areas where air pollution levels constitute serious health risks (cited in Little, 2007).

Racial Inequality in the Educational System

In 1954, the U.S. Supreme Court ruled in *Brown v. Board of Education of Topeka* that racially segregated schools were unconstitutional because they were inherently unequal. School districts around the country were placed under court order to desegregate. But within the past 10 years, courts have lifted desegregation orders in at least three dozen school districts around the country. In 2007, the Supreme Court reversed itself and ruled that public school systems could not try to achieve or maintain integration through actions that take explicit account of students' race. At the time of the ruling, such programs were in place in hundreds of school districts around the country (Greenhouse, 2007b). Some districts have resorted to using integration plans based on children's socioeconomic disadvantage, rather than race, to skirt these restrictions (Bazelon, 2008).

You might assume that the court took this action because desegregation plans based on students' race were no longer needed. However, African American and Latino/a students are actually more isolated from white students today than they were 30 years ago (Orfield & Lee, 2007). The average black and Latino/a student attends a school in which at least 70% of the students are not white. In fact, more than a third of black and Latino/a students attend schools in which at least 90% of the students are not white. In contrast, the average white student attends a school in which almost 80% of the students are white (Orfield & Lee, 2007).

And it's not just students who are segregated. In general, white teachers have very little experience with racial diversity. They are currently teaching in schools where almost 90% of their faculty colleagues are white and more than 70% of the students are white (Frankenberg, 2006).

Schools where the majority of students are not white are likely to be schools where poverty is concentrated. Almost 86% of schools in which black and Latino/a students represent more than 90% of the enrollment are also schools in which more than half the students came from poor families. This is not the case with majority-white schools, which almost always enroll high proportions of middle-class students. Just 12% of schools with less than 10% black and Latino/a students are schools where a majority of students are poor (Frankenberg, 2006).

The racial mix of the classroom has important implications for the quality of the education that students receive. Concentrated poverty tends to be linked to lower educational achievement. Schools in poor communities lack the financial and therefore educational resources that schools in more affluent communities have (see Chapter 10). For instance, poor school districts are less likely than wealthier districts to offer Advanced Placement (AP) programs. And because poor schools tend to be in minority communities, fewer students of color have access to AP courses. So while African Americans make up 14% of high school graduates, they constitute only 8% of those taking AP exams and 4% of those with passing scores (cited in Lewin, 2009). Furthermore, poor schools hire fewer teachers with credentials in the subjects they're teaching and have more unstable enrollments, higher dropout rates, and more students with untreated health problems. Despite attempts to rectify the problem, black and Latino/a students still lag behind white and Asian students at all levels of the educational system (National Center for Education Statistics, 2006; U.S. Bureau of the Census, 2009).

Lack of money isn't the only problem, though. Common institutional practices within the educational system can also lead to unequal outcomes. Consider the widespread use of standardized tests, which are often used as the basis for "tracking" students—that is, as Chapter 5 explains, assigning them to different educational programs based on their intellectual abilities. Standardized tests supposedly measure innate intelligence. Many educational experts agree, however, that these tests are culture bound, tapping an individual's familiarity with a specific range of white, middle-class experiences rather than indicating innate intelligence (Hout & Lucas, 2001). Hence, members of ethnoracial minorities consistently score lower on these tests than Whites (Jencks & Phillips, 1998).

Despite the potential for bias, more and more states across the country are requiring high school students to pass a standardized test to graduate. At the same time, though, many universities and other educational organizations have begun seeking alternative ways to determine eligibility for admission.

For instance, some universities now use a "strivers" approach, whereby college applicants whose SAT scores fall in the borderline range for many selective colleges but who manage to exceed the historical average for students from similar backgrounds by at least 200 points would be deemed "strivers" and given special consideration (Cooper, 1999). The Texas legislature went a step further, ordering the University of Texas system to accept all students who graduate in the top 10% of their class, regardless of their SAT scores. In 1999, a U.S. district court judge ruled that the NCAA (National Collegiate Athletic Association) could no longer use SAT scores to determine athletic eligibility. The court concluded that the test is culturally biased and therefore discriminates against underprivileged students.

These changes indicate a significant effort to undermine institutional racism in the educational system, which is, according to some sociologists, the largest barrier to racial equality that exists in this country today (Jencks & Phillips, 1998).

Remedies for Institutional Racism: Affirmative Action

If tomorrow all people in the United States were to wake up harboring absolutely no hatred, prejudice, or animosity toward other groups, institutional racism would still exist. It is part of the structure of society. Thus, it requires a structural solution.

You have already seen how the educational system is undertaking limited measures to overcome certain types of institutional racism. However, the most far-reaching structural solution to the problem of institutional racism has been ***affirmative action.*** Affirmative action is a governmental policy, developed in the 1960s, that requires organizations to seek out members of minority groups and women for educational or occupational positions from which they had previously been excluded. One assumption is that past discrimination has left certain people ill-equipped to compete with others as equals today. Another assumption is that organizations will not change discriminatory policies unless they are forced to do so.

Contrary to popular belief, employers and university admissions officers are not compelled to institute hiring or admissions quotas or to compromise standards to meet affirmative action goals. They are simply required to gather all relevant information on all qualified applicants, to interview minority candidates, and to make sure minorities have access to needed information. Government agencies and private firms doing business with the government, for instance, are required to publicly announce job openings at least 45 days prior to the cutoff day for applications (Cherry, 1989).

Quotas are used only as a last resort, reserved for situations in which organizations are not making good-faith efforts to seek out qualified minority candidates. If an organization announces a job opening in newspapers that reach only the white community, encourages college applicants only in white-dominated schools, or uses discriminatory procedures to eliminate minorities from consideration, the government can then impose quotas.

For close to half a century, affirmative action policies have been successful in helping members of ethnoracial minorities get ahead (Katel, 2008). Businesses, unions, universities, and local governments accused of discrimination in hiring or admissions have been sued under the 1964 Civil Rights Act. In part because of such actions, more than 40% of U.S. colleges and universities reported enrollment gains among African Americans and Latino/as during the 1990s (cited in Worsnop, 1996). People of color now hold a greater percentage of management, white-collar, and upper-level blue-collar jobs than ever before. Even young black men—historically, the most economically disadvantaged and alienated group in the United States—have made some employment gains (Nasar & Mitchell, 1999). Wages and salaries, relative to those of Whites, have also improved somewhat (though, as we've seen, they still lag behind).

Despite its successes, affirmative action remains highly controversial. In one national survey, for example, 93% of respondents agreed that society has an obligation to help hardworking people overcome disadvantages so they can succeed in life. However, when asked whether a fictitious low-income college applicant who happens to be black should be given preference over a high-income student who happens to be white, only 36% agreed (Carnevale & Rose, 2003).

Opposition to affirmative action comes from all directions. Some politically liberal critics, for example, argue that the lives of people for whom affirmative action policies were originally designed—the poorest and most disadvantaged—remain largely unchanged. Although the percentages of Blacks and Whites earning midrange incomes are roughly the same now, there continues to be a large discrepancy at the top- and bottom-income levels (U.S. Bureau of the Census, 2009). Top U.S. colleges are accepting more students of color today than ever before. But these students tend to come from middle- or upper-class backgrounds. For example, of the 8% of Harvard's undergraduates who are black, only a handful are from poor families in which all four grandparents were born in this country and were descendents of slaves (Rimer & Arenson, 2004). In addition, many schools don't provide enough support to ensure that those students from historically disadvantaged groups actually graduate. The 6-year graduation rate for Native American, Latino/a, and African American students is well below 50%, compared with 60% for white students and 65% for Asian students (Carey, 2005b). Because a college degree is associated with success later in life (bachelor's degree holders earn about twice as much a year as those with high school diplomas), such educational disappointment can have far-reaching social and personal effects.

Conservative critics argue that preferential treatment of any group, even one whose rights have been historically unrecognized, is demeaning to the people it's supposed to help and unfair to everyone else, amounting to a form of "reverse" discrimination. After the Supreme Court's 2007 ruling that barred the use of race in school desegregation plans, the Chief Justice said, "The way to stop discrimination on the basis of race is to stop discriminating on the basis of race" (quoted in Greenhouse, 2007b, p. 1). Some go further, arguing that affirmative action isn't needed because discrimination is already illegal and nothing more is required. And others maintain that it's not working because the problems that disadvantaged people face have more to do with economics or with inherent character flaws than with race (Fish, 2000). After 4 decades of such criticisms, many people have come to believe that affirmative action in all its forms should be abolished.

Ironically, however, other modes of preferential treatment continue to operate with virtually no criticism. For instance, those applicants who are most likely to receive favored treatment when it comes to college admissions are white, affluent "legacies," or children of alumni. Playing favorites with alumni children is a common practice at almost every private college and many public institutions as well. At some highly selective universities, legacies are twice as likely to be accepted as unconnected applicants with similar or better credentials (Larew, 2003). Some schools reserve a certain number of spaces for legacies. In one recent year at Harvard, marginally qualified legacies outnumbered all African American, Mexican American, Puerto Rican, and Native American students combined.

Yet all around the country, voters have been approving bans on race-based affirmative action. Currently, five states—California, Florida, Michigan, Nebraska, and Washington—forbid racial preferences for historically underrepresented groups in college admissions as well as employment. The California case has served as a model for other states considering bans on racial preferences. In 1996, voters there approved Proposition 209, a landmark referendum that bans the consideration of race, ethnicity, and sex in the public sector, including college admissions. Prior to the ban, African Americans, Latino/as, and Native Americans made up 23.1% of first-year students in the University of California system. The first year after the ban went into effect, that figure fell to 10.4% (Bronner, 1998b). In California, Blacks and Latino/as make up 42% of the state's population. However, they accounted for only about 15% of first-year admissions in the University of California system in 2006. At the same time, Asians, who make up about 12% of the state's population, accounted for about half of first-year admissions (Egan, 2007). That year, UCLA had its lowest first-year black enrollment in 30 years (Lewin, 2007).

Clearly, affirmative action remains a divisive issue. In a society with a tradition of racial stratification, what is the best way to overcome institutional inequality? Does it take discriminating in the opposite direction to "make things equal," or is it enough simply to treat people equally from this point on?

In sum, just because opportunities have been equalized in the present doesn't mean that the accumulated disadvantages of the past have been entirely overcome (Shapiro, 2008). Such is the problem we face today. We can legislate hiring and admission policies that do away with unfair advantages to any group, but is that action enough to address a long history of exclusion? For a long time to come, members of certain groups will continue to be underrepresented in traditionally white positions. Can U.S. citizens achieve complete equality without forcing those who have benefited historically to give up some of their advantages? The answer to this question is complex, controversial, and emotionally charged and will have a great impact on the nature of ethnoracial relations in the United States in the foreseeable future.

GLOBAL PERSPECTIVES ON RACISM

Given the focus of this chapter so far, you might be tempted to conclude that racism and racial inequality are purely U.S. phenomena. Certainly, these problems are very obvious in a society such as the United States, which is so ethnically and racially diverse and which has had such a long history of bitter conflict. But ethnoracial tension is the worldwide rule, not the exception.

Like disadvantaged ethnoracial groups in the United States, minority groups in other countries suffer discrimination that ruins their opportunities for success:

- Between 2004 and 2008, negative attitudes toward Jews and Muslims increased significantly in Spain, Poland, Russia, Germany, and France (Pew Global Attitudes Project, 2008).

- During soccer matches all across Europe, black players are routinely subjected to racist taunts, derisive chanting, monkey noises, and hurled bananas from white fans (Longman, 2006).

- Police in Paris, France, stop young Arab and black men for identity checks in train stations about seven times more often than young Whites (Erlanger, 2009).

- In eastern European countries such as Slovakia, Romania, Hungary, and the Czech Republic, discrimination against the Roma—or Gypsies—is the norm. They have been despised for centuries as thieving subhumans with no respect for the law and are stereotyped as loud, dirty, indecent, and sloppy (Erlanger, 2000). As a result of such attitudes, Gypsies suffer disproportionately from poverty, interethnic violence, discrimination, illiteracy, and disease (Wood, 2005).

- In Mexico, all citizens are considered legally equal under the country's constitution. Yet it is a society deeply divided along racial lines, particularly between dark-skinned people of Indian descent and light-skinned people of Spanish descent. Ironically, most Mexicans are of mixed lineage, so nearly all of them could be considered at least part Indian. But Mexicans who are considered Indians are the object of severe discrimination. More than 80% of Mexico's Indian communities suffer high levels of poverty. Nearly half of all Indians are illiterate, and only 14% complete sixth grade (DePalma, 1996).

Sociologists once believed that the global forces of industrialization and modernization would create ethnoracially diverse societies where people's loyalty would be directed to the national society rather than their racial or ethnic community (Deutsch, 1966). But the opposite has happened. At a time when people from every corner of the globe are linked technologically, economically, and ecologically and when mass migrations mix people from different races, religions, and cultures in unprecedented numbers, racial and ethnic hostilities are at an all-time high (Barber, 1992).

So much ethnic conflict is going on in the world today that we might conclude that hostility between groups is among the most universal of human feelings (Schlesinger, 1992). Look at any online news service, and you will see stories of ethnic, religious, or racial conflict: Jews and Palestinians in Israel and Gaza, Chechens and Russians in the former Soviet Union, Janjaweed and Darfurians in Sudan, Hindus and Muslims or Bengalis and Gurkhas in India, the Han and Uighurs in western China, Lendus and Hemas in the Democratic Republic of the Congo, Georgians and Ossetians in Georgia, Sunis and Shiites in Iraq, Tajiks and Pashtun in Afghanistan, and the Ijaw and Itsekiri in Nigeria. In Great Britain, France, and Germany, loud and sometimes violent resentment occurs between the native-born and immigrants from Africa, eastern Europe, and the Middle East. In the United States, such animosity is likely to be directed toward immigrants from Latin America and Asia (see Chapter 13 for more detail). When people feel that their survival is threatened, they often blame others for their problems, particularly newly arrived others who look and act differently. Racial and ethnic hatred costs the lives of millions of people each year.

But global forces don't just increase ethnoracial tension and inequality; sometimes they help resolve it. In South Africa, for example, the end of apartheid in the early 1990s was influenced by an international boycott. In the 1980s, the global media brought the world pictures and stories of the brutal treatment of South African Blacks. When consumers in the United States and other industrial nations stopped buying products from companies that held investments in South Africa, the companies began to withdraw their money. The minority white government felt the sting as domestic economic problems mounted. In part, as a result of these pressures, the white population of South Africa voted to abolish apartheid. Shortly thereafter, the first black president, Nelson Mandela, was elected. In 1996, a new constitution was adopted that officially and peacefully completed South Africa's transition from white supremacy to nonracial democracy. The document renounces the racism of the past and guarantees all South Africans broad freedoms of speech, movement, and political activity (Daley, 1996). Although serious inequalities and animosities remain, the country is on its way toward unity and stability.

More recently, we've seen how political developments in one country can reverberate around the globe. Shortly after the 2008 U.S. presidential election, social observers in Europe began to speculate on how Barack Obama's ascendency to the highest office in the land would influence race relations there. As an editor of a French blog put it, "They always said, 'You think race relations are bad here in France, check out the U.S.' But that argument can no longer stand" (quoted in Erlanger, 2008, p. 1). France's defense minister pondered how Obama's victory might serve as a lesson to the French on dealing with issues of immigration and integration. However, others in Italy, Great Britain, and Germany were more skeptical about the ultimate impact it would have on race relations there. I guess we'll just have to wait and see.

CONCLUSION

On April 16, 1963, the Reverend Martin Luther King Jr. was arrested and jailed for leading a civil rights demonstration in Birmingham, Alabama. At that time, not only were Blacks being subjected to daily doses of fear, violence, and humiliation, but they also had to constantly fight what Dr. King called "a degenerating sense of nobodiness." Torn between the brutal reality of a racist society and a fierce optimism for the future, he wrote from his jail cell,

> Let us all hope that the dark clouds of racial prejudice will soon pass away and the deep fog of misunderstanding will be lifted from our fear-drenched communities and in some not too distant tomorrow the radiant stars of love and brotherhood will shine over our great nation with all of their scintillating beauty. (King, 1991, p. 158)

Close to a half century later, our society—like most societies around the globe—still struggles with the debilitating effects of personal and institutional discrimination based on race, religion, and ethnicity. In the United States, lynchings and state-supported segregation have given way to a form of racism that resides not in bloodshed and flagrant exclusion but in the day-to-day workings of our major social institutions. Despite recent gains, people of color still suffer noticeable disadvantages in economics, education, politics, employment, health care, vulnerability to crime, and many other areas. When opportunities to learn, legislate, and make a living are unequally distributed according to race, all facets of life remain unequal.

Fifty years after racial segregation was ruled unconstitutional in the United States, the complete integration of fundamental social institutions such as public schools, government, and business has only partially been achieved. And some are questioning the very value of integration. One reason why race relations are so problematic today is that public debate over the issue confuses personal racism and institutional racism. Different types of racism require different solutions. We cannot put an end to economic deprivation or massive residential segregation by trying to convince people not to stereotype other groups.

I realize that this chapter has been rather depressing. After reading it, you may have a hard time imagining a society without racial or ethnic stratification, one where skin color is about as relevant in determining people's life chances as eye color.

We must remember, however, that differences do not have to imply inequality. The transformation from difference to disadvantage is a social construction. The people of every society decide which differences should be irrelevant and which should be the primary criteria for making social and legal distinctions between groups of people. The good news is that because we construct these differences, we can tear them down.

CHAPTER HIGHLIGHTS

◆ The history of race and ethnicity in U.S. society is an ambivalent one. Famous sayings about equality conflict with the experiences of most ethnoracial minorities–experiences of oppression, violence, and exploitation. Opportunities for life, liberty, and the pursuit of happiness have always been distributed along racial and ethnic lines.

◆ Personal racism is manifested in the form of bigotry, prejudice, and individual acts of discrimination. Quiet racism is expressed not directly but rather indirectly through anxiety about or avoidance of minorities.

◆ Racism can also be found in a language and norms prescribing differential treatment of certain groups.

◆ Institutional racism exists in established institutional practices and customs that reflect, produce, and maintain ethnoracial inequality. Institutional racism is more difficult to detect than personal racism and hence is more difficult to stop. Because such racism exists at a level above personal attitudes, it will not disappear simply by reducing people's prejudices.

◆ Ethnoracial conflict is not just an American phenomenon. It is a global reality.

KEY TERMS

affirmative action Program designed to seek out members of minority groups for positions from which they had previously been excluded, thereby seeking to overcome institutional racism

colorism Skin color prejudice within an ethnoracial group, most notably between light-skinned and dark-skinned Blacks

discrimination Unfair treatment of people based on some social characteristic, such as race, ethnicity, or sex

ethnicity Sense of community that derives from the cultural heritage shared by a category of people with common ancestry

institutional racism Laws, customs, and practices that systematically reflect and produce racial and ethnic inequalities in a society, whether or not the individuals maintaining these laws, customs, and practices have racist intentions

panethnic labels General terms applied to diverse subgroups that are assumed to have something in common

personal racism Individual expression of racist attitudes or behaviors

prejudice Rigidly held, unfavorable attitudes, beliefs, and feelings about members of a different group, based on a social characteristic such as race, ethnicity, or gender

quiet racism Form of racism expressed subtly and indirectly through feelings of discomfort, uneasiness, and fear, which motivate avoidance rather than blatant discrimination

race Category of people labeled and treated as similar because of some allegedly common biological traits, such as skin color, texture of hair, and shape of eyes

racial transparency Tendency for the race of a society's majority to be so obvious, normative, and unremarkable that it becomes, for all intents and purposes, invisible

racism Belief that humans are subdivided into distinct groups that are different in their social behavior and innate capacities and that can be ranked as superior or inferior

stereotype Overgeneralized belief that a certain trait, behavior, or attitude characterizes all members of some identifiable group

©Dave Etheridge-Barnes/Getty Images

12 The Architecture of Inequality

Sex and Gender

At a women's rights convention held in Seneca Falls, New York, participants created a modified version of the Declaration of Independence. They called it the Declaration of Sentiments and Resolutions. Here are some excerpts from that document:

> We hold these truths to be self-evident: that all men and women are created equal. . . . The history of mankind is a history of repeated injuries . . . on the part of man toward woman, having in direct object the establishment of an absolute tyranny over her:
>
> He has compelled her to submit to laws, in the formation of which she had no voice.
>
> He has monopolized nearly all profitable [occupations], and from those she is permitted to follow, she receives but a scanty remuneration. He closes against her all the avenues to wealth and distinction which he considers most honorable to himself.
>
> He has endeavored, in every way that he could, to destroy her confidence in her own powers, to lessen her self-respect, and to make her willing to lead a dependent and abject life.
>
> In view of their social degradation and in view of the unjust laws above mentioned, and because women do feel themselves aggrieved, oppressed, and fraudulently deprived of the most sacred rights, we insist that they have immediate admission to all the rights and privileges which belong to them as citizens of the United States.

("Declaration of Sentiments and Resolutions," 2001, pp. 449–450)

The women who wrote this declaration were not the women's liberationists of the 1960s and 1970s or the radical feminists of the 1990s and 2000s. They were participants in the first convention in support of women's rights ever held in the United States—in 1848. We tend to think that women of the past were either content with their second-class status or unaware that it could be otherwise. As you can see from the preceding declaration, though, 160 years ago U.S. women were anything but passive, ignorant victims of discrimination.

Many people are also inclined to believe that the battle against gender inequality has been won. Beginning with the civil rights movement of the 1960s and the so-called sexual revolution of the 1970s, a process of liberation has given contemporary U.S. women opportunities that equal men's. After all, almost as many U.S. women as men work in the paid labor force, the majority of college students these days are women, and women play a prominent role in business, politics, and entertainment. In 2009, seven states had female governors, and there were four women in the president's Cabinet. Perhaps you will be surprised to learn in this chapter, then, that women's struggle to overcome economic, legal, and social inequality is no less relevant in the 21st century than it was in 1848.

In Chapter 5, I discussed the difference between sex and gender and how we learn to become boys and girls and men and women within the appropriate social and cultural contexts. Being placed in a gender category affects everything we do in life. But gender is more than just a source of personal identity that sets societal expectations; it is a location in the stratification system and a major criterion for the distribution of important resources in most societies.

In this chapter, I will address several important questions: What are sexism and gender discrimination? How are they expressed and felt at the personal level? How is inequality based on sex and gender supported by cultural beliefs and symbols? At the institutional level, how is inequality related to family and work roles? What are its legal and economic consequences? And finally, how pervasive is gender inequality around the world?

SEXISM AT THE PERSONAL LEVEL

What do you think of when you hear the word *sexism?* The husband who won't let his wife work outside the home? The construction worker who whistles and shouts vulgar comments at female passersby? Perhaps you think of the woman who mocks men's interpersonal skills or their clumsy attempts at romance? Sexism is all those things, to be sure. But sociologically speaking, ***sexism*** refers to a system of beliefs that asserts the inferiority of one sex and that justifies discrimination based on gender—that is, on feminine or masculine roles and behaviors. At the personal level, sexism refers to attitudes and behaviors communicated in everyday interaction.

In male-dominated societies, or ***patriarchies,*** which exist in every quadrant of the globe, cultural beliefs and values typically give higher prestige and importance to men than to women. Throughout such societies, inequality affects girls and women in everything from the perceptions, ambitions, and social interactions of individuals to the organization of social institutions. Above all, gender inequality in a patriarchy provides men with privileged access to socially valued resources and furnishes them with the ability to influence the political, economic, and personal decisions of others. ***Matriarchies,*** which are societies that give preference to women, are rare in the contemporary world.

Even the most democratic societies tend to be patriarchal to some degree. Research on U.S. gender stereotypes, for instance, has shown that they have changed little over the years (Berger & Williams, 1991). Some researchers have shown that women are consistently perceived as more passive, emotional, easily influenced, and dependent than men (Broverman, Vogel, Broverman, Clarkson, & Rosenkrantz, 1972; Deaux & Kite, 1987; Tavris & Offir, 1984). Others have noted the myriad ways personal sexism is expressed in U.S. society, both overtly and subtly, through physical domination, condescending comments, sabotage, and exploitation (Benokraitis & Feagin, 1993). One study found that although some forms of personal sexism are motivated by hostility, others are motivated by benevolence, as when men assume women are helpless and thus feel compelled to offer assistance (Glick & Fiske, 1996). Such attitudes and behaviors not only place women in a lower-status position compared with men but also channel them into less advantageous social opportunities.

Men, of course, aren't the only ones who can be personally sexist. Certainly, many women dislike men, judge them on the basis of stereotypes, hold prejudiced attitudes toward them, objectify them sexually, consider them inferior, and even discriminate against them socially or professionally. We must keep in mind, though, that male sexism occupies a very different place in society from female sexism. The historical balance of power in patriarchal societies has allowed men as a group to subordinate women socially and sometimes legally to protect male interests and privileges. Because men dominate society, their sexism has more cultural legitimacy, is more likely to be reflected in social institutions, and has more serious consequences than women's sexism.

Sexism and Social Interaction

Everyday social life is fraught with reminders of gender imbalances. Men and women interact with each other a lot, but rarely are these interactions between two people who are of equal status (Ridgeway & Smith-Lovin, 1999). The average woman is reminded frequently of her subordinate position, through subtle—and sometimes not so subtle—ways. Men often have a hard time understanding women's reactions to personal encounters between the sexes. Just as white people enjoy racial transparency (see Chapter 11), members of the dominant sex take for granted the social arrangements that serve their interests.

For example, consider the following tongue-in-cheek quote from a female newspaper columnist:

> By whistling and yelling at attractive but insecure young men, we women may actually help them feel better about themselves, and give them new appreciation of their bodies. Some might say women were descending to the level of male street-corner oafs, but I'm willing to take that risk. If, with so little effort, I can bring joy to my fellow man, then I am willing to whistle at cute guys going down the street. (Viets, 1992, p. 5)

If you're a man, you may wonder why the columnist is bothering to make fun of "wolf whistles." The answer simply is that this behavior means different things when directed at men versus women. Unsolicited sexual attention may be an enjoyable, esteem-enhancing experience for men, but it doesn't have the weight of a long tradition of subordination attached to it, nor is it linked in any way to the threat of violence. Men aren't subjected to ***objectification***—that is, to being treated like objects rather than people—in the same way that women are. Sure, women gawk at and swoon over good-looking men from time to time. But men's entire worth is not being condensed into a quick and crude assessment of their physical appearance. For women, who must often fight to be taken seriously in their social, private, and professional lives, whistles and lewd comments serve as a reminder that their social value continues to be based primarily on their looks.

The implicit, nonverbal messages of social interaction—body movements, facial expressions, posture—also have more serious implications and consequences for women than for men. For example, femininity is typically gauged by how little space women take up; masculinity is judged by men's expansiveness and the strength of their gestures. Women's bodily demeanor tends to be restrained and restricted (Henley, 1977). What is typically considered "ladylike"—crossed legs, folded arms—is also an expression of submission. Men's freedom of movement—feet on the desk, legs spread, straddling a chair—conveys power and dominance. Such interactional norms place women who are in authoritative positions in a no-win situation. If, on the one hand, they meet cultural definitions of femininity by being passive, polite, submissive, and vulnerable, they fail to meet the requirements of authority. If, on the other hand, they exercise their authority by being assertive, confident, dominant, and tough, their femininity may be called into question (Mills, 1985).

Women are also routinely exposed to unwelcome leers, comments, requests for sexual favors, and unwanted physical contact in a variety of institutional settings, from schools to workplaces. According to the American Association of University Women (2001), about 83% of girls have been subjected to sexual harassment in elementary, middle, and high school, ranging from the spread of sexual rumors about them to coerced sexual activity. And nearly two thirds of female college students experience sexual harassment at some point during their college careers, though less than 10% tell a university official and an even smaller number file an official complaint (Hill & Silva, 2006).

The U.S. Equal Employment Opportunity Commission (2009) resolved close to 12,000 cases of workplace sexual harassment in 2008, but these figures obviously don't include episodes that are never reported. Some estimate that as many as 70% of women experience some kind of harassment in the workplace ("Sexual Harassment Statistics," 2004). From a conflict perspective, cases of sexual harassment are expressions of and attempts to reinforce positions of dominance and power (Uggen & Blackstone, 2004).

The vast majority of harassment cases involve male assertions of power over women. But women aren't the only victims. Sometimes an overbearing, sexually aggressive female boss may come on to a male subordinate; but more commonly, it's men who create a hostile environment for other men through "bullying," "hazing," "goosing," various sexual insults, and other boorish behaviors. According to the U.S. Equal Employment Opportunity Commission (2009), sexual harassment charges filed by men increased from 11.6% of all cases in 1997 to 15.9% of all cases in 2008.

Sexual Orientation

Prejudices expressed at the personal level often combine gender and sexual orientation. For many decades, gays and lesbians have been rejected, ridiculed, and condemned on moral, religious, criminal, or even psychiatric grounds. Today, homosexuals and bisexuals—as well as people assumed to be or accused of being gay or bisexual—routinely experience discrimination, interpersonal rejection, or violence (Herek, 2000a). Such sexual prejudice varies along gender lines. According to one study (Herek, 2000b), women tend to express fewer antigay attitudes, beliefs, and behaviors than men. But the object of attitudes is also gender-specific. Heterosexual men tend to have more negative attitudes toward and feel more discomfort around gay men than they feel toward lesbians. Heterosexual women, in contrast, hold similar attitudes toward gay men and lesbians. Demonstrating one's heterosexuality and one's conformity to traditional gender roles seems to be of greater concern to men than women, which may explain the heightened male hostility toward gay men.

Often the attitudes are unabashedly virulent. For instance, several years ago, a gay college student in Wyoming, Matthew Shepard, was pistol-whipped, tied to a fence, and left to die. At his funeral, protestors from a church in Topeka, Kansas, held up signs reading "God Hates Fags!" The church's website had a picture of Matthew depicted burning in hell. The same website had a similar photo of a lesbian who was mauled to death by two dogs a few years ago. Above her picture, it read, "God used literal dogs to kill a figurative dog."

But harassment can also occur in settings purported to be more tolerant, such as universities. In a nationwide study of gay, lesbian, and bisexual college students, 89% had been the recipient of derogatory remarks, 49% had received verbal threats, and 2% had been physically assaulted. Close to 20% feared for their physical safety because of their sexual orientation (Rankin, 2003). These students are not only more likely than heterosexuals to be harassed by fellow students, but they're also at greater risk of being harassed by teachers and school employees (Hill & Silva, 2006). In 2009, Congress voted to define antigay violence as a federal hate crime.

Violence Against Women

The epitome of sexual domination expressed at the personal level is sexual violence. Forcible rape and other forms of sexual assault exist throughout the world, in the most democratic societies as well as in the most repressive.

In the United States, rape is the most frequently committed but least reported violent crime (U.S. Department of Justice, 2001). According to the National Crime Victimization Survey—an annual assessment of crime victimization carried out by the U.S. Bureau of Justice Statistics (Rand, 2008)—more than 248,000 women over the age of 12 said they'd been raped or sexually assaulted in 2007, more than double the roughly 92,000 incidents of forcible rape and attempted rape that are officially reported to the police in a given year (U.S. Bureau of the Census, 2009).

Rape is the most personal of violent crimes. In 64% of rapes and sexual assaults, the victim knows the attacker (U.S. Bureau of Justice Statistics, 2009). On college campuses, where about 3% of college women experience a completed or attempted rape during a typical college year, 90% of the victims know their attackers (U.S. Bureau of Justice Statistics, 2001).

Rape as a Means of Social Control

According to the conflict perspective, stratification along sex and gender lines has long distorted our understanding of rape. Throughout history, women have been viewed socially and legally as the property of men, as either daughters or wives. Thus, in the past, rape was defined as a crime against men or, more accurately, against men's property (Siegel, 2004). Any interest a husband took in a sexual assault on his wife probably reflected a concern with his own status, the loss of his male honor, and the devaluation of his sexual possession. Even when women are not seen as men's property, their lives are controlled by rape and sexual assault. Lesbians in South Africa are sometimes raped by men who believe it will "cure" them of their sexual orientation. These violent acts are known as "corrective rapes." As one woman put it,

> We get insults every day, beatings if we walk alone, you are constantly reminded that . . . you deserve to be raped, they yell, "if I rape you then you will go straight . . . you will buy skirts and start to cook because you will have learned how to be a real woman." (quoted in ActionAid, 2009, p. 15)

Globally, rape is a time-tested wartime tactic of terror, revenge, and intimidation, not only against female victims but also against husbands, sons, and fathers whose idea of honor is connected to their ability to protect "their" women (Amnesty International, 2004; Enloe, 1993; Sengupta, 2004). In the Democratic Republic of Congo, for example, bands of soldiers have been "waging a war of rape and destruction against women" since the 1980s (Herbert, 2009, p. A17). Congolese girls and women of all ages have been publicly gang-raped, had their reproductive organs deliberately destroyed, and been violated with loaded guns. Millions have been killed. The devastation of these atrocities extends beyond the psychological humiliation, physical wounds, and deaths of individual victims. Entire families and neighborhoods are traumatized when husbands are forced to watch their wives being raped, parents their daughters, or children their mothers.

According to some feminist sociologists, men have used rape and the threat of rape throughout history to exert control over women (Brownmiller, 1975). The mere existence of rape limits women's freedom of social interaction, denies them the right of self-determination, and makes them dependent on and ultimately subordinate to men (Griffin, 1986). All forms of oppression—whether against ethnic Darfurians in Sudan, peasants in Bolivia, or women in the United States—employ the threat of violence to ensure compliance. The subordination of women depends on the power of men to intimidate and punish them sexually.

The fear of rape goes beyond simply making life terrifying and uncomfortable for women. It also can restrict their economic opportunities. Women may avoid some neighborhoods with affordable housing because of potential danger. If a woman has a job that requires night work, she may be forced to buy a car to avoid walking at night or using public transportation. The threat of sexual assault limits where and when she is able to work, thereby limiting her money-earning choices and perhaps keeping her financially dependent on others.

Women are also harmed by the larger cultural ideology surrounding rape and rapists. I think most of us are inclined to believe that men who rape must be insane or abnormally violent. All one has to do to avoid being raped, then, is to avoid strange guys. However, rapists as a group have not been shown to be any more disturbed or crazy than nonrapists (Griffin, 1986; Warshaw, 1988). In fact, most rapists are quite "normal" by usual societal standards. As I mentioned earlier, about two thirds of them are friends, acquaintances, or relatives of their victims. But when rape is generally perceived to be perpetrated by psychologically defective strangers, it doesn't implicate the dominant culture or established social arrangements. In other words, rape isn't considered the fault of society; it's the fault of flawed men who can't abide by society's rules. This assumption may explain why date or acquaintance rape, marital rape, and other forms of sexual violence that don't fit the typical image have, until quite recently, been ignored or trivialized.

We must therefore examine the crime of rape within a broader cultural context that encourages certain types of behavior between men and women (Jackson, 1995). When we do so, rape becomes less an act of deviance and more an act of overconformity to cultural expectations; less an act of abnormal individuals and more an act of "normal" men taking cultural messages about power and assertiveness to their violent extreme. As one author wrote, rape is the "all-American crime," involving precisely those characteristics traditionally regarded as desirable in American men: strength, power, domination, and control (Griffin, 1989).

Victim Blaming

Globally, cultural beliefs about gender, sexuality, and intimacy influence societal and legal responses to rape and rape victims (Morgan, 1996):

- In Colombia, a man who rapes a woman—whether he knows her or not—can be absolved of all charges if he offers to marry her.

- In Senegal, single women who are rape victims may be killed by their families because as nonvirgins they can no longer command a high dowry; a married woman who's been raped may be killed by her "dishonored" husband.
- In Iran, because Islamic tradition forbids the execution of virgins, any woman condemned to die must first lose her virginity through rape.
- In Afghanistan, women are forbidden by law to refuse to have sex with their husbands.

Arguably, the United States has a more sympathetic reaction to rape victims. But the legal response here still tends to be consistent with men's interests, focusing on women's complicity or blameworthiness. In rape cases, unlike any other crime, victims typically must prove their innocence rather than the state having to prove the guilt of the defendant. Many women who have been victimized come to the conclusion that reporting their experiences would, at best, be embarrassing and useless (Sanday, 1996).

And, to some extent, they may be right. Consider, for example, the way a victim is treated in the immediate aftermath of a rape. When she reports being victimized, she is physically examined, photographed, probed, and swabbed for the assailant's DNA. This process—which can last several hours in a hospital—produces what's known as a "rape kit." The kit is then sent to a crime lab, where, after thorough DNA analysis, it becomes the key piece of physical evidence in criminal proceedings. National studies have found that rape cases in which there is a rape kit containing DNA evidence are significantly more likely to move forward than cases where there is no kit. You would think that the process that produces such an important component of a legal case would be quick and efficient. However, according to a study of rape cases in Los Angeles County, there are more than 12,000 *untested* rape kits sitting in police storage facilities; 450 of them have been there for more than 10 years (Human Rights Watch, 2009). Such delays can be tragic. California has a 10-year statute of limitations for rape (the maximum time period after a crime when a defendant can be prosecuted) that can be lifted only if a rape kit is tested within 2 years of the date of the crime. It's no wonder that so many women are reluctant to report being sexually victimized.

The conflict perspective provides one explanation for the widespread tendency to hold women responsible for their own victimization: The common definition of rape is based on a traditional model of sexual intercourse—penile-vaginal penetration—rather than on the violent context within which the act takes place. The primary focus on the sexual component of the crime requires that information about the intimate circumstances of the act and about the relationship between the people involved be taken into consideration—all of which tends to put female rape victims at a disadvantage during criminal proceedings. Research consistently shows that observers attribute more blame to the victims and minimize the seriousness of the assault when the perpetrator is an acquaintance, date, or steady partner (Bell, Kuriloff, & Lottes, 1994). One study of convicted rapists found that those who assaulted strangers received longer prison sentences than those who were acquaintances or partners of their victims, regardless of the amount of force used or physical injury to the victim (McCormick, Maric, Seto, & Barbaree, 1998).

Rape victims are often expected to provide clear evidence that they were "unwilling" and tried to resist. Anything short of vigorous and repeated resistance can still call the victim's motives into question. Indeed, research suggests that police, prosecutors, and juries are less likely to believe allegations of rape if there is no evidence of violence (McEwan, 2005).

No other serious crime requires that the victim prove lack of consent. People aren't asked if they wanted their house broken into or if they enticed someone to beat them up and steal their wallet. Yet if women cannot prove that they resisted or cannot find someone to corroborate their story, consent (or even latent desire) may be presumed (Siegel, 2004). While in a hospital waiting room after being brutally raped, a woman from Madison, Wisconsin, was required to submit a "statement of nonconsent" swearing that she hadn't given her knife-wielding assailant permission to rape, cut, and rob her (Lueders, 2006).

Certain states are reconsidering the issue of what constitutes consent. In Connecticut and Kansas, for example, a woman may withdraw her consent to have sex at any time, and if the man continues, he is committing rape. However, in North Carolina, once a woman gives consent, she cannot rescind it. Such an understanding of consent rests on the belief that at a certain point during arousal, a man loses the ability to stop (Lee-St. John, 2007).

Public perceptions are slow to change. Many people regard female rape victims as at least partly to blame if they put themselves in risky situations, for instance, by behaving seductively, wearing "provocative" clothing, drinking too much, or telling dirty jokes. In one study, male and female high school students were given a list of statements and asked to indicate the extent to which they agreed with them (Kershner, 1996). Of the male and female subjects, 52% agreed that most women fantasize about being raped by a man, 46% felt that women encourage rape by the way they dress, and 53% said they felt that some women provoke men into raping them. Moreover, 31% agreed that many women falsely report rapes, and 35% felt that the victim should be required to prove her innocence during a rape trial. Research has linked such attitudes to an increased likelihood of holding rape victims responsible (Frese, Moya, & Megías, 2004) as well as a heightened risk of rape and sexual assault on college campuses (Ching & Burke, 1999). The important sociological point of these findings is that many men and even some women don't always define violent sexual assault as a form of victimization. They think it is either something women bring on themselves or something men understandably do under certain circumstances.

As a consequence of victim blaming, women must bear much of the responsibility for preventing rape. I frequently pose this question to students in my introductory sociology class: What can people do to stop rape from occurring? Their responses always echo the standard advice: Don't walk alone at night. Don't get drunk at parties where men are present, and if you do drink, know where your drink is at all times. Don't flirt or engage in foreplay if you have no intention of "going all the way." Don't miscommunicate your intentions. Don't wear revealing clothes. Certainly all these safety measures are smart, sensible things to do. But note how all of these suggestions focus exclusively on things that *women* should avoid in order to prevent rape and say nothing about the things *men* can do to stop it. Confining discussions of rape prevention to women's behavior and vulnerability suggests that if a woman doesn't take these precautions, she is "inviting trouble." And "inviting trouble" implies that violent male behavior either is a natural response to provocation or is likely to happen if precautions aren't taken to discourage it.

Some progress is being made regarding cultural perceptions of rape. Myths are being debunked, the violent sexual exploitation of women in the media is being protested, and the rules governing admissible evidence in rape trials are being changed. The recent increase in attention paid to rape, particularly to rape between acquaintances and intimate partners, has increased public awareness of the problem. Rates of officially reported rapes and attempted rape dropped steadily throughout the 1990s, although they have stabilized somewhat in recent years (U.S. Bureau of the Census, 2009). However, as long as we live in a culture that objectifies women and glorifies male assertiveness, we will continue to have sexual violence.

THE IDEOLOGY OF SEXISM: BIOLOGY AS DESTINY

The domination of one group over another is always endorsed by a set of beliefs that explains and justifies that domination. You saw in the previous chapter that racism is often justified by the belief in innate racial inferiority. With sexism, it is the belief that men and women are biologically and naturally different.

For 19th- and early-20th-century physicians, few facts were more incontestable than the fact that women were the products and prisoners of their anatomy. One French scientist noted a century ago that women have smaller brains than men, which explained their "fickleness, inconstancy, absence of thought and logic, and incapacity to reason" (quoted in Angier & Chang, 2005, p. A1). Even today, there's no shortage of books purporting to show that female tendencies in self-control, risk taking, intuition, empathy, anxiety, aggression, emotions, and even decision making can all be traced to the structure and function of their brains (Baron-Cohen, 2003; Brizendine, 2006; Mansfield, 2006).

Likewise, women's reproductive systems have been the object of scientific attention and concern for centuries (Scull & Favreau, 1986). Everything supposedly known about women that made them different from men—their subordinate place in society, their capacity for affection, their love of children and aptitude for child rearing, their "preference" for domestic work, and so on—could be explained by their uterus and ovaries (Ehrenreich & English, 1979; Scull & Favreau, 1986). Scholars in the past warned that young women who studied too much were struggling against nature, would badly damage their reproductive organs, and would perhaps even go insane in the process (Fausto-Sterling, 1985). So the exclusion of women from higher education was not only justifiable but necessary for health reasons and for the long-term good of society.

Some structural-functionalist sociologists have also used the bodily differences between men and women to explain gender inequality. The fact that men tend to be physically stronger and that women bear and nurse children has created many culturally recognized sex-segregated social roles, especially at work and in the family (Parsons & Bales, 1955). This specialization of roles is the most effective way to maintain societal stability, structural-functionalists believe. By giving birth to new members, by socializing very young children, and by providing affection and nurturing, women make invaluable contributions to the reproduction of society. The common occupations that women have traditionally had outside the home—teacher, nurse, day care provider, maid, social worker, and so on—tend simply to be extensions of their "natural" tendencies.

Similarly, men's physical characteristics have been presumed to better suit them for the roles of economic provider and protector of the family. If it's true that men are "naturally endowed" with traits such as strength, assertiveness, competitiveness, and rationality, then they are best qualified to enter the serious and competitive world of work and politics (Kokopeli & Lakey, 1992). Sociologist Steven Goldberg (1999) argues that because male rule and male dominance seem to characterize the vast majority of human societies, this gender difference must be rooted in evolutionary biology.

The problem with depicting masculinity and femininity as natural, biological phenomena is that it confuses sex with gender. The underlying assumption of sexist ideology—that gender is as unchangeable as sex—overlooks extensive similarities between the sexes and extensive variations within each sex. The distributions of men and women on most personality and behavioral characteristics generally overlap. For instance, men as a group do tend to be more aggressive than women as a group. Yet some women are much more aggressive than the average man, and some men are much less aggressive than the average woman. Indeed, social circumstances may have a greater impact on aggressive behavior than any innate, biological traits. Some studies show that when women are rewarded for behaving aggressively, they can be just as violent as men (Hyde, 1984).

Furthermore, the reliance on biology ignores the wide cultural and historical variation in conceptions of masculinity and femininity. For instance, although every known society has a division of labor based on sex, what's considered "men's work" and "women's work" differs. In most societies, men fish, hunt, clear land, and build boats and houses, but in some societies, women regularly perform these tasks. In most societies, women do the cooking; but in some societies, cooking is typically a male responsibility (Eitzen & Baca Zinn, 1991).

Although women have become prominent in the U.S. workforce, many people still believe that they are less capable than men of performing certain tasks outside the home (Wagner, Ford, & Ford, 1986). Some in the United States still may find female doctors or dentists unusual. Legislators and military officials continue to debate the role of female soldiers in direct ground combat. The controversy in several churches over whether or not women should be ordained as ministers and priests illustrates the depth and intensity of people's feelings about gender-appropriate career pursuits.

The biological rationale for gender inequality is difficult to justify these days. Technological advances—including bottled baby formula, contraceptives that give women more choices over childbearing, and innovations that lessen the need for sheer physical strength—have made it possible for women and men to fulfill many of the same responsibilities. Nevertheless, as long as people believe that gender-linked roles and societal contributions are determined by nature, they will continue to accept inequality in women's and men's opportunities, expectations, and outcomes. If people consider it "natural" for women to play nurturing, weak, and dependent roles, then limiting women to such positions seems neither unfair nor oppressive.

INSTITUTIONS AND GENDER INEQUALITY

The subordination of women that is part of the everyday workings of social institutions (or ***institutional sexism***) has far greater consequences for women as a group than do personal expressions of sexism. When sexism in social institutions becomes part of the ongoing operation of large-scale organizations, it perpetuates and magnifies women's disadvantages, making social equality all the more difficult to attain. But not only can social institutions be sexist, they can also be gendered. In other words, institutions and organizations segregate, exploit, and exclude women solely on the basis of their physical characteristics and then compound the impact of their sexism by incorporating values and practices based on traditional expectations for women and men (Kimmel, 2004).

Masculinized Institutions

More often than not, institutions incorporate masculine values—which is not surprising because, historically, men have developed, dominated, and interpreted most institutions. Take competitive sports, for example. Most of us would agree that to be successful, an athlete must be aggressive, strong, and powerful—attributes typically associated with masculinity. By celebrating these traits, a sport such as football symbolically declares itself an arena that women cannot or should not enter (except, of course, as spectators or cheerleaders). But even sports such as gymnastics and figure skating, which have traditionally valued more "feminine" traits such as grace, beauty, and balance, have now made their judging criteria more masculine. For a woman to be a world-class gymnast or skater these days, she must also be physically strong and exhibit explosive acrobatic power. Indeed, the popularity of women's team sports in this country coincides with the increasing presence of traditionally male traits such as physical strength and competitive vigor in female athletes.

In most high schools, student culture revolves around sports, especially football. In such an environment, privilege and power are conferred on successful male athletes. Some sociologists and educators fear that high schools are now being pressured to apply an equally aggressive, competitive, "masculinized" approach to the curriculum as well, through emphases on academic rigor, high-stakes test taking, zero-tolerance discipline policies, and increased efforts in math, science, and technology (Lesko, 2008).

Similarly, most bureaucracies in institutional areas such as business, politics, and the military operate according to taken-for-granted masculine principles. Successful leaders and organizations are usually portrayed as aggressive, goal oriented, competitive, and efficient—all characteristics associated with masculinity in this society. Rarely are strong governments, prosperous businesses, or efficient military units described as supportive, nurturing, cooperative, kind, and caring (Acker, 1992). When institutions are gendered in these ways, everyday inequalities become apparent.

Gender Inequality in Health and Health Care

Gender inequality has created some curious discrepancies in the way the medical establishment treats men and women. For instance, women pay much higher premiums for individual private health insurance policies than men of the same age. Insurance companies claim they are justified in charging women more because they typically use more health care than men, especially in their child-bearing years. However, the discrepancies exist even for policies that don't cover maternity costs (Pear, 2008b).

Ironically, men tend to have more health problems and a shorter life expectancy than women (Legato, 2006). They occupy more physically demanding jobs and engage in more dangerous physical activity. Hence, they've historically been at greater risk for various bodily injuries and stress-related ailments. According to figures from the U.S. Bureau of the Census (2009), men also have higher rates of most cancers than women.

Yet women have historically been the focus of intrusive medical attention more than men (Rothman, 1984). Women are far more likely than men to undergo surgical and diagnostic procedures. Indeed, the three most common short-stay surgical procedures for women—repair of lacerations during childbirth, cesarean section, and hysterectomy—all deal with female anatomy and physiology. The three most common short-stay procedures for men—cardiac catheterization, reduction of fracture, and coronary artery bypass graft—are not sex-specific (U.S. Bureau of the Census, 2009). Similarly, physicians commonly specialize in *women's* health care, but rarely do they specialize in *men's*. Obstetricians and gynecologists deal exclusively with the reproductive and sexual matters of female patients. There are no comparable specialties of medicine devoted solely to men's reproductive health (urologists address men's reproductive issues, but they also see female patients).

Normal biological events in women's lives—menstruation, pregnancy, childbirth, and menopause—have long been considered problematic conditions in need of medical intervention. For instance, the Board of Trustees of the American Psychiatric Association continues to debate the inclusion of a psychiatric diagnosis called "Premenstrual Dysphoric Disorder" in its official manual of mental disorders. Indisputably, many women around the world experience irritability, moodiness, and other symptoms related to hormonal cycles. The issue, however, is whether these symptoms ought to be labeled as a medical and/or mental problem (Lander, 1988). To do so not only promotes the selling of drugs to healthy women (Bailey, 1993; Figert, 1996) but fosters the belief that women, biologically frail and emotionally erratic because of their hormones, cannot be allowed to work too hard or be trusted in positions of authority (Fausto-Sterling, 1985).

Given the special attention women's health problems receive, it's ironic that, outside obstetrics and gynecology, research on women's general health needs has been rather limited. Twenty years ago, the U.S. Public Health Service reported that a lack of medical research on women limited our understanding of their health concerns (Rothman & Caschetta, 1999). The reason often given for their exclusion from medical studies was that their menstrual cycles complicated the interpretation of research findings. In addition, medical researchers have historically been reluctant to perform research on women of childbearing age because of fears that exposing them to experimental manipulations might harm their reproductive capabilities. In fact, in the 1970s and 1980s, federal policies and guidelines actually called for the blanket exclusion of women of childbearing potential from certain types of drug research. That meant that any woman who was physically capable of becoming pregnant, regardless of her own desire to do so, could be excluded. Concerns were less with threats to women's health than with the possibility of liability if reproductive damage due to exposure to the experimental drug occurred (Hamilton, 1996).

The exclusion of women from medical research became so problematic that Congress passed a law in 1993 stipulating that women must be included in clinical trials in numbers sufficient to provide evidence of the different ways men and women respond to drugs, surgical treatments, and changes in diet or behavior. Nevertheless, a 2000 study found that many researchers were not complying with the law (cited in Pear, 2000). In 2003, the Agency for Healthcare Research and Quality reported that research on coronary heart disease (CHD) still either excluded women entirely or included them only in limited numbers. Consequently, the therapies used to treat women with CHD—a disease that kills 250,000 women a year—are still based on studies conducted primarily on middle-aged men (cited in "Research Findings Affirm," 2003).

Gender Inequality in Families

Much of the inequality women face revolves around the traditional view of their family role: keepers of the household and producers, nurturers, and socializers of children. Although in other times and places, women have had different levels of responsibility for homemaking, they have always been responsible for reproduction.

One of the major consequences of the industrial revolution of the 18th and 19th centuries was the separation of the workplace and the home. Prior to industrialization, most countries were primarily agricultural. People's lives centered on the farm, where husbands and wives were partners not only in making a home but also in making a living (Vanek, 1980). The farm couple were interdependent; each needed the other for survival. It was taken for granted that women provided for the family along with men (Bernard, 1981). Although the relationship between husbands and wives on the farm was never entirely equal—wives still did most if not all of the housekeeping and family care—complete male dominance was offset by women's indispensable contributions to the household economy (Vanek, 1980).

With the advent of industrialization, things began to change. New forms of technology and the promise of new financial opportunities and a good living drew people (mostly men) away from the farms and into cities and factories. For the first time in history, the family economy in some societies was based outside the household. Women no longer found themselves involved in the day-to-day supervision of the family's business as they had once been. Instead, they were consigned to the only domestic responsibilities that remained necessary in an industrial economy: the care and nurturing of children and the maintenance of the household. Because this work was unpaid and because visible goods were no longer being produced at home, women quickly found their labor devalued in the larger society (Hareven, 1992).

However, as we saw in Chapter 7, men weren't the only ones who left home each day to work in factories. At the turn of the century, hundreds of thousands of children worked in mines, mills, and factories (Coontz, 1992). And contrary to popular belief, one fifth of U.S. women worked outside the home in 1900, especially women of color (Staggenborg, 1998).

Today, the devaluation of "women's work" is the result of a separation of the public and private spheres (Sidel, 1990). As long as men dominate the public sphere—the marketplace and the government—they will wield greater economic and political power within society and also be able to translate that power into authority at home. "Women's work" within the relatively powerless private sphere of the home will continue to be hidden and undervalued.

According to the conflict perspective, the problem is not that housewives don't work; it's that they work for free outside the mainstream economy, in which work is strictly defined as something one is paid to do (Ciancanelli & Berch, 1987; Voyandoff, 1990). Ironically, however, domestic work is actually invaluable to the entire economic system.

If a woman were to be paid the minimum going rate for all her labor as mother and housekeeper, including child care, transportation, housecleaning, laundry, cooking, bill paying, and grocery shopping, her yearly salary would be larger than the average salary of full-time male workers. One recent study found that if we apply average hourly wage rates to the typical daily amounts of child care mothers of children under 12 provide, a low-end estimate of the monetary value of this work is about $33,000 a year (Folbre & Yoon, 2006). But because societal and family power is a function of who brings home the cash, such unpaid work does not afford women the prestige it might if it were paid labor.

Despite significant shifts in U.S. attitudes toward gender roles and the accelerated entry of women into the paid labor force in the past few decades, housework continues to be predominantly female (Baxter, 1997; Brines, 1994). Husbands do play a more prominent role in the raising of children than they did two decades ago, and they've increased their contribution to housework somewhat (Bianchi, Robinson, & Milkie, 2006), especially when compared with men in other industrialized countries (Fuwa, 2004). But the household work that husbands do tends to be quite different from the work that wives do. Women's tasks tend to be essential to the daily functioning of the household (Fuwa, 2004); men's chores are typically infrequent, irregular, or optional:

> They take out the garbage, they mow the lawns, they play with children, they occasionally go to the supermarket or shop for household durables, they paint the attic or fix the faucet; but by and large, they do not launder, clean, or cook, nor do they feed, clothe, bathe, or transport children. These . . . most time-consuming activities . . . are exclusively the domain of women. (Cowan, 1991, p. 207)

From a structural-functionalist perspective, one could argue that traditional gendered household responsibilities actually reflect an equitable, functional, interdependent division of labor. That is, the husband works in the paid labor force and supports the family financially; the wife takes care of the household work and child care. Each person provides essential services in exchange for those provided by the other. But research in this area indicates that the gender discrepancy in housework responsibilities does not diminish when women work full-time outside the home. On average, working women spend about 19 hours per week on housework, while men spend only about 10 hours (Bianchi et al., 2006). The hours that women spend on housework are down from 35 hours in the mid-1960s, and men have increased their contribution from 4 hours per week, but still men contribute only half as much time as women do to the maintenance of the household. According to a survey conducted by the U.S. Bureau of Labor Statistics (2008a), employed women spend about an hour a day more than employed men caring for young children. When they have older children, these women spend 6 hours a day on so-called "secondary care," such as shopping with children in tow, while men spend only 4 hours a day on such activities.

Because working women continue to be primarily responsible for housework, they often end up working what amounts to two full-time jobs. Even when a husband is unemployed, he does less housework than a wife who puts in a 40-hour week. Indeed, recently laid-off men tend to take on fewer household tasks—rather than more—when they lose their jobs. In contrast, laid-off women double the time they spend on child care and household chores (Dokoupil, 2009).

The dynamics of retirement, too, are a factor. Because wives, in general, are younger than their husbands, millions of women continue to work for pay after their husbands have retired. These women sometimes come to resent retired husbands, who have lots of free time on their hands but who don't contribute much more around the house than they did while they were employed. One study of retirement-age men and women found that working women whose husbands are retired were the least happy with their marriages of all types of couples; working men whose wives stayed home were the happiest (cited in Leland, 2004).

Gender Inequality in Education

Another institutional setting in which gender inequality persists is education. In elementary school and beyond, teachers are likely to treat their male and female students differently (Sadker, Sadker, Fox, & Salata, 2004):

- Girls receive less teacher attention and less useful feedback than boys.
- Girls talk significantly less in class than boys, and when they do speak up, they are more likely than boys to be reminded to raise their hands.
- Students rarely see mention of the contributions of women in their textbooks, which continue to emphasize male accomplishments.
- Girls are more likely than boys to be the focus of unwanted sexual attention in school.

Over the course of their school careers, such differential treatment takes its toll on girls. Since it is sometimes quite subtle, most people are unaware of the hidden sexist lessons and quiet losses it creates (Sadker & Sadker, 1999).

In elementary school and middle school, girls outperform boys on almost every standard measure of academic achievement (Tyre, 2006). Boys are more likely than girls to repeat a grade, drop out, be put in special education, or be diagnosed as having an emotional problem, a learning disability, or attention-deficit disorder (Lewin, 1998). Yet boys have higher expectations and higher self-esteem than girls, a gap that widens with each passing year in the school system. According to one study, around the ages of 8 and 9, about two thirds of both boys and girls report feeling confident and positive about themselves. By high school, however, the percentage drops to 29% for young women (Freiberg, 1991). As girls make the transition from childhood to adolescence, they are faced with a conflict between the way they see themselves and the way others, particularly teachers, see them (Gilligan, 1990).

These gender-typed patterns pervade high school. Teenage boys' sense of their own masculinity tends to be derived primarily from participation in organized sports (Messner, 2002). Boys are also likely to be encouraged by counselors and teachers to formulate ambitious career goals. In contrast, prestige and popularity for teenage girls are still likely to come largely from their physical appearance and from having a boyfriend (Lott, 1987). Not surprisingly, by the end of high school, boys perform better than girls. For instance, though 54% of all SAT takers are girls, boys' average total score is higher (1526 for boys vs. 1501 for girls; National Center for Fair and Open Testing, 2008).

Gender differences in academic performance are usually a cultural byproduct, as opposed to some innate intellectual difference. Take, for instance, the common belief that boys are naturally better at mathematics than girls. A few years ago, a former Harvard University president famously stated that the reason there are so few female mathematicians is that women lack an "intrinsic aptitude" for math. However, cross-cultural evidence shows that many Asian and Eastern European countries consistently produce girls with highly developed mathematical abilities, while other countries (chiefly the United States) do not (Andreescu, Gallian, Kane, & Mertz, 2008). Even in this country, girls who excel in national and international mathematical competitions are likely to be the daughters of immigrants. Researchers locate the reason for this discrepancy in a culture that doesn't value, actively discourages, or even socially penalizes mathematical excellence in girls.

Gender inequality is evident in postsecondary education, too. Since 1980, more U.S. women than men have enrolled in college (U.S. Bureau of the

Census, 2009). In 2007, about a third of women between the ages of 25 and 29 had a bachelor's degree or more, compared with 26% of men (Yin, 2008). Moreover, college women study more and have higher grade point averages than men. They're also more likely to complete their bachelor's degrees in 4 or 5 years (cited in Lewin, 2006). However, men are more likely to take rigorous courses geared for math and science majors and achieve higher grades in those courses than women (College Board, 1998). Many of the majors that lead to high-paying or high-prestige careers remain male dominated (engineering, economics, mathematics, earth sciences, etc.), whereas women are concentrated in fields such as nursing, education, and social services (Dey & Hill, 2007).

Gender Inequality in the Economy

Because of their difficulty converting educational achievements into high pay, women have historically been prevented from taking advantage of the occupational opportunities and rewards to which most men have had relatively free access. Today, women continue to have much less earning power in the labor market than men (Cohen & Huffman, 2003).

The unequal economic status of women results not only from the personal sexism of potential employers but is tied to larger economic structures and institutional forces. The standard assumptions that drive the typical workplace often work against women. Think of the things one generally has to do to be considered a good worker by a boss: work extra hours, travel to faraway business meetings, go to professional conferences, attend training programs, be willing to work unpopular shifts, or entertain out-of-town clients. These activities assume that employees have the time and the freedom from familial obligations to do them. Because women, especially mothers, still tend to have the lion's share of responsibility at home, they are less able than their male colleagues to "prove" to management that they are good, committed employees. Even if women are able to commit extra time to work, employers frequently assume that, because they are women, they won't.

Such assumptions are even present in professional, academic environments. In its assessment of the underrepresentation of women in science and engineering, the National Academy of Sciences (2007) concluded that the traditional scientific or engineering career rests on the assumption that the faculty member will be thoroughly committed to his or her academic career throughout his or her working life. It found that attention to other obligations, such as family, is often interpreted as a lack of dedication to one's career. Because the burden of family and household care still generally falls more heavily on women than on men—and because women seldom have substantial spousal support—female scientists and engineers experience greater conflict between their family and professional roles than male scientists and engineers.

It's not surprising, therefore, that women in these fields experience widespread bias. It's not just that there are relatively few of them, both in academic positions and in leadership positions, in professional organizations. They also typically receive fewer resources and less institutional support than their male colleagues (National Academy of Sciences, 2007).

Segregation in the Workplace

U.S. women have made remarkable progress in overcoming traditional obstacles to employment. In 1950, a little more than 30% of adult women were employed in the paid labor force; today, that figure is almost 60%, and it increases to 69.3% for married mothers, 71.4% for single mothers, and 80% for widowed, separated, and divorced mothers (U.S. Bureau of the Census, 2009). Close to half of all U.S. workers today are female.

The increase in female labor force participation has been particularly dramatic in traditionally male-dominated fields such as medicine, law, and administration. For instance, in 1983, 15% of lawyers and 16% of physicians in the United States were women; by 2007, those figures had doubled (U.S. Bureau of Labor Statistics, 2008d; U.S. Bureau of the Census, 2004).

Although such a trend is encouraging, sex segregation in the workplace is still the rule. According to the U.S. Bureau of Labor Statistics (2008d), women constitute 96.7% of all secretaries, 91.7% of all registered nurses, 94.6% of all child care workers, 99.2% of all dental hygienists, and 97.3% of all preschool and kindergarten teachers. Despite their increased presence in traditionally male occupations, women are still underrepresented among dentists (28.2%), physicians (30%), engineers and architects (14.4%), lawyers (32.6%), police officers (13.7%), and firefighters (5.3%).

Most of the changes that have taken place in the sex distribution of different occupations have been the result of women entering male lines of work. Although women have entered traditionally male occupations at a steady clip since the 1980s, men have not noticeably increased their representation in female-dominated occupations. The number of male nurses, kindergarten teachers, and secretaries has increased only minimally, if at all (U.S. Bureau of Labor Statistics, 2008d). One study found that some men would rather suffer unemployment than accept "women's jobs," even high-paying ones, because of the potential damage to their sense of masculinity (Epstein, 1989).

This kind of "one-way" occupational shift may cause problems in the long run. Historically, when large numbers of women enter a particular occupation previously closed to them, the number of men in that occupation decreases. Given the fact that greater value is usually awarded to male pursuits, such occupations become less prestigious as men leave them. In fact, the higher the proportion of female workers in an occupation, the less both male and female workers earn in that occupation (Padavic & Reskin, 2002).

Greater female entry into traditionally male lines of work doesn't necessarily mean sexual equality either. Often, sex segregation occurs in jobs *within* a profession. In the field of medicine, for example, female physicians are substantially overrepresented in specialties such as family practice, pediatrics, and obstetrics and gynecology and underrepresented in more prestigious and lucrative areas such as surgery. Seventy-three percent of pediatric residents and 77% of obstetrics/gynecology residents today are women, but only 30% of surgical residents are women (Women Physicians Congress, 2008). Among lawyers, women are promoted at a lower rate than their male counterparts, and they remain underrepresented in private practice, in law firm partnerships, and in high positions such as judges on the federal courts, district courts, and circuit courts of appeals (Hull & Nelson, 2000).

And it's not just in traditionally male occupations that women are relegated to the least lucrative positions. Women who work as salesclerks in department stores are likely to be in the lower-paying departments (e.g., clothing and housewares), whereas men are likely to be in the more lucrative departments (e.g., furniture and large appliances). In 1997, Home Depot, the home improvement discount chain, paid $87.5 million to settle a lawsuit brought by female employees who claimed they were systematically relegated to cash register jobs rather than given higher-paying sales positions.

In sum, although more women than ever work in the paid labor force, we continue to have some jobs that employ almost exclusively women and others that employ almost exclusively men. When people are allocated jobs on the basis of sex rather than ability to perform the work, chances for self-fulfillment are limited (Reskin & Hartmann, 1986). Society also loses, because neither men nor women are free to do the jobs for which they might best be suited. However, segregation is most harmful to individual women, because the occupations they predominantly hold tend to be less prestigious and to pay lower wages than those held predominantly by men.

The Wage Gap

> The Lord spoke to Moses and said, "When a man makes a special vow to the Lord which requires your valuation of living persons, a male between twenty and sixty years old shall be valued at fifty silver shekels. If it is a female, she shall be valued at thirty shekels." (Leviticus 27:1–4)

You don't have to go back to biblical times to find evidence of the practice of setting women's pay at less than men's. Even though the 1963 Equal Pay Act guaranteed equal pay for equal work in the United States, and Title VII of the 1964 Civil Rights Act banned job discrimination on the basis of sex (as well as race, religion, and national origin), a gap in earnings persists. In 2007, the average earnings for all U.S. men working full-time, year round was $46,367. All women working full-time, year round earned an average salary of $35,745 per year (DeNavas-Walt, Proctor, & Smith, 2009). To put it another way, for every dollar a U.S. man earns, a woman earns only about 77 cents. The gap widens with age. Women between 15 and 24 working full-time, year round earn about 94% of what male counterparts earn. But by the time they reach the years leading up to retirement (between the ages of 45 and 64), they earn only 70% of what men earn. That means that over the span of her working career, the average working woman will earn between $700,000 and $2 million less than the average working man (National Committee on Pay Equity, 2008). And because they earn less when employed, women's retirement pensions are also significantly smaller than men's (National Women's Law Center, 2006).

Moreover, the wage gap is especially pronounced for women of color. In 2004, the annual earnings for African American women were $27,730 (or 67% of men's earnings). Latinas earned $23,444 (or 57% of men's earnings). Asian American women were more successful, earning an average of $35,975, 88% of men's pay (National Committee on Pay Equity, 2006).

Why is the wage gap so persistent? One reason, of course, is occupational segregation and the types of jobs women are most likely to have. One study of workers in major U.S. metropolitan areas found that women in female-dominated jobs earn the lowest wages (less than $6.95 per hour), while men in male-dominated jobs earn the highest wages ($11.60 per hour; Cohen & Huffman, 2003). For five of the "most female" jobs in the United States (i.e., those that are around 95% female)—namely, preschool teacher, teacher's assistant, secretary, child care worker, and dental assistant—the overall average weekly salary is $490. For five of the "most male" jobs (those around 95% male)—namely, airplane pilot, firefighter, aircraft engine mechanic, plumber, and steel worker—the overall average weekly salary is $948 (U.S. Department of Labor, 2008). However, even when in the same occupations, men's and women's earnings diverge.

Some economists and policymakers argue that the wage gap is essentially an institutional byproduct that exists because men on the whole have more work experience and training, work more hours per year, and are more likely to work a full-time schedule than women (Dey & Hill, 2007). Now, you will recall from Chapter 10 that due to the recent economic recession, large numbers of both men and women have been forced to work part-time because their employers have cut back (U.S. Bureau of Labor Statistics, 2008b). But women are particularly susceptible to this trend. In 2007, 10.5% of employed men worked part-time, compared with 24.7% of employed women (U.S. Bureau of Labor Statistics, 2008b). Not only do part-time workers earn less, but during hard times, they are usually the first ones pushed out of employment—not because they're women but because their jobs are the most expendable.

However, even when controlling for differences in experience, age, and education—factors that might justify discrepancies in salary—the wage gap between men and women remains (Weinberg, 2007). For instance, the average income of female workers in the United States is significantly lower than that of men with the same level of educational attainment. Men with bachelor's degrees earn, on average, more than 60% more than women with bachelor's degrees. In fact, women with a bachelor's degree can expect to earn only around $4,000 a year more than men with just a high school diploma (mean annual earnings of $43,302 compared with $38,932 for high school-educated men). Similarly, women with doctoral degrees (with mean annual earnings of $77,968) earn only about $8,000 more a year than men with bachelor's degrees (with mean annual earnings of $69,818; U.S. Bureau of the Census, 2009).

One possible remedy for the wage gap is to increase women's access to occupations that have traditionally been closed to them. As I noted earlier, this is already happening, to a certain degree, although sex segregation is still the rule.

Another solution is ***pay equity***. The principle behind this remedy is that the pay for particular jobs shouldn't be less simply because those jobs happen to be filled predominantly by women. Different jobs that are of equal value to society and require equal levels of training ought to have equal pay. In 2007, a bill was introduced in the U.S. Senate called "The Fair Pay Act." It sought to end wage discrimination against those who work in female-dominated jobs by establishing equal pay guidelines for equivalent work. For example, within an individual company, employers could not pay less for jobs that are held predominately by women than for jobs held predominately by men if those jobs were similarly important to the employer (National Committee on Pay Equity, 2007). However, the bill was defeated.

In 2009, President Obama signed into law a stripped-down version of the bill, which makes it easier for women to file equal-pay lawsuits.

THE GLOBAL DEVALUATION OF WOMEN

At first glance, women may seem to be making tremendous advances worldwide—becoming better educated and more economically independent than ever before. For instance, in 1990, 79 girls were enrolled in secondary schools for every 100 boys around the world; by 2006, that figure had risen to 95 (Population Reference Bureau, 2006b). And over the past several decades, women in most regions of the world have increased their representation in most sectors of the paid labor force.

Nevertheless, women remain economically and physically disadvantaged in most societies around the world. In sub-Saharan Africa, women make up close to 60% of all HIV-infected adults (UNAIDS, 2008). About 536,000 women around the world die each year in pregnancy and childbirth, but an astounding 99.5% of these deaths occur in poor, less developed countries (UNICEF, 2009). The chances of a woman in a developed country dying from maternal causes is 1 in 6,000; for a woman in a less developed country, it's 1 in 75 (Population Reference Bureau, 2008b). Women make up the vast majority of global factory workers in multinational corporations, often working under unsafe and unhealthy conditions at extremely low pay. And while women have made significant strides worldwide in access to education, they still lag far behind men in top political and decision-making roles (Hausmann, Tyson, & Zahidi, 2008).

In many countries, women do not have the same legal, familial, and physical protections that men enjoy:

- The Iranian constitution states that the value of a woman's life is half that of a man's. An Iranian woman cannot travel anywhere without her husband's permission (Watson, 2005).

- In Kenya, when a woman's husband dies, she loses her land, her livestock, and all her household property. In addition, a widow is transferred to a male relative of her deceased husband, who takes control of the property (Lacey, 2003).

- In Kyrgyzstan, it's estimated that more than half of all married women were abducted by their soon-to-be husbands in a centuries-old legal custom known as *ala kachuu* (which literally means "grab and run"). If the woman is kept in the man's home overnight, her virginity becomes suspect, her name disgraced, and her future marriage chances destroyed. So most women (about 80%, according to estimates) eventually relent and marry their abductor, often at the urging of their own families (Smith, 2005).

- In Syria, girls who bring dishonor to their families by having premarital sex are sometimes killed by relatives. Under Syrian law, these killings, called *ghasalat al arr* ("washing away the shame"), are not considered murder. If the killer is convicted of the lesser charge of "crime of honor" and sentenced to prison, he is typically released within months (Zoepf, 2007).

- In India, almost 76,000 women were tortured by their husbands or relatives in 2007, and more than 8,000—an average of 19 a day—were killed by their husbands for not providing adequate dowries (National Crime Records Bureau, 2007). Even though dowry (gifts that a woman receives from her parents on marriage) was officially banned in 1961, it is still an essential part of premarital negotiations and now encompasses the wealth that the bride's family pays the groom. Young brides, who by custom live with their new husbands' parents, are commonly subjected to severe abuse if the promised money is not paid. Sometimes dowry harassment ends in suicide or murder.

The public devaluation of women can sometimes hide a very different private reality. For instance, Japanese women have historically occupied a visibly subservient position in society and in families. Wives are still legally prohibited from using different surnames from their husbands'. Women in the workforce suffer discrimination in hiring, salary, and promotion despite the presence of equal-opportunity laws there. Only 40% of women currently work outside the home, even though many economists argue that their inclusion could help boost an economy that has been slumping for decades (French, 2003). They are expected to clean, cook, and tend to the needs of their husbands within the home.

Yet many Japanese wives dominate their husbands. Typically, they control the household finances, giving their husbands monthly allowances as they see fit. If a man wants to withdraw money from the family account, the savings bank will usually phone the wife to get her approval. Japanese men are even starting to take on some of the housework responsibilities, which would have been unthinkable a couple of decades ago.

Women are making significant strides in other parts of the world where they have traditionally suffered. In India, for instance, although rural, lower-caste women still occupy the bottom rungs of the social ladder, approximately one million of them have been elected in recent years to the 500,000 or so *panchayats,* or village councils, that were established in 1993 to help rural villages deal with local political issues (Dugger, 1999b). In most of the Arab world, women occupy a clearly subordinate position. But in Algeria, women now make up 60% of university students, 70% of lawyers, and 60% of judges. They also contribute more to household income than men (Slackman, 2007).

To some extent, the improvement of women's lives in some parts of the world can be attributed to global forces for change, which sometimes spread democratic values and humanitarian principles (Giddens, 2005). In 1979, the United Nations General Assembly adopted a treaty known as the Convention on the Elimination of All Forms of Discrimination Against Women (Division for the Advancement of Women, 2009). By accepting the treaty, countries agreed to take measures to end discrimination against women in all forms by

- incorporating the principle of equality of men and women into their legal systems, abolishing all discriminatory laws, and adopting appropriate ones prohibiting discrimination against women;
- establishing tribunals and other public institutions to ensure the effective protection of women against discrimination; and
- ensuring elimination of all acts of discrimination against women by persons, organizations, or enterprises.

All but 8 of the 192 member countries of the United Nations have ratified this agreement, which legally binds them to put its provisions into practice (Crary, 2009). The only holdouts are Sudan, Somalia, Qatar, Iran, Nauru, Palau, Tonga, . . . and the United States. Some U.S. women's rights groups are optimistic that with recent changes in the White House and in Congress, the agreement has a better chance of being ratified than ever before.

CONCLUSION

Inequality based on sex and gender goes beyond the degrading media and cultural images of women, the face-to-face interactions that reinforce the devaluation of women, and the stereotypical beliefs of individual people. It is woven into the institutional and cultural fabric of societies around the world. In the United States, it is as much a part of the social landscape as baseball, apple pie, and Fourth of July fireworks. Every woman has felt sexism at some level, whether as personal violence, annoying harassment, sexually suggestive leers and comments, fear of going out at night, job discrimination, legal obstacles, or subtle encouragement toward "appropriate" pursuits—whether they be sports, hobbies, or careers.

Men tend to benefit from living in a society where language, identity, intimacy, history, culture, and social institutions are built on gender distinctions, even if the men themselves do not support such inequality. Like most people whose interests are being served by the system, men are largely unaware of the small and large advantages the social structure provides them (Goode, 1981). Thus, most men don't see sex and gender inequality as their problem—it's a "women's issue"—and they are less likely than women to see a need for large-scale social change.

So the first step toward gender equality is that men will have to come to understand their role in the process, even in the absence of blatant, personal sexism. All men are tacitly involved in the oppression of women each time they automatically giggle at sexist jokes, mistake female doctors for nurses, see women in purely physical terms, expect less from women on the job or in school, or expect more of them at home.

The next step will require a fundamental transformation of institutional patterns and cultural values. Such a solution sounds too massive to be possible. But today, we are seeing early steps in that direction: changing conceptions of family roles, women's increasing (though not yet equal) participation in the labor force, their growing (but not yet equal) political power, and greater awareness of sexual exploitation and violence worldwide. How far these changes will take us in the future remains to be seen.

CHAPTER HIGHLIGHTS

◆ Personal sexism is most apparent during the course of everyday interaction in the form of communication patterns and gestures. It can be particularly dangerous when expressed in the form of sexual harassment and sexual violence.

◆ Gender stratification is perpetuated by a dominant cultural ideology that devalues women on the basis of alleged biological differences between men and women. This ideology overlooks the equally important role of social forces in determining male and female behavior.

◆ Institutional sexism exists in the media, in the law, in the family, in the educational system, and in the economy. Women have entered the paid labor force in unprecedented numbers, but they still tend to occupy jobs that are typically considered "female" and still earn significantly less than men.

◆ Not only are social institutions sexist in that women are systematically segregated, exploited, and excluded, they are also "gendered." Institutions themselves are structured along gender lines so that traits associated with success are usually stereotypically male characteristics: tough-mindedness, rationality, assertiveness, competitiveness, and so forth.

◆ Despite recent advances worldwide, women still tend to suffer physically, psychologically, economically, and politically in most societies.

KEY TERMS

institutional sexism Subordination of women that is part of the everyday workings of economics, law, politics, and other social institutions

matriarchy Female-dominated society, which gives higher prestige and value to women than to men

objectification Practice of treating people as objects

patriarchy Male-dominated society, in which cultural beliefs and values give higher prestige and value to men than to women

pay equity Principle that women and men who perform jobs that are of equal value to society and that require equal training ought to be paid equally

sexism System of beliefs that asserts the inferiority of one sex and justifies gender-based inequality

13 Demographic Dynamics

Population Trends

I admit it. I said those seven words I once vowed I'd never say. The ones that permanently tag you as an over-the-hill relic: "I just don't understand you kids today!"

It all started several years ago when I was arguing with my two sons—one 16 at the time, the other 13—over what to watch on television. They wanted to watch the X Games on ESPN; I wanted to watch a rerun of the sixth game of the 1975 World Series on ESPN Classic. I told them that my choice was a priceless piece of U.S. sports history, the best World Series game ever played. Besides, I didn't understand the allure of the X Games. I know it's an annual alternative sports festival based on obscure recreational sports such as skateboarding, in-line skating, Moto X, freestyle BMX, snowboarding, and so on. But I don't care to know the difference between an "airwalk grab" and a "backside disaster." To me, "grinding" is what you do with coffee beans in the morning, a "McTwist" is a pastry you'd buy after eating a Big Mac, and "getting clean air" means moving out of Los Angeles.

They told me that I was a dinosaur and that I had better wake up and smell the 21st century. The X Games, they claimed, was the future. And you know what, they turned out to be right. "Extreme" sports, as they have come to be called, are part of a broader youth subculture with its own hard-edged language, fashion, and music. In fact, the word *extreme* has become a modifying adjective for any activity that pushes beyond what's commonly accepted: extreme camping, extreme bartending, extreme paintball, extreme pumpkin carving, extreme science, extreme chess, and even extreme childbirth.

It would seem that the trend in society today is to eliminate risk for young people. For instance, some cities are installing "managed playgrounds"—public areas where adult "play workers" supervise children's play and guide all their activities (Carey, 2007). Other communities have removed swings and monkey bars from playgrounds to avoid liability in the event of an injury. Extreme sports are self-consciously designed to be the opposite: thrilling, dangerous, subversive, and rebellious. Their appeal lies not so much in grace, strategy, or face-to-face competition as in the chance of disaster striking. "The fact that they're called 'extreme' sports means, if you make a mistake, you die," said one admirer (quoted in Clemmitt, 2009, p. 301).

For the most part, extreme athletes bear little resemblance to athletes in more traditional sports. They tend to despise rules, regulations, and standard conceptions of the competitive spirit. Indeed, many extreme sports don't have objective measures of success—such as finishing first in a race—but are instead judged on their degree of risk and danger.

The allure has been powerful. One survey found that more teens and preteens prefer watching extreme sports on television than watching college basketball, college football, auto racing, hockey, tennis, or golf (Bennett, Henson, & Zhang, 2003). Indeed, the number of Americans who ride skateboards tripled between 1995 and 2005; during that same period, the number of baseball players dropped by 7%. There are now more skateboarders in this country than football players. Worldwide, there are more than 18.5 million snowboarders, ranging in age from 5 to 75 (Clemmitt, 2009). Tens of millions of people now regularly participate in other extreme sports such as wall climbing, mountain biking, and wakeboarding ("Extreme Facts," 2005).

Ironically, although extreme sports appear to be solidly antiestablishment, they have clearly become a marketing gold mine, generating tens of billions of dollars a year (Longman & Higgins, 2005). Corporate America has been scrambling to co-opt the language, image, and culture of extreme athletes in order to tap into a market that is booming. Extreme sports have also achieved a significant degree of societal acceptance. Events such as freestyle skiing, snowboarding, and BMX racing are now in the Olympics. Nevertheless, many older people still fail to understand the appeal of these sports.

What my sons didn't realize was that they had identified one of the most crucial dividing lines in society today. They and I may be members of the same family. We may share the same genes, ethnicity, social class, and political views. But we're also members of two extremely different, sometimes antagonistic, social groups that are distinguished by one simple and unchangeable fact: our ages.

In the past several chapters, I examined various interconnected sources of social stratification: class, race and ethnicity, and sex and gender. You have seen that the distance between the haves and the have-nots—both locally and globally—continues to grow wider as a result of their different levels of access to important cultural, economic, and political resources. But within the United States, as well as most other societies, imbalances between various age groups will also be a defining feature of social life in the decades to come. This chapter examines the relationship between broad population trends—which include not only changing age structure but also population growth and immigration—and everyday life. How are these changes affecting the ability to provide people with the resources they need for a comfortable life? How are important social institutions functioning as a result of these population shifts?

THE INFLUENCE OF BIRTH COHORTS

If you're like most college students, you've no doubt asked yourself questions like the following: What career will I pursue after I graduate? Where will I live? Will I be able to afford a house? Will I have a spouse or lifetime partner? Will I ever be a parent? How will I save for my retirement? The answers to these questions are obviously influenced by your personal desires, traits, values, ambitions, and abilities. And as you've already read in this book so far, your social class, gender, race, religion, ethnicity, not to mention the state of the economy, will shape the answers, too.

But they will also be influenced by your place in the population at a given point in time. ***Birth cohorts*** are sets of people who were born during the same time period and who face similar societal circumstances brought about by their position in the age structure of the population. Birth cohorts affect people's everyday lives in two fundamental ways (Riley, 1971):

- People born within a few years of one another tend to experience life course events or social rites of passage—such as puberty, marriage, childbearing, graduation, entrance into the workforce, and death—at roughly the same time. Sociologists call these experiences ***cohort effects***. The size of your birth cohort, relative to other cohorts, can have a significant impact on your life experiences: It can determine things such as the availability of affordable housing, high-paying jobs, and attractive potential mates and can also affect how satisfied you feel with your own life. One study found that large cohorts in developed countries tend to have higher rates of suicide than small cohorts because people face more economic disadvantage and have more difficulty integrating into their communities when there are large numbers of people in the same age range competing for limited resources (Stockard & O'Brien, 2002).

- Members of the same birth cohort also share a common history. A cohort's place in time tells us a lot about the opportunities and constraints placed on its members. Unexpected historical events (wars, epidemics, natural disasters, economic depressions, etc.), changing political conditions, and major cultural trends, called ***period effects***, contribute to the unique shape and outlook of each birth cohort. Many historians, for instance, believe that a period of drought and famine caused the people of the Mayan civilization to abandon their great cities nearly a thousand years ago. Those who were young when this period began enjoyed comfortable lives, reveled in the high culture of the Mayans, and had tremendous prospects for the future. But for their children, born just a generation later, starvation, death, and social dislocation were the basic facts of life (Clausen, 1986).

Cohort and period effects combine to give each birth cohort its distinctive properties, such as ethnic composition, average life expectancies, and age-specific birthrates. For instance, the birth cohort that experienced the Great Depression during its peak childbearing years had the lowest birthrate of any cohort in the 20th century. Therefore, people born between 1900 and 1910 tended as a group to have smaller families to rely on in their old age, which for them occurred roughly between 1970 and 1990. These experiences contrast sharply with those of people born a mere 10 years later, who were too young to have children during the Great Depression but entered adulthood during the prosperous years after World War II. They tended to have large families and therefore more sources of support in their old age (Soldo & Agree, 1988).

Cohort and period effects also influence your worldview and self-concept. Think how different your goals and ambitions would be had you experienced childhood during a time of economic uncertainty as opposed to a period of relative affluence, such as the late 1990s and early 2000s. Rights and privileges considered unattainable dreams by one cohort are likely to be taken for granted by a different one.

As we grow older, we develop and change in a society that itself is developing and changing. We start our lives in one historical period with a distinct set of social norms, and we end our lives in another. Early in the 20th century, for example, most people went to school for only 6 or 7 years, which yielded an adequate education for the types of jobs their parents and older siblings held. Today, close to 86% of U.S. residents go to school for at least 12 years (U.S. Bureau of the Census, 2009). As a result, older cohorts on the whole tend to score substantially lower on standardized intelligence tests than do younger cohorts. Because of such test results, social scientists long assumed that intelligence declines markedly with age. But we now know that these differences are the result not of aging but of changing societal values regarding education (Clausen, 1986).

As you can see, birth cohorts are more than just a collection of individuals born around the same time; they are distinctive generations tied together by historical circumstances, population trends, and societal changes. However, we must also realize that when many individuals in the same cohort are affected by social events in similar ways, the changes in their collective lives can produce changes in society. Each succeeding cohort leaves its mark on the prevailing culture. In other words, cohorts are not only affected by social changes but contribute to them as well (Riley, Foner, & Waring, 1988).

Baby Boomers

The birth cohort that has received the most national attention is, without a doubt, the Baby Boom generation, those 76 million or so people born between 1946 and 1964. They make up more than 25% of the entire U.S. population (U.S. Bureau of the Census, 2009).

The passing of this massive cohort through the life course has been described metaphorically as "a pig in a python." If you've ever seen one of those nature shows on TV where snakes devour and digest small animals, you know how apt the metaphor is. In 1980, the largest age group in the United States consisted of people between 15 and 24 years of age. In 1990, the largest group was 25- to 34-year-olds. In 2007, it was people between 40 and 49 (U.S. Bureau of the Census, 2009). As this cohort bulge works its way through the life course, it stretches the parameters of the relevant social institutions at each stage. Baby Boomers packed hospital nurseries as infants, school classrooms as children, and college campuses, employment lines, and the housing market as young adults (Light, 1988). In middle age, they are prime movers in the burgeoning markets for adventure travel, diet, nutrition, and wellness products, as well as relaxed-fit fashion, high-tech gadgets, and financial services.

The trend will continue into the future. By the year 2030, there will be more than 72 million Baby Boomers of retirement age, about twice the number of retirees today (U.S. Bureau of the Census, 2009). As they reach their golden years, those programs concerned with later life—pension plans, Social Security, medical and personal care—will be seriously stretched. And sometime in the middle of the 21st century, there will likely be a surge in business for the funeral industry as this generation reaches the end of its collective life cycle (Schodolski, 1993).

Baby Boomers have left a particularly influential mark on the institution of family. Their generation was the first to redefine families to include a variety of living arrangements, such as cohabitation, domestic partnerships, and never-married women with dependent children (Wattenberg, 1986). They were also the first to acknowledge the expectation of paid work as a central feature of women's lives. And they were the first to grow up with effective birth control, enabling delayed childbearing, voluntary childlessness, and low birthrates.

Consequently, as the Baby Boomers reach old age, they will have fewer children to turn to for the kind of help they gave their own grandparents and parents (Butler, 1989). Thus, Baby Boom elders will be more likely than previous generations to turn to social service and health care organizations to care for them.

Generation X

Although Baby Boomers have dominated the cultural spotlight for decades, U.S. society has also taken notice of the next generation to follow them, known in the media as "Generation X." Today, there are almost 62 million U.S. residents who were born between 1965 and 1979 (U.S. Bureau of the Census, 2009). The birthrate during the 1970s, when most of these individuals were born, was about half what it was during the post-World War II years of the Baby Boom.

More Generation Xers—roughly 40% of them—experienced the divorce of their parents than any previous generation. As a result, they are emotionally conflicted about marriage. They are less likely to get married than older generations and more likely to delay marriage and childbearing if they do (Carlson, 2009). In addition, they're more likely to be single—with or without children—than previous generations (Sayer, Casper, & Cohen, 2004).

Even more Generation Xers grew up as so-called latchkey children, the first generation of children to experience the effects of having two working parents. For many of these children, childhood was marked by dependence on secondary relationships—teachers, friends, babysitters, and day care workers.

The Millennium Generation

The 80 million or so individuals born between 1980 and the late 1990s make up the next noticeable cohort, known as the Millennium Generation, Generation Y, or the New Boomers. This generation is comparable to the Baby Boom in size but differs in almost every other way. For one thing, unlike the Baby Boomers, this cohort is not evenly distributed across the nation. Those states that have large minority and immigrant populations (e.g., California, Florida, and Texas) account for a relatively high proportion of the Millennium Generation (Faust, Gann, & McKibben, 1999). Consequently, its members are more ethnically diverse than previous cohorts; one in three is not white (Mather, 2007). They are also more likely than preceding cohorts to grow up in a nontraditional family. One in four lives in a single-parent household; three in four have working mothers.

The Millennium Generation is the most media connected of any generation. According to a Kaiser Family Foundation report (Rideout, Roberts, & Foehr, 2005), children between the ages of 8 and 18 spend more than 8 hours a day with some kind of communication or entertainment medium: watching TV, listening to CDs or MP3 players, playing video games, sending e-mail, and talking or texting on cell phones. Sixty-eight percent have a television in their bedrooms, and two thirds have portable CD or MP3 players.

Although this preoccupation with computers and other forms of technology may create a generation less interpersonally adept than generations of the past, the exposure to other cultures that the Internet provides will make these individuals significantly more worldly than any generation in history. And as the Millennium Generation enters and exits college, it will come to the workforce with unprecedented technological savvy, forcing companies to think more creatively about how to meet its needs (Trunk, 2007). Indeed, some have argued that this cohort's seemingly constant participation in social network sites, online games, and video-sharing sites and its constant use of gadgets such as iPods actually give its members the technological skills they'll need to succeed in the contemporary world. They have also become adept at maintaining and navigating intimate connections in an "always on," full-time technological community via texting, instant messaging, mobile phones, and the Internet (Ito et al., 2008).

Members of the Millennium Generation may be more socially conservative than prior generations. For instance, a nationwide study found that close to 70% of young people today support so-called zero tolerance policies against drugs in high school (cited in Howe & Strauss, 2000). The proportion of high school students who had sexual intercourse within the preceding 3 months decreased from 37.5% in 1991 to 35% in 2007 (Centers for Disease Control and Prevention, 2008b). Indeed, rates of pregnancy, abortion, and births for girls between 15 and 19 have all declined since 1990 (U.S. Bureau of the Census, 2009). At the same time though, members of the Millennium Generation seem even less eager to get married in their early 20s than either the Generation Xers or the Baby Boomers.

As this cohort ages and begins to control important social institutions, these attitudes and behaviors will shape reality for other cohorts in U.S. society.

DEMOGRAPHIC DYNAMICS

Many aspects of our personal lives are influenced by our birth cohort, but our lives are also affected by society-wide and worldwide population trends. Sociologists who study fluctuations in population characteristics are called ***demographers***. Demographers examine several important and interrelated population processes to explain current social problems or to predict future ones: birth or fertility rates, death or mortality rates, and patterns of migration. These three processes influence a population's growth, overall age structure, and geographic distribution.

Population Growth

The most fundamental population characteristic is, of course, size. Changes in population size are mostly a function of birth and death rates. As long as people are dying and being born at similar rates, the size of the population remains stable (barring large changes caused by migration). But when birthrates increase and death rates decrease, the population grows.

It took hundreds of thousands of years, from the beginning of humanity to the early 19th century, for Earth's human population to reach 1 billion. However, it took only an additional 100 years for it to reach 2 billion. Then, 3 billion was reached 30 years later; 4 billion, 16 years later; and 5 billion, a little more than 10 years after that. Today's population is more than 6.8 billion and will likely exceed 9.5 billion by 2050 (United Nations, 2004; U.S. Bureau of the Census, 2009).

Undeniably, the global population is growing at an unprecedented rate. However, people disagree about the consequences of such growth. In the past, large numbers of people were seen as a precious resource. The Bible urged humanity to be fruitful and multiply. One 18th-century British scholar, referring to the strategic importance of a large population, called a high birthrate "the never-failing nursery of Fleets and Armies" (quoted in Mann, 1993, p. 49).

Although few people today sing the praises of massive population growth, some argue that it isn't particularly troublesome. A larger population creates greater division of labor and a larger market to support highly specialized services. More people are available to contribute to the production of needed goods and services.

Others, however, aren't so optimistic. When a particular population is excessively large, individuals are forced to compete for limited food, living space, and jobs. According to some contemporary demographers, population growth can compound, magnify, or even create a wide variety of social problems, such as pollution, environmental degradation, housing shortages, high inflation, energy shortages, illiteracy, and the loss of individual freedom (Weeks, 1995).

Global Imbalances in Population Growth

On a global scale, population growth could widen the gap between rich and poor nations, perpetuate social and economic inequality within nations, give rise to racial and ethnic separatism, and increase the already high levels of world hunger and unemployment (Ehrlich & Ehrlich, 1993). Environmental threats are growing, too. Humanity's use of once plentiful natural resources—fossil fuel, rich soil, and certain plant and animal species—is now 30% higher than Earth's biologically productive capacity. If we continue at this pace, by the mid-2030s we will need two planets to maintain our lifestyles (World Wildlife Fund, 2008).

The problem, however, is not just that the overall population is growing rapidly but also that different countries are experiencing vastly different rates of growth. Populations in poor, developing countries tend to expand rapidly, whereas those in wealthy, developed countries have either stabilized or are declining. The annual growth rate of the world's population is approximately 1.2% (Population Reference Bureau, 2008b). But that figure masks the dramatic regional differences that will exist for several decades to come. Consider these facts:

- In Africa, the rate of natural population increase (i.e., without taking migration into consideration) is about 2.4% each year; Europe, in contrast, sees a *decline* of about 0.1% in population each year. If current trends continue, by the middle of the 21st century, the population of Germany will be 13% smaller, and Bulgaria's population will be 35% smaller than it is today. In contrast, Liberia's population will be 216% bigger, Niger's 261% bigger, and Uganda's 263% bigger (Population Reference Bureau, 2008b).

- In 1950, half of the 10 most populous nations were in the industrialized world. By 2050, demographers predict that the United States will be the only developed country among the world's 10 most populous nations. The rest will be developing countries in Asia, Africa, and South America (Crossette, 2001; Population Reference Bureau, 2008b).

- In 1950, more than 28% of the world's population lived in North America and Europe. Today, it's 16%, and by 2050, about 12% will live in these regions. The rest of the world's population will reside in the developing countries of Africa, Asia, and Latin America (Population Reference Bureau, 2008b; United Nations Population Division, 2005).

These imbalances will influence how people view one another, affect global and domestic policies, and determine the availability of food, energy, and adequate living space (Kennedy, 1993). When the most highly industrialized and economically productive countries begin to experience shrinking populations, their role as major global producers and consumers of goods is thrown into doubt. The result can be economic and political turmoil as other countries jockey for global advantage.

Why would populations in poor, developing countries grow at such a high rate when so many people are already struggling to survive? When societies begin to industrialize, living conditions improve. New technology often means better food supplies and increased knowledge about disease. Societies learn how to keep their water supplies clean and how to dispose of garbage and sewage. So death rates begin to fall.

But for a considerable time after the death rate begins to fall, the birthrate remains high, resulting in a dramatic increase in the size of the population. In sub-Saharan Africa, for instance, women will bear an average of 5.4 children in their lifetimes. By comparison, U.S. women have, on average, 2.1 children. In Canada, the rate is 1.6, and in the countries of Eastern Europe, it's a miniscule 1.4 (Population Reference Bureau, 2008b).

One of the reasons why birthrates are so high in less developed countries is the lack of access to effective contraception. Only 43% of women in these regions use some form of modern contraception, compared with 58% in the more developed world (Population Reference Bureau, 2008b). In sub-Saharan Africa, the figure is 16%. In contrast, close to 68% of U.S. women and 75% of Northern European women use modern contraception. In addition, established laws, customs, and religious norms often continue to exert strong influences on people's reproductive behavior. In developing nations, children are likely to be perceived as productive assets and "social security" for old age (Mann, 1993).

Politics, Culture, and Population Growth

You may have the impression that population growth is a "natural" process working relentlessly and inevitably on unsuspecting populations. Yet human intervention—government intervention, more specifically—has at times purposefully altered the size or even the configuration of a population for political or economic reasons.

Take China, for example. Because of its massive population of more than 1.3 billion and its limited resources, China's leadership has been struggling for decades to limit family size. One of every five humans alive today is Chinese, but China has only 7% of Earth's farmland, much of it of poor quality. In response, the government enacted a strict birth policy in the early 1970s. Couples had to wait until their mid-20s to marry. Provinces and cities were assigned yearly birth quotas. Neighborhood committees determined which married couples could have a baby and when (Ignatius, 1988). Pregnant women who lacked approval to give birth were often subjected to forced abortions (Kahn, 2007). In the 1990s, more than 80% of all Chinese couples of childbearing age were sterilized (Crossette, 1997). Couples who had only one child were rewarded with salary bonuses, better educational opportunities, and housing priorities. Couples who had more than one child faced fines of more than a year's salary, lost access to apartments and schools, or dismissal from their jobs (Ignatius, 1988).

The effectiveness of China's birth policy has amazed population experts. The average number of births per woman has decreased from more than 7 in the 1960s to 1.6 today (Population Reference Bureau, 2008b). In contrast, the average number of births per woman in India, a country with similar population problems, is 2.8. Without the policy, there would be 300 million more Chinese citizens than there are now (Kahn, 2004).

But the success of China's birth policy has created some serious social problems. So few babies are being born now—and so many more elderly people are living longer—that the overall age of the population is growing steadily. Chinese officials fear that the country will likely encounter what is sometimes called the "four-two-one problem"—a generation of only children who will have to find the resources to care for four elderly grandparents and two aging parents ("One Child Left Behind," 2009). Today, there are six Chinese working adults for every one retired person; by 2040, there will be just two (French, 2007). It's estimated that by that same year, China will have an older population than the United States but with only about one fourth the average per capita income (Kahn, 2004). Retirement funds and pension plans are scarce, and the social networks that once supported aging Chinese are no longer there. The problem has become so bad that the city of Shanghai has started a public awareness leaflet campaign urging couples to have a second child ("Shanghai Urges," 2009).

Like China, officials in many other countries are now starting to worry that their populations aren't growing enough. In contemporary Russia, for instance, many couples postpone childbearing or decide not to have children altogether because of severe economic instability and uncertainty about the future. Russia now has one of the world's lowest birthrates. At the same time, because of skyrocketing rates of poverty, stress, and alcoholism, Russians are dying much earlier than the rest of the world. As a result, over the past decade and a half, the Russian population has shrunk by about 700,000 people a year ("Vladimir Putin," 2006). Population experts project that it will decrease by an additional 22% between now and 2050 (Population Reference Bureau, 2008b). Fearing that such a dramatic population decline will lead to economic catastrophe, Russian politicians are promoting a variety of policies to reverse the trend, such as a nationwide ban on abortions, financial incentives for couples to have children, increases in funds for prenatal care and maternity leave, and a tax on childlessness ("Fearing Demographic Abyss," 2006; Karush, 2001).

A few years ago, the French government approved a package of parenting incentives that included generous allowances, tax incentives, housing payments, and "large-family" discounts on public transportation, household goods, and leisure activities for families with three or more children (Schofield, 2005). In Germany—where about 30% of all women are childless—the government now pays new mothers two thirds of their salary for up to a year to stay home with a child (Glazer, 2008). When Australia introduced a "baby bonus" in 2006, whereby families would receive about US$3,000 per child, the country's treasurer encouraged parents to "have one for Mum, one for Dad, and one for the country" (quoted in Balter, 2006, p. 1894).

Cultural tradition also continues to play a powerful role in people's decisions about having children. Some patriarchal cultures express a deep preference for male children because only they can perpetuate the family line. As one Chinese mother put it, "If you have only girls, you don't feel right inside. You feel your status is lower than everyone else" (quoted in Jacobs, 2009, p. 8).

Parents in such cultures may take extreme measures to have sons rather than daughters. In rural China—where the one-child policy, coupled with a tradition of favoring boys over girls, has led many parents to fear they will be left to take care of themselves in old age—the abduction and sale of baby boys has become a thriving business (Jacobs, 2009). Elsewhere, female babies are aborted, killed at birth, abandoned, neglected, or given up for foreign adoption (Kristof, 1993).

Though it is illegal in some countries, couples often seek to determine the sex of their fetus through sonograms, and if it's a girl, they have an abortion. In South Korea, for instance, 1 out of 12 female fetuses—or 30,000 girls a year—is aborted, even though disclosure of the sex of a fetus and abortion are against the law (WuDunn, 1997). In India, as many as 10 million female fetuses have been aborted over the past 20 years as families tried to secure male heirs (Gentleman, 2006).

Such practices have led to a conspicuous shortage of females in many developing countries. Under normal circumstances in every society, there are between 103 and 107 boys born for every 100 girls; but higher male infant mortality works to even the distribution of boys to girls. In India, however, there are 109 males for every 100 females (Gentleman, 2006). In some areas of China, the ratio is 120 males for every 100 females. There are 32 million more Chinese males under 20 than females; in 2005 alone, there were 1.1 million more boys born than girls (Zhu, Lu, & Hesketh, 2009). Demographers have identified similar shortages of females in South Korea, Pakistan, Bangladesh, Nepal, and Papua New Guinea.

Age Structure

In addition to population growth, demographers also study the ***age structure*** of societies, the balance of old and young people. Age structure, like the size of a population, is determined principally by birthrates and life expectancy.

The proportion of the world's population over the age of 60 has been growing steadily for decades. Currently, 7% of the world's population is over 65 (Population Reference Bureau, 2008b). By 2045, that figure is projected to be 15.2% (Sanderson & Scherbov, 2008). During the same period, the proportion of the "oldest old" (those over 80) will increase more than fivefold (United Nations Population Division, 2003).

But as with population growth in general, the global growth of the elderly population is not spread evenly across countries. In developing countries where recent population growth is exceedingly rapid and where life expectancy remains low—as in most countries of Southeast Asia, Latin America, the Indian subcontinent, the Middle East, and especially Africa—the age structure tends to be dominated by young people. Forty-three percent of the population in sub-Saharan Africa is under the age of 15 (Population Reference Bureau, 2008b). The average age of the male population in the four youngest countries in the world (Chad, the Republic of Congo, Uganda, and the Gaza Strip) is between 15 and 16 (Geographic.org, 2005).

In contrast, those developed countries that are experiencing low birthrates coupled with increasing life expectancy have a very different age structure. More old people are living, and fewer people are being born. The average age of the population in the world's four oldest countries (Italy, Japan, Germany, and Finland) is over 40. Demographers project that by 2050 the median age in Europe will be an unprecedented 52.3 years (cited in Bernstein, 2003). Only 16% of Europe's population is under 15 (Population Reference Bureau, 2008b).

The global implications of these different age structures cannot be understated. In some European countries, a decreasing number of young people are paying into a pension system that must support a growing number of older people (Bernstein, 2003). Governments have reacted to the financial pressures caused by the aging of their populations by reducing social services, including the pensions that millions of retirees have been counting on.

In contrast, when young people outnumber the elderly in a particular country, they are likely to overwhelm labor markets and educational systems (Davis, 1976). The result is a steady decline in living standards, which usually means growing political unrest. That unrest can have an impact not only on the country's residents but also on the people who live in countries that depend on the troubled country for certain resources, goods, or services.

The obvious consequence of today's trends is that developing nations will have the burden of trying to accommodate populations dominated by young people, whereas developed nations will have the burden of trying to support millions of people over the age of 65.

Geographic Distribution

In response to these kinds of problems, many people will be motivated to escape through ***migration***, or moving to another place where prospects for a comfortable life are brighter. Through the centuries, migration has played a crucial role in history as people have contended for territory and the resources that go with it ("Workers of the World," 1998). Today, global media expose people more quickly and more consistently than ever to appealing lifestyles elsewhere. Large-scale migration includes both within-country movement and cross-border movement.

Migration Within a Country

Migration trends within a country can have a considerable effect on social life. In the United States, such internal migration usually consists of people moving from cold to warmer climates or from large cities to outer suburbs (Lalasz, 2006). But in less developed countries these days, in-country migration is more likely to reflect ***urbanization***, the process by which people leave rural areas and begin to concentrate in large cities. For instance, in 1950, less than 30% of the world's population lived in cities. In 2008, that figure topped 50% (Population Reference Bureau, 2008b), and it's estimated that by 2050, almost 70% of the world's population will be urban dwellers (United Nations Population Division, 2008). In Asia and Africa today, four times as many people live in cities as did in 1950 (Population Reference Bureau, 2008b). It's estimated that in India alone, 700 million people will move from villages to cities by 2050 (cited in Giridharadas, 2007).

This transformation has changed assumptions about what urban living means worldwide. In the past, cities were meccas of commerce and culture and tended to have higher standards of living and better health conditions than rural areas. But when cities grow rapidly, as many are in the developing world, their economies and infrastructures can't keep up. In sub-Saharan Africa, only about 55% of city dwellers have access to adequate or improved sanitation facilities (Population Reference Bureau, 2006a). Contemporary urban life is also associated with environmental and social devastation. In developing countries, 90% of raw sewage from urban areas pours into streams and oceans. Of India's 3,000 cities, only 8 had full water treatment plants in the mid-1990s (Crossette, 1996). Moreover, cities have much higher rates of poverty, crime, violence, and sexually transmitted diseases than do rural areas.

Migration From One Country to Another

Population movement from one country to another is equally significant. It's estimated that about 200 million people worldwide live outside their countries of birth (cited in DeParle, 2007). Most have left their homelands in search of a better life somewhere else.

International migration is motivated by disparities in opportunities. Poverty, political instability, war, famine, environmental deterioration, high unemployment, and the lure of high wages in richer countries continue to drive the world's poorest people to give up their life savings and risk death to find a better life in more prosperous nations. According to the United Nations, each year, hundreds of thousands of illegal immigrants from poor countries in Africa, Central Asia, and the Middle East try to enter the wealthy nations of Western Europe (cited in Cowell, 2002).

You might think that when people migrate from underdeveloped, overcrowded countries to more developed, technologically advanced countries, everyone would benefit. After all, migration lowers population pressures and unemployment at home while offsetting the problems of negative population growth and an aging workforce in developed destination countries. Indeed, the only way Japan and Western Europe will be able to sustain a stable population in the future is through immigration.

From a sociological point of view, however, international migration often creates conflict. The immigrants, themselves, often experience tension between the values of their new home and the values of their country of origin. Take, for instance, cultural mores regarding virginity and premarital sex. As the Middle Eastern immigrant population in Europe grows, young Muslim women are caught between the relative sexual freedoms of European society and the deep, and often very restrictive, traditions of their parents and grandparents. Although there are no reliable statistics, French cosmetic surgeons report increasing numbers of young Muslim women seeking a surgical procedure called hymenoplasty—the restoration of the hymen, the vaginal membrane that breaks during the first act of intercourse—to give the appearance of virginity (Sciolino & Mekhennet, 2008).

People seeking opportunities can no longer move to uncharted areas but rather must push into territories where other people already live. Instead of seeing immigrants for their contribution to the overall economy, the people already in residence see immigrants as an immediate and personal threat. The immigrants require jobs, housing, education, and medical attention, all of which are in limited supply. They also bring with them foreign habits, traditions, and norms.

Immigration creates a variety of cultural fears: fear that a nation can't control its own borders, fear that an ethnically homogeneous population will be altered through intermarriage, fear of the influx of a "strange" way of life, and fear that newcomers will encroach on property, clog the educational system, and suck up social benefits owned and largely paid for by "natives" (Kennedy, 1993). Many people also express concern that immigrants are responsible for outbreaks of diseases such as AIDS, tuberculosis, measles, and cholera, which strain health care systems and thus create even more resentment. Above all, they fear that immigrants and their offspring may one day become a statistical majority, rendering the "natives" powerless in their own country.

Even though laws in most countries ban discrimination against immigrants, antiforeigner resentment and prejudice are global phenomena. In Great Britain, the antipathy is often directed against immigrants from India and Pakistan; in France, against Algerians and Moroccans; in Germany, Turks; in Sweden, Iraqis and Kurds; in Australia, South and East Asians; in the United States, Latin Americans and Asians; and in Japan, almost anyone not Japanese. Antiforeigner sentiment tends to be more pronounced in places with a large proportion of foreign populations, where economies are less prosperous, and where there is greater support for extreme right-wing political parties (Semyonov & Raijman, 2006).

It's important to note, though, that such hostility is not inevitable. Peaceable contact with immigrants at work, at school, or in the community can reduce feelings of threat and the willingness to expel legal immigrants from the country (McLaren, 2003). In any case, the trend toward greater immigration is unlikely to slow down as long as communication and transportation technologies continue to shrink the globe and economic disparities between countries continue to exist.

POPULATION TRENDS IN THE UNITED STATES

In the United States, two important demographic trends will exert a profound effect on the population in the years to come: the growing proportion of nonwhite, non-English-speaking immigrants and their children and the shifting age structure of the population, marked by a growing proportion of elderly and a shrinking proportion of young people. These two trends together will strain the social fabric, raising questions about the fair distribution of social resources.

Immigration and the Changing Face of the United States

Because the U.S. population is currently growing at a manageable rate, residents may have trouble understanding the impact of population explosions in other countries on their everyday lives here. But as populations burst the seams of national boundaries elsewhere, many of those seeking better opportunities end up in the United States. Newly arrived immigrants believe that chances to get ahead, protection of women's rights, treatment of the poor, and availability of schools are all better here than in their countries of origin (Rieff, 2005). Some arrive legally by plane, boat, or train. Others arrive illegally by foot or are smuggled in the backs of trucks or the holds of cargo ships.

In the mid-1980s, the U.S. Bureau of the Census predicted that by the year 2050, the United States would have a population of 300 million (Pear, 1992). But that number has already been surpassed. Subsequently, the Census Bureau has revised its estimate to 439 million by 2050 (U.S. Bureau of the Census, 2009).

Part of the reason this projection had to be adjusted upward was that immigration increased more than had been anticipated. The share of the

U.S. population that is foreign-born rose from 5% in 1967 to 12.5% in 2006 (U.S. Bureau of the Census, 2009). Although the numbers fluctuate from year to year, between 2000 and 2007, 10.3 million immigrants have arrived—the highest 7-year period of immigration in U.S. history. It's estimated that more than half of the post-2000 arrivals (5.6 million) are here illegally (Passel, Capps, & Fix, 2004).

This isn't the first time the U.S. population has been radically increased by a surge of immigration. In the first decade of the 20th century, nearly 9 million immigrants entered the country. By 1915, foreign-born residents constituted 15% of the population (U.S. Bureau of the Census, 2006b). What makes contemporary immigration different, though, is that fewer of today's newcomers are of European descent.

Not surprisingly, then, the racial and ethnic composition of the United States has changed dramatically over the past century. In 1900, one out of every eight U.S. residents was nonwhite; by 2000, that ratio was one in four (Hobbs & Stoops, 2002). During that time span, the fastest-growing surnames in the United States were Garcia, Rodriguez, Martinez, Hernandez, Lopez, and Gonzalez (Roberts, 2007b). Latino/as currently constitute a little more than 14% of the population, but they accounted for almost half of the population increase between 2000 and 2004 (Haub, 2006). Experts estimate that by the year 2050, one out of four U.S. residents will be Latino/a, and by 2100, one out of three will be Latino/a (Saenz, 2004).

Until quite recently, the non-European immigrant population was not spread evenly across the country. Immigrants tended to settle in large urban areas that serve as ports of entry, such as New York, Los Angeles, Houston, and Miami. In the mid-1980s, for example, two thirds of Mexican immigrants lived in California, and 20% more lived in Texas and Illinois (Thompson, 2009). Of the 20 metropolitan areas with the largest proportion of Asian immigrants, 8 are in California and 6 are cities in the eastern corridor that runs from Boston to Washington, D.C. (Zhao, 2002).

However, Latino/a and Asian immigrants are now settling in towns and cities all across the United States. Since 2000, economic development in the Southeast and Midwest has drawn more and more non-English-speaking immigrants. Consequently, the need for people to teach English as a second language has grown most rapidly in school districts in these regions. Between 1993 and 2002, the number of students in Idaho, Nebraska, Tennessee, and Georgia who speak little if any English tripled. In North Carolina, the number of such students increased sixfold (Zhao, 2002). Students who do not know English represent the fastest-growing group of students in the nation (Thompson, 2009). Questions of how best to integrate immigrants and their children are now being debated in every corner of the country.

The immigrant experience in the United States has changed in other ways, too. Advances in technology and cheaper travel fares mean that many immigrants today can base themselves in the United States—getting a job, finding a place to live, and so on—but maintain vital ties with their homelands. Those with the economic means travel back and forth frequently between their country of origin and the United States.

U.S. residents have always had a love-hate relationship with immigrants. In good times, immigrants have been welcome contributors to the economy. Early in the 20th century, their labor helped build roads and the U.S. rail system. Immigrants have filled unwanted jobs, opened businesses, and improved the lives of many U.S. residents by working cheaply as housekeepers, dishwashers, and gardeners.

When times are bad, however, or when the political winds shift, many U.S. residents are inclined to shut the door and blame immigrants for many of the country's economic and social woes. During these periods, people often describe the influx of immigrants as a "flood," subtly equating their arrival with disaster. As in Europe, immigrants to the United States often find they are the targets of a variety of social anxieties, from economic tension to outright hostility (Sontag, 1992).

The "Graying" of the United States

At the same time that the United States grapples with the changing ethnic and racial configuration of its population, it also must address its shifting age structure. Perhaps the most important and most problematic demographic trend in the United States today involves the increasing average age of the population. Two hundred years ago, the median age for U.S. residents was 16; in 1980, it was 30; today, it is 36.2. And it's expected to be close to 40 by the middle of this century, as the massive Baby Boom cohort reaches old age (U.S. Bureau of the Census, 2009).

Two developments in the past few decades have conspired to alter the U.S. age structure. The first has been a decrease in the number of children being born. In 1960, there were approximately 24 births per 1,000 people in the population. By 2006, the rate had dropped to 14.2 per 1,000 (U.S. Bureau of the Census, 2009). More U.S. women than ever are choosing not to have children at all (Dye, 2008). Like many countries in the developed world, the U.S. fertility rate is barely at the level necessary to replace the current population in the next generation. Most of the conditions that have helped lower fertility—improved work conditions for women and more effective contraception, for example—are not likely to reverse in the future.

The other development has been a rapid increase in the number of people surviving to old age. Technological advances in medicine and nutrition have extended the lives of countless U.S. residents, whose historical counterparts would have routinely died several decades ago. Life expectancy has risen from 67.1 for males and 74.7 for females born in 1970 to 75.2 for males and 80.4 for females born in 2005 (U.S. Bureau of the Census, 2009). By 2050, the United States will have more old people than children. The number of people over 85, an age group for which health care costs are exceptionally high, will grow fastest of all, increasing from 5.1 million today to more than 8 million by 2025 and soaring to more than 19 million by 2050 (U.S. Bureau of the Census, 2009). Some demographers project that by 2050 there will be 10 times the number of centenarians (people living to 100) than we have today (cited in Dominus, 2004).

Why should we be concerned about the "graying" of the U.S. population? The answer is that a society with an aging population will inevitably experience increased demands for pensions, health care, and other social services for the elderly. Although older people in the United States tend to be healthier than their counterparts in the past, a significant proportion suffers from health problems and chronic disease and will eventually need some kind of long-term care (National Institute on Aging, 2006). The ability and willingness of society, and in particular the working population, to bear the additional burden of caring for the growing number of elderly people is an open question.

Political debate rages today over how—or even whether—the Social Security system should be transformed to accommodate the growing number of people who will turn 65 in the coming years. One survey found that 18% of Americans feel that the Social Security system is in crisis, 53% believe it has major problems, and 24% feel it has minor problems. About 60% of people fear that by the time they retire, there will not be enough money in the system to pay the benefits to which they're entitled (Pew Research Center, 2005). Unless elderly Americans are better able to support themselves financially in the future than they are today, the government will have to play an even larger role in providing health care and other services. To do that, it will have to devote more tax dollars to the needs of older citizens.

The graying of the United States is also challenging employers to restructure the workplace. Already, fewer young workers are available to replace retiring workers. Some employers will be forced to pay higher wages or provide additional benefits to attract new workers or will be forced to focus more attention on employee productivity, perhaps turning to machines to replace workers.

On the positive side, however, employers will have to find innovative ways to keep older workers interested in the job. Business owners are beginning to realize that older workers are more stable employees than younger workers. Indeed, the turnover rate for workers under 30 is 10 times higher than the rate for workers over 50. So employers are developing new strategies to recruit older employees. Home Depot, for example, offers its older workers "snowbird specials"—winter jobs in warm-climate regions such as Florida and summer jobs in cooler states such as Maine. Borders bookstores regularly recruits retired teachers to sales positions by promising reading and discussion groups (Freudenheim, 2005). Employers may also have to keep older workers interested in continuing to work by offering substantial bonuses or by creating prestigious and well-paid part-time positions.

CONCLUSION

In discussing current and future demographic trends, I can't help but think about my own children. Their Millennium Generation cohort is the first to reach the teen years during the 21st century. I wonder what kind of impact being born in the late 1980s and growing up in the 1990s and early 2000s will have on their lives. Will the world's population reach the predicted catastrophic proportions, or will we figure out a way to control population growth and enable all people to live quality lives? Will the growing ethnic diversity of U.S. society continue to create tension and conflict, or will Americans eventually learn how to be a truly multicultural nation? What will be the single, most definitive "punctuating" event for my sons' cohort: a war, an assassination, a severe economic depression, a terrorist attack, a natural disaster, a political scandal, or some environmental catastrophe? Or will it be world peace, an end to hunger and homelessness, and a cure for cancer?

I also wonder how well social institutions will serve my children's generation. What will their experience in higher education be like? Will jobs be waiting for them when they're ready to go to work? What will be their share of the national debt? How will they perceive family life? Will marriage be an outdated mode of intimacy by the time they reach adulthood? What will be a desirable family size?

As a parent, of course, I'm more than a little curious about how these questions will be answered. But as a sociologist, I realize that they will emerge only from the experiences and interactions of my kids, and others their age, as they progress through their lives. Herein lies the unique and fundamental message of the sociological perspective.

As powerful and relentless as the demographic and generational forces described in this chapter are in determining my children's life chances, the responsibility for shaping and changing this society in the 21st century ultimately rests in the hands of their generation. This topic—the ability of individuals to change and reconstruct their society—is the theme of the next and final chapter.

CHAPTER HIGHLIGHTS

- Often overlooked in our quest to identify the structural factors that shape our everyday experiences are the effects of our birth cohort. Birth cohorts are more than just a collection of individuals born within a few years of one another; they are distinctive generations tied together by historical events, national and global population trends, and large-scale societal changes.
- Earth's population is growing at an unprecedented rate. But different countries experience different rates of growth. Poor, developing countries are expanding rapidly, whereas the populations in wealthy, developed countries have either stabilized or, in some cases, declined.
- When the population of a country grows rapidly, the age structure is increasingly dominated by young people. In slow-growth countries with low birthrates and high life expectancy, the population is much older, on average.
- As conditions in developing countries grow worse, pressures to migrate increase, creating a variety of cultural, political, and economic fears in countries experiencing high levels of immigration.
- The changing age structure of the U.S. population–more older people and fewer younger people–suggests that a number of adjustments will have to be made in both employment policies and social programs.

KEY TERMS

age structure Population's balance of old and young people

birth cohort Set of people who were born during the same era and who face similar societal circumstances brought about by their shared position in the overall age structure of the population

cohort effect Phenomenon in which members of a birth cohort tend to experience a particular life course event or rite of passage–puberty, marriage, childbearing, graduation, entry into the workforce, death–at roughly the same time

demographer Sociologist who studies trends in population characteristics

migration Movement of populations from one geographic area to another

period effect Phenomenon in which a historical event or major social trend contributes to the unique shape and outlook of a birth cohort

urbanization Process by which people leave rural areas and begin to concentrate in large cities

©David Silverman/Getty Images

14 Architects of Change

Reconstructing Society

Jonathan Simms, a 17-year-old student from a working-class family in Belfast, Northern Ireland, was a gifted soccer player who some felt had a chance of playing professionally. In September 2001, however, things began to change. He seemed to lose interest in soccer, and his play suffered. Around the house, he became clumsy, falling down, dropping things, and so on. He slurred his words. His parents suspected that he was drinking or taking drugs.

Within weeks, Jonathan became so weak that he had to be rushed to the hospital. He was diagnosed with a condition called variant Creutzfeldt-Jakob disease, popularly known as mad cow disease. This malady is a debilitating condition that results from eating infected beef. It can incubate in the body for years, even decades, before manifesting itself by attacking the brain (Belkin, 2003). By the middle of 2002, Jonathan could no longer walk or talk. His parents had to bathe him. Soon he became totally unresponsive, lying in bed in a vegetative state.

Doctors told Jonathan's parents that there was no hope and that he wouldn't live more than a year. But his father, Don, refused to accept the prognosis. And so he set out on a single-minded mission: to save his son's life. Don quit his job and spent all day on the Internet trying to find doctors, researchers, anybody who could commute his son's death sentence.

Don Simms eventually found a researcher, Steven Dealler, who had been experimenting with a powerful and sometimes lethal new drug called pentosan polysulfate (PPS). PPS had shown some effectiveness in treating animals suffering from a similar disease called scrapie but had never been tested on humans. The problem with PPS is that the molecules are so big that it can't be administered by pill or intravenously. Instead, the drug has been injected directly into the brains of the animals it's been used to treat. Most doctors were convinced that injecting this drug directly into a human's brain would be fatal.

So Don embarked on another quest, to find someone who would be willing to use this technique on his son. He found Dr. Nikolai Rainov, a neurosurgeon who was an expert on injecting cancer drugs directly to the brain. Dr. Rainov agreed to treat Jonathan, but the Board of Neurosurgery at Rainov's hospital refused to approve the treatment plan, stating that it was simply too dangerous (Belkin, 2003). Britain's Committee on Safety of Medicines entered the fray, saying that there was no rational basis for prescribing the drug ("Family of VCJD Victim Claim," 2003).

Don didn't give up. He found a hospital in Germany that would allow the PPS treatment. He chartered a medical transport plane—at his own expense—and prepared his son for the trip. But days before the family was set to leave, the German Department of Health blocked them. Germany had no cases of mad cow disease and wanted to keep it that way.

Again, Don refused to give up. He hired a lawyer and took the case to court in Great Britain. Numerous legal battles ensued. But in December 2002, 15 months after the initial diagnosis, a High Court judge ruled that the family could proceed with the treatment.

Jonathan began PPS treatments in February 2003. After several months, his doctors noticed that his heart rhythms were improving, that he had regained his ability to swallow, and that he was more responsive to light and pain. There were none of the adverse side effects that critics had predicted. By all accounts, the disease had been brought under control. In 2008, his condition was upgraded from "critical" to "non–life threatening." It's doubtful that Jonathan will ever be fully "cured," but he is now the world's longest-known survivor of this disease, something no one—except his father—thought possible at the time of his diagnosis.

The message of the Jonathan Simms case is sociologically compelling: An individual was able to overcome the institutional obstacles of a massive international medical establishment to find a solution to a seemingly insoluble problem. As we have seen throughout this book, institutions must operate in a highly structured, standardized, and impersonal way, at a level above the interests and personalities of the individual people they are created to serve. Imagine the chaos that would ensue if the system were set up so that any parent with a terminally ill child could compel researchers, physicians, and hospitals to concoct unique and risky treatments. The entire health care system would quickly collapse. That hasn't stopped some patient advocacy groups from lobbying for laws that would allow the "compassionate use" of not yet approved experimental drugs for seriously ill patients who have run out of other options (Harmon, 2009).

But from an institutional perspective, new drugs must be tested meticulously—and sometimes slowly—to determine their effectiveness and to identify all potentially dangerous side effects before they are made available to the public. A sharp line must be drawn between the need to satisfy the principles of sound scientific method and the desire to help people who are suffering (Rothman & Edgar, 1992). Insurance companies usually won't pay for drugs that have not completed rigorous scientific testing (Harmon, 2009). Indeed, in 2005, the Food and Drug Administration slowed down its drug approval process in response to several reports of unsafe drugs on the market (Harris, 2005a). But Jonathan's story shows that individuals can overcome bureaucratic lethargy and actually change a part of the social structure. As a result of Don Simms's actions, the standard medical approach to treating people infected with mad cow disease changed.

In the past, only the most dedicated individuals, such as Don Simms, were able to become highly involved in medical decisions. Today, however, when a doctor mentions a diagnosis or prescribes a drug, patients can immediately go online and consult one of the thousands of medical websites that offer information (some of it more trustworthy than others) on everything from common colds to exotic diseases. And when they visit their doctors, more and more patients arrive with printouts bearing information downloaded from websites (Kolata, 2000).

By working together, individuals with the same illnesses or medical concerns have also been able to act as their own best advocates. For instance, in the early 1990s, AIDS deaths were mounting while the slow progress of the government drug-approval process kept drugs out of the hands of the people who needed them. But AIDS activists succeeded in changing the way AIDS drugs were developed and regulated.

Potentially helpful treatments are now being produced more quickly and are making an impact.

Mother-to-child transmission of HIV/AIDS in the United States, for example, has been all but eliminated (Santora, 2005). AIDS activists have also successfully pressured pharmaceutical companies to allow developing countries in sub-Saharan Africa to import cheaper, generic anti-AIDS drugs (Swarns, 2001). In 2006, Bristol-Myers agreed to license its newest and most powerful AIDS drugs to drug makers in India and South Africa so it could be made more cheaply (McNeil, 2006). These activists have worked together to enhance the influence none of them could have had acting individually. The reach of their achievements goes beyond sick individuals to global institutions and concerns.

This theme—the power of individuals acting collectively to change the structural elements of their society—guides this final chapter of the book. I have spent the previous 13 chapters discussing how our society and everything in it is socially constructed and how these social constructions, in turn, shape the lives of individuals. You may feel a little helpless when considering how much control culture, bureaucracies, institutions, and systems of social stratification have over our lives. It's only fitting, then, to end this book on a more encouraging note, with a discussion of social change and the ways individuals can reconstruct their society.

SOCIAL CHANGE

Change is the preeminent characteristic of modern human societies, whether it occurs in personal relationships, cultural norms and values, systems of stratification, or institutions. Everywhere you look—your school, your job, your home, your government, and every aspect of your very way of life—institutional and cultural change is the rule, not the exception.

As a result of substantive changes affecting many social institutions simultaneously, the United States and other technologically advanced societies have become what sociologists call ***postindustrial societies***. Economies that once centered around farms and agriculture or factories and the production of material goods now revolve around information and service industries, including communication, mass media, research and development, tourism, insurance, banking and finance, and technology. The everyday lives of ordinary people in these societies are qualitatively different from the lives of those in agricultural or industrial societies.

Change is clear when we look at specific institutions. Consider how the nature of education has changed in the past half-century. If you had taken this sociology course 50 years ago, your instructor would have needed only a few tools: a good collection of books on the subject, a manual typewriter, some pencils, a ditto machine, a stack of carbon paper, and a love of the discipline. Good instructors today still need a love of the discipline (I hope!), but it's becoming difficult to teach interestingly, effectively, and efficiently without taking advantage of state-of-the-art technology: a high-speed computer; in-class access to the Internet; e-mail; online databases, blogs, and course materials; computerized test banks; a DVD library; and access to photocopy and fax machines. My university goes so far as to offer financial incentives to professors who want to revise their courses to incorporate the latest technology. Indeed, technological advances have made similar inroads into almost every occupation—as well as almost every social institution.

Family life in the United States has also changed considerably over the past 50 years. Divorce rates were low in the 1950s, skyrocketed in the 1960s to 1970s, stabilized in the 1980s to 1990s, and have dropped a bit in the 2000s. Women have entered the workforce in unprecedented numbers. People are waiting longer to marry, and once they do, they are having fewer children. Cultural concerns about gender equality have altered the way men and women relate to one another inside and outside the home. Social and sexual rules that once seemed permanent and natural have disintegrated: Unmarried couples can live openly together, unmarried women can have and keep their babies without community condemnation, and remaining single and remaining childless have become acceptable lifestyle options (Skolnick & Skolnick, 1992). In short, today's family bears little resemblance to the cultural ideal of the 1950s.

These changes have, in turn, affected other institutions. Because so many families are headed by dual-earner couples these days, children spend less time with their parents than they did in the past, forcing families to depend on others to look after their children: paid caregivers, friends, neighbors, and/or teachers. More parents than ever rely on professional day care centers to watch over their preschool-age children. Many of these centers require that children be toilet trained before they enroll, compelling parents to exert premature pressure on their children to comply. As a result, many pediatricians report an increase in children with toilet-training problems, such as lack of daytime and nighttime urine control (Goode, 1999).

Schools are also being called on to address many of the problems that families used to deal with at home. They now routinely provide students with training in moral values, technological and financial "literacy," adequate nutrition, and practical instruction to help them avoid drug and alcohol abuse, teen pregnancy, and sexually transmitted diseases.

Not surprisingly, the very nature of childhood is also changing. Contemporary social critics argue that childhood has all but disappeared in the modern world. In the United States, children are exposed to events, devices, images, and ideas that would have been inconceivable to their Baby Boom grandparents or Generation X parents when they were young. Moreover, the increasingly competitive nature of childhood is making some parents feel obligated to give their young children every conceivable edge to help them succeed. Some parents fight to get their 2- and 3-year-olds into one of the limited spots in top preschools, where tuition can run well over $10,000 a year (Scherzer, 2007).

More seriously, children are increasingly having trouble getting along in society. A 2005 nationwide study found that about 7 out of every 1,000 three- and four-year-old preschoolers are expelled each year for misbehavior, a rate more than three times as high as for K-12 students (Gilliam, 2005). We read about 12-year-olds becoming pregnant and 7-year-olds being tried for crimes such as rape and drug smuggling. In Pensacola, Florida, a 5-year-old girl faced assault charges for beating a 51-year-old school counselor. In Columbus, Ohio, an 8-year-old girl was charged with attempted murder for allegedly pouring poison into her great-grandmother's drink because the two didn't get along. A 6-year-old in Michigan shot and killed a classmate. A 7-year-old boy in Tampa beat his 7-month-old sister to death with a two-by-four (Chachere, 2005).

The National Longitudinal Study of Adolescent Health found that one in four young people between the ages of 12 and 17 has used a gun or a knife or has been in a situation where someone was injured by a weapon in the past year ("Study Finds Increase," 2000). Between 1998 and 2002, some 90,000 teachers nationwide were the victims of violent crimes, and about 1 out of every 10 elementary and secondary school teachers was threatened with injury by a student (DeVoe et al., 2004). No wonder that since the late 1980s, 44 states have adopted new laws enabling courts to try more children as adults. Between 1990 and 2008, the number of juveniles sent to adult jails and prisons increased by more than 300% (Minton & Sabol, 2009).

The state of childhood is even more precarious in other parts of the world. For instance, 830,000 children around the globe die each year from preventable accidents, such as drowning, burns, car crashes, poisoning, and falls (cited in McNeil, 2008). According to United Nations estimates, more than 49 million children under 14 in sub-Saharan Africa work as miners, construction workers, pesticide sprayers, street vendors, haulers, prostitutes, and so on. Some are as young as 5 or 6. Often, they're not even paid for their labor (Wines, 2006). In addition, more than 250,000 children have been exploited as child soldiers and are taking part in armed conflicts in places such as Sudan, Colombia, Myanmar, Iraq, and Afghanistan (United Nations, 2007). Clearly, social change has made children's lives less carefree than we would wish.

The Speed of Social Change

In the distant past, societies tended to change slowly, almost imperceptibly, during the course of one's lifetime. Family and community traditions typically spanned many generations. Although the traditional societies that exist today still change relatively slowly, change in postindustrial societies is particularly fast paced. Even while writing this book, I've had to revise several examples at the last minute because some things changed so abruptly. The early 2000s already seem like a long-gone era.

Because we live in a world that seems to be in a constant state of flux, we're often tempted to believe that rapid social change is an exclusively contemporary issue. Keep in mind, however, that sociologists and other scholars have long expressed deep concern over the effects that social change has on people. The 19th-century sociologist Émile Durkheim (1897/1951) argued that rapid social change creates a vacuum in norms, which he called ***anomie,*** where the old cultural rules no longer apply. When things change quickly—through sudden economic shifts, wars, natural disasters, population explosions, or rapid transitions from a traditional to a modern society—people become disoriented and experience anomie as they search for new guidelines to govern their lives.

Widespread anomie affects the larger society as well. When rapid change disrupts social norms, it unleashes our naturally greedy impulses. Without norms to constrain our unlimited aspirations and with too few resources to satisfy our unlimited desires, we are in a sense doomed to a frustrating life of striving for unattainable goals (Durkheim, 1897/1951). The result, Durkheim felt, is higher rates of suicide and criminal activity as well as weakened ties to family, neighborhood, and friends.

But rapid change isn't always bad. Sometimes rapid change is necessary to effectively address shifting social conditions. For instance, over the span of a few years in the late 1990s, school districts around the country drastically modified their curricula in response to the sudden ascendancy of the Internet in students' everyday lives, forever changing the face of U.S. education. In the wake of the September 11, 2001, attacks and the subsequent military action in Iraq and Afghanistan, universities around the country scrambled to offer more courses on Islam and the politics of the Middle East.

The velocity of change today has affected the way sociologists go about their work, too. When U.S. society was understood to be relatively stable, sociological study was fairly straightforward. Most social researchers in the 1950s believed that one could start a 5- or 10-year study of some social institution, say the family or higher education, and assume that the institution would still be much the same when the study ended (Wolfe, 1991). Today, such assumptions about the staying power of institutions are dubious at best.

There is no such thing as a permanent social institution. Thus, sociologists, like everyone else in contemporary society, have had to adjust their thinking and their methods to accommodate the rapid pace of social change.

Causes of Social Change

The difficulty of pinning down any aspect of society when change is so rapid has led sociologists to study change itself. Following in the footsteps of Durkheim, they ask, What causes all these technological, cultural, and institutional changes? On occasion, massive change—in the private lives of individuals as well as in entire social institutions—can result from a single dramatic historical event, such as the attacks of September 11, 2001, Hurricane Katrina, or the global economic meltdown of 2008. We can be thankful that such colossal events are relatively rare. Sociologists who focus on change tell us that institutional transformations are more likely to be caused over time by a variety of social forces, including environmental and population pressures, cultural innovation, and technological and cultural diffusion.

Environmental and Population Pressures

As you saw in Chapter 13, the shifting size and shape of the population—globally and locally—is enough by itself to create change in societies. As populations grow, more and more people move either into urban areas, where jobs are easier to find, or into previously uninhabited areas, where natural resources are plentiful.

Environmental sociologists note the complex interplay among people, social structure, and natural resources as previously undeveloped territories are settled. For instance, one social scientist has argued that many civilizations throughout history—such as the Easter Islanders, the Mayans, and the Norse colony in Greenland—collapsed because deforestation led to soil erosion, which led to food shortages and ultimately political and social collapse (Diamond, 2005).

Even when new areas are developed for food production, environmental damage often occurs. Of course, improved food supplies have had obvious benefits for societies around the world. Fewer and fewer people today die from famine and malnutrition than ever before. But the positive effects of a growing global food supply have been tempered by the serious environmental harm that new production techniques have caused. For instance, pesticide use has increased 17-fold over the past several decades, threatening the safety of water supplies. Some insects have developed resistance, which leads to increased pesticide use. New crop varieties often require more irrigation than old varieties, which has been accompanied by increased erosion and water runoff. As demand for meat products increases, cattle ranches expand, destroying natural habitats, displacing native animal species, and polluting water sources. Modern factory farming practices have helped spread mad cow disease throughout England (Cowley, 2003).

More broadly, the clearing of forests and the burning of fossil fuels, such as coal, oil, and natural gas, have been implicated as the chief cause of ***global warming***—a steady rise in Earth's average temperature as a result of increasing amounts of carbon dioxide in the atmosphere. We are already seeing the consequences of global warming: Polar ice caps and glaciers are melting; sea levels are rising; plants and animals are being forced out of their habitats; certain diseases, such as malaria, are spreading to higher altitudes; and the number of severe storms, heat waves, and droughts is increasing. Many scientists believe that the long-term effects of global warming may lead to unprecedented worldwide catastrophe.

Cultural and Technological Innovation

But population and environmental pressures have the potential to create more positive social change in the form of cultural and technological innovation. For example, natural disasters, such as earthquakes, hurricanes, and tornadoes, often inspire improvements in emergency response technology, home safety products, and architectural design that improve everyone's lives. Likewise, concerns about pollution and global warming have fostered innovative changes in people's behavior (e.g., recycling and conserving energy), the creation of environmentally safe products and services (low-watt light bulbs, low-flow showerheads, and biodegradable detergent), and the development of energy-efficient hybrid vehicles and nonpolluting energy sources, such as solar power and wind power. The result is felt not only on an individual level but also on a societal level, as eco-efficient and environmentally sustainable businesses grow around these innovations and attract investors. The Apollo Alliance (2009), a coalition of business, labor, environmental, and community groups, estimates that a $500 billion investment over 10 years will produce 5 million jobs in renewable energy, hybrid cars, and infrastructure replacement. Many companies and even city governments now employ full-time "sustainability directors" to look for cost-saving ways to minimize the wasting of electricity and natural gas, improve energy efficiency, and reduce harmful greenhouse gases (Greenblatt, 2009).

Sometimes, these scientific discoveries and technological inventions spur further innovations within a society. Improvements in motor vehicle safety, such as air bags, safety belts, child safety seats, and motorcycle helmets, have contributed to large reductions in motor vehicle deaths and fundamentally changed the way we drive. Water fluoridation is credited for a 40% to 60% reduction in tooth loss in adults. Safer and healthier foods have all but eliminated nutritional deficiency diseases such as rickets, goiter, and pellagra in the United States (Centers for Disease Control and Prevention, 1999).

Often, revolutionary innovations seem insignificant at first. Imagine what life would be like without the invention of corrective eyeglasses, which dramatically extended the activities of near- and far-sighted people and fostered the belief that physical limitations could be overcome with a little ingenuity. The invention of indoor plumbing, the internal combustion engine, television, the microchip, nuclear fusion, and effective birth control have been instrumental in determining the course of human history. Sometimes the smallest innovation has the largest impact: According to one author, without the machine-made precision screw—the most durable way of attaching one object to another—entire fields of science would have languished, routine maritime commerce would have been impossible, and there would have been no machine tools and hence no industrial products and no industrial revolution (Rybczynski, 1999).

But social institutions can sometimes be slow to adjust to scientific and technological innovations. Consider, for instance, the medical treatment of infertility. Artificial insemination, in vitro fertilization, surrogate motherhood, and other medical advances have increased the number of previously infertile people who can now bear and raise children. Yet these technological developments were changing the face of parenthood well before society began to recognize and address the ethical, moral, and legal issues they raised. For instance, close to half a million embryos created through in vitro fertilization are kept frozen at fertility clinics around the country. Many of them belong to couples that no longer need them because they are finished having children. But it's unclear exactly what should be done with the embryos. Some couples are opposed to destroying them for moral or religious reasons. Most couples don't want to donate them to other couples because of genetic links to their own children. (In fact, state and federal regulations make donation to other couples difficult because they require donors to come back to the clinics to be tested for infectious diseases.) Still others would like to donate them for research, but that option is not always available (Grady, 2008).

Parental responsibility can also become complicated when technology plays a role in childbearing. Surrogacy—an arrangement in which a woman agrees to become pregnant and give birth to a child others will raise—divides motherhood into three distinct roles, which may be occupied by three separate people: the *genetic* mother (the one who supplies the egg from which the fetus develops), the *gestational* mother (the one who becomes pregnant and gives birth), and the *social* mother (the one who raises the child). In such situations, legal parenthood can be unclear. There is little uniformity between states about whether to recognize and enforce surrogacy agreements. Some states grant preference to surrogacy agreements; others assume the woman giving birth to the child is the mother and will reverse that determination only when the commissioning couple files a prebirth order to legally adopt the child after he or she is born (Shapo, 2006).

Diffusion of Technologies and Cultural Practices

Another cause of social change is ***cultural diffusion:*** the process by which beliefs, technology, customs, and other cultural items are spread from one group or society to another. You may not realize it, but most of the taken-for-granted aspects of our daily lives originally came from somewhere else. For instance, pajamas, clocks, toilets, glass, coins, newspapers, and soap were initially imported into Western cultures from elsewhere (Linton, 1937). Even a fair amount of the English language has been imported, as can be seen from the following examples:

algebra (Arabic)
anatomy (Greek)
bagel (Yiddish)
barbeque (Taino)
boondocks (Filipino Tagalog)
catamaran (Tamil)
coyote, poncho (Spanish)
dynamite (Swedish)
medicine (Latin)
safari (Swahili)
sherbet (Turkish)
tycoon (Chinese)
vogue (French)

Diffusion often occurs because one society considers the culture or technology of another society to be useful. However, the diffusion process is not always friendly, as you may recall from the discussion of colonization in Chapter 10. When one society's territory is taken over by another society, the indigenous people may be required to adapt to the customs and beliefs of the invaders. When Europeans conquered the New World, Native American peoples were forced to abandon their traditional ways of life and become more "civilized." Hundreds of thousands of Native Americans died in the process, not only from violent conflict but also from malnutrition and new diseases inadvertently brought by their conquerors. Whether diffusion is invited or imposed, the effect is the same: a chain reaction of social changes that affect both individuals and the larger social structure.

SOCIAL MOVEMENTS

One danger of talking about the sources of social change or its cultural, environmental, and institutional consequences is that we then tend to see change as a purely macrolevel structural phenomenon, something that happens to us rather than something we create. But social change is not some huge, invisible hand that descends from the heavens to arbitrarily alter our routine way of life. It is, in the end, a phenomenon driven by human action.

Collective action by large numbers of people has always been a major agent of social change, whether it takes the form of mothers marching on Washington, D.C., to demand gun control legislation; people holding a pray-in outside the Capitol building to encourage lawmakers to pass a budget "that is more reflective of the moral values of our nation" ("Religious Groups Gather," 2005); or a sit-in by students in the Harvard University president's house to demand higher wages for the school's blue-collar workers. When people organize and extend their activities beyond the immediate confines of the group, they may become the core of a ***social movement*** (Zurcher & Snow, 1981).

Underlying all social movements is a concern with social change: the desire to enact it, stop it, or reverse it. That desire may be expressed in a variety of ways, from peaceful activities such as signing petitions, participating in civil demonstrations, donating money, and campaigning during elections to violent activities such as rioting and overthrowing a government.

Types of Social Movements

Social movements can be categorized, depending on the magnitude of their goals, as reform movements, countermovements, or revolutionary movements. A ***reform movement*** attempts to change limited aspects of a society but does not seek to alter or replace major social institutions. Take the U.S. civil rights movement of the 1960s. It did not call for an overhaul of the U.S. economic system (capitalism) or political system (two-party democracy). Instead, it advocated a more limited change: opening existing institutions to full and equal participation by members of minority groups (DeFronzo, 1991). Similarly, the anti–Vietnam War movement questioned government policy (and in the process brought down two presidents—Lyndon Johnson and Richard Nixon), but it didn't seek to change the form of government itself (Fendrich, 2003). Other recent examples of reform movements include the women's movement, the nuclear freeze movement, the labor union movement, the school prayer movement, and the environmental movement.

Because reform movements seek to alter some aspect of existing social arrangements, they are usually opposed by some people and groups. ***Countermovements*** are designed to prevent or reverse the changes sought or accomplished by an earlier movement. A countermovement is most likely to emerge when the reform movement against which it is reacting becomes large and effective in pursuing its goals and therefore comes to be seen as a threat to personal and social interests (Chafetz & Dworkin, 1987; Mottl, 1980).

For instance, the emergence in the 1980s and 1990s of a conservative social countermovement often called the "religious right" or the "Christian right" was provoked by a growing perception among its members of enormous social upheaval in U.S. society: the breakdown of traditional roles and values and a concerted challenge to existing institutions such as education, religion, and the family. Although members of the religious right blamed these changes on the civil rights, antiwar, student, and women's movements of the 1960s and 1970s (Klatch, 1991), they perceived the women's movement as particularly dangerous. Indeed, the leaders of the religious right were the first, in modern times, to articulate the notion that the push for women's equality is responsible for the unhappiness of many individual women and the weakening of the American family (Faludi, 1991). Access to legal abortion, the high divorce rate, and the increased number of children who grow up with working mothers are often offered as proof that the moral bases of family life are eroding (Klatch, 1991).

Over the past few decades, the religious right has had some success in shifting the political and social mood of the country. It first gained legitimacy in 1980, when presidential candidate Ronald Reagan and several Senate candidates who were supported by the group won the election. It reasserted its influence in 1994 with the takeover of Congress by conservative Republicans. And it gained even more power and visibility with the election and reelection of George W. Bush, who promoted many religious right themes.

In the late 2000s, the religious right has turned its focus to opposing the increasing visibility of homosexuality in U.S. society. Through organizations such as the Eagle Forum, the Christian Coalition, the Family Research Council, the Traditional Values Coalition, Concerned Women for America, Focus on the Family, the Alliance for Marriage, and many smaller groups around the United States, it has achieved some notable triumphs at the state and local levels. It has succeeded in influencing public school curricula as well as promoting anti-gay-rights legislation and defense of marriage acts at the city and state levels.

Over the years, the religious right has been especially effective in limiting access to abortion. Even though the majority of U.S. citizens still favor the legal right to abortion, virtually every state in the nation has enacted new restrictions on abortion since 1996, such as mandatory waiting periods and parental notification. About 87% of all U.S. counties (and 97% of rural counties) have no abortion provider. Nationwide, the number of abortion providers decreased by 37% between 1982 and 2001 (Henshaw & Finer, 2003) and another 2% between 2000 and 2005 (Kaiser Family Foundation, 2008). Few medical schools or residency programs in obstetrics and gynecology provide training in abortion techniques, although pressure from medical student advocacy groups has led some programs to reinstate abortion in the curriculum (cited in

Edwards, 2001). In addition, those abortion clinics that do exist have been picketed, blockaded, vandalized, and, on occasion, destroyed. In 2009, George Tiller, a Wichita doctor who performed abortions, was shot and killed during worship services at a church where he served as an usher. Given such an environment, it's not surprising that rates of legal abortion have declined steadily over the past 2 decades. In 1980, there were about 29 abortions per 1,000 women between the ages of 15 and 44; today, that figure is 19 per 1,000 (Alan Guttmacher Institute, 2008).

The women's movement, the gay rights movement, and the religious right all remain quite active today, creating numerous colorful conflicts in the national political arena. However, it is important to remember that all these movements are pursuing their interests within the existing social system—as do all reform movements and countermovements. In contrast, ***revolutionary movements*** attempt to overthrow the entire system itself, whether it is the government or the existing social structure, in order to replace it with another (Skocpol, 1979). The American Revolution of 1776, the French Revolution of 1789, the Russian Revolution of 1917, the Iranian Revolution of 1979, and the Afghan Revolution of 1996 are examples of movements that toppled existing governments and created a new social order.

Revolutionary change in basic social institutions can be brought about through nonviolent means, such as peaceful labor strikes, democratic elections, and civil disobedience. However, most successful revolutions have involved some level of violence on the part of both movement participants and groups opposing the revolution (DeFronzo, 1991).

Elements of Social Movements

Whichever type they are, social movements occur when dissatisfied people see their condition as resulting from society's inability to meet their needs. Movements typically develop when certain segments of the population conclude that society's resources—access to political power, higher education, living wages, legal justice, medical care, a clean and healthy environment, and so on—are distributed unequally and unfairly (Brown, 1986). People come to believe that they have a moral right to the satisfaction of their unmet expectations and that this satisfaction cannot or will not occur without some effort on their part. This perception is often based on the experience of past failures of working within the system.

As individuals and groups who share this sense of frustration and unfairness interact, the existing system begins to lose its perceived legitimacy (Piven & Cloward, 1977). Individuals who ordinarily might have considered themselves helpless come to believe that as a social movement they have the capacity to change things and significantly alter their lives and the lives of others:

- In 2006, a website called MomsRising.org was launched, bringing mothers together to talk about ways to change public policy. In "house parties" all across the country, small groups of mothers meet regularly to discuss ways to lobby legislators on issues such as family leave, health insurance, child care, and after-school activities. They now have 90,000 members nationwide and have helped change paid family leave policies in several states (St. George, 2007).

- In the early 2000s, tens of thousands of janitors all around the country went on strike to demand health insurance and better wages. Typically, janitors are among the most invisible and least appreciated workers. But in Chicago, they banded together to block downtown traffic. In Los Angeles, they walked off their jobs. In New York, they marched down Park Avenue. In San Diego, some went on a hunger strike. In several cities, the janitors won new contracts.

- In several dozen cities across the country, day laborers—typically immigrants who congregate at well-known locations such as street corners or parking lots, waiting for building contractors, landscapers, plumbers, or other potential employers to offer a day's work—have organized to set their own minimum wages (Greenhouse, 2006).

Ideology

Any successful social movement must have an ***ideology***, a coherent system of beliefs, values, and ideas that justifies its existence (Turner & Killian, 1987; Zurcher & Snow, 1981). An ideology fulfills several functions. First, it helps frame the issue in moral terms. Once people perceive the moral goodness of their position, they become willing to risk arrest, personal financial costs, or more for the good of the cause. Second, the ideology defines the group's interests and helps identify people as either supporters or detractors, creating identifiable "good guys" and "villains." Finally, an ideology provides participants with a collective sense of what the specific goals of the movement are or should be.

Consider the antiabortion (or pro-life) movement. Its ideology rests on several assumptions about the nature of childhood and motherhood (Luker, 1984). For instance, it assumes that each conception is an act of God and so abortion violates God's will. The ideology also states that life begins at conception, the fetus is an individual who has a constitutional right to life, and every human life should be valued (Michener, DeLamater, & Schwartz, 1986). This ideology reinforces the view among adherents that abortion is immoral, evil, and self-indulgent.

The power of an ideology to mobilize support for a social movement often depends on the broader cultural and historical context in which the movement exists. For instance, it would have seemed in the 2003 buildup to the invasion of Iraq that antiwar activists would be able to make a strong case against going to war by using an ideology based on a portrayal of the United States as a hostile aggressor. After all, the country we were set to invade, Iraq, posed no direct threat to the United States, hadn't undertaken a large-scale military mobilization, wasn't involved in planning or carrying out the 9/11 attacks that precipitated our military action, and wasn't harboring those who were involved. Internationally, the sympathetic response that we received from other countries immediately after the attacks was short-lived, replaced by a growing perception that the United States was a global bully whose policies ignore the interests of people in other countries (Pew Research Center, 2005). The vast majority of nations around the world—foes and allies alike—were strongly opposed to the invasion.

But the post-9/11 cultural atmosphere in this country was a mixture of anger, fear, lingering shock, and heightened patriotism, which made an ideology of military restraint intolerable to many Americans. Enduring memories of earlier antiwar protestors' hostility toward soldiers returning from Vietnam during the late 1960s and early 1970s complicated the task. Reluctant to disrespect those individuals in Iraq who were willing to put their lives at risk, antiwar activists had to walk a thin line between opposing U.S. aggression and expressing support for the young men and women who were being asked to carry out that aggression on the frontlines. Against such a backdrop, the ideology of the 2003 antiwar movement—which advocated a diplomatic, reflective, and measured approach—sounded unpatriotic, weak, and inadequate, not to mention disloyal to the thousands who died in the 9/11 attacks. Not surprisingly, the movement failed to prevent the onset of war.

Although an ideology might be what attracts people to a movement, it must be spread through social networks of friends, family, coworkers, and other contacts (Zurcher & Snow, 1981). For some people, in fact, the ideology of the movement is secondary to other social considerations. Potential participants are unlikely to join without being introduced to the movement by someone they know. The ideological leaders of a social movement might want to believe that participants are there because of "the cause," but chances are that the participants have a friend or acquaintance who persuaded them to be there (Gerlach & Hine, 1970; Stark & Bainbridge, 1980).

Sometimes the activities required to promote or sustain a particular movement run counter to the ideological goals of the movement itself. The leaders of successful political revolutions, for example, soon realize that to run the country they now control, they must create highly structured bureaucracies not unlike the ones they have overthrown.

Individuals in reform movements may also have to engage in behaviors that conflict with the ideological beliefs of the movement. The religious right movement's profamily, promotherhood positions are clearly designed to turn back the feminist agenda. However, early in the movement, it became clear that to be successful it would have to enlist high-profile women to campaign against feminist policies. Women on the religious right frequently had to leave their families, travel the country to make speeches, and display independent strength—characteristics that were anything but the models of traditional womanhood they were publicly promoting.

Ironically, social movements sometimes require the involvement of individuals from outside the group of people whose interests the movement represents. For example, many of the people who fought successfully for Blacks' right to vote in Alabama and Mississippi during the civil rights movement of the 1950s and 1960s were middle-class white college students from the North. Similarly, it wasn't until mainstream religious organizations, labor groups, and college students got involved that the *living wage movement*—an effort to require cities and counties to pay its low-wage workers an amount above the federal minimum wage—became successful. As of 2006, 140 cities had passed living wage laws (Living Wage Resource Center, 2006). In 2006, the Chicago City Council passed an ordinance requiring large retail stores, such as Wal-Mart and Home Depot, to pay a minimum wage that was almost twice as high as the federal minimum wage (Eckholm, 2006a). In 2007, Maryland became the first state to require a living wage for all state employees.

The ideology of a social movement gains additional credibility when voiced by those whose interests seem contrary to its goals. Opposition to the war in Iraq gained some traction not because people took a second look at its original ideology or because street protests and rallies suddenly gained their attention. Instead, it grew because many U.S. soldiers who fought there and saw the conditions firsthand started speaking out in opposition, often under the threat of disciplinary action (Houppert, 2005). Combatants knew the reality of war in ways that civilian protestors never could (Utne, 2006). Some even spoke out while on the frontlines, posting daily blogs that criticized the condition of military equipment and resources, our lack of understanding of Iraqi insurgents, and ultimately our very involvement in the war (Finer, 2005). Membership in organizations with names such as Operation Truth, Gold Star Families for Peace, and Iraq and Afghanistan Veterans of America grew during the early years of the war (Banerjee, 2005).

Furthermore, people who are already disadvantaged by particular social conditions may not be as effective as others in promoting their cause, because they lack the money, time, skills, and connections that successful movements require. For instance, the people who would stand to benefit the most from environmental improvement—individuals in poor, polluted communities—have historically been uninvolved in the environmental movement. Residents tend to see environmentalists as middle- and upper-middle-class outsiders whose own neighborhoods are relatively unpolluted and who don't appreciate the community's concerns (Bullard, 1993). Nobody wants garbage dumps, landfills, incinerators, or polluting factories in their backyards. But if these are the only ventures that will provide steady employment for residents, poor communities are left with little choice but to support them. Consequently, they often fear that outside environmentalists will take away their jobs and economic livelihoods. Recently, however, many members of poor communities have joined the environmental movement, motivated not by a "Save the Earth" ideology but by a more immediately relevant one that emphasizes the unfairness and discrimination to which they are exposed. As one successful local activist recently put it, "People here aren't going to install solar panels on their roofs or drive a Prius, but they can demand institutional change and decent business practices" (quoted in Breslau, 2007, p. 69). In some developing nations, poor communities have mobilized resistance to commercial tree plantations, oil drilling, mining, or dam construction when these developments are perceived to constitute a threat to people's livelihoods (Martinez-Alier, 2003).

Resource Mobilization

At any given point, numerous problems in a society need to be fixed, and people's grievances remain more or less constant from year to year. Yet relatively few major social movements exist at any one time. If widespread dissatisfaction and frustration were all that is needed to sustain a social movement, "the masses would always be in revolt" (Trotsky, 1930/1959). What else is needed for a social movement to get started, gain support, and achieve its goals?

According to *resource mobilization theory*, the key ingredient is effective organization. No social movement can exist unless it has an organized system for acquiring needed resources: money, labor, participants, legal aid, access to the media, and so on (McCarthy & Zald, 1977). How far a movement goes in attaining its goals depends on its ability to expand its ranks, build large-scale public support, and transform those who join into committed participants (Zurcher & Snow, 1981).

Most large, long-term social movements involve a national, and even international, coalition of groups. Such widespread organization makes the movement more powerful by making recruiting and fundraising more efficient. For example, most of us first heard of the movement against corporate globalization in 1999, when thousands of people in Seattle protested against a meeting of the World Trade Organization (WTO). News reports of the event gave the impression that the protesters were a bunch of renegade anarchists who spontaneously took to the streets to vandalize local outlets of corporate giants such as McDonald's and Starbucks. Although a few of the protesters were, in fact, destructive, the vast majority were longtime nonviolent supporters of the movement. The mobilization that was required to get so many people involved was accomplished by various established organizations, such as the AFL-CIO, Sierra Club, Humane Society, Global Exchange, Public Citizen, and Rainforest Action Network. In fact, more than 1,200 labor, environmental, consumer, religious, farm, academic, and human rights groups from more than 90 nations had already been working to halt the expansion of the WTO long before the Seattle protest took place (Nichols, 2000; Rothschild, 2000).

Moreover, those movements that historically have lasted the longest—the women's movement, the antiabortion movement, the civil rights movement, the environmental movement—are those that are supported by large bureaucratic organizations. The National Organization for Women, the Christian Coalition, the National Association for the Advancement of Colored People (NAACP), the Sierra Club, and the like have full-time lobbyists or political action committees in Washington that connect them to the national political system. Few movements can succeed without such connections because achieving social change often requires changing laws or convincing courts to interpret laws in particular ways.

Another important feature of highly organized social movements is an established network of communication (McCarthy & Zald, 1977). Movements need an effective system both for getting information to all participants and for recruiting and fundraising (Tarrow, 1994). The ability to quickly mobilize large numbers of people for, say, a march to the nation's capital depends on the ability to tell them what is going to happen and when and where it will happen. Websites, blogs, direct mailing strategies, and networked phone and computer systems are all used by modern movements.

In 2009, a crowd of more than 10,000 youth in Moldova gathered to protest against the country's communist leadership. Protestors ransacked government buildings and clashed with the police. To older observers and government officials, the sea of young people seemed to materialize out of nowhere. What they didn't realize was that the protest organizers mobilized participants through Twitter, the social-messaging network (Barry, 2009). Similar technological mobilization occurred in Iran in 2009, as hundreds of thousands of young people took to the streets to protest what they considered to be the fraudulent results of that country's presidential election. And because the Iranian government barred foreign journalists from covering the protests, images of them taken on people's cell phones were disseminated worldwide through Flickr and YouTube.

The mass media play an equally important part in the success of a social movement by validating and enlarging the scope of its cause. In other words, the media play a key role in constructing a particular social reality useful to the movement. The media spotlight sends the message that the movement's concerns are valid and that the movement is an important force in society. A small group of people disrupting a town hall meeting on health care reform is, for all intents and purposes, a nonevent without media coverage. Media recognition is often a necessary condition before those who are the targets of influence respond to the movement's claims and demands (Gamson & Wolfsfeld, 1993).

In sum, movements that succeed in enacting substantial social change are not necessarily those with the most compelling ideological positions or the greatest emotional appeal (Ferree, 1992). Instead, they are the ones with the necessary high-level organization and communication networks to mobilize supporters and the necessary media access to neutralize the opposition and transform the public into sympathizers.

Bureaucratization

It makes sense that the most successful social movements are the ones that are the best organized. However, high-level organization can backfire if it leads to rigidity and turf wars, common to any bureaucracy. When organizations within a movement differ in their philosophies and tactics, tremendous infighting and bickering may break out among organizations ostensibly working toward the same goal.

For instance, the U.S. civil rights movement during the 1950s and 1960s included many diverse, seemingly incompatible organizations. The NAACP was large, racially integrated, legalistic, and bureaucratic in form; the Student Non-Violent Coordinating Committee (SNCC) was younger and more militant in its tactics and after a while excluded Whites from participation; the Southern Christian Leadership Conference (SCLC) was highly structured, had a religious ideology, and was dominated by male clergy; the Black Muslims and the Black Panthers advocated violent methods to achieve civil rights. The ideologies and methods of these diverse civil rights groups often conflicted, which arguably slowed down the extension of civil rights to African Americans.

No matter what their shape, size, or motive, social movements require sustained activity over a long period (Turner & Killian, 1987). Thus, unlike riots, which are of limited duration, social movements may become permanent fixtures in the political and social environment. Ironically, a social movement whose goal is the large-scale alteration of some aspect of society can, in time, become so large and bureaucratic itself that it becomes part of the establishment it seeks to change. For instance, Sinn Féin was a movement founded in 1905 to end British rule in Ireland. Among its offshoots over the years was the Irish Republican Army, which carried out a bombing and terror campaign in Northern Ireland and England for decades. In recent years, most of the violence has been stopped, and the people of Ireland have won some autonomy. Sinn Féin is now the third-largest political party in Ireland, with its own news organization, a highly structured network of local branches, and representatives in both the Irish Parliament and the European Parliament.

In addition, people who devote their lives to a movement come to depend on it for their own livelihood. Hence, social movements organized for the purposes of enacting social change actually provide structure and order in the lives of their members, acting as sources of opportunities, careers, and rewards (Hewitt, 1988).

Political Opportunity Structure

Social movements also depend on conditions outside their reach. One such condition is the structure of existing political institutions. Political systems are more or less vulnerable and more or less receptive to challenge at different times (McAdam, McCarthy, & Zald, 1988). These ebbs and flows of political opportunities produce cycles of protest and movement activity. When political systems are firm, unyielding, and stable, people have to deal individually with their problems or air their grievances through existing channels. But when a system opens and people realize it is vulnerable—that they can actually make a difference—movements are likely to develop.

Sometimes these opportunities are unintentional and exist quite independently of the actions of movement members. For instance, similar antinuclear movements arose about the same time in the 1970s in (what was then West) Germany and France. The movements had similar ideologies and used similar mobilization techniques. However, the German movement flourished and remains highly influential in national politics today. The French movement was weak and quickly died off. Why were the outcomes of these two movements so different? In West Germany, the government procedure for reviewing nuclear power facilities provided opportunities for those opposed to nuclear power to legally intervene. The procedure in place in France was closed and unresponsive to public sentiment (Nelkin & Pollak, 1981). Similarly, the emergence in the 1970s of the contemporary environmental movement in the United States was possible because government agencies were already sympathetic to environmental concerns (Gale, 1986).

The idea that unintentional political opportunities can encourage social movements for change was dramatically supported by the 1989 prodemocracy movement in the former Soviet Union and Eastern Europe. In the mid-1980s, the Soviet government under Mikhail Gorbachev embarked on a massive program of economic and structural reforms (*perestroika*) as well as a relaxation of constraints on freedom of expression (*glasnost*). The ensuing liberties encouraged open criticism of the political order and created new opportunities for political action (Tarrow, 1994). Protest movements took advantage of these opportunities, leading to the sometimes violent struggles for independence on the part of small, ethnically homogeneous republics that we saw during the 1990s and continue to see today in a few remaining areas. In other words, only when the political structure became less repressive could these monumental changes take place.

Political instability can sometimes spawn less dramatic reform movements. The changing fortunes of a government can create uncertainty among supporters and encourage challengers to try to take advantage of the situation. Consider once more the civil rights movement in the United States in the 1950s and 1960s. During the 1950s, as the first calls for racial equality were being heard, many conservative Southern Democrats defected to the Republican Party, where their segregationist leanings had more support. The ensuing decline of Southern white backing for the Democratic Party, coupled with the movement of African Americans to large cities in the North, where they were more likely to vote, forced the Democrats to seek black support in the presidential election of 1960. The black vote is widely credited with John Kennedy's narrow victory that year (McAdam, 1982). Hence, the Kennedy administration (and later the Johnson administration) felt compelled to campaign for civil rights (Tarrow, 1994). Increased political power, in turn, enhanced the bargaining position of civil rights forces, culminating in two landmark pieces of legislation: the Civil Rights Act of 1964 and the Voting Rights Act of 1965.

At other times, existing political regimes intentionally create or actively support structural opportunities for change. For example, from the beginning, the George W. Bush administration accepted political and financial support from Christian fundamentalist groups and organizations. In return, it made some efforts to support things such as school prayer, the teaching of "intelligent design" in science classes, and funding for faith-based organizations, as well as efforts to limit abortion access, prohibit same-sex marriage, and prevent stem cell research. The success of these initiatives further fortified the growth and development of the religious groups and organizations and cemented their political power on the national scene.

Similarly, the U.S. anti-drunk-driving movement is strong and influential today because it enjoys substantial support from federal, state, and local governments; state and federal highway agencies; and state and local police departments (McCarthy & Wolfson, 1992). When in the 1980s the movement advocated a national drinking age of 21, many state legislatures balked, fearing a backlash from powerful alcohol producers, distributors, and retailers. However, the federal government enacted legislation threatening to withhold significant amounts of federal highway funds from states that didn't establish a drinking age of 21—a strong incentive for states to pass such a law.

Political opportunities provide the institutional framework within which social movements operate. Movements form when ordinary citizens respond to changes in the opportunity structure that lower the costs of involvement and reveal where the authorities are vulnerable. Unlike money and power, these conditions are external to the movement. If political opportunities exist, then even groups with fairly mild grievances or few resources can develop a successful movement (see also Jenkins & Perrow, 1977). In contrast, groups with deep grievances and ample resources—but few political opportunities—may never get their movements off the ground (Tarrow, 1994).

THE SOCIOLOGICAL IMAGINATION REVISITED

In the summer of 1981 with my brand-new bachelor's degree in hand, I had the good fortune to visit Florence, Italy. While there, I made a point of visiting the Galleria dell' Accademia, the museum where one of my favorite works of art, Michelangelo's statue of David, resides. To my eye, it is truly a masterpiece of sculpture, nearly flawless in its detail. I stood there admiring this amazing work of art for close to 2 hours. As I left, I noticed several sculptures that had escaped my attention when I first entered the museum. I soon discovered that they, too, were created by Michelangelo. What made them particularly interesting was that they were all unfinished. Some were obviously near completion, but others looked to me like shapeless blocks of granite. As I looked closer, I could see the actual chisel marks that the great sculptor had made. I imagined the plan Michelangelo had in his head as he worked. I envisioned him toiling to bring form to the heavy stone.

These imperfect slabs of rock showed evidence of human creation in a way that the perfect, finished statue of David never could. At that moment, I saw Michelangelo as a real person who fashioned beauty from formlessness. I began to admire the genius of the creator and not just the creation. I went back to look at David again with a newfound appreciation.

Society isn't nearly as perfect as Michelangelo's David, yet we can still fall into the trap of seeing social structure as a product that exists on its own and not as something that people have collectively chiseled. We sometimes forget that many of the realities of our lives that we take for granted were the result, at some point in history, of the handiwork of individuals. One generation's radical changes become another's common features of everyday life. The fact that you can't be forced to work 70 or 80 hours a week, can't be exposed to dangerous working conditions without your knowledge, and are entitled to a certain number of paid holidays a year is a result of the actions of real people in early labor union movements.

Because we take many of our freedoms, rights, and desires for granted, we may not only overlook the struggles of those who came before us but also downplay the extent to which inequities and injustices existed in the past. For instance, many young women today have never even considered that they are only a generation or two removed from a time when they might have been prohibited from attending the college or pursuing the career of their choice, when they might have been expected to abandon their own dreams and ambitions to provide the support their husbands needed to succeed, or when they might have had to take sole responsibility for household chores and their children's daily care while their husbands focused on work and the outside world. The majority of young women polled in a survey a few years ago indicated that they didn't know that abortion was once illegal (Zernike, 2003). Like most beneficiaries of past movements, young women today simply take their freedoms and opportunities for granted, sometimes even expressing contempt for the women's movement responsible for the rights they so casually enjoy (Stacey, 1991). The irony of social movements, then, is that the more profound and far-reaching their accomplishments, the more likely we are to eventually forget the original inequities that fostered them and the efforts of the individuals who produced them.

Fundamentally, societies remain stable because enough individuals define existing conditions as satisfactory, and societies change because enough individuals define situations that were once tolerable as problems that must be acknowledged and solved. Some influential acts of individuals may at first blush appear rather insignificant. Early in 1960, four black students at North Carolina Agricultural & Technical State University, in Greensboro, engaged in a series of discussions in their dormitory room about the state of the civil rights movement. They came to the conclusion that things weren't progressing quickly enough in the still segregated South and that it was time for action. So they decided to go to the lunch counter at the local Woolworth's store and order coffee and doughnuts. Now that might not sound like much. But in the early-1960s South, public eating facilities that were reserved for Whites were forbidden by law to serve Blacks.

After purchasing some school supplies in another part of the store, the four students sat down at the lunch counter and placed their orders. As anticipated, the reply was "I'm sorry, we don't serve you here" (McCain, 1991, p. 115). They remained seated for 45 minutes, citing the fact that they had been served in another part of the store without any difficulty. They were subjected to the verbal taunts, racial slurs, and even violence of angry Whites in the store.

Their actions attracted the attention of area religious leaders, community activists, and students from other local colleges, both black and white. Despite the abuses they knew awaited them, these four young men returned to Woolworth's a few days later, only this time with more demonstrators. At one point, they and their fellow protestors occupied 63 of the 65 seats available at the lunch counter. This was the first social movement covered by television, too, so word of their actions spread quickly. They received endorsements from religious organizations such as the North Carolina Council of Churches. Within weeks, young African Americans and sympathetic Whites had engaged in similar acts in 9 states and 54 cities in the South as well as several areas in the North, where stores were picketed. After several months of protests, Woolworth's integrated its lunch counter.

Some historians argue that many of the political movements for change that burst onto the scene in the 1960s—including the women's movement, the antiwar movement, and the student free speech movement—could trace their philosophical and tactical roots to this small act by four students (Cluster, 1979). Admittedly, the participants in all these movements might have developed the sit-in as a tactic on their own, even if in 1960 the four students *had* been served coffee and doughnuts at Woolworth's. The point is, though, that the collective movement that arose from the actions of these seemingly insignificant individuals in 1960 had an enormous impact on the massive changes that occurred in the United States over the next 40 years and probably beyond.

We recreate society not only through acts of defiance and organized social movements but also through our daily interactions. The driving theme throughout this book has been that society and its constituent elements are simultaneously human creations and phenomena that exist independently of us, influencing and controlling our private experiences at every turn.

Organizations and institutions exist and thrive because they implicitly or explicitly discourage individuals from challenging the rules and patterns of behavior that characterize them. Imagine what would happen to the system of higher education if you and others like you challenged the authority of the university. You could establish a new order in which students would dictate the content of courses, take control of the classroom, abolish grading or any other evaluative mechanism used for assessing student performance, do away with tuition, and so on. But because you have an education and a career to gain from the institutional structure as it stands, you're not very likely to do something to jeopardize it.

Are we then to believe that we are all leaves in the wind, buffeted here and there by the powerful and permanent forces of a structure that dwarfs us? To some extent, the answer is yes. I subscribe to the sociological imagination and strongly believe that to fully understand our lives, we must acknowledge that processes larger than ourselves determine some of our private experiences. Along the way, though, we sometimes lose sight of our important role as shapers of society. Although society presents itself as largely unchangeable, U.S. culture is based at least in part on the "can-do" attitude. I recall, as a child in 1969, sitting in a darkened living room with my parents on a warm July evening. The only light in the room came from the gray-blue glow of our little black-and-white television. I watched with great amazement the fuzzy, almost imperceptible image of astronaut Neil Armstrong taking the first tentative steps on the moon and stating, "That's one small step for man, one giant leap for mankind." I didn't realize at the time how far beyond the space program the power of that statement stretched. But since then, I have come to realize that people do indeed leave footprints on the world in which they live.

CONCLUSION AND FAREWELL

Sociology is not one of those disciplines that draws from a long-standing body of scientific facts and laws. We do have some useful explanations for why certain important social phenomena happen, and we can make reasonable predictions about future developments. But sociology is not inherently a discipline of answers. It's a discipline of questions, one that provides a unique and useful method for identifying the puzzles of your life and your society.

This discipline scrutinizes, analyzes, and dissects institutional order and its effects on our thinking. It exposes the vulnerable underbelly of both objective and official reality and, by doing so, prods us into taking a closer look at ourselves and our private worlds, not an easy thing to do. Sociology makes life an unsafe place. I don't mean that it makes people violent or dangerous; I mean that it makes perceptions of social stability unstable or at least fair game for analysis. It's not easy to admit that our reality may be a figment of our collective minds and just one of many possible realities. We live under a belief system that tells us that our unchallenged assumptions are simply the way things are.

Sociology is thus a "liberating" perspective (Liazos, 1985). It forces us to look at the social processes that influence our thoughts, perceptions, and actions and helps us see how social change occurs and the impact we can have on others. In doing so, sociology also points out the very limits of liberation. We become aware of the chains that restrict our "movements." But sociology also gives us the tools to break those chains. The sociological imagination gives us a glimpse of the world both as it is and as it could be. To be a sociologically astute observer of the world as it is, you must be able to strip away fallacies and illusions and see the interconnected system underneath. Only then can you take full advantage of your role as a cocreator of society.

I leave you with one final thought: If you now look at your life and the lives of those around you differently, if you now question things heretofore unquestionable, if you now see where you fit in the bigger societal picture, if you now see orderly patterns in areas you previously thought were chaotic, or chaos in areas you previously thought were orderly, then you are well on your way to understanding the meaning—and the promise—of sociology.

CHAPTER HIGHLIGHTS

◆ Whether at the personal, cultural, or institutional level, change is the preeminent feature of modern societies.

◆ Social change is not some massive, impersonal force that arbitrarily disrupts our routine way of life; it is a human creation.

◆ Social change has a variety of causes: adaptation to environmental pressures, internal population changes, technological discoveries and innovations, and the importation of cultural practices from other countries.

◆ Social movements are long-term collective actions that address an issue of concern to large numbers of people.

◆ Societies remain stable because enough people define existing conditions as satisfactory and they change because enough people define the once accepted conditions as problems that must be solved.

KEY TERMS

anomie Condition in which rapid change has disrupted society's ability to adequately regulate and control its members and the old rules that governed people's lives no longer seem to apply

countermovement Collective action designed to prevent or reverse changes sought or accomplished by an earlier social movement

cultural diffusion Process by which beliefs, technology, customs, and other elements of culture spread from one group or society to another

global warming Steady rise in the Earth's average temperature as a result of increasing amounts of carbon dioxide in the atmosphere

ideology Coherent system of beliefs, values, and ideas

postindustrial society Society in which knowledge, the control of information, and service industries are more important elements of the economy than agriculture or manufacturing and production

reform movement Collective action that seeks to change limited aspects of a society but does not seek to alter or replace major social institutions

revolutionary movement Collective action that attempts to overthrow an entire social system and replace it with another

social movement Continuous, large-scale, and organized collective action motivated by the desire to enact, stop, or reverse change in some area of society

Glossary

absolute poverty Inability to afford the minimal requirements for sustaining a reasonably healthy existence

absolutism Approach to defining deviance that rests on the assumption that all human behavior can be considered either inherently good or inherently bad

account Statement designed to explain unanticipated, embarrassing, or unacceptable behavior after the behavior has occurred

achieved status Social position acquired through our own efforts or accomplishments or taken on voluntarily

affirmative action Program designed to seek out members of minority groups for positions from which they had previously been excluded, thereby seeking to overcome institutional racism

age structure Population's balance of old and young people

agents of socialization Various individuals, groups, and organizations who influence the socialization process

aligning action Action taken to restore an identity that has been damaged

analysis of existing data Type of unobtrusive research that relies on data gathered earlier by someone else for some other purpose

anomie Condition in which rapid change has disrupted society's ability to adequately regulate and control its members and the old rules that governed people's lives no longer seem to apply

anticipatory socialization Process through which people acquire the values and orientations found in statuses they will likely enter in the future

ascribed status Social position acquired at birth or taken on involuntarily later in life

authority Possession of some status or quality that compels others to obey one's directives or commands

back stage Area of social interaction away from the view of an audience, where people can rehearse and rehash their behavior

birth cohort Set of people who were born during the same era and who face similar societal circumstances brought about by their shared position in the overall age structure of the population

bureaucracy Large hierarchical organization governed by formal rules and regulations and having clearly specified work tasks

caste system Stratification system based on heredity, with little movement allowed across strata

coalition Subgroup of a triad, formed when two members unite against the third member

cohort effect Phenomenon in which members of a birth cohort tend to experience a particular life course event or rite of passage—puberty, marriage, childbearing, graduation, entry into the workforce, death—at roughly the same time

collectivist culture Culture in which personal accomplishments are less important in the formation of identity than group membership

colonization Process of expanding economic markets by invading and establishing control over a weaker country and its people

colorism Skin color prejudice within an ethnoracial group, most notably between light-skinned and dark-skinned Blacks

competitive individualism Cultural belief that those who succeed in society are those who work the hardest and have the best abilities and that those who suffer don't work hard enough or lack the necessary traits or abilities

conflict perspective Theoretical perspective that views the structure of society as a source of inequality, which always benefits some groups at the expense of other groups

content analysis Form of unobtrusive research that studies the content of recorded messages, such as books, speeches, poems, songs, television shows, websites, and advertisements

cooling out Gently persuading someone who has lost face to accept a less desirable but still reasonable alternative identity

countermovement Collective action designed to prevent or reverse changes sought or accomplished by an earlier social movement

criminalization Official definition of an act of deviance as a crime

cultural diffusion Process by which beliefs, technology, customs, and other elements of culture spread from one group or society to another

cultural relativism Principle that people's beliefs and activities should be interpreted in terms of their own culture

culture Language, values, beliefs, rules, behaviors, and artifacts that characterize a society

demographer Sociologist who studies trends in population characteristics

dependent variable Variable that is assumed to be caused by, or to change as a result of, the independent variable

deterrence theory Theory of deviance positing that people will be prevented from engaging in deviant acts if they judge the costs of such an act to outweigh its benefits

deviance Behavior, ideas, or attributes of an individual or group that some people in society find offensive

disclaimer Assertion designed to forestall any complaints or negative reactions to a behavior or statement that is about to occur

discrimination Unfair treatment of people based on some social characteristic, such as race, ethnicity, or sex

division of labor Specialization of different people or groups in different tasks, characteristic of most bureaucracies

dramaturgy Study of social interaction as theater, in which people ("actors") project images ("play roles") in front of others ("the audience")

dyad Group consisting of two people

embarrassment Spontaneous feeling that is experienced when the identity someone is presenting is suddenly and unexpectedly discredited in front of others

empirical research Research that operates from the ideological position that questions about human behavior can be answered only through controlled, systematic observations in the real world

endogamy Marriage within one's social group

estate system (feudal system) Stratification system in which high-status groups own land and have power based on noble birth

ethnicity The cultural heritage shared by a category of people with common ancestry

ethnocentrism Tendency to judge other cultures using one's own as a standard

eugenics Control of mating to ensure that "defective" genes of troublesome individuals will not be passed on to future generations

exogamy Marriage outside one's social group

experiment Research method designed to elicit some sort of behavior, typically conducted under closely controlled laboratory circumstances

extended family Family unit consisting of the parent-child nuclear family and other relatives, such as grandparents, aunts, uncles, and cousins

false consciousness Situation in which people in the lower classes come to accept a belief system that harms them; the primary means by which powerful classes in society prevent protest and revolution

family Two or more persons, including the householder, who are related by birth, marriage, or adoption and who live together as one household

feminist perspective Theoretical perspective that focuses on gender as the most important source of conflict and inequality in social life

field research Type of social research in which the researcher observes events as they actually occur

folkway Informal norm that is mildly punished when violated

free-rider problem Tendency for people to refrain from contributing to the common good when a resource is available without requiring any personal cost or contribution

front stage Area of social interaction where people perform and work to maintain appropriate impressions

game stage Stage in the development of self during which a child acquires the ability to take the role of a group or community (the generalized other) and conform his or her behavior to broad, societal expectations

gender Psychological, social, and cultural aspects of maleness and femaleness

generalized other Perspective of the larger society and its constituent values and attitudes

global warming Steady rise in the Earth's average temperature as a result of increasing amounts of carbon dioxide in the atmosphere

globalization Process through which people's lives all around the world become economically, politically, environmentally, and culturally interconnected

group Set of people who interact more or less regularly and who are conscious of their identity as a unit

heteronormative culture Culture in which heterosexuality is accepted as the normal, taken-for-granted mode of sexual expression

hierarchy of authority Ranking of people or tasks in a bureaucracy from those at the top, where there is a great deal of power and authority, to those at the bottom, where there is very little power and authority

historical analysis Form of social research that relies on existing historical documents as a source of data

household Living arrangement composed of one or more people who occupy a housing unit

hypothesis Researchable prediction that specifies the relationship between two or more variables

identity Essential aspect of who we are, consisting of our sense of self, gender, race, ethnicity, and religion

ideology Coherent system of beliefs, values, and ideas

impression formation The process by which we define others based on observable cues such as age, ascribed status characteristics such as race and gender, individual attributes such as physical appearance, and verbal and nonverbal expressions

impression management Act of presenting a favorable public image of oneself so that others will form positive judgments

incorrigible proposition Unquestioned cultural belief that cannot be proved wrong no matter what happens to dispute it

independent variable Variable presumed to cause or influence the dependent variable

indicator Measurable event, characteristic, or behavior commonly thought to reflect a particular concept

individualist culture Culture in which personal accomplishments are a more important component of one's self-concept than group membership

individualistic explanation Tendency to attribute people's achievements and failures to their personal qualities

in-groups Those groups we belong to and toward which we feel a sense of loyalty

institutional racism Laws, customs, and practices that systematically reflect and produce racial and ethnic inequalities in a society, whether or not the individuals maintaining these laws, customs, and practices have racist intentions

institutional sexism Subordination of women that is part of the everyday workings of economics, law, politics, and other social institutions

institutionalized norm Pattern of behavior within existing social institutions that is widely accepted in a society

intersexuals Individuals in whom sexual differentiation is either incomplete or ambiguous

labeling theory Theory stating that deviance is the consequence of the application of rules and sanctions to an offender; a deviant is an individual to whom the identity "deviant" has been successfully applied

latent function Unintended, unrecognized consequences of activities that help some part of the social system

looking-glass self Sense of who we are that is defined by incorporating the reflected appraisals of others

macrolevel Way of examining human life that focuses on the broad social forces and structural features of society that exist above the level of individual people

manifest function Intended, obvious consequences of activities designed to help some part of the social system

material culture Artifacts of a society that represent adaptations to the social and physical environment

matriarchy Female-dominated society, which gives higher prestige and value to women than to men

means of production Land, commercial enterprises, factories, and wealth, which form the economic basis of class societies

medicalization Definition of behavior as a medical problem, mandating the medical profession to provide some kind of treatment for it

microlevel Way of examining human life that focuses on the immediate, everyday experiences of individuals

middle class In a society stratified by social class, a group of people who have an intermediate level of wealth, income, and prestige, such as managers, supervisors, executives, small business owners, and professionals

migration Movement of populations from one geographic area to another

monogamy The practice of being married to only one person at a time

more Highly codified, formal, systematized norm that brings severe punishment when violated

multinational corporation Company that has manufacturing, production, and marketing divisions in multiple countries

near-poor Individuals or families whose earnings are between 100% and 125% of the poverty line (see also **working poor**)

neolocal residence Living arrangement in which a married couple sets up residence separate from either spouse's family

nonmaterial culture Knowledge, beliefs, customs, values, morals, and symbols that are shared by members of a society and that distinguish the society from others

nonparticipant observation Form of field research in which the researcher observes people without directly interacting with them and without letting them know that they are being observed

norm Culturally defined standard or rule of conduct

nuclear family Family unit consisting of at least one parent and one child

objectification Practice of treating people as objects

oligarchy System of authority in which many people are ruled by a privileged few

organization Large, complex network of positions created for a specific purpose and characterized by a hierarchical division of labor

out-groups The groups we don't belong to and toward which we feel a certain amount of antagonism

panethnic labels General terms applied to diverse subgroups that are assumed to have something in common

participant observation Form of field research in which the researcher interacts with subjects, sometimes hiding his or her identity

patriarchy Male-dominated society, in which cultural beliefs and values give higher prestige and value to men than to women

pay equity Principle that women and men who perform jobs that are of equal value to society and that require equal training ought to be paid equally

period effect Phenomenon in which a historical event or major social trend contributes to the unique shape and outlook of a birth cohort

personal racism Individual expression of racist attitudes or behaviors

play stage Stage in the development of self during which a child develops the ability to take a role but only from the perspective of one person at a time

polygamy Marriage of one person to more than one spouse at the same time

poor In a society stratified by social class, a group of people who work for minimum wage or are chronically unemployed

postindustrial society Society in which knowledge, the control of information, and service industries are more important elements of the economy than agriculture or manufacturing and production

poverty line Amount of yearly income a family requires to meet its basic needs, according to the federal government

poverty rate Percentage of people whose income falls below the poverty line

power Ability to affect decisions in ways that benefit a person or protect his or her interests

prejudice Rigidly held, unfavorable attitudes, beliefs, and feelings about members of a different group, based on a social characteristic such as race, ethnicity, or gender

prestige Respect and honor given to some people in society

primary group Collection of individuals who are together over a relatively long period, whose members have direct contact with and feel emotional attachment to one another

probabilistic Capable of identifying only those forces that have a high likelihood, but not a certainty, of influencing human action

qualitative research Sociological research based on nonnumerical information (text, written words, phrases, symbols, observations) that describes people, actions, or events in social life

quantitative research Sociological research based on the collection of numerical data that uses precise statistical analysis

quiet racism Form of racism expressed subtly and indirectly through feelings of discomfort, uneasiness, and fear, which motivate avoidance rather than blatant discrimination

race Category of people labeled and treated as similar because of some allegedly common biological traits, such as skin color, texture of hair, and shape of eyes

racial transparency Tendency for the race of a society's majority to be so obvious, normative, and unremarkable that it becomes, for all intents and purposes, invisible

racism Belief that humans are subdivided into distinct groups that are different in their social behavior and innate capacities and that can be ranked as superior or inferior

reactivity A problem associated with certain forms of research in which the very act of intruding into people's lives may influence the phenomenon being studied

reflexive behavior Behavior in which the person initiating an action is the same as the person toward whom the action is directed

reform movement Collective action that seeks to change limited aspects of a society but does not seek to alter or replace major social institutions

relative poverty Individuals' economic position compared with the living standards of the majority in the society

relativism Approach to defining deviance that rests on the assumption that deviance is socially created by collective human judgments and ideas

representative Typical of the whole population being studied

resocialization Process of learning new values, norms, and expectations when an adult leaves an old role and enters a new one

revolutionary movement Collective action that attempts to overthrow an entire social system and replace it with another

role conflict Frustration people feel when the demands of one role they are expected to fulfill clash with the demands of another role

role Set of expectations—rights, obligations, behaviors, duties—associated with a particular status

role strain Situations in which people lack the necessary resources to fulfill the demands of a particular role

role taking Ability to see oneself from the perspective of others and to use that perspective in formulating one's own behavior

sample Subgroup chosen for a study because its characteristics approximate those of the entire population

sanction Social response that punishes or otherwise discourages violations of a social norm

secondary group Relatively impersonal collection of individuals that is established to perform a specific task

self Unique set of traits, behaviors, and attitudes that distinguishes one person from the next; the active source and passive object of behavior

self-fulfilling prophecy Assumption or prediction that in itself causes the expected event to occur, thus seeming to confirm the prophecy's accuracy

sex Biological maleness or femaleness

sexism System of beliefs that asserts the inferiority of one sex and justifies gender-based inequality

sexual dichotomy Belief that two biological sex categories, male and female, are permanent, universal, exhaustive, and mutually exclusive

sick role Set of norms governing how one is supposed to behave and what one is entitled to when sick

slavery Economic form of inequality in which some people are legally the property of others

social class Group of people who share a similar economic position in a society, based on their wealth and income

social construction of reality Process through which the members of a society discover, make known, reaffirm, and alter a collective version of facts, knowledge, and "truth"

social dilemma Potential for a society's long-term ruin because of individuals' tendency to pursue their own short-term interests

social institution Stable set of roles, statuses, groups, and organizations—such as the institutions of education, family, politics, religion, health care, or the economy—that provides a foundation for behavior in some major area of social life

social mobility Movement of people or groups from one class to another

social movement Continuous, large-scale, and organized collective action motivated by the desire to enact, stop, or reverse change in some area of society

social structure Framework of society—social institutions, organizations, groups, statuses and roles, cultural beliefs, and institutionalized norms—which adds order and predictability to our private lives

socialization Process through which one learns how to act according to the rules and expectations of a particular culture

society Population of people living in the same geographic area who share a culture and a common identity and whose members fall under the same political authority

socioeconomic status Prestige, honor, respect, and lifestyle associated with different positions or groups in society

sociological imagination Ability to see the impact of social forces on our private lives

sociology Systematic study of human societies

spurious relationship A false association between two variables that is actually due to the effect of some third variable

status Any named social position that people can occupy

stereotype Overgeneralized belief that a certain trait, behavior, or attitude characterizes all members of some identifiable group

stigma Deeply discrediting characteristic that is viewed as an obstacle to competent or morally trustworthy behavior

stratification Ranking system for groups of people that perpetuates unequal rewards and life chances in society

structural-functionalist perspective Theoretical perspective that posits that social institutions are structured to maintain stability and order in society

subculture Values, behaviors, and artifacts of a group that distinguish its members from the larger culture

survey Form of social research in which the researcher asks subjects a series of questions, either verbally, online, or on paper

symbol Something used to represent or stand for something else

symbolic interactionism Theoretical perspective that explains society and social structure through an examination of the *micro*level, personal, day-to-day exchanges of people as individuals, pairs, or groups

theory Set of statements or proposition that seeks to explain or predict a particular aspect of social life

total institution Place where individuals are cut off from the wider society for an appreciable period and where together they lead an enclosed, formally administered life

tragedy of the commons Situation in which people acting individually and in their own interest use up commonly available (but limited) resources, creating disaster for the entire community

transsexuals People who identify with a different sex and sometimes undergo hormone treatment and surgery to change their sex

triad Group consisting of three people

unobtrusive research Research technique in which the researcher, without direct contact with the subjects, examines the evidence of social behavior that people create or leave behind

upper class In a society stratified by social class, a group of people who have high income and prestige and who own vast amounts of property and other forms of wealth, such as owners of large corporations, top financiers, rich celebrities and politicians, and members of prestigious families

urbanization Process by which people leave rural areas and begin to concentrate in large cities

value Standard of judgment by which people decide on desirable goals and outcomes

variable Any characteristic, attitude, behavior, or event that can take on two or more values or attributes

working class In a society stratified by social class, a group of people who have a low level of wealth, income, and prestige, such as industrial and factory workers, office workers, clerks, and farm and manual laborers

working poor Employed people who consistently earn wages but do not make enough to survive (see also **near-poor**)

References

Abelson, R., & Freudenheim, M. (2008, May 4). Even the insured feel the strain of health costs. *New York Times.*

Acitelli, L. (1988). When spouses talk to each other about their relationship. *Journal of Social and Personal Relationships, 5,* 185–199.

Acker, J. (1992). From sex roles to gendered institutions. *Contemporary Sociology, 21,* 565–569.

A continuing abomination. (2008, November 1). *The Economist.*

ActionAid. (2009). *Hate crimes: The rise of "corrective" rape in South Africa.* Retrieved June 3, 2009, from www.actionaid.org/assets/pdf/CorrectiveRapeRep_final.pdf

Aday, D. P. (1990). *Social control at the margins.* Belmont, CA: Wadsworth.

Adler, P. (1985). *Wheeling and dealing.* New York: Columbia University Press.

Administration for Children and Families. (2009). *Child maltreatment 2007.* Washington, DC: U.S. Department of Health and Human Services. Retrieved May 6, 2009, from www.acf.hhs.gov/programs/cb/pubs/cm07/cm07.pdf

AFL-CIO. (2009). *2009 executive pay watch.* Retrieved May 27, 2009, from www.aflcio.org/corporatewatch/paywatch/

Ainlay, S. C., Becker, G., & Coleman, L. M. (1986). *The dilemma of difference.* New York: Plenum Press.

AIS Health. (2004). *Medco says pediatric drug costs soar, driven by ADHD, depression.* Retrieved June 3, 2005, from www.aishealth.com/DrugCosts/DCMRMedcoPediatricCosts.html

Alan Guttmacher Institute. (2008). *Facts on induced abortion in the United States.* Retrieved June 10, 2009, from www.guttmacher.org/pubs/fb_induced_abortion.html

Allport, G. (1954). *The nature of prejudice.* Reading, MA: Addison-Wesley.

Alter, J. (2005, February 7). The end of "pay to praise." *Newsweek.*

Alter, J. (2007, May 7). Trials of the truth seekers. *Newsweek.*

Altman, D. (2003, April 26). Does a dollar a day keep poverty away? *New York Times.*

Amato, P. R. (2000). The consequences of divorce for adults and children. *Journal of Marriage and the Family, 62,* 126–288.

Amato, P. R., & Sobolewski, J. M. (2001). The effects of divorce and marital discord on adult children's psychological well-being. *American Sociological Review, 66,* 900–921.

American Association of University Women. (2001). *Hostile hallways: Teasing and sexual harassment in school.* Retrieved July 31, 2004, from www.aauw.org/research/girls_education/hostile.cfm

American Lung Association. (2008). *State of tobacco control: 2008.* Retrieved January 14, 2009, from www.stateoftobaccocontrol.org/2008/ALA_SOTC_08.pdf

American Psychiatric Association. (2000). *Diagnostic and statistical manual of mental disorders IV-TR.* Washington, DC: Author.

American Society of Plastic Surgeons. (2009). *2000/2007/2008 National plastic surgery statistics: Cosmetic and reconstructive procedure trends.* Retrieved May 15, 2009, from www.plasticsurgery.org/media/statistics.html

American Sociological Association. (2002). *Statement of the American Sociological Association on the importance of collecting data and doing social scientific research on race.* Retrieved June 18, 2003, from www.asanet.org/governance/racestmt.htm

American Sociological Association. (2005, July). *Race, ethnicity, and the health of Americans* (ASA Series on How Race and Ethnicity Matter). Washington, DC: Author.

Ammerman, N. T. (1987). *Bible believers: Fundamentalists in the modern world.* New Brunswick, NJ: Rutgers University Press.

Amnesty International. (2004). *Rape as a tool of war: A fact sheet.* Retrieved September 4, 2009, from www.amnestyusa.org/women/pdf/rapeinwartime.pdf

Anderson, D. J. (2003). The impact on subsequent violence of returning to an abusive partner. *Journal of Comparative Family Studies, 34,* 93–112.

Andreescu, T., Gallian, J. A., Kane, J. M., & Mertz, J. E. (2008). Cross-cultural analysis of students with exceptional talent in mathematical problem solving. *Notices of the American Mathematical Society, 55,* 1248–1260.

Andrews, E. L. (2007, January 8). Bush tax cuts offer most for very rich, study finds. *New York Times.*

Andriote, J. M. (2005, March). *HIV/AIDS and African Americans: A "state of emergency"* (PRB Report). Washington, DC: Population Reference Bureau. Retrieved March 16, 2005, from www.prb.org

Ang, A. (2004, December 13). Pageant is paean to plastic surgery. *Indianapolis Star.*

Angier, N. (1997a, May 13). New debate over surgery on genitals. *New York Times.*

Angier, N. (1997b, March 14). Sexual identity not pliable after all, report says. *New York Times.*

Angier, N., & Chang, K. (2005, January 24). Gray matter and the sexes: Still a scientific gray area. *New York Times.*

Ansell, A. E. (2000). The new face of race: The metamorphosis of racism in the post-civil rights era United States. In P. Kivisto & G. Rundblad (Eds.), *Multiculturalism in the United States.* Thousand Oaks, CA: Pine Forge Press.

Antill, J. K., Goodnow, J. J., Russell, G., & Cotton, S. (1996). The influence of parents and family context on children's involvement in household tasks. *Sex Roles, 34,* 215–236.

Anti-Muslim incidents increase. (2004, May 4). *New York Times.*

Apollo Alliance. (2009). *The New Apollo Program: Clean energy, good jobs.* Retrieved June 9, 2009, from www.apolloalliance.org/category/new-appolo-program/the-full-report/

Appiah, K. A. (2007, March 18). A slow emancipation. *New York Times Magazine.*

Arendell, T. (1995). *Fathers and divorce.* Thousand Oaks, CA: Sage.

Ariès, P. (1962). *Centuries of childhood: A social history of family life.* New York: Vintage Books.

Associated Press. (2007). *Deployed troops fight for lost custody of kids.* Retrieved June 14, 2007, from www.msnbc.msn.com/id/18506417

Astbury, J. (1996). *Crazy for you: The making of women's madness.* Melbourne, Victoria, Australia: Oxford University Press.

Babbie, E. (1986). *Observing ourselves: Essays in social research.* Belmont, CA: Wadsworth.

Babbie, E. (1992). *The practice of social research.* Belmont, CA: Wadsworth.

Babbie, E. (2007). *The practice of social research* (11th ed.). Belmont, CA: Wadsworth.

Baca Zinn, M., & Eitzen, D. S. (1996). *Diversity in families* (4th ed.). New York: HarperCollins.

Bagdikian, B. H. (1991). Missing from the news. In J. H. Skolnick & E. Currie (Eds.), *Crisis in American institutions.* New York: HarperCollins.

Bagdikian, B. H. (2000). *The media monopoly* (6th ed.). Boston: Beacon Press.

Bai, M. (2009, May 24). Queer developments. *New York Times Magazine.*

Bailey, B. L. (1988). *From front porch to back seat: Courtship in 20th century America.* Baltimore: Johns Hopkins University Press.

Bailey, C. A. (1993). Equality with difference: On androcentrism and menstruation. *Teaching Sociology, 21,* 121–129.

Bailey, J. (2007, March 18). Airlines learn to fly on a wing and an apology. *New York Times.*

Bailey, W. C. (1990). Murder, capital punishment, and television: Execution publicity and homicide rates. *American Sociological Review, 55,* 628–633.

Bainbridge, W. L. (2005, February 5). Longer school year would benefit students. *Columbus Dispatch.*

Bajaj, V., & Fessenden, F. (2007, November 4). What's behind the race gap? *New York Times.*

Bajaj, V., & Nixon, R. (2006, February 22). For minorities, signs of trouble in foreclosures. *New York Times.*

Ballard, C. (1987). A humanist sociology approach to teaching social research. *Teaching Sociology, 15,* 7–14.

Balter, M. (2006). The baby deficit. *Science, 312,* 1894–1897.

Bandura, A., & Walters, R. H. (1963). *Social learning and personality development.* New York: Holt, Rinehart & Winston.

Banerjee, N. (2005, January 23). Aided by elders and Web, Iraq veterans turn critics. *New York Times.*

Banks, J., Marmot, M., Oldfield, Z., & Smith, J. P. (2006). Disease and disadvantage in the United States and in England. *Journal of the American Medical Association, 295,* 2037–2045.

Baptists seek to "convert" Mormons. (2000, January 22). *New York Times.*

Barber, B. (1992, March). Jihad vs. McWorld. *Atlantic Monthly,* pp. 53–65.

The Barna Group. (2007). *Barna's annual tracking study shows Americans stay spiritually active, but biblical views wane.* Retrieved September 4, 2009, from www.barna.org/barna-update/article/18-congregations/103-barnas-annual-tracking-study-shows-americans-stay-spiritually-active-but-biblical-views-wane

Barnard, A. (2009, January 9). In attacks on Latinos, seeing a pattern of hate. *New York Times.*

Baron-Cohen, S. (2003). *The essential difference: Men, women, and the extreme male brain.* London: Allen Lane.

Barrionuevo, A. (2007, June 16). Globalization in every loaf. *New York Times.*

Barro, R. J., & McCleary, R. M. (2003). Religion and economic growth across countries. *American Sociological Review, 68,* 760–781.

Barry, E. (2009, April 8). Protests in Moldova explode, with a call to arms on Twitter. *New York Times.*

Barstow, D. (2003, December 22). U.S. rarely seeks charges for deaths in workplace. *New York Times.*

Barstow, D., & Stein, R. (2005, March 13). Is it news or public relations? Under Bush, lines are blurry. *New York Times.*

Baxter, J. (1997). Gender equality and participation in housework: A cross-national perspective. *Journal of Comparative Family Studies, 28,* 220–247.

Bazelon, E. (2008, July 20). The next kind of integration. *New York Times Magazine.*

Beaman, A. L., Klentz, B., Diener, E., & Svanum, S. (1979). Objective self-awareness and transgression in children: A field study. *Journal of Personality and Social Psychology, 37,* 1835–1846.

Becker, H. (1963). *The outsiders.* New York: Free Press.

Becker, H. & Geer, B. (1958). The fate of idealism in medical school. *American Sociological Review, 23,* 50–56.

Belkin, L. (2003, May 11). Why is Jonathan Simms still alive? *New York Times Magazine.*

Bell, S. T., Kuriloff, P. J., & Lottes, I. (1994). Understanding attributions of blame in stranger rape and date rape situations: An examination of gender, race, identification, and students' social perceptions of rape victims. *Journal of Applied Social Psychology, 24,* 1719–1734.

Bellah, R., Madsen, R., Sullivan, W. M., Swidler, A., & Tipton, S. M. (1985). *Habits of the heart.* New York: Harper & Row.

Belluck, P. (2001, January 20). A nation's voices: Concern and solace, resentment and redemption. *New York Times.*

Belluck, P. (2002, January 15). Doctors' new practices offer deluxe service for deluxe fee. *New York Times.*

Belluck, P. (2004, November 14). To avoid divorce, move to Massachusetts. *New York Times.*

Bennett, G., Henson, R. K., & Zhang, J. (2003). Generation Y's perceptions of the action sports industry segment. *Journal of Sports Management, 17,* 95–115.

Bennett, J. (2008, February 25). Say "cheese" and now say "airbrush." *Newsweek.*

Benokraitis, N. V., & Feagin, J. R. (1993). Sex discrimination: Subtle and covert. In J. Henslin (Ed.), *Down-to-earth sociology* (7th ed.). New York: Free Press.

Ben-Yehuda, N. (1990). *The politics and morality of deviance.* Albany: State University of New York Press.

Berenson, A. (2005, May 31). Despite vow, drug makers still withhold data. *New York Times.*

Berenson, A. (2008, December 8). Weak patchwork of oversight lets bad hospitals stay open. *New York Times.*

Berg, B. (1992). The guilt that drives working mothers crazy. In J. Henslin (Ed.), *Marriage and family in a changing society.* New York: Free Press.

Berger, D. L., & Williams, J. E. (1991). Sex stereotypes in the United States revisited: 1972–1988. *Sex Roles, 24,* 413–423.

Berger, J. (2004, October 24). Pressure to live by an outmoded tradition is still felt among Indian immigrants. *New York Times.*

Berger, P. L. (1963). *Invitation to sociology.* Garden City, NY: Anchor Books.

Berger, P. L., & Kellner, H. (1964). Marriage and the construction of reality: An exercise in the micro-sociology of knowledge. *Diogenes, 46,* 1–23.

Berger, P. L., & Luckmann, T. (1966). *The social construction of reality.* Garden City, NY: Anchor Books.

Bernard, J. (1972). *The future of marriage.* New York: Bantam Books.

Bernard, J. (1981). The good provider role: Its rise and fall. *American Psychologist, 36,* 1–12.

Berndt, T. J., & Heller, K. A. (1986). Gender stereotypes and social inferences. *Journal of Social and Personality Psychology, 50,* 889–898.

Bernstein, R. (2003, June 29). Aging Europe finds its pension is running out. *New York Times.*

Berthelsen, C. (1999, July 28). Suit says advanced-placement classes show bias. *New York Times.*

Bhattacharya, J., DeLeire, T., Haider, S., & Currie, J. (2003). Heat or eat? Cold-weather shocks and nutrition in poor American families. *American Journal of Public Health, 93,* 1149–1154.

Bianchi, S. M., Robinson, J. P., & Milkie, M. A. (2006). *Changing rhythms of American family life.* New York: Russell Sage Foundation.

Bibbins-Domingo, K. (2009). Racial differences in incident heart failure among young adults. *New England Journal of Medicine, 360,* 1179–1190.

Billings, A. C., Angelini, J. R., & Eastman, S. T. (2005). Diverging discourses: Gender differences in televised golf announcing. *Mass Communication and Society, 8,* 155–171.

Billitteri, T. J. (2007). Curbing CEO pay. *CQ Researcher, 17,* 217–239.

Birenbaum, A., & Sagarin, E. (1976). *Norms and human behavior.* New York: Praeger.

Black Health Care.com. (2003). *Sickle-cell anemia: Description.* Retrieved June 17, 2003, from www.blackhealthcare.com/BHC/SickleCell/Description.asp

Blanton, K. (2007, March 16). A "smoking gun" on race, subprime loans. *Boston Globe.*

Blau, P. M., & Meyer, M. W. (1987). The concept of bureaucracy. In R. T. Schaeffer & R. P. Lamm (Eds.), *Introducing sociology.* New York: McGraw-Hill.

Blauner, R. (1992). The ambiguities of racial change. In M. L. Anderson & P. H. Collins (Eds.), *Race, class and gender: An anthology.* Belmont, CA: Wadsworth.

Blow, C. M. (2008, August 9). Racism and the race. *New York Times.*

Blow, C. M. (2009, February 21). A nation of cowards? *New York Times.*

Blumstein, E., & Schwartz, P. (1983). *American couples.* New York: Morrow.

Bocian, D. G., Ernst, K. S., & Li, W. (2006). *Unfair lending: The effect of race and ethnicity on the price of subprime mortgages.* Durham, NC: Center for Responsible Lending. Retrieved October 10, 2007, from www.responsiblelending.org

Bonilla-Silva, E. (2003). *Racism without racists: Color-blind racism and the persistence of racial inequality in the United States.* Lanham, MD: Rowman & Littlefield.

Bonilla-Silva, E. (2008). "New racism," color-blind racism, and the future of whiteness in America. In S. J. Ferguson (Ed.), *Mapping the social landscape.* New York: McGraw-Hill.

Bonner, R., & Fessenden, F. (2000, September 22). States with no death penalty share lower homicide rates. *New York Times.*

Bonner, R., & Lacey, M. (2000, September 12). Pervasive disparities found in the federal death penalty. *New York Times.*

Booth, A., Johnson, D. R., Branaman, A., & Sica, A. (1995). Belief and behavior: Does religion matter in today's marriage? *Journal of Marriage and the Family, 57,* 661–671.

Boshara, R. (2002, September 29). Poverty is more than a matter of income. *New York Times.*

Bosman, J. (2009, February 20). Newly poor swell lines at nation's food banks. *New York Times.*

Bradsher, K. (1993, July 22). Mark Twain would understand the water crisis that's corrupting Iowans. *New York Times.*

Bragg, R. (1998, January 4). Proposal to ban sofas from porches creates culture clash. *Indianapolis Star.*

Bramlett, M. D., & Mosher, W. D. (2002). *Cohabitation, marriage, divorce, and remarriage in the United States.* Hyattsville, MD: National Center for Health Statistics. Retrieved August 11, 2006, from www.cdc.gov/nchs/data/series/sr_23/sr23_022.pdf

Braun, D. (1997). *The rich get richer: The rise of income inequality in the United States and the world.* Chicago: Nelson-Hall.

Breaking the rules of engagement. (2002, July/August). *American Demographics.*

Breslau, K. (2007, December 25). Majora Carter. *Newsweek.*

Brines, J. (1994). Economic dependency, gender and the division of labor at home. *American Journal of Sociology, 100,* 652–688.

Brizendine, L. (2006). *The female brain.* New York: Broadway.

Bronner, E. (1998a, January 10). Inventing the notion of race. *New York Times.*

Bronner, E. (1998b, April 1). U of California reports big drop in black admission. *New York Times.*

Brookings Institution. (2006). *From poverty, opportunity: Putting the market to work for lower income families.* Retrieved July 18, 2006, from www.brookings.edu/metro/pubs/20060718_PovOp.pdf

Broverman, I., Vogel, S., Broverman, D., Clarkson, F., & Rosenkrantz, P. (1972). Sex role stereotypes: A current appraisal. *Journal of Social Issues, 28,* 59–78.

Brown, P. (1998). Biology and the social construction of the "race" concept. In J. Ferrante & P. Brown (Eds.), *The social construction of race and ethnicity in the United States.* New York: Longman.

Brown, R. (1986). *Social psychology.* New York: Free Press.

Brown, R. (2009, January 23). Nashville won't make English official language. *New York Times.*

Brownmiller, S. (1975). *Against our will: Men, women, and rape.* New York: Simon & Schuster.

Brutus, D. (1999). Africa 2000 in the new global context. In T. J. Gallagher (Ed.), *Perspectives: Introductory sociology.* St. Paul, MN: Coursewise.

Bullard, R. D. (1993). Anatomy of environmental racism and the environmental justice movement. In R. D. Bullard (Ed.), *Confronting environmental racism.* Boston: South End Press.

Bullard, R. D. (2001). Decision making. In L. Westra & B. E. Lawson (Eds.), *Faces of environmental racism: Confronting issues of global justice.* Lanham, MD: Rowman & Littlefield.

Bullington, B. (1993). All about Eve: The many faces of United States drug policy. In F. Pearce & M. Woodiwiss (Eds.), *Global crime connections.* Toronto, Ontario, Canada: University of Toronto Press.

Burke, T. W., & Owen, S. S. (2006, January-February). Same-sex domestic violence: Is anyone listening? *Gay & Lesbian Review, 8*(1), 6–7.

Burning through oil, or conserving it. (2008, April 20). *New York Times.*

Butler, R. (1989). A generation at risk: When the baby boomers reach Golden Pond. In W. Feigelman (Ed.), *Sociology full circle.* New York: Holt, Rinehart & Winston.

Butterfield, F. (1999, January 10). Eliminating parole boards isn't a cure-all, experts say. *New York Times.*

Butterfield, F. (2000, April 26). Racial disparities seen as pervasive in juvenile justice. *New York Times.*

Cameron, P. (2003). Domestic violence among homosexual partners. *Psychological Reports, 93,* 410–416.

Campbell, A. (1987). Self-definition by rejection: The case of gang girls. *Social Problems, 34,* 451–466.

Campbell, A., Converse, P. E., & Rodgers, W. L. (1976). *The quality of American life.* New York: Russell Sage Foundation.

Campbell, M. E., & Troyer, L. (2007). The implications of racial misclassification by observers. *American Sociological Review, 72,* 750–765.

Campo-Flores, A. (2008). A gay marriage surge. *Newsweek Online.* Retrieved May 18, 2009, from www.newsweek.com/id/172399/output/print

Canadian Broadcasting Corporation. (2003). *What border? The Americanization of Canada.* Retrieved May 27, 2003, from www.tv.cbc.ca/national/pgminfo/border/culture.html

Caplan, P. J. (1995). *They say you're crazy: How the world's most powerful psychiatrists decide who's normal.* Reading, MA: Addison-Wesley.

Carey, B. (2005a, June 7). Most will be mentally ill at some point, study says. *New York Times.*

Carey, B. (2005b, June 21). Some politics may be etched in genes. *New York Times.*

Carey, B. (2007, January 14). Can Johnny come out and (be taught to) play? *New York Times.*

Carey, B. (2008, April 1). April fool! The purpose of pranks. *New York Times.*

Carey, B. (2009, April 7). When all you have left is your pride. *New York Times.*

Carlson, E. (2009). 20th-century U.S. generations. *Population Bulletin, 64,* 1–17.

Carmichael, M. (2008, December 1). Katrina kids: Sickest ever. *Newsweek.*

Carnevale, A. P., & Rose, S. J. (2003). *Socioeconomic status, race/ethnicity, and selective college admissions.* Washington, DC: Century Foundation. Retrieved September 4, 2009, from www.tcf.org/Publications/Education/carnevale_rose.pdf

Carter, H., & Glick, P. C. (1976). *Marriage and divorce: A social and economic study.* Cambridge, MA: Harvard University Press.

Cast, A. D. (2004). Role taking and interaction. *Social Psychology Quarterly, 67,* 296–309.

Catalano, S. (2006). *Intimate partner violence in the United States.* Washington, DC: Bureau of Justice Statistics. Retrieved June 18, 2010, from http://www.ojp.usdoj.gov/content/intimate/ipv.cfm

Center for Public Integrity. (2008). *Iraq: The war card.* Retrieved May 3, 2009, from www.publicintegrity.org/projects/entry/276

Center for Responsive Politics. (2008). *Personal finances: Overview.* Retrieved May 28, 2009, from www.opensecrets.org/pfds/index.php

Centers for Disease Control and Prevention. (1999). Ten great public health achievements in the United States, 1900–1999. *Mortality and Morbidity Weekly Report, 48,* 241–243.

Centers for Disease Control and Prevention. (2006). *Intimate partner violence: Fact sheet.* Retrieved August 4, 2006, from www.cdc.gov/ncipc/factsheets/ipvfacts.htm

Centers for Disease Control and Prevention. (2008a). Smoking-attributable mortality, years of potential life lost, and productivity losses—United States 2000–2004. *Morbidity and Mortality Weekly Report, 57,* 1226–1228.

Centers for Disease Control and Prevention. (2008b). Youth risk behavior surveillance: United States, 2007. Surveillance Summaries. *Morbidity and Mortality Weekly Report, 48* (No. SS-4).

Chachere, V. (2005, June 3). Young killers a quandary for states. *Indianapolis Star.*

Chafetz, J. S. (1978). *A primer on the construction and testing of theories in sociology.* Itasca, IL: Peacock.

Chafetz, J. S., & Dworkin, A. G. (1987). In the face of threat: Organized anti-feminism in comparative perspective. *Gender & Society, 1,* 33–60.

Chambliss, W. (1964). A sociological analysis of the law of vagrancy. *Social Problems, 12,* 66–77.

Charon, J. (1992). *Ten questions: A sociological perspective.* Belmont, CA: Wadsworth.

Charon, J. (1998). *Symbolic interactionism.* Upper Saddle River, NJ: Prentice Hall.

Chase-Dunn, C., & Rubinson, R. (1977). Toward a structural perspective on the world system. *Politics and Society, 7,* 453–476.

Chaudhry, L. (2006, April 7). Acting your race. *In These Times.*

Chen, E., Matthews, K. A., & Boyce, W. T. (2002). Socioeconomic differences in children's health: How and why do these relationships change with age? *Psychological Bulletin, 128,* 295–329.

Cherlin, A. (1992). *Marriage, divorce, remarriage.* Cambridge, MA: Harvard University Press.

Cherlin, A., Furstenberg, F. F., Chase-Landale, P. L., Kiernan, K. E., Robins, P. K., Morrison, D. R., & Teitler, J. O. (1991). Longitudinal studies of effects of divorce on children in Great Britain and the United States. *Science, 252,* 1386–1389.

Cherry, R. (1989). *Discrimination: Its economic impact on Blacks, women and Jews.* Lexington, MA: Lexington Books.

China changes death penalty law. (2006, October 31). *New York Times.*

Ching, C. L., & Burke, S. (1999). An assessment of college students' attitudes and empathy toward rape. *College Student Journal, 33,* 573–584.

Christakis, N. A., & Fowler, J. H. (2007). The spread of obesity in a large social network over 32 years. *New England Journal of Medicine, 357,* 370–379.

Ciancanelli, P., & Berch, B. (1987). Gender and the GNP. In B. B. Hess & M. M. Ferree (Eds.), *Analyzing gender: A handbook of social science research.* Newbury Park, CA: Sage.

Clark, C. (1997). *Misery and company: Sympathy in everyday life.* Chicago: University of Chicago Press.

Clausen, J. A. (1986). *The life course: A sociological perspective.* Englewood Cliffs, NJ: Prentice Hall.

Clear Channel Communications. (2003). *Clear Channel Radio.* Retrieved July 3, 2003, from www.clearchannel.com/radio

Clemmitt, M. (2009). Extreme sports. *CQ Researcher, 19,* 297–320.

Clinard, M. B., & Meier, R. F. (1979). *Sociology of deviant behavior.* New York: Holt, Rinehart & Winston.

Cluster, D. (1979). *They should have served that cup of coffee.* Boston: South End Press.

CNN.com. (2009). *Most blacks say MLK's vision fulfilled, poll finds.* Retrieved August 13, 2009, from http://edition.cnn.com/2009/POLITICS/01/19/king.poll/

Coe, R. M. (1978). *Sociology of medicine.* New York: McGraw-Hill.

Cohen, A. K. (1955). *Delinquent boys: The culture of the gang.* New York: Free Press.

Cohen, A. K. (1966). *Deviance and control.* Englewood Cliffs, NJ: Prentice Hall.

Cohen, F. G. (1986). *Treaties on trial: The continuing controversy over Northwest Indian fishing rights.* Seattle: University of Washington Press.

Cohen, J., & Agiesta, J. (2008, June 22). 3 in 10 Americans admit to race bias. *Washington Post.*

Cohen, N. (2006, August 6). So English is taking over the globe. So what? *New York Times.*

Cohen, P. (2009, March 7). Doctoral candidates anticipate hard times. *New York Times.*

Cohen, P. N., & Huffman, M. L. (2003). Occupational segregation and the devaluation of women's work across U.S. labor markets. *Social Forces, 81,* 881–908.

College Board. (1998). *SAT and gender differences* (Research Summary RS-04). Retrieved August 13, 2009, from http://professionals.collegeboard.com/profdownload/pdf/rs04_3960.pdf

Collegiate Employment Research Institute. (2009). *Recruiting trends 2008–2009: Executive summary.* Retrieved June 18, 2010, from www.ceri.msu.edu/wp-content/uploads/2010/06/rt8-9final.pdf

Collins, R. (1971). Functional and conflict theories of educational stratification. *American Sociological Review, 36,* 1002–1019.

Collins, R. (1981). On the microfoundations of macro-sociology. *American Journal of Sociology, 86,* 984–1014.

Comer, J. P., & Poussaint, A. F. (1992). *Raising black children.* New York: Plume.

Conant, E. (2009, May 4). Rebranding hate in the age of Obama. *Newsweek.*

Conrad, P. (1975). The discovery of hyperkinesis: Notes on the medicalization of deviant behavior. *Social Problems, 23,* 12–21.

Conrad, P. (2005). The shifting engines of medicalization. *Journal of Health and Social Behavior, 46,* 3–14.

Conrad, P., & Leiter, V. (2004). Medicalization, markets, and consumers. *Journal of Health and Social Behavior, 45,* 158–176.

Conrad, P., & Schneider, J. W. (1992). *Deviance and medicalization: From badness to sickness.* Philadelphia: Temple University Press.

Cookson, P., & Persell, C. (1985). *Preparing for power.* New York: Basic Books.

Cooley, C. H. (1902). *Human nature and social order.* New York: Scribner.

Coontz, S. (1992). *The way we never were.* New York: Basic Books.

Coontz, S. (2005). *Marriage, a history: From obedience to intimacy, or how love conquered marriage.* New York: Viking.

Cooper, K. J. (1999). Admissions models for inclusion. *Black Issues in Higher Education, 16,* 3–5.

Cose, E. (2009, February 2). Revisiting "The rage of the privileged class." *Newsweek.*

Coser, R. L. (1960). Laughter among colleagues: A study of the social functions among staff of a mental hospital. *Psychiatry, 23,* 81–95.

Coulson, M. A., & Riddell, C. (1980). *Approaching sociology.* London: Routledge & Kegan Paul.

Cowan, R. (1991). More work for mother: The postwar years. In L. Kramer (Ed.), *The sociology of gender.* New York: St. Martin's Press.

Cowell, A. (2002, April 28). Migrants feel chill in a testy Europe. *New York Times.*

Cowell, A. (2007, March 8). Commons moves again to erode nobles' power in Britain. *New York Times.*

Cowley, G. (1997, May 9). Gender limbo. *Newsweek.*

Cowley, G. (2003, May 5). How progress makes us sick. *Newsweek.*

Coyle, M. (2003). *Race and class penalties in crack cocaine sentencing* (Sentencing Project Report No. 5077). Retrieved September 4, 2009, from www.sentencingproject.org/doc/publications/5077.pdf

Crandall, M., Nathens, A. B., Kernic, M. A., Holt, V. L., & Rivara, F. P. (2004). Predicting future injury among women in abusive relationships. *Journal of Trauma: Injury, Infection, and Critical Care, 56,* 906–912.

Crary, D. (2007, June 3). TB case raises ethical questions. *Indianapolis Star.*

Crary, D. (2009, March 8). Women's rights pact worries right, left. *Indianapolis Star.*

Cross, J., & Guyer, M. (1980). *Social traps.* Ann Arbor: University of Michigan Press.

Crossette, B. (1996, June 3). Hope, and pragmatism, for U.N. cities conference. *New York Times.*

Crossette, B. (1997, November 2). How to fix a crowded world: Add people. *New York Times.*

Crossette, B. (2001, February 28). Against a trend, U.S. population will bloom, UN says. *New York Times.*

Croteau, D., & Hoynes, W. (2000). *Media/society: Industries, images, and audiences.* Thousand Oaks, CA: Pine Forge Press.

Crystal, D. (2003). *English as a global language.* Cambridge, UK: Cambridge University Press.

Curra, J. (2000). *The relativity of deviance.* Thousand Oaks, CA: Sage.

Cushing, R., & Bishop, B. (2005, July 20). The rural war. *New York Times.*

Cushman, J. H. (1993, November 19). U.S. to weigh Blacks' complaints about pollution. *New York Times.*

Dahrendorf, R. (1959). *Class and class conflict in industrial society.* Stanford, CA: Stanford University Press.

Daley, S. (1996, May 9). A new charter wins adoption in South Africa. *New York Times.*

Daley, S. (2000, April 9). More and more, Europeans find fault with U.S. *New York Times.*

Davis, D. B. (2006). *Inhuman bondage: The rise and fall of slavery in the New World.* New York: Oxford.

Davis, F. J. (1991). *Who is black?* University Park: Pennsylvania State University Press.

Davis, K. (1937). The sociology of prostitution. *American Sociological Review, 2,* 744–755.

Davis, K. (1976). The world's population crisis. In R. K. Merton & R. Nisbett (Eds.), *Contemporary social problems.* New York: Harcourt Brace Jovanovich.

Davis, K., & Moore, W. (1945). Some principles of stratification. *American Sociological Review, 10,* 242–247.

Dawes, R. M., & Messick, D. M. (2000). Social dilemmas. *International Journal of Psychology, 35,* 111–116.

Death Penalty Information Center. (2009). *Facts about the death penalty.* Retrieved June 18, 2010, from www.deathpenaltyinfo.org/FactSheet.pdf

Deaux, K., & Kite, M. E. (1987). Thinking about gender. In B. B. Hess & M. M. Ferree (Eds.), *Analyzing gender: A handbook of social science research.* Newbury Park, CA: Sage.

DeCastro, J. M. (1994). Family and friends produce greater social facilitation of food-intake than other companions. *Physiology and Behavior, 56,* 445–455.

DeCastro, J. M. (2000). Eating behaviors: Lessons from the real world of humans. *Ingestive Behavior and Obesity, 16,* 800–813.

Declaration of sentiments and resolutions, Seneca Falls Convention, 1848. (2001). In P. S. Rothenberg (Ed.), *Race, class, and gender in the United States.* New York: Worth.

DeFronzo, J. (1991). *Revolutions and revolutionary movements.* Boulder, CO: Westview Press.

DeLeire, T. (2000). The unintended consequences of the Americans with Disabilities Act. *Regulation, 23,* 21–24.

DeNavas-Walt, C., Proctor, B. D., & Smith, J. C. (2009). *Income, poverty, and health insurance coverage in the United States: 2008* (U.S. Census Bureau, Current Population Reports, P60–236). Retrieved May 7, 2010, from www.census.gov/prod/2009pubs/p60-236.pdf

Denzin, N. (1977). *Childhood socialization: Studies in the development of language, social behavior, and identity.* San Francisco: Jossey-Bass.

Denzin, N. (1989). *The research act: A theoretical introduction to sociological methods.* Englewood Cliffs, NJ: Prentice Hall.

DePalma, A. (1996, January 13). For Mexico's Indians, new voice but few gains. *New York Times.*

DeParle, J. (2007, April 22). A good provider is one who leaves. *New York Times Magazine.*

DeParle, J. (2009, February 2). Welfare system failing to grow as economy lags. *New York Times.*

DePaulo, B. (2006). *Singled out: How singles are stereotyped, stigmatized, and ignored, and still live happily ever after.* New York: St. Martin's Press.

Derber, C. (1979). *The pursuit of attention.* New York: Oxford University Press.

Deutsch, K. W. (1966). *Nationalism and social communication.* Cambridge: MIT Press.

DeVoe, J. F., Peter, K., Kaufman, P., Miller, A., Noonan, M., Snyder, T. D., & Baum, K. (2004). *Indicators of school crime and safety: 2004.* Retrieved June 21, 2005, from www.ojp.usdoj.gov/bjs/pub/pdf/iscs04ex.pdf

Dewan, S. (2008, May 7). Releases from Death Row raise doubts about quality of defense. *New York Times.*

Dey, J. G., & Hill, C. (2007). *Behind the pay gap.* Washington, DC: American Association of University Women Educational Foundation. Retrieved April 1, 2007, from www.aauw.org

Diamond, J. (2005). *How societies choose to succeed or fail.* New York: Viking.

Diekman, A. B., & Murnen, S. K. (2004). Learning to be little women and little men: The inequitable gender equality of nonsexist children's literature. *Sex Roles, 50,* 373–385.

Diekmann, A., & Engelhardt, H. (1999). The social inheritance of divorce: Effects of parent's family type in postwar Germany. *American Sociological Review, 64,* 78–93.

Diller, L. H. (1998). *Running on Ritalin.* New York: Bantam Books.

Dillon, S. (2008, September 1). Hard times hitting students and schools in double blow. *New York Times.*

DiMaggio, P. J., & Powell, W. W. (1983). The iron cage revisited: Institutional isomorphism and collective rationality in organizational fields. *American Sociological Review, 48,* 147–160.

DiMaggio, P. J., & Powell, W. W. (1991). Introduction. In W. W. Powell & P. J. DiMaggio (Eds.), *The new institutionalism in organizational analysis.* Chicago: University of Chicago Press.

Dion, K., Berscheid, E., & Walster, E. (1972). What is beautiful is good. *Journal of Personality and Social Psychology, 24,* 285–290.

Division for the Advancement of Women. (2009). *Convention on the elimination of all forms of discrimination against women: Overview of the convention.* New York: Author. Retrieved June 4, 2009, from www.un.org/womenwatch/daw/cedaw/

Dixon, T. L., & Linz, D. (2000). Race and the misrepresentation of victimization on local television news. *Communication Research, 27,* 547–573.

Dobash, R. E., & Dobash, R. P. (1979). *Violence against wives: A case against the patriarchy.* New York: Free Press.

Dokoupil, T. (2009, March 2). Men will be men. *Newsweek.*

Domhoff, G. W. (1983). *Who rules America now? A view for the eighties.* Englewood Cliffs, NJ: Prentice Hall.

Domhoff, G. W. (1998). *Who rules America? Power and politics in the year 2000.* Mountain View, CA: Mayfield.

Domino's. (2008). *Franchise with Domino's Pizza.* Retrieved April 15, 2009, from www.dominosbiz.com/Biz-Public-EN/Site+Content/Secondary/Franchise/

Dominus, S. (2004, February 22). Life in the age of old, old age. *New York Times Magazine.*

Dugger, C. W. (1996, February 29). Immigrant cultures raising issues of child punishment. *New York Times.*

Dugger, C. W. (1999a, April 25). India's poorest are becoming its loudest. *New York Times.*

Dugger, C. W. (1999b, May 3). Lower-caste women turn village rule upside down. *New York Times.*

Dugger, C. W. (2004a, December 28). Supermarket giants crush Central American farmers. *New York Times.*

Dugger, C. W. (2004b, July 28). World Bank challenged: Are the poor really helped? *New York Times.*

Duncan, G. J. (2007). School readiness and later achievement. *Developmental Psychology, 43,* 1428–1446.

Duncan, G. J., & Chase-Landale, P. L. (2001). For better and for worse: Welfare reform and the well-being of children and families. In G. J. Duncan & P. L. Chase-Landale (Eds.), *For better and for worse.* New York: Russell Sage Foundation.

Durkheim, É. (1947). *The division of labor in society* (G. Simpson, Trans.). Glencoe, IL: Free Press. (Original work published 1893)

Durkheim, É. (1951). *Suicide.* New York: Free Press. (Original work published 1897)

Durkheim, É. (1954). *The elementary forms of religious life* (J. Swain, Trans.). New York: Free Press. (Original work published 1915)

Durkheim, É. (1958). *Rules of sociological method* (G. E. G. Catlin, Ed.; A. Solovay & J. H. Mueller, Trans.). Glencoe, IL: Free Press. (Original work published 1895)

Dye, J. L. (2008). *Fertility of American women: 2006* (U.S. Census Bureau, Current Population Reports, P20–558). Retrieved September 4, 2009, from www.census.gov/prod/2008pubs/p20–558.pdf

Ebaugh, H. R. F. (1988). *Becoming an ex.* Chicago: University of Chicago Press.

Eckholm, E. (2001, February 18). Psychiatric abuse by China reported in repressing sect. *New York Times.*

Eckholm, E. (2006a, July 27). Chicago orders "big box" stores to raise wages. *New York Times.*

Eckholm, E. (2006b, March 20). Plight deepens for black men, study warns. *New York Times.*

Eckholm, E. (2009, March 11). As jobs vanish, motel rooms become home. *New York Times.*

Edidin, P. (2005, March 6). How to shake hands or share a meal with an Iraqi. *New York Times.*

Edney, J. (1979, August). Free riders en route to disaster. *Psychology Today,* 80–102.

The Education Trust. (2002). *The funding gap: Low-income and minority students receive fewer dollars.* Retrieved January 16, 2003, from www.edtrust.org

Edwards, T. M. (2000, August 28). Flying solo. *Time.*

Edwards, T. M. (2001, May 7). How med students put abortion back in the classroom. *Time.*

Egan, T. (1999, February 28). The war on crack retreats, still taking prisoners. *New York Times.*

Egan, T. (2007, January 7). Little Asia on the hill. *New York Times.*

Ehrenreich, B. (1990). Is the middle class doomed? In B. Ehrenreich (Ed.), *The worst years of our lives*. New York: Harper & Row.

Ehrenreich, B., & English, D. (1979). *For her own good: 150 years of the experts' advice to women*. Garden City, NY: Anchor Books.

Ehrlich, P. R., & Ehrlich, A. H. (1993). World population crisis. In K. Finsterbusch & J. S. Schwartz (Eds.), *Sources: Notable selections in sociology*. Guilford, CT: Dushkin.

Eitzen, D. S., & Baca Zinn, M. (1991). *In conflict and order: Understanding society*. Boston: Allyn & Bacon.

Elder, G. H., & Liker, J. K. (1982). Hard times in women's lives: Historical influences across 40 years. *American Journal of Sociology, 88*, 241–269.

Eldridge, R. I., & Sutton, P. D. (2007, May). *Births, marriages, divorces, and deaths: Provisional data for October 2006* (National Vital Statistics Reports, Vol. 55, pp. 1–6). Hyattsville, MD: National Center for Health Statistics.

England, P., & Thomas, R. J. (2007). The decline of the date and the rise of the college hook-up. In A. S. Skolnick & J. H. Skolnick (Eds.), *Family in transition*. Boston: Allyn & Bacon.

Enloe, C. (1993). *The morning after: Sexual politics at the end of the cold war*. Berkeley: University of California Press.

Epstein, C. F. (1989). Workplace boundaries: Conceptions and creations. *Social Research, 56*, 571–590.

Erikson, K. (1966). *Wayward Puritans*. New York: Wiley.

Erlanger, S. (2000, April 2). Across a new Europe, a people deemed unfit for tolerance. *New York Times*.

Erlanger, S. (2008, November 12). After U.S. breakthrough, Europe looks in mirror. *New York Times*.

Erlanger, S. (2009, June 30). Study says Blacks and Arabs face bias from Paris police. *New York Times*.

Evans, L., & Davies, K. (2000). No sissy boys here: A content analysis of the representation of masculinity in elementary school reading textbooks. *Sex Roles, 42*, 255–270.

Evans, T., & Nichols, M. (2009, March 22). Waiting for help in Indy. *Indianapolis Star*.

Evered, R. (1983). The language of organizations: The case of the Navy. In L. R. Pondy, P. J. Frost, G. Morgan, & T. C. Dandridge (Eds.), *Organizational symbolism*. Greenwich, CT: JAI Press.

Extreme facts. (2005, June 4). *Indianapolis Star*.

Faludi, S. (1991). *Backlash: The undeclared war against women*. New York: Crown.

Family of VCJD victim claim untried treatment is a success. (2003). *Vegsource Newsletter*. Retrieved June 30, 2003, from www.vegsource.com/talk/madcow/messages/422.html

Farb, P. (1983). *Word play: What happens when people talk*. New York: Bantam Books.

Farley, J. (1982). *Majority-minority relations*. Englewood Cliffs, NJ: Prentice Hall.

Farmer, R. (2002, Spring). Same sex couples face post–September 11 discrimination. *National NOW Times*.

Faust, K., Gann, M., & McKibben, J. (1999). The boomlet goes to college. *American Demographics, 21*, 4–5.

Fausto-Sterling, A. (1985). *Myths of gender: Biological theories about women and men*. New York: Basic Books.

Fausto-Sterling, A. (2000). *Sexing the body: Gender politics and the construction of sexuality*. New York: Basic Books.

Feagin, J. R. (1975). *Subordinating the poor*. Englewood Cliffs, NJ: Prentice Hall.

Feagin, J. R., & McKinney, K. D. (2003). *The many costs of racism*. New York: Rowman & Littlefield.

Fearing demographic abyss, Putin promises mums more money. (2006, May 10). *Agence France Presse—English*.

Fears, D., & Deane, C. (2001, July 5). Biracial couples report tolerance. *Washington Post*.

Federal Interagency Forum on Child and Family Statistics. (2007). *America's children: Key national indicators of well-being, 2007*. Retrieved July 20, 2007, from www.childstats.gov/pdf/ac2007/ac_07.pdf

Federal Bureau of Investigation. (2008). *Hate crime statistics, 2007: Incidents and offenses*. Retrieved May 29, 2009, from www.fbi.gov/ucr/hc2007/incidents.htm

Feldmann, L., Marlantes, L., & Bowers, F. (2003, March 14). The impact of Bush linking 9/11 and Iraq. *Christian Science Monitor*.

Felmlee, D., Sprecher, S., & Bassin, E. (1990). The dissolution of intimate relationships: A hazard model. *Social Psychology Quarterly, 53*, 13–30.

Fendrich, J. M. (2003). The forgotten movement: The Vietnam antiwar movement. *Sociological Inquiry, 73*, 338–358.

Ferguson, N. (2004, April 4). Eurabia? *New York Times Magazine*.

Ferree, M. M. (1992). The political context of rationality. In A. D. Morris & C. M. Mueller (Eds.), *Frontiers in social movement theory*. New Haven, CT: Yale University Press.

Festinger, L., Riecken, H., & Schacter, S. (1956). *When prophecy fails.* New York: Harper & Row.

Feuer, A. (2004, May 15). Vatican discourages marriage with Muslims for Catholic women. *New York Times.*

Fields, J. (2003). *Children's living arrangements and characteristics: March 2002* (U.S. Census Bureau, Current Population Reports, P20–547). Washington, DC: Government Printing Office.

Fields, J. (2004). *America's families and living arrangements: 2003* (U.S. Census Bureau, Current Population Reports, P20–553). Retrieved September 4, 2009, from www.census.gov/prod/2004pubs/p20–553.pdf

Fiese, B. H., & Skillman, G. (2000). Gender differences in family stories: Moderating influence of parent gender role and child gender. *Sex Roles, 43*(5/6), 267–283.

Figert, A. (1996). *Women and the ownership of PMS.* New York: Aldine de Gruyter.

Fincham, F., & Bradbury, T. N. (1987). The impact of attributions in marriage: A longitudinal analysis. *Journal of Personality and Social Psychology, 53,* 510–517.

Finer, J. (2005, August 12). The new Ernie Pyles: Sgtlizzie and 67cshdocs. *Washington Post.*

Fish, S. (2000). The nifty nine arguments against affirmative action in higher education. *Journal of Blacks in Higher Education, 27,* 79–81.

Folbre, N., & Yoon, J. (2006, January 5). *The value of unpaid child care in the U.S. in 2003.* Paper presented at the Meeting of the Allied Social Science Association, Boston (cited with permission of author).

Forman, T. A., Williams, D., & Jackson, J. (1997). Race, place, and discrimination. *Perspectives on Social Problems, 9,* 231–261.

Fox, J. A., & Zawitz, M. W. (2007). *Homicide trends in the United States.* Washington, DC: U.S. Bureau of Justice Statistics. Retrieved June 18, 2010, from www.ojp.usdoj.gov/content/homicide/hontrend.cfm

Frank, A. G. (1969). *Capitalism and under-development in Latin America.* New York: Monthly Review Press.

Frankenberg, E. (2006). *The segregation of American teachers.* Cambridge, MA: Civil Rights Project at Harvard University.

Franklin, D. (2006, August 15). Patient power: Making sure your doctor really hears you. *New York Times.*

Freedman, V. A., Martin, L. G., & Schoeni, R. F. (2004). Disability in America. *Population Bulletin, 59,* 1–32.

Freiberg, P. (1991). Self-esteem gender gap widens in adolescence. *APA Monitor, 22,* 29.

French, H. W. (1999a, November 15). "Japanese only" policy takes body blow in court. *New York Times.*

French, H. W. (1999b, October 12). Japan's troubling trend: Rising teen-age crime. *New York Times.*

French, H. W. (2000, May 3). Japan unsettles returnees, who yearn to leave again. *New York Times.*

French, H. W. (2002, September 23). Educators try to tame Japan's blackboard jungles. *New York Times.*

French, H. W. (2003, July 25). Japan's neglected resource: Female workers. *New York Times.*

French, H. W. (2007, March 22). China scrambles for stability as its workers age. *New York Times.*

Frese, B., Moya, M., & Megías, J. L. (2004). Social perception of rape: How rape myth acceptance modulates the influence of situational factors. *Journal of Interpersonal Violence, 19,* 143–161.

Freudenheim, M. (2005, March 23). More help wanted: Older workers please apply. *New York Times.*

Freund, P. E. S., & McGuire, M. B. (1991). *Health, illness, and the social body: A cultural sociology.* Englewood Cliffs, NJ: Prentice Hall.

Friedman, T. L. (2005, April 3). It's a flat world after all. *New York Times Magazine.*

Furstenberg, F. F., & Harris, K. M. (1992). The disappearing American father? Divorce and the waning significance of biological parenthood. In S. J. South & S. E. Tolnay (Eds.), *The changing American family: Sociological and demographic perspectives.* Boulder, CO: Westview Press.

Fuwa, M. (2004). Macro-level gender inequality and the division of household labor in 22 countries. *American Sociological Review, 69,* 751–767.

Gale, R. P. (1986). Social movements and the state: The environmental movement, countermovement and governmental agencies. *Sociological Perspectives, 29,* 202–240.

Galinsky, E., Bond, J. T., Kim, S. S., Backon, L., Brownfield, E., & Sakai, K. (2006). *Overwork in America: When the way we work becomes too much.* New York: Families and Work Institute. Retrieved July 19, 2006, from www.familiesandwork.org/summary/overwork2005.pdf

Galles, G. M. (1989, June 8). What colleges really teach. *New York Times.*

Galliher, J. M., & Galliher, J. F. (2002). A "commonsense" theory of deterrence and the "ideology" of science: The New York State death penalty debate. *Journal of Criminal Law and Criminology, 92,* 307–333.

Gamson, W. A., & Wolfsfeld, G. (1993). Movements and media as interactive systems. *Annals of the American Academy of Political and Social Science, 528,* 114–125.

Gans, H. (1971, July/August). The uses of poverty: The poor pay for all. *Social Policy,* pp. 20–24.

Gans, H. (1996). Positive functions of the undeserving poor: Uses of the underclass in America. In J. Levin & A. Arluke (Eds.), *Snapshots and portraits of society.* Thousand Oaks, CA: Pine Forge Press.

Gans, H. (2005). Race as class. *Contexts, 4,* 17–21.

Garcia-Moreno, C., Jansen, H., Ellsberg, M., Heise, L., & Watts, C. H. (2006). Prevalence of intimate partner violence: Findings from the WHO multi-country study on women's health and domestic violence. *Lancet, 368,* 1260–1269.

Garfinkel, J. (2003, February 24). Boutique medical practices face legal, legislative foes. *Cincinnati Business Courier.* Retrieved July 12, 2004, from www.bizjournals.com/cincinnati/stories/2003/02/24/focus2.html

Garment, L. (1996, June 27). Holier than us? *New York Times.*

Gates, H. L. (2007, November 18). Forty acres and a gap in wealth. *New York Times.*

Gaubatz, K. T. (1995). *Crime in the public mind.* Ann Arbor: University of Michigan Press.

Gelles, R. J., & Straus, M. A. (1988). *Intimate violence.* Newbury Park, CA: Sage.

Gentleman, A. (2006, January 10). Millions of abortions of female fetuses reported in India. *New York Times.*

Gentleman, A. (2007, June 3). Indian shepherds stoop to conquer caste system. *New York Times.*

Geographic.org. (2005). *Median age: Total 2004.* Retrieved June 19, 2005, from www.photius.com/rankings/population/median_age_total_2004_1.html

Gergen, K. J. (1991). *The saturated self.* New York: Basic Books.

Gerlach, P., & Hine, V. H. (1970). *People, power, change: Movements of social transformation.* Indianapolis, IN: Bobbs-Merrill.

Getlin, J., & Wilkinson, T. (2003, April 3). "Embedded" reporters are mixed blessing for the military. *Seattle Times.*

Giddens, A. (1984). *The construction of society: Outline of the theory of structuration.* Berkeley: University of California Press.

Giddens, A. (2005). The global revolution in family and personal life. In A. S. Skolnick & J. H. Skolnick (Eds.), *Family in transition.* Boston: Allyn & Bacon.

Gillen, B. (1981). Physical attractiveness: A determinant of two types of goodness. *Personality and Social Psychology Bulletin, 7,* 277–281.

Gilliam, W. S. (2005). *Prekindergarteners left behind: Expulsion rates in state prekindergarten systems.* New York: Foundation for Child Development. Retrieved May 17, 2005, from www.fcd-us.org/PDFs/NationalPreKExpulsionPaper03.02_new.pdf

Gilligan, C. (1990). Teaching Shakespeare's sister: Notes from the underground of female adolescence. In C. Gilligan, N. P. Lyons, & T. J. Hanmer (Eds.), *Making connections.* Cambridge, MA: Harvard University Press.

Gimpel, J. G. (2009). *Latino voting in the 2008 election: Part of a broader electoral movement.* Washington, DC: Center for Immigration Studies. Retrieved May 31, 2009, from www.cis.org/latinovoting

Ginzel, L. E., Kramer, R. M., & Sutton, R. I. (2004). Organizational impression management as a reciprocal influence process: The neglected role of the organizational audience. In M. J. Hatch & M. Schultz (Eds.), *Organizational identity.* New York: Oxford University Press.

Giridharadas, A. (2007, November 25). Rumbling across India: Stories of urban migration. *New York Times.*

Gitlin, T. (1979). Prime time ideology: The hegemonic process in television entertainment. *Social Problems, 26,* 251–266.

Glater, J. D. (2006, December 3). Straight "A" students? Good luck making partner. *New York Times.*

Glazer, S. (2008). Declining birthrates. *CQ Researcher, 18,* 961–984.

Glick, P., & Fiske, S. T. (1996). The ambivalent sexism inventory: Differentiating hostile and benevolent sexism. *Journal of Personality and Social Psychology, 70,* 491–512.

Godson, R., & Olson, W. J. (1995). International organized crime. *Society, 32,* 18–29.

Goffman, A. (2009). On the run: Wanted men in a Philadelphia ghetto. *American Sociological Review, 74,* 339–357.

Goffman, E. (1952). On cooling the mark out: Some aspects of adaptation to failure. *Psychiatry, 15,* 451–463.

Goffman, E. (1959). *The presentation of self in everyday life.* Garden City, NY: Doubleday.

Goffman, E. (1961). *Asylums.* Garden City, NY: Doubleday.

Goffman, E. (1963). *Stigma: Notes on the management of spoiled identity.* Englewood Cliffs, NJ: Prentice Hall.

Goffman, E. (1967). *Interaction ritual.* Chicago: Aldine-Atherton.

Goldberg, C. (2001, April 22). In some states, sex offenders serve more than their time. *New York Times.*

Goldberg, S. (1999). The logic of patriarchy. *Gender Issues, 17,* 53–69.

Goleman, D. (1989, October 10). Sensing silent cues emerges as key skill. *New York Times.*

Goleman, D. (1990, December 25). The group and the self: New focus on a cultural rift. *New York Times.*

Goleman, D. (1993, May 4). Therapists find some patients are just hateful. *New York Times.*

Golway, T. (2004, August 2–9). Redrafting America. *America.*

Gomstyn, A. (2009). Good P.R. or guilt? Rich get discreet. *ABC News.* Retrieved April 28, 2009, from http://abcnews.go.com/Business/Economy/story?id=6823310&page=1

Goode, Erica. (1999, January 12). Pediatricians renew battle over toilet training. *New York Times.*

Goode, Erich. (1989). *Drugs in American society.* New York: McGraw-Hill.

Goode, Erich. (1994). *Deviant behavior.* Englewood Cliffs, NJ: Prentice Hall.

Goode, W. J. (1971). World revolution and family patterns. *Journal of Marriage and the Family, 33,* 624–635.

Goode, W. J. (1981). Why men resist. In B. Thorne & M. Yalom (Eds.), *Rethinking the family: Some feminist questions.* New York: Longman.

Goodman, P. S. (2008, April 18). Workers get fewer hours, deepening the downturn. *New York Times.*

Goodman, P. S., & Healy, J. (2009, April 4). 660,000 more jobs lost: Total surpasses 5 million. *New York Times.*

Goodnough, A. (2005, April 27). Florida expands right to use deadly force in self-defense. *New York Times.*

Goodstein, L. (2003, September 11). Survey finds slight rise in Jews' intermarrying. *New York Times.*

Gorbis, E., & Kholodenko, Y. (2005, September 1). Plastic surgery addiction in patients with body dysmorphic disorder. *Psychiatric Times.*

Gordon, M. M. (1964). *Assimilation in American life.* New York: Oxford University Press.

Gordon, R. G. (2005). *Ethnologue: Languages of the world* (15th ed.). Dallas, TX: SIL International.

Gott, N. (2004, November 6). Textbooks ok'd after marriage redefined. *Indianapolis Star.*

Gould, S. J. (1981). *The mismeasure of man.* New York: Norton.

Gould, S. J. (1997, June). Dolly's fashion and Louis's passion. *Natural History.*

Gove, W., Hughes, M., & Geerkin, M. R. (1980). Playing dumb: A form of impression management with undesirable effects. *Social Psychology Quarterly, 43,* 89–102.

Gove, W., Style, C. B., & Hughes, M. (1990). The effect of marriage on the well-being of adults. *Journal of Family Issues, 11,* 34–35.

Gracey, H. L. (1991). Learning the student role: Kindergarten as academic boot camp. In J. Henslin (Ed.), *Down-to-earth sociology.* New York: Free Press.

Grady, D. (2008, December 4). Parents torn over extra frozen embryos from fertility procedures. *New York Times.*

Graham, L. O. (1999). *Our kind of people: Inside America's black upper class.* New York: HarperCollins.

Grall, T. S. (2007). *Custodial mothers and fathers and their child support: 2005* (U.S. Census Bureau, Current Population Reports, P60–234). Retrieved September 4, 2009, from www.census.gov/prod/2007pubs/p60–234.pdf

Greenblatt, A. (2009). Confronting warming. *CQ Researcher, 19,* 1–24.

Greencastle Banner Graphic. (1992, March 7). Letter to the editor.

Greenhouse, L. (2005, June 7). Justices say U.S. may prohibit the use of medical marijuana. *New York Times.*

Greenhouse, L. (2007a, June 12). Court to weigh disparities in cocaine laws. *New York Times.*

Greenhouse, L. (2007b, June 29). Justices, 5–4, limit use of race for school integration plans. *New York Times.*

Greenhouse, S. (2004, March 7). If you're a waiter, the future is rosy. *New York Times.*

Greenhouse, S. (2006, July 14). On dusty corner, laborers band together for more pay. *New York Times.*

Greenhouse, S., & Leonhardt, D. (2006, August 28). Real wages fail to match a rise in productivity. *New York Times.*

Griffin, S. (1986). *Rape: The power of consciousness.* New York: Harper & Row.

Griffin, S. (1989). Rape: The all-American crime. In L. Richardson & V. Taylor (Eds.), *Feminist frontiers II.* New York: Random House.

Griswold, W. (1994). *Cultures and societies in a changing world.* Thousand Oaks, CA: Pine Forge Press.

Gross, E., & Etzioni, A. (1985). *Organizations and society.* Englewood Cliffs, NJ: Prentice Hall.

Gross, E., & Stone, G. P. (1964). Embarrassment and the analysis of role requirements. *American Journal of Sociology, 70,* 1–15.

Gross, J. (2004, February 24). Older women team up to face future together. *New York Times.*

Gross, J. (2006, July 16). Checklist for camp: Bug spray. Sunscreen. Pills. *New York Times.*

Gusfield, J. R. (1963). *Symbolic crusade: Status politics and the American temperance movement.* Urbana: University of Illinois Press.

Hacker, A. (1992). *Two nations: Black and white, separate, hostile, unequal.* New York: Scribner.

Hacker, A. (1994, October 31). White on white. *New Republic.*

Hafferty, F. W. (1991). *Into the valley: Death and socialization of medical students.* New Haven, CT: Yale University Press.

Hagan, J. (2000). The poverty of a classless criminology: The American Society of Criminology 1991 presidential address. In R. D. Crutchfield, G. S. Bridges, J. G. Weis, & C. Kubrin (Eds.), *Crime readings.* Thousand Oaks, CA: Pine Forge Press.

Halbfinger, D. M., & Holmes, S. A. (2003, March 30). Military mirrors a working-class America. *New York Times.*

Hall, W. (1986). Social class and survival on the *S.S. Titanic. Social Science and Medicine, 22,* 687–690.

Hallin, D. C. (1986). We keep America on top of the world. In T. Gitlin (Ed.), *Watching television.* New York: Pantheon Books.

Hamermesh, D. S., & Biddle, J. E. (1994). Beauty and the labor market. *American Economic Review, 84,* 1174–1194.

Hamill, S. D. (2009, April 29). 2 white youths on trial for killing of a Mexican. *New York Times.*

Hamilton, D. L. (1981). Cognitive processes in stereotyping and intergroup behavior. Hillsdale, NJ: Erlbaum.

Hamilton, J. A. (1996). Women and health policy: On the inclusion of women in clinical trials. In C. F. Sargent & C. B. Brettell (Eds.), *Gender and health: An international perspective.* Upper Saddle River, NJ: Prentice Hall.

Haney López, I. E. (1996). *White by law: The legal construction of race.* New York: New York University Press.

Harden, B. (2000, April 6). Africa's gems: Warfare's best friend. *New York Times.*

Harden, B. (2001, August 12). The dirt in the new machine. *New York Times Magazine.*

Hardin, G., & Baden, J. (1977). *Managing the commons.* New York: Freeman.

Hareven, T. K. (1978). *Transitions: The family and the life course in historical perspective.* New York: Academic Press.

Hareven, T. K. (1992). American families in transition: Historical perspectives on change. In A. S. Skolnick & J. H. Skolnick (Eds.), *Family in transition* (7th ed.). New York: HarperCollins.

Harmon, A. (2009, May 17). Fighting for a last chance at life. *New York Times.*

Harris, G. (2003, December 7). If shoe won't fit, fix the foot? Popular surgery raises concern. *New York Times.*

Harris, G. (2005a, August 6). F.D.A. responds to criticism with new caution. *New York Times.*

Harris, G. (2005b, October 19). Sleeping pill use by youths soars, study says. *New York Times.*

Harris, G. (2009, January 12). F.D.A. is lax on oversight during trials, inquiry finds. *New York Times.*

Harris, M. C. (1996). Doctors implicated in Tutsi genocide. *Lancet, 347,* 684.

Hart, T. C. (2003). *Violent victimization of college students* (Bulletin NCJ 196143). Washington, DC: Bureau of Justice Statistics. Retrieved June 18, 2007, from www.ojp.usdoj.gov/bjs/pub/pdf/vvcs00.pdf

Hass, N. (1995, September 10). Margaret Kelly Michaels wants her innocence back. *New York Times Magazine.*

Haub, C. (2006). *Hispanics account for almost one-half of U.S. population growth.* Washington, DC: Population Reference Bureau. Retrieved February 24, 2006, from www.prb.org

Hausmann, R., Tyson, L. D., & Zahidi, S. (2008). *The global gender gap report: 2008.* Geneva, Switzerland: World Economic Forum. Retrieved June 3, 2009, from www.weforum.org/pdf/gendergap/report2008.pdf

Health Grades. (2009). *The sixth annual Health Grades Patient Safety in American Hospitals Study.* Retrieved May 22, 2009, from www.healthgrades.com/media/DMS/pdf/PatientSafetyinAmericanHospitalsStudy2009.pdf

Health Resources and Services Administration. (2004). *What is behind HRSA's projected supply, demand, and shortage of registered nurses?* Retrieved June 21, 2007, from ftp://ftp.hrsa.gov/bhpr/workforce/behindshortage.pdf

Health Resources and Services Administration. (2005). *Nursing education in five states: 2005.* Retrieved June 21, 2007, from http://bhpr.hrsa.gov/healthworkforce/reports/nursing/nursinged5/default.htm

Hebel, S. (2007, March 23). The graduation gap. *Chronicle of Higher Education.* Retrieved August 8, 2007, from http://chronicle.com/weekly/v53/i29/29a02001.htm

Helmreich, W. B. (1992). The things they say behind your back: Stereotypes and the myths behind them. In H. E. Lena, W. B. Helmreich, & W. McCord (Eds.), *Contemporary issues in sociology.* New York: McGraw-Hill.

Henderson, J. J., & Baldasty, G. J. (2003). Race, advertising, and prime-time television. *Howard Journal of Communications, 14,* 97–112.

Henley, N. (1977). *Body politics.* Englewood Cliffs, NJ: Prentice Hall.

Henriques, D. B. (1999, August 24). New take on perpetual calendar. *New York Times.*

Henriques, D. B. (2009, June 30). Madoff, apologizing, is given 150 years. *New York Times.*

Henshaw, S. K., & Finer, L. B. (2003). The accessibility of abortion services in the United States, 2001. *Perspectives on Sexual and Reproductive Health, 35,* 16–24.

Herbert, B. (2007, May 15). The right to paid sick days. *New York Times.*

Herbert, B. (2009, February 21). The invisible war. *New York Times.*

Herek, G. M. (2000a). The psychology of sexual prejudice. *Current Directions in Psychological Science, 9,* 19–22.

Herek, G. M. (2000b). Sexual prejudice and gender: Do heterosexuals' attitudes toward lesbians and gay men differ? *Journal of Social Issues, 56,* 251–266.

Hewitt, J. P. (1988). *Self and society: A symbolic interactionist social psychology.* Boston: Allyn & Bacon.

Hewitt, J. P., & Hewitt, M. L. (1986). *Introducing sociology: A symbolic interactionist perspective.* Englewood Cliffs, NJ: Prentice Hall.

Hewitt, J. P., & Stokes, R. (1975). Disclaimers. *American Sociological Review, 40,* 1–11.

Hibbler, D. K., & Shinew, K. J. (2005). The social life of interracial couples. In R. H. Lauer & J. C. Lauer (Eds.), *Sociology: Windows on society.* Los Angeles: Roxbury.

Higginbotham, E., & Weber, L. (1992). Moving up with kin and community: Upward social mobility for black and white women. *Gender & Society, 6,* 416–440.

Hill, C., & Silva, E. (2006). *Drawing the line: Sexual harassment on campus.* Washington, DC: American Association of University Women. Retrieved September 5, 2009, from www.aauw.org/research/upload/DTLFinal.pdf

Hill, M. E. (2000). Color differences in the socioeconomic status of African American men: Results from a longitudinal study. *Social Forces, 78,* 1437–1460.

Hill, N. E. (1997). Does parenting differ based on social class? African American women's perceived socialization for achievement. *American Journal of Community Psychology, 25,* 67–97.

Hills, S. (1980). *Demystifying social deviance.* New York: McGraw-Hill.

Hirschi, T. (1969). *Causes of delinquency.* Berkeley: University of California Press.

Hitt, J. (2005, August 21). The new Indians. *New York Times Magazine.*

Hobbs, E., & Stoops, N. (2002). *Demographic trends in the 20th century* (Census 2000 Special Reports, Series CENSR-4). Washington, DC: Government Printing Office.

Hochschild, A. R. (1983). *The managed heart.* Berkeley: University of California Press.

Hochschild, A. R. (1997). *The time bind: When work becomes home and home becomes work.* New York: Metropolitan Books.

Hofferth, S. L., & Sandberg, J. F. (2001). How American children spend their time. *Journal of Marriage and the Family, 63,* 295–308.

Hoffman, J. (1997, January 16). Crime and punishment: Shame gains popularity. *New York Times.*

Holtzworth-Munroe, A., & Jacobson, N. S. (1985). Causal attributions of married couples: When do they search for causes? What do they conclude when they do? *Journal of Personality and Social Psychology, 48,* 1398–1412.

Hooks, G., & Smith, C. L. (2004). The treadmill of destruction: National sacrifice areas and Native Americans. *American Sociological Review, 69,* 558–575.

Horon, I. L., & Cheng, D. (2001). Enhanced surveillance for pregnancy-associated mortality—Maryland, 1993–1998. *Journal of the American Medical Association, 285,* 1455–1459.

Horwitz, A. V. (2002). *Creating mental illness.* Chicago: University of Chicago Press.

Houppert, K. (2005, March 28). The new face of protest? *The Nation.*

House, J. (1981). Social structure and personality. In M. Rosenberg & R. H. Turner (Eds.), *Social psychology: Sociological perspectives.* New York: Basic Books.

Hout, M., & Lucas, S. R. (2001). Narrowing the income gap between rich and poor. In P. Rothenberg (Ed.), *Race, class, and gender in the United States.* New York: Worth.

Howard, J. A., & Hollander, J. (1997). *Gendered situations, gendered selves.* Thousand Oaks, CA: Sage.

Howe, N., & Strauss, W. (2000). *Millennials rising: The next great generation.* New York: Vintage Books.

Hu, W. (2008, May 24). Too busy to eat, students get a new required course: Lunch. *New York Times.*

Huber, J., & Form, W. H. (1973). *Income and ideology.* New York: Free Press.

Hughes, D., & Chen, L. (1997). When and what parents tell children about race: An examination of race-related socialization among African American families. *Applied Developmental Science, 1,* 200–214.

Hull, K. E., & Nelson, R. L. (2000). Assimilation, choice, or constraint? Testing theories of gender differences in the careers of lawyers. *Social Forces, 79,* 229–264.

Human Rights Campaign. (2009). *Marriage equality and other relationship recognition laws.* Retrieved May 18, 2009, from www.hrc.org/documents/Relationship_Recognition_Laws_Map.pdf

Human Rights Watch. (2001). *Caste discrimination: A global concern.* Retrieved June 16, 2004, from www.hrw.org/reports/2001/globalcaste

Human Rights Watch. (2009). *Testing justice: The rape kit backlog in Los Angeles City and County.* Retrieved June 18, 2010, from http://www.hrw.org/en/reports/2009/03/31/testing-justice

Hunsinger, D. (2009, March 15). New college grads scramble for jobs. *Indianapolis Star.*

Hunt, J. (1985). Police accounts of normal force. *Urban Life, 13,* 315–341.

Hyde, J. S. (1984). How large are gender differences in aggression? A developmental meta-analysis. *Developmental Psychology, 20,* 722–736.

Ignatius, A. (1988, July 14). China's birthrate is out of control again as one-child policy fails in rural areas. *Wall Street Journal.*

INEGI. (2007). *Personal ocupado en la industria maquiladora de exportación según tipo de ocupación* [People employed in the maquiladora export industry according to type of occupation]. Retrieved June 14, 2007, from www.inegi.gob.mx/est/contenidos/espanol/rutinas/ept/asp?t=emp75&c=1811

Institute of Medicine. (1999). *To err is human: Building a safer health care system.* Washington, DC: Committee on Quality of Health Care in America, National Academy Press.

International Centre for Prison Studies. (2007). *Entire world: Prison population rates per 100,000 of the national population.* Retrieved May 20, 2009, from www.kcl.ac.uk/depsta/law/research/icps/worldbrief/wpb_stats.php?area=all&category=wb_poprate

Is there a Santa Claus? (1897, September 21). *New York Sun.*

Issenberg, S. (2007). *The sushi economy.* New York: Gotham Books.

Ito, M., Horst, H., Bittanti, M., Boyd, D., Herr-Stephenson, B., Lange, P. G., Pascoe, C.J., & Robinson, L. (2008). *Living and learning with new media: Summary of findings from the Digital Youth Project* (Reports on Digital Media and Learning). Chicago: MacArthur Foundation. Retrieved June 7, 2009, from http://digitalyouth.ischool.berkeley.edu/files/report/digitalyouth-WhitePaper.pdf

Jackson, S. (1995). The social context of rape: Sexual scripts and motivation. In P. Searles & R. J. Berger (Eds.), *Rape and society.* Boulder, CO: Westview Press.

Jacobs, A. (2009, April 5). Rural China's hunger for sons fuels traffic in abducted boys. *New York Times.*

Jamail, D. (2007). *Another casualty: Coverage of the Iraq war.* New York: Global Policy Forum. Retrieved September 5, 2009, from http://globalpolicy.org/component/content/article/168-general/36698.html

Jefferson, T. (1955). *Notes on the State of Virginia.* Chapel Hill: University of North Carolina Press. (Original work published 1781)

Jencks, C., & Phillips, M. (1998). *The black-white test score gap.* Washington, DC: Brookings Institute.

Jencks, S. F., Williams, M. V., & Coleman, E. A. (2009). Rehospitalizations among patients in the Medicare fee-for-service program. *New England Journal of Medicine, 360,* 1418–1428.

Jenkins, H. (1999, July). Professor Jenkins goes to Washington. *Harper's Magazine.*

Jenkins, J. C., & Perrow, C. (1977). Insurgency of the powerless: Farm worker movements (1946–1972). *American Sociological Review, 42,* 249–268.

Johnson, R. (1987). *Hard time: Understanding and reforming the prison.* Pacific Grove, CA: Brooks/Cole.

Johnston, D. (2002, April 7). Affluent avoid scrutiny on taxes even as I.R.S. warns of cheating. *New York Times.*

Jones, E. E., Farina, A., Hastorf, A. H., Markus, H., Miller, D. T., & Scott, R. A. (1984). *Social stigma: The psychology of marked relationships.* New York: Freeman.

Jones, E. E., & Pittman, T. S. (1982). Toward a general theory of strategic self-presentation. In J. Suls (Ed.), *Psychological perspectives on the self* (Vol. 1). Hillsdale, NJ: Lawrence Erlbaum.

Jones, J. M. (1986). The concept of racism and its changing reality. In B. P. Bowser & R. G. Hunt (Eds.), *Impacts of racism on white Americans*. Beverly Hills, CA: Sage.

Jones, M. (2006, January 15). Shutting themselves in. *New York Times Magazine*.

Jost, K. (2006a). Transgender issues. *CQ Researcher, 16,* 385–408.

Jost, K. (2006b). Understanding Islam. *CQ Researcher, 16,* 913–936.

Joyce, A. (2005, June 6). Workplace improves for gay, transgender employees, rights group says. *Washington Post*.

Juergensmeyer, M. (1996, November). Religious nationalism: A global threat? *Current History*.

Justice Policy Institute. (2002). *Cellblocks or classrooms? The funding of higher education and corrections and its impact on African American men*. Retrieved September 5, 2009, from www.justicepolicy.org/images/upload/02–09_REP_CellblocksClassrooms_BB-AC.pdf

Kagay, M. R., & Elder, T. (1992, August 9). Numbers are no problem for pollsters. Words are. *New York Times*.

Kahn, J. (2004, May 30). The most populous nation faces a population crisis. *New York Times*.

Kahn, J. (2007, May 22). Harsh birth control steps fuel violence in China. *New York Times*.

Kahneman, D., Krueger, A. B., Schkade, D., Schwartz, N., & Stone, A. A. (2006). Would you be happier if you were richer? A focusing illusion. *Science, 312,* 1908–1910.

Kain, E. (1990). *The myth of family decline*. Lexington, MA: Lexington Books.

Kaiser Family Foundation. (2008). *Abortion in the U.S.: Utilization, financing, and access*. Retrieved September 5, 2009, from www.kff.org/womenshealth/upload/3269–02.pdf

Kaiser Family Foundation. (2009). *Rising unemployment, Medicaid, and the uninsured* (Publication No. 7850). Retrieved June 7, 2009, from www.kff.org/uninsured/7850.cfm

Kalmijn, M. (1994). Assortive mating by cultural and economic occupational status. *American Journal of Sociology, 100,* 422–452.

Kalmijn, M., & Flap, H. (2001). Assortive meeting and mating: Unintended consequences of organized settings for partner choices. *Social Forces, 79,* 1289–1312.

Kantor, J. (2006, December 26). Nanny hunt can be a "slap in the face" for Blacks. *New York Times*.

Karp, D. A., & Yoels, W. C. (1976). The college classroom: Some observations on the meanings of student participation. *Sociology and Social Research, 60,* 421–439.

Karush, S. (2001, May 6). Russia's population drain could open a floodgate of consequences. *Los Angeles Times*.

Katel, P. (2006). War on drugs. *CQ Researcher, 16,* 649–672.

Katel, P. (2008). Affirmative action. *CQ Researcher, 18,* 841–864.

Katz, J. (1975). Essences as moral identities: Verifiability and responsibility in imputations of deviance and charisma. *American Journal of Sociology, 80,* 1369–1390.

Kearl, M. C. (1980). Time, identity and the spiritual needs of the elderly. *Sociological Analysis, 41,* 172–180.

Kearl, M. C., & Gordon, C. (1992). *Social psychology*. Boston: Allyn & Bacon.

Keith, V. M., & Herring, C. (1991). Skin tone and stratification in the black community. *American Journal of Sociology, 97,* 760–778.

Kelley, R. (2008, November 17). A letter to my son on election night. *Newsweek*.

Kells, T. (2009). *Layoffs list: Job losses in 2008 and 2009 (ongoing)*. Retrieved May 26, 2009, from www.nowpublic.com/tech-biz/ layoffs-list-job-losses-2008-and-2009-ongoing

Kennedy, P. (1993). *Preparing for the 21st century*. New York: Random House.

Kent, M., & Lalasz, R. (2006, June). *In the news: Speaking English in the United States*. Washington, DC: Population Reference Bureau. Retrieved July 20, 2006, from www.prb.org

Kerbo, H. R. (1991). *Social stratification and inequality*. New York: McGraw-Hill.

Kershaw, S. (2004, July 21). It's a long, lonely search for men looking for love in Alaska. *New York Times*.

Kershaw, S. (2005, January 26). Old law shielding a woman's virtue faces an updating. *New York Times*.

Kershaw, S. (2008, October 30). Move over, my pretty, ugly is here. *New York Times*.

Kershner, R. (1996). Adolescent attitudes about rape. *Adolescence, 31,* 29–33.

Kessler, S. J., & McKenna, W. (1978). *Gender: An ethnomethodological approach*. Chicago: University of Chicago Press.

Kessler-Harris, A. (1982). *Out to work: A history of wage-earning women in the United States.* New York: Oxford University Press.

Khalema, N. E., & Wannas-Jones, J. (2003). Under the prism of suspicion: Minority voices in Canada post-September 11. *Journal of Muslim Minority Affairs, 23,* 25–39.

Kilborn, P. T. (1999, September 16). Bias worsens for minorities buying homes. *New York Times.*

Kimmel, M. S. (2004). *The gendered society.* New York: Oxford University Press.

King, M. L., Jr. (1991). Letter from Birmingham City jail. In C. Carson, D. J. Garrow, G. Gill, V. Harding, & D. Clark Hine (Eds.), *The eyes on the prize civil rights reader.* New York: Penguin Books.

Kirp, D. L. (2006, July 23). After The Bell Curve. *New York Times Magazine.*

Kishor, S., & Johnson, K. (2004). *Profiling domestic violence: A multi-country study.* Retrieved June 1, 2005, from www.measuredhs.com/pubs/pdf/OD31/DV.pdf

Klatch, R. (1991). Complexities of conservatism: How conservatives understand the world. In A. Wolfe (Ed.), *America at century's end.* Berkeley: University of California Press.

Kleck, R. (1968). Physical stigma and nonverbal cues emitted in face-to-face interaction. *Human Relations, 21,* 19–28.

Kleck, R., Ono, H., & Hastorf, A. (1966). The effects of physical deviance and face-to-face interaction. *Human Relations, 19,* 425–436.

Klevens, R. M., Edwards, J. R., Richards, C. L., Horan, T. C., Gaynes, R. P., Pollock, D. A., & Cardo, D. M (2007). Estimating health care-associated infections and deaths in the U.S. hospitals, 2002. *Public Health Reports, 122,* 160–166. www.cdc.gov/ncidod/dhqp/pdf/hicpac/infections_deaths.pdf. Accessed September 5, 2009.

Knight, D. (2006, May 21). Hiring frenzy. *Indianapolis Star.*

Kobrin, F. E. (1976). The fall in household size and the rise of the primary individual in the United States. *Demography, 31,* 127–138.

Koch, K. (1999, October 22). Rethinking ritalin. *CQ Researcher* [Special issue].

Kochhar, R., Gonzalez-Barrera, A., & Dockterman, D. (2009). *Through boom and bust: Minorities, immigrants, and homeownership* (PHC Report). Washington, DC: Pew Hispanic Center. Retrieved September 5, 2009, from http://pewhispanic.org/files/reports/109.pdf

Kocieniewski, D. (2006, October 10). A history of sex with students, unchallenged over the years. *New York Times.*

Koeppel, B. (1999, November 8). Cancer Alley, Louisiana. *The Nation.*

Kohlberg, L. A. (1966). A cognitive-developmental analysis of children's sex-role concepts and attitudes. In E. Maccoby (Ed.), *The development of sex differences.* Stanford, CA: Stanford University Press.

Kohn, M. L. (1979). The effects of social class on parental values and practices. In D. Reiss & H. A. Hoffman (Eds.), *The American family: Dying or developing.* New York: Plenum Press.

Kohut, A. (1999, December 3). Globalization and the wage gap. *New York Times.*

Kokopeli, B., & Lakey, G. (1992). More power than we want: Masculine sexuality and violence. In M. L. Anderson & P. H. Collins (Eds.), *Race, class and gender: An anthology.* Belmont, CA: Wadsworth.

Kolata, G. (2000, March 6). Web research transforms visit to the doctor. *New York Times.*

Kosmin, B. A., & Keysar, A. (2009). *American religious identification survey (ARIS 2008).* Hartford, CT: Trinity College. Retrieved May 6, 2009, from www.livinginliminality.files.wordpress.com/2009/03/aris_report_2008.pdf

Kreider, R. M. (2005). *Number, timing, and duration of marriages and divorces: 2001* (U.S. Census Bureau, Current Population Reports, P70–97). Washington, DC: Government Printing Office.

Kress, M. (2005, April 20). Mormonism is booming in the U.S. and overseas. *Ft. Wayne News Sentinel.*

Kristof, N. D. (1993, July 21). Peasants of China discover new way to weed out girls. *New York Times.*

Krueger, A. B. (2002, November 14). The apple falls close to the tree, even in the land of opportunity. *New York Times.*

Krugman, P. (2008, February 18). Poverty is poison. *New York Times.*

Kurtz, L. R. (1995). *Gods in the global village.* Thousand Oaks, CA: Pine Forge Press.

Labaton, S. (2005, April 15). House passes bankruptcy bill; overhaul now awaits president's signature. *New York Times.*

Lacey, M. (2003, March 5). Rights group calls for end to inheriting African wives. *New York Times.*

Lacey, M. (2006, December 14). Rwandan priest sentenced to 15 years for allowing deaths of Tutsi in church. *New York Times.*

LaCoste-Caputo, J. (2007, June 21). Academic ratings, teacher pay tied. *San Antonio Express-News.*

Lakshmi, R. (2005, February 27). India call centers suffer storm of 4–letter words. *Washington Post.*

Lalasz, R. (2006). *Americans flocking to outer suburbs in record numbers.* Washington, DC: Population Reference Bureau. Retrieved May 9, 2006, from www.prb.org

Lamont, M. (1992). *Money, morals and manners: The culture of the French and American upper middle class.* Chicago: University of Chicago Press.

Lander, L. (1988). *Images of bleeding: Menstruation as ideology.* New York: Orlando.

Landler, M. (1996, September 10). Corporate insurer to cover cost of spin doctors. *New York Times.*

Landler, M. (2002, December 1). For Austrians, HoHoHo is no laughing matter. *New York Times.*

Landler, M., & Barbaro, M. (2006, August 2). No, not always. *New York Times.*

Lang, S. (1998). *Men as women, women as men: Changing gender in Native American cultures.* Austin: University of Texas Press.

Langman, L. (1988). Social stratification. In M. B. Sussman & S. K. Steinmetz (Eds.), *Handbook of marriage and the family.* New York: Plenum Press.

Lanvers, U. (2004). Gender in discourse behaviour in parent-child dyads: A literature review. *Child: Care, Health, and Development, 30,* 481–493.

Lapchick, R. (2009). *The 2009 racial and gender report card: Major league baseball.* Orlando, FL: Institute for Diversity & Ethics in Sport. Retrieved May 29, 2009, from http://web.bus.ucf.edu/documents/sport/2009_rgrcmlb.pdf

Lareau, A. (2003). *Unequal childhoods: Class, race, and family life.* Berkeley: University of California Press.

Larew, J. (2003). Why are droves of unqualified, unprepared kids getting into our top colleges? Because their dads are alumni. In K. E. Rosenblum & T. C. Travis (Eds.), *The meaning of difference: American constructions of race, sex and gender, social class, and sexual orientation.* New York: McGraw-Hill.

Larson, L. E., & Goltz, J. W. (1989). Religious participation and marital commitment. *Review of Religious Research, 30,* 387–400.

Lasch, C. (1977). *Haven in a heartless world.* New York: Basic Books.

Lauer, R., & Handel, W. (1977). *Social psychology: The theory and application of symbolic interactionism.* Boston: Houghton Mifflin.

Leape, L. L., & Bates, D. W. (1995). Systems analysis of adverse drug events. *Journal of the American Medical Association, 274,* 35–43.

LeBesco, K. (2004). *Revolting bodies? The struggle to redefine fat identity.* Amherst: University of Massachusetts Press.

Lee, S. M. (1993). Racial classifications in the U.S. Census: 1890–1990. *Ethnic and Racial Studies, 16,* 75–94.

Lee-St. John, J. (2007, February 12). A time limit on rape. *Time.*

Legato, M. J. (2006, June 17). The weaker sex. *New York Times.*

Lehigh, S. (2005, January 19). The case for longer school days. *Boston Globe.*

Leland, J. (1996, February 19). Tightening the knot. *Newsweek.*

Leland, J. (2004, March 23). He's retired, she's working, they're not happy. *New York Times.*

Lemert, E. (1972). *Human deviance, social problems, and social control.* Englewood Cliffs, NJ: Prentice Hall.

Leonhardt, D. (2009, April 12). Richly undeserved. *New York Times Magazine.*

Leonhardt, D., & Fabrikant, G. (2009, August 21). After 30-year run, rise of the super-rich hits a sobering wall. *New York Times.*

Leonnig, C. D. (2005, June 8). Tobacco escapes huge penalty. *New York Times.*

Lerner, M. (1970). The desire for justice and reactions to victims. In J. Macauley & L. Berkowitz (Eds.), *Altruism and helping behavior.* New York: Academic Press.

Lesko, N. (2008). Our guys/good guys: Playing with high school privilege and power. In S. J. Ferguson (Ed.), *Mapping the social landscape.* New York: McGraw-Hill.

Lester, W. (2005, January 8). Poll: 29% in U.S. give tsunami aid. *Indianapolis Star.*

Levine, H. G. (1992). Temperance cultures: Concern about alcohol problems in Nordic and English-speaking cultures. In M. Lader, G. Edwards, & D. C. Drummond (Eds.), *The nature of alcohol and drug-related problems.* New York: Oxford University Press.

Levinson, D. (1989). *Family violence in cross-cultural perspective.* Newbury Park, CA: Sage.

Levy, A. (2006, May 29). Dirty old women. *New York Magazine.* Retrieved September 5, 2009, from http://nymag.com/news/features/17064/index1.html

Lewin, T. (1998, December 13). How boys lost out to girl power. *New York Times.*

Lewin, T. (2000, April 11). Disabled student is suing over test-score labeling. *New York Times.*

Lewin, T. (2001, October 21). Shelters have empty beds: Abused women stay home. *New York Times.*

Lewin, T. (2006, July 9). At colleges, women are leaving men in the dust. *New York Times.*

Lewin, T. (2007, January 26). Colleges regroup after voters ban race preferences. *New York Times.*

Lewin, T. (2009, February 5). A.P. program is growing, but black students lag. *New York Times.*

Lewis, M. (1978). *The culture of inequality.* New York: New American Library.

Lewis, M. M. (1948). *Language in society.* New York: Social Science Research Council.

Lewis, P. H. (1998, August 15). Too late to say "extinct" in Ubykh, Eyak or Ona. *New York Times.*

Lewis, R., & Yancey, G. (1997). Racial and nonracial factors that influence spouse choice in black/white marriages. *Journal of Black Studies, 28,* 60–78.

Liazos, A. (1985). *Sociology: A liberating perspective.* Boston: Allyn & Bacon.

Liben, L. S., & Bigler, R. S. (2002). The developmental course of gender differentiation: Conceptualizing, measuring, and evaluating constructs and pathways. *Monographs of the Society for Research in Child Development, 67,* 1–112.

Lichtblau, E. (2003, March 18). U.S. lawsuit seeks tobacco profits. *New York Times.*

Lichtblau, E. (2008, April 9). In justice shift, corporate deals replace trials. *New York Times.*

Light, P. (1988). *Baby boomers.* New York: Norton.

Lindesmith, A. R., Strauss, A. L., & Denzin, N. K. (1991). *Social psychology.* Englewood Cliffs, NJ: Prentice Hall.

Link, B. G., Mirotznik, J., & Cullen, F. T. (1991). The effectiveness of stigma-coping orientations: Can negative consequences of mental illness labeling be avoided? *Journal of Health and Social Behavior, 32,* 302–320.

Link, B. G., & Phelan, J. C. (2001). Conceptualizing stigma. *Annual Review of Sociology, 27,* 363–385.

Lino, M. (2008). *Expenditures on children by families, 2007* (Miscellaneous Publication No. 1528–2007). Alexandria, VA: U.S. Department of Agriculture, Center for Nutrition Policy and Promotion. Retrieved September 5, 2009, from www.cnpp.usda.gov/Publications/CRC/crc2007.pdf

Linton, R. (1937). One hundred percent American. *American Mercury, 40,* 427–429.

Lippmann, L. W. (1922). *Public opinion.* New York: Harcourt Brace Jovanovich.

Lips, H. M. (1993). *Sex and gender: An introduction.* Mountain View, CA: Mayfield.

Liptak, A. (2006, August 7). 15 states expand victims' rights on self-defense. *New York Times.*

Little, A. G. (2007, September 2). Not in whose backyard? *New York Times Magazine.*

Living Wage Resource Center. (2006). *Living wage wins.* Brooklyn, NY: Author. Retrieved June 10, 2009, from www.livingwagecampaign.org/index.php?id=1959

Loe, V. (1997, September 21). New nuptial license gets cool reception. *Indianapolis Star.*

Lofland, L. H. (1973). *A world of strangers: Order and action in urban public space.* New York: Basic Books.

Lohr, S. (2005, June 24). Cutting here, but hiring over there. *New York Times.*

Longman, J. (2006, June 4). Surge in racist mood raises concerns on eve of World Cup. *New York Times.*

Longman, J., & Higgins, M. (2005, August 3). Rad dudes of the world, unite. *New York Times.*

Lopez, M. H. (2008). *How Hispanics voted in the 2008 election.* Washington, DC: Pew Research Center. Retrieved June 2, 2009, from http://pewresearch.org/pubs/1024/exit-poll-analysis-hispanics

Lorber, J. (1989). Dismantling Noah's Ark. In B. J. Risman & P. Schwartz (Eds.), *Gender in intimate relationships: A microstructural approach.* Belmont, CA: Wadsworth.

Lorber, J. (2000). *Gender and the social construction of illness.* Walnut Creek, CA: AltaMira Press.

Lott, B. (1987). *Women's lives: Themes and variations in gender learning.* Pacific Grove, CA: Brooks/Cole.

Lowenstein, R. (2009, July 26). The new joblessness. *New York Times Magazine.*

Lueders, B. (2006). *Cry rape: The true story of one woman's harrowing quest for justice.* Madison, WI: Terrace Books.

Luker, K. (1984). *Abortion and the politics of motherhood.* Berkeley: University of California Press.

Luo, M. (2007, July 22). God '08: Whose, and how much, will voters accept? *New York Times.*

Luo, M. (2009, May 28). Still working, but making do with less. *New York Times.*

Lyall, S. (2000, July 8). Irish now face the other side of immigration. *New York Times.*

Lyman, R. (2005, April 4). Gay couples file suit after Michigan denies benefits. *New York Times.*

Macgillivray, I. K. (2000). Educational equity for gay, lesbian, bisexual, transgendered, and queer/questioning students: The demands of democracy and social justice for America's schools. *Education and Urban Society, 32,* 303–323.

Mann, C. C. (1993, February). How many is too many? *Atlantic Monthly.*

Manning, W. D., & Smock, P. J. (1999). New families and nonresident father-child visits. *Social Forces, 78,* 87–117.

Mannon, J. (1997). *Measuring up.* Boulder, CO: Westview Press.

Mansfield, H. (2006). *Manliness.* New Haven, CT: Yale University Press.

Marger, M. N. (1994). *Race and ethnic relations: American and global perspectives.* Belmont, CA: Wadsworth.

Marger, M. N. (2005). The mass media as a power institution. In S. J. Ferguson (Ed.), *Mapping the social landscape.* New York: McGraw-Hill.

Marmot, M. (2004). *The status syndrome: How social standing affects our health and longevity.* New York: Times Books.

Martin, C. L., & Ruble, D. (2004). Children's search for gender cues. *Current Directions in Psychological Science, 13,* 67–70.

Martinez-Alier, J. (2003). *The environmentalism of the poor.* Cheltenham, UK: Edward Elgar.

Marx, K. (1963). *The 18th Brumaire of Louis Bonaparte.* New York: International. (Original work published 1869)

Marx, K., & Engels, F. (1982). *The communist manifesto.* New York: International. (Original work published 1848)

Mataloni, R. J. (2007). *Operations of U.S. multinational companies in 2005.* Washington, DC: Bureau of Economic Analysis. Retrieved May 24, 2009, from www.bea.gov/scb/pdf/2007/11%20November/1107_mnc.pdf

Mather, M. (2007). *The new generation gap.* Washington, DC: Population Reference Bureau. Retrieved May 19, 2007, from www.prb.org/Articles/2007/NewGenerationGap.aspx

Mather, M., & Adams, D. (2006). *The risk of negative child outcomes in low-income families.* Washington, DC: Population Reference Bureau. Retrieved July 27, 2006, from www.prb.org/pdf06/RiskNegOut_Families.pdf

Mathews, L. (1996, July 6). More than identity rides on a new racial category. *New York Times.*

MBA vs. prison. (1999, May/June). *American Prospect.*

McAdam, D. (1982). *Political process and the development of black insurgency, 1930–1970.* Chicago: University of Chicago Press.

McAdam, D., McCarthy, J. D., & Zald, M. N. (1988). Social movements. In N. J. Smelser (Ed.), *Handbook of sociology.* Newbury Park, CA: Sage.

McCain, F. (1991). Interview with Franklin McCain. In C. Carson, D. J. Garrow, G. Gill, V. Harding, & D. Clark Hine (Eds.), *The eyes on the prize civil rights reader.* New York: Penguin Books.

McCall, G. J., & Simmons, J. L. (1978). *Identities and interactions.* New York: Free Press.

McCarthy, J. D., & Wolfson, M. (1992). Consensus movements, conflict movements, and the cooptation of civic and state infrastructures. In A. D. Morris & C. M. Mueller (Eds.), *Frontiers in social movement theory.* New Haven, CT: Yale University Press.

McCarthy, J. D., & Zald, M. N. (1977). Resource mobilization and social movements: A partial theory. *American Journal of Sociology, 82,* 1212–1241.

McCarthy, T. (2001, May 14). He makes a village. *Time.*

McCormick, J. S., Maric, A., Seto, M. C., & Barbaree, H. E. (1998). Relationship to victim predicts sentence length in sexual assault cases. *Journal of Interpersonal Violence, 13,* 413–420.

McEwan, J. (2005). Proving consent in sexual cases: Legislative change and cultural evolution. *International Journal of Evidence and Proof, 9,* 1–28.

McIntosh, P. (2001). White privilege: Unpacking the invisible knapsack. In P. Rothenberg (Ed.), *Race, class, and gender in the United States.* New York: Worth.

McKenry, P. C., & Price, S. J. (1995). Divorce: A comparative perspective. In B. B. Ingoldsby & S. Smith (Eds.), *Families in multicultural perspective.* New York: Guilford Press.

McLaren, L. M. (2003). Anti-immigrant prejudice in Europe: Contact, threat perception, and preferences for the exclusion of migrants. *Social Forces, 81,* 909–936.

McLean, R. (2005, January 12). Spaniards dare to question the way the day is ordered. *New York Times.*

McLean, R. (2006, January 21). In the new year, a novel idea for Spanish government workers: A literal lunch hour. *New York Times.*

McLoyd, V. C., Cauce, A. M., Takeuchi, D., & Wilson, L. (2000). Marital processes and parental socialization in families of color: A decade review of research. *Journal of Marriage and the Family, 62,* 1070–1094.

McNeil, D. G. (2006, February 15). Bristol-Myers allows 2 major AIDS drugs to be sold cheaply. *New York Times.*

McNeil, D. G. (2008, December 10). Report sounds alarm on child accidents. *New York Times.*

McPhee, J. (1971). *Encounters with the archdruid.* New York: Noonday.

McPherson, M., Smith-Lovin, L., & Brashears, M. E. (2006). Social isolation in America: Changes in core discussion networks over two decades. *American Sociological Review, 71,* 353–375.

Mead, G. H. (1934). *Mind, self and society.* Chicago: University of Chicago Press.

Meier, B. (2004, June 15). Group is said to seek full drug-trial disclosure. *New York Times.*

Merton, R. (1948). The self-fulfilling prophecy. *Antioch Review, 8,* 193–210.

Merton, R. (1957). *Social theory and social structure.* New York: Free Press.

Messick, D. M., & Brewer, M. B. (1983). Solving social dilemmas: A review. In L. Wheeler & P. Shaver (Eds.), *Review of personality and social psychology.* Beverly Hills, CA: Sage.

Messner, M. (2002). Boyhood, organized sports, and the construction of masculinities. In D. M. Newman & J. O'Brien (Eds.), *Sociology: Exploring the architecture of everyday life (Readings).* Thousand Oaks, CA: Pine Forge Press.

Meyer, J. W., & Rowan, B. (1977). Institutionalized organizations: Formal structure as myth and ceremony. *American Journal of Sociology, 83,* 340–363.

Miall, C. E. (1989). The stigma of involuntary childlessness. In A. S. Skolnick & J. H. Skolnick (Eds.), *Family in transition.* Boston: Little, Brown.

Michaels, K. (1993). Eight years in Kafkaland. *National Review, 45,* 36–38.

Michels, R. (1949). *Political parties.* Glencoe, IL: Free Press. (Original work published 1911)

Michener, H. A., DeLamater, J. D., & Schwartz, S. H. (1986). *Social psychology.* San Diego, CA: Harcourt Brace Jovanovich.

Milbank, D., & Deane, C. (2003, September 6). Hussein link to 9/11 lingers in many minds. *Washington Post.*

Miller, E., & Almon, J. (2009). *Crisis in the kindergarten: Why children need to play in school.* College Park, MD: Alliance for Childhood.

Miller, L. (2008, May 5). An algorithm for Mr. Right. *Newsweek.*

Mills, C. W. (1940). Situated actions and vocabularies of motive. *American Sociological Review, 5,* 904–913.

Mills, C. W. (1956). *The power elite.* New York: Oxford University Press.

Mills, C. W. (1959). *The sociological imagination.* New York: Oxford University Press.

Mills, J. L. (1985, February). Body language speaks louder than words. *Horizons.*

Minton, T. D., & Sabol, W. J. (2009). *Jail inmates at midyear 2008: Statistical tables* (NCJ225709). Washington, DC: Bureau of Justice Statistics. Retrieved June 18, 2010, from http://bjs.ojp.usdoj.gov/content/pub/pdf/jim08st.pdf

Mishel, L., Bernstein, J., & Allegretto, S. (2007). *The state of working America: 2006/2007.* Washington, DC: Economic Policy Institute.

Mishel, L., Bernstein, J., & Shierholz, H. (2009). *The state of working America 2008/2009.* Washington, DC: Economic Policy Institute.

Mobius, M. M., & Rosenblat, T. S. (2006). Why beauty matters. *American Economic Review, 96,* 222–235.

Moffatt, M. (1989). *Coming of age in New Jersey.* New Brunswick, NJ: Rutgers University Press.

Mokhiber, R. (1999, July/August). Crime wave! The top 100 corporate criminals of the 1990s. *Multinational Monitor,* 1–9.

Mokhiber, R. (2000, July/August). White collar crime spree. *Multinational Monitor,* 38.

Mokhiber, R., & Weissman, R. (2004, December). The ten worst corporations of 2004. *Multinational Monitor,* 8–21.

Mokhiber, R., & Weissman, R. (2006, November/December). J'accuse: The 10 worst corporations of 2006. *Multinational Monitor.* Retrieved September 5, 2009, from www.multinationalmonitor.org/mm2006/112006/mokhiber.html

Molotch, H., & Lester, M. (1974). News as purposive behavior: On the strategic use of routine events, accidents, and scandals. *American Sociological Review, 39,* 101–112.

Montopoli, B. (2009). Poll: Support of same-sex marriage grows. *CBS News.* Retrieved May 18, 2009, from www.cbsnews.com/blogs/2009/04/27/politics/politicalhotsheet/entry4972643.shtml

Moore, R. B. (1992). Racist stereotyping in the English language. In M. L. Anderson & P. H. Collins (Eds.), *Race, class and gender: An anthology.* Belmont, CA: Wadsworth.

Moore, S. (2009. March 3). Study shows high cost of criminal corrections. *New York Times.*

Morgan, G. (1986). *Images of organizations.* Newbury Park, CA: Sage.

Morgan, M. (1982). Television and adolescents' sex role stereotypes: A longitudinal study. *Journal of Personality and Social Psychology, 48,* 1173–1190.

Morgan, M. (1987). Television sex role attitudes and sex role behavior. *Journal of Early Adolescence, 7,* 269–282.

Morgan, R. (1996). *Sisterhood is global.* New York: Feminist Press at the City University of New York.

Morrongiello, B. A., & Hogg, K. (2004). Mothers' reactions to children misbehaving in ways that can lead to injury: Implications for gender differences in children's risk taking and injuries. *Sex Roles, 50,* 103–118.

Mottl, T. L. (1980). The analysis of countermovements. *Social Problems, 27,* 620–635.

Murdock, G. P. (1949). *Social structure.* New York: Macmillan.

Murdock, G. P. (1957). World ethnography sample. *American Anthropologist, 59,* 664–687.

Murguia, E., & Telles, E. E. (1996). Phenotype and schooling among Mexican Americans. *Sociology of Education, 69,* 276–289.

Murphy, K. (2008, May 31). Job climate for the class of 2008 is a bit warmer than expected. *New York Times.*

Mydans, S. (1995, February 12). A shooter as vigilante, and avenging angel. *New York Times.*

Mydans, S. (2007, April 9). Across cultures, English is the word. *International Herald Tribune.*

Nanda, S. (1994). *Cultural anthropology.* Belmont, CA: Wadsworth.

Nasar, S., & Mitchell, K. B. (1999, May 23). Booming job market draws young black men into the fold. *New York Times.*

National Academy of Sciences. (2007). *Beyond bias and barriers: Fulfilling the potential of women in academic science and engineering.* Washington, DC: National Academies Press.

National Association of Colleges and Employers. (2009). *Salary offers to college class of 2009 are flat.* Bethlehem, PA: Author. Retrieved February 26, 2009, from www.naceweb.org/press/display.asp?year=&prid=296

National Center for Education Statistics. (2006). *2005 Trial urban district results.* Washington, DC: Author. Retrieved July 5, 2007, from http://nces.ed.gov/nationsreportcard/nrc/tuda_reading_mathematics_2005/

National Center for Fair and Open Testing. (2008). *2007 college-bound seniors average SAT scores.* Boston: Author. Retrieved May 27, 2009, from www.fairtest.org/files/SATScores2007Chart.pdf

National Committee on Pay Equity. (2006). *The wage gap over time: In real dollars, women see a continuing gap.* Washington, DC: Author. Retrieved July 17, 2006, from www.pay-equity.org/info-time.html

National Committee on Pay Equity. (2007). *Current legislation.* Washington, DC: Author. Retrieved July 11, 2007, from www.pay-equity.org/info-leg.html

National Committee on Pay Equity. (2008). *The wage gap over time: In real dollars, women see a continuing gap.* Washington, DC: Author. Retrieved June 5, 2009, from www.pay-equity.org/info-time.html

National Conference of State Legislatures. (2009). *State laws regarding marriage between first cousins.* Washington, DC: Author. Retrieved April 28, 2009, from www.ncsl.org/programs/cyf/cousins.htm

National Crime Records Bureau. (2007). *Crime in India: 2007* (Table 5(A)). New Delhi, India: Author. Retrieved September 5, 2009, from http://ncrb.nic.in/cii2007/home.htm

National Fair Housing Alliance. (2009). *Fair housing enforcement: Time for a change: 2009 fair housing trends report.* Washington, DC: Author. Retrieved May 31, 2009, from www.nationalfairhousing.org/Portals/33/2009Trends/2009 FairHousingTrendsReport.pdf

National Institute of Mental Health. (2008). *Mental disorders cost society billions in unearned income.* Retrieved May 11, 2009, from www.nimh.nih.gov/science-news/2008/mental-disorders-cost-society-billions-in-unearned-income.shtml

National Institute of Mental Health. (2009). *Statistics.* Retrieved September 5, 2009, from www.nimh.nih.gov/health/ topics/ statistics/index.shtml

National Institute on Aging. (2006). *Dramatic changes in U.S. aging highlighted in new Census, NIH report.* Bethesda, MD: Author. Retrieved July 31, 2006, from www.nia.nih.gov/NewsAndEvents/PressReleases/PR2006030965PLusReport.htm

National Institute on Alcohol Abuse and Alcoholism. (2007). *What colleges need to know now: An update on college drinking research* (NIH Publication 07–5010). Bethesda, MD: Author. Retrieved September 5, 2009, from www .collegedrinkingprevention.gov/1College_Bulletin-508_361C4E.pdf

National Institute on Drug Abuse. (2003). *Drug use among racial/ethnic minorities* (NIH Publication 03–3888). Retrieved June 18, 2010, from http://archives.drugabuse.gov/pdf/minorities03.pdf.

National Labor Committee for Worker and Human Rights. (2001). *Shah Haksdum Garments Factory, Dhaka, Bangladesh.* Pittsburgh, PA: Author. Retrieved June 16, 2003, from www.nlcnet.org/campaigns/shahmakhdum/0502/sm0201.shtml

National Public Radio. (2007). *Bunk busters unravel the art of spin.* Washington, DC: Author. Retrieved September 5, 2009. from www.npr.org/templates/story/story.php?storyId=10416827

National Urban League. (2004). *The state of black America 2004.* New York: Author. Retrieved April 6, 2005, from www.nul.org/pdf/sobaexec.pdf

National Urban League. (2009). *The state of black America 2009: Message to the President. Executive Summary.* Retrieved September 5, 2009, from www.nul.org/thestateofblackamerica.html

National Women's Law Center. (2006). *The Paycheck Fairness Act: Helping to close the wage gap for women.* Washington, DC: Author. Retrieved September 5, 2009, from www.pay-equity.org/PDFs/PaycheckFairnessActApr06.pdf

Nelkin, D., & Pollak, M. (1981). *The atom besieged.* Cambridge: MIT Press.

Neubeck, K. (1986). *Social problems: A critical approach.* New York: Random House.

Neuman, W. L. (1994). *Social research methods: Qualitative and quantitative approaches.* Boston: Allyn & Bacon.

Newman, D. (2007). *Identities and inequalities: Exploring the intersections of race, class, gender, and sexuality.* New York: McGraw-Hill.

Newman, D. (2009). *Families: A sociological perspective.* New York: McGraw-Hill.

Newman, K. (2005). Family values against the odds. In A. S. Skolnick & J. H. Skolnick (Eds.), *Family in transition* (13th ed.). Boston: Allyn & Bacon.

Nichols, J. (2000, January). Now what? WTO Protests: Seattle is just a start. *Progressive.*

Niebuhr, G. (1998, April 12). Makeup of American religion is looking more like a mosaic, data say. *New York Times.*

Nord, M., Andrews, M., & Carlson, S. (2006). *Household food security in the United States, 2005* (Economic Research Report No. 29). Washington, DC: USDA. Retrieved August 7, 2007, from www.ers.usda.gov/publications/err29

Nugman, G. (2002). *World divorce rates.* Washington, DC: Heritage Foundation. Retrieved July 6, 2003, from www.divorcereform.org/gul.html

O'Connell Davidson, J. (2002). The practice of social research. In D. M. Newman & J. O'Brien (Eds.), *Sociology: Exploring the architecture of everyday life (Readings).* Thousand Oaks, CA: Pine Forge Press.

Oldenburg, R., & Brissett, D. (1982). The third place. *Qualitative Sociology, 5,* 265–284.

Olds, J., & Schwartz, R. S. (2009). *The lonely American: Drifting apart in the twenty-first century.* Boston: Beacon Press.

Olsen, M. (1965). *The logic of collective action.* Cambridge, MA: Harvard University Press.

Omi, M., & Winant, H. (1992). Racial formations. In P. S. Rothenberg (Ed.), *Race, class and gender in the United States.* New York: St. Martin's Press.

One child left behind. (2009, March/April). *UTNE Reader.*

Onishi, N. (2004a, March 30). On U.S. fast food, more Okinawans grow super-sized. *New York Times.*

Onishi, N. (2004b, December 16). Tokyo's flag law: Proud patriotism, or indoctrination? *New York Times.*

Orfield, G., & Lee, C. (2007). *Historical reversals, accelerating resegregation, and the need for new integration strategies.* Los Angeles: The Civil Rights Project. Retrieved September 5, 2009, from www.civilrightsproject.ucla.edu/research/deseg/reversals_reseg_need.pdf

Organ Procurement and Transplant Network. (2009). *Data reports.* Washington, DC: USDHSS. Retrieved June 2, 2009, from http://optn.transplant.hrsa.gov/latestdata/viewDataReports.asp

O'Sullivan-See, K., & Wilson, W. J. (1988). Race and ethnicity. In N. Smelser (Ed.), *Handbook of sociology.* Newbury Park, CA: Sage.

Padavic, I., & Reskin, B. (2002). *Women and men at work* (2nd ed.). Thousand Oaks, CA: Sage.

Pager, D. (2003). The mark of a criminal record. *American Journal of Sociology, 108,* 937–975.

Parenti, M. (1986). *Inventing reality.* New York: St. Martin's Press.

Parenti, M. (1995). *Democracy for the few.* New York: St. Martin's Press.

Parenti, M. (2006). Mass media: For the many, by the few. In P. S. Rothenberg (Ed.), *Beyond borders: Thinking critically about global issues.* New York: Worth.

Parrott, S. (2008). *Recession could cause large increases in poverty and push millions into deep poverty.* Washington, DC: Center on Budget and Policy Priorities. Retrieved May 26, 2009, from www.cbpp.org/cms/index.cfm?fa=view&id=1290

Parrott, S., & Sherman, A. (2006). *TANF at 10: Program results are more mixed than often understood.* Washington, DC: Center on Budget and Policy Priorities. Retrieved September 5, 2009, from www.cbpp.org/files/8-17-06tanf.pdf

Parsons, T. (1951). *The social system.* New York: Free Press.

Parsons, T., & Bales, R. F. (1955). *Family, socialization and interaction process.* Glencoe, IL: Free Press.

Parsons, T., & Smelser, N. (1956). *Economy and society.* New York: Free Press.

Passel, J. S., Capps, R., & Fix, M. (2004). *Undocumented immigrants: Facts and figures.* Retrieved April 6, 2005, from www.urban.org/UPLoadedPDF/1000587_undoc_immigrants_facts.pdf

Payer, L. (1988). *Medicine and culture.* New York: Penguin Books.

Pear, R. (1992, December 4). New look at U.S. in 2050: Bigger, older and less white. *New York Times.*

Pear, R. (2000, April 30). Studies find research on women lacking. *New York Times.*

Pear, R. (2008a, March 23). Gap in life expectancy widens for the nation. *New York Times.*

Pear, R. (2008b, October 30). Women buying health policies pay a penalty. *New York Times.*

Pearce, D. (1979). Gatekeepers and homeseekers: Institutional patterns in racial steering. *Social Problems, 26,* 325–342.

Pearce, L. D., & Axinn, W. G. (1998). The impact of family religious life on the quality of mother child relations. *American Sociological Review, 63,* 810–828.

Perez-Peña, R. (2003, April 19). Study finds asthma in 25% of children in central Harlem. *New York Times.*

Perlez, J. (1991, August 31). Madagascar, where the dead return, bringing joy. *New York Times.*

Perlin, S. A., Sexton, K., & Wong, D. W. S. (1999). An examination of race and poverty for populations living near industrial sources of air pollution. *Journal of Exposure Analysis and Environmental Epidemiology, 9,* 29–48.

Perlman, D., & Fehr, B. (1987). The development of intimate relationships. In D. Perlman & S. Duck (Eds.), *Intimate relationships: Development, dynamics and deterioration.* Newbury Park, CA: Sage.

Pescosolido, B. A. (1986). Migration, medical care and the lay referral system: A network theory of role assimilation. *American Sociological Review, 51,* 523–540.

Pescosolido, B. A., Grauerholz, E., & Milkie, M. A. (1997). Culture and conflict: The portrayal of Blacks in U.S. children's picture books through the mid- and late-twentieth century. *American Sociological Review, 62,* 443–464.

Peterson, R. D., & Bailey, W. C. (1991). Felony murder and capital punishment: An examination of the deterrence question. *Criminology, 29,* 367–395.

Peterson, S. B., & Lach, M. A. (1990). Gender stereotypes in children's books: Their prevalence and influence in cognitive and affective development. *Gender and Education, 2,* 185–197.

Pew Forum on Religion and Public Life. (2004). *The American religious landscape and politics, 2004.* Washington, DC: Pew Research Center. Retrieved December 31, 2004, from www.pewforum.org/publications/surveys/green.pdf

Pew Global Attitudes Project. (2008). *Unfavorable views of Jews and Muslims on the increase in Europe.* Washington, DC: Pew Research Center. Retrieved June 18, 2010, from http://pewglobal.org/2008/09/17/unfavorable-views-of-jews-and-muslims-on-the-increase-in-europe/

Pew Research Center. (2005). *Social security polling: Cross-currents in opinion about private accounts.* Washington, DC: Author. Retrieved September 5, 2009, from http://people-press.org/commentary/pdf/106.pdf

Pew Research Center. (2007a). *Muslim Americans: Middle class and mostly mainstream.* Washington, DC: Author. Retrieved September 5, 2009, from http://pewresearch.org/assets/pdf/muslim-americans.pdf

Pew Research Center. (2007b). *Trends in political values and core attitudes: 1987–2007.* Washington, DC: Author. Retrieved September 5, 2009, from http://people-press.org/reports/pdf/312.pdf

Pfohl, S. J. (1994). *Images of deviance and social control.* New York: McGraw-Hill.

Phillips, K. (2002). *Wealth and democracy.* New York: Broadway Books.

Piore, A. (2003, March 17). Home alone. *Newsweek.*

Piper, A. (1992). Passing for white, passing for black. *Transition, 58,* 4–32.

Piven, F. F., & Cloward, R. A. (1977). *Poor people's movements: Why they succeed, how they fail.* New York: Vintage Books.

Pizza must go through: It's the law in San Francisco. (1996, July 14). *New York Times.*

Polgreen, L. (2005, December 27). Ghana's uneasy embrace of slavery's diaspora. *New York Times.*

Pope exalts women for roles as wife, mom. (2003, June 7). *Indianapolis Star.*

Popenoe, D. (1993). American family decline, 1960–1990: A review and appraisal. *Journal of Marriage and the Family, 55,* 527–555.

Population Reference Bureau. (2006a). *2006 World population data sheet.* Washington, DC: Author. Retrieved September 5, 2009, from http://www.prb.org/pdf06/06WorldDataSheet.pdf

Population Reference Bureau. (2006b). *The world's youth: 2006 data sheet.* Washington, DC: Author. Retrieved April 1, 2007, from www.prb.org

Population Reference Bureau. (2008a). *Female genital mutilation/cutting: Data and trends.* Washington, DC: Author. Retrieved May 3, 2009, from www.prb.org/pdf08/fgm-wallchart.pdf

Population Reference Bureau. (2008b). *2008 world population data sheet.* Washington, DC: Author. Retrieved May 27, 2009, from www.prb.org/pdf08/08WPDS_Eng.pdf

Porter, E. (2006, October 17). Law on overseas brides is keeping couples apart. *New York Times.*

Powell, M. (2009a, May 31). On diverse force, blacks still face special peril. *New York Times.*

Powell, M. (2009b, June 7). Suit accuses Wells Fargo of steering blacks to subprime mortgages in Baltimore. *New York Times.*

Powell, M., & Roberts, J. (2009, May 15). Minorities affected most as New York foreclosures rise. *New York Times.*

Prah, P. M. (2006). Domestic violence. *CQ Researcher, 16,* 1–24.

President's Council on Bioethics. (2003). *Beyond therapy: Biotechnology and the pursuit of happiness.* Washington, DC: Government Printing Office.

Price paid in military lives equal to 9/11 toll. (2006, September 23). *Banner Graphic.*

Project for Excellence in Journalism. (2005). *Embedded reporters: What are Americans getting?* Washington, DC: Pew Research Center. Retrieved September 5, 2009, from www.journalism.org/sites/journalism.org/files/pejembedreport.pdf

Project for Excellence in Journalism. (2006). *Change in stations owned by top companies: 1999–2005.* Washington, DC: Pew Research Center. Retrieved June 18, 2007, from www.journalism.org/node/1325

Prothero, S. (2007). *Religious literacy.* San Francisco: Harper.

Pugliesi, K. (1987). Deviation in emotion and the labeling of mental illness. *Deviant Behavior, 8,* 79–102.

Putnam, R. D. (1995). Bowling alone: America's declining social capital. *Journal of Democracy, 6,* 65–78.

Quinney, R. (1970). *The social reality of crime.* Boston: Little, Brown.

Rabin, R. C. (2008, December 16). Living with in-laws linked to heart risks in Japanese women. *New York Times.*

Raley, S., & Bianchi, S. (2006). Sons, daughters, and family processes: Does gender of children matter? *Annual Review of Sociology, 32,* 401–421.

Rand, M. R. (2008). *Criminal victimization, 2007* (NCJ224390). Washington, DC: Bureau of Justice Statistics. Retrieved June 3, 2009, from www.ojp.usdoj.gov/bjs/pub/pdf/CV07.pdf

Rankin, S. R. (2003). *Campus climate for gay, lesbian, bisexual, and transgender people: A national perspective.* Washington, DC: National Gay and Lesbian Task Force. Retrieved September 5, 2009, from www.thetaskforce.org/downloads/reports/reports/CampusClimate.pdf

Reddy, G. (2005). *With respect to sex: Negotiating hijra identity in South Asia.* Chicago: University of Chicago Press.

Reiman, J. (2007). *The rich get richer and the poor get prison.* Boston: Allyn & Bacon.

Relethford, J. H., Stern, M. P., Caskill, S. P., & Hazuda, H. P. (1983). Social class, admixture, and skin color variation in Mexican Americans and Anglo Americans living in San Antonio, Texas. *American Journal of Physical Anthropology, 61,* 97–102.

Religious groups gather for "Justice Wednesday" pray in. (2005, April 26). *Worldwide Faith News.* Retrieved July 24, 2005, from www.wfn.org/2005/04/msg00274.html

Rennison, C. M., & Welchans, S. (2000). *Intimate partner violence* (Special Report No. NCJ 178247). Washington, DC: United States Bureau of Justice Statistics.

Research findings affirm health of women hinges on reform of clinical research. (2003, August 14). *Women's Health Weekly.*

Reskin, B., & Hartmann, H. (1986). *Women's work, men's work: Sex segregation on the job.* Washington, DC: National Academy Press.

Reyes, L., & Rubie, P. (1994). *Hispanics in Hollywood: An encyclopedia of film and television.* New York: Garland Press.

Rice, A. (2009, April 12). Mission from Africa. *New York Times Magazine.*

Rideout, V., Roberts, D. E., & Foehr, U. G. (2005). *Generation M: Media in the lives of 8–18 year olds.* Retrieved Retrieved June 18, 2010, from www.kff.org/entmedia/upload/8010.pdf

Ridgeway, C. L., & Smith-Lovin, L. (1999). The gender system and interaction. *Annual Review of Sociology, 25,* 191–216.

Rieff, D. (2005, November 6). Migrant worry. *New York Times Magazine.*

Rieff, D. (2006, July 2). America the untethered. *New York Times Magazine.*

Riesman, D. (1950). *The lonely crowd.* New Haven, CT: Yale University Press.

Riley, M. W. (1971). Social gerontology and the age stratification of society. *Gerontologist, 11,* 79–87.

Riley, M. W., Foner, A., & Waring, J. (1988). Sociology of age. In N. J. Smelser (Ed.), *Handbook of sociology.* Newbury Park, CA: Sage.

Rimer, S. (2002, June 4). Suspects lacking lawyers are freed in Atlanta. *New York Times.*

Rimer, S., & Arenson, K. W. (2004, June 24). Top colleges take more blacks, but which ones? *New York Times.*

Robbins, A. (2004). *Pledged: The secret life of sororities.* New York: Hyperion.

Robert Wood Johnson Foundation. (2005). *Characteristics of the uninsured: A view from the states.* Retrieved September 5, 2009, from www.rwjf.org/files/research/Full_SHADAC.pdf

Roberts, S. (2006, February 12). So many men, so few women. *New York Times.*

Roberts, S. (2007a, January 16). 51% of women are now living without spouse. *New York Times.*

Roberts, S. (2007b, November 17). In the U.S. name count, Garcias are catching up with the Joneses. *New York Times.*

Robinson, B. A. (1999). *Facts about inter-faith marriages.* Retrieved July 6, 2003, from www.religioustolerance.org/ifm_facthtm

Robinson, R. V., & Bell, W. (1978). Equality, success and social justice in England and the United States. *American Sociological Review, 43,* 125–143.

Robinson, R. V., & Kelley, J. (1979). Class as conceived by Marx and Dahrendorf: Effects on income inequality and politics in the United States and Great Britain. *American Sociological Review, 44,* 38–58.

Rodriguez, C. E., & Cordero-Guzman, H. (2004). Placing race in context. In C. A. Gallagher (Ed.), *Rethinking the color line: Readings in race and ethnicity.* New York: McGraw-Hill.

Roethlisberger, E. J., & Dickson, W. J. (1939). *Management and the worker.* Cambridge, MA: Harvard University Press.

Rohter, L. (2004, December 29). Learn English, says Chile, thinking upwardly global. *New York Times.*

Rohter, L. (2005, January 30). Divorce ties Chile in knots. *New York Times.*

Roland, A. (1988). *In search of self in India and Japan.* Princeton, NJ: Princeton University Press.

Romero, S. (1999, July 24). Cashing in on security woes. *New York Times.*

Roscigno, V. J., Karafin, D. L., & Tester, G. (2009). The complexities and processes of racial housing discrimination. *Social Problems, 56,* 49–69.

Rosenbaum, D. E. (2005, April 14). True to ritual, house votes for full repeal of estate tax. *New York Times.*

Rosenblatt, P. C., Karis, T. A., & Powell, R. D. (1995). *Multiracial couples.* Thousand Oaks, CA: Sage.

Rosenbloom, S. (2009, June 20). Big retailers shift strategy in a recession. *New York Times.*

Rosenfeld, M. J. (2005). A critique of exchange theory in mate selection. *American Journal of Sociology, 110,* 1284–1325.

Rosenthal, R., & Jacobson, L. (1968). *Pygmalion in the classroom.* New York: Holt, Rinehart & Winston.

Ross, C. E., Mirowsky, J., & Goldstein, K. (1990). The impact of family on health: The decade in review. *Journal of Marriage and the Family, 52,* 1059–1078.

Rossi, A. (1968). Transition to parenthood. *Journal of Marriage and the Family, 30,* 26–39.

Rothenberg, P. S. (Ed.). (1992). *Race, class and gender in the United States.* New York: St. Martin's Press.

Rothman, B. K. (1984). Women, health and medicine. In J. Freeman (Ed.), *Women: A feminist perspective.* Palo Alto, CA: Mayfield.

Rothman, B. K., & Caschetta, M. B. (1999). Treating health: Women and medicine. In S. J. Ferguson (Ed.), *Mapping the social landscape: Readings in sociology.* Mountain View, CA: Mayfield.

Rothman, D. J., & Edgar, H. (1992). Scientific rigor and medical realities: Placebo trials in cancer and AIDS research. In E. Fee & D. M. Fox (Eds.), *AIDS: The making of a chronic disease.* Berkeley: University of California Press.

Rothschild, M. (2000, January). Soothsayers of Seattle. *Progressive.*

Rothstein, R. (2001, December 12). An economic recovery will tell in the classroom. *New York Times.*

Rubin, L. (1994). *Families on the fault line.* New York: HarperCollins.

Rucker, P. (2009, April 8). Some link economy with spate of killings. *New York Times.*

Rusbult, C. E., Zembrodt, I. M., & Iwaniszek, J. (1986). The impact of gender and sex-role orientation on responses to dissatisfaction in close relationships. *Sex Roles, 15,* 1–20.

Rybczynski, W. (1999, April 18). One good turn. *New York Times Magazine.*

Sabol, W. J., Minton, T. D., & Harrison, P. M. (2007). *Prison and jail inmates at midyear 2006* (NCJ217675). Washington, DC: Bureau of Justice Statistics. Retrieved June 18, 2010, from http://bjs.ojp.usdoj.gov/content/pub/pdf/pjim06.pdf

Sack, K. (2009, May 11). Despite recession, personalized health care remains in demand. *New York Times.*

Sadker, M., & Sadker, D. (1999). Failing at fairness: Hidden lessons. In S. Ferguson (Ed.), *Mapping the social landscape.* Mountain View, CA: Mayfield.

Sadker, M., Sadker, D., Fox, L., & Salata, M. (2004). Gender equity in the classroom: The unfinished agenda. In M. S. Kimmel (Ed.), *The gendered society reader.* New York: Oxford University Press.

Saenz, R. (2004, August). *Latinos and the changing face of America* (PRB Report). Washington, DC: Population Reference Bureau. Retrieved September 3, 2004, from www.prb.org

Safer, D. J., Zito, J. M., & dosReis, S. (2003). Concomitant psychotropic medication for youths. *American Journal of Psychiatry, 160,* 438–449.

Safire, W. (1995, July 17). News about Jews. *New York Times.*

Safire, W. (2008, May 25). Emoticons. *New York Times Magazine.*

Sanday, P. R. (1996). *A woman scorned: Acquaintance rape on trial.* New York: Doubleday.

Sanderson, W., & Scherbov, S. (2008). Rethinking age and aging. *Population Bulletin, 63,* 1–16.

Santora, M. (2005, January 30). U.S. is close to eliminating AIDS in infants, officials say. *New York Times.*

Sapir, E. (1949). *Selected writings* (D. G. Mandelbaum, Ed.). Berkeley: University of California Press.

Saul, L. (1972). Personal and social psychopathology and the primary prevention of violence. *American Journal of Psychiatry, 128,* 1578–1581.

Saulny, S. (2009, February 25). They stand when called upon, and when not. *New York Times.*

Saunders, J. M. (1991). Relating social structural abstractions to sociological research. *Teaching Sociology, 19,* 270–271.

Sayer, L., Casper, L., & Cohen, P. (2004, October). *Women, men, and work* (PRB Report). Washington, DC: Population Reference Bureau. Retrieved December 30, 2004, from www.prb.org

Scherzer, L. (2007, August 7). With pre-school tuition soaring, parents seek alternatives. *SmartMoney.* Retrieved September 3, 2009, from www.smartmoney.com/spending/deals/with-preschool-tuition-soaring-parents-seek-alternatives-21648/

Schlesinger, A. (1992). *The disuniting of America.* New York: Norton.

Schodolski, V. J. (1993, December 26). Funeral industry, pitching videos, 2-for-1 specials to baby boomers. *Indianapolis Star.*

Schoenborn, C. A. (2004). Marital status and health: United States, 1999–2002. Centers for Disease Control and Prevention. *Vital and Health Statistics, 351.* Retrieved September 5, 2009, from http://www.cdc.gov/nchs/data/ad/ad351.pdf

Schofield, H. (2005, September 22). France announces new measures to encourage large families. *Agence France Presse—English.*

Schooler, C. (1996). Cultural and social structural explanations of cross-national psychological differences. *Annual Review of Sociology, 22,* 323–349.

Schuman, H., & Krysan, M. (1999). A historical note on Whites' beliefs about racial inequality. *American Sociological Review, 64,* 847–855.

Schur, E. M. (1984). *Labeling women deviant: Gender, stigma and social control.* New York: Random House.

Schwartz, C. R., & Mare, R. D. (2005). Trends in educational assertive marriage from 1940 to 2003. *Demography, 42,* 621–646.

Schwartz, J., Revkin, A. C., & Wald, M. L. (2005, September 12). In reviving New Orleans, a challenge of many tiers. *New York Times.*

Sciolino, E., & Mekhennet, S. (2008, June 11). Muslim world and virginity: 2 worlds collide. *New York Times.*

Scott, J., & Leonhardt, D. (2005, May 15). Class in America: Shadowy lines that still divide us. *New York Times.*

Scott, L. D. (2003). The relation of racial identity and racial socialization to coping with discrimination among African American adolescents. *Journal of Black Studies, 33,* 520–538.

Scott, M., & Lyman, S. (1968). Accounts. *American Sociological Review, 33,* 46–62.

Scull, A., & Favreau, D. (1986). A chance to cut is a chance to cure: Sexual surgery for psychosis in three nineteenth-century societies. In S. Spitzer & A. T. Scull (Eds.), *Research in law, deviance and social control* (Vol. 8). Greenwich, CT: JAI Press.

Segal, D. (2009, March 12). Financial fraud rises as target for prosecutors. *New York Times.*

Semyonov, M., & Raijman, R. (2006). The rise of anti-foreigner sentiment in European societies, 1988–2000. *American Sociological Review, 71,* 426–449.

Sengupta, S. (2004, October 26). Relentless attacks on women in West Sudan draw an outcry. *New York Times.*

Sennett, R. (1984). *Families against the city: Middle-class homes in industrial Chicago.* Cambridge, MA: Harvard University Press.

Sex offender's case denied in court. (2001, January 16). *Associated Press Online.* Retrieved January 30, 2001.

Sexual harassment statistics in the workplace and in education. (2004). Retrieved July 31, 2004, from http://womensissues.about.com/cs/goverornews/a/sexharassstats.htm

Shah, A. (2009). Poverty facts and statistics. *Global Issues.* Retrieved May 28, 2009, from www.globalissues.org/article/26/poverty-facts-and-stats#src1

Shakin, M., Shakin, D., & Sternglanz, S. H. (1985). Infant clothing: Sex labeling for strangers. *Sex Roles, 12,* 955–964.

Shanghai urges "two child" policy. (2009, July 24). *BBC News.* Retrieved September 2, 2009, from http://news.bbc.co.uk/2/hi/asia-pacific/8166413.stm

Shapiro, T. M. (2008). The hidden cost of being African American. In S. J. Ferguson (Ed.), *Mapping the social landscape.* New York: McGraw-Hill.

Shapo, H. S. (2006). Assisted reproduction and the law: Disharmony on a divisive social issue. *Northwestern University Law Review, 100,* 465–479.

Shipler, D. K. (2004). *The working poor: Invisible in America.* New York: Knopf.

Shugart, H. A. (2003). She shoots, she scores: Mediated construction of contemporary female athletes in coverage of the 1999 U.S. Women's soccer team. *Western Journal of Communication, 67,* 1–31.

Shweder, R. A. (1997, March 9). It's called poor health for a reason. *New York Times.*

Sidel, R. (1986). *Women and children last.* New York: Penguin Books.

Sidel, R. (1990). *On her own: Growing up in the shadow of the American dream.* New York: Penguin Books.

Siegel, R. B. (2004). A short history of sexual harassment. In C. A. MacKinnon & R. B. Siegel (Eds.), *Directions in sexual harassment law.* New Haven, CT: Yale University Press.

Signorielli, N. (1990). Children, television, and gender roles. *Journal of Adolescent Health Care, 11,* 50–58.

Silverman, D. (1982). *Secondary analysis in social research: A guide to data sources and methods with examples.* Boston: Allen & Unwin.

Simmel, G. (1950). *The sociology of Georg Simmel* (K. Wolff, Ed.). New York: Free Press. (Original work published 1902)

Simon, S. (2009, April 13). Education board in Texas faces curbs. *Wall Street Journal.*

Simons, M. (2001, April 30). An awful task: Assessing 4 roles in death of thousands in Rwanda. *New York Times.*

Simpson, I. H. (1979). *From student to nurse: A longitudinal study of socialization.* Cambridge, UK: Cambridge University Press.

Sinclair Broadcast Group. (2005). *Company profile.* Hunt Valley, MD: Author. Retrieved May 24, 2005, from www.sbgi.net/about/profile.shtml

Sindelar, R. (2004). *Recess: Is it needed in the 21st century?* Champaign, IL: Clearinghouse on Early Education and Parenting. Retrieved May 23, 2009, from http://ceep.crc.uiuc.edu/poptopics/recess.html

Skocpol, T. (1979). *States and social revolutions: A comparative analysis of France, Russia and China.* New York: Cambridge University Press.

Skolnick, A. S. (1991). *Embattled paradise.* New York: Basic Books.

Skolnick, A. S., & Skolnick, J. H. (Eds.). (1992). *Family in transition* (7th ed.). New York: HarperCollins.

Slackman, M. (2006, August 6). The fine art of hiding what you mean to say. *New York Times.*

Slackman, M. (2007, May 26). A quiet revolution in Algeria: Gains by women. *New York Times.*

Smith, C. S. (2002, May 5). Risking limbs for height and success in China. *New York Times.*

Smith, C. S. (2005, April 30). Abduction, often violent, a Kyrgyz wedding rite. *New York Times.*

Smith, W. (2002, April 5). Eroica trio offers beauty of more than one kind. *Indianapolis Star.*

Snell, T. L. (2008). *Capital punishment, 2007* (NCJ224528). Washington, DC: Bureau of Justice Statistics. Retrieved May 20, 2009, from www.ojp.usdoj.gov/bjs/pub/html/cp/2007/cp07st.htm#2007tables

Sniderman, P. M., & Tetlock, P. E. (1986). Symbolic racism: Problems of motive attribution in political analysis. *Social Forces, 42,* 129–150.

Snipp, C. M. (1986). American Indians and natural resource development. *American Journal of Economics and Sociology, 45,* 457–474.

Soldo, B. J., & Agree, E. M. (1988). America's elderly. *Population Bulletin, 43,* 1–45.

Sontag, D. (1992, December 11). Across the U.S., immigrants find the land of resentment. *New York Times.*

Soukup, E. (2004, August 2). Till blog do us part. *Newsweek.*

South, S. J., & Lloyd, K. M. (1995). Spousal alternatives and marital dissolution. *American Sociological Review, 60,* 21–35.

Springen, K. (2006, February 27). States: Time to stub out smoking. *Newsweek.*

St. George, D. (2007, May 13). Pushing the motherhood cause. *Washington Post.*

St. John, W. (2006, June 2). Sports, songs, and salvation on Faith Night at the stadium. *New York Times.*

Stacey, J. (1991). Backward toward the postmodern family. In A. Wolfe (Ed.), *America at century's end.* Berkeley: University of California Press.

Staggenborg, S. (1998). *Gender, family, and social movements.* Thousand Oaks, CA: Pine Forge Press.

Staples, R. (1992). African American families. In J. M. Henslin (Ed.), *Marriage and family in a changing society.* New York: Free Press.

Starbucks. (2008). *Fiscal 2008 annual report.* Central Islip, New York: Author. Retrieved September 5, 2009, from http://media.corporate-ir.net/media_files/irol/99/99518/AR2008.pdf

Stark, R., & Bainbridge, W. S. (1980). Networks of faith: Interpersonal bonds and recruitment in cults and sects. *American Journal of Sociology, 85,* 1376–1395.

Starr, P. (1982). *The social transformation of American medicine.* New York: Basic Books.

Stein, R. (2007, May 27). Critical care without consent. *Washington Post.*

Steinberg, J. (2002, May 2). More family income committed to college. *New York Times.*

Steinhauer, J. (2005, May 29). When the Joneses wear jeans. *New York Times.*

Steinhauer, J. (2006, October 30). With the House in the balance, Pelosi serves as a focal point for both parties. *New York Times.*

Steinmetz, S. K., Clavan, R., & Stein, K. F. (1990). *Marriage and family realities: Historical and contemporary perspectives.* New York: Harper & Row.

Steuerle, C. E. (2007). *Crumbs for children?* Washington, DC: Urban Institute. Retrieved June 24, 2007, from www.urban.org/publications/901068.html

Stevenson, B., & Wolfers, J. (2007). *Marriage and divorce: Changes and their driving forces* (Working Paper No. 12944). Cambridge, MA: National Bureau of Economic Research. Retrieved May 12, 2007, from http://bpp.wharton.upenn.edu/jwolfers/Papers/MarriageandDivorce(JEP).pdf

Stewart, A. J., Copeland, A. P., Chester, A. L., Malley, J. E., & Barenbaum, N. B. (1997). *Separating together: How divorce transforms families.* New York: Guilford Press.

Stewart, J. E. (1980). Defendant's attractiveness as a factor in the outcome of criminal trials: An observational study. *Journal of Applied Social Psychology, 10,* 348–361.

Stille, A. (2002, June 29). Textbook publishers learn to avoid messing with Texas. *New York Times.*

Stinnett, N., & DeFrain, J. (1985). *Secrets of strong families.* Boston: Little, Brown.

Stockard, J., & O'Brien, R. M. (2002). Cohort effects on suicide rates: International variation. *American Sociological Review, 67,* 854–872.

Stokes, R., & Hewitt, J. P. (1976). Aligning actions. *American Sociological Review, 41,* 837–849.

Stolberg, S. G. (1998, April 5). Live and let die over transplants. *New York Times.*

Stolberg, S. G., & Connelly, M. (2009, April 29). Obama nudging views on race, a survey finds. *New York Times.*

Stone, G. P. (1981). Appearance and the self: A slightly revised version. In G. P. Stone & H. A. Farberman (Eds.), *Social psychology through symbolic interaction.* New York: Wiley.

Straus, M. A. (1977). A sociological perspective on the prevention and treatment of wife beating. In M. Roy (Ed.), *Battered women.* New York: Van Nostrand Reinhold.

Straus, M. A., & Gelles, R. J. (1990). How violent are American families? Estimates from the National Family Violence Resurvey and other studies. In M. A. Straus & R. J. Gelles (Eds.), *Physical violence in American families.* New Brunswick, NJ: Transaction.

Strom, S. (2005, January 13). U.S. charity overwhelmed by disaster aid. *New York Times.*

Strube, M. J., & Barbour, L. S. (1983). The decision to leave an abusive relationship: Economic dependence and psychological commitment. *Journal of Marriage and the Family, 45,* 785–793.

Stryker, J. (1997, July 13). The age of innocence isn't what it once was. *New York Times.*

Stryker, S. (1980). *Symbolic interactionism.* Menlo Park, CA: Benjamin/Cummings.

Student performance, poverty link seen again. (2007, June 7). *Banner Graphic.*

Study finds increase in weapons use. (2000, November 30). *New York Times.*

Suarez, Z. (1998). The Cuban-American family. In C. H. Mindel, R. W. Habenstein, & R. Wright (Eds.), *Ethnic families in America: Patterns and variations.* Upper Saddle River, NJ: Prentice Hall.

Sudarkasa, N. (2001). Interpreting the African heritage in Afro-American family organization. In S. Ferguson (Ed.), *Shifting the center: Understanding contemporary families.* Mountain View, CA: Mayfield.

Sudnow, D. (1965). Normal crimes: Sociological features of the penal code in a public defender's office. *Social Problems, 12,* 255–264.

Sullivan, R. (2006, June 25). A slow-road movement. *New York Times Magazine.*

Sutherland, E., & Cressey, D. (1955). *Criminology.* Philadelphia: Lippincott.

Swanson, G. (1992). Doing things together: On some basic forms of agency and structuring in collective action and on some explanations for them. *Social Psychology Quarterly, 55,* 94–117.

Swarns, R. L. (2001, April 20). Drug makers drop South Africa suit over AIDS medicines. *New York Times.*

Swarns, R. L. (2004, October 24). Hispanics resist racial grouping by census. *New York Times.*

Swarns, R. L. (2008a, September 2). Bipartisan calls for new federal poverty measure. *New York Times.*

Swarns, R. L. (2008b, August 25). Blacks debate civil rights risk in Obama's rise. *New York Times.*

Sykes, G., & Matza, D. (1957). Techniques of neutralization: A theory of delinquency. *American Sociological Review, 22,* 664–670.

Takayama, H. (2003, January 13). The Okinawa way. *Newsweek.*

Talbot, M. (2000, February 27). A mighty fortress. *New York Times Magazine.*

Tarrow, S. (1994). *Power in movement.* New York: Cambridge University Press.

Tavris, C., & Offir, C. (1984). *The longest war: Sex differences in perspective.* New York: Harcourt Brace Jovanovich.

Teachman, J. D. (1991). Contributions to children by divorced fathers. *Social Problems, 38,* 358–371.

Tejada-Vera, B., & Sutton, P. D. (2009). Births, marriages, divorces, and deaths: Provisional data for July 2008. *National Vital Statistics Reports, 57,* 13. Retrieved May 18, 2009, from www.cdc.gov/nchs/data/nvsr/nvsr57/nvsr57_13.htm

Telles, E. E., & Murguia, E. (1990). Phenotypic discrimination and income differences among Mexican Americans. *Social Science Quarterly, 71,* 682–696.

Thoits, P. (1985). Self-labeling process in mental illness: The role of emotional deviance. *American Journal of Sociology, 91,* 221–249.

Thompson, G. (2003, February 13). Behind roses' beauty, poor and ill workers. *New York Times.*

Thompson, G. (2009, March 15). Where education and assimilation collide. *New York Times.*

Thompson, T. L., & Zerbinos, E. (1995). Gender roles in animated cartoons: Has the picture changed in 20 years? *Sex Roles, 32,* 651–673.

Thomson, D. S. (2000). The Sapir-Whorf hypothesis: Worlds shaped by words. In J. Spradley & D. W. McCurdy (Eds.), *Conformity and conflict.* Boston: Allyn & Bacon.

Thornton, M. (1997). Strategies of racial socialization among black parents: Mainstreaming, minority, and cultural messages. In R. Taylor, J. Jackson, & L. Chatters (Eds.), *Family life in black America.* Thousand Oaks, CA: Sage.

Thurlow, C. (2001). Naming the "outsider within": Homophobic pejoratives and the verbal abuse of lesbian, gay, and bisexual high-school pupils. *Journal of Adolescence, 24,* 25–38.

Tietz, J. (2006, April 20). The killing factory. *Rolling Stone.*

Timms, E., & McGonigle, S. (1992, April 5). Psychological warfare. *Indianapolis Star.*

Tjaden, P., & Thoennes, N. (2000). *Extent, nature, and consequences of intimate partner violence* (NCJ 181867). Washington, DC: Bureau of Justice Statistics. Retrieved September 5, 2009, from www.ncjrs.gov/pdffiles1/nij/181867.pdf

Tobin, J. J., Wu, D. Y. H., & Davidson, D. H. (1989). *Preschool in three cultures: Japan, China and the United States.* New Haven, CT: Yale University Press.

Tönnies, F. (1957). *Community and society*, C. P. Loomis (Ed.). East Lansing: Michigan State University Press. (Original work published 1887)

Towell, L. (2007, November 18). Patients without borders. *New York Times Magazine.*

Triandis, H. C., McCusker, C., & Hui, C. H. (1990). Multimethod probes of individualism and collectivism. *Journal of Personality and Social Psychology, 59,* 1006–1020.

Trotsky, L. (1959). *The history of the Russian Revolution* (F. W. Dupee, Ed.). Garden City, NY: Doubleday. (Original work published 1930)

Trotter, R. T., & Chavira, J. A. (1997). *Curanderismo: Mexican American folk healing.* Athens: University of Georgia Press.

Trunk, P. (2007, July 16). What Gen Y really wants. *Time.*

Tumin, M. (1953). Some principles of stratification: A critical analysis. *American Sociological Review, 18,* 387–393.

Turkheimer, E., Haley, A., Waldron, M., D'Onofrio, B., & Gottesman, I. I. (2003). Socioeconomic status modifies heritability of IQ in young children. *Psychological Science, 14,* 623–628.

Turner, E. H., Matthews, A. M., Linardatos, E., Tell, R. A., & Rosenthal, R. (2008). Selective publication of antidepressant trials and its influence on apparent efficacy. *New England Journal of Medicine, 358,* 252–260.

Turner, J. H. (1972). *Patterns of social organization.* New York: McGraw-Hill.

Turner, R. W., & Killian, L. M. (1987). *Collective behavior.* Englewood Cliffs, NJ: Prentice Hall.

Tyagi, A. W. (2004, March 22). Why women have to work. *Time.*

Tyre, P. (2006, January 30). The trouble with boys. *Newsweek.*

Uchitelle, L. (2005, January 13). College degree still pays, but it's leveling off. *New York Times.*

Uchitelle, L. (2006a, December 20). Raising the floor on pay. *New York Times.*

Uchitelle, L. (2006b, November 27). Very rich are leaving the merely rich behind. *New York Times.*

Uchitelle, L. (2008, April 20). The wage that meant middle class. *New York Times.*

Uggen, C., & Blackstone, A. (2004). Sexual harassment as a gendered expression of power. *American Sociological Review, 69,* 64–92.

UNAIDS. (2008). *2008 report on the global AIDS epidemic.* Geneva, Switzerland: Author. Retrieved September 5, 2009, from http://data.unaids.org/pub/GlobalReport/2008/JC1511_GR08_ExecutiveSummary_en.pdf

UNICEF. (2009). *The state of the world's children 2009.* Geneva, Switzerland: Author. Retrieved September 5, 2009, from www.unicef.org/sowc09/docs/SOWC09-FullReport-EN.pdf

United Nations. (2004). *World population to 2300.* Geneva, Switzerland: Author. Retrieved June 18, 2010, from www.un.org/esa/population/publications/longrange2/WorldPop2300final.pdf

United Nations. (2007). *Situations of concern.* Geneva, Switzerland: Office of the Special Representative of the Secretary-General for Children and Armed Conflict. Retrieved September 5, 2009, from www.un.org/children/conflict/english/conflicts2.html

United Nations Population Division. (2003). *World population prospects: The 2002 revision.* Geneva, Switzerland: Author. Retrieved June 26, 2003, from www.un.org/esa/population/publications/wpp2002/wpp2002-highlightsrev1.pdf

United Nations Population Division. (2005). *World population prospects: The 2004 revision population database.* Geneva, Switzerland: Author. Retrieved July 15, 2005, from http://esa.un.org/unpp/index.asp?panel=2

United Nations Population Division. (2008). *World urbanization prospects: The 2007 revision.* Geneva, Switzerland: Author. Retrieved June 18, 2010, from www.un.org/esa/population/publications/wup2007/2007WUP_Highlights_web.pdf

United States Bureau of Justice Statistics. (2001). *The sexual victimization of college women* [Press release]. Washington, DC: Author. Retrieved June 18, 2010, from http://bjs.ojp.usdoj.gov/content/pub/press/svcw.pr

United States Bureau of Justice Statistics. (2009). *Growth in prison and jail populations slowing: 16 states report declines in the number of prisoners.* Washington, DC: Author. Retrieved September 5, 2009, from www.ojp.usdoj.gov/bjs/pub/press/pimjim08stpr.htm

United States Bureau of Labor Statistics. (2007). *Consumer expenditures in 2005* (Report No. 998). Washington, DC: Author. Retrieved September 5, 2009, from www.bls.gov/cex/csxann05.pdf

United States Bureau of Labor Statistics. (2008a). *American time use survey. Tables 8–10*. Washington, DC: Author. Retrieved September 5, 2009, from www.bls.gov/news.release/pdf/atus.pdf

United States Bureau of Labor Statistics. (2008b). *Involuntary part-time work on the rise. Summary 08–08*. Washington, DC: Author. Retrieved September 5, 2009, from www.bls.gov/opub/ils/pdf/opbils71.pdf

United States Bureau of Labor Statistics. (2008c). *May 2008 national occupational employment and wage estimates: United States*. Washington, DC: Author. Retrieved May 29, 2009, from www.bls.gov/oes/2008/may/oes_nat.htm#600–0000

United States Bureau of Labor Statistics. (2008d). *Women in the labor force: A databook 2008*. Washington, DC: Author. Retrieved September 5, 2009, from www.bls.gov/cps/wlf-databook2008.htm

United States Bureau of Labor Statistics. (2009). Ranks of discouraged workers and others marginally attached to the labor force rise during recession. *Issues in Labor Statistics,* Summary 09–04. Washington, DC: Author. Retrieved September 5, 2009, from www.bls.gov/opub/ils/pdf/opbils74.pdf

United States Bureau of Labor Statistics (2010). *The employment situation,* April 2010 (USDL-10-0394). Washington, DC: Author. Retrieved May 2, 2010, from www.bls.gov/news.release/empsit.nr0.htm

United States Bureau of the Census. (2004). *Statistical abstract of the United States*. Washington, DC: Author. Retrieved June 15, 2005, from www.census.gov/prod/www/statistical-abstract-04.html

United States Bureau of the Census. (2005). *Current population survey (CPS): Definitions and explanations*. Washington, DC: Author. Retrieved September 21, 2005, from www.census.gov/population/www/cps/cpsdef.html

United States Bureau of the Census. (2006a). *Black-owned firms: 2002*. SB02–00CS-BLK (RV). Washington, DC: Author. Retrieved July 4, 2007, www.census.gov/prod/ec02/sb0200csblk.pdf

United States Bureau of the Census. (2006b). *Special edition: 300 million*. Washington, DC: Author. Retrieved July 12, 2007, from www.census.gov/Press-Release/www/releases/archives/facts_for_features_special_editions/007276.htm

United States Bureau of the Census. (2007). *Statistical abstract of the United States*. Washington, DC: Author. Retrieved March 29, 2007, from www.census.gov/prod/2006pub/07statab/pop.pdf

United States Bureau of the Census. (2008). *America's families and living arrangements: 2008*. Washington, DC: Author. Retrieved May 18, 2009, from www.census.gov/population/socdemo/hh-fam/cps2008/tabC3-all.xls

United States Bureau of the Census. (2009). *Statistical abstract of the United States*. Washington, DC: Author. Retrieved June 18, 2010, from www.census.gov/compendia/statab/2009/2009edition.html

United States Commission on Human Rights. (1992). Indian tribes: A continuing quest for survival. In P. S. Rothenberg (Ed.), *Race, class and gender in the United States*. New York: St. Martin's Press.

United States Department of Agriculture. (2001). *USDA estimates child rearing costs. June 17, 2001*. Washington, DC: Author.

United States Department of Health and Human Services. (2006). *Sustaining state programs for tobacco control: Data highlights 2006*. Retrieved September 5, 2009, from www.cdc.gov/tobacco/data_statistics/state_data/data_highlights/2006/pdfs/dataHighlights06rev.pdf

United States Department of Justice. (2001). *Criminal victimization in United States, 1999 statistical tables* (NCJ 184938). Washington, DC: Bureau of Justice Statistics. Retrieved September 5, 2009, from www.ojp.usdoj.gov/bjs/pub/pdf/cvus99.pdf

United States Department of Justice. (2008). *Criminal victimization in the United States, 2006 statistical tables* (Table 27) (NCJ 223436). Washington, DC: Author. Retrieved September 5, 2009, from www.ojp.usdoj.gov/bjs/pub/pdf/cvus06.pdf

United States Department of Justice. (2009). *UBS enters into deferred prosecution agreement*. Washington, DC: Author. Retrieved May 21, 2009, from www.usdoj.gov/opa/pr/2009/February/09-tax-136.html

United States Department of Labor. (2004). *The Americans with Disabilities Act of 1990*. Washington, DC: Author. Retrieved December 14, 2004, from www.dol.gov

United States Department of Labor. (2008). *Median weekly earnings of full-time wage and salary workers by detailed occupation and sex*. Washington, DC: Author. Retrieved October 20, 2009, from www.bls.gov/cps/cpsaat39.pdf

United States Divorce Statistics. (2006). *Divorce Magazine*. Retrieved August 16, 2006, from www.divorcemag.com/statistics/statsUS.shtml

United States Equal Employment Opportunity Commission. (2009). *Sexual harassment charges: EEOC & FEPAs combined* (FY1997–2008). Washington, DC: Author. Retrieved June 18, 2010, from www.eeoc.gov/eeoc/statistics/enforcement/sexual_harassment.cfm

United States Sentencing Commission. (2008). *U.S. Sentencing Commission 2008 Annual Report.* Washington, DC: Author. Retrieved May 22, 2009, from www.ussc.gov/ANNRPT/2008/Chap5_08.pdf

Upton, R. L. (in press). *The next one changes everything.* Ann Arbor: University of Michigan Press.

Urbina, I. (2009, February 25). In push to end death penalty, some states cite cost-cutting. *New York Times.*

Utne, L. (2006, March/April). Soldiers for peace. *Utne Reader.*

Van Ausdale, D., & Feagin, J. R. (2001). *The first R: How children learn race and racism.* Lanham, MD: Rowman & Littlefield.

Van den Haag, E. (1975). *Punishing criminals: Concerning a very old and painful question.* New York: Basic Books.

Vanek, J. (1980). Work, leisure and family roles: Farm households in the United States: 1920–1955. *Journal of Family History, 5,* 422–431.

Van Ryn, M., & Burke, J. (2000). The effect of patient race and socio-economic status on physicians' perceptions of patients. *Social Science and Medicine, 50,* 813–820.

Vaughan, D. (1986). *Uncoupling.* New York: Vintage Books.

Vedantam, S. (2005, June 26). Patients' diversity is often discounted. *Washington Post.*

Viets, E. (1992, November 29). Give a whistle, he'll love it. *St. Louis Post-Dispatch.*

Virning, B. A. (2008). Associating insurance status with cancer stage at diagnosis. *Lancet Oncology, 9,* 189–191.

Vladimir Putin on raising Russia's birth rate. (2006). *Population and Development Review, 32,* 385–389.

Vogeler, I. (2003). *Maquiladoras.* Eau Claire: University of Wisconsin. Retrieved September 5, 2009, from www.uwec.edu/geography/Ivogeler/w188/border/maquil.htm

Von Zielbauer, P. (2005, June 17). Race a factor in job offers for ex-convicts. *New York Times.*

Voyandoff, P. (1990). Economic distress and family relations: A review of the eighties. *Journal of Marriage and Family, 52,* 1099–1115.

Wade, N. (2002, July 30). Race is seen as real guide to track roots of disease. *New York Times.*

Wagner, D. G., Ford, R. S., & Ford, T. W. (1986). Can gender inequalities be reduced? *American Sociological Review, 51,* 47–61.

Wahl, O. (1999). *Telling is risky business.* New Brunswick, NJ: Rutgers University Press.

Waite, L. J., & Gallagher, M. (2000). *The case for marriage: Why married people are happier, healthier, and better off financially.* New York: Doubleday.

Waldman, A. (2003, March 28). Broken taboos doom lovers in an Indian village. *New York Times.*

Walton, J. (1990). *Sociology and critical inquiry.* Belmont, CA: Wadsworth.

Wansink, B. (2006). *Mindless eating: Why we eat more than we think.* New York: Bantam.

Ward, L. M., & Friedman, K. (2006). Using TV as a guide: Associations between television viewing and adolescents' sexual attitudes and behavior. *Journal of Research on Adolescence, 16,* 133–156.

Warren, E., & Tyagi, A. W. (2007). Why middle-class mothers and fathers are going broke. In A. S. Skolnick & J. H. Skolnick (Eds.), *Family in transition.* Boston: Allyn & Bacon.

Warshaw, R. (1988). *I never called it rape.* New York: Harper & Row.

Wartik, N. (2003, September 9). Muting the obsessions over perceived flaws. *New York Times.*

Waters, M. C. (2008). Optional ethnicities: For whites only? In D. Newman & J. O'Brien (Eds.), *Sociology: Exploring the architecture of everyday life (Readings).* Thousand Oaks, CA: Pine Forge Press.

Watson, I. (2005, June 13). As elections near, Iranian women stage protest. NPR *(Morning Edition).* Retrieved June 13, 2005, from www.npr.org/templates/story/story.php?storyID=4700486

Wattenberg, E. (1986). The fate of baby boomers and their children. *Social Work, 31,* 20–28.

Watzlawick, P. (1976). *How real is real?* Garden City, NY: Doubleday.

Watzlawick, P. (1984). Self-fulfilling prophecies. In P. Watzlawick (Ed.), *The invented reality: How do we know what we believe we know? Contributions to constructivism.* New York: Norton.

Waxman, S. (2007, June 9). What's in a slur? A new play searches for answers. *New York Times.*

Weber, M. (1946). Bureaucracy. In H. H. Gerth & C. W. Mills (Eds.), *From Max Weber: Essays in sociology.* New York: Oxford University Press.

Weber, M. (1947). *The theory of social and economic organization.* New York: Free Press.

Weber, M. (1970). *From Max Weber: Essays in sociology,* H. H. Gerth & C. W. Mills (Eds.). New York: Oxford University Press.

Weber, M. (1977). *The Protestant ethic and the spirit of capitalism.* New York: Macmillan. (Original work published 1904)

Weber, M. (1978). *Economy and society* (G. Roth & C. Wittich, Trans.). Berkeley: University of California Press. (Original work published 1921)

Weeks, J. (1995). *Population: An introduction to concepts and issues* (Rev. 5th ed.). Belmont, CA: Wadsworth.

Wehrfritz, G., & Cochrane, J. (2005, January 17). Charity and chaos. *Newsweek.*

Weil, E. (2006, September 24). What if it's (sort of) a boy and (sort of) a girl? *New York Times Magazine.*

Weinberg, D. H. (2007, July/August). Earnings by gender: Evidence from Census 2000. *Monthly Labor Review,* 26–34.

Weitzman, L., Eifler, D., Hodada, E., & Ross, C. (1972). Sex-role socialization in picture books for preschool children. *American Journal of Sociology, 77,* 1125–1150.

Welch, H. G., Schwartz, L., & Woloshin, S. (2007, January 2). What's making us sick is an epidemic of diagnoses. *New York Times.*

Weller, C. E., & Logan, A. (2008). *America's middle class still losing ground.* Washington, DC: Center for American Progress. Retrieved September 5, 2009, from www.americanprogress.org/issues/2008/07/pdf/middleclasssqueeze.pdf

West, H. C., & Sabol, W. J. (2009). *Prison inmates at midyear 2008: Statistical tables* (NCJ225619). Washington, DC: Bureau of Justice Statistics. Retrieved June 18, 2010, from http://bjs.ojp.usdoj.gov/content/pub/pdf/pim08st.pdf

Whalen, C. K., & Henker, B. (1977). The pitfalls of politicization: A response to Conrad's "The discovery of hyperkinesis: Notes on the medicalization of deviance." *Social Problems, 24,* 590–595.

What is coltan? (2002, January 21). *ABCNews.com.* Retrieved September 5, 2009, from http://abcnews.go.com/Nightline/story?id=128631&page=1

White, L., & Brinkerhoff, D. (1981). The sexual division of labor: Evidence from childhood. *Social Forces, 60,* 170–181.

Whorf, B. (1956). *Language, thought and reality.* Cambridge: MIT Press.

Whyte, M. K. (1990). *Dating, mating and marriage.* New York: Aldine de Gruyter.

Wilcox, W. B. (2000). Conservative Protestant child discipline: The case of parental yelling. *Social Forces, 79,* 856–891.

Wildman, S. M., & Davis, A. D. (2002). Making systems of privilege visible. In P. S. Rothenberg (Ed.), *White privilege: Essential readings on the other side of racism.* New York: Worth.

Wilford, J. N. (2007, September 19). Languages die, but not their last words. *New York Times.*

Wilkinson, L. C., & Marrett, C. B. (1985). *Gender influences in classroom interaction.* Orlando, FL: Academic Press.

Williams, W. L. (1992). *The spirit and the flesh: Sexual diversity in American Indian culture.* Boston: Beacon Press.

Williamson, R. C. (1984). A partial replication of the Kohn-Gecas-Nye thesis in a German sample. *Journal of Marriage and the Family, 46,* 971–979.

Wilson, D. (2009a, August 30). Race, ethnicity, and care. *New York Times.*

Wilson, D. (2009b, June 12). Senate approves tight regulation over cigarettes. *New York Times.*

Wines, M. (2006, August 24). Africa adds to miserable ranks of child workers. *New York Times.*

Winter, G. (2002, May 19). Workers contend Coke sent old soda to poor neighborhoods. *New York Times.*

Witt, S. (2005). How television shapes children's gender roles. In R. H. Lauer & J. C. Lauer (Eds.), *Sociology: Windows on society.* Los Angeles: Roxbury.

Wolfe, A. (1991). *America at century's end.* Berkeley: University of California Press.

Women Physicians Congress. (2008). *Statistics and history.* Chicago: Author. Retrieved June 5, 2009, from www.ama-assn.org/ama/pub/about-ama/our-people/member-groups-sections/women-physicians-congress/statistics-history.shtml

Wood, N. (2005, February 6). Eight nations agree on plan to lift status of Gypsies. *New York Times.*

Workers of the world. (1998, January 30). *Economist.*

World Bank. (2006). *Global monitoring report 2006.* Washington, DC: Author. Retrieved August 9, 2007, from http://web.worldbank.org

World Wildlife Fund. (2008). *Living planet report 2008.* Retrieved September 5, 2009, from http://assets.panda.org/downloads/living_planet_report_2008.pdf

Worsnop, R. (1996, February 23). Getting into college. *CQ Researcher.*

Wright, E. O. (1976). Class boundaries in advanced capitalist societies. *New Left Review, 98,* 3–41.

Wright, E. O., Costello, C., Hachen, D., & Sprague, J. (1982). The American class structure. *American Sociological Review, 47,* 709–726.

Wright, E. O., & Perrone, L. (1977). Marxist class categories and income inequality. *American Sociological Review, 42,* 32–55.

Wright, J. D., & Wright, S. R. (1976). Social class and parental values for children: A partial replication and extension of the Kohn thesis. *American Sociological Review, 41,* 527–537.

Wrong, D. (1988). *Power: Its forms, bases, and uses.* Chicago: University of Chicago Press.

Wu, F. H. (2002). *Yellow: Race in America beyond black and white.* New York: Basic Books.

WuDunn, S. (1996a, January 23). In Japan, even toddlers feel the pressure to excel. *New York Times.*

WuDunn, S. (1996b, September 11). A taboo creates a land of Romeos and Juliets. *New York Times.*

WuDunn, S. (1997, January 14). Korean women still feel demands to bear a son. *New York Times.*

Wuthnow, R. (1994). *Sharing the journey.* New York: Free Press.

Xiao, H. (2000). Class, gender, and parental values in the 1990s. *Gender & Society, 14,* 785–803.

Yardley, W. (2007, August 28). When wildfires threaten, wealthy get extra shield. *New York Times.*

Yi, C.-C., Chang, C.-E., & Chang, Y.-H. (2004). The intergenerational transmission of family values: A comparison between teenagers and parents in Taiwan. *Journal of Comparative Family Studies, 35,* 523–545.

Yin, S. (2008). *Popwire. A higher share of young women than men have earned B.A.'s.* Washington, DC: Population Reference Bureau. Retrieved February 16, 2008, from www.prb.org/Articles/2008/popwirefeb2008.aspx?p=1

Yoshino, K. (2006). *Covering: The hidden assault on our civil rights.* New York: Random House.

Yum! Brands. (2008). *Yum! financial data: Restaurant counts.* Dallas, TX: Author. Retrieved May 3, 2009, from www.yum.com/investors/restcounts.asp

Zernike, K. (2003, January 20). 30 years after *Roe v. Wade,* new trends but the old debate. *New York Times.*

Zernike, K. (2004, December 19). Does Christmas need to be saved? *New York Times.*

Zhao, Y. (2002, August 5). Wave of pupils lacking English strains schools. *New York Times.*

Zhu, W. X., Lu, L., & Hesketh, T. (2009). China's excess males, sex selective abortion, and one child policy: Analysis of data from 2005 national intercensus survey. *British Medical Journal, 338,* 1211–1213.

Zimbardo, P. (2007). *The Lucifer effect: Understanding how good people turn evil.* New York: Random House.

Zoepf, K. (2007, September 23). A dishonorable affair. *New York Times Magazine.*

Zola, I. (1986). Medicine as an institution of social control. In P. Conrad & R. Kern (Eds.), *The sociology of health and illness.* New York: St. Martin's Press.

Zoll, R. (2005, June 7). Poll reveals U.S. leads in religious devotion. *Indianapolis Star.*

Zuger, A. (2005, October 30). For a retainer, lavish care by "boutique doctors." *New York Times.*

Zurcher, L. A., & Snow, D. A. (1981). Collective behavior: Social movements. In M. Rosenberg & R. H. Turner (Eds.), *Social psychology: Sociological perspectives.* New York: Basic Books.

Zwerdling, D. (2004). U.S. military whistle blowers face retribution. *National Public Radio Online.* Retrieved June 19, 2007, from www.npr.org/templates/story/story.php?storyId=1905858

Index